MW01030629

Native American Food Plants

Native American Food Plants

An Ethnobotanical Dictionary

DANIEL E. MOERMAN

Timber Press
Portland • London

This abridged work is based on the author's *Native American Ethnobotany*
published by Timber Press Inc. in 1998.

Facts stated in this book are to the best of the author's knowledge true;
however, the author and publisher can take no responsibility for any illness
or damage that might result from use of the materials described herein.

The botanical drawings in this volume were obtained from the U.S. Department
of Agriculture Natural Resources Conservation Service's PLANTS Database
(http://plants.usda.gov, Baton Rouge, La.: National Plant Data Center).
These drawings were originally published in *An Illustrated Flora of the Northern
United States, Canada and the British Possessions* by N. L. Britton and A. Brown
(3 vols., 1913. New York: Scribner's Sons). The ornamental geranium initial capitals
and other elements throughout were drawn by Jennifer Sontchi.

The Haseltine Building
133 S.W. Second Avenue, Suite 450
Portland, Oregon 97204-3527
www.timberpress.com

2 The Quadrant
135 Salusbury Road
London NW6 6RJ
www.timberpress.co.uk

Printed in the United States of America

Library of Congress Cataloging-in-Publication Data

Moerman, Daniel E.
    Native American food plants : an ethnobotanical dictionary / Daniel E. Moerman.
        p. cm.
    "This abridged work is based on the author's Native American ethnobotany published by
Timber Press, Inc. in 1998."
    Includes bibliographical references and index.
    ISBN 978-1-60469-189-4
    1. Plants, Edible—North America—Dictionaries. 2. Indians of North America—Food—
Dictionaries. 3. Indians of North America—Ethnobotany—Dictionaries. 4. Ethnobotany—
North America—Dictionaries. I. Title.
    QK98.5.N57M64 2011
    581.6'32097—dc22

                                                                                    2010016021

A catalog record for this book is also available from the British Library.

For Owen, with love

Contents

Preface

I am pleased to introduce the second abridged edition of *Native American Ethnobotany* in a new format and with a new title: *Native American Food Plants.* This volume contains more than 11,000 food uses of some 1866 plant species from the original volume with the relevant references.

I believe that this is the most comprehensive and authoritative listing of Native North American plant use for foods available anywhere. There is a range of food types from staples to sweets, breakfast to vegetables. They represent uses from native peoples living all over North America, from the Arctic Eskimo to the Florida Seminoles, from the Canadian Algonquin to the southwestern Navajo and Hopi.

The original encyclopedia, *Native American Ethnobotany*, had a long history. It started with medicines. In 1970, I was in the Sea Islands of South Carolina doing anthropological fieldwork for my Ph.D. dissertation in a rural black community. I was surprised to learn that sometimes when people were ill, they gathered various wild plants as medicines. Although I had not intended to do so, I began to inquire into the matter. In time, I had identified about 35 species of plants, from *Allium* to *Zanthoxylum*, which were so used. I then asked what seemed at the time to be a few simple questions: How had these people learned of these plants? Did it do any good to take them? Had anyone else ever used them, and if so, for what?

In asking these questions I found I was in the company of some of the great American students of ethnobotany of the past—Huron H. Smith, Francis Densmore, Melvin Randolf Gilmore, Matilda Coxe Stevenson, Gladys Tantaquidgeon, and many others. Their fascinating works, too often overlooked, were found with the help of reference librarians in the recesses of one library or another across the continent. Most of the works have long been out of print or were published in specialist journals and were very difficult to find.

Once found, many of the works were difficult to use. Most were not indexed, or at least not very well indexed. To answer a seemingly simple question such as "Who used *Allium* and for what?" took hours of digging. I decided to try to coordinate the information. I bought a few hundred index cards, the kind with sorting holes around the edges, and started filling them in. Soon I had more cards than would fit on the sorting pin. I had to start new boxes of subcategories to store the cards. Once I dropped a stack of cards on the floor. It was very discouraging. Eventually I transferred the information to cards that could be fed into the hopper at the computing center at the University of Michigan–Dearborn. The material was then read into a database using the TAXIR (Taxonomic Information Retrieval) system available on the university mainframe computer.

In 1975, with a summer stipend from the National Endowment for the Humanities, I filled out thousands of code sheets with material from the works by Smith, Tantaquidgeon, and others. With funds provided by the university, I hired keypunch operators to produce the thousands of cards needed for computing. The first version of the database was published in 1977 as *American Medical Ethnobotany: A Reference Dictionary* (New York: Garland Publishing). That book included 1288 plant species from 531 genera from 118 families used in 4869 different ways in 48 different societies. There was no index, but each of the 4869 items appeared in the book four times—one list organized by genus, one by family, one by use, and one by tribe.

Even though that book had more than 500 pages, it was far from a comprehensive list of Native American medicinal plant use. I had not had time or resources to code several other available sources (for example, Francis Elmore on the Navajo and Erna Gunther on the Northwest Coast peoples). And at the time there were no sources available on two major groups, the Cherokee and Iroquois. With the help of several reference librarians, I continued to add to my collection of ethnobotanical works, published and unpublished. Paul Hamel and Mary Chiltoskey's *Cherokee Plants and Their Uses* and James Herrick's monumental *Iroquois Medical Botany* appeared later in the 1970s (those two sources alone had more items in them, 4875, than all the rest of my original database).

Improvements in database technology and important grants from the National Endowment for the Humanities and the National Science Foundation helped further my work over the decades. *Medicinal Plants of Native America* was published in 1986 by the University of Michigan Museum of Anthropology. Subsequent funding from the National Science Foundation to do serious analysis of the data and to include nonmedicinal plants (for food, dye, fiber, construction, and so on) led to *Native American Ethnobotany* published in 1998 by Timber Press, which dwarfs the present volume in size with its 47,000 uses of 3860 plant species. All the information in that book is available online at herb.umd.umich.edu thanks to the support of the University of Michigan–Dearborn.

This book incorporates all the parts of *Native American Ethnobotany* dealing specifically with food uses, and it is an effort to provide an affordable and portable alternative for those especially interested in the uses of plants as foods. Many of the entries are short and even cryptic: "Plant used as food" or "Roots eaten." But others are much richer and more amusing. For example, consider the Inupiat Eskimo uses of black crowberry listed under *Empetrum nigrum*. Bon appétit!

Acknowledgments

So many people and organizations have contributed materially and otherwise to this project that it is not feasible to list them all. Foundations, universities, libraries and librarians, colleagues, students, friends, and family have all been indispensible to a project that took approximately 25 years to complete. Here I thank them all without naming any, for to name one would require me to name them all, and I would surely miss someone. Thank you all.

The current abridged editions were made possible by Neal Maillet of Timber Press, who conceived the project, and Lisa DiDonato Brousseau, who did most of the work. I deeply appreciate their confidence in this project.

Anthropologists are often and rightly criticized for taking from the lives of other people and not giving very much back. In a small effort to address that criticism, I decided some time ago to find funds sufficient to purchase a copy of the original book to give to each of the 1100 or so registered American Indian tribes and Canadian First Nations. With the help of many individuals and companies, we originally managed to give books to about half of the tribes. Then, Mike Balick of the New York Botanical Garden interested the Force for Good Foundation in the project. The foundation is funded by the Nu Skin Company of Provo, Utah, a cosmetics company with a rich corporate conscience. Their support allowed us to complete the project, sending copies of the book to all 1100 groups.

On a more personal level, my wife, Claudine Farrand, is a true partner. She provided context for this work by making life fun. My daughter, Jennifer Sontchi, did the lettered geranium illustrations seen throughout the book, and I thank her for them. She also provided grandson Owen Daniel Sontchi, to whom this volume is dedicated.

But our deepest debt is to those predecessors of ours on the North American continent who, through glacial cold in a world populated by mammoths and saber-toothed tigers, seriously, deliberately, and thoughtfully studied the flora of a new world, learned its secrets, and encouraged the next generations to study more closely and to learn more. Their diligence and energy, their insight and creativity, are the marks of true scientists, dedicated to gaining meaningful and useful knowledge from a complex and confusing world. That I cannot list them individually by name in no way diminishes my sense of obligation to them.

Plant Use by Native Americans

Native American peoples had a remarkable amount of knowledge of the world in which they lived. In particular, they knew a great deal about plants. There are in North America more than 31,000 kinds (species, subspecies, varieties, and so on) of vascular plants: seed plants, including the flowering plants (angiosperms) and conifers (gymnosperms), and spore-bearing plants, including the ferns, club mosses, spike mosses, and horsetails (pteridophytes). North America is defined here as North America north of Mexico plus Hawaii and Greenland. American Indians used more than 1500 of these species as foods. *Native American Food Plants* also contains information on nonvascular plants (algae, fungi, lichens, liverworts, and mosses). The data for nonvascular plants are much less complete than those for vascular plants, however.

Native American Food Plants includes information on plant use by Native American people. Most of the plants used are native to North America, but some are not. Some are plants that were introduced into North America—some perhaps in pre-Columbian times and some certainly thereafter—and became naturalized, growing spontaneously. Other plants are introductions that were kept in cultivation. The information in *Native American Food Plants* documents plant usage no doubt dating back to very early times and passed down through generations as traditional knowledge, as well as innovations in response to much more recent plant introductions.

Plants Used as Foods

There are more than 1500 species included in *Native American Food Plants* that were used for food by Native Americans. They are an extremely diverse assortment of species. The listing of Food Usage Categories toward the end of this chapter defines the many sorts of food use that appear in the Catalog of Plants. The 10 plants with the greatest number of uses as foods by Native Americans are *Prunus virginiana*, common chokecherry (163); *Yucca baccata*, banana yucca (126); *Zea mays*, corn (121); *Amelanchier alnifolia*, Saskatoon serviceberry (117); *Prosopis glandulosa*, honey mesquite (79); *Rubus idaeus*, American red raspberry (74); *Carnegia gigantea*, saguaro (72); *Rubus spectabilis*, salmonberry (72); *Rubus parviflorus*, thimbleberry (71); and *Typha latifolia*, broadleaf cattail (71).

Is there a relationship between food plants and medicinal plants? Many medicines are plant substances that are toxic; they often serve plants by being herbicides or insecticides or the like. It is not at all uncommon for medicines to be poisonous. In most societies, medicines are considered dangerous, or powerful, or are associated with strong powers in nature. They are often under the control of people with elaborate and esoteric training, for example, shamans and physicians. In Western culture, medicines are often only available by prescription, presumably because they are dangerous, or poisonous, or addicting. In any event, it seems a reasonable prediction that foods and drugs would be quite different.

Quite surprisingly, food and drug plants are not so discrete. There is a remarkable overlap of the two categories. (Much of the interpretation of such overlap that follows is based on a mathematical and statistical argument, details of which are complex and do not require full explanation here. Aficionados can read more about the background of this argument by consulting a paper of mine: An Analysis of the Food Plants and Drug Plants of Native North America. Journal of Ethnopharmacology 1996; 52: 1–22.)

A number of plant families have disproportionate shares of both kinds of plants, among which are the parsley family (Apiaceae), honeysuckle family (Caprifoliaceae), heath family (Ericaceae), oak family (Fagaceae), pine family (Pinaceae), and rose family (Rosaceae). These plants may produce nutritious and edible parts (often fruits or seeds) that attract animals, probably to facilitate plant dispersal. At the same time, however, they may produce noxious and poisonous substances to protect other aspects of their integrity.

The Rosaceae, an excellent example of this proposition, includes apples (*Pyrus*) and almonds, cherries, peaches, and pears (all *Prunus*) yet is also characterized by what we may think of as a "poisoned apple syndrome." Many members of the rose family produce nutritious and attractive fruits; they also produce quite toxic substances in the leaves, bark, and pits of the fruits of many species. Among these chemicals are a class of cyanogenic glucosides. Their toxicity occurs because they release cyanide gas when combined with certain enzymes; usually this occurs if the appropriate plant parts are crushed or chewed. Amygdalin is one of several cyanogenic glucosides produced by various species of Rosaceae that "can give rise to cyanide poisoning. Usually this is only moderate, with distress, but occasionally more serious poisoning gives rise to loss of consciousness, and serious respiratory trouble. Apnoeia and fatal collapse are exceptional, but have occurred" (F. Bodin and C. F. Cheinisse, page 162 in Poisons. New York: McGraw-Hill. 1970).

People have died eating apple pits; "poisoned apple" is redundant. In this manner the plants can attract various browsers to them to aid in dispersion of the seeds but simultaneously protect the seeds from being destroyed. At the same time, in moderation, people have made medicinal use of these chemicals, as the rose family is an important source of plant medicines. Of 836 North American species of Rosaceae, 56 (7%) have been used medicinally by Native Americans, 23 (3%) have been used as food, and a significantly larger number, 77 (9%), as both food and medicine.

Members of the honeysuckle family (Caprifoliaceae) also produce significant quantities of cyanogenic glycosides. One genus, *Sambucus* (elderberry), has been shown to produce a whole series of them, including holocalin, prunasin, sambunigrin, and zierin. *Sambucus* also produces a series of alkaloids, most of which probably act to inhibit excessive browsing by birds. Some species of *Sambucus* provide edible fruits. The earliest recipe of which I am aware that calls for elder is from Apicius's cookbook, written during the reign of Tiberius, C.E. 14–37. He recommended a sort of omelet of eggs, elderberries, pepper, wine, and *liquamen* (a sauce made of fish and salt, of the order of Worcestershire). Elderberries are generally cooked, dried, or fermented before they are eaten to moderate the effects of several emetic alkaloids. These substances are probably responsible for the common use of the plants as emetics, cathartics, or laxatives. Although most of the food uses of elder reported in *Native American Food Plants* involve such cooking or drying, in a number of cases it is reported that the berries were eaten raw!

It is often the case, however, that for species used for both food and medicine, different plant parts are used. For those cases in which the plant part used can be identified, it is far more likely for a root to be used for a medicine than for a food. Likewise, it is far more likely for a fruit to be used for a food than for a medicine. So the food–drug situation is complex, and simple assertions ("foods and medicines are different" or "foods and medicines are the same") just will not do.

Appreciating the Common Knowledge of Our Past

There is an enormous amount of real human knowledge contained in *Native American Food Plants*. People have been experimenting with nature since the earliest of times, learning what could be eaten and how it can be prepared. Cooking, fermenting, drying, mixing, aging, roasting, and boiling are only a few of the ways that people have dramatically expanded the number of plants suitable for human food. People first came to the Americas about 15,000 years ago and have been studying the plants of the two continents, and their preparation, ever since. Given that the floras of North America and China are remarkably alike, it is possible that the earliest Asian immigrants to North America saw recognizable plants when they got here.

Much of this accumulated knowledge of useful plants, slowly wrung from nature over millennia, has in a few centuries been lost, at least lost as a part of normal human life. There are specialists—primarily anthropologists and ethnobotanists—who are aware of some portions of what this book contains. But in past times this was to a large degree the knowledge of ordinary people. Surely there were specialists, people who were more interested than others in these matters, and they may even have developed esoteric knowledge that they kept to themselves for personal profit. But generally this was normal human knowledge, part and parcel of everyday life. People walked in the world and saw plants they knew to be useful for various purposes. Their children learned of these matters as naturally as our children learn the names of baseball teams or athletic shoes or rock bands. One needs not seek out edible roots and berries in order to appreciate them, any more than a bird-watcher needs to eat a curlew to enjoy it. But when one knows something of the uses people have made of thousands of the wild plants around us, the plants take on a new meaning, a new value greater than their beauty or their cooling shade or their pleasant scent. And few things taste as good as a handful of freshly picked wild blueberries or wild strawberries, a tiny fraction of the size of our currently plum-sized supermarket strawberries.

Sources of Information on Plant Usages

Native American Food Plants is based on the research of hundreds of scholars. I have accumulated the material included here over a period of more than 25 years. In that period, any time I saw an item containing useful information, I made a note of it. In addition, in 1993 I did an intensive search of the literature using traditional techniques such as reading bibliographies as well as using computerized search techniques. I examined approximately 500 possible sources. The information gathered here is based on material from 206 of those sources, enumerated in the Bibliography.

The criteria for selecting a source to be included were fairly simple. First, the material had to be primary, that is, based on original work with Native Americans who used the plants. I excluded all secondary material, that is, material based on prior published work. If I found an interesting secondary source I examined its bibliography to identify original sources that had yet to be consulted. In a few cases the primary source was not written by the individual who actually did the fieldwork. For example, source 59, by Catherine Fowler, is based on primary research done many years earlier by Willard Z. Park with the Northern Paiute, work that was not published at the time. As a second criterion, the source had to have reasonably clear scientific plant names, the plant identifications preferably having been made by professional botanists. Third, at least some of the information had to come from Native Americans living north of the Rio Grande. Fourth, information was coded only once even if it was published several times. In such cases I tried to use the earliest publication, but sometimes I used a later one if it had better plant identifications. The average number of plant usages coming from each source is 217.5, but the range is from 1 to 2947. The oldest source was published in 1840, the most recent in 1993.

Although sources were used in which care had been taken with regard to scientific plant names, no doubt some plants were misidentified and thus misnamed. Or, in some cases, if the plant were reidentified now, another identification might be made because, for example, what may have been recognized as one species at the time the plant was originally identified may now be recognized as two similar species. Which of those two (or both) species was used cannot be determined without a reidentification. Such reidentification is possible when a sample of the plant was dried, pressed, and preserved in an herbarium for reexamination. Such specimens are called vouchers. Although vouchers exist in various herbaria for some of the sources, unfortunately some sources' identifications do not rest on vouchered collections. "Suspect" identifications must be reverified by recourse to vouchers, when they exist.

And there is further work to do on the plants themselves, as documented in *Native American Food Plants*. For example, sometimes plants were originally identified in the sources only to the level of genus; these include the "sp." entries under various genera in the Catalog of Plants. The particular species (one or more than one species) may yet be identified, if vouchers exist. Apart from the matter of the accuracy of identification, the precision of identification in *Native American Food Plants* depends on that in the original sources. For example, in some species different subspecies or varieties may be recognized. If one source reported a plant named only to the level of species, and another source reported a plant to the level of subspecies or variety (or used a name that can be attributed to a particular subspecies or variety), then the usages will be listed in the Catalog of Plants under the species, or under the subspecies or variety, respectively. Thus the usages of *Rhus trilobata* by the Kiowa were reported in two sources, and because the sources used plant names that can be determined to different levels of precision, some uses are reported under the entry for *R. trilobata*, and others under that for *R. trilobata* var. *trilobata*.

Food Usage Categories

There are 32 different plant usage categories in *Native American Food Plants*. Some care needs to be exercised in the interpretation of certain categories. Not all people organize meals in terms of courses (ordinarily, we do not organize breakfast that way). In addition, not all people organize food into three meals per day. In a number of societies one can find that an evening meal is quite significant, and leftovers constitute breakfast. In many societies, a midday meal is the primary one. This means that, if an original author was not specific about these culinary details, we could not be either. In several cases of what seem to be fairly explicitly Western meal concepts (*breakfast, dessert*, and *snack*), those terms are used only when the author of the source used it first. In addition, it is common for a source to report that a particular plant is eaten but not specify in any more detail regarding how, what part, in what form, or when. Such usages are classified under Unspecified. "Unspecified" is a very large category, including 2203 reports.

Appetizer. Food or drink that stimulates the appetite and is usually served before
   a meal.
Baby Food. Food prepared especially for babies or children.
Beverage. Beverages include beer, cider, coffee, intoxicants, tea, wine, and other
   drinks.
Bread & Cake. All biscuits, breads, cakes, cookies, doughnuts, dumplings, muffins,
   pancakes, stuffings, pones, rolls, and tortillas.
Breakfast Food. This category is used when the source specifically mentions the term
   breakfast.
Candy. Candies, chewing gums, confections, and taffy.
Cooking Agent. Cooking oils, curdling agents, flavorings, food colorings, food thickeners, pectin, vinegars, and yeast.
Dessert. This category is used when the source specifically mentions the term *dessert*.
Dietary Aid. Plant parts added to food to make it more digestible, to benefit the diet, to
   improve the (normal) appetite, or as a good source of vitamins.
Dried Food. Food sun or fire dried and usually stored for future use.
Fodder. Food fed to animals by people.
Forage. Food sought out by animals, usually by grazing or browsing.

Frozen Food. Food frozen and stored for future use.

Fruit. Fruit used fresh with no significant preparation.

Ice Cream. This category is used only when the source specifically mentions the term *ice cream*.

Pie & Pudding. Savory or sweet pies and puddings. Basically, a pie is a pudding with a crust.

Porridge. A soft food made by boiling grain or legume meal in a liquid until thick, including atole, boiled hot cereal, gruel, hominy, mucilaginous mass, mush, and paste.

Preservative. Food additive used to protect against decay, discoloration, or spoilage.

Preserves. Conserves, fruit butters, jams, jellies, marmalades, nut butters, pastes, and preserves.

Sauce & Relish. Condiments, dips, gravies, ice cream toppings, relishes, sauces, sweet pickles, and syrups.

Snack Food. This category is used when the source specifically states the food was used for nibbles, refreshments, snacks, or tidbits. It is also used for popcorn.

Soup. Broths, chowders, pottages, soups, and stews.

Sour. Foods said to have acidic, bitter, sour, or tart tastes.

Special Food. Ceremonial foods, delicacies, rations, and food used for ritual meals and feasts.

Spice. Used to flavor, marinate, or season foods.

Staple. Foods used regularly, including cereals, flours, meals, pinoles, sugars, hominies, and rice. This category is also used when the source states that the item was used as a dependable, important, main, principal, or staple food.

Starvation Food. Food said to be used in times of emergency, famine, food shortage, or need but generally avoided in ordinary times.

Substitution Food. Food used to take the place of another food when the latter was unavailable.

Sweetener. Nectars, sugars, sweetening flavors, and syrups.

Unspecified. A very large category with 2203 items. In many sources it is common to see something such as "the root of this plant was eaten" or "the inner bark was used for food." When the food use was not specified any more clearly, it has been classified as unspecified.

Vegetable. All foods described in the source as being greens, vegetables, or the like, for example, "the flower stalks were eaten as greens."

Winter Use Food. Stored foods used during the winter months.

Native Americans

The naming of Native American or American Indian groups is a complicated matter. Even the term *American Indian* is problematic. Christopher Columbus and his followers were naive about the location of "India." And so, many people now seem to prefer the term *Native American*. But it is also the case that indigenous peoples were here long before the continents of the New World were named after the Italian navigator Amerigo Vespucci. In Canada, the generic term most often used in the past was *Native People*, but today the terms *First Nations* or *First Nations People* are most common. Yet the fact remains that many people have been quite happy with the term *Indian*. One of the radical movements of the 1960s, for example, was known as AIM, the American Indian Movement. Because these names often have political significance, it is for all practical purposes impossible to refer generically to the indigenous population of the Americas without offending someone, but such is not the intention here.

There are similar problems with tribal names. A classic case is the name Eskimo. The word is, apparently, an English mispronunciation of a French mispronunciation of a Montagnais or Micmac word *ayashkimew*, which seems to have meant something like "eaters of raw meat," intended as a nasty insult. The Eskimo people generally call themselves Inuit or Innuit, meaning "people." I am unaware of the Inuit name for the Micmac, but my guess is that it was equally insulting. Such derived names are not always insults, however. The name Navaho or Navajo is a Spanish variation on a Tewa word meaning "large arroyo with cultivated fields," a place name. The Navajo name for themselves is Dene, meaning "people," but many Navajo also call themselves Navajo. Again, the names used to refer to particular Native American tribes can occasion political debate. Referring to one group by a term that means "people" implicitly asserts that other groups are something other than people, for example. Names used in *Native American Food Plants* are not intended in any way to offend anyone. I have elected to use the names for peoples reported in the original sources. This means that material for "the same people" is sometimes listed under different designations, but rarely is it for the same people at the same time. There are 221 groups mentioned in *Native American Food Plants*, as listed below. The parenthetical reference numbers below correspond to the sources enumerated in the Bibliography, from which information on each of the peoples was obtained.

Abnaki. St. François du Lac, about 100 miles (160 km) northwest of Montreal, Quebec (144).
Acoma. A pueblo in west-central New Mexico (32, 200). See also Keresan, and Keres, Western.
Alaska Native. Alaska (85).
Algonquin, Quebec. Western Quebec (18).
Algonquin, Tête-de-Boule. Manouan, about 260 miles (420 km) north of Montreal, Quebec (132).
Anticosti. On the Ile d'Anticosti in the St. Lawrence River, north of the Gaspé Peninsula, Quebec (143).
Apache. Various Apache groups live in Arizona and New Mexico (17, 32, 47, 121, 138).
Apache, Chiricahua & Mescalero. Chiricahua Apache ranged through western New Mexico, southeastern Arizona, and southward into Mexico; their eastern boundary began at the Rio Grande. The Mescalero Apache were principally located in New Mexico; the Rio Grande was their western boundary (33).

Apache, Mescalero. Southern New Mexico, western Texas, and northern Chihuahua, Mexico (14, 17).

Apache, San Carlos. The San Carlos Reservation is in eastern Arizona (95).

Apache, Western. Fort Apache Reservation, Arizona (26).

Apache, White Mountain. White Mountains, Arizona (136).

Apalachee. In the sixteenth and seventeenth centuries, the Apalachee lived in Spanish Florida, what is now northern Florida and southern Georgia (81).

Arapaho. Between the Platte and Arkansas Rivers in eastern Colorado and southeastern Wyoming (19, 118, 121).

Atsugewi. North of the Sierra Nevada and south of the Pit River in northeastern California (61).

Bellabella. The village of Bella Bella, British Columbia, is about 250 miles (400 km) northwest of Vancouver (184).

Bella Coola. The village of Bella Coola, British Columbia, is near the mouth of the Bella Coola River, about 250 miles (400 km) north northwest of Vancouver (74, 150, 184). See also Kimsquit.

Blackfoot. The Blackfoot hunted over the region of Montana, Alberta, and Saskatchewan. Blackfoot is a common spelling in Canada, whereas Blackfeet is more common in the United States (82, 86, 97, 114, 118, 121).

Cahuilla. Southern California (15).

California Indian. California (19, 118).

Canadian Indian. British Columbia, Alberta, and Saskatchewan (97).

Carrier. Near Fort St. James and Anahim Lake in central and northern British Columbia (31, 89, 184).

Chehalis. Central coast of Washington (79).

Cherokee. The Cherokees are found throughout much of western North Carolina (particularly in Graham and Cherokee Counties) and in northwestern Georgia. There are also many Cherokees in Oklahoma (80, 126, 169, 177, 203, 204).

Cheyenne. Montana and Oklahoma (19, 75, 76, 82, 83, 97).

Chinook, Lower. Southern coast of Washington (79).

Chippewa. Also known as the Ojibwa, the Chippewa are located in the upper Midwest and southern Ontario. Source 51 describes the Ojibwa of northern Minnesota, primarily the Leech Lake, Red Lake, and White Earth Reservations but also including a consultant from the Bois Fort Reservation. Source 53 describes the Ojibwa of north-central Minnesota and the Manitou Rapids Reserve in Ontario. Source 71 describes people from Pinconning and Lapeer, Michigan, and Sarnia, Ontario. See also Ojibwa.

Choctaw. St. Tammany Parish, Louisiana, on the northern shore of Lake Pontchartrain, is a center of the Choctaw region. Information in source 28 was collected by Gideon Lincecum during the years 1800–1835 in Mississippi (25, 28, 158, 177).

Clallam. Olympic Peninsula, Washington (57).

Coahuilla. Southern California coast (13).

Cochiti. Pueblo Indians of New Mexico (32). See also Keresan.

Cocopa. Southwestern Arizona and Baja California and Sonora, Mexico, generally along the lower Colorado River (37, 64).

Cocopa & Yuma. Lower Colorado River in Arizona (37).

Cocopa, Maricopa, Mohave & Yuma. The Cocopa, Mohave, and Yuma are located on the lower Colorado River in Arizona, and the Maricopa are located on the Gila River in Arizona (37).

Coeur d'Alene. The Coeur d'Alene Reservation is in northern Idaho (89, 178).

Comanche. The Comanche Indian Reservation is near Indiahoma, Comanche County, Oklahoma (29, 32, 99).

Concow. The Round Valley Indian Reservation is in Mendocino County, California, and stretches as a band about 60 miles (100 km) broad for 84 miles (135 km) along the coast, about midway between San Francisco and the Oregon border to the north (41). See also Numlaki.

Costanoan. The territory once occupied by the Costanoan Indians is in the Coast Ranges of central California. Their territory extended from San Francisco south to Big Sur and from the Pacific coast inland to the Diablo Range foothills (21).

Costanoan (Olhonean). Central California (117).

Cowichan. Southeastern coast of Vancouver Island, British Columbia (182, 186).

Cowlitz. South-central Washington (79).

Cree. The Cree range from the Northwest Territories (16) through central Alberta and southwestern Saskatchewan (97) to Montana (82).

Cree, Plains. Montana and North Dakota (113).

Cree, Woodlands. Saskatchewan (109).

Crow. A Siouan tribe living in southwestern Montana and northern Wyoming (19, 82).

Dakota. The Dakota, also known as the Lakota or Sioux, live on a number of reservations in Montana, the Dakotas, Nebraska, and Minnesota (69, 70, 97, 121). See also Lakota and Sioux.

Delaware. The Delaware originally lived on the East Coast. Today, some live in Ontario, but most are in Oklahoma (176).

Diegueño. The Diegueño live throughout southernmost California, notably on the Santa Ysabel Indian Reservation in San Diego County (15, 37, 84, 88).

Eskimo. There are many communities of Inuit or Eskimo people across the Arctic regions of Alaska, Canada, and Greenland. Some sources describe individual villages, whereas others are more general in their coverage. Source 149 describes some Alaskan Inuit, and source 181 describes people living at Hudson Bay.

Eskimo, Alaska. Nelson Island, on the Bering Sea coast of the Yukon-Kuskokwim Delta, western Alaska (1), villages along the northern Bering Sea and Arctic Alaska (4), western and southwestern Alaska (128), and Kodiak, Alaska (149).

Eskimo, Arctic. Central Canadian Arctic and sub-Arctic (127, 128).

Eskimo, Greenland. Greenland (128).

Eskimo, Inuktitut. Alaska, Canada, and Greenland (202).

Eskimo, Inupiat. Kotzebue in northwestern Alaska (98).

Flathead. An Interior Salish tribe located in western Montana and Idaho, north of the

Gallatin River, between the Rocky Mountains in the west and the Little Belt Range in the east (19, 82, 89, 97).

Gitksan. The Gitksan live along the northern coast of British Columbia and along the Skeena River (43, 73, 74, 150).

Gosiute. In desert territory bordering the Great Salt Lake in Utah on the south and extending westward into eastern Nevada (39).

Great Basin Indian. Uintah-Ouray Reservation, Fort Duchesne, Utah (121).

Green River Group. South of Seattle, Washington (79).

Gros Ventre. An Algonquian tribe living in the Milk River area of northern Montana (19, 82, 118).

Hahwunkwut. Northern California (117).

Haida. The Haida live along the northern coast of British Columbia into southern Alaska as well as on the Queen Charlotte Islands off the coast of British Columbia (43, 79).

Haihais. Central coast of British Columbia (43).

Haisla. Central coast of British Columbia (43, 73, 74).

Haisla & Hanaksiala. Central coast of British Columbia (43).

Hanaksiala. Central coast of British Columbia (43).

Havasupai. Cataract Canyon, a side branch of the Grand Canyon in northwestern Arizona (17, 162, 197, 200).

Hawaiian. Hawaii (2, 112).

Heiltzuk. Central coast of British Columbia (43).

Hesquiat. Coast of British Columbia and Hesquiat Harbor, Vancouver Island, British Columbia (43, 185, 186).

Hoh. Hoh Village is near the mouth of the Hoh River on the western side of the Olympic Peninsula, Washington (137).

Hopi. The Hopi live in several villages on the Hopi Reservation in northeastern Arizona. The Hopi Reservation is surrounded by the Navajo Reservation (17, 32, 34, 36, 42, 56, 101, 120, 138, 190, 200, 205).

Houma. Louisiana (158).

Hualapai. Northwestern Arizona (195).

Hupa. Northern California (117, 118, 148).

Huron. The Huron lived in southern Ontario and Michigan until the early nineteenth century. Now they live in Wisconsin (3).

Iroquois. The Iroquois live throughout upstate New York and in southern Quebec (87, 124, 141, 142, 196).

Isleta. The Isleta pueblo is located on the western bank of the Rio Grande, 12 miles (19 km) south of Albuquerque, New Mexico (32, 100).

Jemez. The Jemez pueblo is located on the Jemez River about 45 miles (72 km) northwest of Albuquerque, New Mexico (17, 32, 44, 100, 200).

Kamia. Imperial Valley in southeastern California (62).

Karok. The Karok are located along the Klamath River in an area paralleling the California coast from above Bluff Creek in Humboldt County to Happy Camp in Siskiyou County (6, 117, 148).

Kawaiisu. East of Bakersfield in southeastern California (206).

Keresan. There are seven pueblos near Albuquerque, New Mexico, where the languages are classified as Keresan. The Eastern Keresan pueblos are Cochiti, San Felipe, Santa Ana, Santo Domingo, and Sia. The Western Keresan pueblos are Acoma and Laguna. All of these but Santa Ana and Santo Domingo are treated separately in this book (198). See also Acoma; Cochiti; Keres, Western; Laguna; San Felipe; Sia.

Keres, Western. The Acoma and Laguna pueblos (171). See also Keresan.

Kimsquit. Bella Coola, British Columbia (184). See also Bella Coola.

Kiowa. Southern plains near the Arkansas and Red Rivers (19, 192).

Kitasoo. Central coast of British Columbia (43).

Klallam. Southern coast of Vancouver Island, British Columbia, and the north-central Olympic Peninsula, Washington (78, 79).

Klamath. South-central Oregon (45, 46, 117, 118, 163).

Koyukon. Huslia and Hughes, Alaska (119).

Kutenai. Montana (82).

Kwakiutl. Northern Vancouver Island and north of Vancouver Island on the mainland coast of British Columbia (20, 182, 183).

Kwakiutl, Southern. Central coast of British Columbia and northeastern coast of Vancouver Island, British Columbia (183, 184).

Kwakwaka'wakw. Central coast of British Columbia (43).

Laguna. The Laguna pueblo is in New Mexico (32). See also Keresan, and Keres, Western.

Lakota. Standing Rock Reservation is located on the central border of North Dakota and South Dakota (106); Rosebud Reservation is in Todd County, South Dakota (106, 139). The Lakota are also known as Dakota and Sioux. See also Dakota and Sioux.

Lillooet. British Columbia (89).

Luiseño. Southern California near San Juan Capistrano (15, 155).

Lummi. Northwestern border of Washington, near British Columbia (79).

Mahuna. Southwestern California (140).

Makah. Northwestern tip of the Olympic Peninsula, Washington (43, 67, 79, 186).

Malecite. New Brunswick, Canada (116, 160).

Mandan. North Dakota along the Missouri River near the mouth of the Heart River (19, 70).

Maricopa. South-central Arizona (32, 37, 47, 95).

Maricopa & Mohave. The Maricopa are located on the Gila River in Arizona; the Mohave are located on the lower Colorado River in Arizona (37).

Mendocino Indian. Mendocino County, California, halfway between San Francisco and the Oregon border (41).

Menominee. Wisconsin (54, 151).

Meskwaki. Tama, Iowa (152).

Mewuk. Central California (117).

Micmac. Nova Scotia, Prince Edward Island, New Brunswick east of the St. John River, and part of the Gaspé Peninsula, Quebec (40, 116, 145, 156, 159, 194).

Midoo. Central California (117).

Miwok. The Sierra Nevada together with the western foothills and a relatively small portion of the adjacent Sacramento–San Joaquin Valley, California (12).

Modesse. Northern California (117).

Modoc. Northern California and southern Oregon along the Lost River, as well as Tule, Klamath, and Clear Lakes (45).

Mohave. Lower Colorado River valley (32, 37, 168).

Mohegan. Connecticut (30, 174, 176).

Montagnais. Montagnais live throughout eastern Quebec, Lac-St.-Jean (24), the northern coast of the Gulf of St. Lawrence and the lower St. Lawrence River (156), and Labrador (174).

Montana Indian. Montana (19, 82).

Nanaimo. Vancouver Island, British Columbia (182).

Navajo. Arizona, New Mexico, and Utah (17, 23, 32, 47, 55, 56, 90, 97, 100, 110, 136, 138, 165, 200).

Navajo, Kayenta. Northeastern Arizona, near Monument Valley (205).

Navajo, Ramah. Western New Mexico (191).

Neeshenam. Bear River, Placer County, California (129).

Nevada Indian. Nevada (118, 121).

Nez Perce. Along the lower Snake River and its tributaries in western Idaho, north-eastern Oregon, and southwestern Washington (19, 82, 97).

Nisqually. South of Puget Sound, Washington (79).

Nitinaht. Southwestern coast of Vancouver Island, British Columbia, from near Jordan River to Pachena Point, extending inland along Nitinat Lake (67, 185, 186).

Northwest Indian. Oregon and Washington (19, 118).

Numlaki. Round Valley Indian Reservation is in Mendocino County, California, mid-way between San Francisco and the Oregon border (41). See also Concow.

Nuxalkmc. Valley of the Bella Coola River, South Bentinck Arm, Tallio Inlet, and Kim-squit in west-central British Columbia (43).

Oglala. South Dakota (70).

Ojibwa. Also known as the Chippewa, Ojibwas are located in the upper Midwest and southern Ontario. Source 5 describes the Ojibwa north of Lakes Superior and Hu-ron in Ontario. Source 96 describes people on Parry Island, located on the east-central side of Georgian Bay, Ontario. The Fort Bois Ojibwa described in source 135 live on a reservation 140 miles (225 km) northwest of Duluth, Minnesota. People described in source 153 live in northern Wisconsin. See also Chippewa.

Okanagan-Colville. Okanagan is the Canadian spelling. The Okanagan occupied the Okanagan and Similkameen River valleys and the shores of Lake Okanagan on both sides of the U.S.–Canadian border. The Colville are located on the Colville Reservation in northeastern Washington (74, 188). See also Okanagon.

Okanagon. Okanagon is the American spelling. The Okanagon are found on the

Colville Reservation in Washington and on various reserves in British Columbia (125, 164, 178). See also Okanagan-Colville.

Omaha. Nebraska (58, 68, 70).

Oregon Indian. Oregon (118).

Oregon Indian, Warm Springs. Warm Springs, Oregon (104, 118).

Oweekeno. Central coast of British Columbia (43).

Paiute. Paiutes generally live in the Great Basin region, although some live in California and Oregon. People described in sources 15 and 104 are from Surprise Valley, California. Source 111 describes the Warm Springs Reservation, Oregon. The remaining sources (32, 118, 121, 167, 180) generally describe people living in Nevada.

Paiute, Nevada. Nevada (121).

Paiute, Northern. Western Nevada (59, 60).

Paiute, Southern. Northern Arizona, southern Utah, and southern Nevada and adjacent areas of California (15).

Papago. In desert regions south of the Gila River of Arizona and extending into Sonora, Mexico (17, 32, 34, 36, 47, 95, 118, 146).

Papago & Pima. Arizona (35).

Pawnee. Missouri River region (70).

Penobscot. Northern New England and the maritime provinces of Canada. There is a Penobscot Reservation in Maine (156, 174).

Pima. Gila and Salt River valleys of southern Arizona (17, 32, 36, 47, 95, 146).

Pima, Gila River. From north of Jalisco, Mexico, to Phoenix, Arizona (133).

Pima, Lehi. Lehi, Arizona (47).

Poliklah. Northern California (117).

Pomo. Sonoma, Mendocino, and Lake Counties, California (9, 11, 41, 66, 117, 118).

Pomo, Kashaya. Coast of Sonoma County, California (72).

Ponca. The Northern Ponca are located in Nebraska and South Dakota, whereas the Southern band is located in Oklahoma (70, 94).

Potawatomi. Wisconsin (154).

Pueblo. New Mexico and Arizona (32, 34).

Puyallup. Southeastern side of Puget Sound, Washington (79).

Quileute. Western coast of the Olympic Peninsula, Washington (67, 79, 137).

Quinault. Southwestern coast of the Olympic Peninsula, Washington (79, 201).

Rappahannock. Virginia (30, 161).

Ree. Montana (19).

Rocky Boy. Rocky Boy Reservation, Montana (118).

Round Valley Indian. Round Valley in northern California, 200 miles (320 km) north of San Francisco (41).

Saanich. Southeastern side of Vancouver Island, British Columbia (182).

Salish. North of Vancouver Island on the mainland coast of British Columbia (178, 182, 183, 185).

Salish, Coast. North-central side of Vancouver Island and north of Vancouver Island on the mainland of British Columbia (182, 183).

Salish, Straits. Vancouver Island, British Columbia (186).

Samish. Northern coast of Washington, near the British Columbia border (79).

Sanel. Mendocino County, California (41).

San Felipe. The San Felipe pueblo is in New Mexico (32). See also Keresan.

San Ildefonso. The San Ildefonso pueblo is located about 20 miles (32 km) north of Santa Fe, New Mexico, on the eastern bank of the Rio Grande (138).

Sanpoil. South of the Columbia River in northeastern Washington (89, 131, 188).

Sanpoil & Nespelem. South of the Columbia River in northeastern Washington (131, 188).

Santa Clara. The Santa Clara pueblo is about 25 miles (40 km) north of Santa Fe, New Mexico, on the western bank of the Rio Grande (138).

Seminole. Southern Florida (169).

Seri. Isla Tiburon in the Gulf of California, Mexico (50).

Shasta. Along the Klamath River in northern California near the Oregon border (93, 117).

Shoshoni. Most Shoshoni are in Nevada, but they extend into Montana and central California (82, 97, 117, 118, 121, 180).

Shuswap. Southern interior plateau of British Columbia (89, 123, 178).

Sia. Sia (sometimes Zia) is a Keresan pueblo near Albuquerque, New Mexico (199). See also Keresan.

Sierra. California (41).

Sioux. The Sioux, also known as the Dakota or Lakota, hunted buffalo across the Great Plains from Minnesota to Wyoming and Montana (19, 82, 118, 153). See also Dakota and Lakota.

Skagit. Northwestern Washington (79).

Skagit, Upper. Northern Cascade Range, Washington (179).

Skokomish. West-central side of Puget Sound, Washington (79).

Snohomish. Northeastern side of Puget Sound, Washington (79).

Snuqualmie. Central Washington (79).

Southwest Indians. Southwestern United States (17).

Spanish American. Southwestern United States (32).

Spokan. The Spokan and Colville Reservations are in eastern Washington, and the Coeur d'Alene Reservation is in northwestern Idaho (178).

Squaxin. South of Puget Sound, Washington (79).

Swinomish. Northern coast of Washington (79).

Tanana, Upper. Alaska between Anchorage and Fairbanks (77, 102, 115).

Tewa. Near Santa Fe, New Mexico (17, 32, 42, 138).

Tewa of Hano. Near Santa Fe, New Mexico (138).

Thompson. Southwestern British Columbia (89, 125, 164, 178, 187).

Thompson, Lower. On the lower Fraser River in British Columbia (89).

Thompson, Upper (Lytton Band). Lytton, British Columbia (164).

Thompson, Upper (Nicola Band). Along the Nicola River from a few miles above Spences Bridge to above Nicola Lake in British Columbia (164).

Thompson, Upper (Spences Bridge). Along the Thompson River from Lytton to Ashcroft, British Columbia (164).

Tolowa. Northwestern California (6).

Tsimshian. Northern coast of British Columbia into the southeastern portion of the Alaska panhandle (43, 73, 74, 79).

Tubatulabal. California (193).

Umatilla. Along the Umatilla and Columbia Rivers in Oregon (45, 89).

Ute. Western Colorado and eastern Utah (32, 34, 38, 45, 118).

Wailaki. Round Valley Reservation is in Mendocino County, northern California (41, 118).

Walapai. Cataract Canyon, a side branch of the Grand Canyon in northwestern Arizona (17, 162, 197).

Warihio. Lower Colorado River valley (37).

Washo. Near Lake Tahoe on the California–Nevada border (10, 118, 121, 180).

Wet'suwet'en. East of the central coast of British Columbia (73).

Winnebago. Originally living near Green Bay, Wisconsin, the Winnebago now occupy reservations in Wisconsin and Nebraska (70, 130).

Wintoon. Central California (117).

Yana. Northern California (147).

Yaqui. Guadalupe, Arizona (47).

Yavapai. Western Arizona (17, 63, 65).

Yokia. Ukiah, Mendocino County, northern California (41).

Yokut. Central California (117).

Yuki. Round Valley, Mendocino County, northern California (9, 41, 48, 49, 103, 118).

Yuma. Lower Colorado River valley in Arizona (32, 34, 37).

Yurok. Northwestern California (6).

Yurok, South Coast (Nererner). Northwestern California (117).

Zuni. The Zuni pueblo is about 40 miles (64 km) southwest of Gallup, New Mexico (17, 27, 32, 34, 136, 166).

Organization of the Information in *Native American Food Plants*

Scientific Plant Names

The information in *Native American Food Plants* is organized in the Catalog of Plants alphabetically by the scientific names of the plants. Scientific plant names have a very particular form, for example, *Abies balsamea* for balsam fir. *Abies* is the genus and *balsamea* the species name, in combination called a binomial.

Some plant names are more complex than the example just given. In some species, botanists recognize a number of subspecies or naturally occurring varieties. Usually the rank of subspecies *or* variety is recognized in a particular species, but sometimes both ranks are used and then a subspecies may comprise more than one variety. For the purpose of completeness, the subspecies (abbreviated here as ssp.) and variety (var.) names are both given in this book, for example, for the full name of New Mexico giant hyssop, a plant used in a dozen or so ways by a number of Southwestern tribes, *Agastache pallidiflora* ssp. *neomexicana* var. *neomexicana*.

When reference is made to an unknown species of a particular genus, the abbreviation sp., for species, is used. A source may have referred to one unknown species of a genus or to more than one unknown species; sp. is used here for both kinds of references.

Species that are known to result from hybridization have a multiplication sign added to their names, for example, *Arctostaphylos* ×*cinerea*, formed by the hybridization *Arctostaphylos canescens* × *A. viscida*.

Common Plant Names

Although a correctly identified plant can be assigned one unique scientific name, common names for the plant may be several to many. Unlike scientific names, there are no rules of nomenclature governing common names, and different people in the same place or people in different places have bestowed their own names on plants. Not all names so applied have been adopted by others and have been forgotten, and some plants do not have truly commonly used names at all. The common name included in the Catalog of Plants is not necessarily the one used by ethnobotanists reporting on usage. And because various ethnobotanists may have used different common names for the various usages of the plant, usually more than one common name appears in the original sources. When one is available, what has generally been chosen is, instead, a relatively standard common name established by the U.S. Department of Agriculture Natural Resources Conservation Service. The common names used by the various ethnobotanists are cross-referenced in the Index of Common Names, however, so that the information on Native American plant use may be found even if one does not know the scientific name of the plant.

Unfortunately, with few exceptions the names applied to plants by Native Americans, their common names for the plants, have not been recorded in the sources and are not indexed. With so many Native American languages, it would require a separate, large book to treat the American Indian names of plants as comprehensively as their uses are cataloged here.

Ethnobotanical Information

Under each plant name, food usages are divided alphabetically by tribe, all the names of which are listed in the previous chapter under Native Americans. Following the tribe name are all the uses of the plant, listed alphabetically according to the categories defined in the previous chapter under Food Usage Categories.

The statement or statements on usage are followed by an abbreviated reference, for example, (184:197). The reference applies to all preceding statements, even if the reference is separated from the particular statement, for example, by the italicized name of a different usage category or the boldfaced name of a different tribe. The number preceding the colon refers to the source from which the information came, and sources are enumerated in the Bibliography. The number following the colon is the page number in that original source. When the original source used a plant name differing from that adopted in the Catalog of Plants, that is, the source cited a synonymous name, the plant name used in the source is also given within the parentheses, for example, within the entry for *Lens culinaris* (as *L. esculenta* 34:33). When differences are minor, however, such as insignificant differences in spelling, these variations are not given.

Two comprehensive Plant Usage Indexes are provided so that the information collected in the Catalog of Plants can be found in ways other than by plant name. In the Index of Tribes, plant usages are listed under the names of Native American groups, which are arranged alphabetically. Particular food usages are listed alphabetically. Plants are identified to the level of species. If subspecies or varieties appear in the Catalog of Plants, check under those names, too, for all usages given. For example, one may find Thompson in the index and under Candy see that *Agoseris glauca* was used. The specific ethnobotanical information and the sources from which the information was obtained may be found by turning to *Agoseris glauca* and *Agoseris glauca* var. *dasycephala* in the Catalog of Plants.

In the Index of Usages, plants are listed under the categories of food usage and then alphabetically by the particular usage. Plants are identified to the level of genus. For all usages given, check all entries under that genus in the Catalog of Plants. For example, one may find Fruit and see that *Aronia* was used by the Abnaki and Potawatomi. The specific ethnobotanical information and the sources from which the information was obtained may be found by turning to *Aronia* in the Catalog of Plants and examining Fruit under the entries for that genus.

Catalog of Plants

Abies amabilis, Pacific Silver Fir
Haisla *Unspecified* Cambium used for food.
(73:151) **Kitasoo** *Unspecified* Inner bark used
for food. (43:316) **Nitinaht** *Candy* Hardened
pitch chewed for pleasure. (186:71)

Abies balsamea, Balsam Fir
Micmac *Beverage* Bark used to make a beverage. (159:258)

Abies grandis, Grand Fir
Nitinaht *Candy* Hardened pitch chewed for
pleasure. (186:71) **Shuswap** *Beverage* Gum
from inside the bark, next to the trunk, made
into a drink. *Candy* Gum from inside the bark,
next to the trunk, chewed. (123:50) **Thompson**
Beverage Branch tips sometimes steeped to
make a tea-like beverage. (187:97)

Abies lasiocarpa, Subalpine Fir
Blackfoot *Candy* Cones pulverized into a fine
powder, mixed with back fat and marrow, and
eaten as a confection. The fragments of the
cones were left by squirrels and chipmunks and
gathered by the Indians to make the confection.
The confection was distributed during social
gatherings and meetings. It was an aid to diges-
tion as well as a delicacy. (86:100) Resin
chewed for bad breath and pleasure. (86:123)
Shuswap *Unspecified* Seeds used for food.
(123:50) **Thompson** *Unspecified* Inner bark
used for food. (187:97)

Abronia fragrans, Snowball Sand
  Verbena
Acoma *Unspecified* Roots ground, mixed with

cornmeal, and eaten. **Laguna** *Unspecified*
Roots ground, mixed with cornmeal, and eaten.
(32:39)

Abronia latifolia, Coastal Sand Verbena
Clallam *Unspecified* Roots used for food.
(57:201) **Klallam** *Unspecified* Roots used for
food. **Makah** *Unspecified* Roots eaten in the
fall. (79:29)

Acacia greggii, Catclaw Acacia
Cahuilla *Porridge* Dried pods ground into flour
and used to make mush or cakes. *Vegetable*
Pods eaten fresh. (15:29) **Diegueño** *Fodder*
Used to feed domesticated animals. (88:218)
Havasupai *Bread & Cake* Seeds stored, roasted,
ground, and made into bread. (197:225) **Pima**
Unspecified Beans formerly used for food.
(146:76) **Pima, Gila River** *Starvation Food*
Seeds used as "starvation food." (133:7) **Seri**
Porridge Beans ground into a meal, mixed with
water or sea lion oil, and eaten. (50:136)

Acer circinatum, Vine Maple
Clallam *Dried Food* Sap eaten dried. *Unspecified* Sap eaten fresh. (57:197)

Acer glabrum, Rocky Mountain Maple
Blackfoot *Spice* Dried, crushed leaves used to
spice stored meat. (86:100)

Acer glabrum var. **neomexicanum**, New Mexico Maple
Apache, Chiricahua & Mescalero *Sweetener*
Sap collected and boiled to obtain syrup and
sugar. (as *A. neomexicana* 33:44)

Acer macrophyllum, Bigleaf Maple
Clallam *Dried Food* Sap eaten dried. *Unspecified* Sap eaten fresh. (57:197) **Costanoan** *Unspecified* Seeds used for food. (21:248) **Cowichan** *Spice* Leaves used in steaming pits to flavor deer, seal, or porpoise meat. **Saanich** *Spice* Leaves used in steaming pits to flavor deer, seal, or porpoise meat. **Salish, Coast** *Unspecified* Cambium eaten in small quantities with oil. (182:77) **Thompson** *Sauce & Relish* Sap boiled to make a type of maple syrup. *Unspecified* Raw shoots used for food. *Vegetable* Sprouted seeds boiled and eaten as green vegetables. The sprouted seeds were generally bitter, but the young shoots were considered to be quite sweet and juicy. (187:147)

Acer negundo, Box Elder
Apache, Chiricahua & Mescalero *Dried Food* Inner bark scrapings dried and kept for winter use. *Sweetener* Inner bark boiled until sugar crystallizes out of it. (33:44) **Cheyenne** *Candy* Sap mixed with shavings from inner sides of animal hides and eaten as candy. (82:4) Sap boiled, added to animal hide shavings, and eaten as a relished candy. (83:13) **Dakota** *Sweetener* Sap used to make sugar. (69:366)

Acer negundo

Montana Indian *Sauce & Relish* Sap boiled or frozen and used as a sweet syrup. (82:4) **Ojibwa** *Beverage* Sap mixed with the sap of the sugar maple and used as a beverage. (153:394) **Omaha** *Sweetener* Sap boiled to make sugar and syrup. (68:329) Sap used to make sugar. **Pawnee** *Sweetener* Sap used to make sugar. **Ponca** *Sweetener* Sap used to make sugar. **Winnebago** *Sweetener* Sap used to make sugar. (70:101)

Acer negundo* var. *interius, Box Elder
Cree *Sweetener* Sap used to make sugar. (97:44)

Acer negundo* var. *negundo, Box Elder
Sioux *Staple* Sap boiled down in the spring and made into sugar. (as *Negundo aceroides* 19:16)

Acer nigrum, Black Maple
Ojibwa *Sweetener* Sap used to make sugar. (as *A. saccharinum* var. *nigrum* 135:234)

Acer pensylvanicum, Striped Maple
Micmac *Beverage* Bark used to make a beverage. (159:258)

Acer rubrum, Red Maple
Abnaki *Sweetener* Used as a sweetener. (144:152) Sap used to make sugar. (144:170) **Algonquin, Quebec** *Sauce & Relish* Sap used to make syrup. *Sweetener* Sap used to make sugar. (18:99) **Iroquois** *Bread & Cake* Bark dried, pounded, sifted, and made into bread. (as *A. rubra* 196:119)

Acer saccharinum, Silver Maple
Chippewa *Sweetener* Sap used to make sugar. (71:136) **Dakota** *Sweetener* Sap used to make sugar. (70:100) **Iroquois** *Beverage* Sap, thimbleberries, and water used to make a drink for home consumption and longhouse ceremonies. (196:142) Sap fermented and used as an intoxicant. (196:146) *Bread & Cake* Bark dried, pounded, sifted, and made into bread. (196:119) *Sweetener* Sap used to make sugar. (196:142) **Ojibwa** *Sweetener* Sap used to make sugar. (135:234) **Omaha** *Sweetener* Sap boiled

to make sugar and syrup. (68:328) Sap used to make sugar. **Ponca** *Sweetener* Sap used to make sugar. **Winnebago** *Sweetener* Sap used to make sugar. (70:100)

Acer saccharum, Sugar Maple
Algonquin, Quebec *Sauce & Relish* Sap used to make syrup. *Sweetener* Sap used to make sugar. (18:98) **Cherokee** *Sweetener* Juice used to make sugar. (80:44) Sap used to make sugar. (126:32) **Dakota** *Sweetener* Sap formerly used to make sugar. (70:100) **Iroquois** *Beverage* Sap made into sugar and used to make beer. (as *A. saccharophorum* 141:52) Sap, thimble-berries, and water used to make a drink for home consumption and longhouse ceremonies. (196:142) Sap fermented and used as an intoxicant. (196:146) *Bread & Cake* Bark dried, pounded, sifted, and made into bread. (196:119) *Sweetener* Sap used to make sugar. (as *A. saccharophorum* 141:52) Sap used to make sugar. (196:142) **Malecite** *Sauce & Relish* Used to make maple syrup. *Sweetener* Used to make maple syrup and sugar. (160:6) **Menominee** *Sweetener* Boiled sap made into maple sugar and used in almost every combination of cookery. (151:61) **Meskwaki** *Sweetener* Maple sugar used instead of salt as seasoning in cooking. (152:255) **Micmac** *Beverage* Bark used to make a beverage. *Sauce & Relish* Sap used to make maple syrup and maple sugar. (159:258) **Mohegan** *Sweetener* Sap used as a sweetening agent and to make maple syrup. (176:69) **Ojibwa** *Beverage* Sap saved to drink as it comes from the tree, alone or mixed with box elder or birch sap. *Sour* Sap allowed to sour to make vinegar and mixed with maple sugar to cook sweet and sour meat. *Sweetener* Maple sugar used to season all kinds of meats, replaced now with salt. Smith describes in detail the process by which the Ojibwe make maple syrup. Although now (1932) they use iron kettles, originally the sap and storage vessels were "made of birch bark, sewed with boiled basswood fiber or the core of the jack pine root." The vessels are rendered waterproof by the application of pitch secured by boiling jack pine cones. (153:394) **Potawatomi** *Beverage* Maple sap, as

it came from the tree, drunk by children. *Candy* Children made taffy by cooling the maple sap in the snow. *Sour* Maple sap not only furnished the sugar for seasoning material but also furnished the vinegar. Sap that was allowed to become sour made a vinegar to be used in cooking venison which was afterwards sweetened with maple sugar. This corresponds somewhat to the German "sweet and sour" style of cooking. *Sweetener* Maple sugar used, instead of salt, to season all cooking. The sugar maple and the black sugar maple are found all over Wisconsin and were considered to be the most valuable trees in the forest because they furnished them their seasoning material. While they do use salt today, it is an acquired ingredient and most of the old people would prefer to have sugar for their seasoning. (154:92)

Achillea millefolium, Common Yarrow
Blackfoot *Beverage* Leaves and flowers used to make a pleasant tea. (86:100) **Haisla & Hanaksiala** *Forage* Plant eaten by bears. (43:220) **Klamath** *Preservative* Stem, leaf, and flower placed inside fish cavity as a preservative. (45:105)

Acorus calamus, Calamus
Abnaki *Unspecified* Roots used for food. (144:175) **Dakota** *Unspecified* Dried root chewed for the agreeable taste. (69:359) **Lakota** *Unspecified* Leaves and stalks used for food. (139:26) **Micmac** *Beverage* Used to make a beverage. (159:258)

Adenostoma sparsifolium,
    Redshank
Cahuilla *Unspecified* Seeds used for food. (15:30) **Coahuilla** *Unspecified* Seeds used for food. (13:77)

Aesculus californica, California
    Buckeye
Costanoan *Fruit* Fruit used for food. (21:252) **Kawaiisu** *Bread & Cake* Seeds pounded, leached, boiled into a mush, made into a cake, and eaten with meat. (206:10) **Mendocino Indian** *Forage* Fruits eaten by squirrels as forage.

Fruit Fruits roasted and eaten cold without salt. (41:366) **Miwok** *Soup* Roasted, peeled nuts ground into a meal and used to make soup. *Winter Use Food* Nuts stored for long periods and resorted to only when the acorn crop failed. (12:148) **Modesse** *Starvation Food* Nuts eaten in times of need. (117:223) **Pomo, Kashaya** *Unspecified* Boiled nuts eaten with baked kelp, meat, and seafood. Nuts were put into boiling water to loosen the husk. After the husk was removed, the nutmeat was returned to boiling water and cooked until it was soft like cooked potatoes. The nutmeat was then mashed with a mortar stone. The grounds could be strained at this stage or strained after soaking. The grounds would be soaked and leached a long time to remove the poisonous tannin. An older method was to peel the nuts and roast them in ashes until they were soft. They were then crushed and the meal was put in a sandy leaching basin beside a stream. For about 5 hours, the meal was leached with water from the stream. When the bitterness disappeared it was ready to eat without further cooking. (72:27) **Tubatulabal** *Unspecified* Nuts used for food. (193:15) **Yana** *Staple* Nuts ground into a fine meal and eaten. (147:251) **Yuki** *Unspecified* Nutmeats mashed and used for food. (49:85)

Agaricus campestris
Delaware *Unspecified* Salted, boiled, or fried in fat and used for food. (176:60) **Pomo, Kashaya** *Vegetable* Baked on hot rocks or in the oven or fried. (72:130)

Agaricus silvicola, Deer Mushroom
Pomo, Kashaya Plant top cooked on a flat hot rock and eaten. (72:129)

Agastache foeniculum, Blue Giant Hyssop
Cheyenne *Beverage* Leaves used to make tea. (as *A. anethiodora* 76:186) **Cree, Woodlands** *Beverage* Leaves added to store bought tea to improve the flavor. (109:26) **Dakota** *Beverage* Leaves used to make a hot, tea-like beverage taken with meals. *Sweetener* Plant used as a sweetening flavor in cooking. (as *A. anethio-*

Agastache foeniculum

dora 70:113) **Lakota** *Beverage* Used to make tea. (139:49) **Omaha** *Beverage* Leaves used to make a hot, tea-like beverage taken with meals. *Sweetener* Plant used as a sweetening flavor in cooking. **Pawnee** *Beverage* Leaves used to make a hot, tea-like beverage taken with meals. *Sweetener* Plant used as a sweetening flavor in cooking. **Ponca** *Beverage* Leaves used to make a hot, tea-like beverage taken with meals. *Sweetener* Plant used as a sweetening flavor in cooking. **Winnebago** *Beverage* Leaves used to make a hot, tea-like beverage taken with meals. *Sweetener* Plant used as a sweetening flavor in cooking. (as *A. anethiodora* 70:113)

Agastache pallidiflora ssp. neo-mexicana var. neomexicana, New Mexico Giant Hyssop
Acoma *Spice* Leaves used for flavoring. (as *A. neo-mexicana* 32:34) **Apache** *Staple* Used as one of the most important foods. **Comanche** *Staple* Used as one of the most important foods. (as *A. neo-mexicana* 32:10) **Keres, Western** *Spice* Leaves mixed with meat for seasoning. (as *Agastrache neo-mexicana* 171:24) **Laguna** *Spice* Leaves used for flavoring. (as *Agastache neo-mexicana* 32:34) **Mohave** *Staple* Used as one of the most important foods. **Paiute** *Staple*

Used as one of the most important foods. **Papago** *Staple* Used as one of the most important foods. **Ute** *Staple* Used as one of the most important foods. **Yuma** *Staple* Used as one of the most important foods. (as *A. neo-mexicana* 32:10)

Agastache urticifolia, Nettleleaf Giant Hyssop
Gosiute *Unspecified* Seeds formerly used for food. (as *Lophanthus urticifolius* 39:374)

Agave americana, American Century Plant
Apache *Dried Food* Heads and young leaves roasted, sun dried, and used immediately or stored. *Staple* Used as one of the most important foods. (32:10) **Apache, White Mountain** *Beverage* "Hearts" and roots pit baked, crushed, and fermented into an intoxicating beverage. (136:145) *Unspecified* Tubers pit baked and eaten. (136:155) *Winter Use Food* Tubers pit baked and stored for future use. (136:145) **Comanche** *Staple* Used as one of the most important foods. **Mohave** *Staple* Used as one of the most important foods. **Paiute** *Staple* Used as one of the most important foods. **Papago** *Staple* Used as one of the most important foods. (32:10) *Unspecified* Pit baked and extensively used for food. (34:16) Pit baked and used for food. (36:61) *Vegetable* Crowns with leaves removed eaten as greens in winter. Central flowering stalks eaten as greens in spring before they emerged. (34:14) Flower stalks eaten as greens. (34:16) Pit baked and used as greens. Flower stalks roasted in ashes and eaten as greens. (34:46) **Pima** *Dried Food* Fruit heads roasted, centers sun dried and used for food. *Sauce & Relish* Juice boiled and used as a syrup. *Starvation Food* Used for food in times of famine. (146:70) **Ute** *Staple* Used as one of the most important foods. **Yuma** *Staple* Used as one of the most important foods. (32:10)

Agave decipiens, False Sisal
Apache, White Mountain *Beverage* Heart and tubers used to make a fermented drink. *Unspecified* Tubers pit baked and eaten. (136:155)

Agave deserti, Desert Agave
Cahuilla *Dried Food* Flowers parboiled to release the bitterness and dried for future use. Baked leaves dried and stored for future use. Roasted, pounded stalks and leaves made into cakes and sun dried. *Unspecified* Flowers parboiled to release the bitterness and eaten. Baked leaves eaten. Roasted stalks used for food. (15:31) **Cocopa** *Unspecified* Crowns gathered and pit baked. (37:202) **Diegueño** *Unspecified* Roots and stalks baked overnight in a pit oven and used for food. (84:13) **Papago** *Unspecified* Pit baked and used for food. (36:61) **Pima** *Candy* Heads baked, sliced, dried, and eaten like candy. *Unspecified* Heads pit baked and eaten with pinole. (47:48) **Pima, Gila River** *Candy* Plant dried and used as sweets. (133:6) *Dried Food* Hearts dried and stored indefinitely. (133:4) *Staple* Hearts pit roasted and used as a staple food. (133:7)

Agave palmeri, Palmer's Century Plant
Apache, Western *Beverage* Juice fermented into a drink. Crowns cooked, fermented in a vessel, ground, boiled, and the liquor again fermented. Juice strained and mixed with "tiswin water," a liquor of fermented maize. Flower stalk baked and chewed for juice. *Candy* Heart of the crown eaten by children as candy. *Dried Food* Plant eaten dried. *Substitution Food* Used in absence of other foods. *Unspecified* Crowns used for food. (26:169) **Papago** *Unspecified* Pit baked and used for food. (36:61)

Agave parryi, Parry's Agave
Apache *Dried Food* Heads and young leaves roasted, sun dried, and used immediately or stored. Heads and young leaves roasted, sun dried, and used immediately or stored. *Staple* Used as one of the most important foods. (32:10) *Unspecified* Roots baked and eaten. (32:13) **Apache, Chiricahua & Mescalero** *Unspecified* Bulbous crowns baked in pits, pulpy centers released, pounded into thin sheets, and eaten. The Mescalero Apache were named for the food they made from mescal. In the pits where the crowns were baked, the largest rock was placed in the center and a cross

made on it from black ashes. While the mescal baked, the women were supposed to stay away from their husbands, and if the crown was not completely roasted when removed from the pit, they were believed to have disobeyed. (33:35) Stalks roasted, boiled, or eaten raw. *Vegetable* Stalks boiled, dried, and stored to be used as vegetables. (33:38) **Apache, Mescalero** *Bread & Cake* Leaf bases pit cooked, made into cakes, dried, and used for food. (14:30) **Apache, Western** *Beverage* Juice fermented into a drink. Crowns cooked, fermented in a vessel, ground, boiled, and the liquor again fermented. Juice strained and mixed with "tiswin water," a liquor of fermented maize. Flower stalk baked and chewed for juice. *Candy* Heart of the crown eaten by children as candy. *Dried Food* Plant eaten dried. Plant eaten dried. *Substitution Food* Used in absence of other foods. Used in absence of other foods. *Unspecified* Crowns used for food. (26:169) **Comanche** *Staple* Used as one of the most important foods. **Mohave** *Staple* Used as one of the most important foods. **Paiute** *Staple* Used as one of the most important foods. **Papago** *Staple* Used as one of the most important foods. **Ute** *Staple* Used as one of the most important foods. **Yuma** *Staple* Used as one of the most important foods. (32:10)

Agave schottii, Schott's Century Plant
Papago *Unspecified* Pit baked and used for food. (36:61)

Agave utahensis, Utah Agave
Havasupai *Beverage* Plant used to make a drink. (197:66)

Agoseris aurantiaca, Orange Agoseris
Karok *Candy* Root juice used for chewing gum. (as *A. gracilens* 148:389)

Agoseris aurantiaca* var. *aurantiaca, Orange Agoseris
Gosiute *Unspecified* Leaves used for food. (as *Troximon aurantiacum* 39:383)

Agoseris glauca, Pale Agoseris
Thompson *Candy* Milky juice chewed as gum. (as *A. villosa* 164:493)

Agoseris glauca* var. *dasycephala, Pale Agoseris
Okanagan-Colville *Candy* Latex dried and used as chewing gum. (188:74) **Thompson** *Candy* Milky latex used as chewing gum. (187:167)

Agoseris retrorsa, Spearleaf Agoseris
Kawaiisu *Vegetable* Green leaves boiled and eaten. Whole plant above the ground boiled, washed in cold water to remove bitterness, and fried in grease. (206:10)

***Agropyron* sp.**, Wheat Grass
Paiute *Unspecified* Species used for food. (167:243)

Agrostis perennans, Upland Bentgrass
Klamath *Unspecified* Seeds used for food. (45:91)

Alaria marginata, Short Kelp
Hesquiat *Dried Food* Stipes and fronds with attached herring eggs dried for later use. (185:24)

Alectoria fremontii, Black Moss
Montana Indian *Starvation Food* Long, black, hair-like lichen used as a famine food. (19:5)

Alectoria jubata
Coeur d'Alene *Unspecified* Formerly used for food. (black tree moss 178:91) **Spokan** *Unspecified* Species used for food. (black tree moss 178:344) **Thompson** *Unspecified* Plant cooked and eaten. (black moss 164:482)

Alectoria nigricans, Caribou Moss
Eskimo, Inuktitut *Fodder* Plant given to fawns to try to get them to eat from their hands. (202:191)

Alectoria nitidula, Caribou Moss
Eskimo, Inuktitut *Fodder* Plant given to fawns

to try to get them to eat from their hands. (202:191)

Alectoria ochroleuca, Caribou Moss
Eskimo, Inuktitut *Fodder* Plant given to fawns to try to get them to eat from their hands. (202:191)

Aletes anisatus, Rocky Mountain Indian Parsley
Isleta *Sauce & Relish* Leaves eaten fresh as a relish. (as *Pseudocymopterus aletifolius* 32:47) Raw leaves eaten as a relish. (as *Pseudocymopterus aletifolius* 100:40) *Vegetable* Leaves cooked and used as greens. (as *Pseudocymopterus aletifolius* 32:47) Cooked leaves eaten as greens. (as *Pseudocymopterus aletifolius* 100:40)

Alisma plantago-aquatica, American Water Plantain
Iroquois *Beverage* Plant made into a tea and used by forest runners. (141:65)

Allenrolfea occidentalis, Iodine Bush
Cahuilla *Beverage* Ground seed flour and water made into a drink. *Bread & Cake* Ground seed flour dampened, shaped, dried, and eaten as a cookie. *Porridge* Ground seed flour and water made into a mush. (15:36) **Maricopa** *Staple* Seeds harvested, winnowed, parched, ground, and the meal eaten. **Mohave** *Staple* Seeds harvested, winnowed, parched, ground, and the meal eaten. (37:187) **Pima** *Unspecified* Ripe seeds winnowed, roasted, ground, water added, cooked, and used for food. (47:69) **Pima, Gila River** *Starvation Food* Seeds used as "starvation food." (133:6) *Unspecified* Seeds used for food. (133:7) **Yuma** *Staple* Seeds harvested, winnowed, parched, ground, and the meal eaten. (37:187)

Allium acuminatum, Tapertip Onion
Gosiute *Unspecified* Bulbs eaten in spring and early summer. (39:360) **Hoh** *Unspecified* Bulbs pit baked and used for food. (137:59) **Karok** *Unspecified* Bulbs relished by only old men and old women. (148:380) **Paiute** *Sauce & Relish*

Leaves eaten as a relish. *Unspecified* Bulbs roasted and used for food. Seeded heads placed in hot ashes for a few minutes, seeds extracted and eaten. (104:102) *Vegetable* Onions eaten raw, boiled, or baked in a pit. (111:55) **Quileute** *Unspecified* Bulbs pit baked and used for food. (137:59) **Salish, Coast** *Unspecified* Strongly flavored bulbs eaten with other foods. (182:74) **Thompson** *Unspecified* Thick coated, spherical bulbs eaten. (164:482) Bulbs dug in the spring and used for food. (187:117) **Ute** *Unspecified* Bulbs and leaves used for food. (38:32)

Allium anceps, Twinleaf Onion
Paiute, Northern *Bread & Cake* Bulbs cooked on hot rocks, squeezed into cakes, and eaten. *Unspecified* Bulbs roasted in the sand and eaten. (59:44)

Allium bisceptrum, Twincrest Onion
Apache, White Mountain *Unspecified* Bulbs eaten raw and cooked. (136:155) **Gosiute** *Unspecified* Bulbs eaten in spring and early summer. (39:360) **Paiute** *Sauce & Relish* Leaves eaten as a relish. *Unspecified* Seeded heads placed in hot ashes for a few minutes, seeds extracted and eaten. Bulbs roasted and used for food. (104:102) **Ute** *Unspecified* Bulbs and leaves used for food. (38:32)

Allium bisceptrum var. ***palmeri***, Aspen Onion
Havasupai *Starvation Food* Bulbs eaten only when very hungry. (as *A. palmeri* 197:211)

Allium bolanderi, Bolander's Onion
Karok *Unspecified* Bulbs relished by only old men and old women. (148:380) **Mendocino Indian** *Unspecified* Corms used for food. (41:322)

Allium canadense, Meadow Garlic
Cherokee *Vegetable* Boiled bulbs fried with grease and greens. (126:46) **Iroquois** *Vegetable* Cooked and seasoned with salt, pepper, or butter. Bulb, consisting of the fleshy bases of the leaves, eaten raw. (196:118) **Menominee**

Unspecified Small, wild onion used for food. (151:69) **Meskwaki** *Spice* Dried bulb used for seasoning. *Winter Use Food* Dried bulb used for winter cookery. (152:262) **Potawatomi** *Soup* Very strong flavor of this plant, a valuable wild food, used in soup. (154:104)

Allium canadense var. *mobilense*,
Meadow Garlic

Dakota *Sauce & Relish* Fresh, raw bulbs used as a relish. *Spice* Bulbs used as a flavor for meat and soup. *Unspecified* Fried bulbs used for food. **Omaha** *Sauce & Relish* Fresh, raw bulbs used as a relish. *Spice* Bulbs used as a flavor for meat and soup. *Unspecified* Fried bulbs used for food. **Pawnee** *Sauce & Relish* Fresh, raw bulbs used as a relish. *Spice* Bulbs used as a flavor for meat and soup. *Unspecified* Fried bulbs used for food. **Ponca** *Sauce & Relish* Fresh, raw bulbs used as a relish. *Spice* Bulbs used as a flavor for meats and soups. *Unspecified* Fried bulbs used for food. **Winnebago** *Sauce & Relish* Fresh, raw bulbs used as a relish. *Spice* Bulbs used as a flavor for meat and soup. *Unspecified* Fried bulbs used for food. (as *A. mutabile* 70:71)

Allium cepa, Garden Onion
Haisla & Hanaksiala *Vegetable* Bulbs used for

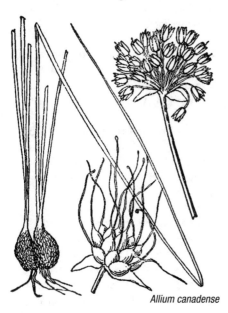

Allium canadense

food. (43:194) **Havasupai** *Unspecified* Bulbs used for food. (197:212) **Navajo** *Unspecified* Onions singed, to remove the strong taste, and eaten immediately. *Winter Use Food* Onions singed, to remove the strong taste, dried, and stored for winter use. (55:31) **Navajo, Ramah** *Unspecified* Species used for food. (191:20) **Neeshenam** *Unspecified* Eaten raw, roasted, or boiled. (129:377) **Oweekeno** *Unspecified* Bulbs used for food. (43:77) **Seminole** *Unspecified* Plant used for food. (169:505)

Allium cernuum, Nodding Onion
Apache, Chiricahua & Mescalero *Spice* Onions used to flavor soups and gravies. *Vegetable* Onions occasionally eaten raw. (33:47) **Bella Coola** *Unspecified* Bulbs eaten fresh. (184:199) **Blackfoot** *Spice* Bulbs and leaves used as flavoring. *Vegetable* Bulbs and leaves eaten raw. (97:23) **Cherokee** *Unspecified* Bulbs used for food. (80:47) **Clallam** *Unspecified* Bulbs eaten raw, cooked in pits, or fried with meat. (57:196) **Cree** *Vegetable* Species used for food. (16:485) **Flathead** *Sauce & Relish* Bulbs used as condiments. *Staple* Bulbs used as a staple food. (82:10) **Haisla & Hanaksiala** *Vegetable* Bulbs cooked and eaten and the tops eaten fresh with meat. (43:193) **Hoh** *Unspecified* Bulbs pit baked and used for food. (137:59) **Hopi** *Spice* Used for flavoring before the introduction of the cultivated onion. (200:70) *Unspecified* Eaten raw with cornmeal dumplings or fresh piki bread. (120:20) **Isleta** *Vegetable* Bulbs eaten fresh, uncooked, or boiled. *Winter Use Food* Bulbs stored for future use. (100:20) **Keres, Western** *Vegetable* Bulbs used for food. (171:25) **Klallam** *Unspecified* Bulbs used for food. (79:24) **Kutenai** *Sauce & Relish* Bulbs used as condiments. *Staple* Bulbs used as a staple food. (82:10) **Kwakiutl, Southern** *Unspecified* Bulbs cooked and used for food. (183:272) **Makah** *Unspecified* Bulbs used for food. (67:338) Bulbs eaten sparingly. (79:24) **Navajo** *Sauce & Relish* Bulbs used to make gravies. *Soup* Bulbs used to make soup. *Spice* Leaves finely chopped and used like chives in salads or sauces. (110:29) *Unspecified* Onions singed, to remove the strong taste, and eaten

immediately. (55:31) *Vegetable* Bulbs cooked with other vegetables. Roasted bulbs eaten with salt and pepper. (110:29) *Winter Use Food* Onions singed, to remove the strong taste, dried, and stored for winter use. (55:31) **Navajo, Ramah** *Dried Food* Bulbs, never the tops, dried for the winter. *Unspecified* Bulbs, never the tops, eaten raw, with fried or boiled meat. (191:20) **Nitinaht** *Unspecified* Bulbs used for food. (67:338) **Ojibwa** *Vegetable* Used in the spring as an article of food, the small wild onion was sweet. (153:406) **Okanagan-Colville** *Dried Food* Bulbs dried and stored for winter use. *Vegetable* Bulbs pit cooked and eaten. (188:38) **Okanagon** *Staple* Roots used as a principal food. (178:238) *Unspecified* Bulbs and leaves used for food. (125:37) **Oweekeno** *Unspecified* Bulbs used for food. (43:76) **Quileute** *Unspecified* Bulbs pit baked and used for food. (137:59) **Quinault** *Unspecified* Bulbs used for food. (79:24) **Salish, Coast** *Unspecified* Strongly flavored bulbs eaten with other foods. (182:74) **Shuswap** *Forage* Bulbs eaten by sheep and cattle. *Spice* Bulbs used to flavor dried salmon heated with dried bread on an open fire. (123:54) **Thompson** *Dried Food* Bulbs tied in bundles, partially dried, pit cooked, and used for food. Bulbs dried for winter storage. The dried bulbs were sprinkled with water and became just like fresh bulbs or they were soaked overnight in water. *Special Food* Cooked bulbs considered a delicacy. (187:117) *Unspecified* Bulbs and leaves used for food. (125:37) Thick bulbs cooked and eaten. (164:481)

Allium cernuum var. *obtusum*, Nodding Onion

Acoma *Unspecified* Bulbs used for food. (as *A. recurvatum* 32:15) **Blackfoot** *Spice* Bulbs used for flavoring. *Vegetable* Bulbs eaten raw. (as *A. recurvatum* 114:278) **Hopi** *Unspecified* Dipped in water with broken wafer bread and eaten raw. (as *A. recurvatum* 32:15) Bulbs washed and eaten raw with broken wafer bread dipped in water. (as *A. recurvatum* 138:53) **Isleta** *Unspecified* Bulbs eaten raw or boiled. **Laguna** *Unspecified* Bulbs used for food. **Tewa** *Unspec-*

ified Dipped in water with broken wafer bread and eaten raw. (as *A. recurvatum* 32:15) Bulbs washed and eaten raw with broken wafer bread dipped in water. (as *A. recurvatum* 138:53)

Allium dichlamydeum, Coastal Onion

Pomo, Kashaya *Vegetable* Greens and bulb eaten raw or cooked with potatoes or meats for flavoring. (72:86)

Allium douglasii, Douglas's Onion

Okanagan-Colville *Dried Food* and *Vegetable* Bulbs dried, pit cooked, and eaten. (188:38)

Allium drummondii, Drummond's Onion

Cheyenne *Spice* Boiled with meat, when salt scarce, to flavor the food. (as *A. nuttallii* 76:171) *Unspecified* Bulbs formerly boiled with meat and used for food. (as *A. nuttalii* 83:12) Species used for food. (as *A. nuttallii* 83:45) **Lakota** *Unspecified* Species used for food. (139:27) **Navajo, Ramah** *Unspecified* Bulbs boiled with meat. (191:20)

Allium falcifolium, Scytheleaf Onion

Shoshoni *Spice* Bulbs used for seasoning. (118:14)

Allium geyeri, Geyer's Onion

Apache *Unspecified* Bulbs used for food. (32:15) **Apache, Chiricahua & Mescalero** *Spice* Onions used to flavor soups and gravies. *Vegetable* Onions occasionally eaten raw. (33:47) **Hopi** *Spice* Used for flavoring before the introduction of the cultivated onion. (200:70) *Unspecified* Eaten raw with cornmeal dumplings or fresh piki bread. (120:20) **Okanagan-Colville** *Dried Food* and *Vegetable* Bulbs dried, pit cooked, and eaten. (188:38)

Allium geyeri var. *tenerum*, Bulbil Onion

Keres, Western *Spice* Bulbs used largely for seasoning. (as *A. sabulicola* 171:25) **Pueblo** *Spice* Bulbs used for seasoning. (as *A. sabulicola* 32:15)

Allium hyalinum, Glassy Onion
Tubatulabal *Unspecified* Leaves, stalks, and heads used for food. (193:12)

Allium lacunosum, Pitted Onion
Tubatulabal *Unspecified* Leaves, stalks, and heads used for food. (193:12)

Allium macropetalum, Largeflower Wild Onion
Navajo *Dried Food* Bulbs rubbed in hot ashes, dried, and stored for winter use. *Unspecified* Bulbs rubbed in hot ashes and eaten. (as *A. deserticolum* 32:15) Onions singed, to remove the strong taste, and eaten immediately. (as *A. deserticola* 55:31) *Vegetable* Entire plant eaten raw or cooked with meat. (as *A. deserticola* 165:221) *Winter Use Food* Onions singed, to remove the strong taste, dried, and stored for winter use. (as *A. deserticola* 55:31)

Allium nevadense, Nevada Onion
Paiute, Northern *Unspecified* Whole plant eaten raw. (59:44)

Allium parvum, Small Onion
Paiute, Northern *Dried Food* Bulbs dried and eaten. *Soup* Bulbs dried, ground, and cooked in soup. (59:44)

Allium peninsulare, Mexicali Onion
Tubatulabal *Unspecified* Leaves, stalks, and heads used for food. (193:12)

Allium platycaule, Broadstemmed Onion
Paiute *Sauce & Relish* Leaves eaten as a relish. *Unspecified* Bulbs roasted and used for food. Seeded heads placed in hot ashes for a few minutes, seeds extracted and eaten. (104:102)

Allium pleianthum, Manyflower Onion
Paiute *Sauce & Relish* Green leaves eaten as a relish. (104:102)

Allium sativum, Cultivated Garlic
Algonquin, Tête-de-Boule *Spice* Bulbs mixed with food and eaten. (132:118)

Allium schoenoprasum, Wild Chives
Alaska Native *Unspecified* Bulbs used sparingly. (85:113) **Cree, Woodlands** *Spice* Leaves added to boiled fish for flavor. *Unspecified* Fresh leaves used for food. (109:26) **Eskimo, Inuktitut** *Spice* Used as a soup condiment. (202:182) **Eskimo, Inupiat** *Soup* Bulbs and leaves used to make soup. *Vegetable* Leaves eaten cooked or raw with seal oil, meat, and fish. Leaves used like raw green onions or garlic in a salad. Leaves fried with meat, fat, other greens, vinegar, salt, and pepper and eaten as a hot salad. (98:28) **Koyukon** *Unspecified* Plant eaten raw, alone or with fish. (119:56) **Tanana, Upper** *Frozen Food* Stems and bulbs frozen for future use. *Unspecified* Stems and bulbs eaten raw, fried, or boiled. (102:15)

Allium schoenoprasum* var. *sibiricum, Wild Chives
Anticosti *Soup* Leaves salted and added to soup. (143:69) **Cheyenne** *Spice* Boiled with meat, when salt scarce, to flavor the food. (as *A. sibiricum* 76:171) *Unspecified* Species used for food. (as *A. sibiricum* 83:45) Bulbs formerly boiled with meat and used for food. (as *A. sibiricum* L. 83:12) **Great Basin Indian** *Unspecified* Bulbs used for food. (as *A. sibiricum* 121:46)

Allium textile, Textile Onion
Lakota *Soup* Bulbs cooked in stews. *Unspecified* Bulbs eaten fresh or stored for future use. (106:50)

Allium tricoccum, Wild Leek
Cherokee *Unspecified* Species used for food. (80:52) Young plants boiled, fried, and eaten. (204:251) *Vegetable* Bulbs and leaves cooked like poke, with or without eggs. (126:47) **Iroquois** *Vegetable* Cooked and seasoned with salt, pepper, or butter. Bulb, consisting of the fleshy bases of the leaves, eaten raw. (196:118) **Menominee** *Winter Use Food* Large, wild onion dried for winter use. (151:69) **Ojibwa** *Dried Food* Large, bitter, wild leek gathered in spring and dried for future use. (153:406) **Potawatomi** *Vegetable* Large, wild onion used for food. (154:104)

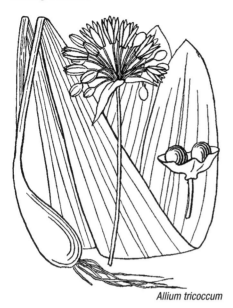

Allium tricoccum

Allium unifolium, Oneleaf Onion
Mendocino Indian *Unspecified* Bulbs and leaf bases fried and eaten. (41:323) **Papago** *Unspecified* Bulbs used for food. (32:15) **Pomo** *Spice* Bulbs cooked with other bulbs as a seasoning. *Unspecified* Bulbs eaten raw or baked. (11:89) **Yuki** *Unspecified* Bulbs eaten raw or fried. (49:86)

Allium validum, Pacific Onion
Cahuilla *Spice* Bulbs used as a flavoring ingredient for other foods. *Vegetable* Bulbs eaten raw. (15:37)

Allium vineale, Wild Garlic
Hopi *Unspecified* Bulb used for food. (190:159)

Alnus rhombifolia, White Alder
Costanoan *Unspecified* Inner bark used for food. (21:248) **Karok** *Preservative* Wood used to smoke salmon, eels, and deer meat. (148:382)

Alnus rubra, Red Alder
Clallam *Sweetener* Sap mixed with soapberry whip as a sweetener. (57:198) **Haisla & Hanaksiala** *Preservative* Wood used to smoke fish and meat. (43:224) **Salish, Coast** *Unspecified*

Cambium eaten fresh with oil in spring. (182:79) **Skagit, Upper** *Unspecified* Sap used for food. (179:42) **Swinomish** *Unspecified* Sap taken from the inside of the bark only with the incoming tide and used as food. (as *A. oregona* 79:27)

Alnus viridis* ssp. *crispa, American Green Alder
Tanana, Upper *Preservative* Wood used to smoke fish. (as *A. crispa* 102:5)

Aloysia wrightii, Wright's Beebrush
Havasupai *Beverage* Leaves boiled into tea. (197:238) Twigs boiled to make tea. (197:66)

Amaranthus acanthochiton, Greenstripe
Hopi *Starvation Food* Used numerous times to ward off famines. (as *Acanthochiton wrightii* 200:74) *Vegetable* Cooked as greens. (as *Acanthochiton wrightii* 32:10) Cooked with meat and eaten as greens. (as *Acanthochiton wrightii* 200:74)

Amaranthus albus, Prostrate Pigweed
Apache, Chiricahua & Mescalero *Bread & Cake* Seeds winnowed, ground into flour and used to make bread. (as *A. graecizans* 33:48) *Unspecified* Eaten without preparation or cooked with green chile and meat or animal bones. (as *A. graecizans* 33:46) **Apache, White Mountain** *Unspecified* Seeds used for food. (136:155) **Cochiti** *Vegetable* Young plants eaten as greens. (as *A. graecizans* 32:16) **Navajo, Ramah** *Staple* Threshed seeds ground into flour. (as *A. graecizans* 191:25)

Amaranthus arenicola, Sandhill Amaranth
Hopi *Unspecified* Leaves boiled and eaten with meat. (as *A. torreyi* 56:18) Boiled with meat. Boiled with meat. (as *Amblogyne torreyi* 190:162)

Amaranthus blitoides, Mat Amaranth
Acoma *Dried Food* Young plants boiled and dried for winter use. (32:15) *Staple* Seeds ground into meal. (32:22) *Vegetable* Young

plants boiled and eaten as greens. (32:15) **Apache, White Mountain** *Unspecified* Seeds used for food. (136:155) **Hopi** *Porridge* Ground seeds used to make mush. (190:162) *Unspecified* Seeds used as food. (32:22) Seeds formerly prized as a food. (56:18) Seeds eaten for food. *Vegetable* Cooked and eaten as greens. (200:74) **Klamath** *Unspecified* Seeds used for food. (45:96) **Laguna** *Dried Food* Young plants boiled and dried for winter use. (32:15) *Staple* Seeds ground into meal. (32:22) *Vegetable* Young plants boiled and eaten as greens. (32:15) **Montana Indian** *Unspecified* Seeds formerly used as articles of the diet. *Vegetable* Used as a potherb. (19:6) **Navajo** *Forage* Plant used as sheep forage. *Porridge* Seeds ground into meal and made into stiff porridge or mixed with goat's milk and made into gruel. *Staple* Seeds ground into a meal and used for food. (55:45) *Vegetable* Boiled and eaten like spinach, boiled and fried in lard, or canned. **Pueblo** *Vegetable* Boiled and eaten like spinach, boiled and fried in lard, or canned. **Spanish American** *Vegetable* Boiled and eaten like spinach, boiled and fried in lard, or canned. (32:15) **Tewa** *Unspecified* Boiled or fried and used for food. (138:53) **Zuni** *Bread & Cake* Seeds originally eaten raw, but later ground with black cornmeal, made into balls, and eaten. (166:65)

Amaranthus caudatus, Love-lies-bleeding
Cocopa *Unspecified* Fresh plants baked and eaten. *Vegetable* Plants cooked and eaten as greens. *Winter Use Food* Plants cooked, rolled into a ball, baked, and stored. **Mohave** *Unspecified* Fresh plants baked and eaten. *Vegetable* Plants cooked and eaten as greens. *Winter Use Food* Plants cooked, rolled into a ball, baked, and stored for future use. (37:200)

Amaranthus cruentus, Red Amaranth
Hopi *Cooking Agent* Plant used as a red coloring for paper bread distributed at kachina exhibitions. (as *A. paniculatus* 56:18) Heads dried and used as a brilliant pink dye for wafer bread. (200:74) **Keresan** *Vegetable* Leaves eaten as greens. (as *A. paniculatus* 198:558) **Navajo,**

Ramah *Staple* Threshed seeds ground into flour. (191:25) **Sia** *Unspecified* Seeds used for food. *Vegetable* Leaves used as greens. (*Amaranthus paniculatus* 199:107) **Zuni** *Cooking Agent* Feathery part of plant ground into a fine meal and used to color ceremonial bread red. (as *A. hybridus paniculatus* 166:87)

Amaranthus fimbriatus, Fringed Amaranth
Cahuilla *Porridge* Parched seeds ground into a flour and used to make mush. *Vegetable* Boiled leaves eaten as greens or used as potherbs. (15:37)

Amaranthus hybridus, Slim Amaranth
Acoma *Dried Food* Young plants boiled and dried for winter use. *Vegetable* Young plants boiled and eaten as greens. (32:16) **Havasupai** *Bread & Cake* Seeds parched, ground fine, boiled, thickened, made into balls, and eaten as dumplings. (197:66) *Porridge* Seeds parched, ground, and used to make mush. *Soup* Seeds parched, ground, and used to make soup. (197:67) Leaves and squash flowers boiled, ground, and fresh or dried corn and water added to make soup. (197:74) *Unspecified* Seeds used for food. *Vegetable* Leaves of young plants cooked like spinach. (197:218) Young, fresh, tender leaves boiled, drained, balled into individual portions, and served. (197:66) **Keres, Western** *Unspecified* Seeds collected and ground with meal for food. *Vegetable* Young, tender plants used for greens like spinach. *Winter Use Food* Plant used as winter food by boiling and drying for winter storage. (171:26) **Laguna** *Dried Food* Young plants boiled and dried for winter use. *Vegetable* Young plants boiled and eaten as greens. (32:16)

Amaranthus palmeri, Careless Weed
Cocopa *Unspecified* Fresh plants baked and eaten. *Vegetable* Plants cooked and eaten as greens. *Winter Use Food* Plants cooked, rolled into a ball, baked, and stored. **Mohave** *Unspecified* Fresh plants baked and eaten. *Vegetable* Plants cooked and eaten as greens. *Winter Use*

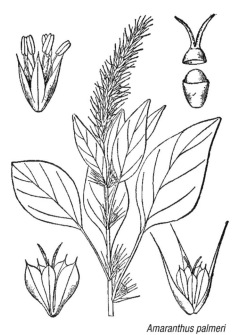

Amaranthus palmeri

Food Plants cooked, rolled into a ball, baked, and stored. (37:200) **Navajo** *Staple* Seeds ground into a meal and used for food. *Sweetener* Parched, ground seeds chewed to obtain sugar. (55:46) **Papago** *Dried Food* Seeds basket winnowed, parched, sun dried, cooked, stored, and used for food. (34:24) *Staple* Seeds ground and used as food. (32:23) *Unspecified* Seeds used for food. (36:62) *Vegetable* Leaves eaten as greens in midsummer. (34:14) Boiled and used for greens. (34:46) Greens used for food. (36:61) **Pima** *Unspecified* Leaves boiled and eaten with pinole. *Vegetable* Young, tender leaves cooked and eaten as greens. (47:47) **Pima, Gila River** *Dried Food* Leaves dried and stored for year-round use. (133:5) *Unspecified* Leaves boiled and eaten. (133:7) *Vegetable* Leaves used as greens. (133:5) **Yuma** *Staple* Seeds parched and ground into meal. (37:189) *Unspecified* Fresh plants baked and eaten. *Vegetable* Plants cooked and eaten as greens. *Winter Use Food* Plants cooked, rolled into a ball, baked, and stored for future use. (37:200)

Amaranthus powellii, Powell's Amaranth

Hopi *Unspecified* Seeds used for food. *Vegetable* Leaves used as greens. (42:283)

Amaranthus retroflexus, Redroot Amaranth

Acoma *Dried Food* Young plants boiled and dried for winter use. *Vegetable* Young plants boiled and eaten as greens. (32:15) **Apache, Chiricahua & Mescalero** *Bread & Cake* Seeds winnowed, ground into flour, and used to make bread. (33:48) *Unspecified* Leaves eaten without preparation or cooked with green chile and meat or animal bones. (33:46) **Cochiti** *Vegetable* Young plants eaten as greens. (32:16) **Iroquois** *Vegetable* Cooked and seasoned with salt, pepper, or butter. (196:117) **Isleta** *Vegetable* Fresh, tender, young leaves eaten as greens. (100:21) **Jemez** *Unspecified* Young plant used for food many generations ago. (44:20) **Keres, Western** *Unspecified* Seeds collected and ground with meal for food. *Vegetable* Young, tender plants used for greens like spinach. *Winter Use Food* Plant boiled and dried for winter storage. (171:26) **Laguna** *Dried Food* Young plants boiled and dried for winter use. *Vegetable* Young plants boiled and eaten as greens. (32:15) **Mendocino Indian** *Staple* Small, shiny black seeds used to make pinole. (41:346) **Mohegan** *Vegetable* Combined with mustard, plantain, dock, and nettle and used as mixed greens. (176:83) **Navajo** *Bread & Cake* Seeds ground, boiled, mixed with corn flour, and made into dumplings. *Porridge* Seeds ground, boiled, and mixed with corn flour into a gruel. (165:222) *Unspecified* Seeds used for food. Leaves and seeds mixed with grease and eaten. (55:46) *Vegetable* Boiled and eaten like spinach, boiled and fried in lard, or canned. (32:15) Leaves boiled and eaten like spinach. *Winter Use Food* Leaves boiled and canned. (55:46) **Navajo, Ramah** *Bread & Cake* Seeds winnowed, ground with maize, made into bread, and used as a ceremonial food in Nightway. *Special Food* Seeds winnowed, ground with maize, made into bread, and used as a ceremonial food in Nightway. *Vegetable* Leaves used as spring greens, boiled with meat, boiled alone, or boiled and fried with meat or fat. *Winter Use Food* Seeds stored for winter use. (191:26) **Pueblo** *Vegetable* Boiled and eaten like spinach, boiled and fried in lard, or canned. **Spanish American** *Vegetable* Boiled and eaten like spinach, boiled and fried in lard, or canned. (32:15) **Tewa** *Unspecified* Boiled or fried and used for food. (138:53)

Ambrosia tenuifolia, Slimleaf Burr Ragweed

Papago *Dried Food* Surplus of roots sun dried on roofs and used for food. *Staple* Roots used as a staple crop. (as *Franseria tenuifolia* 34:17) *Unspecified* Roots used for food. (*Franseria tenuifolia* 36:60) *Vegetable* Stalks eaten as greens in the summer. (as *Franseria tenuifolia* 34:14)

Amelanchier alnifolia, Saskatoon Serviceberry

Atsugewi *Dried Food* Dried, stored berries soaked in water and eaten. *Porridge* Ripe, mashed fruit added to water to form a paste and eaten without cooking. (61:139) **Bella Coola** *Fruit* Berries used for food. (184:208) **Black-foot** *Dessert* Berries and buffalo fat used to make a soup eaten as a dessert at feasts. (97:37) *Dried Food* Berries dried and stored, some with back fat, for future use. (86:100) Berries dried for future use. (97:37) *Fruit* Crushed berries, animal fat, and dried meat used to make pemmican. Berries and fat stuffed into an intestine, boiled, and eaten like a sausage. Dried berries used to make sausages. (86:100) *Preserves* Berries used to make preserves. (86:26) *Snack Food* Berries and red osier dogwood berries used as a favorite snack reserved for men. (86:100) Berries used to make tasty snacks. (86:26) *Soup* Dried berries used to make soups. Crushed leaves mixed with blood, dried, and used to make a rich broth in winter. (86:100) *Special Food* Berries used in ritual meals. Berry soup used for most ceremonial events. (86:26) *Staple* Berries used as a staple food. *Winter Use Food* Crushed berries mixed with flour for winter storage. (86:100) **Cheyenne** *Beverage* Leaves used to make tea.

(76:176) Leaves used to make a red beverage tea. *Pie & Pudding* Fruits boiled, sugar and flour added, and eaten as a pudding. (83:34) *Special Food* Berries stewed for feasts. *Winter Use Food* Berries dried for winter use. (76:176) **Cree, Plains** *Dried Food* Berries crushed, dried, and stored for future use. (113:202) **Cree, Woodlands** *Dried Food* Sun dried fruit eaten cooked in water or raw as a sweet snack. Sun dried fruit eaten boiled or pounded into a pemmican. *Fruit* Fruit eaten fresh. Sun dried fruit eaten boiled or pounded into a pemmican. *Preservative* Barked split sticks, 4 inches long, boiled in sturgeon oil to keep the oil fresh during storage. *Snack Food* Sun dried fruit eaten raw as a sweet snack. (109:28) **Dakota** *Fruit* Prized berries used for food. (70:87) **Flathead** *Pie & Pudding* Dried berries mixed with flour, sugar, and water and eaten as a sweet pudding. (82:9) **Gosiute** *Dried Food* Berries mashed and dried in large quantities for winter use. *Fruit* Berries used in season. (39:361) **Great Basin Indian** *Dried Food* Berries eaten dried. *Fruit* Berries eaten fresh or added to elk or deer meat to make pemmican. (121:48) **Hesquiat** *Forage* Berries eaten by bears. *Fruit* Berries used for food. (185:72) **Karok** *Dried Food* Berries dried and stored in big baskets. *Fruit*

Amelanchier alnifolia

Berries eaten fresh. (148:385) **Kitasoo** *Fruit* Fruit used for food. (43:341) **Klamath** *Fruit* Fresh berries used for food. *Unspecified* Seeds chewed for pleasure. *Winter Use Food* Dried berries stored for winter use. (45:97) **Kwakiutl, Southern** *Fruit* Berries used for food. (183:288) **Lakota** *Beverage* Petals, leaves, and small stems used to make a drink. *Fruit* Berries eaten fresh. (106:36) Fruits eaten for food. (139:56) *Starvation Food* Berries dried and eaten during famines. (106:36) **Mendocino Indian** *Fruit* Black, glaucous berries eaten fresh. (41:355) **Modesse** *Fruit* Berries used for food. (117:223) **Montana Indian** *Beverage* Berries used to make wine. (19:6) Fruits used to make wine. *Bread & Cake* Fruits sun dried, pounded, formed into patties, and stored for winter use. *Forage* Berries eaten by bears and grouse. Young stems and leaves eaten by elk, deer, moose, and mountain sheep. (82:9) *Fruit* Berries spiced and eaten. *Pie & Pudding* Berries used to make pies. (19:6) Fruits made into pies and eaten. (82:9) *Preserves* Berries used to make jam. (19:6) Fruits made into jams and jellies. *Soup* Fruits sun dried and eaten in meat stews. (82:9) *Winter Use Food* Large quantities of berries gathered and dried for winter use. (19:6) **Navajo** *Fruit* Fruits eaten for food. (55:52) **Okanagan-Colville** *Dried Food* Berries dried for future use. *Frozen Food* Berries frozen for future use. *Fruit* Berries eaten fresh, with sugar or cooked. *Pie & Pudding* Berries used to make pies and puddings. *Sweetener* Dried berries used to sweeten "Indian ice cream." *Winter Use Food* Berries canned for future use. (188:120) **Okanagon** *Bread & Cake* Berries pressed into cakes and used for food. (125:38) *Staple* Berries used as a principal food. (178:238) **Omaha** *Fruit* Prized berries used for food. **Ponca** *Fruit* Prized berries used for food. (70:87) **Saanich** *Fruit* Berries eaten in late summer. **Salish, Coast** *Fruit* Berries eaten in late summer. (182:86) **Shuswap** *Fruit* Berries used for food. (123:65) **Thompson** *Beverage* Twigs used to make a tea-like beverage. (187:253) *Bread & Cake* Berries pressed into cakes and used for food. (125:38) Berries dried into cakes. *Dried Food* Berries dried

loose like raisins. *Frozen Food* Berries frozen for future use. (187:253) *Fruit* Fruits eaten fresh in large quantities. (164:489) Berries eaten fresh or boiled. *Pie & Pudding* Dried berries and many other ingredients used to make a special pudding. The dried berries with bitterroot, flour, butter, cream, sugar, and sometimes tiger lily bulbs, avalanche lily corms, deer fat, black tree lichen, and salmon eggs were used to make a special pudding. *Preserves* Berries jammed. *Spice* Berry juice used to marinate other foods. *Sweetener* Dried berry cakes used as a sweetener for other foods. (187:253) *Unspecified* Drupes eaten wherever found. (164:487) *Winter Use Food* Fruits preserved for future use. (164:489) Berries frozen or canned for future use. (187:253) **Ute** *Dried Food* Berries dried for winter use. *Fruit* Berries used in season. (38:32) **Winnebago** *Fruit* Prized berries used for food. (70:87)

Amelanchier alnifolia var. *alnifolia*, Saskatoon Serviceberry
Haisla *Fruit* Berries combined with other fruits and eaten. **Hanaksiala** *Dried Food* Berries dried and eaten. (43:263) **Oweekeno** *Fruit* Berries used for food. (43:107)

Amelanchier alnifolia var. *cusickii*, Cusick's Serviceberry
Paiute *Candy* Mashed berries formed into cakes, sun dried, and eaten as candy. *Dried Food* Berries eaten dried. *Fruit* Berries eaten fresh. *Winter Use Food* Mashed berries formed into cakes, sun dried for winter use, boiled, and eaten. (as *A. cusickii* 111:83)

Amelanchier alnifolia var. *semiintegrifolia*, Pacific Serviceberry
Alaska Native *Bread & Cake* Berries used to make muffins. *Dried Food* Berries dried and used in place of raisins or currants. *Fruit* Berries eaten raw. *Pie & Pudding* Berries used to make puddings and pies. (as *A. florida* 85:75) **Chehalis** *Fruit* Fruits eaten fresh. *Spice* Fruits dried and used as seasoning in soup or with meats. (as *A. florida* 79:38) **Hoh** *Fruit* Fruits eaten for food. (as *A. florida* 137:64) **Lummi**

Dried Food Berries dried, boiled with dog salmon, and eaten at feasts. (as *A. florida* 79:38) **Quileute** *Fruit* Fruits eaten for food. (as *A. florida* 137:64) **Sanpoil & Nespelem** *Bread & Cake* Berries dried whole or mashed, formed into cakes, and dried. *Fruit* Berries eaten raw or cooked with salmon. (as *A. florida* 131:101) **Skagit** *Fruit* Berries eaten fresh. (as *A. florida* 79:38) **Skagit, Upper** *Dried Food* Berries mashed and dried for winter use. *Fruit* Berries eaten fresh. (as *A. florida* 179:38) **Swinomish** *Dried Food* Fruits dried and eaten during the winter. *Fruit* Fruits eaten fresh. (as *A. florida* 79:38)

Amelanchier arborea, Common Serviceberry
Cherokee *Fruit* Berries used for food. (80:54)

Amelanchier arborea var. *arborea*, Common Serviceberry
Blackfoot *Dried Food* Berries dried for winter use. *Soup* Berries used with stews and soups. *Unspecified* Berries used with meats. (as *A. oblongifolia* 114:277)

Amelanchier canadensis, Canadian Serviceberry
Chippewa *Dried Food* Fruit dried for winter use. *Fruit* Fruit eaten fresh. (71:132) **Iroquois** *Bread & Cake* Fruit mashed, made into small cakes, and dried for future use. *Dried Food* Raw or cooked fruit sun or fire dried and stored for future use. *Fruit* Dried fruit taken as a hunting food. *Sauce & Relish* Dried fruit cakes soaked in warm water and cooked as a sauce or mixed with corn bread. (196:128)

Amelanchier canadensis ssp. *laevis*, Canadian Serviceberry
Menominee *Winter Use Food* Berries dried for winter use. (151:70)

Amelanchier canadensis var. *oblongifolda*, Canadian Serviceberry
Ojibwa *Fruit* Fruit used for food. (135:236)

Amelanchier laevis, Allegheny Serviceberry
Cherokee *Fruit* Fruit used for food. (80:21) Fresh fruit used for food. (126:55) **Menominee** *Winter Use Food* Berries dried for winter use. (151:70) **Ojibwa** *Dried Food* Berries used for food and dried for winter use, the Indians preferred them to blueberries. (153:408)

Amelanchier pallida, Pale Serviceberry
Cahuilla *Dried Food* Berries dried for future use. *Fruit* Berries eaten fresh. (15:38) **Costanoan** *Fruit* Raw fruits used for food. (21:249) **Kawaiisu** *Fruit* Fruit eaten sparingly while fresh. (206:11)

Amelanchier sanguinea var. *sanguinea*, Roundleaf Serviceberry
Menominee *Winter Use Food* Berries dried for winter use. (as *A. huronensis* 151:70)

Amelanchier stolonifera, Running Serviceberry
Potawatomi *Dried Food* Berries dried for winter use. *Fruit* Berries relished as a fresh food. *Winter Use Food* Berries dried and canned for winter use. (as *A. spicata* 154:107)

Amelanchier utahensis, Utah Serviceberry
Havasupai *Forage* Fruit eaten by deer. (197:222) **Isleta** *Fruit* Fruit formerly used for food. (as *A. prunifolia* 100:21) **Navajo** *Dried Food* Berries dried for winter use. (90:148) *Fruit* Fruits eaten fresh. (as *A. prunifolia* 55:52) Berries eaten fresh. (90:148) *Winter Use Food* Fruits dried and preserved for winter use. (as *A. prunifolia* 55:52) **Paiute** *Dried Food* Berries crushed, dried, and used for food. *Fruit* Berries eaten fresh. (as *A. venulosa* 104:100)

Amelanchier utahensis ssp. *utahensis*, Utah Serviceberry
Navajo, Ramah *Fruit* Berries eaten raw or sometimes cooked. (as *A. mormonica* 191:30)

Ammannia coccinea, Valley Redstem
Mohave *Unspecified* Seeds gathered and prepared as food. **Yuma** *Unspecified* Seeds gathered and prepared as food. (37:187)

Amoreuxia palmatifida, Mexican
Yellowshow
Pima, Gila River *Unspecified* Roots used for
food. (133:7)

Amorpha canescens, Lead Plant
Oglala *Beverage* Leaves used to make a hot tea.
(70:93)

Amphicarpaea bracteata, American
Hogpeanut
Cherokee *Bread & Cake* Underground fruit
used to make bean bread. (126:45) *Unspecified*
Roots used for food. (80:38) *Vegetable* Underground fruit cooked like pinto beans or added
to cornmeal and hot water. (126:45) **Chippewa**
Fruit Fruit used for food. (as *Amphicarpa
monoica* 71:134) *Unspecified* Roots boiled and
used for food. (as *Falcata comosa* 53:320)
Dakota *Unspecified* Beans used for the agreeable taste and nutritive value. (as *Falcata comosa* 70:95) **Meskwaki** *Unspecified* Nuts gathered and stored in heaps by the mice, taken by
the Meskwaki and used. (as *Amphicarpa
monoica* 152:259) **Ojibwa** *Unspecified* Roots
cooked, although really too small to be considered of much importance. *Vegetable* Beans
cooked, unusual flavor imparted and eaten.
(as *Amphicarpa pitcheri* 153:405) **Omaha** *Unspecified* Roots peeled, boiled, and eaten. (as
Amphicarpaea monoica 58:341) Beans used
for the agreeable taste and nutritive value. (as
Falcata comosa 70:95) *Winter Use Food* Roots
gathered from the storehouses of field mice and
stored in skin bags during the winter. (as *Amphicarpaea monoica* 58:341) **Pawnee** *Unspecified* Beans used for the agreeable taste and
nutritive value. **Ponca** *Unspecified* Beans used
for the agreeable taste and nutritive value.
Winnebago *Unspecified* Beans used for the
agreeable taste and nutritive value. (as *Falcata
comosa* 70:95)

Amsinckia lycopsoides, Tarweed
Fiddleneck
Atsugewi *Bread & Cake* Parched, ground seeds
made into cakes and eaten without cooking. (as
Amsinkia parviflora 61:139) **Mendocino Indian** *Unspecified* Fresh, juicy shoots formerly
used for food. (41:382)

Amsinckia spectabilis, Woolly
Breeches
Pima *Unspecified* Young leaves rolled into balls
and eaten raw. (95:264)

Amsinckia tessellata, Bristly
Fiddleneck
Gosiute *Unspecified* Seeds formerly used for
food. (39:361) **Kawaiisu** *Vegetable* Leaves
bruised by rubbing between the hands and eat-
en with salt. (206:11) **Pima** *Unspecified* Leaves
eaten raw. (95:264)

Ananas comosus, Pineapple
Seminole *Unspecified* Plant used for food.
(169:500)

Anaphalis margaritacea, Western
Pearlyeverlasting
Anticosti *Beverage* Flowers used to scent alco-
hol. (143:68)

Andromeda polifolia, Bog Rosemary
Tanana, Upper *Beverage* Leaves used to make
tea. (102:8)

**Andromeda polifolia var.
glaucophylla**, Bog Rosemary
Ojibwa *Beverage* Fresh or dried leaves and tips
boiled for a beverage tea. (as *A. glaucophylla*
153:400)

Androsace sp., Pinetorum
Isleta *Beverage* Leaves steeped in water to
make a beverage. (100:22)

Anemone narcissiflora, Narcissus
Anemone
Alaska Native *Unspecified* Upper root ends
used for food. (85:151) **Eskimo, Alaska** *Ice*

Cream Leaves, other salad greens, and oil beaten to a creamy consistency and frozen into "ice cream." *Unspecified* Leaves prepared in oil together with other salad greens and beaten to a creamy consistency. (4:715)

Anemopsis californica, Yerba Mansa
Kamia *Bread & Cake* Pulverized seeds used for bread. *Porridge* Pulverized seeds cooked as mush. (62:24)

Angelica archangelica, Norwegian
   Angelica
Eskimo, Greenland *Vegetable* Tender, young leaf stalks and peeled, young flowering stems eaten raw. (128:28)

Angelica arguta, Lyall's Angelica
Shuswap *Spice* Young stems eaten and used to flavor salmon heated with dried bread over an open fire. *Vegetable* Young stems, with a celery flavor, eaten in May. (123:56)

Angelica genuflexa, Kneeling Angelica
Hanaksiala *Unspecified* Leaves and stems used for food. (43:211)

Angelica lucida, Wild Celery
Alaska Native *Unspecified* Young stems and tender stalks of young leaves peeled and the juicy inside eaten raw. *Vegetable* Leaves cooked as a green vegetable or boiled with fish. (85:11)
Bella Coola *Unspecified* Formerly used for food. (184:201) **Eskimo, Alaska** *Unspecified* Stalks, with the outer sheet peeled off, eaten raw by children and adults. Only young plants were considered good to eat because older plant became fibrous and strong tasting. Young leaves eaten with seal oil. (1:37) *Vegetable* Used like celery. (as *Coelopleurum gmelini* 4:715)
Eskimo, Inuktitut *Unspecified* Young stems used for food. (202:184) **Eskimo, Inupiat** *Unspecified* Peeled stems and young leaves stored in seal oil for future use. (98:16) **Makah** *Unspecified* Peeled petioles used for food. (67:292)

Angelica lucida

Angelica tomentosa, Woolly Angelica
Karok *Vegetable* Leaves eaten raw as greens. (148:387) **Pomo, Kashaya** *Unspecified* Young, green shoots eaten raw. (72:20) **Yana** *Unspecified* Peeled stems eaten raw. (147:251)

Angelica tomentosa var. hendersonii, Henderson's Angelica
Mewuk *Unspecified* Young stems eaten raw. (as *A. hendersoni* 117:366)

Annona glabra, Pond Apple
Seminole *Unspecified* Plant used for food. (169:509)

Annona reticulata, Custard Apple
Seminole *Unspecified* Plant used for food. (169:495)

Antennaria parvifolia, Smallleaf
   Pussytoes
Navajo, Kayenta *Vegetable* Used for greens in foods. (as *A. aprica* 205:44)

Antennaria rosea, Rosy Pussytoes
Blackfoot *Candy* Leaves chewed by children for the flavor. (97:56)

Anthemis sp.
Navajo *Beverage* Fresh or dried plant used to
make tea. (as *Cota*, Navajo tea 110:20)

Anthoxanthum odoratum, Sweet
Vernalgrass
Hesquiat *Forage* Cattle used this plant for for-
age. (185:56)

Apiaceae sp.
Yana *Unspecified* Roots roasted and eaten. (as
Umbelliferae 147:251)

Apiastrum angustifolium, Mock
Parsley
Cahuilla *Unspecified* Hair-like plant provided
a small seasonal food source in wet years.
(15:39)

Apios americana, Groundnut
Cherokee *Substitution Food* Uncooked seeds
substituted for pinto beans in bean bread. (as
Glycine apios 126:46) *Vegetable* Beans used for
food. (80:24) Roots cooked like potatoes. (as
Glycine apios 126:46) **Chippewa** *Vegetable*
Tubers eaten. (as *A. tuberosa* 71:133) **Dakota**
Unspecified Roasted or boiled tubers used for
food. (as *Glycine apios* 70:94) **Delaware**
Bread & Cake Roots dried, ground into flour,
and made into bread. *Unspecified* Roots boiled
and eaten as the cultivated potato. *Winter Use
Food* Tuberous roots used as winter food. (as *A.
tuberosa* 176:59) **Huron** *Starvation Food*
Roots used with acorns during famine. (as *A.
tuberosa* 3:63) **Iroquois** *Unspecified* Tubers
eaten. (as *A. uberosa* 196:120) **Menominee**
Vegetable Roots cooked with maple sugar and
superior to candied yams. *Winter Use Food*
Peeled, parboiled, sliced roots dried for winter
use. (as *A. tuberosa* 151:68) **Meskwaki** *Vegetable* Root stocks eaten raw. *Winter Use Food*
Root stocks peeled, parboiled, sliced, and dried
for winter use. (as *A. tuberosa* 152:259) **Mohegan** *Cooking Agent* Dried roots ground into a
flour and used for thickening stews. *Unspecified*
Fresh or dried roots cooked and used for food.
(as *A. tuberosa* 176:83) **Omaha** *Unspecified*
Thickened root boiled until the skin came off

and used for food. (as *A. apios* 68:325) Roasted
or boiled tubers used for food. (as *Glycine apios*
70:94) *Vegetable* Nuts boiled, peeled, and eaten
as a vegetable. (as *A. tuberosa* 58:341) **Pawnee**
Unspecified Roasted or boiled tubers used for
food. **Ponca** *Unspecified* Roasted or boiled tubers used for food. (as *Glycine apios* 70:94)
Potawatomi *Vegetable* Wild potato was appreciated. (as *A. tuberosa* 54:103) **Seminole**
Unspecified Plant used for food. (169:492)
Winnebago *Unspecified* Roasted or boiled tubers used for food. (as *Glycine apios* 70:94)

Apios tuberosum, Potato Bean
Cheyenne *Unspecified* Species used for food.
(as *Alycine apios* 83:45) *Vegetable* Roots used
for food. (as *Alycine apios* 76:179)

Apium graveolens, Wild Celery
Cahuilla *Vegetable* Used as a potherb. (15:39)
Luiseño *Vegetable* Plant used for greens.
(155:230)

Aplectrum hyemale, Adam and Eve
Cherokee *Fodder* Roots added to the slop to
make hogs fat. (80:51)

Apocynum cannabinum, Indian
Hemp
Isleta *Candy* Gummy latex mixed with clean
clay and used as chewing gum. (as *A. angustifolium* 32:31) Gum mixed with clean clay and
used for chewing gum. (as *A. angustifolium*
100:22) **Karok** *Unspecified* Seeds eaten raw.
(as *A. androsaemifolium* var. *nevadense*
148:388) **Kiowa** *Candy* Milky latex used as
chewing gum. After the latex was squeezed from
the plant, it was allowed to stand overnight,
whereupon it hardened into a "white gum." Two
kinds of gum were recognized: that which was
left overnight, and that which was chewed only
a few hours after it had been extracted from the
plant. (192:47)

Aquilegia formosa, Western Columbine
Hanaksiala *Candy* Flowers sucked by children
for the sweet nectar. (43:262) **Yurok** *Unspecified* Sweet nectaries inside the sepal spurs

bitten off and savored mostly by the younger people. (6:17)

Aquilegia formosa var. *formosa*,
Crimson Columbine
Miwok *Vegetable* Early spring greens boiled and eaten. (as *A. truncata* 12:159) **Thompson** *Forage* Flowers used as sources of nectar by hummingbirds. (as *A. truncata* 164:516)

Arabis glabra, Tower Rockcress
Cheyenne *Beverage* Infusion of plant used as a beverage. (76:174)

Arabis lyrata, Lyrate Rockcress
Alaska Native *Vegetable* Rosettes of lobed leaves added to tossed salads or cooked and served as a green vegetable. (85:13)

Arachis hypogaea, Peanut
Huron *Starvation Food* Roots used with acorns during famine. (3:63) **Seminole** *Unspecified* Plant used for food. (169:483)

Aralia nudicaulis, Wild Sarsaparilla
Algonquin, Quebec *Beverage* Berries used to make wine. (18:115) **Bella Coola** *Beverage* Roots boiled and used as a beverage. (184:201) **Iroquois** *Beverage* Fruits used to make wine.

Aralia nudicaulis

(142:96) **Kwakiutl, Southern** *Unspecified* Roots roasted, broken into pieces, mixed with oulachen (candlefish) grease, and used for food. (183:277) **Micmac** *Beverage* Used to make a beverage. (159:258) **Montagnais** *Beverage* Dark berries fermented in cold water and used to make a wine. *Forage* Roots eaten by rabbits. (as *A. medicalis* 156:315)

Aralia racemosa, American Spikenard
Menominee *Unspecified* An aboriginal Menomini dish was spikenard root, wild onion, wild gooseberry, and sugar. (151:62) **Potawatomi** *Soup* Young tips were relished in soups. Soup was a favorite aboriginal dish and still is among the Indians. Being expandable, it fits in well with the well-known Indian hospitality. After a meal is started, several more guests may arrive and they are always welcome. (154:96)

Arbutus menziesii, Pacific Madrone
Costanoan *Fruit* Fruit eaten in small quantities. (21:252) **Karok** *Dried Food* Berries steamed, dried, and stored for future use. *Frozen Food* Berries steamed, dried, stored, and soaked in warm water before eating. (148:387) *Fruit* Berries used for food. (6:17) **Mendocino Indian** *Forage* White, globular flowers eaten by doves, wild pigeons, and turkeys. Fruits eaten by deer. Leaves eaten by cows when green grass scarce. (41:374) **Miwok** *Beverage* Berries crushed for sweet, unfermented cider. *Winter Use Food* Dried berries stored for winter consumption, chewed but never swallowed. (12:161) **Pomo** *Fruit* Fruits eaten for food. (41:374) **Pomo, Kashaya** *Fruit* Berries eaten fresh or roasted. *Winter Use Food* Berries parched and stored for the winter. (72:67) **Wailaki** *Fruit* Fruits eaten for food. (41:374) **Yuki** *Fruit* Berries used for food. (49:87) **Yurok** *Fruit* Berries roasted over an open fire and eaten. (6:17)

Arctium lappa, Greater Burrdock
Iroquois *Dried Food* Roots dried by the fire and stored away for winter use. *Soup* Dried roots soaked and boiled into a soup. (196:120) *Vegetable* Young leaves cooked and seasoned with salt, pepper, or butter. (196:118)

Arctostaphylos alpina, Alpine Bearberry

Alaska Native *Fruit* Berries used for food. Berry was juicy but rather insipid in flavor. Not usually available in large quantities. Picked in poor berry years and mixed with blueberries. Flavor was much improved with cooking. (85:77) **Eskimo, Alaska** *Fruit* Fruit used for food. (4:715) **Eskimo, Arctic** *Forage* Berries eaten greedily by bears and ptarmigan. (128:23) **Eskimo, Inupiat** *Fruit* Berries, other berries, and sugar cooked and eaten. (98:108) **Koyukon** *Winter Use Food* Berries stored in grease or oil and eaten with fish or meat. (119:55)

Arctostaphylos canescens, Hoary Manzanita

Karok *Beverage* Berries used to make a drink. *Dried Food* Berries dried and stored in storage baskets for future use. *Fruit* Dried berries pounded, mixed with salmon eggs, cooked in a basket with a hot rock, and eaten. (148:388)

Arctostaphylos ×cinerea, Del Norte Manzanita

Tolowa *Bread & Cake* Berries mixed with salmon roe and sugar, formed into patties, and baked in rocks. **Yurok** *Fruit* Berries used for food. (6:18)

Arctostaphylos glandulosa, Eastwood's Manzanita

Cahuilla *Beverage* Mashed fruit mixed with water and strained into a drink. *Dried Food* Berries sun dried and stored for future use. *Fruit* Berries eaten fresh. *Porridge* Dried berries ground into flour and used to make mush. *Sauce & Relish* Berries used to make a gelatinous substance and eaten like aspic. *Staple* Seeds ground into a meal and used to make mush or cakes. (15:40) **Pomo, Kashaya** *Dried Food* Dried, pounded berries stored for later use and made into pinole, cakes, or mixed with water. (72:68)

Arctostaphylos glauca, Bigberry Manzanita

Cahuilla *Beverage* Mashed fruit mixed with water and strained into a drink. *Dried Food* Berries sun dried and stored for future use. *Porridge* Dried berries ground into flour and used to make mush. *Sauce & Relish* Berries used to make a gelatinous substance and eaten like aspic. *Staple* Seeds ground into a meal and used to make mush or cakes. (15:40) **Diegueño** *Fruit* Fruit used for food. (88:219) **Kawaiisu** *Beverage* Berries used to make a beverage. Berries were covered with a thin layer of dirt and sifted in a yaduci, a winnowing tray, so that the dirt fell through. Then they were sprinkled with water, kneaded with the hands, mashed, and soaked "in the sun" for about a half day. The yaduci was used as a sieve to remove the berry pulp from the infusion which could be drunk thus or mixed with chia. Water could be drained through the berry pulp a second time. The liquid was said to be sweet and fattening. *Fruit* Berries eaten fresh. (206:11)

Arctostaphylos manzanita, White-leaf Manzanita

Karok *Beverage* Berries used to make a drink. *Dried Food* Berries dried and stored in storage baskets for future use. *Fruit* Dried berries pounded, mixed with salmon eggs, cooked in a basket with a hot rock, and eaten. (148:388) **Mendocino Indian** *Beverage* Ripe berries used to make cider. *Forage* Fruits eaten by bears as forage. *Fruit* Green fruits eaten in small quantities to quench thirst. Ripe fruits eaten raw or cooked. *Unspecified* Globular, waxy flowers sucked or eaten by children. *Winter Use Food* Ripe berries stored as a winter use food. (41:375) **Miwok** *Beverage* Berries crushed for sweet, unfermented cider. *Winter Use Food* Dried berries stored for winter consumption, chewed but never swallowed. (12:161) **Numlaki** *Bread & Cake* Fruits made into bread and eaten. *Porridge* Fruits made into mush and eaten. *Staple* Fruits eaten like pinole. (41:375) **Yuki** *Beverage* Ripe fruits crushed, strained, and used to make cider. *Fruit* Ripe berries eaten raw. *Staple* Ripe berries parched and used in pinole. (49:85)

Arctostaphylos nevadensis, Pine Mat Manzanita
Karok *Beverage* Berries pulverized and made into a drink. (6:18) Berries used to make a drink. *Dried Food* Berries dried and stored in storage baskets for future use. (148:388) *Fruit* Berries used for food. (6:18) Dried berries pounded, mixed with salmon eggs, cooked in a basket with a hot rock, and eaten. (148:388) **Paiute** *Fruit* Berries used for food. (111:101) **Tolowa** *Bread & Cake* Berries mixed with salmon roe and sugar, formed into patties, and baked in rocks. (6:18)

Arctostaphylos parryana, Parry Manzanita
Luiseño *Fruit* Ground berry pulp used for food. (as *A. parryi* 155:230)

Arctostaphylos patula, Greenleaf Manzanita
Atsugewi *Beverage* Berries made into cakes and eaten plain or put into water and drunk. Cider was made by adding water to pounded berries and was conveyed to the mouth with a deer tail sop. *Bread & Cake*, and *Winter Use Food* Berries made into flour, molded into cakes, and stored for later use. (61:138) **Karok** *Dried Food* Berries dried and eaten. (148:388) **Klamath** *Fruit* Berries used for food. (45:102) **Midoo** *Fruit* Berries used for food during an acorn crop failure. (117:308) **Navajo, Kayenta** *Fruit* Berries eaten raw. (205:35) **Paiute** *Forage* Berries eaten by bears and deer. (111:102) **Wintoon** *Fruit* Berries used for food. (117:263)

Arctostaphylos pringlei, Pringle Manzanita
Navajo *Beverage* Crushed berries used to make a beverage. *Fruit* Berries eaten raw or cooked. *Porridge* Seeds ground into a mush. *Preserves* Berries used to make jelly. (110:23)

Arctostaphylos pumila, Sandmat Manzanita
Costanoan (Olhonean) *Beverage* Berries used to make cider. (117:373)

Arctostaphylos pungens, Pointleaf Manzanita
Cahuilla *Beverage* Mashed fruit mixed with water and strained into a drink. *Dried Food* Berries sun dried and stored for future use. *Fruit* Berries eaten fresh. *Porridge* Dried berries ground into flour and used to make mush. *Sauce & Relish* Berries used to make a gelatinous substance and eaten like aspic. *Staple* Seeds ground into a meal and used to make mush or cakes. (15:40) **Yavapai** *Beverage* Fresh or stored pulverized berries put in mouth, solid matter spat out, and juice sucked. Sometimes the liquid was expressed by squeezing the moistened pulverized mass with the two hands. (63:213) Berries used to make a beverage. *Fruit* Berries chewed and used for food. (65:256)

Arctostaphylos rubra, Red Fruit Bearberry
Eskimo, Arctic *Forage* Berries eaten greedily by bears and ptarmigan. (128:23) **Eskimo, Inupiat** *Winter Use Food* Berries and salmonberries stored in barrels for future use. (98:109) **Tanana, Upper** *Fruit* Berries used for food. (102:10)

Arctostaphylos tomentosa, Woollyleaf Manzanita
Mendocino Indian *Beverage* Berries used to make cider. (41:377) **Miwok** *Beverage* Berries crushed for sweet, unfermented cider. *Winter Use Food* Dried berries stored for winter consumption, chewed but never swallowed. (12:161) **Pomo** *Dried Food* Seeds ground, molded into biscuits, and sun dried. *Porridge* Seeds ground into meal and rock boiled to make mush. (11:81)

Arctostaphylos uva-ursi, Kinnikinnick
Bella Coola *Special Food* Berries formerly mixed with melted mountain goat fat and served to chiefs at feasts. (184:204) **Blackfoot** *Beverage* Crushed leaves used to make tea. *Dried Food* Berries dried and later soaked with sugar. *Fruit* Berries eaten fresh. (86:101) Berries eaten raw. (97:49) Berries eaten raw or mashed in

fat and fried. (114:276) *Winter Use Food* Berries preserved for later use. (97:49) **Carrier** *Fruit* Berries mixed with salmon eggs as a palatable and nutritious food. *Soup* Berries used to make soup. (89:12) **Cherokee** *Fruit* Fruit used for food. (80:25) **Chinook, Lower** *Dried Food* Berries dried in bags, mixed with oil, and eaten. *Fruit* Berries eaten fresh. (79:44) **Chippewa** *Spice* Berries cooked with meat to season the broth. (53:318) **Coeur d'Alene** *Dried Food* Berries dried and used for food. *Fruit* Berries eaten fresh. *Soup* Berries dried, boiled with roots, and eaten as soup. (178:90) **Cree, Woodlands** *Fruit* Fruit cooked in grease, pounded, mixed with raw fish eggs, and eaten. Approximate proportions of ingredients were 1 tablespoon grease, 1½ cups fruit, and 2 tablespoons whitefish eggs separated from the adhering membranes. A little sugar was added for flavor. After the fruits were lightly cooked in grease, they were pounded until they were crumbly. They were then placed in a heavy cloth folded to make a sack and pounded with the back of an ax head. The fish eggs moistened the pounded fruit. (109:29) **Eskimo, Arctic** *Fruit* Berries cooked and eaten. (128:23) **Eskimo, Inupiat** *Frozen Food* Berries frozen for future use. *Fruit*

Berries eaten with salmon eggs, to prevent the eggs from sticking to the teeth. Berries and oil eaten with dry meat. *Ice Cream* Berries stored in bear fat and cracklings or in seal oil and used to make ice cream. *Winter Use Food* Berries stored in seal oil, fish oil, or rendered bear fat. (98:99) **Flathead** *Sauce & Relish* Berries dried, powdered, and used as a condiment with deer liver. (82:40) **Hanaksiala** *Fruit* Berries mashed, mixed with grease, and eaten. *Special Food* Berries mixed with high-bush cranberries or Pacific crabapples and featured at winter feasts. (43:239) **Kimsquit** *Dried Food* Berries formerly dried, boiled, mixed with boiled dumplings, and used for food. (184:204) **Koyukon** *Winter Use Food* Berries stored in grease or oil and eaten with fish or meat. (119:55) **Kwakiutl, Southern** *Fruit* Dry, mealy berries formerly used for food. (183:282) **Makah** *Fruit* Berries used for food. (67:297) **Montana Indian** *Dried Food* Fruit eaten fresh and dried. *Fruit* Fresh fruit used for food. (19:7) *Soup* Berries boiled and used to make a broth. *Starvation Food* Berries eaten raw or fried during famines. (82:40) **Nitinaht** *Forage* Fruits eaten by grouse. *Fruit* Fruits formerly eaten fresh. (186:104) **Nuxalkmc** *Fruit* Berries used for food. (43:239) **Okanagan-Colville** *Fruit* Berries used for food. (188:101) **Okanagon** *Fruit* Insipid fruits eaten fresh. *Soup* Insipid fruits boiled in soups. (as *Arvtostaphylos uva-ursi* 125:38) *Staple* Berries used as a principal food. (178:239) **Oweekeno** *Fruit* Berries used for food. (43:239) **Salish, Coast** *Fruit* Berries eaten raw or cooked. (182:82) **Sanpoil & Nespelem** *Dried Food* Berries dried and stored for future use. (188:101) *Soup* Dried berries used in soups. (131:102) **Skokomish** *Fruit* Berries eaten with salmon eggs. (79:44) **Spokan** *Fruit* Berries used for food. (178:343) **Squaxin** *Fruit* Berries occasionally eaten. (79:44) **Tanana, Upper** *Fruit* Fruit used for food. (77:28) Raw berries mixed with grease, dried or fresh, raw whitefish eggs, and eaten. Berries warmed in grease and eaten. *Winter Use Food* Raw berries mixed with grease, dried or fresh, raw whitefish eggs, and stored for later use. (102:10) **Thompson** *Beverage* Leaves

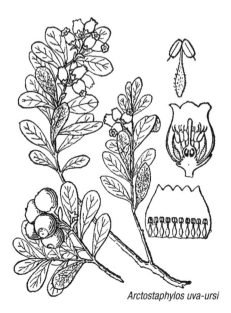

Arctostaphylos uva-ursi

and young stems boiled and drunk as a tea. (164:493) *Forage* Fruits eaten by deer. (164:514) *Fruit* Insipid fruits eaten fresh. (as *Arvtostaphylos uva-ursi* 125:38) Drupes eaten fresh. (164:486) Dry, mealy fruits eaten with bear fat or fish oil because of the dryness. Washed berries fried in hot lard or salmon oil and used for food. The berries would crackle and pop "just like popcorn." They were the only berries prepared in this manner. (187:211) *Soup* Insipid fruits boiled in soups. (as *Arvtostaphylos uva-ursi* 125:38) Drupes boiled in soups. (164:486) **Tolowa** *Bread & Cake* Berries mixed with salmon roe and sugar, formed into patties, and baked in rocks. **Yurok** *Fruit* Berries used for food. (6:18)

Arctostaphylos viscida, Sticky White-leaf Manzanita
Mewuk *Beverage* Berries used to make cider. *Fruit* Berries used for food. (117:336) **Midoo** *Fruit* Berries pounded and eaten. (117:311) **Miwok** *Beverage* Berries crushed for sweet, unfermented cider. *Winter Use Food* Dried berries stored for winter consumption, chewed but never swallowed. (12:161) **Wintoon** *Fruit* Berries used for food. (117:263)

Arctostaphylos viscida ssp. *mariposa*, Mariposa Manzanita
Mewuk *Beverage* Berries used to make cider. *Fruit* Berries used for food. (as *A. mariposa* 117:336) **Midoo** *Fruit* Berries pounded and eaten. (as *A. mariposa* 117:311)

Ardisia escallonoides, Island Marlberry
Seminole *Unspecified* Plant used for food. (169:470)

Argentina anserina, Silverweed Cinquefoil
Montana Indian *Vegetable* Roots, tasted like sweet potatoes, used for food. (as *Potentilla anserina* 19:19) **Okanagon** *Staple* Roots used as a principal food. (as *Potentilla anserina* 178:238) *Unspecified* Roots eaten either raw or cooked. (as *Pontentilla anserina* 125:37)

Shuswap *Unspecified* Roasted roots used for food. (as *Potentilla anserina* 123:66) **Thompson** *Unspecified* Roots eaten either raw or cooked. (as *Potentilla anserina* 164:480) Roots eaten raw, but more often cooked. (as *Potentilla anserina* ssp. *anserina* 187:262)

Argentina egedii ssp. *egedii*, Eged's Pacific Silverweed
Alaska Native *Vegetable* Roots eaten raw, boiled, or roasted like potatoes. (as *Potentilla pacifica* 85:127) **Bella Coola** *Unspecified* Roots used for food. (as *Potentilla pacifica* 184:209) **Haisla & Hanaksiala** *Unspecified* Roots used for food. (as *Potentilla anserina* ssp. *pacifica* var. 43:270) **Hesquiat** *Unspecified* Boiled or steamed roots eaten with oil or "stink salmon-eggs" (fermented eggs). (as *Potentilla pacifica* 185:73) **Kitasoo** *Unspecified* Roots mixed with sugar and oolichan (candlefish) grease and eaten. (as *Potentilla anserina* ssp. *pacifica* 43:344) **Kwakiutl, Southern** *Dried Food* Roots dried, steamed, and eaten with oil at large feasts. *Special Food* Roots dried, steamed, and eaten with oil at large feasts. (as *Potentilla pacifica* 183:289) **Makah** *Unspecified* Roots used for food. (as *Potentilla pacifica* 67:265) **Nitinaht** *Dessert* Long, fleshy roots steam cooked, dipped in oil, and eaten fresh like a dessert. *Dried Food* Roots steam cooked, dried for winter storage, soaked, briefly steamed, and eaten like dessert. (as *Potentilla pacifica* 186:118) *Unspecified* Peeled roots eaten raw or steamed. (as *Potentilla pacifica* 67:265) Roots eaten as accompaniments to cooked duck. (as *Potentilla pacifica* 186:131) Roots formerly used as an important food. (as *Potentilla pacifica* 186:63) **Oweekeno** *Unspecified* Roots used for food. (as *Potentilla anserina* ssp. *pacifica* 43:110) **Quileute** *Unspecified* Roots steamed, dipped in whale oil, and eaten. (as *Potentilla pacifica* 79:37) **Salish, Coast** *Unspecified* Fleshy taproots used for food. (as *Potentilla pacifica* 182:87)

Arisaema triphyllum, Jack in the Pulpit
Potawatomi *Unspecified* Thinly sliced roots

cooked in a pit oven for 3 days to eliminate the poison. (154:95)

Aristida purpurea var. *longiseta*, Fendler Threeawn
Navajo, Ramah *Fodder* Used for horse feed, if better forage was not available. Recognized as poor sheep or horse feed. (as *A. longiseta* 191:15)

Armillaria ponderosa
Karok *Unspecified* Species used for food. **Yurok** *Unspecified* Species used for food. (6:18)

Armoracia rusticana, Horseradish
Cherokee *Sauce & Relish* Root used as a condiment. (as *A. lapathifolia* 126:36)

Arnoglossum atriplicifolium, Armoglossum
Cherokee *Spice* Powdered leaves used as seasoning. (as *Cacalia atriplicifolia* 80:58)

Aronia melanocarpa, Black Chokeberry
Abnaki *Fruit* Fruit used for food. (144:152) *Unspecified* Species used for food. (144:168) **Potawatomi** *Fruit* Berries used for food. (as *Pyrus melanocarpa* 154:107)

Artemisia biennis, Biennial Wormwood
Gosiute *Unspecified* Seeds formerly gathered and used for food. (39:362) **Iroquois** *Forage* Plants eaten by turkeys. (142:102)

Artemisia campestris ssp. *pacifica*, Pacific Wormwood
Navajo, Kayenta *Unspecified* Seeds made into mush and used for food. (as *A. pacifica* 205:45)

Artemisia cana, Silver Sagebrush
Blackfoot *Forage* Plant used as fall and winter forage for horses. (97:56) **Lakota** *Forage* Best sage for winter browse by livestock and game. (139:35)

Artemisia carruthii, Carruth's Sagewort
Apache, White Mountain *Unspecified* Species used for food. (as *A. wrightii* 136:155) **Navajo** *Bread & Cake* Seeds ground and made into bread and dumplings. *Porridge* Seeds ground and made into gruel. (as *A. wrightii* 165:223) *Unspecified* Seeds used for food. (as *A. wrightii* 55:82) **Zuni** *Bread & Cake* Ground seeds mixed with water, made into balls, steamed, and used for food. (as *A. wrightii* 166:65) *Unspecified* Seeds considered among the most important food plants when the Zuni reached this world. (*A. wrightii* 32:21)

Artemisia dracunculus, Wormwood
Apache, Chiricahua & Mescalero *Beverage* Leaves and young stems boiled to make a non-intoxicating beverage. (as *A. aromatica* 33:53) **Luiseño** *Unspecified* Seeds used for food. (155:228)

Artemisia dracunculus ssp. *dracunculus*, Wormwood
Gosiute *Unspecified* Oily and nutritious seeds formerly used for food. (39:363) **Hopi** *Unspecified* Leaves boiled or roasted between hot, flat stones and eaten. (32:25) Leaves baked between hot stones, dipped in salted water, and eaten. (56:19) **Shoshoni** *Spice* Steeped seeds added to dishes for flavoring. (118:29)

Artemisia filifolia, Sand Sagebrush
Navajo *Fodder* Used as stock feed. (55:81)

Artemisia frigida, Fringed Sagewort
Blackfoot *Spice* Crushed leaves mixed with stored meat to maintain a good odor. (86:101) **Hopi** *Spice* Used with sweet corn when roasting. (190:167) **Isleta** *Forage* Plant considered excellent grazing plant for sheep and cattle. (100:22)

Artemisia ludoviciana, Louisiana Sagewort
Apache, Chiricahua & Mescalero *Spice* Sage used to flavor meats. (33:47) **Blackfoot** *Candy* Leaves chewed as a confection. (86:101)

Artemisia ludoviciana ssp. *incompta*, Mountain Sagewort
Gosiute *Unspecified* Seeds formerly used for food. (as *A. discolor* 39:362)

Artemisia tilesii, Tilesius's Wormwood
Eskimo, Alaska *Unspecified* Raw shoots peeled and eaten with seal oil. (1:38)

Artemisia tridentata, Big Sagebrush
Apache, White Mountain *Beverage* Used to make tea. *Spice* Used as a seasoning. (136:155) **Paiute** *Staple* Seeds roasted, ground into flour, and eaten with water. *Starvation Food* Seeds used, generally mixed with other seeds, in times of food shortages. (167:243) **Paiute, Northern** *Candy* Gum chewed. (59:53)

Artemisia tripartita ssp. *tripartita*, Idaho Threetip Sagebrush
Gosiute *Unspecified* Seeds formerly used for food. (as *A. trifida*. 39:362)

Arthrocnemum subterminale, Parish's Glasswort
Cahuilla *Staple* Seeds ground into a meal. (as *Salicornia subterminalis* 15:135)

Artocarpus altilis, Breadfruit
Hawaiian *Fruit* Fruit cooked and eaten. (as *A. incisa* 2:38)

Asarum canadense, Canadian Wild-ginger
Chippewa *Spice* Root used as an appetizer in all cooked foods. (53:318) **Meskwaki** *Spice* Root used as seasoning for mud catfish, to destroy the mud taste and to render them palatable. Root used to cook with an animal that had died, to remove the danger of ptomaine poisoning. (152:255) **Ojibwa** *Dietary Aid* Roots render any meat dish digestible by anyone, even if they are sick. *Spice* Roots processed in lye water and used to season food and take muddy taste away from fish. (153:397) **Potawatomi** *Spice* Root flavored meat or fish and rendered otherwise inedible food, palatable. (154:96)

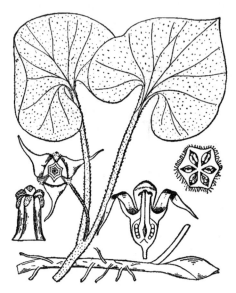

Asarum canadense

Asclepias asperula ssp. *capricornu*, Antelope Horns
Gosiute *Candy* Latex used as a chewing gum. (as *Asclepiodora decumbens* 39:363)

Asclepias californica, California Milkweed
Kawaiisu *Candy* Milky juice boiled until thick and chewed like chewing gum. Leaves roasted under hot ashes and chewed. (206:13)

Asclepias cordifolia, Heartleaf Milkweed
Karok *Candy* Latex boiled, condensed, and chewed. **Yurok** *Candy* Dried latex chewed by the older people at their leisure. (6:19)

Asclepias eriocarpa, Woollypod Milkweed
Karok *Candy* Milk stirred, heated, mixed with salmon fat or deer grease, and used for chewing gum. (148:388) **Luiseño** *Candy* Stem sap boiled in water until coagulation and used as chewing gum. (155:196) **Mendocino Indian** *Forage* Sweet-scented flowers used by bees as a source of nectar. (41:379)

Asclepias erosa, Desert Milkweed
Coahuilla *Candy* Sap collected, set aside to solidify, heated over the fire, and used as a chewing gum. (13:75) **Tubatulabal** *Candy* Juice roasted until congealed and used as chewing gum. (193:19)

Asclepias fascicularis, Mexican
Whorled Milkweed
Miwok *Cooking Agent* Boiled greens added to thicken manzanita cider. *Vegetable* Boiled greens used for food. (as *A. mexicana* 12:159) **Paiute** *Unspecified* Species used for food. (as *A. mexicana* 167:244) **Yokia** *Unspecified* Young blossoms occasionally eaten in small quantities. (as *A. mexicana* 41:380)

Asclepias incarnata, Swamp
Milkweed
Menominee *Soup* Heads, deer broth, or fat used to make soup. *Unspecified* Heads added to cornmeal mush. *Winter Use Food* Cut, dried heads stored for winter use. (as *Ascepias incarnata* 151:62)

Asclepias involucrata, Dwarf
Milkweed
Zuni *Forage* Plant favored by jackrabbits. (166:65)

Asclepias speciosa, Showy Milkweed
Acoma *Candy* Milky latex allowed to harden and used as chewing gum. (32:31) **Apache, Chiricahua & Mescalero** *Candy* "Milk" squeezed from leaves and stems and chewed as gum. (33:45) **Cheyenne** *Candy* Dried, hardened milk used for chewing gum. (76:184) Milky juice allowed to harden and used as chewing gum. (82:66) Milky juice hardened and chewed as gum. (83:14) *Fruit* Inner layer of fruit used for food. (76:184) Immature fruits peeled and inner layer eaten. (82:66) Green, immature fruits peeled and the inner layer eaten raw. (83:14) *Sauce & Relish* Flowers boiled with soup or meat, flour added, and eaten as a gravy. (82:66) *Soup* Whole buds boiled with meat or in water to make soup. (76:184) *Unspecified* Young, unopened buds boiled with

meat, grease, gravy, or soup and used for food. Tender, spring shoots eaten raw. (83:46) Young, unopened buds boiled with meat, grease, gravy, or soup and eaten. Tender stalks cooked, sweetened, and used for food. (83:14) **Crow** *Sauce & Relish* Flowers boiled with soup or meat, flour added, and eaten as a gravy. (82:66) *Unspecified* Flowers boiled for food. Seeds eaten raw. (19:7) **Hopi** *Unspecified* Boiled with meat. (190:164) **Keres, Western** *Candy* Milky juice used as chewing gum. (171:30) **Laguna** *Candy* Milky latex allowed to harden and used as chewing gum. (32:31) **Lakota** *Cooking Agent* Floral bud clusters used to thicken soup. *Preserves* Open flowers cut up for a sort of preserve. *Unspecified* Blossoms boiled, mixed with flour, and eaten. (139:34) **Paiute** *Candy* Dried sap chewed as gum. (111:105) *Unspecified* Species used for food. (167:242) **Shoshoni** *Candy* Milk rolled in hand and used for gum. (118:56)

Asclepias subverticillata, Whorled
Milkweed
Apache, White Mountain *Unspecified* First buds eaten by children. (as *A. galioides* 136:155) **Jemez** *Unspecified* Roots and unripe pods eaten raw. (as *A. galioides* 32:17) **Keres, Western** *Candy* Ripe seed silk mixed with grease and used as chewing gum. (as *A. galioides* 171:30) **Zuni** *Unspecified* Buds eaten by little boys. (as *A. galioides* 166:65)

Asclepias syriaca, Common Milkweed
Chippewa *Appetizer* Plant eaten before a feast to increase the appetite. *Preserves* Flowers cut up, stewed, and eaten like preserves. (53:320) *Vegetable* Tender leaves, young green seedpods, sprouts, and tops cooked as greens. (71:140) **Dakota** *Unspecified* Sprouts used in early spring for food. (69:363) **Iroquois** *Vegetable* Stalks eaten as greens in spring. (124:93) Tender stems, leaves, and immature flower clusters cooked and seasoned with salt, pepper, or butter. (196:117) **Meskwaki** *Soup* Buds used in soups. *Vegetable* Buds cooked with meat or added to cornmeal mush, tastes like okra. *Winter Use Food* Dried buds stored away in paper bags for winter use. (152:256) **Mohegan**

Unspecified Cooked and used for food. (176:83) **Ojibwa** *Unspecified* Young pods cooked with salt and vinegar. *Vegetable* Young shoots and flower buds cooked like spinach. (5:2205) Fresh flowers and shoot tips, mucilaginous like okra when cooked, used in meat soups. *Winter Use Food* Dried flowers, freshened in the wintertime, made into soup. (153:397) **Omaha** *Vegetable* Tender shoots boiled and eaten as a vegetable. (58:341) Young shoots used for food like asparagus. Inflorescence, before the flower buds opened, and young fruits used as greens. (68:325) Boiled young sprouts, floral bud clusters, and young, firm green fruits used for food. **Pawnee** *Vegetable* Boiled young sprouts, floral bud clusters, and young, firm green fruits used for food. **Ponca** *Vegetable* Boiled young sprouts, floral bud clusters, and young, firm green fruits used for food. (70:109) **Potawatomi** *Soup* Flowers and buds used to thicken meat soups and to impart a very pleasing flavor to the dish. (154:96) **Winnebago** *Vegetable* Boiled young sprouts, floral bud clusters, and young, firm green fruits used for food. (70:109)

Asclepias verticillata, Whorled Milkweed
Hopi *Unspecified* Leaves and young shoots boiled with meat and eaten. (56:18)

Asclepias viridiflora, Green Milkweed
Blackfoot *Soup* Root pieces stored for winter soups. *Spice* Plant used to spice soups. *Unspecified* Fresh roots used for food. (86:101)

Asimina triloba, Common Pawpaw
Cherokee *Fruit* Fruit used for food. (80:47) **Iroquois** *Bread & Cake* Fruit mashed, made into small cakes, and dried for future use. *Dried Food* Raw or cooked fruit sun or fire dried and stored for future use. *Fruit* Dried fruit taken as a hunting food. *Sauce & Relish* Dried fruit cakes soaked in warm water and cooked as a sauce or mixed with corn bread. (196:129)

Asparagus officinalis, Garden Asparagus
Cherokee *Vegetable* Species used for food. (80:24) **Iroquois** *Vegetable* Stalks eaten as greens in spring. (124:93) **Isleta** *Unspecified* Uncultivated but used as food when found in the wild. (32:17) *Vegetable* Boiled, seasoned spears used for food. (100:23)

Aster dumosus, Rice Button Aster
Tewa *Fruit* Small fruits eaten. (as *Sericotheca dumosa* 138:49)

Aster laevis var. geyeri, Geyer's Smooth Aster
Keres, Western *Unspecified* Flowers mixed with parched corn and eaten. (as *A. geyeri* 171:30)

Aster macrophyllus, Bigleaf Aster
Algonquin, Quebec *Vegetable* Leaves used for greens. (18:108) **Ojibwa** *Soup* Roots used as a soup material. *Unspecified* Young and tender leaves eaten and act as a medicine at the same time that they are food. (153:398)

Astragalus australis, Indian Milkvetch
Canadian Indian *Unspecified* Roots used for food. (as *A. aboriginum* 97:39)

Astragalus canadensis, Canadian Milkvetch
Blackfoot *Staple* Root considered a staple. *Unspecified* Roots eaten fresh or boiled in blood or broth. (86:101) Roots eaten raw or boiled. (97:39) **Lakota** *Fodder* Seeds eaten by horses. (139:45)

Astragalus canadensis var. canadensis, Canadian Milkvetch
Blackfoot *Unspecified* Roots eaten raw or boiled. (as *A. carolinianus* 114:278)

Astragalus ceramicus, Painted Milkvetch
Hopi *Candy* Sweet roots eaten by children. (42:291)

Astragalus ceramicus var. ceramicus, Painted Milkvetch
Hopi Roots eaten as a sweet. (as *A. pictus filifolius* 56:16)

Astragalus ceramicus var. filifolius, Painted Milkvetch
Hopi *Unspecified* Sweet roots dug up and eaten by children. (200:79)

Astragalus crassicarpus, Groundplum Milkvetch
Dakota *Unspecified* Plant sometimes eaten raw and fresh. (69:365) **Lakota** *Fruit* Fruits eaten for food. (139:46)

Astragalus crassicarpus var. crassicarpus, Groundplum Milkvetch
Montana Indian *Unspecified* Fleshy, plum-like pods eaten raw, boiled, and used for pickles. (as *A. caryocarpus* 19:7)

Astragalus cyaneus, Cyanic Milkvetch
Keres, Western *Unspecified* Tubers eaten. (as *A. jemensis* 171:31)

Astragalus giganteus, Giant Milkvetch
Thompson *Fodder* Used as a rich horse and deer feed. (164:514)

Astragalus lentiginosus var. diphysus, Speckledpod Milkvetch
Acoma *Unspecified* Fleshy roots eaten fresh. (as *A. diphysus* 32:17) **Apache, White Mountain** *Fruit* Pea fruit eaten raw and cooked. (as *A. diphysus* 136:155) **Jemez** *Unspecified* Pods eaten raw or cooked. **Laguna** *Unspecified* Fleshy roots eaten fresh. (as *A. diphysus* 32:17) **Zuni** *Dried Food* Pods dried for winter use. *Unspecified* Pods eaten fresh, boiled, and salted. (as *A. diphysus* 166:65)

Astragalus miser, Weedy Milkvetch
Okanagan-Colville *Unspecified* Seeds used for food. (188:105) **Thompson** *Unspecified* Plant placed at the top of the cooking pit in the absence of black tree lichen and wild onion. (187:222)

Astragalus miser var. decumbens, Prostrate Loco Milkvetch
Thompson *Fodder* Used as a rich horse and deer feed. (as *A. decumbens* 164:514)

Astragalus mollissimus var. matthewsii, Matthews's Woolly Milkvetch
Navajo, Ramah *Forage* Plant and roots eaten by sheep. (as *A. matthewsii* 191:32)

Astragalus polaris, Polar Milkvetch
Eskimo, Alaska *Unspecified* Tiny peas eaten raw or cooked. (1:36)

Astragalus purshii, Woollypod Milkvetch
Thompson *Forage* Used as a common forage plant. (164:516)

Asyneuma prenanthoides, California Harebell
Costanoan *Winter Use Food* Bulbs eaten in winter and early spring. (as *Campanula prenanthoides* 21:254)

Athyrium filix-femina, Common Ladyfern
Quileute *Unspecified* Rhizomes roasted, peeled, and the centers eaten. **Quinault** *Unspecified* Rhizomes roasted, peeled, and the centers eaten. (79:14) **Salish, Coast** *Unspecified* New shoots and rhizomes used for food. (182:68)

Atriplex argentea, Silverscale Saltbush
Acoma *Fruit* Fruits eaten for food. (32:18) **Hopi** *Unspecified* Leaves boiled and eaten with fat. (56:21) Boiled with meat. (190:160) *Vegetable* Young, tender leaves cooked and eaten as greens. (200:73) **Isleta** *Vegetable* Young leaves boiled and eaten as greens. (32:18) **Keres, Western** *Forage* Plant used as forage for cattle. *Unspecified* Seeds and expanded calyx eaten for food and the salty taste. (171:31) **Laguna** *Fruit* Fruits eaten for food. (32:18) **Paiute, Northern** *Porridge* Seeds parched, ground into a flour, and made into mush. (59:47) **Pueblo** *Spice* Boiled alone or with plant products and

Atriplex argentea

meats for flavoring. Boiled alone or with plant products and meats for flavoring. (as *A. cornuta* 32:18)

Atriplex argentea ssp. *expansa*,
Silverscale Saltbush
Navajo *Fodder* Plant used, for the salt, and stored for the winter as fodder. *Forage* Plant used, for the salt, to pasture sheep in the summer. (as *A. expansa* 55:43)

Atriplex canescens, Fourwing Saltbush
Gosiute *Unspecified* Seeds used for food. (39:363) **Hopi** *Substitution Food* Ashes used instead of baking soda. (as *Calligonum canescens* 190:160) **Navajo** *Fodder* Plant used in the winter to provide salt for the sheep. *Forage* Plant used as forage for cattle, sheep, and goats, especially when other forage was scarce. (55:43) *Pie & Pudding* Flowers used to make puddings. (90:148) **Navajo, Ramah** *Fodder* Used for sheep feed. *Spice* Leaves placed on coals in pit for roasting corn, to impart a salty taste. (191:24) **Tewa of Hano** *Cooking Agent* Ashes stirred into dough to give it a greenish blue color. (138:54)

Atriplex confertifolia, Shadscale
Saltbush
Gosiute *Unspecified* Seeds formerly used for food. (39:363) **Hopi** *Pie & Pudding* Scented leaves boiled and water mixed with cornmeal to make a pudding. (32:17) Leaves boiled in water, the water mixed with cornmeal, and baked into a pudding. (56:20) *Spice* Plant used as flavoring with meat or other vegetables. (as *A. jonesii* 42:293) *Unspecified* Boiled with meat. (as *Obione confertifolia* 190:160) *Vegetable* Plant used for greens. (as *A. jonesii* 42:293) Young, tender leaves cooked and eaten as greens. (200:73)

Atriplex coronata, Crownscale
Pima *Cooking Agent* Boiled with dried cane cactus to counteract its acidic flavor. (32:36) *Spice* Plants boiled with other foods for their salty flavor. *Unspecified* Plants roasted in pits with cactus fruits and eaten. (146:69)

Atriplex elegans, Wheelscale Saltbush
Pima *Cooking Agent* Boiled with dried cane cactus to counteract its acidic flavor. (32:36) *Spice* Plants boiled with other foods for their salty flavor. *Unspecified* Plants roasted in pits with cactus fruits and eaten. (146:69) **Pima, Gila River** *Unspecified* Leaves boiled and eaten. (133:7)

Atriplex lentiformis, Big Saltbush
Cahuilla *Porridge* Seeds ground into a flour and used to make mush or small cakes. (15:45) **Papago** *Unspecified* Seeds used for food. (36:62) **Pima** *Dried Food* Seeds roasted, dried, parched, and stored. (32:23) *Porridge* Seeds pounded into meal, cooked, mixed with water, and eaten as mush. (95:263) Seeds pit roasted, dried, parched, added to water, and eaten as a thick gruel. (146:78) *Starvation Food* Tiny seeds formerly roasted and eaten during famines. (47:66) **Pima, Gila River** *Starvation Food* Seeds used as "starvation food." (133:6) *Unspecified* Seeds used for food. (133:7) **Yuma** *Porridge* Seeds boiled to make a mush. (37:187) *Unspecified* Seeds pounded, pit baked, ground, mixed with water to form stiff dough, and eaten raw. (37:200)

Atriplex nuttallii, Nuttall's Saltbush
Pima *Bread & Cake* Stems used as stuffing for
roast rabbit. (146:77) *Spice* Young stems and
flower heads used as flavoring. *Unspecified*
Stems cut in short lengths and used as a stuffing
in cooked rabbits. (32:18) Stems boiled with
wheat and used for food. (146:77)

Atriplex obovata, Mound Saltbush
Hopi *Spice* Plant used as flavoring with meat or
other vegetables. *Vegetable* Plant used for
greens. (42:293) Young, tender leaves cooked
and eaten as greens. (200:73)

Atriplex polycarpa, Cattle Saltbush
Pima *Bread & Cake* Seeds made into bread and
used for food. *Forage* Used as an important forage plant. *Starvation Food* Seeds formerly
roasted, ground, and eaten during famines.
(47:67) **Yuma** *Unspecified* Seeds separated
from hulls and eaten. (37:187)

Atriplex powellii, Powell's Saltweed
Cochiti *Vegetable* Young plants eaten as greens.
Hopi *Unspecified* Salty leaves boiled and eaten
with fat. (as *A. philonitra* 32:18) *Vegetable*
Young, tender leaves cooked and eaten as
greens. (200:73) **Keres, Western** *Vegetable*
Young plants used for greens. (as *A. philonitra*
171:31) **Navajo, Kayenta** *Substitution Food*
Used as a greens and salt substitute in foods.
(205:20) **Pueblo** *Vegetable* Young plants eaten
as greens. (as *A. philonitra* 32:18) **Zuni** *Porridge* Seeds mixed with ground corn to make a
mush. (32:22) Seeds eaten raw before the presence of corn and afterwards, ground with cornmeal and made into a mush. (166:66)

Atriplex rosea, Tumbling Saltweed
Navajo, Ramah *Fodder* Used for sheep and
horse feed and harvested for winter use. *Porridge* Seeds of dried plants threshed on a blan-
ket, winnowed, ground, and made into a mush
or used like maize. (191:24)

Atriplex saccaria, Sack Saltbush
Hopi *Vegetable* Young, tender leaves cooked
and eaten as greens. (200:73)

Atriplex semibaccata, Australian
  Saltbush
Cahuilla *Fruit* Berries gathered and eaten
fresh. (15:45)

Atriplex serenana, Bractscale
Kawaiisu *Vegetable* Leaves boiled, fried in
grease, and eaten. (206:15) **Pima** *Cooking
Agent* Boiled with dried cane cactus to counteract its acidic flavor. (as *A. bracteosa* 32:36)
Spice Plants boiled with other foods for their
salty flavor. *Unspecified* Plants roasted in pits
with cactus fruits and eaten. (as *A. bracteosa*
146:69)

Atriplex torreyi, Torrey's Saltbush
Kamia *Staple* Pulverized seeds made into a
meal. (62:24)

Atriplex truncata, Wedgescale Saltbush
Gosiute *Unspecified* Seeds used for food.
(39:363)

Atriplex wrightii, Wright's Saltbush
Papago *Soup* Mixed with roasted cholla buds
and eaten as a vegetable stew. (34:16) *Spice*
Branches used as seasoning in cooking or in
pit baking. (34:15) *Vegetable* Branches eaten
as greens in summer. (34:14) Greens used for
food. (36:61) **Pima** *Vegetable* Leaves boiled,
strained, fried in grease, and eaten as greens.
(47:69) **Pima, Gila River** *Unspecified* Leaves
boiled and eaten. (133:7)

Avena barbata, Slender Oat
Cahuilla *Unspecified* Small seeds used for
food. (15:46) **Miwok** *Porridge* Parched, stone
boiled seeds pulverized and eaten as a mush.
Soup Parched, stone boiled seeds pulverized
and eaten as a soup. (12:152)

Avena fatua, Wild Oat
Cahuilla *Porridge* Parched seeds ground into
flour and used to make mush. (15:46) **Diegueño** *Porridge* Moistened, hulled kernels
boiled and eaten as hot cereal. (84:15)
Kawaiisu *Unspecified* Seeds pounded in a bedrock mortar hole, boiled, and eaten. (206:15)

Luiseño *Staple* Seeds ground into a flour and used for food. (155:234) **Mendocino Indian** *Staple* Seeds parched, ground, and the flour eaten dry. (41:311) **Pomo** *Staple* Seeds used to make pinoles. (11:87) *Unspecified* Seeds used for food. (41:311) Parched, pounded seeds used for food. *Winter Use Food* Seeds stored for later use. (66:11)

Avena sativa, Common Oat
Haisla & Hanaksiala *Unspecified* Grains used for food. (43:205) **Karok** *Unspecified* Species used for food. (148:380) **Navajo** *Fodder* Used for hay. (55:25) **Navajo, Ramah** *Fodder* Fed to horses without being thrashed and in a bad winter fed to sheep and goats. (191:15) **Pomo** *Unspecified* Seeds parched in a circular coiled basket and used for food. (66:11)

Avena fatua

Baccharis salicifolia, Mule's Fat
Mohave *Starvation Food* Young shoots roasted and eaten as a famine food. **Yuma** *Starvation Food* Young shoots roasted and eaten as a famine food. (as *B. glutinosa* 37:201)

Baccharis sarothroides, Desert Broom
Papago *Beverage* Seeds steeped and used as tea-like drinks for refreshment. (34:27)

Balsamorhiza deltoidea, Deltoid Balsamroot
Atsugewi *Bread & Cake* Parched, winnowed, ground seeds made into cakes and eaten without cooking. (61:139) **Karok** *Unspecified* Peduncles used for food. (6:20) **Klamath** *Unspecified* Roasted, ground seeds used for food. (45:106)

Balsamorhiza hookeri, Hooker's Balsamroot
Atsugewi *Bread & Cake* Parched, winnowed, ground seeds made into cakes and eaten without cooking. (61:139) **Gosiute** *Unspecified* Seeds used for food. (39:363) **Okanagan-Colville** *Unspecified* Roots pit cooked and eaten. (188:80) **Paiute, Northern** *Unspecified* Roots used for food. (59:43)

Balsamorhiza incana, Hoary Balsamroot
Nez Perce *Unspecified* Thick roots eaten raw. (19:7)

Balsamorhiza sagittata, Arrowleaf Balsamroot
Atsugewi *Bread & Cake* Parched, winnowed, ground seeds made into cakes and eaten without cooking. (61:139) **Flathead** *Unspecified* Young, immature flower stems peeled and eaten

raw. Roots pit baked and used for food. (82:20) **Gosiute** *Cooking Agent* Seeds a highly prized source of oil. *Unspecified* Leaves and petioles boiled and eaten. Seeds a highly prized source of food. (39:363) **Klamath** *Unspecified* Roasted, ground seeds used for food. (45:106) **Kutenai** *Unspecified* Young, immature flower stems peeled and eaten raw. (82:20) **Miwok** *Unspecified* Cracked seeds pulverized, winnowed, and eaten. (12:152) **Montana Indian** *Staple* Roasted seeds ground into a flour. (19:8) *Unspecified* Plant heated, fermented, and eaten. (19:26) Roots eaten raw and cooked. *Vegetable* Young stems and leaves eaten raw as a salad. (19:8) **Nez Perce** *Unspecified* Young, immature flower stems peeled and eaten raw. Seeds roasted, ground, grease added, and mixture eaten. (82:20) **Okanagan-Colville** *Dried Food* Seeds oven dried for future use. *Unspecified* Young shoots eaten raw or baked in the ground or oven. Flower bud stems peeled and succulent inner portion eaten raw or boiled. Powdered seeds eaten alone or mixed with deer grease, pine nuts, saskatoon berries, or fir sugar. (188:80) **Okanagon** *Staple* Seeds used as a principal food. (178:239) Roots used as a principal food. (178:238) *Unspecified* Young plants used for food. Old, large roots cooked and used for food. (125:36) Roots used as an important food. (178:237) Seeds roasted in baskets with hot stones and eaten. (178:240) **Paiute** *Beverage* Juice from the stems sucked when thirsty. *Candy* Root pitch chewed as gum. (111:117) *Pie & Pudding* Ground seed meal and juniper berries used to make a pudding. (118:26) *Porridge* Roasted, ground seeds made into flour and used to make mush. *Unspecified* Blooming stems peeled and eaten. *Winter Use Food* Roasted, ground seeds made into flour and stored for winter use. (111:117) **Sanpoil** *Special Food* Shoots mixed with chocolate tips and used in the "first roots" ceremony. (188:80) **Shuswap** *Unspecified* Roots steamed and eaten. (123:59) **Thompson** *Bread & Cake* Seeds mixed with deer fat or grease, boiled, cooled, and made into small cakes. (164:491) *Dessert* Dried roots cooked and eaten as a "sort of dessert" after meals. *Dried Food* Cooked roots hung on strings,

dried, and then stored on the strings or in baskets. (187:175) *Staple* Seeds pounded and flour mixed with other foods. (164:491) *Starvation Food* Dried seed flour eaten as porridge, especially in times of famine. The seeds were laid on mats, sun dried, placed in buckskin bags, and pounded into a flour. The resulting flour was made into a porridge and eaten, especially in times of famine. One informant said that the seeds were "choky" and difficult to swallow if eaten alone. (187:175) *Unspecified* Young plants used for food. Old, large roots cooked and used for food. (125:36) Plant used for food. (164:480) Young stems eaten as a favorite food. Stalks soaked in water, peeled, and eaten raw. Crowns chewed or sucked. (164:484) Ripe seeds eaten raw. (164:491) Roots used as an important food. (178:237) Loose or skewered roots cooked overnight in a steaming pit and used for food. Young shoots chewed while eating fish. Young leafstalks, leaves, young bud stems, and fruits used for food. Root crown, with the young undeveloped leaves, used for food. (187:175) **Ute** *Unspecified* Young shoots, leaves, and roots used for food. (38:32)

Balsamorhiza ×*terebinthacea*, Balsamroot
Paiute *Dried Food* Dried roots eaten raw. *Unspecified* Fresh roots roasted, ground, and pounded or eaten raw. (104:103)

Barbarea orthoceras, American Yellowrocket
Alaska Native *Vegetable* Rosettes of dark green shiny leaves cooked as a green vegetable or eaten raw in a mixed salad. (85:17)

Barbarea verna, Early Yellowrocket
Cherokee *Unspecified* Plant boiled, fried, and eaten. (204:252) *Vegetable* Leaves parboiled, rinsed, seasoned with grease and salt, and cooked until tender as potherbs. Leaves used in salads. (126:36)

Barbarea vulgaris, Garden Yellowrocket
Cherokee *Unspecified* Plant boiled, fried, and

eaten. (204:252) *Vegetable* Leaves parboiled, rinsed, seasoned with grease and salt, and cooked until tender as potherbs. Leaves used in salads. (126:36)

Beckmannia syzigachne, American Sloughgrass
Klamath *Unspecified* Seeds used for food. (as *B. erucaeformis* 45:91) **Montana Indian** *Unspecified* Seeds used for food. (as *B. erucaeformis* 19:8) **Navajo, Ramah** *Fodder* Used as sheep and horse feed. (191:15)

Berberis fendleri, Colorado Barberry
Jemez *Fruit* Berries used for food. (32:19) Berries used for food. (44:21)

Berlandiera lyrata, Lyreleaf Greeneyes
Acoma *Spice* Flowers mixed with sausage as seasoning. (32:19) **Keres, Western** *Spice* Flowers mixed with sausage as seasoning. (171:33) **Laguna** *Spice* Flowers mixed with sausage as seasoning. (32:19)

Berula erecta, Cutleaf Waterparsnip
Apache, White Mountain *Unspecified* Leaves and blossoms used for food. (136:155)

Beta vulgaris, Common Beet
Anticosti *Beverage* Bulbs used to make wine. (143:65) **Cherokee** *Unspecified* Species used for food. (80:25)

Betula alleghaniensis var. *alleghaniensis*, Yellow Birch
Algonquin, Quebec *Substitution Food* Sap mixed with maple sap if the latter is not available in sufficient quantities. (as *B. lutea* 18:80) **Ojibwa** *Beverage* Sap and maple sap used for a pleasant beverage drink. (as *B. lutea* 153:397)

Betula lenta, Sweet Birch
Iroquois *Beverage* Twigs steeped into a beverage. (196:148)

Betula papyrifera, Paper Birch
Algonquin, Quebec *Sauce & Relish* Sap used to make syrup. (18:80) **Cree, Woodlands** *Pre-*

servative Soft, rotten wood burned to make a slow, smoky fire to smoke cure meat and fish. *Sauce & Relish* Sap collected, made into syrup, and eaten on bannock. *Substitution Food* Root bark used as a tea substitute. *Unspecified* Cambium eaten fresh from the tree trunk. (109:32) **Montagnais** *Dietary Aid* Inner bark grated and eaten to benefit the diet. (156:313) **Ojibwa** *Preservative* Birch bark keeps the food stored in it from spoiling. (as *B. alba* var. *papyrifera* 153:416) **Tanana, Upper** *Unspecified* Raw sap, sometimes mixed with fish grease, used for food. Sap used for food. (102:5)

Bidens amplectens, Kokolau
Hopi *Beverage* Used to make coffee. (as *B. gracilis* 190:168)

Bidens laevis, Smooth Beggartick
Paiute *Unspecified* Species used for food. (167:244)

Blechnum spicant, Deer Fern
Haisla & Hanaksiala *Forage* Plant eaten by mountain goats and deer. (43:153) **Hesquiat** *Starvation Food* Young, tender stalks peeled and center portion eaten when hungry and there is nothing to eat. (185:29) **Makah** *Spice* Fronds used for flavor in cooking by placing them under the items to be cooked. (67:219) **Nitinaht** *Starvation Food* Fronds eaten to relieve hunger when lost in the bushes. (186:63)

Blennosperma nanum, Common Stickyseed
Neeshenam *Bread & Cake* Seeds parched, ground into flour, and used to make bread. *Porridge* Seeds parched, ground into flour, and used to make mush. *Staple* Seeds parched, ground into flour, and used for food. (as *B. californicum* 129:377)

Bloomeria crocea, Common Goldenstars
Cahuilla *Unspecified* Corms eaten raw any time of the year. (15:47)

Bloomeria crocea var. *aurea*,
Common Goldenstars
Luiseño *Unspecified* Bulb used for food. (as *B. aurea* 155:233)

Boisduvalia densiflora, Denseflower
Spike Primrose
Mendocino Indian *Bread & Cake* Seeds used to make bread. *Staple* Seeds eaten as a pinole. (41:370) **Miwok** *Unspecified* Parched, pulverized, dried seeds used for food. Stored, unparched seeds used for food. (12:152) **Pomo** *Staple* Seeds used to make pinoles. (11:86)

Boisduvalia stricta, Brook Spike
Primrose
Miwok *Unspecified* Parched, pulverized seeds used for food. (12:152)

Boletus edulis, Timber Mushroom
Pomo, Kashaya *Vegetable* Cooked on hot stones, baked in the oven, or fried. (72:132)

Boschniakia hookeri, Vancouver
Groundcone
Hesquiat *Unspecified* Peeled roots eaten raw. (185:70) **Luiseño** *Unspecified* Roots used for food. (as *Orobanche tuberosa* 155:229)

Boschniakia rossica, Northern
Groundcone
Tanana, Upper *Fodder* Raw roots or above ground portion of plant diced, mixed with other food, and used for puppy and dog food. (102:15)

Boschniakia strobilacea, California
Groundcone
Karok *Unspecified* Eaten when young. **Yurok** *Unspecified* Species used for food. (6:20)

Bouteloua curtipendula var.
curtipendula, Sideoats Grama
Kiowa *Fodder* Recognized as a good fodder. (as *Atheropogon curtipendula* and *Chloris curtipendula* 192:14)

Bouteloua gracilis

Bouteloua gracilis, Blue Grama
Apache, Western *Porridge* Seeds ground, mixed with cornmeal and water and made into a mush. (26:189) **Apache, White Mountain** *Bread & Cake* Seeds ground and used to make bread and pones. *Porridge* Seeds ground, mixed with meal, and water and eaten as mush. (136:149) **Hopi** *Forage* Used as an important forage grass. (200:64) **Keres, Western** *Forage* Grass used for grazing purposes. (as *B. cligostachya* 171:33) **Montana Indian** *Forage* Grass used for forage. (as *B. oligostachya* 19:8) **Navajo, Ramah** *Forage* Important forage grass. (191:15)

Bouteloua hirsuta, Hairy Grama
Kiowa *Fodder* Very good fodder for horses and mules. (192:14)

Bouteloua simplex, Matted Grama
Navajo, Ramah *Forage* Important forage grass for a short season. (191:16)

Brassica napus, Rape
Cherokee *Vegetable* Leaves boiled and served with drippings, or boiled, fried with other greens, and eaten. (as *B. napa* 204:253)

Brassica nigra, Black Mustard
Diegueño *Vegetable* Young, spring leaves
boiled and eaten as greens. (84:15) **Hoh** *Spice*
Used for flavoring. *Vegetable* Plants eaten as
greens. (137:61) **Iroquois** *Vegetable* Cooked
and seasoned with salt, pepper, or butter.
(196:117) **Luiseño** *Vegetable* Plant used for
greens. (155:232) **Mohegan** *Vegetable* Combined with pigweed, plantain, dock, and nettle
and used as mixed greens. (176:83) **Quileute**
Spice Used for flavoring. *Vegetable* Plants eaten
as greens. (137:61)

Brassica oleracea, Cabbage
Cherokee *Vegetable* Leaves used for food.
(80:28) **Haisla & Hanaksiala** *Vegetable* Species used for food. (43:227) **Kitasoo** *Vegetable*
Leaves used for food. (43:328) **Lakota** *Vegetable* Leaves eaten as greens. (106:34) **Okanagan-
Colville** *Vegetable* Heads used for food.
(188:92) **Seminole** *Unspecified* Plant used for
food. (169:485)

Brassica rapa, Rape Mustard
Haisla & Hanaksiala *Vegetable* Roots used for
food. (43:227) **Kitasoo** *Vegetable* Roots used
for food. (43:329) **Okanagan-Colville** *Vegetable* Roots used for food. (188:92) **Oweekeno**
Unspecified Roots used for food. (43:89)

Brassica rapa var. rapa, Birdrape
Cherokee *Vegetable* Leaves cooked with turnip
greens, creaseys (probably *Lepidium virginicum*), and sochan (*Rudbeckia laciniata*) and
eaten. (as *B. campestris* 204:253) **Mendocino
Indian** *Vegetable* Young leaves eaten as greens
in imitation of the first white settlers who first
ate them. (as *B. campestris* 41:352)

Brickellia californica, California
    Brickellbush
Sanel *Substitution Food* Leaves used as a substitute for tea. (as *Coleosanthus californicus*
41:393)

Brickellia grandiflora, Tasselflower
    Brickellbush
Gosiute *Cooking Agent* Seeds and other seeds
made into a meal and used as "baking powder"
to improve the cakes. (39:364)

Brodiaea coronaria, Harvest
    Clusterlily
Atsugewi *Unspecified* Roots boiled in water or
cooked in earth oven and used for food.
(61:138) **Mendocino Indian** *Forage* Corms
eaten by sheep. *Unspecified* Corms roasted and
used for food. (as *Hookera coronaria* 41:326)
Miwok *Unspecified* Bulbs steamed in earth ov-
en and eaten without salt. (12:156) **Pomo** *Unspecified* Corms roasted and eaten. (as *Hookera
coronaria* 11:89) **Pomo, Kashaya** *Vegetable*
Baked or boiled corms eaten like baked or
boiled potatoes. (72:27)

Brodiaea elegans, Elegant Clusterlily
Yurok *Vegetable* Bulbs baked in sand with a
fire built over them. (6:21)

Brodiaea minor, Vernalpool Clusterlily
Yana *Unspecified* Roots steamed and eaten.
(147:251)

Bromus anomalus, Nodding Brome
Navajo, Ramah *Fodder* Used for horse feed.
(191:16)

Bromus carinatus, California Brome
Neeshenam *Bread & Cake* Seeds parched,
ground into flour and used to make bread. *Porridge* Seeds parched, ground into flour, and
used to make mush. *Staple* Seeds parched,
ground into flour, and used for food. (as *Pro-
mus virens* 129:377)

Bromus catharticus, Rescue Grass
Kiowa *Fodder* Grass recognized as an important fodder. Grass recognized as an important
fodder. (as *B. unioloides* 192:14)

Bromus diandrus, Ripgut Brome
Karok *Porridge* Seeds parched, pounded into
a meal, and mixed with water into a gruel. (as

B. rigidus 148:380) **Luiseño** *Unspecified* Seeds used for food. (as *B. maximus* 155:234) **Miwok** *Unspecified* Pulverized seeds made into pinole. (as *B. rigidus* var. *gussonei* 12:152)

Bromus hordeaceus, Soft Brome
Karok *Porridge* Seeds parched, pounded into a meal, and mixed with water into a gruel. (148:379)

Bromus marginatus, Mountain Brome
Mendocino Indian *Staple* Seeds formerly used for pinole. (41:312)

***Bromus marginatus* var. brevia-ristatus**, Mountain Brome
Gosiute *Unspecified* Seeds formerly eaten. (as *B. breviaristatus* 39:364)

Bromus tectorum, Cheat Grass
Cahuilla *Starvation Food* Seeds, a famine food, cooked into a gruel during food shortages. (15:48) **Navajo, Ramah** *Fodder* Used for sheep and horse feed. (191:16)

Buchloe dactyloides, Buffalo Grass
Blackfoot *Forage* Used as an excellent fall and winter pasture for horses. (97:20)

Caesalpinia jamesii, James's Holdback
Comanche *Unspecified* Raw or boiled tubers used for food. (as *Hoffmanseggia jamesii* 29:522)

Calandrinia ciliata, Fringed Redmaids
Costanoan *Staple* Seeds, in great quantities, used for pinole. *Unspecified* Raw foliage used for food. (21:251) **Luiseño** *Unspecified* Seeds used for food. *Vegetable* Tender plant used for greens. (as *C. caulescens* 155:232) **Miwok** *Unspecified* Oily, pulverized seeds pressed into balls and cakes for eating. (as *C. caulescens* var. *mensiesii* 12:152) **Numlaki** *Staple* Tiny, jet-black seeds eaten as pinole. (as *C. elegans* 41:346)

Calocedrus decurrens, Incense Cedar
Round Valley Indian *Spice* Dense leaflets used as flavoring in leaching acorn meal. (as *Libocedrus decurrens* 41:306)

Calochortus amabilis, Short Lily
Pomo, Kashaya *Vegetable* Baked or boiled bulbs eaten like baked or boiled potatoes. (72:32)

Calochortus aureus, Golden Mariposa Lily
Hopi *Unspecified* Roots eaten raw. (56:18) Bulbs and flowers eaten. (190:159) **Navajo** *Unspecified* Bulbs gathered in early spring, peeled, and eaten raw. (55:32) **Navajo, Ramah** *Unspecified* Bulbs used for food. (as *C. nuttallii* var. *aureus* 191:20)

Calochortus catalinae, Santa Catalina Mariposa Lily
Cahuilla *Unspecified* Bulbs roasted in hot ash pits or steamed prior to eating. (15:50)

Calochortus concolor, Goldenbowl Mariposa Lily
Cahuilla *Unspecified* Bulbs roasted in hot ash pits or steamed prior to eating. (15:50)

Calochortus flexuosus, Winding
  Mariposa Lily
Cahuilla *Unspecified* Bulbs roasted in hot ash
pits or steamed prior to eating. (15:50)

Calochortus gunnisonii, Gunnison's
  Mariposa Lily
Cheyenne *Dried Food* Bulbs dried and used as
a winter food. (83:12) *Porridge* Dried bulbs
pounded fine and meal boiled into a sweet porridge or mush. (76:172) *Unspecified* Bulbs
cooked fresh and used for food. Young buds
used for food. (83:12) Species used for food.
(83:45) *Winter Use Food* Dried bulbs stored for
winter use. (76:172) **Navajo, Ramah** *Unspecified* Bulbs eaten raw or gathered in the fall and
boiled. (191:20)

Calochortus leichtlinii, Smoky
  Mariposa
Paiute, Northern *Dried Food* Roots dried and
eaten. *Soup* Roots dried and eaten or ground
and cooked in soup. *Vegetable* Roots and tubers
peeled and eaten roasted or raw. (59:44)

Calochortus luteus, Yellow Mariposa
  Lily
Miwok *Unspecified* Roasted bulbs used for

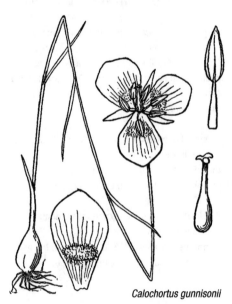

Calochortus gunnisonii

food. (12:157) **Navajo** *Unspecified* Bulbs gathered in early spring, peeled, and eaten raw.
(55:32) **Pomo, Kashaya** *Vegetable* Baked
bulbs eaten like baked potatoes. (72:64)

Calochortus macrocarpus, Sage-
  brush Mariposa Lily
Klamath *Unspecified* Species used for food.
(45:93) **Okanagan-Colville** *Unspecified* Bulbs
eaten raw or pit cooked with other roots.
(188:41) **Okanagon** *Staple* Roots used as a
principal food. (178:238) *Unspecified* Corms
formerly cooked and used for food. Sweet flower
buds used for food. (125:37) **Paiute** *Unspecified* Bulbs skinned and eaten fresh in spring.
(104:102) *Vegetable* Bulbs eaten raw, boiled, or
roasted. (111:58) **Shuswap** *Forage* Plant eaten
by cattle and sheep. *Unspecified* Roots eaten
either raw or cooked. (123:54) **Thompson** *Unspecified* Corms formerly cooked and used for
food. Sweet flower buds used for food. (125:37)
Coated, starchy corms used for food. (164:481)
Sweet buds eaten. Unopened flowers eaten raw.
(164:483) Corms used for food, usually raw, but
sometimes cooked. (187:119)

Calochortus nuttallii, Sego Lily
Gosiute *Dried Food* Bulbs formerly dried and
preserved for winter use. *Unspecified* Bulbs formerly used for food. (39:364) **Great Basin
Indian** *Winter Use Food* Bulbs used for food
during the winter. (121:47) **Havasupai** *Unspecified* Bulbs eaten with bread and mescal.
(197:212) **Hopi** *Candy* Raw roots filled with
sugar and eaten by children in early spring. *Unspecified* Seeds and flowers ground to make yellow pollen. (42:295) **Navajo** *Baby Food* Bulbs,
a children's food, eaten by children while playing. (55:32) *Starvation Food* Bulbs formerly
used for food in times of scarcity. *Unspecified*
Bulbs eaten raw. (as *Calochortus nuttali*
110:24) **Paiute, Nevada** *Unspecified* Bulbs
used for food during the spring. (121:47) **Paiute,
Northern** *Dried Food* Roots dried and eaten.
Soup Roots dried and eaten or ground and
cooked in soup. *Vegetable* Roots and tubers
peeled and eaten roasted or raw. (59:44) **Ute**
Starvation Food Bulbs used for food in starving

times. (118:15) *Unspecified* Bulbs formerly
used for food. (38:33)

Calochortus palmeri, Palmer's
Mariposa Lily
Cahuilla *Unspecified* Bulbs roasted in hot
ash pits or steamed prior to eating. (15:50)
Tubatulabal *Unspecified* Bulbs used for food.
(193:15)

Calochortus pulchellus, Mount
Diablo Globelily
Karok *Unspecified* Bulbs baked in the earth
oven and eaten. (148:380) **Mendocino Indian**
Unspecified Corms eaten raw or roasted.
(41:323) **Pomo** *Unspecified* Corms eaten raw
or roasted. (11:89)

Calochortus tolmiei, Tolmie Startulip
Mendocino Indian *Unspecified* Corms eaten
mostly by children. (as *C. maweanus* 41:323)
Pomo, Kashaya *Vegetable* Baked or boiled
bulbs eaten like baked or boiled potatoes.
(72:31) **Yuki** *Unspecified* Sweet corms eaten
raw. (as *C. caeruleus* var. *maweanus* 49:85)

Calochortus venustus, Butterfly
Mariposa Lily
Miwok *Unspecified* Roasted bulbs used for
food. (12:157) **Tubatulabal** *Unspecified* Bulbs
used for food. (193:15)

Calochortus vestae, Coast Range
Mariposa Lily
Pomo *Unspecified* Bulbs eaten for food. (as *C.
luteus* var. *oculatus* 11:90) **Pomo, Kashaya**
Vegetable Baked bulbs eaten like baked pota-
toes. (72:63)

Caltha palustris, Yellow Marshmarigold
Abnaki *Unspecified* Leaves boiled with lard
and eaten. (144:166) *Vegetable* Seeds used for
food. (144:152) **Alaska Native** *Unspecified*
Leaves and thick fleshy smooth slippery stems
cooked and eaten. Roots boiled and eaten.
(85:19) **Chippewa** *Vegetable* Leaves cooked
and used as greens. (71:130) **Iroquois** *Vegetable* Young plants boiled and eaten as greens.

(124:93) Cooked and seasoned with salt, pepper, or butter. (196:117) **Menominee** *Vegetable*
Leaves used as greens. (151:70) **Mohegan** *Unspecified* Cooked and used for food. (176:83)
Ojibwa *Unspecified* Leaves cooked with pork in
the springtime. (153:408)

Caltha palustris var. *flabelli-*
folia, Yellow Marshmarigold
Eskimo, Alaska *Unspecified* Leaves and stalks
boiled and eaten with seal oil. The leaves and
stalks were collected before the plants flowered
because after flowering commenced, the plant
was apparently inedible. But boiling the plant
broke down the poisonous protoanemonin that
it contained, rendering it edible. (1:35)

Caltha palustris var. *palustris*,
Yellow Marshmarigold
Eskimo, Alaska Leaves eaten fresh. (as *C.
asarifolia* 4:715)

Calylophus lavandulifolius,
Lavenderleaf Sundrops
Apache, Chiricahua & Mescalero *Unspeci-
fied* Pods cooked and eaten by children. (as
Galpinsia lavandulaefolia 33:45)

Camassia leichtlinii, Large Camas
Cowichan *Special Food* Bulbs formerly served
to guests at potlatches or winter dances.
(186:83) **Klamath** *Pie & Pudding* Bulbs used
to make pies. (as *Quamasia leichtlinii* 45:93)
Kwakiutl, Southern *Unspecified* Bulbs pit
steamed and used for food. (183:272) **Nitinaht**
Dried Food Bulbs steam cooked, flattened, and
dried for future food use. *Vegetable* Bulbs formerly steam cooked, dipped in whale or seal
oil, and eaten as vegetables. (186:83) **Round
Valley Indian** *Unspecified* Bulbs roasted or
cooked and used for food. (as *Quamasia
leichtlinii* 41:326) **Salish** *Vegetable* Bulbs used
for food. (185:55) **Salish, Coast** *Dried Food*
Bulbs pit steamed, slightly dried, and used for
food. *Vegetable* Bulbs pit steamed and eaten immediately as the most important vegetable food.
(182:74) **Yuki** *Unspecified* Bulbs cooked and
used for food. (as *Quamasia leichtlinii* 41:326)

Camassia quamash, Small Camas

Blackfoot *Bread & Cake* Roots pit roasted and made into loaves. (97:24) *Unspecified* Bulbs roasted and eaten. (82:14) Roots pit roasted and boiled with meat. (97:24) *Special Food* Bulbs boiled and given in soup on special events. (86:101) *Winter Use Food* Roots kept dry and preserved for future use. (97:24) **Chehalis** *Soup* Bulbs smashed, pressed together like cheese, and boiled in a stew with salmon. (79:24) **Clallam** *Unspecified* Bulbs cooked in pits with meat. (57:196) **Cowichan** *Special Food* Bulbs formerly served to guests at potlatches or winter dances. (186:83) **Flathead** *Beverage* Boiled and used as a sweet, hot beverage. *Sauce & Relish* Boiled with flour and eaten as a thick gravy. *Soup* Simmered with moss in blood into a soup and used for food. *Unspecified* Bulbs roasted and eaten. (82:14) **Hesquiat** *Vegetable* Steamed or boiled bulbs dipped in dogfish oil or whale oil before being eaten. (185:54) **Hoh** *Unspecified* Bulbs pit baked and used for food. (as *Quamasia quamash* 137:59) **Karok** *Vegetable* Bulbs used for food. Bulbs were dug up with a stick and placed in a pit 2 feet in diameter. Leaves of *Vitis californica* were placed on the bottom, a layer of bulbs, and then another layer of *V. californica* leaves. Finally a layer of dirt was added and a fire built on top. The mush formed was pure white and eaten by itself. (6:21) **Klamath** *Dried Food* Bulbs stored for future use. *Unspecified* Steamed bulbs used for food. (as *Quamasia quamash* 45:93) **Kutenai** *Unspecified* Bulbs roasted and eaten. (82:14) **Kwakiutl, Southern** *Unspecified* Bulbs pit steamed and used for food. (183:272) **Makah** *Unspecified* Bulbs pit cooked and eaten. (67:338) **Montana Indian** *Bread & Cake* Oven baked bulbs squeezed into little cakes or pulverized, formed into round loaves, and stored. *Staple* Bulbs formerly fire baked and used as a sweet and nutritious staple. *Sweetener* Bulbs formerly used as a sweetening agent. (82:14) **Nisqually** *Dried Food* Bulbs cooked, sun dried, and stored for future use as food. (79:24) **Nitinaht** *Dried Food* Bulbs steam cooked, flattened, and dried for future food use. *Vegetable* Bulbs formerly steam cooked, dipped in whale or seal oil, and eaten as vegetables. (186:83) **Okanagan-Colville** *Dried Food* Bulbs pit cooked, dried, and stored for future use. *Sauce & Relish* Bulbs pit cooked, dried, ground, and mixed with water and butter to make a "gravy." *Unspecified* Bulbs pit cooked, boiled with dried bitterroots, and eaten. (188:41) **Okanagon** *Unspecified* Bulbs baked and used for food. (as *Quamasia quamash* 125:37) **Paiute** *Dried Food* Roots cooked overnight, dried, and used for food. (104:102) *Pie & Pudding* Dried, ground bulbs made into a pudding. (111:56) *Unspecified* Roots cooked overnight and eaten. (104:102) *Winter Use Food* Bulbs prepared, preserved in numerous ways, and stored for winter use. (111:56) **Quileute** *Unspecified* Bulbs pit baked and used for food. (as *Quamasia quamash* 137:59) **Salish** *Vegetable* Bulbs used for food. (185:54) **Salish, Coast** *Dried Food* Bulbs pit steamed, slightly dried, and used for food. *Vegetable* Bulbs pit steamed and eaten immediately as the most important vegetable food. (182:74) **Skagit, Upper** *Unspecified* Bulbs steamed in an earth oven and eaten. (179:40) **Thompson** *Unspecified* Bulbs baked and used for food. (as *Quamasia quamash* 125:37) Bulbs cooked and eaten. (as *Quamasia quamash* 164:481) **Yuki** *Unspecified* Bulbs pit cooked and eaten. (49:86)

Camassia scilloides, Atlantic Camas

Blackfoot *Unspecified* Roots baked and eaten. (as *C. esculenta* 114:278) **Coeur d'Alene** *Vegetable* Roots used as a principal vegetable food. (as *C. esculenta* 178:88) **Comanche** *Unspecified* Raw roots used for food. (as *C. esculenta* 29:520) **Gosiute** *Unspecified* Bulbs roasted in pits lined with hot stones and eaten. *Winter Use Food* Bulbs formerly preserved for winter use. (as *C. esculenta* 39:364) **Montana Indian** *Unspecified* Bulbs boiled for eating fresh or preserved. *Winter Use Food* Bulbs baked in the ground by hot stones and dried for winter use. (as *C. esculenta* 19:9) **Okanagon** *Staple* Roots used as a principal food. (as *C. esculenta* 178:238) *Unspecified* Roots used as an important food. (as *C. esculenta* 178:237) **Spokan** *Unspecified* Roots used for food. (as *C. escu-*

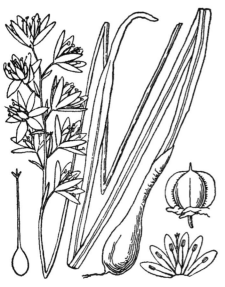

Camassia scilloides

lenta 178:343) **Thompson** *Unspecified* Roots used as an important food. (as *C. esculenta* 178:237)

Camelina microcarpa, Littlepod Falseflax
Apache, Chiricahua & Mescalero *Bread & Cake* Seeds threshed, winnowed, ground, and the flour used to make bread. *Unspecified* Seeds boiled and eaten. (33:49)

Camellia sinensis, Tea
Haisla & Hanaksiala *Beverage* Leaves used to make tea. (as *Thea sinensis* 43:294) **Oweekeno** *Beverage* Leaves used to make tea. (as *Thea sinensis* 43:119)

Camissonia brevipes* ssp. *brevipes, Golden Suncup
Mohave *Unspecified* Seeds used for food. (as *Oenothera brevipes* 37:187)

Camissonia claviformis* ssp. *claviformis, Browneyes
Cahuilla *Vegetable* Leaves used for greens. (as *Oenothera clavaeformis* 15:94)

Camissonia ovata, Goldeneggs
Costanoan *Unspecified* Raw, boiled, or steamed foliage used for food. (as *Oenothera ovata* 21:250)

Canotia holacantha, Crucifixion Thorn
Apache, San Carlos *Fruit* Berries used for food. (95:258) **Apache, Western** *Fruit* Berries eaten raw. (26:191)

Cantharellus cibarius, Chantarelle
Pomo, Kashaya *Vegetable* Baked on hot stones or fried with onions. (72:128)

Capsella bursa-pastoris, Shepherd's Purse
Apache, Chiricahua & Mescalero *Bread & Cake* Seeds winnowed, dried, stored, ground into flour, and used to make bread. *Unspecified* Seeds roasted without grinding and combined with other foods. (33:48) *Vegetable* Tops cooked alone or with meat and used as greens. (33:47) **Cahuilla** *Unspecified* Seeds gathered for food. *Vegetable* Leaves used for greens. (15:51) **Cherokee** *Spice* Mixed into other greens for flavoring. (204:253) *Vegetable* Leaves cooked and eaten as greens. (80:54) **Mendocino Indian** *Staple* Seeds eaten as a pinole. (as *Bursa bursa-pastoris* 41:352) **Thompson** *Vegetable* Leaves soaked in water overnight and eaten raw or cooked as a green vegetable. (187:194)

Capsicum annuum, Cayenne Pepper
Hopi *Dried Food* Fruits strung and dried for winter use. *Spice* Dried peppers crushed and used as flavoring for food. (200:88) **Keresan** *Soup* Used in stews. (198:560) **Navajo** *Unspecified* Chile peppers used for food. (165:221) **Papago** *Unspecified* Species used for food. **Pima** *Unspecified* Species used for food. (36:121) **Pima, Gila River** *Fruit* Fruits eaten raw and boiled. *Staple* Fruits used as a staple food. (133:7) **Sia** *Unspecified* Cultivated and eaten almost daily or sometimes at more than one meal per day. (199:106)

Capsicum annuum **var.** *annuum*, Cayenne Pepper

Navajo, Ramah *Spice* Pepper used extensively as a condiment in soups and stews. (as *C. frutescens* var. *longum* 191:42) **Pima** *Spice* Used for seasoning. (as *C. frutescens* var. *baccatum* 36:121)

Capsicum annuum **var.** *frutescens*, Cayenne Pepper

Papago *Special Food* Added to meat and eaten as a delicacy. (as *C. frutescens* var. *baccatum* 34:47) *Spice* Berries used as a seasoning. (as *C. frutescens* 34:19)

Cardamine concatenata, Cutleaf Toothwort

Iroquois *Unspecified* Roots eaten raw with salt or boiled. (as *Dentaria laciniata* 196:120)

Cardamine diphylla, Crinkle Root

Abnaki *Sauce & Relish* Used as a condiment. (*Dentaria diphylla* 144:152) *Unspecified* Species used for food. (as *Dentaria diphylla* 144:167) **Algonquin, Quebec** *Sauce & Relish* Ground root put into vinegar for use as a relish. (as *Dentaria diphylla* 18:86) **Cherokee** *Vege-*

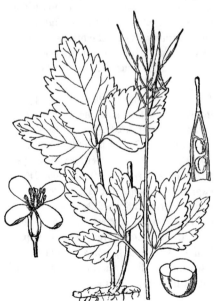

Cardamine diphylla

table Leaves and stems parboiled, rinsed, added to hot grease, salt, and water, and boiled until soft as potherbs. Leaves used in salads. (as *Dentaria diphylla* 126:37) **Iroquois** *Unspecified* Roots eaten raw with salt or boiled. (as *Dentaria diphylla* 196:120) **Ojibwa** *Sauce & Relish* Ground roots mixed with salt, sugar, or vinegar and used as a condiment or relish. (as *Dentaria diphylla* 5:2207)

Cardamine maxima, Large Toothwort

Menominee *Vegetable* Roots fermented for 4 or 5 days to sweeten and cooked with corn. (as *Dentaria maxima* 151:65) **Ojibwa** *Vegetable* Favored wild potatoes cooked with corn and deer meat or beans and deer meat. (as *Dentaria maxima* 153:399)

Carduus **sp.**, Thistle

Luiseño *Unspecified* Raw buds eaten for food. *Vegetable* Plant used as greens. (155:228)

Carex aquatilis, Water Sedge

Alaska Native *Unspecified* Stem bases eaten raw. (85:129)

Carex atherodes, Slough Sedge

Thompson *Fodder* Grass used for animal feed. *Forage* Roots sometimes eaten by muskrats. (187:114)

Carex douglasii, Douglas's Sedge

Kawaiisu *Unspecified* Raw stems used for food. (206:17)

Carex microptera, Smallwing Sedge

Navajo, Ramah *Forage* Plant browsed by sheep. (as *C. festivella* 191:19)

Carex nebrascensis, Nebraska Sedge

Blackfoot *Forage* Leaves thought to be a favorite food of the buffalo. (97:22) Favorite grass of the buffalo. (114:277)

Carex obnupta, Slough Sedge

Thompson *Fodder* Grass used for animal feed. *Forage* Roots sometimes eaten by muskrats. (187:114)

Carex rostrata, Beaked Sedge
Thompson *Fodder* Grass used for animal feed. (187:114) *Forage* Used as a forage plant. (164:514) Roots sometimes eaten by muskrats. *Unspecified* Bulbs used for food. (187:114)

Carex utriculata, Northwest Territory
Sedge
Gosiute *Unspecified* Lower, tender stems and root parts eaten by children. (39:365)

Carex vicaria, Western Fox Sedge
Mendocino Indian *Forage* Foliage cut for hay and used for forage. (41:314)

Carica papaya, Papaya
Hawaiian *Fruit* Fruit used for food. (2:43)
Seminole *Unspecified* Plant used for food. (169:486)

Carnegia gigantea, Saguaro
Apache, Chiricahua & Mescalero *Fruit* Fruit used for food. (33:40) *Substitution Food* Syrup used in the absence of sugar to sweeten an intoxicating drink. (33:50) **Apache, San Carlos** *Bread & Cake* Fruits sun dried, made into large cakes, and used for food. *Fruit* Fruits eaten raw. (as *Cereus giganteus* 95:257) **Apache, Western** *Beverage* Juice used as a drink. *Bread & Cake* Squeezed pulp dried and made into cakes. *Dried Food* Seeds washed and dried. *Fruit* Fruit eaten raw. *Pie & Pudding* Seeds ground with corn into a pudding. *Porridge* Seeds roasted, ground, and mixed with water to make a mush. (26:178) **Apache, White Mountain** *Fruit* Fruit used for food. (as *Cereus gigantea* 136:156) *Preserves* Fruit used to make a kind of butter. (as *Cercus gigantea* 136:147) **Maricopa** *Beverage* Juice fermented to make an intoxicating drink. (as *Cereus gigantea* 37:204) **Papago** *Beverage* Pulp boiled with water, strained, boiled again, and used as a ceremonial drink. (34:20) Juice mixed with water, fermented, and used as an intoxicating drink in ceremonies to bring rain. (34:26) *Bread & Cake* Seeds parched, stored, and used to make meal cakes. *Cooking Agent* Seeds parched, ground, water added, and oil extracted. (34:20) *Dried Food*

Fruits dried, stored in jars, and used as sweets. (34:46) *Fodder* Seeds parched and used as a chicken feed. (34:20) *Fruit* Fruits used as an important article of diet. *Preserves* Fruits made into a conserve. (32:19) Juice made into cactus jam and used as the most important sweet in the diet. Pulp boiled to a sweet, sticky mass and used like raspberry jam. (34:20) Fruits made into jam. (34:46) *Sauce & Relish* Fruits boiled to make a syrup. (32:19) Fruits made into a syrup. (34:46) *Staple* Seeds ground into flour. (32:19) Seeds made into flour and used for food. (34:20) Used as a staple food. (34:45) *Unspecified* Oil extracted from the seeds. (32:19) Pulp eaten fresh. (34:20) Fruits and seeds used for food. (36:59) **Papago & Pima** *Candy* Used to make candy. (35:17) *Fruit* Fruit used for food. (35:11) *Preserves* Fruit boiled, without sugar, to make preserves. (35:17) *Sauce & Relish* Fruit used to make syrup. (35:11) **Pima** *Beverage* Ripe, dried fruits shaped into balls, boiled, fermented, and used to make wine. (47:53) Fruits boiled, fermented, and used as an intoxicating liquor. *Bread & Cake* Seeds ground, put into water, meal combined with other meal and baked to make bread. (as *Cereus giganteus* 146:71) *Dessert* Pulp eaten as dessert. (47:53) *Dried Food* Ripe fruits made into balls and dried for future use. (32:20) Fruits dried in balls and used for food. (as *Cereus giganteus* 146:71) *Fodder* Seeds fed to chickens. (47:53) *Fruit* Ripe fruits eaten fresh. (32:20) Ripe fruits eaten raw. (as *Cereus giganteus* 146:71) *Porridge* Seeds dried, roasted, ground, and eaten as a moist and sticky mush. (47:53) Fresh or dried fruits boiled, residue ground into an oily paste and eaten. (as *Cereus giganteus* 146:71) *Sauce & Relish* Fresh or dried fruits boiled to make a syrup. (32:20) Pulp boiled, seeds strained, boiled again, and sealed in jars until thick as honey. Ripe, dried fruits shaped into balls, boiled, and used to make a syrup. (47:53) Fresh or dried fruits boiled and used as a syrup. *Staple* Seeds ground, put into water, and eaten as pinole. (as *Cereus giganteus* 146:71) *Substitution Food* Seeds ground, passed through a sieve or left mixed with husks, and used as a substitute for lard.

(47:53) *Unspecified* Seeds eaten raw. (as *Cereus giganteus* 146:71) **Pima, Gila River** *Beverage* Pulp made into a syrup and fermented for the annual wine feast, an elaborate liturgical celebration intended to bring rain and to continue it through the growing season. Ripe fruit used to make a cold drink. (133:4) *Candy* Fruits used as sweets. (133:6) *Dried Food* Pulp dried whole for future use. *Porridge* Seeds ground, mixed with grains, and used to make a porridge. *Preserves* Pulp used to make jam. Seeds ground, mixed with grains, and used to make a paste resembling peanut butter. *Sauce & Relish* Pulp used to make syrup. (133:4) *Staple* Fruits used as a staple food. (133:7) **Seri** *Fruit* Fruits eaten for food. *Porridge* Seeds ground to a powder and made into a meal or paste. (50:134) **Southwest Indians** *Fruit* Fruit used for food. (17:15) **Yavapai** *Beverage* Fruit mixed with water and liquid scooped with hand. Dried fruit pressed into bricks and kept for later use, pieces broken off and stirred in water. *Bread & Cake* Dried, parched, seeds ground to consistency of peanut butter and squeezed into cakes. *Dried Food* Dried fruit smeared with fresh fruit juice, made into slabs, and dried for later use. Dried fruit pressed into bricks and kept for later use. *Fruit* Fruit used for food. (as *Cereus giganteus* 65:260)

Carpobrotus aequilateralus, Baby Sunrose

Luiseño *Fruit* Fruit used for food. (as *Mesembryanthemum aequilaterale* 155:232) **Pomo** *Fruit* Raw fruit used for food. (as *Mesembryanthemum aequilaterale* 66:13) **Pomo, Kashaya** *Fruit* Fruit eaten raw. (as *Mesembryanthemum chilense* 72:48)

Carthamus tinctorius, Safflower

Hopi *Cooking Agent* Flowers used as a yellow coloring for paper bread. (56:20) Flowers used to color wafer bread yellow. (200:95)

Carum carvi, Caraway

Cree, Woodlands *Spice* Seeds added as a flavoring to bannock. *Staple* Seeds ground into flour. (109:34)

Carya alba, Mockernut Hickory

Cherokee *Unspecified* Species used for food. (as *C. tomentosa* 80:38) **Choctaw** *Soup* Pounded nutmeat boiled, made into a paste, and eaten as a broth or soup. (as *Juglans squamosa* 25:8)

Carya cordiformis, Bitternut Hickory

Iroquois *Beverage* Fresh nutmeats crushed, boiled, and liquid used as a drink. *Bread & Cake* Fresh nutmeats crushed and mixed with bread. (124:99) Nuts crushed, mixed with cornmeal and beans or berries, and made into bread. (196:123) *Pie & Pudding* Fresh nutmeats crushed and mixed with corn pudding. (124:99) *Sauce & Relish* Nuts pounded, boiled, resulting oil seasoned with salt and used as gravy. *Soup* Nutmeats crushed and added to corn soup. (196:123) *Special Food* Fresh nutmeats crushed, boiled, and oil used as a delicacy in corn bread and pudding. (124:99) Nutmeat oil added to the mush used by the False Face Societies. *Staple* Nutmeats crushed and added to hominy. *Unspecified* Nutmeats, after skimming off the oil, seasoned and mixed with mashed potatoes. (196:123)

Carya illinoinensis, Pecan

Comanche *Unspecified* Nuts used for food. (29:520) *Winter Use Food* Nuts stored for winter use. (29:531)

Carya laciniosa, Shellbark Hickory

Cherokee *Unspecified* Species used for food. (80:38)

Carya ovata, Shagbark Hickory

Dakota *Soup* Nuts used to make soup. *Sweetener* Sap used to make sugar. Hickory chips boiled to make sugar. *Unspecified* Nuts eaten plain or with honey. (as *Hicoria ovata* 70:74) **Iroquois** *Baby Food* Fresh nutmeats crushed, boiled, and oil used as a baby food. *Beverage* Fresh nutmeats crushed, boiled, and liquid used as a drink. *Bread & Cake* Fresh nutmeats crushed and mixed with bread. (124:99) Nuts crushed, mixed with cornmeal and beans or berries, and made into bread. (196:123) *Pie &*

Pudding Fresh nutmeats crushed and mixed with corn pudding. (124:99) *Sauce & Relish* Nuts pounded, boiled, resulting oil seasoned with salt and used as gravy. *Soup* Nutmeats crushed and added to corn soup. (196:123) *Special Food* Fresh nutmeats crushed, boiled, and oil used as a delicacy in corn bread and pudding. (124:99) Nutmeat oil added to the mush used by the False Face Societies. *Staple* Nutmeats crushed and added to hominy. *Unspecified* Nutmeats, after skimming off the oil, seasoned and mixed with mashed potatoes. (196:123) **Lakota** *Unspecified* Nuts used for food. (139:49) **Meskwaki** *Winter Use Food* Nuts stored for winter use. (152:259) **Ojibwa** *Unspecified* Edible nuts were appreciated. (153:405) **Omaha** *Soup* Nuts used to make soup. *Sweetener* Sap used to make sugar. Hickory chips boiled to make sugar. *Unspecified* Nuts eaten plain or with honey. **Pawnee** *Soup* Nuts used to make soup. *Sweetener* Sap used to make sugar. Hickory chips boiled to make sugar. *Unspecified* Nuts eaten plain or with honey. **Ponca** *Soup* Nuts used to make soup. *Sweetener* Sap used to make sugar. Hickory chips boiled to make sugar. *Unspecified* Nuts eaten plain or with honey. (as *Hicoria ovata* 70:74) **Potawatomi** *Winter Use Food* Hickory nuts

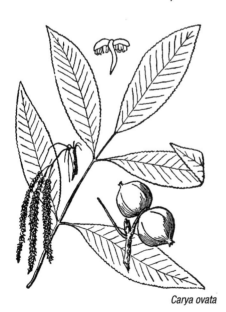

Carya ovata

gathered for winter use. (154:103) **Winnebago** *Soup* Nuts used to make soup. *Sweetener* Sap used to make sugar. Hickory chips boiled to make sugar. *Unspecified* Nuts eaten plain or with honey. (as *Hicoria ovata* 70:74)

Carya pallida, Sand Hickory
Cherokee *Unspecified* Species used for food. (80:38)

Castanea dentata, American Chestnut
Cherokee *Bread & Cake* Nuts ground into a meal and used to make bread. (126:39) *Substitution Food* Used as a coffee substitute. *Unspecified* Nuts boiled, pounded with corn, kneaded, wrapped in a green corn blade, boiled, and eaten. (80:29) **Iroquois** *Beverage* Fresh nutmeats crushed, boiled, and liquid used as a drink. *Bread & Cake* Fresh nutmeats crushed and mixed with bread. (124:99) Nuts crushed, mixed with cornmeal and beans or berries, and made into bread. (196:123) *Pie & Pudding* Fresh nutmeats crushed and mixed with corn pudding. (124:99) *Sauce & Relish* Nuts pounded, boiled, resulting oil seasoned with salt and used as gravy. *Soup* Nutmeats crushed and added to corn soup. (196:123) *Special Food* Fresh nutmeats crushed, boiled, and oil used as a delicacy in corn bread and pudding. (124:99) Nutmeat oil added to the mush used by the False Face Societies. (196:123) *Spice* Meats dried, pounded into flour and mixed with bread for flavoring. (124:99) *Staple* Nutmeats crushed and added to hominy. *Unspecified* Nutmeats, after skimming off the oil, seasoned and mixed with mashed potatoes. (196:123)

Castanopsis chrysophylla, Golden Chinkapin
Karok *Unspecified* "Nuts" roasted in coals and eaten. (as *Chrysolepis chrysophila* 6:24) Nuts used for food. *Winter Use Food* Nuts stored for winter use. (148:383) **Klamath** *Unspecified* Nuts used for food. (45:94) **Mendocino Indian** *Unspecified* Nuts sometimes used for food. (41:333) **Paiute** *Beverage* Leaves used to make tea. (111:65) **Pomo** *Dried Food* Nuts stored for later use. *Unspecified* Raw nuts used for food.

(66:12–13) **Pomo, Kashaya** *Unspecified* Nuts eaten raw, roasted, or pounded into a meal. *Winter Use Food* Nuts stored in their shell for winter. (72:34) **Tolowa** *Unspecified* "Nuts" shaken out of the dried fruits, rolled over hot coals, and eaten. **Yurok** *Unspecified* "Nuts" used for food. (as *Chrysolepis chrysophila* 6:24)

Castanopsis sempervirens, Sierran Chinkapin

Kawaiisu *Unspecified* Raw seeds eaten by hunters when in the field. (as *Chrysolepis sempervirens* 206:20)

Castilleja applegatei var. *pinetorum*, Wavyleaf Indian Paintbrush

Miwok *Beverage* Flowers sipped sporadically and as a pastime. (as *Castilleia pinetorum* 12:163)

Castilleja foliolosa, Texas Indian Paintbrush

Cahuilla *Sweetener* Flowers picked by children to suck the nectar. (15:51)

Castilleja hispida, Harsh Indian Paintbrush

Nitinaht *Candy* Sweet nectar sucked by children. (186:127)

Castilleja linariifolia, Wyoming Indian Paintbrush

Hopi *Unspecified* Flowers eaten as food. (190:166)

Castilleja lineata, Marshmeadow Indian Paintbrush

Navajo *Special Food* Flowers sucked for the honey, a delicacy. (55:76)

Castilleja miniata, Scarlet Indian Paintbrush

Kwakiutl, Southern *Unspecified* Flower nectar formerly sucked by children. (183:292) **Nitinaht** *Candy* Sweet nectar sucked by children. (186:127) **Thompson** *Fodder* Plant used as hummingbird feed. (187:284)

Castilleja parviflora var. *douglasii*, Mountain Indian Paintbrush

Miwok *Beverage* Flowers sipped sporadically and as a pastime. (12:163)

Castilleja sessiliflora, Downy Paintedcup

Cheyenne *Unspecified* Flower nectar sucked in spring. (83:39)

Catabrosa aquatica, Water Whorlgrass

Crow *Unspecified* Seeds used for food. (as *Glyceria aquatica* 19:12) **Gosiute** *Unspecified* Seeds used for food. (as *Glyceria aquatica* 39:370)

Caulanthus coulteri, Coulter's Wild Cabbage

Kawaiisu *Vegetable* Leaves gathered in early spring before the flowers appear, boiled, salted, fried in grease, and eaten. (206:17)

Caulanthus inflatus, Desert Candle

Kawaiisu *Unspecified* Soft upper section of the stem roasted in a pit oven covered with dirt and eaten. (206:17)

Ceanothus americanus, New Jersey Tea

Dakota *Beverage* Leaves used to make a tea-like beverage. (70:102) **Menominee** *Beverage* and *Substitution Food* Dried leaves used as a substitute for Ceylon black tea. (151:70) **Meskwaki** *Beverage* Leaves used as a beverage. (152:263) **Omaha** *Beverage* Leaves used to make tea. (58:342) Leaves used to make a hot, aqueous, tea-like beverage. (68:329) Leaves used to make a tea-like beverage. **Pawnee** *Beverage* Leaves used to make a tea-like beverage. **Ponca** *Beverage* Leaves used to make a tea-like beverage. **Winnebago** *Beverage* Leaves used to make a tea-like beverage. (70:102)

Ceanothus cuneatus, Buck Brush

Mendocino Indian *Forage* Leaves eaten by deer as forage. Seeds eaten by squirrels as forage. (41:367)

Ceanothus fendleri, Fendler's Ceanothus

Acoma *Fruit* Berries sweetened with sugar and used for food. (32:21) **Keres, Western** *Fruit* Berries sweetened with sugar and used for food. (171:35) **Laguna** *Fruit* Berries sweetened with sugar and used for food. (32:21) **Navajo, Ramah** *Unspecified* Inner bark strips eaten in summer. (191:36)

Ceanothus herbaceus, Jersey Tea

Lakota *Beverage* Leaves used to make tea. (139:56)

Ceanothus integerrimus, Deerbrush

Concow *Staple* Seeds eaten as a pinole. (41:368) **Karok** *Forage* Plant eaten by deer. (148:386)

Ceanothus sanguineus, Redstem Ceanothus

Okanagan-Colville *Forage* Buds and branches considered an important food for deer. (188:119)

Ceanothus velutinus, Snowbrush Ceanothus

Okanagan-Colville *Forage* Bush eaten by deer. (188:120) **Paiute** *Forage* Plant eaten by

deer. (111:89) **Thompson** *Forage* Shrub extensively eaten by deer. (164:516) Plant considered a favorite food of deer. (187:252)

Celastrus scandens, American Bittersweet

Menominee *Starvation Food* Palatable inner bark would sustain life when food was hard to get. (151:63) **Ojibwa** *Soup* Inner bark used to make a thick soup when other food unobtainable in the winter. The Ojibwe name of the bittersweet is "manidobima' kwit," which means "spirit twisted" and "refers to the twisted intestines of the their culture hero, Winabojo." (153:398) **Potawatomi** *Starvation Food* Inner bark cooked in times of food scarcity, not highly commended as a food but valued. (154:97)

Celtis laevigata, Sugarberry

Comanche *Fruit* Fruits beaten to a pulp, mixed with fat, rolled into balls, and roasted over fire. (29:521) **Seminole** *Unspecified* Plant used for food. (169:489)

Celtis laevigata var. *brevipes*, Sugarberry

Yavapai *Unspecified* Ground, boiled, and used for food. (65:256)

Celtis laevigata var. *reticulata*, Netleaf Hackberry

Acoma *Fruit* Berries extensively used as food. (as *C. reticulata* 32:21) **Apache, Chiricahua & Mescalero** *Bread & Cake* Fruit ground, caked, and dried for winter use. *Fruit* Fruit eaten fresh. *Preserves* Fruit used to make jelly. (as *C. reticulata* 33:46) **Hualapai** *Dried Food* Fruit dried for winter use. *Fruit* Fruit eaten fresh. (as *C. reticulata* 195:6) **Laguna** *Fruit* Berries extensively used as food. (as *C. reticulata* 32:21) **Navajo** *Fruit* Berries ground and eaten. (as *C. reticulata* 55:41) **Papago** *Fruit* Fruits eaten for food. **Pueblo** *Fruit* Berries used for food. (as *C. reticulata* 32:21) **Tewa** *Fruit* Berries eaten. (as *C. reticulata* 138:39)

Ceanothus americanus

Celtis occidentalis, Common Hackberry
Dakota *Spice* Dried fruit pounded to make a
condiment used for seasoning meat in cooking.
(69:362) Berries used to flavor meat. (70:76)
Keres, Western *Fruit* Berries used extensively
for food. (171:35) **Meskwaki** *Porridge* Ground,
hard berries made into a mush. (152:265)
Omaha *Fruit* Berries used occasionally for
food. **Pawnee** *Fruit* Berries pounded fine,
mixed with a little fat, and parched corn and
used for food. (70:76)

**Celtis occidentalis var. occiden-
talis**, Western Hackberry
Kiowa *Fruit* Berries pounded into a paste-like
consistency, molded onto a stick, and baked
over an open fire. (192:23)

Cercis canadensis, Eastern Redbud
Cherokee *Unspecified* Blossoms eaten by children. (203:74)

Cercis canadensis var. texensis,
California Redbud
Navajo *Unspecified* Pods roasted in ashes and
seeds eaten. (as *C. occidentalis* 32:21) Seeds
roasted and eaten. (as *C. occidentalis* 55:56)
Navajo, Kayenta *Unspecified* Pods roasted in
ashes and seeds eaten. (as *C. occidentalis*
205:28)

Cercocarpus montanus, True Mountain Mahogany
Navajo *Forage* Whole plant used by sheep for
forage. (55:53)

Cereus sp.
Apache, White Mountain *Fruit* Fruit used for
food. *Preserves* Fruit used to make a kind of
butter. (136:156)

Cetraria crispa, Shield Lichen
Eskimo, Inuktitut *Spice* Used as a soup condiment. (202:183)

Cetraria cucullata, Curled Shield Lichen
Eskimo, Inuktitut *Sauce & Relish* Used as a
condiment for fish or duck soup. (202:188)

Chaenactis glabriuscula, Yellow
Chaenactis
Cahuilla *Porridge* Parched seeds ground into
flour, mixed with other seeds, and used to form
a mush. (15:52)

Chamaebatiaria millefolium,
Fernbush
Navajo, Ramah *Fodder* Used as sheep, goat,
and deer feed and not eaten by cattle. (191:30)

Chamaedaphne calyculata, Leather
Leaf
Ojibwa *Beverage* Fresh or dried leaves used as
a beverage tea. (153:400)

**Chamaesyce serpyllifolia ssp.
serpyllifolia**, Thymeleaf Sandmat
Apache, White Mountain *Beverage* Roots
used to make a fermented, intoxicating drink.
(as *Euphorbia serpyllifolia* 136:151) *Cooking
Agent* Roots chewed and used as a yeast preparation for the wedding cake. *Dried Food* Roots
dried for future use. (as *Euphorbia serpyllifolia*
136:148) **Zuni** *Candy* Leaves chewed for the
pleasant taste. *Sweetener* Root pieces used to
sweeten cornmeal. After the mouth had been
thoroughly cleansed, the women who sweetened
the corn placed a piece of it in their mouths.
The root remained in the mouth for 2 days, except to take refreshment and to sleep. Each time
the root was removed from the mouth, the
mouth was cleansed with cold water before re-
turning the root to it. Finally, when they began
sweetening the corn, either yellow or black corn
was used. The women, with their fingers, placed
as much cornmeal as possible into their mouths
and held it there, without chewing, until the ac-
cumulation of saliva forced ejection of the mass.
(as *Euphorbia serpyllifolia* 166:67)

Chasmanthium latifolium, Indian
Woodoats
Cocopa *Porridge* Seeds dried, ground, and
made into mush. (as *Uniola palmeri* 37:187)
Unspecified Seeds used for food. *Winter Use
Food* Seeds stored for later use. (as *Uniola
palmeri* 64:267)

Cheilanthes covillei, Coville's Lipfern

Kawaiisu *Beverage* Stems and leaves used to make tea. (206:19)

Cheilanthes fendleri, Fendler's Lipfern

Apache, Chiricahua & Mescalero *Beverage* Leaves and young stems boiled to make a nonintoxicating beverage. (33:53)

Chelone glabra, White Turtlehead

Cherokee *Unspecified* Young shoots and leaves boiled, fried, and eaten. (204:253)

Chenopodium album, Lamb's Quarters

Alaska Native *Dietary Aid* Fresh leaves, properly cooked, furnished significant amounts of vitamins C and A. *Substitution Food* Young, tender leaves and stems used as a substitute for spinach or other greens. *Vegetable* Young, tender leaves and stems cooked in a small amount of boiling water and eaten. (85:21) **Apache** *Vegetable* Young plants cooked as greens. (32:16) **Apache, Chiricahua & Mescalero** *Unspecified* Eaten without preparation or cooked with green chile and meat or animal bones. (as *C. alba* 33:46) **Cherokee** *Spice* Young growth mixed with mustard leaves, morning glory leaves, or potato leaves for flavoring. *Unspecified* Young growth parboiled, fried, and eaten. (204:253) *Vegetable* Leaves mixed with other leaves, parboiled, and cooked in grease until tender. Leaves mixed with other leaves and used for greens. (126:32) **Dakota** *Soup* Young, tender plant cooked as pottage. (70:78) *Unspecified* Young plants boiled for food. (as *C. albidum* 69:361) **Diegueño** *Vegetable* Leaves cooked and eaten as greens. (84:17) **Eskimo, Inupiat** *Dried Food* Leaves and stems dried for future use. *Frozen Food* Leaves and stems frozen for future use. *Vegetable* Leaves and stems eaten raw or cooked as hot greens with beans. (98:64) **Hopi** *Porridge* Ground seeds used to make mush. (190:160) *Unspecified* Leaves cooked with meat. (32:16) Leaves boiled and eaten with fat. (56:18) Boiled and eaten with other foods. (200:73) **Iroquois** *Vegetable* Cooked and seasoned with salt, pep-

per, or butter. (196:117) **Kawaiisu** *Vegetable* Upper leaves boiled, "rinsed" in cold water, and fried in grease and salt. (206:19) **Lakota** *Vegetable* Used as cooked greens. (139:43) **Luiseño** *Vegetable* Leaves used as greens. (155:233) **Mendocino Indian** *Vegetable* Young leaves boiled and eaten as greens. (41:346) **Miwok** *Dried Food* Boiled greens dried and stored for later use. *Vegetable* Boiled greens used for food. (12:159) **Mohegan** *Unspecified* Cooked and used for food. (176:83) **Montana Indian** *Staple* Seeds ground into flour and made into bread. *Vegetable* Young plant used as a potherb. (19:9) **Navajo** *Dried Food* Seeds dried and used like corn. (55:43) *Staple* Seeds ground and eaten as a nutrient. (90:149) *Vegetable* Young, tender plants eaten raw, boiled as herbs alone or with other foods. (55:43) **Navajo, Ramah** *Bread & Cake*, and *Special Food* Seeds winnowed, ground with maize, made into bread, and used as a ceremonial food in Nightway. *Winter Use Food* Seeds stored for winter use. (191:24) **Ojibwa** *Vegetable* Young plant cooked as greens. (5:2209) Leaves eaten as greens. (135:240) **Omaha** *Soup* Young, tender plant cooked as pottage. (70:78) **Paiute** *Staple* Seeds parched, ground, and eaten as meal. (104:98) *Unspecified* Species used for food. (167:244)

Chenopodium album

Papago *Soup* Mixed with roasted cholla buds and eaten as a vegetable stew. (as *C. alba* 34:16) **Pawnee** *Soup* Young, tender plant cooked as pottage. (70:78) **Pima, Gila River** *Unspecified* Leaves used for food. (133:7) **Potawatomi** *Vegetable* Leaves used as a relish food for salads and spring greens. (154:98) **Pueblo** *Vegetable* Young plants cooked as greens. (32:16) **Shuswap** *Vegetable* Leaves boiled with butter, salt, and pepper and used for greens. (123:61) **Spanish American** *Vegetable* Young plants cooked as greens. (32:16) **Thompson** *Vegetable* Boiled leaves eaten as greens. (187:203) **Zuni** *Vegetable* Young plants cooked as greens. (32:16)

Chenopodium californicum, California Goosefoot
Cahuilla *Candy* Milky sap used to make gum. *Staple* Parched seeds ground into flour. *Vegetable* Boiled shoots and leaves eaten as greens. (15:52) **Luiseño** *Unspecified* Seeds used for food. (155:233)

Chenopodium capitatum, Blite Goosefoot
Alaska Native *Dietary Aid* Leaves properly cooked and used as a good source of vitamins C and A. *Vegetable* Young, tender leaves used in raw salad mixture or cooked like garden spinach. (85:23) **Gosiute** *Unspecified* Seeds used for food. (39:366)

Chenopodium carinatum, Tasmanian Goosefoot
Atsugewi *Bread & Cake* Parched, ground seeds made into cakes and eaten without cooking. (61:139)

Chenopodium fremontii, Frémont's Goosefoot
Cahuilla *Vegetable* Boiled shoots and leaves eaten as greens. (15:52) **Cocopa** *Vegetable* Young shoots boiled as greens. (37:202) **Havasupai** *Bread & Cake* Seeds used to make bread. (197:66) **Hopi** *Porridge* Ground seeds used to make mush. (190:161) *Spice* Leaves used as flavoring with meat or other vegetables. *Vegetable*

Leaves cooked alone as greens or boiled and eaten with a number of other foods. (42:300) **Klamath** *Unspecified* Roasted, ground seeds used for food. (45:95–96) **Mohave** *Vegetable* Young shoots boiled as greens. (37:202) **Navajo** *Bread & Cake* Seeds used to make tortillas and bread. (55:44) **Paiute** *Unspecified* Species used for food. (167:243) **Paiute, Northern** *Staple* Seeds ground into a meal and eaten. (59:48)

Chenopodium graveolens, Fetid Goosefoot
Hopi *Bread & Cake* Seeds ground, mixed with cornmeal, and made into small dumplings wrapped in corn husks. (as *C. cornutum* 56:18)

Chenopodium humile, Marshland Goosefoot
Cahuilla *Vegetable* Boiled shoots and leaves eaten as greens. (15:52)

Chenopodium incanum, Mealy Goosefoot
Apache, Western *Unspecified* Species used for food. (26:192) **Apache, White Mountain** *Unspecified* Seeds ground and used for food. Young sprouts boiled with meat and eaten. (136:156) **Hopi** *Vegetable* Young, tender leaves cooked and eaten as greens. (200:73) **Navajo, Ramah** *Bread & Cake*, and *Special Food* Seeds winnowed, ground with maize, made into bread, and used as a ceremonial food in Nightway. *Winter Use Food* Seeds stored for winter use. (191:25)

Chenopodium leptophyllum, Narrowleaf Goosefoot
Apache *Vegetable* Young plants cooked as greens. (32:16) **Apache, Western** *Unspecified* Species used for food. (26:192) **Apache, White Mountain** *Unspecified* Seeds ground and used for food. Young sprouts boiled with meat and eaten. (136:156) **Gosiute** *Unspecified* Seeds used for food. (39:366) **Hopi** *Porridge* Ground seeds used to make mush. (190:161) **Navajo, Ramah** *Unspecified* Seeds used for food. (191:25) **Pueblo** *Vegetable* Young plants

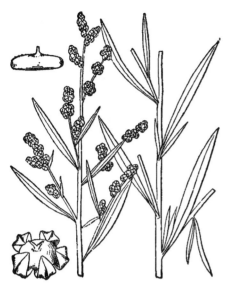

Chenopodium leptophyllum

cooked as greens. **Spanish American** *Vegetable* Young plants cooked as greens. (32:16) **Zuni** *Bread & Cake* Ground seeds mixed with cornmeal and salt, made into a stiff batter, formed into balls, and steamed. The Zuni say that upon reaching this world, the seeds were prepared without the meal because there was no corn. Now the young plants are boiled, either alone or with meat, and are greatly relished. (166:66) *Unspecified* Seeds considered among the most important food plants when the Zuni reached this world. (32:21) Young plants boiled alone or with meat and used for food. (166:66) *Vegetable* Young plants cooked as greens. (32:16)

Chenopodium murale, Nettleleaf
  Goosefoot
Cahuilla *Vegetable* Boiled shoots and leaves eaten as greens. (15:52) **Mohave** *Vegetable* Young shoots boiled as greens. (37:202) **Papago** *Unspecified* Seeds used for food. (36:62) *Vegetable* Stalks eaten as greens in the summer. (34:14) **Pima** *Staple* Seeds parched, ground, and eaten as a pinole in combination with other meal. (32:23) Seeds parched, ground, and eaten as pinole. (146:73)

Chenopodium nevadense, Nevada
  Goosefoot
Paiute *Staple* Seeds parched, ground, and eaten as meal. (104:98) **Paiute, Northern** *Unspecified* Seeds used for food. (59:48)

Chenopodium pratericola, Desert
  Goosefoot
Pima, Gila River *Unspecified* Leaves boiled and eaten. (as *C. desiccatum* var. *leptophylloides* 133:7)

Chenopodium rubrum, Red
  Goosefoot
Gosiute *Unspecified* Seeds used for food. (39:366)

Chenopodium watsonii, Watson's
  Goosefoot
Navajo, Ramah *Unspecified* Seeds used for food. (191:25)

Chilopsis linearis, Desert Willow
Cahuilla *Unspecified* Blossoms and seedpods used for food. (15:53)

Chimaphila maculata, Striped
  Prince's Pine
Cherokee *Snack Food* Leaves used for a nibble. (126:38)

Chimaphila umbellata* ssp. *occidentalis, Pipsissewa
Thompson *Beverage* Stem and roots boiled and drunk as a tea. Leaves made into a tea. (164:494)

Chloracantha spinosa, Spiny
  Chloracantha
Mohave *Starvation Food* Young shoots roasted and eaten as a famine food. (as *Aster spinosus* 37:201) **Navajo** *Candy* Stems chewed for gum. (as *Aster spinosus* 55:83)

Chlorogalum parviflorum, Smallflower Soapplant
Luiseño *Unspecified* Bulb used for food. (155:233)

Chlorogalum pomeridianum,
Wavyleaf Soapplant

Cahuilla *Vegetable* Young, spring shoots used as a potherb. (15:54) **Costanoan** *Unspecified* Leaves of immature plant used for food. (21:255) **Karok** *Unspecified* Bulbs roasted and eaten. (148:380) **Mendocino Indian** *Unspecified* Young shoots used for food. (41:319) **Miwok** *Unspecified* Soaproot used for food. *Winter Use Food* Stored, dried bulbs used for food. (12:157) **Yuki** *Forage* Bulbs eaten by pigs. (49:93)

Chlorogalum pomeridianum var. divaricatum, Wavyleaf Soapplant
Neeshenam *Unspecified* Eaten raw, roasted, or boiled. (as *C. divaricatum* 129:377)

Chrysobalanus icaco, Icaco Coco Plum
Seminole *Unspecified* Plant used for food. (169:484)

Chrysophyllum oliviforme,
Satinleaf

Seminole *Unspecified* Plant used for food. (169:481)

Chrysothamnus nauseosus, Rubber Rabbitbrush
Blackfoot *Forage* Plant used as a fall and winter forage for horses. (97:56) **Kawaiisu** *Spice* Sharpened twig, stripped of bark and leaves, threaded with pinyon nuts to improve their flavor. (206:20) **Navajo** *Forage* Plants browsed by animals. (90:159) **Paiute** *Candy* Roots used as chewing gum. (111:115) **Paiute, Northern** *Candy* Root bark chewed like gum. (59:53)

Chrysothamnus nauseosus ssp. bigelovii, Rubber Rabbitbrush
Apache, White Mountain *Unspecified* Seeds ground and used for food. (as *C. bigelovii* 136:156) **Navajo, Kayenta** *Unspecified* Cooked with cornmeal mush and used for food. (205:46)

Chrysothamnus nauseosus ssp. consimilis, Rubber Rabbitbrush
Paiute *Candy* Roots chewed until gummy as a "chewing gum." (104:104)

Chrysothamnus viscidiflorus,
Green Rabbitbrush

Gosiute *Candy* Roots used as chewing gum. (as *Bigelovia douglasii* 39:364) **Hopi** *Spice* Plant used as an herb. (42:302) **Paiute** *Candy* Roots used as chewing gum. (111:115)

Cicer arietinum, Chick Pea
Papago *Dried Food* Threshed, dried on the ground or roofs, stored, and used for food. (34:33) *Unspecified* Species used for food. **Pima** *Unspecified* Species used for food. (36:120)

Cicuta virosa, Mackenzie's Water Hemlock
Eskimo, Inuktitut *Unspecified* Leaves boiled with fresh fish. (as *Cicuta mackenziana* 202:192)

Cinna arundinacea, Sweet Woodreed
Gosiute *Unspecified* Seeds used for food. (as *C. arundinaceae* var. *pendula* 39:366)

Cirsium brevistylum, Clustered Thistle
Cowichan *Unspecified* Large taproots peeled and eaten raw or cooked. (182:81) **Hesquiat** *Unspecified* Flower heads chewed to get the nectar. (185:61) **Saanich** *Unspecified* Large taproots peeled and eaten raw or cooked. (182:81)

Cirsium californicum, California Thistle
Kawaiisu *Unspecified* Spring stems skinned and eaten raw. (206:20)

Cirsium congdonii, Rosette Thistle
Kawaiisu *Unspecified* Spring stalks peeled and eaten raw. (206:20)

Cirsium drummondii, Dwarf Thistle
Atsugewi *Unspecified* Young, raw stalks used for food. (61:139) **Cahuilla** *Unspecified* Bud, at the base of the thistle, used for food. (15:55) **Gosiute** *Unspecified* Stems formerly used for food. (as *Cnicus drummondi* 39:366)

Cirsium eatonii, Eaton's Thistle
Gosiute *Unspecified* Stems used for food. (as *Cnicus eatoni* 39:366)

Cirsium edule, Edible Thistle
Cheyenne *Special Food* Young stems eaten raw as a "luxury food." (83:20) *Unspecified* Peeled stem used for food. (76:191) Tender, spring shoots eaten raw. (83:46) **Hoh** *Vegetable* Young shoots eaten as greens. (as *Carduus edulis* 137:69) **Okanagon** *Unspecified* Roots boiled and used for food. (as *Carduus edulis* 125:36) **Quileute** *Vegetable* Young shoots eaten as greens. (as *Carduus edulis* 137:69) **Thompson** *Dried Food* Roots dried and stored for future use. *Soup* Dried roots rehydrated, scraped, chopped, and cooked in stews. (187:178) *Unspecified* Roots boiled and used for food. (as *Carduus edulis* 125:36) Fresh roots eaten cooked. (187:178)

Cirsium hookerianum, White Thistle
Okanagon *Unspecified* Roots boiled and used for food. (as *Carduus hookerianus* 125:36) **Thompson** *Dried Food* Roots dried and stored for future use. Dried roots rehydrated, scraped, chopped, and cooked in stews. (187:178) *Unspecified* Roots boiled and used for food. (as *Carduus hookerianus* (125:36) Deep, thick roots cooked and eaten. (164:480) Fresh roots eaten cooked. (187:178)

Cirsium horridulum, Yellow Thistle
Houma *Unspecified* Tender, white hearts eaten raw. (158:57)

Cirsium neomexicanum, New Mexico Thistle
Yavapai *Unspecified* Raw, peeled stems used for food. (65:256)

Cirsium occidentale, Cobwebby Thistle
Kawaiisu *Unspecified* Spring stems skinned and eaten raw. (206:20) **Tubatulabal** *Unspecified* Stalks used extensively for food. (193:15)

Cirsium ochrocentrum, Yellowspine Thistle
Kiowa *Unspecified* Roots used for food. (192:58)

Cirsium pallidum, Pale Thistle
Apache, Chiricahua & Mescalero *Bread & Cake* Seeds threshed, winnowed, ground, and the flour used to make bread. *Unspecified* Seeds boiled and eaten. (33:49)

Cirsium pastoris, Snowy Thistle
Paiute *Unspecified* Stems peeled and eaten raw. (as *C. occidentale* var. *candidissimum* 104:103)

Cirsium scariosum, Meadow Thistle
Flathead *Unspecified* Roots eaten raw or pit baked. **Kutenai** *Unspecified* Roots eaten raw or pit baked. **Nez Perce** *Unspecified* Roots eaten raw or pit baked. (82:13)

Cirsium tioganum* var. *tioganum, Tioga Thistle
Paiute *Unspecified* Roots eaten raw or roasted. (as *C. acaulescens* 104:103)

Cirsium undulatum, Wavyleaf Thistle
Comanche *Unspecified* Raw roots used for food. (29:521) **Gosiute** *Unspecified* Stems used

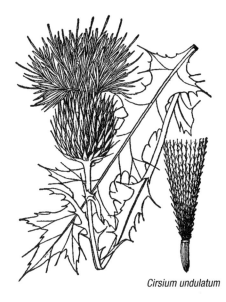

Cirsium undulatum

for food. (as *Cnicus undulatus* 39:366) **Montana Indian** *Vegetable* Early spring roots eaten raw or cooked with meat. Young, summer stalks eaten like asparagus and greens. (as *Cnicus eriocephalus* 19:10) **Okanagon** *Staple* Roots used as a principal food. (as *Cnicus undulatus* 178:238) **Shuswap** *Unspecified* Young roots roasted and eaten. (123:59) **Spokan** *Unspecified* Roots used for food. (as *Cnicus undulatus* 178:343) **Thompson** *Dried Food* Dried roots rehydrated, scraped, chopped, and cooked in stews. Roots dried and stored for future use. (187:178) *Unspecified* Root cooked and eaten. (164:480) Fresh roots eaten cooked. (187:178)

Cirsium vulgare, Bull Thistle
Hesquiat *Unspecified* Flower heads chewed to get the nectar. (185:61) **Thompson** *Dried Food* Dried roots rehydrated, scraped, chopped, and cooked in stews. Roots dried and stored for future use. *Unspecified* Fresh roots eaten cooked. (187:178)

Cistanthe monandra, Common Pussypaws
Kawaiisu *Unspecified* Seeds used for food. (as *Calyptridium monandrum* 206:16)

Citrullus lanatus, Watermelon
Apalachee *Fruit* Fruit used for food. (81:98)

Citrullus lanatus var. *lanatus*, Watermelon
Cahuilla *Fruit* Eaten fresh. *Winter Use Food* Cut, peeled into strips, and dried for winter use. (as *C. vulgaris* 15:55) **Cherokee** *Unspecified* Species used for food. (as *C. vulgaris* 80:61) **Cocopa** *Dried Food* Dried, whole seeds used for food. *Fruit* Ripe melon scooped with fingers and used for food. *Winter Use Food* Ripe and green melons stored in pits and the green melons ripened in storage. (as *C. vulgaris* 64:266) **Havasupai** *Fruit* Fruit eaten fresh. (as *C. vulgaris* 197:66) *Porridge* Seeds parched and ground to make sumkwin (mush) and other dishes. (as *C. vulgaris* 197:243) **Hopi** *Cooking Agent* Seeds ground and used to oil the "piki"

stones. *Staple* Eaten and considered to be almost a staple food. *Unspecified* Seeds parched and eaten with parched corn and "piki." (as *C. vulgaris* 200:92) **Iroquois** *Bread & Cake* Fresh or dried flesh boiled, mashed, and mixed into the paste when making corn bread. *Dried Food* Flesh cut into strips, dried, and stored away. *Special Food* Squash eaten at feasts of ceremonial importance and longhouse ceremonies. *Vegetable* Flesh boiled, baked in ashes or boiled, mashed with butter and sugar, and eaten. Flesh fried and sweetened or seasoned with salt, pepper, and butter. (as *Cucurbita citrullus* 196:113) **Kamia** *Unspecified* Species used for food. (as *Citrullus vulgaris* 62:21) **Meskwaki** *Unspecified* Melon used for food. (as *C. citrullus* 152:257) **Navajo** *Dried Food* Fruit cut into strips, wound upon sticks in the form of a rope, sun dried, and stored for months. (as *C. vulgaris* 165:222) **Navajo, Ramah** *Unspecified* Watermelon cultivated and used for food. *Winter Use Food* Watermelon sliced into strips, dried, and stored for winter use. (as *C. vulgaris* 191:46) **Okanagan-Colville** *Unspecified* Species used for food. (as *C. vulgaris* 188:98) **Pima** *Fruit* Fruits eaten as one of the most important foods. (as *C. vulgaris* 146:75) **Seminole** *Unspecified* Plant used for food. (as *C. vulgaris* 169:479) **Sia** *Unspecified* Cultivated watermelons used for food. (as *C. vulgaris* 199:106)

Citrus aurantifolia, Key Lime
Seminole Plant used for food. (169:513)

Citrus aurantium, Sour Orange
Seminole Plant used for food. (169:511)

Citrus limon, Lemon
Haisla & Hanaksiala *Fruit* Fruit used for food. (43:284) **Seminole** *Unspecified* Plant used for food. (169:512) **Thompson** *Fruit* Fruit much prized for food after it became available. (187:275)

Citrus medica, Citron
Thompson *Fruit* Fruit much prized for food after it became available. (187:275)

Citrus ×paradisi, Paradise Citrus
Seminole *Unspecified* Plant used for food.
(169:512)

Citrus reticulata, Tangerine
Seminole *Unspecified* Plant used for food.
(169:512)

Citrus sinensis, Sweet Orange
Haisla & Hanaksiala *Fruit* Fruit used for
food. (43:284) **Seminole** *Unspecified* Plant
used for food. (169:513) **Thompson** *Fruit* Fruit
much prized for food after it became available.
(187:275)

Cladonia rangiferina
Abnaki *Forage* Plant eaten by caribou.
(144:152)

Clarkia amoena* ssp. *amoena,
Farewell to Spring
Miwok *Unspecified* Parched, pulverized dry
seeds used for food. (as *Godetia amoena*
12:153)

Clarkia biloba* ssp. *biloba, Twolobe
Fairyfan
Miwok Parched, pulverized seeds used for
food. (as *Godetia biloba* 12:154)

***Clarkia purpurea* ssp. *quadri-
vulnera***, Winecup Fairyfan
Mendocino Indian *Staple* Seeds eaten as a
pinole. (as *Godetia albescens* 41:370)

Clarkia purpurea* ssp. *viminea,
Winecup Fairyfan
Miwok *Unspecified* Dried, pulverized, uncooked seeds used for food. (as *Godetia
viminea* 12:154) *Vegetable* Seeds considered
one of the most prized vegetable foods. (as
Godetia viminea 12:137)

Clarkia rhomboidea, Diamond
Fairyfan
Yana *Unspecified* Seeds eaten raw or parched
and finely pounded. (147:251)

Clarkia unguiculata, Elegant Fairyfan
Miwok *Unspecified* Parched, pulverized seeds
eaten dry with acorn mush. (as *C. elegans*
12:153)

Claytonia acutifolia, Bering Sea
Springbeauty
Alaska Native *Unspecified* Fresh roots eaten
raw or cooked with seal oil. (85:115) **Eskimo,
Alaska** *Unspecified* Fleshy taproots used for
food. (4:715)

Claytonia caroliniana, Carolina
Springbeauty
Gosiute *Unspecified* Bulbs used for food.
(39:366) **Ute** *Unspecified* Bulbs formerly used
for food. (38:33)

Claytonia cordifolia, Heartleaf
Springbeauty
Montana Indian *Sauce & Relish* Eaten raw as
a relish. (as *Montia asarifolia* 19:16)

Claytonia lanceolata, Lanceleaf
Springbeauty
Blackfoot *Vegetable* Tubers boiled and eaten.
(114:278) **Montana Indian** *Fodder* Roots "better for fattening hogs than the best feed." (19:10)
Forage Rootstocks eaten by marmots, ground
squirrels, and grizzly bears. (82:29) *Unspecified* Roots eaten raw and roasted. (19:10) Crisp,
tuber-like corms eaten fresh or boiled. (82:29)
Okanagan-Colville *Unspecified* Corms used
for food. *Winter Use Food* Corms stored for future use. (188:113) **Okanagon** *Unspecified*
Corms boiled and used for food. (125:38)
Thompson *Bread & Cake* Corms made into
cakes and dried for future use. (187:239) *Unspecified* Corms boiled and used for food.
(125:38) Small, oval corms eaten. (164:482)
Corms rubbed clean, cooked in pits or steamed,
and eaten. *Winter Use Food* Corms buried fresh
in underground caches and stored for winter
use. (187:239)

Claytonia lanceolata* var. *sessili-folia, Lanceleaf Springbeauty
Okanagon *Staple* Roots used as a principal food. (as *C. sessilifolia* 178:238)

Claytonia multicaulis, Ground Nut
Montana Indian *Fodder* Roots "better for fattening hogs than the best feed." *Unspecified* Roots eaten raw and roasted. (19:10)

Claytonia parviflora, Streambank Springbeauty
Montana Indian *Sauce & Relish* Eaten raw as a relish. (as *Montia parviflora* 19:16)

Claytonia perfoliata, Miner's Lettuce
Costanoan *Unspecified* Raw foliage used for food in early spring and boiled or steamed when eaten later in the season. (21:251)
Kawaiisu *Vegetable* Leaves eaten as greens. (206:21) **Mendocino Indian** *Unspecified* Plants eaten raw. *Vegetable* Plants cooked with salt and pepper and eaten as greens. (41:346) **Neeshenam** *Vegetable* Leaves eaten as greens. (129:377)

Claytonia perfoliata* ssp. *perfoliata, Miner's Lettuce
Diegueño *Vegetable* Young leaves, picked in the spring before the flowers appear, boiled once and eaten as greens. (84:17)

Claytonia perfoliata* ssp. *perfoliata* var. *perfoliata, Miner's Lettuce
Cahuilla *Vegetable* Leaves eaten fresh or boiled as greens. (as *Montia perfoliata* 15:89) **Luiseño** *Vegetable* Plant used for greens or eaten raw. (as *Montia perfoliata* 155:232) **Miwok** *Unspecified* Raw stems, leaves, and blossoms used for food. (as *Montia perfoliata* 12:160) **Montana Indian** *Sauce & Relish* Eaten raw as a relish. (as *Montia perfoliata* 19:16) **Paiute, Northern** *Vegetable* Leaves eaten raw. (as *Montia perfoliata* 59:49)

Claytonia sibirica, Siberian Springbeauty
Alaska Native *Dietary Aid* Leaves properly pre-

pared and used as a good source of vitamin C and provitamin A. *Vegetable* Leaves added raw to mixed salads or cooked as a green vegetable. (85:25) **Yurok** *Unspecified* Shoot tops eaten raw. (6:25)

Claytonia spathulata* var. *spathulata, Pale Springbeauty
Cahuilla *Vegetable* Leaves eaten fresh or boiled as greens. (as *Montia spathulata* 15:89)

Claytonia tuberosa, Tuberous Springbeauty
Alaska Native *Dietary Aid* Green, fresh leaves eaten raw as a source of vitamins C and A. *Soup* Corms cooked and added to stews. *Vegetable* Corms roasted and used for food. Basal leaves added to other greens and eaten raw or cooked. (85:117) **Eskimo, Arctic** *Vegetable* Tubers boiled and eaten. (128:31)

Claytonia umbellata, Great Basin Springbeauty
Paiute, Northern *Unspecified* Roots roasted in the sand and eaten. (59:43)

Claytonia virginica, Virginia Springbeauty
Algonquin, Quebec *Vegetable* Corm cooked and eaten like potatoes. (18:84) **Iroquois** *Unspecified* Roots used for food. (196:120)

Clematis ligusticifolia, Western White Clematis
Lakota *Forage* Leaves eaten by horses. (139:55)

Cleome isomeris, Bladderpod Spiderflower
Diegueño *Unspecified* Seeds and flowers used as food. (as *Isomeris arborea* var. *angustata* 88:217) **Kawaiisu** *Unspecified* Flowers eaten boiled or sun baked. (as *Isomeris arborea* 206:35)

Cleome multicaulis, Slender Spiderflower
Navajo *Sauce & Relish* Leaves used to make a gravy. *Soup* Leaves used to make a watery stew.

Special Food Leaves made into tea and taken at a general feast after finishing the masks for the Night Chant. *Vegetable* Leaves used for greens. (as *C. sonorae* 55:51)

Cleome serrulata, Rocky Mountain Beeplant

Acoma *Porridge* Seeds cooked well, dried, and made into mush before use. (32:22) **Apache, Western** *Vegetable* Leaves and whole, young plants used as greens. (26:192) **Havasupai** *Unspecified* Seeds used for food. (197:221) **Hopi** *Unspecified* Leaves and flowers boiled and used for food. (as *C. integrifolia* 56:16) Young plants boiled for food. (200:77) *Vegetable* Plants boiled and eaten like spinach. (32:24) **Isleta** *Bread & Cake* Seeds made into a meal and used to make bread. (32:22) Large seeds formerly used to make a flour for bread. *Vegetable* Leaves used as greens. (100:26) **Jemez** *Bread & Cake* Green parts boiled, fibrous material removed, molded into cakes, and fried in grease, a delicacy. *Vegetable* Young and tender plants eaten as greens. (as *Peritoma serrulatum* 44:26) **Keres, Western** *Porridge* Dried seeds cooked into a mush and eaten. *Vegetable* Leaves and shoots used for food as greens. (171:37) **Keresan** *Unspecified* Seeds cooked and eaten. *Vegetable* Leaves cooked as greens. (as *Peritoma serrulatum* 198:559) **Laguna** *Porridge* Seeds cooked well, dried, and made into mush before use. (32:22) **Navajo** *Bread & Cake* Dried leaves and meat or tallow used to make dumplings. (55:50) *Dried Food* Young plants boiled, pressed, rolled into balls, dried, and stored for winter use. (32:24) Leaves dried and stored for winter use. (110:13) Young shoots boiled, rolled into small balls, and dried for winter use. (165:223) *Soup* Plant made into stew with wild onions, wild celery, tallow, or bits of meat. (32:24) Leaves, onions, wild celery, and tallow or meat used to make stew. (55:50) Dried leaves used to make stew. (110:13) *Spice* Used as a seasoning. (90:149) *Unspecified* Young plants boiled, pressed, rolled into balls, and eaten. (32:24) Pods used for food. (55:50) *Vegetable* Young plants boiled with a pinch of salt and eaten as greens. (32:24) Leaves boiled like spinach. Young plants boiled and rolled into balls and eaten. (55:50) Young shoots eaten as greens. Young shoots boiled, rolled into small balls, and eaten fresh with or without mutton. (165:223) *Winter Use Food* Young plants boiled, rolled into balls, dried, and stored for the winter. (55:50) **Navajo, Ramah** *Dried Food* Young plants boiled twice and dried in small balls for later use. *Fodder* Young plants used for sheep and horse feed. *Unspecified* Young plants boiled twice and meat added or plants removed and fried. (191:29) **Pueblo** *Staple* Used as one of the most important food plants. **San Felipe** *Unspecified* Flower buds salted and eaten as food. (32:24) **Sia** *Unspecified* Seeds used for food. *Vegetable* Leaves cooked as greens. (as *Peritoma serrulatum* 199:107) **Tewa** *Unspecified* Young plants boiled, dried, soaked in hot water, fried in grease, and used for food. (as *Peritoma serrulatum* 138:58) *Vegetable* Plants boiled and eaten like spinach. (32:24) **Zuni** *Dried Food* Leaves gathered in large quantities and hung indoors to dry for winter use. (as *Peritoma serrulatum* 166:69) *Unspecified* Young plants cooked with corn strongly flavored with chile. (32:24) Tender leaves usually boiled with corn, on or off the cob, and highly seasoned with chile. (as *Peritoma serrulatum* 166:69)

Cleome serrulata

Clermontia arborescens, 'Oha Wai
  Nui
Hawaiian *Fruit* Fruit used for food. (2:30)

Clintonia uniflora, Bride's Bonnet
Bella Coola *Forage* Berries eaten by wolves.
(184:199)

Coccoloba diversifolia, Tietongue
Seminole *Unspecified* Plant used for food. (as
Coccolobis laurifolia 169:475)

Cochlearia officinalis, Common
  Scurvygrass
Alaska Native *Vegetable* Leaves eaten raw in
mixed salads or cooked as greens. (85:27)

Cocos nucifera, Coconut Palm
Seminole *Unspecified* Plant used for food.
(169:503)

Coix lacryma-jobi, Job's Tears
Cherokee *Bread & Cake* Seeds used to make
bread. (80:41)

Coleogyne ramosissima, Blackbrush
Havasupai *Fodder* Plant used as a good feed
for stock in the absence of grass. (197:223)

Colocasia esculenta, Coco Yam
Hawaiian *Unspecified* Roots beaten into poi
and eaten. Plant mixed with coconut meat and
eaten. *Vegetable* Leaves and stems cooked and
eaten as greens. (as *Arum esculentum* 112:67)
Seminole *Unspecified* Plant used for food.
(169:465)

Comandra umbellata, Bastard
  Toadflax
Okanagan-Colville *Sweetener* Flowers sucked
by children for the sweet nectar. (188:138)

***Comandra umbellata* ssp.
  *pallida***, Pale Bastard Toadflax
Navajo, Kayenta *Unspecified* Seeds used for
food. (as *Commandra pallida* 205:18) **Okanagon** *Staple* Seeds or nuts used as a principal
food. (as *Comandra pallida* 178:239) **Paiute**

Unspecified Small, round seeds eaten as nuts by
children. (as *C. pallida* 111:66)

Comarum palustre, Purple Marshlocks
Eskimo, Alaska *Beverage* Dried leaves used to
make a hot, tea-like beverage before the availability of imported tea. (as *Potentilla palustris*
1:36)

Comptonia peregrina, Sweet Fern
Chippewa *Beverage* Leaves used to make a hot,
tea-like beverage. (as *Myrica asplenifolia*
71:127) **Ojibwa** *Preservative* Leaves used to
line buckets when picking blueberries and
cover them to prevent spoiling. (as *Myrica
asplenifolia* 153:420)

Condalia globosa, Bitter Snakewood
Papago *Fruit* Fruits eaten raw. (as *Condolis
spathulata* 34:19)

Condalia hookeri* var. *hookeri,
  Hooker's Bluewood
Maricopa *Fruit* Fruits eaten raw. (as *C. obovata* 95:262) Black berries used for food. (as *C.
obovata* 95:265) **Pima** *Fruit* Fruits eaten raw.
Fruits roasted and used for food. *Sauce & Relish* Berries cooked, strained, and juice boiled
to make syrup. (as *C. obovata* 95:262)

Conioselinum gmelinii, Pacific
  Hemlockparsley
Haihais *Unspecified* Roots used for food.
Haisla *Unspecified* Roots used for food. (as *C.
pacificum* 43:83) **Haisla & Hanaksiala** *Unspecified* Roots steamed and eaten with oolichan (candlefish) grease. (as *C. pacificum*
43:213) **Hanaksiala** *Unspecified* Roots used
for food. **Heiltzuk** *Unspecified* Roots used for
food. (as *C. pacificum* 43:83) **Kitasoo** *Vegetable* Roots used for food. (as *C. pacificum*
43:325) **Kwakwaka'wakw** *Unspecified* Roots
used for food. **Nuxalkmc** *Unspecified* Roots
used for food. **Oweekeno** *Unspecified* Roots
used for food. (as *C. pacificum* 43:83)

Conioselinum scopulorum, Rocky
   Mountain Hemlockparsley
Navajo, Kayenta *Unspecified* Leaves cooked
with meat and used for food. (205:34)

**Conyza canadensis var. cana-
densis**, Canadian Horseweed
Miwok *Vegetable* Raw, pulverized leaves and
tender tops, flavor similar to onions, used for
food. (as *Erigeron canadensis* 12:159)

Cordylanthus sp., Sunflower
Yavapai *Unspecified* Parched, ground seeds
eaten dry or dampened. (65:256)

Cordyline fruticosa, Tiplant
Hawaiian *Beverage* Roots fermented into a
very powerful alcohol. *Unspecified* Roots
cooked and used for food. (as *C. terminalis*
2:49) Roots pit baked and eaten. (as *C. terminalis* 112:68)

Coreopsis bigelovii, Bigelow's
   Tickseed
Kawaiisu *Sweetener* Stems chewed for the
sweet juice. *Vegetable* Whole plant eaten fresh
or cooked and fried in grease and salt. Raw,
bruised leaves eaten boiled or with salt. (206:21)
Tubatulabal *Unspecified* Leaves used extensively for food. (193:15)

Coreopsis tinctoria, Golden Tickseed
Lakota *Beverage* Used to make tea. (139:37)

**Coreopsis tinctoria var. tincto-
ria**, Golden Tickseed
Zuni *Beverage* Plant formerly used to make a
hot beverage until the introduction of coffee by
traders. The plant was folded while fresh, a
number of folds being attached one below the
other, and hung on the wall to dry. When the
beverage was desired, a fold was detached from
the wall and used to make a hot beverage. (as *C.
cardaminefolia* 166:66)

Coriandrum sativum, Chinese Parsley
Hopi *Sauce & Relish* Plant dipped into a stew
and eaten as a condiment. (56:20) *Spice* Used

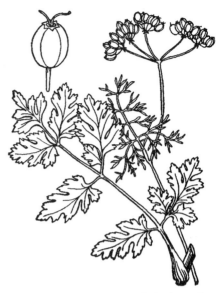

Coriandrum sativum

as flavoring in cooking. (200:86) *Unspecified*
Dipped into water, eaten raw and green.
(190:164) **Keresan** *Spice* Seeds used to flavor
soups and stews. (198:560) **Zuni** *Sauce & Relish* Powdered seeds ground with chile and used
a condiment with meat. *Vegetable* Leaves used
as a salad. (166:66)

Cornicularia divergens, Caribou
   Moss
Eskimo, Inuktitut *Fodder* Plant given to fawns
to try to get them to eat from their hands.
(202:191)

Cornus canadensis, Bunchberry
   Dogwood
Abnaki *Fruit* Fruits eaten for food. (144:170)
Algonquin, Quebec *Snack Food* Berries used
as a nibble food. (18:102) **Chippewa** *Fruit* Berries eaten raw. (53:321) **Cree, Woodlands**
Snack Food Fruit eaten as a fresh nibble.
(109:36) **Eskimo, Alaska** *Fruit* Gathered and
mixed with other berries. (4:715) **Haisla &
Hanaksiala** *Dessert* Berries mashed, mixed
with oolichan (candlefish) grease, and eaten as
a dessert. *Dried Food* Berries dried for winter
use. (43:234) **Hesquiat** *Special Food* Raw ber-

ries eaten with dogfish oil by the elders of the village at a big feast. (185:63) **Kwakiutl, Southern** *Fruit* Pulpy berries extensively used for food. (183:281) **Makah** *Fruit* Berries eaten fresh. (79:43) **Nitinaht** *Fruit* Berries eaten fresh and raw. (186:102) **Potawatomi** *Fruit* Berries used for food. (154:98) **Salish** *Fruit* Berries used for food. (182:81)

Cornus sericea, Red Osier Dogwood
Thompson *Dessert* Fruit eaten as dessert. *Dried Food* Berries and saskatoon berries smashed together, dried, rehydrated, and eaten in the winter. The berries were also pounded with chokecherries, seeds and all, and used for food. *Fruit* Bitter, seedy fruits eaten alone or mashed with dried, "white" saskatoon berries. (187:204)

Cornus sericea ssp. *occidentalis*, Western Dogwood
Nitinaht *Fruit* Berries eaten fresh. (as *C. stolonifera* var. *occidentalis* 186:103) **Okanagon** *Staple* Berries used as a principal food. (as *C. pubescens* 178:238) **Sanpoil & Nespelem** *Fruit* Berries eaten fresh. (as *C. pubescens* 131:102) **Spokan** *Fruit* Berries used for food. (as *C. pubescens* 178:343) **Thompson** *Unspecified* Little, white drupes eaten occasionally. (as *C. pubescens* 164:490)

Cornus sericea ssp. *sericea*, Red Osier Dogwood
Blackfoot *Fruit* Berries eaten ripe. (as *C. stolonifera* 86:102) *Snack Food* Berries and saskatoon berries used as a favorite snack reserved for men. (as *C. stolonifera* 86:100) **Flathead** *Fruit* Berries occasionally eaten raw. Berries mixed with serviceberries and sugar and eaten as a "sweet and sour" dish. (as *C. stolonifera* 82:21) **Haisla & Hanaksiala** *Forage* Berries eaten by bears. (43:233) **Hesquiat** *Dessert* Berries, sugar, and water whipped with salal branches until foamy and eaten as a confectionery dessert. (as *Shepherdia stolonifera* 185:64) **Kutenai** *Fruit* Berries occasionally eaten raw. Berries mixed with serviceberries and sugar and eaten as a "sweet and sour" dish. (as *C. stolonifera* 82:21) **Okanagan-Colville** *Forage*

Berries eaten by black bears. *Fruit* Berries pounded, mixed with chokecherries or saskatoon berries, or boiled and eaten alone. (as *C. stolonifera* 188:96) **Shuswap** *Fruit* Berries used for food. *Preservative* Used with narrow leaf cottonwood to smoke salmon. *Spice* Scraped wood, tasted like salt, used for barbecuing meat. (as *C. stolonifera* 123:61)

Cornus suecica, Lapland Cornel
Eskimo, Alaska *Fruit* Fresh, ripe berries used for food. (1:37) Gathered and mixed with other berries. (4:715)

Cornus unalaschkensis, Western Cordilleran Bunchberry
Bella Coola *Fruit* Ripe berries eaten with sugar and grease. (184:204) **Haisla & Hanaksiala** *Dessert* Berries mashed, mixed with oolichan (candlefish) grease, and eaten as a dessert. *Dried Food* Berries dried for winter use. (43:234) **Kitasoo** *Fruit* Fruit used for food. (43:331) **Oweekeno** *Forage* Berries eaten by bears. *Fruit* Berries used for food. (43:93)

Corydalis aurea, Scrambledeggs
Navajo, Ramah *Fodder* Used for sheep feed. (191:28)

Corydalis aurea ssp. *occidentalis*, Scrambledeggs
Navajo, Ramah *Fodder* Used for sheep feed. (191:28)

Corylus americana, American Hazelnut
Cherokee *Unspecified* Nuts used for food. (80:37) **Chippewa** *Unspecified* Nuts used for food in season. *Winter Use Food* Nuts stored for winter use. (71:127) **Dakota** *Soup* Nuts used as a body for soup. *Unspecified* Nuts eaten raw with honey. (70:74) **Iroquois** *Beverage* Fresh nutmeats crushed, boiled, and liquid used as a drink. *Bread & Cake* Fresh nutmeats crushed and mixed with bread. (124:99) Nuts crushed, mixed with cornmeal and beans or berries, and made into bread. (196:123) *Pie & Pudding* Fresh nutmeats crushed and mixed with corn

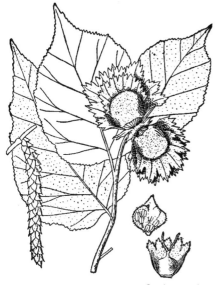

Corylus americana

pudding. (124:99) *Sauce & Relish* Nuts pounded, boiled, resulting oil seasoned with salt and used as gravy. *Soup* Nutmeats crushed and added to corn soup. (196:123) *Special Food* Fresh nutmeats crushed, boiled, and oil used as a delicacy in corn bread and pudding. (124:99) Nutmeat oil added to the mush used by the False Face Societies. *Staple* Nutmeats crushed and added to hominy. *Unspecified* Nutmeats, after skimming off the oil, seasoned and mixed with mashed potatoes. (196:123) **Menominee** *Unspecified* Nuts, in the milk stage, eaten. *Winter Use Food* Nuts, in the milk stage, dried for winter use. (151:63) **Meskwaki** *Unspecified* Nuts eaten in the milk stage or ripe. *Winter Use Food* Nuts stored for winter use. (152:256) **Ojibwa** *Unspecified* Nuts eaten as food and newly gathered nuts before the kernel had hardened were favored. (153:397) **Omaha** *Soup* Nuts used as a body for soup. (70:74) *Unspecified* Nuts eaten plain or mixed with honey. (68:326) Nuts eaten raw with honey. **Ponca** *Soup* Nuts used as a body for soup. *Unspecified* Nuts eaten raw with honey. **Winnebago** *Soup* Nuts used as a body for soup. *Unspecified* Nuts eaten raw with honey. (70:74)

Corylus cornuta, Beaked Hazelnut
Algonquin, Quebec *Unspecified* Nuts used for food. (18:79) **Cree, Woodlands** *Unspecified* Nuts used for food. *Winter Use Food* Nuts collected in quantity to use at a later time. (109:37) **Iroquois** *Fruit* Fruit roasted and eaten. (142:85) **Salish, Coast** *Unspecified* Nuts used for food. (182:79) **Thompson** *Snack Food* Nuts eaten for refreshments. (187:190)

Corylus cornuta var. *californica*,
California Hazelnut
Chehalis *Unspecified* Nuts eaten fresh. *Winter Use Food* Nuts eaten during the winter. (as *C. californica* 79:27) **Costanoan** *Unspecified* Nuts used for food but only late in season. (21:248) **Cowlitz** *Winter Use Food* Nuts eaten during the winter. (as *C. californica* 79:27) **Karok** *Unspecified* Nuts used for food. (6:25) **Klamath** *Unspecified* Nuts used for food. (as *C. californica* 45:94) **Lummi** *Unspecified* Nuts eaten fresh. (as *C. californica* 79:27) **Okanagon** *Unspecified* Species used for food. (as *C. californica* 125:39) **Paiute** *Unspecified* Nutmeat eaten raw. *Winter Use Food* Nutmeat stored for future use. (as *C. californica* 111:64) **Sanpoil & Nespelem** *Unspecified* Nuts stored without removing the shells. Nutmeat eaten whole or pulverized before use. (as *C. californica* 131:104) **Shuswap** *Unspecified* Nuts used for food. (as *C. californica* 123:60) **Skagit** *Unspecified* Nuts cracked with stones and eaten fresh. (as *C. californica* 79:27) **Skagit, Upper** *Unspecified* Nuts eaten fresh. *Winter Use Food* Nuts stored for winter use. (as *C. californica* 179:42) **Snohomish** *Unspecified* Nuts eaten fresh. **Squaxin** *Unspecified* Nuts used for food. **Swinomish** *Unspecified* Nuts eaten fresh. (as *C. californica* 79:27) **Thompson** *Unspecified* Species used for food. (as *C. californica* 125:39) **Tolowa** *Dried Food* Nuts dried and stored for winter use. *Unspecified* Nuts eaten fresh. **Yurok** *Unspecified* Nuts eaten fresh. (6:25)

Corylus cornuta var. *cornuta*,
Beaked Hazelnut
Karok *Unspecified* Nuts used for food. *Winter Use Food* Nuts stored for winter use. (as *C.*

rostrata var. *californica* 148:382) **Miwok** *Unspecified* Nuts used for food. (as *C. rostrata* var. *californica* 12:153) **Ojibwa** *Unspecified* Species used for food. (as *C. rostrata* 135:242) Nuts eaten as a food. (as *C. rostrata* 153:398) **Potawatomi** *Winter Use Food* Mature or "in the milk" nut gathered and used as a favorite food during the winter. (as *C. rostrata* 154:97) **Yuki** *Unspecified* Nuts eaten raw. (as *C. rostrata* var. *californica* 49:87)

Costaria costata, Short Kelp
Hesquiat *Dried Food* Stipes and fronds with attached herring eggs dried for later use. (185:24)

Crataegus calpodendron, Pear Hawthorn
Meskwaki *Fruit* Fruit eaten raw and cooked. (as *C. tomentosa* 152:263)

Crataegus chrysocarpa, Fireberry Hawthorn
Blackfoot *Fruit* Berries used for food. Certain conditions had to be met before the berries were eaten. Otherwise, they would cause stomach cramps. The procedure was to offer the tree a gift, for boys a little bow and arrow made from the thorns, for girls a pair of miniature moccasins fashioned from the leaves. In return, the tree would not allow its berries to "bite" the stomach. The gifts were placed on the tree and the berries collected. (86:102) **Lakota** *Fruit* Fruits eaten for food. (139:56) **Ojibwa** *Fruit* Fruit used for food. (as *C. coccinea* 135:236) **Omaha** *Beverage* Twigs used to make a hot, aqueous, tea-like beverage. (as *C. coccinea* 68:329) *Fruit* Fruit eaten by children fresh from the hand. (as *C. coccinea* 68:326) Fruit sometimes used for food, but mostly as a famine food. (70:87) *Starvation Food* Fruit eaten by adults in times of famine. (as *C. coccinea* 68:326) Fruit sometimes used for food, but mostly as a famine food. **Ponca** *Fruit* and *Starvation Food* Fruit sometimes used for food, but mostly as a famine food. (70:87) **Potawatomi** *Fruit* Fruit eaten by deer, bears, and sometimes the Indians. (as *C. rotundifolia* var. *bicknellii*

154:107) **Winnebago** *Fruit* and *Starvation Food* Fruit sometimes used for food, but mostly as a famine food. (70:87)

Crataegus columbiana, Columbian Hawthorn
Montana Indian *Fruit* Fruit eaten fresh. *Winter Use Food* Fruit mixed with chokecherries and serviceberries pressed into cakes and dried for winter use. (19:11) **Okanagan-Colville** *Bread & Cake* Berries mashed and formed into cakes, dried, and eaten like cookies. *Fruit* Berries eaten fresh. (188:123) **Okanagon** *Fruit* Fruits eaten for food. (125:38) **Oregon Indian** *Fruit* Fresh or dried fruit used for food. (118:22) **Sanpoil & Nespelem** *Fruit* Whole berries eaten fresh or mashed in a mortar. (131:103) **Thompson** *Fruit* Fruits eaten for food. (125:38) *Unspecified* Scarlet, pear-shaped pomes eaten. (164:487)

Crataegus douglasii, Black Hawthorn
Bella Coola *Fruit* Berries used for food. (184:208) **Cheyenne** *Dried Food* Fruits dried and used as a winter food. *Fruit* Fresh fruits cooked and used for food. (83:34) *Winter Use Food* Pulverized, dried berries saved for winter use. (76:176) **Kwakiutl, Southern** *Fruit* Ber-

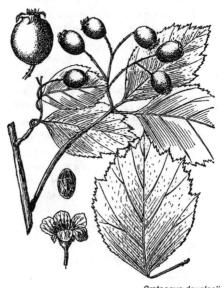

Crataegus douglasii

ries used for food. (183:288) **Okanagan-Colville** *Bread & Cake* Berries mashed and dried into thin, hard cakes. Sometimes the cakes were decorated. The dried cakes were eaten as a snack on winter evenings and were used as crackers to dip into deer marrow soup to soak up the fat. *Forage* Berries eaten by bears and other animals. (188:124) **Okanagon** *Fruit* Fruits eaten for food. (125:38) **Paiute** *Dried Food* Berries formerly dried and eaten. *Fruit* Berries formerly eaten fresh. (104:100) Fruit eaten raw or boiled. (111:84) **Salish, Coast** *Fruit* Dry, sweetish fruits eaten in late fall. (182:86) **Sanpoil & Nespelem** *Dried Food* Berries boiled, dried, and stored. *Fruit* Berries eaten raw. (as *C. brevispina* 131:103) **Shuswap** *Preserves* Berries used to make jelly. (123:66) **Thompson** *Dried Food* Mashed fruit dried for winter use. (187:258) *Fruit* Fruits eaten for food. (125:38) Fruit, without the seeds, eaten fresh or pureed. *Preserves* Fruit made into jam or jelly. (187:258) *Unspecified* Pomes eaten. (164:486)

Crataegus douglasii var. *douglasii*, Douglas's Hawthorn
Haisla & Hanaksiala *Fruit* Fruit used for food. (43:263)

Crataegus erythropoda, Cerro Hawthorn
Apache, Chiricahua & Mescalero *Bread & Cake* Fruit pressed into pulpy cakes, dried, and stored. *Fruit* Fruits eaten fresh. *Winter Use Food* Fruit pressed into pulpy cakes, dried, and stored for winter use. (as *C. cerronis* 33:44)

Crataegus macrosperma, Bigfruit Hawthorn
Cherokee *Fruit* Fresh fruit used for food. (126:56)

Crataegus mollis, Arnold Hawthorn
Omaha *Beverage* Twigs used to make a hot, aqueous, tea-like beverage. (68:329) *Fruit* Fruit eaten by children fresh from the hand. *Starvation Food* Fruit eaten by adults in times of famine. (68:326)

Crataegus pruinosa, Waxyfruit Hawthorn
Iroquois *Bread & Cake* Fruit mashed, made into small cakes, and dried for future use. (196:128) Used to make bread. (196:82) *Dried Food* Raw or cooked fruit sun or fire dried and stored for future use. *Fruit* Dried fruit taken as a hunting food. *Sauce & Relish* Dried fruit cakes soaked in warm water and cooked as a sauce or mixed with corn bread. (196:128)

Crataegus rivularis, River Hawthorn
Okanagon *Staple* Berries used as a principal food. (178:238)

Crataegus submollis, Quebec Hawthorn
Iroquois *Bread & Cake* Fruit mashed, made into small cakes, and dried for future use. (196:128) Used to make bread. (196:82) *Dried Food* Raw or cooked fruit sun or fire dried and stored for future use. *Fruit* Dried fruit taken as a hunting food. *Sauce & Relish* Dried fruit cakes soaked in warm water and cooked as a sauce or mixed with corn bread. (196:128)

Crepis acuminata, Longleaf Hawksbeard
Karok *Vegetable* Stems peeled and eaten raw as greens. (148:389)

Crepis occidentalis, Largeflower Hawksbeard
Paiute *Unspecified* Leaves eaten raw. (104:103)

Crepis runcinata ssp. *glauca*, Fiddleleaf Hawksbeard
Gosiute *Unspecified* Leaves used for food. (as *C. glauca* 39:367)

Croton setigerus, Croton
Mendocino Indian *Forage* Shiny, bean-like seeds eaten by wild mourning doves and turkeys. (41:363)

Croton texensis, Texas Croton
Hopi *Fodder* Used as food for wild doves. (200:84)

Cryptantha cinerea var. *jamesii*,
James's Catseye
Navajo, Ramah *Fodder* Used for sheep feed.
(as *C. jamesii* 191:40)

Cryptantha fendleri, Sanddune
Catseye
Navajo, Ramah *Fodder* Used for sheep feed,
a nuisance because the ripe fruits stick in the
wool. (191:40)

Cucumis melo, Cantaloupe
Hopi *Dried Food* Rind removed, meat pressed
flat or stripped, wrapped into bundles, and
dried. *Unspecified* Eaten fresh. (200:93) **Iroquois** *Bread & Cake* Fresh or dried flesh
boiled, mashed, and mixed into the paste when
making corn bread. *Dried Food* Flesh cut into
strips, dried, and stored away. *Special Food*
Squash eaten at feasts of ceremonial importance and longhouse ceremonies. *Vegetable*
Flesh boiled, baked in ashes or boiled, mashed
with butter and sugar, and eaten. Flesh fried
and sweetened or seasoned with salt, pepper,
and butter. (as *Cucurbita melo* 196:113) **Keresan** *Spice* Seeds ground on metate to remove
the hulls and used to flavor various foods, especially rabbit stews. (198:560) **Navajo** *Dried
Food* Fruit cut into strips, wound upon sticks
in the form of a rope, sun dried, and stored for
months. *Sauce & Relish* Dried fruit boiled with
sugar and eaten like apple sauce. (165:222)
Navajo, Ramah *Unspecified* Muskmelon cultivated and used for food. (191:46) **Okanagan-
Colville** *Unspecified* Species used for food.
(188:98) **Seminole** *Unspecified* Plant used for
food. (169:480) **Sia** *Unspecified* Cultivated can-
taloupes used for food. (199:106) **Thompson**
Fruit Fruit used for food. (187:206)

Cucumis sativus, Garden Cucumber
Iroquois *Bread & Cake* Fresh or dried flesh
boiled, mashed, and mixed into the paste when
making corn bread. *Dried Food* Flesh cut into
strips, dried, and stored away. *Special Food*
Squash eaten at feasts of ceremonial importance and longhouse ceremonies. *Vegetable*
Flesh boiled, baked in ashes or boiled, mashed

with butter and sugar, and eaten. Fruit preserved in brine made with salt and sheep sorrel.
Flesh fried and sweetened or seasoned with salt,
pepper, and butter. (as *Cucurbita sativus*
196:113) **Ojibwa** *Vegetable* Cucumbers eaten
raw and sometimes flavored with maple sap vinegar and powdered maple sugar. (153:399)
Seminole *Unspecified* Plant used for food.
(169:478)

Cucurbita digitata, Fingerleaf Gourd
Pima, Gila River *Snack Food* Seeds roasted
and eaten as a snack food. (133:7)

Cucurbita foetidissima, Missouri
Gourd
Cahuilla *Porridge* Seeds ground into a flour and
used to make mush. (15:57) **Isleta** *Fruit* Fruit
formerly used for food. (100:27) **Luiseño** *Unspecified* Seeds used for food. (155:229) **Pima**
Unspecified Seeds roasted and eaten. (146:70)

Cucurbita maxima, Winter Squash
Hopi *Unspecified* Species used for food.
(200:93) **Iroquois** *Bread & Cake* Fresh or
dried flesh boiled, mashed and mixed into the
paste when making corn bread. *Dried Food*
Flesh cut into strips, dried, and stored away.
Special Food Squash eaten at feasts of ceremo-

Cucurbita foetidissima

nial importance and longhouse ceremonies. *Vegetable* Flesh boiled, baked in ashes or boiled, mashed with butter and sugar, and eaten. Flesh fried and sweetened or seasoned with salt, pepper, and butter. (196:113) **Navajo, Ramah** *Spice* Blossoms used as seasoning for soup. *Unspecified* Squash cultivated and used for food. *Winter Use Food* Squash peeled, cut into strips, sun dried, and stored in cellars or ground holes for winter use. (191:46) **Ojibwa** *Dried Food* Squash rings dried for winter use. (153:399) **Papago** *Fruit* Fruit grown for food. **Pima** *Fruit* Fruit grown for food. (36:101) **Sia** *Unspecified* Cultivated pumpkins used for food. (199:106)

Cucurbita moschata, Crookneck Squash

Cahuilla *Dried Food* Cooked, cut into strips, and dried. *Unspecified* Cooked and eaten fresh. (15:58) **Havasupai** *Dried Food* Seeds dried, parched, shelled, and eaten. *Porridge* Seeds ground to form a paste or mixed with corn into a mush. (197:244) *Soup* Seeds parched, ground, and used to make soup or mush. (197:67) Flowers and amaranth leaves boiled, ground, and fresh or dried corn and water added to make soup. (197:74) *Vegetable* Fruit baked and the flesh eaten. (197:66) **Hopi** *Cooking Agent* Seeds used to oil the "piki" stones. *Dried Food* Meat cut spirally, wound into long bundles, tied in pairs, and dried for winter use. *Special Food* Flowers used to make special foods. *Unspecified* Meat boiled or baked. Seeds roasted and eaten. (200:93) **Iroquois** *Bread & Cake* Fresh or dried flesh boiled, mashed, and mixed into the paste when making corn bread. *Dried Food* Flesh cut into strips, dried, and stored away. *Special Food* Squash eaten at feasts of ceremonial importance and longhouse ceremonies. *Vegetable* Flesh boiled, baked in ashes or boiled, mashed with butter and sugar, and eaten. Flesh fried and sweetened or seasoned with salt, pepper, and butter. (196:113) **Maricopa** *Dried Food* Fruit peeled, cut spirally into strips, dried, and stored. Fruit cut spirally into strips, dried, and stored. *Fruit* Fruits cut into pieces and boiled with mesquite pods. *Vegetable*

Pumpkin eaten as a cooked, mushy vegetable. (37:111) **Navajo** *Dried Food* Fruit cut into strips and dried for future use, could be kept for years. *Preserves* Dried fruit boiled with large amounts of sugar into a preserve. *Sauce & Relish* Dried fruit boiled and eaten with sugar as a sauce. (165:221) **Papago** *Dried Food* Rind hung in long spirals from house roofs to dry, tied in bundles, stored, and used for food. (34:36) *Fruit* Fruit grown for food. (36:101) **Pima** *Dried Food* Seeds parched and eaten. (146:71) *Fruit* Fruit grown for food. (36:101) **Seminole** *Unspecified* Plant used for food. (169:490) **Sia** *Unspecified* Cultivated pumpkins used for food. (199:106) **Yuma** *Dried Food* Seed sun dried, parched, cracked, and the meat eaten. (37:111)

Cucurbita pepo, Field Pumpkin

Apache, White Mountain *Bread & Cake* Blossoms baked as parts of certain kinds of cakes. *Unspecified* Flesh used for food. Blossoms used for food. (136:156) **Cherokee** *Unspecified* Species used for food. (80:51) *Vegetable* Flesh used for food. (80:21) **Cocopa** *Dried Food* Dried flesh strips stored and mixed with flesh of stored whole pumpkins to improve flavor. *Unspecified* Parched seeds used for food. *Vegetable* Fresh flesh boiled with rind on and sometimes mixed with maize meal. Roasted flesh eaten with fingers. (64:266) **Iroquois** *Bread & Cake* Fresh or dried flesh boiled, mashed, and mixed into the paste when making corn bread. Dried flesh pounded, sifted, soaked in cold water, sweetened, grease added, and baked into cakes. *Dried Food* Flesh cut into strips, dried and stored away. *Pie & Pudding* Flesh boiled, cornmeal, and sugar added and eaten as a pudding with sugar and milk. *Sauce & Relish* Dried flesh pounded into a fine meal or flour, boiled, sweetened, grease added, and used as a sauce. *Special Food* Squash eaten at feasts of ceremonial importance and longhouse ceremonies. *Vegetable* Flesh boiled, baked in ashes or boiled, mashed with butter and sugar, and eaten. Fresh or dried flesh boiled, mashed, and sweetened, or boiled with green beans, butter, and salt, and eaten. Flesh fried and sweetened or seasoned with salt, pepper, and butter. (196:113) **Kamia** *Unspecified* Species used for food. (62:21) **Meskwaki** *Winter Use Food* Squash sliced into rings, sun dried, pressed, and stored for winter use. (152:257) **Navajo** *Vegetable* Fruit pulp and seeds used for food. (90:150) **Navajo, Ramah** *Spice* Blossoms used as seasoning for soup. *Unspecified* Pumpkin cultivated and used for food. *Winter Use Food* Pumpkin peeled, cut into strips, sun dried, and stored in cellars or ground holes for winter use. (191:47) **Ojibwa** *Dried Food* Pumpkin rings dried for winter use. (153:400) **Okanagan-Colville** *Unspecified* Species used for food. (188:98) **Papago** *Dried Food* Rind hung in long spirals from house roofs to dry, tied in bundles, stored, and used for food. (34:36) *Fruit* Fruit grown for food. (36:101) *Staple* Seeds parched, sun dried, stored, ground into flour, and used as a staple food. (34:45) **Pima** *Fruit* Fruit grown for food. (36:101) *Unspecified* Seeds roasted, cracked, and the kernels eaten. (47:72) **Rappahannock** *Snack Food* Seeds eaten as "tid-bits." (161:30) **Zuni** *Dried Food* Fresh squash cut into spiral strips, folded into hanks, and hung up to dry for winter use. *Special Food* Blossoms cooked in grease and used as a delicacy in combination with other foods. *Unspecified* Fresh squash, either whole or in pieces, roasted in ashes and used for food. (166:67)

Cucurbita pepo var. *melopepo*, Field Pumpkin
Menominee *Winter Use Food* Squash cut into strips or rings and dried for winter use. (151:65)

Cupressus sp., Cypress
Navajo *Bread & Cake* Berries ground into a meal and mixed with bread dough. Leaf ash mixed with breads. *Fruit* Berries eaten raw or roasted. *Porridge* Leaf ash mixed with cornmeal mush. (as Cupressaceae sp. 110:22)

Cuscuta sp., Dodder
Navajo *Unspecified* Parched seeds used for food. (55:70)

Cycloloma atriplicifolium, Winged Pigweed
Apache, White Mountain *Staple* Seeds used to make flour. (as *C. artriplicifolium* 136:156) **Hopi** *Porridge* Ground seeds used to make mush. (as *Salsola atriplicifolia* 190:161) **Zuni** *Porridge* Seeds mixed with ground corn to make a mush. (32:22) *Staple* Tiny seeds ground, mixed with cornmeal, and made into steamed cakes. (166:67)

Cycloloma cornutum
Hopi *Unspecified* Seeds and flowers used as food. (32:22)

Cymopterus acaulis, Plains Spring-parsley
Comanche *Unspecified* Rootstocks used for food. (29:521) **Navajo** *Dried Food* Plant dried for future use. (as *C. glomeratus* 110:28) *Soup* Used with the Rocky Mountain bee plant to make stew. (as *C. glomeratus* 32:24) *Spice* Dried plant used as an herb for mutton stew. (as *C. glomeratus* 110:28)

Cymopterus acaulis var. *fendleri*, Fendler's Springparsley
Apache, Chiricahua & Mescalero *Spice* Leaves used with other green plant parts to flavor soups and meats. (as *C. fendleri* 33:48) *Unspecified* Roots eaten raw. (as *C. fendleri* 33:47) Raw roots eaten for food. (as *C. fendleri* 33:48) **Keres, Western** *Vegetable* Plant eaten much as celery. (as *C. fendleri* 171:40) **Navajo** *Dried Food* Leaves rubbed through hot ash to remove the strong taste and dried for winter use. *Spice* Leaves used as a seasoning for cornmeal mush, gruel, and boiled meat. *Vegetable* Leaves rubbed through hot ash to remove the strong taste and eaten fresh. (as *C. fendleri* 165:221)

Cymopterus bulbosus, Bulbous Springparsley
Acoma *Vegetable* Eaten like celery. **Cochiti** *Vegetable* Eaten like celery. **Laguna** *Vegetable* Eaten like celery. (as *Phellopterus bulbosus* 32:39) **Navajo, Ramah** *Dried Food* Dried,

ground root cooked with milk. *Unspecified* Root eaten raw or roasted in ashes. *Winter Use Food* Root dried for winter use. (191:38)

Cymopterus longipes, Longstalk Springparsley

Gosiute *Unspecified* Leaves boiled and used for food. (39:367) **Ute** *Unspecified* Leaves formerly boiled and eaten. (38:33)

Cymopterus montanus, Mountain Springparsley

Gosiute *Unspecified* Seeds and underground parts used for food. (39:367) **Navajo** *Substitution Food* Roots peeled, baked, and ground as an occasional substitute for cornmeal. (as *Phellopterus montanus* 55:68) *Unspecified* Cooked with dried wild desert onions in the winter. (as *Phellopterus montanus* 32:15) Cooked in the winter with wild carrot roots. (as *Phellopterus montanus* 32:26) Raw roots used for food. Peeled stems used for food. (as *Phellopterus montanus* 55:68)

Cymopterus multinervatus, Purplenerve Springparsley

Hopi *Unspecified* Roots eaten in spring. (42:305)

Cymopterus montanus

Cymopterus newberryi, Sweetroot Springparsley

Hopi *Unspecified* Sweet roots peeled and eaten by children. (200:86) **Navajo, Kayenta** *Vegetable* Eaten as greens with meat. (205:34)

Cymopterus purpureus, Purple Springparsley

Navajo *Spice* Plant used as a potherb in seasoning mush and soup. (55:67)

Cynoglossum grande, Pacific Hound's Tongue

Yuki *Unspecified* Roots cooked and used for food. (41:382)

Cyperus erythrorhizos, Redroot Flatsedge

Kamia *Porridge* Pulverized seeds cooked as mush. (62:24)

Cyperus esculentus, Chufa Flatsedge

Costanoan *Unspecified* Tubers eaten. (21:255) **Paiute, Northern** *Dried Food* Roots dried, ground, and mixed with other foods. *Unspecified* Roots eaten raw. (59:44) **Pomo, Kashaya** *Vegetable* Tubers on the rootstock eaten raw, baked, or boiled like potatoes. (72:78)

Cyperus fendlerianus, Fendler's Flatsedge

Apache, Chiricahua & Mescalero *Fodder* Flowers salted and fed to horses. Seeds salted and fed to horses. *Unspecified* Tubers eaten raw or peeled and cooked. (33:47)

Cyperus odoratus, Fragrant Flatsedge

Cocopa *Unspecified* Seeds used for food. **Mohave** *Unspecified* Seeds used for food. (as *C. ferax* 37:192) **Pima** *Unspecified* Tubers eaten. (as *C. ferax* 47:99)

Cyperus rotundus, Nut Grass

Paiute *Porridge* Tubers made into meal and cooked as cereal. *Unspecified* Raw tubers used for food. (118:16)

Cyperus schweinitzii, Schweinitz's
  Flatsedge
Kiowa *Fodder* Considered an excellent fodder
for fattening horses. (192:17)

Cyperus squarrosus, Bearded
  Flatsedge
Acoma *Unspecified* Small, tuberous roots eaten
as food. (as *C. inflexus* 32:25) **Keres, Western**

Vegetable Tubers eaten. (as *C. inflexus* 171:41)
Laguna *Unspecified* Small, tuberous roots eat-
en as food. (as *C. inflexus* 32:25)

***Cypripedium* sp.**, Lady Slipper
Lakota *Unspecified* Species used for food.
(139:28)

Dalea candida* var. *candida, White
  Prairieclover
Navajo *Special Food* Roots eaten as a delicacy
by little children and sheepherders. (as *Petalostemon candidus* 55:57) **San Ildefonso** *Unspecified* Roots eaten raw. **Santa Clara** *Special
Food* Plant chewed by women and children as a
delicacy. (as *Pentalostemum candidus* 138:58)

Dalea candida* var. *oligophylla,
  White Prairieclover
Acoma *Staple* Roots dried and ground into
meal. (as *Petalostemon oligophyllus* 32:33)
Keres, Western *Staple* Dried roots ground
into flour. *Sweetener* Roots eaten for the sweetness. (as *Petalostemon cliogophyllus* 171:58)
Keresan *Unspecified* Roots chewed in the
spring before the leaves come out. (as *Petalostemon oligophyllus* 198:560) **Kiowa** *Unspecified* Peeled stems used for food. (as *Petalostemon oligophyllum* 192:33) **Laguna** *Staple*
Roots dried and ground into meal. **San Felipe**
Staple Roots dried and ground into meal. (as
Petalostemon oligophyllus 32:33) **San Ildefonso** *Unspecified* Roots eaten raw. **Santa
Clara** *Special Food* Plant chewed by women and
children as a delicacy. (as *Pentalostemum oligophyllum* 138:58)

Dalea candida var. oligophylla

Dalea lanata, Woolly Prairieclover
Hopi *Candy* Scraped roots eaten as a sweet.
(56:16) *Sweetener* Root eaten and regarded as
sugar. (190:163)

Dalea lasiathera, Purple Prairieclover
Zuni *Candy* Root chewed, especially by children, and greatly enjoyed. *Spice* Flowers
crushed by hand and sprinkled into meat stew

as a flavoring after cooking. (as *Parosela lasianthera* 166:69)

Dalea purpurea, Purple Prairieclover
Navajo *Beverage* Leaves used to make tea. (as *Petalostemum purpureum* 90:154)

Dalea purpurea* var. *purpurea,
  Violet Prairieclover
Comanche *Candy* Roots chewed for sweet flavor. (as *Petalostemum purpureum* 29:523)
Lakota *Candy* Roots chewed as a gum. (as *Petalostemon purpureum* 139:47) **Oglala** *Beverage* Leaves sometimes used to make a tea-like beverage. **Ponca** *Candy* Root chewed for the pleasant taste. (as *Petalostemum purpureum* 70:94)

Darmera peltata, Indian Rhubarb
Karok *Vegetable* Young shoots eaten raw as green vegetables. (as *Peltiphyllum peltatum* 148:384) **Miwok** *Cooking Agent* Pulverized root mixed with acorn meal to whiten it. (as *Peltiphyllum peltatum* 12:144)

Dasylirion texanum, Texas Sotol
Southwest Indians *Bread & Cake* Crowns pit baked, dried, pounded into flour and made into cakes. (17:57)

Dasylirion wheeleri, Common Sotol
Apache, Chiricahua & Mescalero *Beverage* Crowns pit baked, removed, peeled, crushed, mixed with water, fermented, and used as a beverage. (33:52) *Bread & Cake* Crowns baked in pits, stripped, pounded to a pulp, spread out to dry, and eaten like cake. *Unspecified* Stalks roasted, boiled, or eaten raw. *Vegetable* Stalks boiled, dried, and stored to be used as vegetables. (33:38) **Apache, Mescalero** *Beverage* Pounded and used as a drink. *Bread & Cake* Plants pit cooked, formed into cakes, dried, and used for food. (14:41) *Dried Food* Crowns baked, pounded, and dried for winter use. (17:58) *Soup* Head hearts cooked with bones to make soup. *Unspecified* Fresh, young stalks used for food. (14:41) **Papago** *Vegetable* Crowns with leaves removed and central flowering stalks eaten as

greens in May. (34:14) Flower stalks eaten as greens. (34:16) Flower stalks roasted in ashes and eaten as greens. (34:46) **Southwest Indians** *Bread & Cake* Crowns pit baked, dried, pounded into flour, and made into cakes. (17:57)

Datura discolor, Desert Thornapple
Pima *Beverage* Infusion of leaves and mescal used as a dangerously intoxicating brew. (47:85)

Datura wrightii, Sacred Thornapple
Apache, White Mountain *Beverage* Juice or powdered roots used to make a fermented, intoxicating drink. (as *D. meteloides* 136:151) **Navajo** *Dried Food* Fruits dried and used in the winter after soaking and boiling. *Fruit* Fruits ground and eaten without further preparation. (as *D. meteloides* 32:26) *Special Food* Seeds eaten in ceremonies. (as *D. meteloides* 55:74) **Papago** *Beverage* Roots ground, infused, and used as a beverage. (as *D. meteloides* 34:26)

Daucus carota, Queen Anne's Lace
Haisla & Hanaksiala *Vegetable* Roots used for food. (43:214) **Kitasoo** *Vegetable* Roots used for food. (43:325) **Oweekeno** *Unspecified* Roots used for food. (43:83) **Sanpoil & Nespelem** *Dried Food* Dried roots stored for winter use. *Vegetable* Steamed or boiled root used for food. (131:100)

Daucus pusillus, American Wild Carrot
Clallam *Unspecified* Carrots eaten raw or cooked in pits. (57:204) **Cowichan** *Unspecified* Roots eaten raw or steamed. (182:89) **Navajo** *Dried Food* Roots dried and cooked in the winter with wild celery. *Unspecified* Roots eaten fresh. (32:26) Roots eaten raw or cooked with or without wild celery. *Winter Use Food* Roots dried for winter use. (55:67) **Saanich** *Unspecified* Roots eaten raw or steamed. **Salish, Coast** *Unspecified* Roots eaten raw or steamed. (182:89)

Delphinium hesperium, Foothill
  Larkspur
Miwok *Vegetable* Boiled leaves and flowers used for food. (12:159)

Dendromecon rigida, Tree Poppy
Kawaiisu *Unspecified* Seeds used for food. (206:25)

Dentaria sp., Toothwort
Cherokee *Unspecified* Plants cooked with other greens and used for food. (204:252)

Dentinum repandum, Hedgehog Mushroom
Pomo, Kashaya *Vegetable* Baked on hot stones, in the oven, or fried. (72:130)

Deschampsia cespitosa, Tufted Hairgrass
Gosiute *Unspecified* Seeds used for food. (39:367)

Deschampsia danthonioides, Annual Hairgrass
Kawaiisu *Porridge* Seeds pounded, cooked into a mush and eaten. (206:26)

Descurainia incana ssp. incana, Mountain Tansymustard
Paiute, Northern *Beverage* Seeds dried, cooked, ground, water added, kneaded, water added to make a fine batter, and drunk. *Unspecified* Seeds roasted, cooled, ground, mixed with cold water, and eaten. *Winter Use Food* Seeds stored for winter use. (as *D. richardsonii* 59:47)

Descurainia incana ssp. incisa, Mountain Tansymustard
Apache, Chiricahua & Mescalero *Bread & Cake* Seeds threshed, winnowed, ground, and the flour used to make bread. *Unspecified* Seeds boiled and eaten. (as *Sophia incisa* 33:49) **Klamath** *Unspecified* Parched, ground seeds used for food. (as *Sisymbrium incisum* 45:96–97) **Montana Indian** *Unspecified* Parched seeds ground for food. (as *Sisymbrium incisum* 19:24)

Descurainia obtusa, Blunt Tansymustard
Cocopa *Vegetable* Young plants boiled as greens. (37:187) **Hopi** *Vegetable* Plant used as greens. (42:309)

Descurainia pinnata, Western Tansymustard
Cahuilla *Spice* Ground seeds used to flavor soups or used as a condiment with corn. *Vegetable* Leaves used as potherbs. (15:66) **Cocopa** *Staple* Seeds harvested, winnowed, parched, ground, and the meal eaten. (37:187) **Hopi** *Spice* Plant used as flavoring with meat or other vegetables. *Vegetable* Plant cooked alone as greens. (42:310) Greens pit baked, cooled and served in salted water with corn dumplings, boiled bread, or piki bread. (120:19) **Kawaiisu** *Beverage* Seeds parched, pounded, sifted, mixed with cold water, and taken as a nourishing beverage. *Winter Use Food* Pounded or raw seeds stored for future use. (206:26) **Navajo, Ramah** *Bread & Cake* Ground seeds used to make cakes. *Fodder* Used as sheep feed. (191:28) **Paiute, Northern** *Beverage* Seeds dried, cooked, ground, water added, kneaded, water added to make a fine batter, and drunk. *Unspecified* Seeds roasted, cooled, ground, mixed with cold water, and eaten. *Winter Use Food* Seeds stored for winter use. (59:47) **Pima, Gila River** *Beverage* Seeds mixed with water to make a drink. *Porridge* Seeds used to make a mucilaginous mass and eaten. *Staple* Seeds ground, parched and used to make pinole. (133:5) *Unspecified* Seeds mixed with water and eaten. (133:7)

Descurainia pinnata ssp. halictorum, Western Tansymustard
Navajo *Porridge* Parched seeds ground, made into a gruel, and used to dip bread in. (as *Sophia halictorum* 165:223) **Pueblo** *Dried Food* Young plants boiled, pressed, rolled into balls, dried, and stored for winter use. *Soup* Plant made into a stew with wild onions, wild celery, tallow, or bits of meat. *Unspecified* Young plants boiled, pressed, rolled into balls, and eaten. *Vegetable* Young plants boiled with a pinch of salt and eaten as greens. (as *Sophia halictorum* 32:25)

Descurainia pinnata ssp. *pinnata*, Western Tansymustard

Atsugewi *Bread & Cake* Parched, winnowed, ground seeds made into cakes and eaten without cooking. (as *Sisymbrium pinnatum* 61:139) **Gosiute** *Porridge* Seeds used to make a mush. (as *Sisymbrium canescens* 39:382) **Hopi** *Unspecified* Leaves boiled or roasted between hot, flat stones and eaten. (as *Sisymbrium canescens* 32:25) Leaves boiled or roasted and eaten. (as *Sisymbrium canescens* 56:15) *Vegetable* Plant, salty in flavor, eaten as greens in the spring. (as *Sisymbrium canescens* 42:310) Eaten as greens in the spring. (as *Sophia pinnata* (200:77) **Papago** *Beverage* Seeds steeped and used as tea-like drinks for refreshment. (as *Sophia pinnata* 34:27) *Dried Food* Seeds basket winnowed, parched, sun dried, cooked, stored, and used for food. (as *Sophia pinnata* 34:24) *Unspecified* Seeds used for food. (as *Sophia pinnata* 36:62) **Pima** *Dried Food* Seeds parched, ground, and eaten mixed with hot or cold water. (as *Sophia pinnata* 95:263) *Staple* Seeds parched, ground, mixed with water, and eaten as pinole. (as *Sophia pinnata* 146:77)

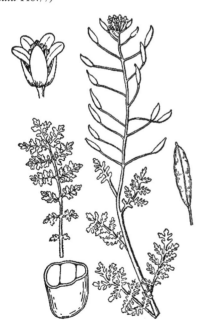

Descurainia pinnata ssp. *pinnata*

Descurainia sophia, Herb Sophia

Kawaiisu *Beverage* Seeds parched, pounded, sifted, mixed with cold water, and taken as a nourishing beverage. *Winter Use Food* Pounded or raw seeds stored for future use. (206:26) **Navajo, Ramah** *Bread & Cake* Ground seeds used to make cakes. *Fodder* Used as sheep feed. (191:28) **Paiute** *Beverage* Roasted, ground seeds mixed with water and used as a cooling beverage for hot weather. (111:74) *Ice Cream* Seeds mixed with snow and eaten as ice cream. *Staple* Seeds parched, ground, and eaten as meal. (as *Sisymbrium sophia* 104:98) **Paiute, Northern** *Beverage* Seeds dried, cooked, ground, water added, kneaded, water added to make a fine batter, and drunk. *Unspecified* Seeds roasted, cooled, ground, mixed with cold water, and eaten. *Winter Use Food* Seeds stored for winter use. (59:47) **Pueblo** *Dried Food* Young plants boiled, pressed, rolled into balls, dried, and stored for winter use. *Soup* Plant made into a stew with wild onions, wild celery, tallow, or bits of meat. *Unspecified* Young plants boiled, pressed, rolled into balls, and eaten. *Vegetable* Young plants boiled with a pinch of salt and eaten as greens. (as *Sophia sophia* 32:25)

Dichanthelium oligosanthes var. *scribnerianum*, Scribner's Rosette Grass

Kiowa *Fodder* Used to fatten horses very quickly. (as *Panicum scribnerianum* 192:16)

Dichelostemma multiflorum, Roundtooth Snakelily

Atsugewi *Unspecified* Cooked in earth oven and used for food. (as *Brodiaea multiflora* 61:138) **Karok** *Unspecified* Raw bulbs used for food. (6:27)

Dichelostemma pulchellum, Congested Snakelily

Apache, San Carlos *Unspecified* Bulbs eaten raw or cooked in spring. Blue flowers eaten raw. (as *Dichelostemma*, var. *brodiaca, capitata pauciflora* 95:258) **Cahuilla** *Unspecified* Corms eaten raw or cooked. (as *Brodiaea pul-*

chella 15:47) **Karok** *Unspecified* Bulbs used for food. (6:27) **Luiseño** *Unspecified* Bulb used for food. (as *Brodiaea capitata* 155:233) **Mendocino Indian** *Unspecified* Bulbs eaten raw or cooked. (as *D. capitatum* 41:323) **Miwok** *Unspecified* Bulbs steamed in earth oven and eaten. (as *Brodiaea pulchella* 12:156) **Neeshenam** *Unspecified* Eaten raw, roasted, or boiled. (as *Brodiaea congesta* 129:377) **Paiute** *Dried Food* Roots dried and stored. *Staple* Roots roasted and ground into flour. *Unspecified* Fresh roots eaten raw. (as *Brodiaea capitata* 167:245) **Papago** *Unspecified* Bulbs eaten raw in spring before other crops appeared. (as *Brodiaea capitata* var. *pauciflora* 34:17) Bulbs eaten raw in early spring before other foods available. (as *Brodiaea capitata* var. *pauciflora* 36:60) **Pima, Gila River** *Baby Food* Raw roots eaten primarily by children. (133:7) *Snack Food* Bulbs eaten primarily by children as snack food. (133:5) **Pomo** *Unspecified* Bulbs eaten raw or cooked. (as *D. capitatum* 11:90) **Pomo, Kashaya** *Vegetable* Baked or boiled corms eaten like baked or boiled potatoes. (as *Brodiaea pulchella* 72:26) **Yuki** *Unspecified* Sweet bulbs used for food. (as *Brodiaea pulchella* 49:86)

Dichelostemma volubile, Twining Snakelily

Neeshenam *Unspecified* Eaten raw, roasted, or boiled. (as *Brodiaea volubilis* 129:377) **Pomo** *Unspecified* Bulbs eaten for food. (as *Hookera volubilis* 11:90)

Digitaria cognata, Carolina Crabgrass

Hopi *Staple* Seeds ground into meal. (as *Panicum autumnale* 190:158)

Digitaria cognata var. *cognata*, Fall Witchgrass

Hopi *Staple* Seeds ground into meal. (as *Leptoloma cognatum* 190:158)

Dimorphocarpa wislizeni, Touristplant

Navajo *Forage* Plant used by sheep for forage. (as *Dithyrea wislizeni* 55:49)

Dioscorea bulbifera, Air Yam

Hawaiian *Fruit* Bitter fruit cooked, grated, washed several times, strained, and eaten. (112:68)

Dioscorea pentaphylla, Fiveleaf Yam

Hawaiian *Unspecified* Tubers oven cooked and eaten. (112:68)

Diospyros texana, Texas Persimmon

Comanche *Fruit* Fruits eaten for food. (as *Brayodendron texanum* 29:520)

Diospyros virginiana, Common Persimmon

Cherokee *Fruit* Fruit used for food. *Pie & Pudding* Fruit used to make pudding. (126:38) **Comanche** *Fruit* Fruits eaten for food. (29:521) **Rappahannock** *Beverage* Fruits rolled in cornmeal, brewed in water, drained, baked, and mixed with hot water to make a beer. (161:25) **Seminole** *Unspecified* Plant used for food. (169:495)

Diplazium meyenianum, Meyen's Twinsorus Fern

Hawaiian *Unspecified* Young shoots used for food. (as *Dilazium arnottii* 2:44)

Disporum hookeri, Drops of Gold

Thompson *Fruit* Fruit occasionally used for food, but not considered important. (187:121)

Disporum hookeri var. *oreganum*, Oregon Drops of Gold

Nitinaht *Forage* Berries eaten by wolves. (186:86)

Disporum smithii, Largeflower Fairybells

Karok *Forage* Berries eaten by squirrels. (148:381)

Disporum trachycarpum, Roughfruit Fairybells

Blackfoot *Fruit* Berries used for food. (86:102) Berries eaten raw. (97:25) Berries eaten raw. (114:277) **Shuswap** *Fruit* Berries used for food. (123:54)

Distichlis spicata, Inland Saltgrass
Cahuilla *Spice* Leaves burned into ashes to remove the salt and used as a condiment. (15:66) **Kawaiisu** *Beverage* Dried grass cakes used to make a beverage. Green grass immersed in cold water, strained, and used as a beverage. (206:26) **Tubatulabal** *Unspecified* Leaves and stems used extensively for food. (193:15)

Dodecatheon hendersonii,
   Mosquito Bills
Yuki *Unspecified* Leaves and roots formerly roasted in ashes and eaten. (41:378)

Dracocephalum parviflorum,
   American Dragonhead
Apache, Chiricahua & Mescalero *Spice* Leaves used as flavoring. (33:47) **Gosiute** *Unspecified* Seeds used for food. (39:367)

Dryopteris arguta, Coastal Woodfern
Costanoan *Unspecified* Rhizomes gathered in spring and eaten. (21:247) **Thompson** *Unspecified* Rootstocks used for food. (187:88) **Yurok** *Cooking Agent* Leaves used to clean meats and to lay over meat to keep the flies off. (6:28)

Dryopteris campyloptera, Mountain Woodfern
Eskimo, Inuktitut *Ice Cream* Boiled roots added to "Eskimo ice cream." (as *D. dilatata* ssp. *americana* 202:193) **Kwakiutl, Southern** *Unspecified* Rhizomes cooked in steaming pits and used for food. (as *D. austriaca* 183:264) **Salish, Coast** *Unspecified* Rhizomes used for food. (as *D. austriaca* 182:69)

Dryopteris carthusiana, Spinulose Woodfern
Alaska Native *Unspecified* Old leaf stalks on the underground stem roasted, peeled, and the inner portion eaten. *Vegetable* Young, curled fronds boiled or steamed and eaten like asparagus with butter, margarine, or cream sauce. (as *D. spinulosa* 85:29)

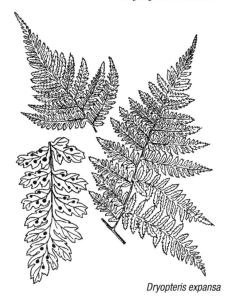

Dryopteris expansa

Dryopteris expansa, Spreading Woodfern
Clallam *Unspecified* Rhizomes used for food. (as *D. dilatata* 57:194) **Cowlitz** *Unspecified* Rhizomes pit baked overnight and the insides used for food. (as *D. dilatata* 79:14) **Eskimo, Alaska** *Soup* Fiddleheads, with the chaffy coverings removed, added to soups. *Unspecified* Fiddleheads, with the chaffy coverings removed, boiled and eaten with seal oil and dried fish. (as *D. dilatata* 1:34) **Thompson** *Unspecified* Rootstocks used for food. (as *D. assimilis* 187:88)

Dryopteris filix-mas, Male Fern
Bella Coola *Dietary Aid* Rhizomes eaten raw for losing weight. *Unspecified* Rhizomes eaten raw or steamed. (184:197)

Dudleya lanceolata, Lanceleaf Liveforever
Neeshenam *Vegetable* Leaves eaten raw as greens. (as *Echeveris lanceolata* 129:377)

Dudleya pulverulenta, Chalk Liveforever
Diegueño *Unspecified* Leaves chewed, with or without salt, by children. (84:19)

Dugaldia hoopesii, Owlsclaws
Navajo *Candy* Roots used as a chewing gum.
(as *Helenium hoopesii* 55:87)

Dyssodia papposa, Fetid Marigold
Apache, Chiricahua & Mescalero *Bread &
Cake* Seeds winnowed, dried, stored, ground
into flour, and used to make bread. *Unspecified*

Seeds roasted without grinding and combined
with other foods. (33:48) *Vegetable* Tops
cooked alone or with meat and used as greens.
(33:47) **Dakota** *Forage* Plant considered a
choice prairie dog food. (as *Boebera papposa*
69:369). Plant eaten by prairie dogs. (as *Boebera papposa* 70:132)

Echinocactus polycephalus,
  Cottontop Cactus
Cahuilla *Staple* Berries and stems were an im-
portant and dependable food source. (15:49)

Echinocereus coccineus, Scarlet
  Hedgehog Cactus
Apache, Chiricahua & Mescalero *Fruit* Raw
fruit used for food. (33:41) **Navajo, Ramah**
Fruit Fruit used for food. (191:37)

Echinocereus engelmannii, Saints
  Cactus
Pima *Fruit* Ripe fruits freed from spines and
eaten raw. (47:57) **Pima, Gila River** *Snack
Food* Fruit eaten primarily by children as a
snack food. (133:5) **Yavapai** *Fruit* Raw fruit
used for food. *Unspecified* Boiled buds used for
food. (as *Cereus engelmanni* 65:256)

**Echinocereus engelmannii var.
  chrysocentrus**, Saints Cactus
Apache, Chiricahua & Mescalero *Fruit* Raw
fruit used for food. (33:41)

Echinocereus fendleri, Pinkflower
  Hedgehog Cactus
Apache, Chiricahua & Mescalero *Fruit* Raw
fruit used for food. (33:41) **Cochiti** *Unspecified*
Stems pit roasted and eaten. (32:26) **Hopi**

Sweetener Fruits dried and used as a source of
sweetening. (200:85)

Echinocereus polyacanthus,
  Mojave Mound Cactus
Apache, Chiricahua & Mescalero *Fruit* Raw
fruit used for food. (33:41)

Echinocereus rigidissimus, Rain-
  bow Hedgehog Cactus
Apache, Chiricahua & Mescalero *Fruit* Raw
fruit used for food. (33:41)

Echinocereus triglochidiatus,
  Kingcup Cactus
Isleta *Beverage* Water extracted from pulp in
emergencies. (100:27) *Bread & Cake* Pulp macerated and cooked with sugar to make cakes.
(32:26) Pulp baked with sugar and used to
make cakes. (100:27) *Candy* Pulp baked with
sugar to make candy. (32:26) Pulp baked with
sugar and used to make candy. (100:27) *Fruit*
Fruits, with spines removed by burning, eaten
fresh. (32:26) Fruit eaten fresh. (100:27) *Preserves* Fruits, with spines removed by burning,
made into a conserve. (32:26) Fruit eaten as
conserves. (100:27) *Sauce & Relish* Pulp baked
with sugar to make sweet pickles. *Unspecified*
Pulp sliced and baked like squash. (32:26) *Vegetable* Sliced pulp baked like squash and used

for food. Pulp baked with sugar and used to make a sweet pickle. (100:27)

Echinocereus triglochidiatus var. *triglochidiatus*, Kingcup Cactus

Cochiti *Unspecified* Stems pit roasted and eaten. **Isleta** *Bread & Cake* Pulp macerated and cooked with sugar to make cakes. *Candy* Pulp baked with sugar to make candy. *Fruit* Fruits, with spines removed by burning, eaten fresh. *Preserves* Fruits, with spines removed by burning, made into a conserve. *Sauce & Relish* Pulp baked with sugar to make sweet pickles. *Unspecified* Pulp sliced and baked like squash. (as *E. gonocanthus* 32:26) **Keres, Western** *Fruit* Tunas used for food. (as *E. gonacanthus* 171:42)

Echinochloa colona, Jungle Rice

Cocopa *Porridge* Seeds parched, ground, and the flour cooked into a mush. *Staple* Seeds parched, ground, and the flour eaten dry. (as *E. colonum* 37:187)

Echinochloa crus-galli, Barnyard Grass

Cocopa *Unspecified* Seeds used for food. *Winter Use Food* Seeds stored for later use. (as *E. crusgalli* 64:267) **Paiute** *Unspecified* Species used for food. (as *E. crusgalli* 167:243) **Tubatulabal** *Unspecified* Used extensively for food. (193:15) **Yuma** *Porridge* Seeds pounded, winnowed, ground, made into mush, and used to cook with fish. *Staple* Seeds pounded, winnowed, parched, and ground into a meal. (as *E. crusgalli* 37:187) *Unspecified* Wild seeds eaten for food. (as *E. crusgalli* 37:173)

Echinochloa crus-pavonis var. *macera*, Gulf Cockspur Grass

Navajo, Ramah *Fodder* Used for horse feed. (as *E. crusgalli* var. *zelayensis* 191:16)

Egregia menziesii, Boa Kelp

Bella Coola *Dried Food* Whole plants with attached herring spawn dried and used as a winter food. *Unspecified* Whole plants with at-

tached herring spawn eaten fresh. (184:195) **Haisla & Hanaksiala** *Dried Food* Plant used to collect herring roe, dried, and eaten with the roe. (43:125) **Kitasoo** *Unspecified* Plant eaten with herring roe. (43:302) **Oweekeno** *Dried Food* Plant and herring eggs dried for future use. *Unspecified* Plant eaten with herring roe. *Winter Use Food* Plant and herring eggs salted and stored for future use. (43:44)

Elaeagnus commutata, Silverberry

Alaska Native *Fruit* Berries fried in moose fat and eaten. (85:144) **Blackfoot** *Candy* Peeled berries mixed with grease, stored in a cool place, and eaten as a confection. *Fruit* Peeled berries used for food. *Soup* Peeled berries used to make soups and broths. (86:102) **Cree** *Beverage* Berries used to make wine. *Fruit* Berries used for food. (as *Eleagnus argentea* 16:485) **Montana Indian** *Fruit* Fruit used for food. (as *Elaeagnus argentea* 19:11) **Okanagan-Colville** *Fruit* Berries used for food. (188:99) **Okanagon** *Staple* Seeds used as a principal food. (as *E. argentea* 178:239) **Paiute** *Unspecified* Seeds used for food. (as *Eleagnus asgentea* 167:244) **Tanana, Upper** *Fruit* Berries mixed with grease, cooked, and eaten. Berries eaten raw. *Soup* Berries used to make soup. (102:13)

Eleocharis palustris, Common Spikerush

Paiute, Northern *Unspecified* Sap eaten. (59:49)

Elymus canadensis var. *canadensis*, Canada Wildrye

Kiowa *Fodder* Foliage and lemmas used as a palatable fodder for livestock. (as *E. robustus* 192:15)

Elymus elymoides, Bottlebrush Squirreltail

Navajo, Ramah *Fodder* Young plants used for sheep and horse feed, mature plants made animals' mouths sore. (as *Sitanion hystrix* 191:17)

Elymus glaucus, Blue Wildrye

Karok *Porridge* Seeds parched, pounded into

a flour, and mixed with water into a paste. (148:380)

Elymus glaucus ssp. *glaucus*, Blue Wildrye
Costanoan *Staple* Seeds used in pinole. (21:255)

Elymus multisetus, Big Squirreltail
Kawaiisu *Porridge* Seeds parched, pounded, and cooked into a thin mush. (as *Sitanion jubatum* 206:64)

Elymus sibiricus, Siberian Wildrye
Gosiute *Unspecified* Seeds formerly used for food. (39:368)

Elymus trachycaulus ssp. *trachycaulus*, Slender Wheatgrass
Navajo, Ramah *Fodder* Used for horse feed and sometimes harvested for winter use. (as *Agropyron trachycaulum* 191:15) **Thompson** *Fodder* Cut and fed to horses as hay. (as *Agropyron tenerum* 164:515)

Elytrigia repens var. *repens*, Quack Grass
Apache, White Mountain *Fodder* Plant used for hay. *Unspecified* Seeds used for food. (as *Agropyron repens* 136:155) **Gosiute** *Unspecified* Seeds formerly eaten. (as *Agropyron repens* 39:360)

Empetrum nigrum, Black Crowberry
Alaska Native *Pie & Pudding* Berries mixed with other berries and used to make pie. *Preserves* Berries mixed with other berries and used to make jelly. (as *Empertrum nigrum* 85:79) **Cree, Woodlands** *Fruit* Fruit eaten in the fall. (109:38) **Eskimo, Alaska** *Fruit* Fruit used for food. (4:715) **Eskimo, Arctic** *Frozen Food* Berries stored frozen and eaten with seal blubber or oil. *Fruit* Berries eaten fresh. (128:21) **Eskimo, Inupiat** *Dessert* Berries cooked with sourdock and eaten as a dessert. *Fruit* Berries eaten with oil and sugar or mixed with other berries, sourdock, ice cream, or fish livers. This was a favorite food made just the

same way and still just as good as it had been for centuries. It was one food one could eat all one wanted, for any meal, day after day, and still like it. It was good fresh or leftover and as a main meal, side dish, or dessert. The sweet acidic berries and fat fish livers balanced each other and also were exceptionally nutritious. The only limiting factor in how much one ate was picking enough berries and catching enough fish to have the ingredients. The recipe was as follows: pick clean, ripe blackberries, at least 1 gallon. Save the livers from four large, freshly caught fall trout. Pinch out the bile sack, without breaking it, and discard. Soak the livers in a bowl of cold water while you finish caring for the fish. Rinse the livers, throw out the soak water. Simmer the livers in clean water until just done, 5 to 10 minutes. Lift the livers out to drain and cool. They could be stored a few days this way in the refrigerator. Skim the oil off the broth and save to add. Mash the livers thoroughly in a bowl, every tiny lump, using your hand or a fork. Mix in a little water as you mash to make a smooth paste, like thick hot cake batter. Stir in the whole blackberries until all the paste was taken up coating the berries. No salt or sugar was ever used or needed. Newcomers would prefer trout livers, which were mild, but after a while began to crave the stronger taste

Empetrum nigrum

and more satisfying oiliness of tom cod livers. *Pie & Pudding* Berries, cornstarch, water, and butter used to make pie. Berries cooked with blueberries and used to make pie and ice cream. *Winter Use Food* Berries mixed with salmonberries and stored for winter use. Berries stored in seal oil, a sealskin poke, or plastic bag for future use. (98:92) **Koyukon** *Beverage* Berries eaten by hunters to quench their thirst in the waterless high country. (119:55) **Ojibwa** *Fruit* Fruit used for food. (135:243) **Tanana, Upper** *Frozen Food* Berries frozen for future use. (102:12) *Fruit* Fruit used for food. (77:28) Berries eaten raw, plain, or mixed raw with sugar, grease, or the combination of the two. Berries fried in grease with sugar or dried fish eggs. Berries boiled with sugar and flour to thicken. *Pie & Pudding* Berries used to make pies. *Preserves* Berries used to make jam and jelly. *Winter Use Food* Berries preserved alone or in grease and stored in a birch bark basket in an underground cache. (102:12) **Tsimshian** *Fruit* Berries used for food. (43:332)

Empetrum nigrum ssp. hermaphroditum, Black Crowberry
Eskimo, Alaska *Fruit* Berries eaten alone. *Ice Cream* Berries added to ice cream. *Winter Use Food* Berries preserved in seal oil for use in fall and winter. (1:37)

Encelia farinosa, Goldenhills
Papago *Candy* Gum secretions chewed by children. (34:28) **Pima** *Candy* Resin used as a primitive chewing gum. (47:102) Amber-colored gum used for chewing gum. (95:265)

Encelia frutescens var. resinosa, Button Brittlebush
Navajo, Kayenta *Spice* Used as a seasoning for broth. (205:47)

Enteromorpha intestinalis, Tubular Green Alga
Hesquiat *Forage* Plants float upright during high tide and the brant geese like to pick at them. (185:23)

Ephedra californica, California Jointfir
Kawaiisu *Beverage* Stems used to make tea. *Unspecified* Seeds formerly used for food. (206:27)

Ephedra fasciculata, Arizona Jointfir
Havasupai *Beverage* Upper portions of plant boiled into tea. (197:207) **Pima** *Beverage* Ends of branches boiled and made into a beverage. **Pima, Lehi** *Beverage* Roots used as a tea. (47:76)

Ephedra nevadensis, Nevada Jointfir
Apache, White Mountain *Beverage* Stems used to make tea. (136:157) **Cahuilla** *Beverage* Fresh or dried twigs boiled to make tea. (15:70) **Coahuilla** *Beverage* Used to make a pleasant and refreshing beverage. (13:73) **Havasupai** *Beverage* Upper portions of plant boiled into tea. (197:207) **Kawaiisu** *Beverage* Stems used to make tea. *Unspecified* Seeds formerly used for food. (206:27) **Papago** *Beverage* Seeds steeped and used as tea-like drinks for refreshment. (34:27) **Zuni** *Beverage* Plant without the root occasionally used to make a hot, tea-like beverage. (166:67)

Ephedra torreyana, Torrey's Jointfir
Havasupai *Beverage* Upper portions of plant boiled into tea. (197:207) **Navajo** *Beverage* Branches used to make tea. (55:24)

Ephedra viridis, Mormon Tea
Havasupai *Beverage* Upper portions of plant boiled into tea. (197:207) Twigs boiled into a tea. (197:66) **Kawaiisu** *Beverage* Stems used to make tea. *Unspecified* Seeds formerly used for food. (206:27) **Navajo** *Beverage* Roasted stems used to make tea. Stems chewed to relieve thirst when on the move and away from water supplies. (110:19) **Paiute** *Beverage* Leafless needles boiled into a drink. (167:245) **Paiute, Northern** *Beverage* Stems used to make tea. (59:128) Stalks boiled in water to make tea. (59:53) **Tubatulabal** *Unspecified* Leaves and stalks used for food. (as *E. viridis* 193:15)

Epilobilum angustifolium,
Fireweed

Alaska Native *Dietary Aid* Young, tender greens, properly prepared, used as a good source of vitamin C and provitamin A. *Unspecified* Young stems peeled and eaten raw. *Vegetable* Young shoots mixed with other greens and eaten. (85:31) **Bella Coola** *Vegetable* Young shoots eaten as greens in spring. (184:207) **Blackfoot** *Unspecified* Fresh roots used for food. (86:102) **Clallam** *Beverage* Roots boiled and used as a drink. (57:201) **Eskimo, Alaska** *Unspecified* Young shoots eaten raw or blanched, with seal oil. (1:36) Young shoots gathered, boiled, and mixed with other plants and sometimes bacon. (4:715) **Eskimo, Inuktitut** *Unspecified* Young shoots used for food. (202:192) **Eskimo, Inupiat** *Sweetener* Pith used as a berry sweetener and eaten by children. *Vegetable* Violet stems, with dark purple leaves, used in salads. Pink stems with leaves boiled and eaten or steamed and served with cream sauce or cheese sauce. *Winter Use Food* Violet stems, with dark purple leaves, preserved in seal oil. (98:23) **Gitksan** *Unspecified* Shoots and stems used for food in summer. **Haisla** *Unspecified* Shoots and stems used for food in summer. (73:154) **Okanagan-Colville** *Forage*

Epilobium angustifolium

Plant eaten by horses and deer. (188:110) **Okanagon** *Unspecified* Young shoots eaten raw. (125:38) **Saanich** *Beverage* Young leaves boiled to make a refreshing tea. (182:85) **Tanana, Upper** *Fodder* Shoots cooked with fish for dog feed. *Preservative* Used for smoking fish and as a mosquito repellent. *Unspecified* Shoots eaten raw or boiled. (102:16) **Thompson** *Fodder* Stalks used for pig feed. (187:235) *Unspecified* Young shoots eaten raw. (125:38) Young shoots peeled and eaten. Stalks eaten raw like celery, boiled, or steamed. (187:235) **Wet'suwet'en** *Unspecified* Shoots and stems used for food in summer. (73:154)

Epilobium angustifolium ssp. circumvagum, Fireweed
Haisla & Hanaksiala *Unspecified* Young shoots used for food. (43:257) **Oweekeno** *Unspecified* Young shoots eaten as a spring food. (43:106)

Epilobium canum ssp. latifolium, Hummingbird Trumpet
Karok *Unspecified* Blossoms sucked for the nectar. (as *Zauschneria latifolia* 148:386)

Epilobium latifolium, Dwarf Fireweed
Alaska Native *Vegetable* Young, tender greens, properly prepared, used as a good source of vitamin C and provitamin A. (85:33) **Eskimo, Arctic** *Vegetable* Flowers eaten raw as a salad. Leaves cooked and eaten. **Eskimo, Greenland** *Vegetable* Flowers and leaves eaten raw with seal blubber. (128:25) **Eskimo, Inuktitut** *Unspecified* Young shoots used for food. (202:192) **Eskimo, Inupiat** *Unspecified* Leaves preserved in seal oil and eaten within 48 hours with walrus blubber. (98:26)

Epixiphium wislizeni, Balloonbush
Apache, Chiricahua & Mescalero *Unspecified* Pods eaten fresh or boiled. (as *Maurandia wislizeni* 33:45)

Equisetum arvense, Field Horsetail
Chinook, Lower *Unspecified* Young shoots used as food. (79:15) **Eskimo, Alaska** *Unspec-*

ified Black, edible nodules attached to roots used for food. The effort of collecting the nodules was considerable and therefore rarely done. However, these nodules were often obtained from underground caches of roots and tubers collected by lemmings and other tundra rodents. The caches were raided by the people and the "mouse nuts" were used for food. (1:33) **Haisla & Hanaksiala** *Forage* Plant eaten by geese. (43:156) **Hesquiat** *Vegetable* Tender, young, vegetative shoots peeled and eaten raw. These shoots were green but had not yet branched out, and the segments were still very close together. The leaf sheaths were peeled off two at a time and the succulent stems eaten raw. They were "nothing but juice." The Hesquiat people traveled up towards Esteven Point especially to get these shoots, and sometimes they would collect 20 or more kilograms of them at a time. When they returned home, the harvesters would call together all their relatives and friends and have a feast of horsetail shoots. The white, fertile shoots were apparently not eaten, although they are in other areas of the Northwest Coast. (185:28) **Meskwaki** *Fodder* Plant fed to captive wild geese to make them fat in a week. (152:272) **Ojibwa** *Fodder* Plant gathered to feed domesticated ducks and fed to ponies to make their coats glossy. (153:400) **Okanagan-Colville** *Fodder* Used in winter for fodder during hay shortage. (188:17) **Saanich** *Unspecified* Tender, young shoots eaten raw or boiled. (182:68) **Tanana, Upper** *Unspecified* Tubers eaten. (102:9) **Tewa** *Forage* Plant eaten by horses. (138:68)

Equisetum byemale, Scouringrush Horsetail

Blackfoot *Beverage* Blades boiled to make a drink. (114:276) **Cowlitz** *Dried Food* Stalk tops dried, mashed, mixed with salmon eggs, and eaten. (79:15) **Hoh** *Dried Food* Rootstocks dried and used for food. *Special Food* Rootstocks eaten during puberty ceremonies. *Unspecified* Rootstocks used for food. (137:57) **Lakota** *Fodder* Plant given to horses to fatten them. (139:25) **Meskwaki** *Fodder* Plant fed to ponies to make them fat in a week. (152:273)

Okanagan-Colville *Fodder* Used in winter for fodder during hay shortage. (188:17) **Quileute** *Dried Food* Rootstocks dried and used for food. *Special Food* Rootstocks eaten during puberty ceremonies. *Unspecified* Rootstocks used for food. (137:57)

Equisetum laevigatum, Smooth Horsetail

Hoh *Dried Food* Rootstocks dried and used for food. *Special Food* Rootstocks eaten as a delicacy. Rootstocks eaten during puberty ceremonies. (137:57) **Isleta** *Fodder* Plant used for horse feed. (100:28) **Okanagan-Colville** *Fodder* Used in winter for fodder during hay shortage. *Unspecified* Heads used for food. (188:17) **Quileute** *Dried Food* Rootstocks dried and used for food. *Special Food* Rootstocks eaten as a delicacy. Rootstocks eaten during puberty ceremonies. (137:57) **San Felipe** *Porridge* Plant dried and ground to make mush. (32:27)

Equisetum pratense, Meadow Horsetail

Eskimo, Inupiat *Unspecified* Raw roots eaten with seal oil. *Winter Use Food* Roots stored in oil for future use. (98:121)

Equisetum scirpoides, Dwarf Scouringrush

Haisla & Hanaksiala *Forage* Plant eaten by grizzly bears. (43:156)

Equisetum telmateia, Giant Horsetail

Clallam *Unspecified* Sprouts peeled and eaten raw or pit baked and eaten. (57:193) **Cowlitz** *Unspecified* Root stock bulbs cooked and eaten. Bulbs eaten raw. (79:15) **Klallam** *Unspecified* Reproductive and vegetative sprouts used for food. (78:197) **Makah** *Unspecified* Young stems peeled and eaten raw. (79:15) **Nitinaht** *Substitution Food* Hollow, water-filled stem segments used when water scarce. *Unspecified* Young shoots eaten in spring. (186:60) **Quileute** *Fodder* Used as fodder for horses. *Unspecified* Young stems peeled and eaten raw. **Quinault** *Fodder* Used as fodder for horses. *Unspecified* Young stems peeled and eaten raw. Roots eaten with whale or seal oil. (79:15) **Saanich** *Unspecified* Tender, young shoots eaten raw or boiled. (182:68) **Swinomish** *Unspecified* Bulbs eaten raw. (79:15)

Equisetum telmateia var. *braunii*, Giant Horsetail

Makah *Unspecified* Young, sterile or fertile shoots peeled, washed, or soaked in cold water and eaten raw. Strobili boiled in water for 10 minutes and eaten. **Nitinaht** *Beverage* Vegetative shoots used as a source of drinking water when traveling. *Unspecified* Fertile and sterile shoots used for food. (67:215) **Yurok** *Unspecified* Very small, fresh sprouts used for food. (6:29)

Equisetum variegatum, Variegated Scouringrush

Mendocino Indian *Forage* Used as an occasional forage food for horses. (41:304)

Eragrostis mexicana, Mexican Lovegrass

Cocopa *Porridge* Seeds parched, ground, and the flour cooked into a mush. *Staple* Seeds parched, ground, and the flour eaten dry. (37:187)

Eragrostis secundiflora, Red Lovegrass

Paiute *Unspecified* Species used for food. (167:243)

Eremalche exilis, White Mallow

Pima, Gila River *Unspecified* Leaves boiled and eaten. (133:7) *Vegetable* Leaves boiled, or boiled, strained, refried, and eaten as greens. (133:5)

Ericameria parishii, Parish's Heath-goldenrod

Luiseño *Unspecified* Seeds used for food. (as *Haplopappus parishii* 155:228)

Erigeron philadelphicus, Philadelphia Fleabane

Ojibwa *Forage* Plant eaten by deer and cows. (153:398)

Eriochloa aristata, Bearded Cupgrass

Cocopa *Porridge* Seeds parched, ground, and the flour cooked into a mush. *Staple* Seeds parched, ground, and the flour eaten dry. (37:187)

Eriodictyon californicum, California Yerbasanta

Karok *Beverage* Decoction of leaves and *Pinus lambertiana* pitch or leaves chewed and water taken as soothing drink. (6:30)

Eriodictyon lanatum, San Diego Yerbasanta

Diegueño *Candy* Decoction of leaves and honey boiled down into a syrup or candy and used by children. *Dried Food* Leaves dried, stored indefinitely, and used for colds, coughs, candy, and with soap to wash hair. (as *E. trichocalyx* ssp. *lanatum* 84:21)

Eriodictyon trichocalyx, Hairy Yerbasanta

Cahuilla *Beverage* Fresh or dried leaves boiled into tea. (15:71)

Eriogonum alatum, Winged Buckwheat

Navajo *Unspecified* Roots used for food. (55:42) **Navajo, Ramah** *Porridge* Ground seeds made into a mush with milk. *Unspecified* Root chewed by children. (191:23)

Eriogonum angulosum, Anglestem Buckwheat

Kawaiisu *Unspecified* Seeds pounded in a bedrock mortar hole and eaten "without boiling." (206:29)

Eriogonum baileyi, Bailey's Buckwheat

Kawaiisu *Beverage* Seeds pounded into a meal, mixed with water, and used as a beverage. *Staple* Seeds pounded into a meal and eaten dry. (206:29)

Eriogonum cernuum, Nodding
  Buckwheat
Navajo, Kayenta *Porridge* Seeds made into a
mush and used for food. (205:19)

Eriogonum corymbosum, Crispleaf
  Buckwheat
Hopi *Bread & Cake* Leaves boiled, mixed with
water and cornmeal, and baked into a bread.
(56:21) *Dried Food* Boiled stalks pressed into
cakes, dried, and eaten with salt. (190:159)

Eriogonum davidsonii, Davidson's
  Buckwheat
Kawaiisu *Staple* Seeds pounded into a meal
and eaten dry. (206:29)

Eriogonum flavum, Yellow Eriogonum
Blackfoot *Unspecified* Roots used for food.
(97:33)

Eriogonum hookeri, Hooker's
  Buckwheat
Hopi *Spice* Boiled with mush for flavor.
(190:160)

Eriogonum inflatum, Native American
  Pipeweed
Havasupai *Vegetable* Leaves boiled for 5 to 10
minutes and eaten. (197:216) Young, fresh, tender leaves boiled, drained, balled into individual portions, and served. (197:66) **Kawaiisu**
Porridge Seeds pounded into a meal and eaten
mixed with water. *Staple* Seeds pounded into a
meal and eaten dry. (206:29)

Eriogonum latifolium, Seaside
  Buckwheat
Mendocino Indian *Unspecified* Young stems
eaten by children in early summer. (41:345)

Eriogonum longifolium, Longleaf
  Buckwheat
Kiowa *Unspecified* Root used for food. (192:25)

Eriogonum microthecum, Slender
  Buckwheat
Havasupai *Beverage* Used to make tea.
(197:217)

Eriogonum nudum, Naked Buckwheat
Karok *Vegetable* Sour tasting, young stems eat-
en raw as greens. (148:383) **Miwok** *Vegetable*
Raw greens, sour flavor, used for food. (12:159)

***Eriogonum nudum* var. *oblongi-
  folium***, Naked Buckwheat
Karok *Unspecified* Young shoots used for food.
(6:30) *Vegetable* Sour tasting, young stems eaten
raw as greens. (148:383)

***Eriogonum nudum* var. *pubiflo-
  rum***, Naked Buckwheat
Kawaiisu *Unspecified* Dried flowers mixed
with valley stickweed seeds and eaten. (206:30)

Eriogonum plumatella, Yucca
  Buckwheat
Kawaiisu *Porridge* Seeds pounded, cooked
into a mush, and eaten. (206:30)

Eriogonum pusillum, Yellowturbans
Kawaiisu *Staple* Seeds pounded and eaten dry.
Unspecified Flowers mixed with valley stick-
weed seeds and eaten. (206:30)

Eriogonum racemosum, Redroot
  Buckwheat
Navajo, Kayenta *Unspecified* Leaves and stems
eaten raw. (205:19)

Eriogonum roseum, Wand Buckwheat
Kawaiisu *Beverage* Seeds pounded into a
meal, mixed with water, and used as a beverage.
Staple Seeds pounded into a meal and eaten
dry. (206:30)

Eriogonum rotundifolium, Roundleaf Buckwheat
Navajo *Unspecified* Stems used for food.
(90:150)

Eriogonum umbellatum var. *majus*, Sulphurflower Buckwheat
Blackfoot *Beverage* Leaves boiled to make tea. (as *E. subalpinum* 97:33)

Eriogonum wrightii, Bastardsage
Kawaiisu *Beverage* Seeds pounded into a meal, mixed with water, and used as a beverage. *Staple* Seeds pounded into a meal and eaten dry. (206:30)

Eriophorum angustifolium, Tall Cottongrass
Alaska Native *Unspecified* Stem bases eaten raw with seal oil. "Mouse nuts" found in mice caches, cooked and eaten with seal oil. (85:131) **Eskimo, Inupiat** *Unspecified* Roots eaten raw or boiled. *Winter Use Food* Roots stored in seal oil for future use. (98:119)

Eriophorum angustifolium ssp. *subarcticum*, Tall Cottongrass
Eskimo, Inuktitut *Unspecified* "Female" stems used for food. (202:184)

Eriophyllum ambiguum, Beautiful Woollysunflower
Kawaiisu *Dried Food* Seeds parched, pounded, and eaten dry. (206:30)

Eriophyllum confertiflorum, Yellow Yarrow
Cahuilla *Staple* Parched seeds ground into flour. (15:72)

Erodium cicutarium, Redstem Stork's Bill
Costanoan *Unspecified* Raw stems used for food. (21:252) **Diegueño** *Vegetable* Leaves picked early in the spring before the flowers appeared and cooked as greens. (84:21) **Hopi** *Candy* Roots chewed by children, sometimes as gum. (42:313) **Isleta** *Forage* High moisture content of leaves and stems made it a good grazing plant for livestock. (100:28) **Kawaiisu** *Forage* Plant eaten by horses, cows, and rabbits. (206:31) **Navajo, Ramah** *Fodder* Used for sheep feed. (191:34)

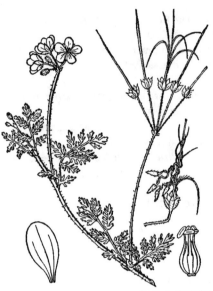

Erodium cicutarium

Erythronium grandiflorum, Dogtooth Lily
Blackfoot *Soup* Bulbs eaten with soup. *Unspecified* Bulbs eaten fresh. (86:102) **Montana Indian** *Forage* Plants eaten by bears and ground squirrels. (82:24) *Unspecified* Bulb-like roots used for food. (19:11) Bulbs occasionally eaten raw or boiled. (82:24) **Okanagan-Colville** *Dried Food* Corms dried for future use. *Unspecified* Corms eaten fresh. (188:45) **Okanagon** *Staple* Roots used as a principal food. (178:238) *Unspecified* Steamed and eaten as a sweet, mealy, and starchy food. (125:37) Roots used as an important food. (178:237) **Shuswap** *Winter Use Food* Roots dried for winter use. (123:54) **Thompson** *Candy* Small root ends of corms eaten as candy by children. *Dried Food* Raw corms dried for future use in soups or stews. The corms were laid out loosely on a scaffold and allowed to partially dry until they had wilted so that they would not split when strung. Then they were strung with needles onto long strings or thin sticks and allowed to dry completely. The strings were tied at the ends to make a large necklace-like loop which could be hung up for storage. *Pie & Pudding* Corms used to make a traditional kind of pudding. The pudding was

made by boiling together such traditional ingredients as dried black tree lichen, dried saskatoon berries, cured salmon eggs, tiger lily bulbs, or bitterroot and deer fat. Some of these ingredients, including avalanche lily corms, were optional. Nowadays flour is often used as a substitute for black tree lichen and sugar is added. *Soup* Raw, dried corms used in soups and stews. (187:121) *Unspecified* Steamed and eaten as a sweet, mealy, and starchy food. (125:37) Corms cooked and eaten. (164:481) Roots used as an important food. (178:237) Corms considered an important traditional food source. Because raw corms were considered poisonous, most of the corms were pit cooked, either immediately after harvesting or at a later date after they had been strung and dried. In the latter case, they were soaked for a few minutes in lukewarm water until they had regained about two-thirds of their moisture before being placed in the cooking pit. They could be eaten immediately or redried for later use, when they could be could again very quickly. One informant confirmed that the corms cooked and eaten immediately after harvesting were not as sweet and good as those that had been stored first. Corms eaten with meat and fish as the vegetable portion of a meal, like potatoes. Deep-fried corms used for food. (187:121)

Erythronium grandiflorum ssp. grandiflorum, Yellow Avalanche Lily
Thompson *Unspecified* Corms cooked and eaten. (164:481)

Erythronium mesochoreum, Midland Fawnlily
Winnebago *Unspecified* Raw plant, freshly dug in springtime, eaten avidly by children. (70:71)

Erythronium oregonum, Giant White Fawnlily
Kwakiutl *Dried Food* Bulbs dried and used for food. *Unspecified* Bulbs eaten raw, baked, or boiled. (182:75)

Erythronium revolutum, Mahogany Fawnlily
Kwakiutl, Southern *Dried Food* Bulbs sun dried, boiled, mixed with grease, and eaten at large feasts. *Unspecified* Bulbs eaten raw, baked, or steamed. (183:272)

Eschscholzia californica, California Poppy
Luiseño *Candy* Flowers chewed with chewing gum. *Vegetable* Leaves used as greens. (155:232)
Mendocino Indian *Vegetable* Leaves eaten as greens. (as *Eschscholtzia douglasii* 41:351)
Neeshenam *Vegetable* Leaves boiled or roasted, laid in water, and eaten as greens. (as *Escholtzia californica* 129:377)

Escobaria missouriensis var. missouriensis, Missouri Foxtail Cactus
Crow *Fruit* Red, ripe fruit eaten. (as *Mamillaria missouriensis* 19:15)

Escobaria vivipara var. vivipara, Spinystar
Blackfoot *Candy* Fruit eaten as a confection. (as *Mammilaria vivipara* 86:103) *Fruit* Fruits eaten for food. (as *Mamillaria viviparia* 97:45)
Cheyenne *Dried Food* Fruits dried, boiled, and eaten. *Fruit* Fruits boiled fresh and eaten. (as *Coryphantha vivipara* 83:16)

Eupatorium purpureum, Sweet-scented Joepyeweed
Cherokee *Spice* Root ash used as salt. (126:33)

Euphorbia marginata, Snow on the Mountain
Kiowa *Candy* Used for chewing gum. (as *Lepadena marginata* 192:36)

Exobasidium sp., Ghost Ear Fungus
Haisla & Hanaksiala *Unspecified* Galls used for food. (43:135)

Fagus grandifolia, American Beech
Algonquin, Quebec *Unspecified* Nuts used,
mainly by men working in the bush, for food.
(18:80) **Chippewa** *Unspecified* Nuts used for
food. People sought stores of beechnuts that
had been put away by chipmunks. These hoards
saved the labor not only of gathering, but also
of shucking, and were certain to contain only
sound nuts. The people had observed that chipmunks never stored any that were not good.
(71:128) **Iroquois** *Beverage* Fresh nutmeats
crushed, boiled, and liquid used as a drink.
Bread & Cake Fresh nutmeats crushed and
mixed with bread. (124:99) Nuts crushed, mixed
with cornmeal and beans or berries, and made
into bread. (196:123) *Pie & Pudding* Fresh nutmeats crushed and mixed with corn pudding.
(124:99) *Sauce & Relish* Nuts pounded, boiled,
resulting oil seasoned with salt, and used as
gravy. *Soup* Nutmeats crushed and added to
corn soup. (196:123) *Special Food* Fresh nutmeats crushed, boiled, and oil used as a delicacy in corn bread and pudding. (124:99) Nut-

meat oil added to the mush used by the False
Face Societies. *Staple* Nutmeats crushed and
added to hominy. *Unspecified* Nutmeats, after
skimming off the oil, seasoned and mixed with
mashed potatoes. (196:123) **Menominee** *Winter Use Food* Beechnuts stored for winter use.
(151:66) **Ojibwa** *Unspecified* Sweet nuts much
appreciated and never enough to store for winter. (153:401) **Potawatomi** *Unspecified* Beechnuts used for food. The hidden stores of the
small deer mouse was what the Indians relied
upon. The deer mouse is outdone by no other
animal in laying up winter stores. Its favorite
food is the beechnut. It will lay up, in some safe
log or hollow tree, from 4 to 8 quarts, shelled
in the most careful manner. The Indians easily
found the stores, when the snow was on the
ground, by the refuse on the snow. (154:100)

Ferocactus coulteri, Barrelcactus
Seri *Beverage* Plant provided drinking water.
(50:136)

**Ferocactus cylindraceus var.
  cylindraceus**, California Barrelcactus
Cahuilla *Beverage* Plant used to obtain water.
The barrel cactus provided a desert reservoir,
one which had long been familiar to many desert travelers at times of emergency. To obtain
water, the top of the cactus was sliced off, a portion of the pulp was removed to create a depression, and then the pulp was squeezed by hand in
the depression until water was released from
the spongy mass. *Dried Food* Buds sun dried for
storage. Flowers sun dried for storage. (as *Echinocactus acanthodes* 15:67) *Staple* Berries and
stems were an important and dependable food
source. (as *Echinocactus acanthodes* 15:49)
Unspecified Buds eaten fresh, parboiled, or
baked in a pit. Flowers eaten fresh, parboiled,
or baked in a pit. (as *Echinocactus acanthodes*
15:67)

Fagus grandifolia

Ferocactus cylindraceus var.
lecontei, Leconte's Barrelcactus
Pima *Beverage* Juice extracted from pulp and used to quench thirst. *Candy* Used to make cactus candy. (as *Echinocactus lecontei* 47:55) *Unspecified* Plants sliced, cut into small pieces, boiled with mesquite beans, and eaten as a sweet dish. (as *Echinocactus lecontei* 47:56)

Ferocactus wislizeni, Candy Barrel-
cactus
Apache, San Carlos *Beverage* Juice used for extreme thirst. *Porridge* Small, black seeds parched, ground, boiled, and eaten as mush. (as *Echinocereus wislizeni* 95:257) **Papago** *Beverage* Plant tops pounded and the juice used as a drink. (as *Echinocactus wislizeni* 34:17) *Vegetable* Pulp eaten as greens in May. (as *Echinocactus wislizeni* 34:14) **Pima** *Beverage* Juice extracted from pulp and used to quench thirst. *Candy* Used to make cactus candy. (as *Echinocactus wislizeni* 47:55) *Substitution Food* Pulp used in lieu of water for thirst. (as *Echinocactus wislizeni* 146:77) *Unspecified* Plants sliced, cut into small pieces, boiled with mesquite beans, and eaten as a sweet dish. (as *Echinocactus wislizeni* 47:56) Pulp cut in strips, boiled, and used for food. (as *Echinocactus wislizeni* 146:77) **Seri** *Beverage* Plant provided drinking water. (50:136)

Ferula dissoluta
Okanagon *Staple* Roots used as a principal food. (178:238)

Festuca brachyphylla ssp.
brachyphylla, Alpine Fescue
Gosiute *Unspecified* Seeds used for food. (as *F. ovina* var. *brevifolia* 39:369)

Ficus aurea, Florida Strangler Fig
Seminole *Candy* Plant used for chewing gum. *Unspecified* Plant used for food. (169:481)

Ficus carica, Common Fig
Havasupai *Beverage* Plant used to make a drink. (197:66) *Dried Food* Fruit sun dried and stored in sacks for winter use. *Fruit* Fruit eaten

fresh. *Winter Use Food* Fallen fruit ground, mixed with water into a thick paste, dried in sheets, and eaten during the winter. (197:216)

Forestiera pubescens var. pube-
scens, Stretchberry
Apache, Chiricahua & Mescalero *Fruit* Raw fruits occasionally eaten as food. (as *F. neomexicana* 33:44)

Fortunella sp., Kumquat
Seminole *Unspecified* Plant used for food. (169:513)

Fouquieria splendens, Ocotillo
Cahuilla *Beverage* Fresh blossoms soaked in water and used to make a summer drink. *Porridge* Parched seeds ground into a flour and used to make mush or cakes. *Unspecified* Fresh blossoms used for food. (as *Fourquieria splendens* 15:74) **Papago** *Special Food* Nectar pressed out of blossoms, hardened like rock candy, and chewed as a delicacy. (34:28) **Yavapai** *Snack Food* Flowers sucked by children for nectar. (65:256)

Fragaria ×ananassa var. cunei-
folia, Hybrid Strawberry
Chehalis *Fruit* Berries eaten fresh. (as *F. cuneifolia* 79:36) **Klallam** *Fruit* Berries used for food. Fruits eaten fresh in early summer. (as *F. cuneifolia* 78:197) Berries eaten fresh. **Squaxin** *Fruit* Berries eaten fresh. (as *F. cuneifolia* 79:36)

Fragaria chiloensis, Beach Strawberry
Alaska Native *Dietary Aid* Berries used as a rich source of vitamin C. *Fruit* Berries eaten raw. *Preserves* Berries made into a jam. (85:81) **Clallam** *Fruit* Berries eaten fresh. (57:202) **Hesquiat** *Fruit* Berries used for food. (185:72) **Hoh** *Fruit* Fruits eaten raw. Fruits stewed and used for food. (137:63) **Kitasoo** *Fruit* Fruit used for food. (43:342) **Makah** *Fruit* Fruit eaten fresh. (67:262) Berries eaten fresh immediately after picking. (79:36) *Preserves* Fruit used to make jams and jellies. (67:262) **Nitinaht** *Fruit* Berries eaten fresh. (186:117) **Oweekeno**

Fruit Berries eaten fresh. *Preserves* Berries used to make jam. (43:108) **Pomo, Kashaya** *Fruit* Berries eaten fresh. (72:109) **Quileute** *Fruit* Berries eaten after fish. (79:36) Fruits eaten raw. Fruits stewed and used for food. (137:63) **Quinault** *Special Food* Berries served by young women to their guests at parties. (79:36) **Salish, Coast** *Beverage* Leaves dried and used to make tea. *Fruit* Fruits eaten fresh. (182:86) **Tolowa** *Fruit* Fresh fruit used for food. **Yurok** *Fruit* Fresh fruit used for food. (6:31)

Fragaria chiloensis ssp. *lucida*,
Beach Strawberry
Haisla & Hanaksiala *Fruit* Berries eaten fresh. *Preserves* Berries used to make jam. (43:264)

Fragaria chiloensis ssp. *pacifica*,
Pacific Beach Strawberry
Haisla & Hanaksiala *Fruit* Berries eaten fresh. *Preserves* Berries used to make jam. (43:264)

Fragaria vesca, Woodland Strawberry
Bella Coola *Fruit* Berries used for food. (184:208) **Clallam** *Fruit* Berries eaten fresh. (57:202) **Gosiute** *Fruit* Berries used for food in season. (39:370) **Hesquiat** *Fruit* Berries used for food. (185:72) **Kitasoo** *Fruit* Fruit used for

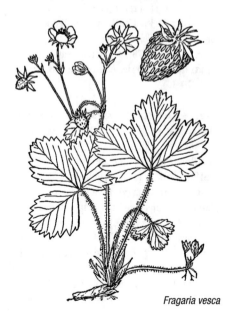

Fragaria vesca

food. (43:342) **Lakota** *Fruit* Fruits eaten fresh. Fruits eaten with other foods. (106:37) Fruits eaten for food. (139:56) **Nitinaht** *Fruit* Berries eaten fresh. (186:117) **Okanagan-Colville** *Fruit* Berries eaten fresh. *Winter Use Food* Berries canned for future use. (188:125) **Oweekeno** *Fruit* Berries eaten fresh. *Preserves* Berries used to make jam. (43:108) **Potawatomi** *Dried Food* Berries sometimes dried for winter use. *Winter Use Food* Berries sometimes dried and at other times preserved for winter use. (154:107) **Salish, Coast** *Beverage* Leaves dried and used to make tea. *Fruit* Fruits eaten fresh. (182:86) **Thompson** *Dried Food* Berries, if plentiful, dried for future use. *Fruit* Berries eaten fresh. (187:259)

Fragaria vesca ssp. *americana*,
Woodland Strawberry
Chippewa *Fruit* Strawberries considered an important part of the diet. (as *F. americana* 71:132) **Dakota** *Fruit* Fruit used for food. (as *F. americana* 70:84) **Iroquois** *Bread & Cake* Fruit mashed, made into small cakes and dried for future use. *Dried Food* Raw or cooked fruit sun or fire dried and stored for future use. *Fruit* Dried fruit taken as a hunting food. *Sauce & Relish* Dried fruit cakes soaked in warm water and cooked as a sauce or mixed with corn bread. (196:127) **Omaha** *Fruit* Fruit used for food. **Pawnee** *Fruit* Fruit used for food. **Ponca** *Fruit* Fruit used for food. (as *F. americana* 70:84) **Thompson** *Fruit* Large, wild berries eaten as a favorite food. (as *F. vesca americana* 164:487) **Winnebago** *Beverage* Young leaves used to make a tea-like beverage. *Fruit* Fruit used for food. (as *F. americana* 70:84)

Fragaria vesca ssp. *bracteata*,
Woodland Strawberry
Apache *Special Food* Fruits eaten as a delicacy. (as *F. bracteata* 32:29) **Apache, Chiricahua & Mescalero** *Fruit* Raw fruits occasionally eaten as food. (as *F. bracteata* 33:44) **Cochiti** *Special Food* Fruits eaten as a delicacy. (as *F. bracteata* 32:29) **Cowlitz** *Beverage* Leaves used for a beverage. *Dried Food* Berries dried and used for food. *Fruit* Berries eaten fresh. (as *F. brac-*

teata 79:36) **Haisla & Hanaksiala** *Fruit* Berries eaten fresh. *Preserves* Berries used to make jam. (43:264) **Isleta** *Fruit* Flavorful fruit considered a delicacy. (as *F. bracteata* 100:29) *Special Food* Fruits eaten as a delicacy. **Navajo** *Special Food* Fruits eaten as a delicacy. (as *F. bracteata* 32:29) Fruits used for food and considered a delicacy. (as *F. bracteata* 55:53) **Swinomish** *Fruit* Berries eaten fresh. (as *F. bracteata* 79:36)

Fragaria vesca ssp. *californica*,
California Strawberry

Cahuilla *Fruit* Fruit always eaten fresh. (as *F. californica* 15:74) **Coeur d'Alene** *Fruit* Berries eaten fresh. Berries mashed and eaten. (as *F. californica* 178:90) **Diegueño** *Fruit* Fruit eaten fresh with cream. (84:21) **Karok** *Fruit* Fresh fruit used for food. (6:31) Berries used for food. (as *F. californica* 148:384) **Mendocino Indian** *Fruit* Berries eaten fresh by children. (as *F. californica* 41:354) **Navajo, Ramah** *Unspecified* Very small fruit, hard to find, used for food. (as *F. californica* 191:31) **Okanagon** *Staple* Berries used as a principal food. (as *F. californica* 178:239) **Pomo** *Fruit* Raw berries used for food. (as *F. californica* 66:13) **Pomo, Kashaya** *Fruit* Berries eaten fresh. (as *F. californica* 72:110) **Spokan** *Fruit* Berries used for food. (as *F. californica* 178:343) **Thompson** *Dried Food* Berries washed, dried, and stored for winter use. *Fruit* Berries eaten fresh. (as *F. californica* 164:488) *Spice* Flowers and stems used to flavor roots. (as *F. californica* 164:478) **Yurok** *Fruit* Fresh fruit used for food. (6:31)

Fragaria virginiana, Virginia
Strawberry

Abnaki *Fruit* Fruits eaten for food. (144:169) **Algonquin, Quebec** *Fruit* Fruit gathered, cultivated, and eaten fresh. *Preserves* Fruit gathered, cultivated, and preserved. (18:91) **Algonquin, Tête-de-Boule** *Fruit* Berries used for food. (132:128) **Bella Coola** *Fruit* Berries used for food. (184:208) **Blackfoot** *Beverage* Leaves used to make tea. *Fruit* Fruits eaten raw. (97:38) **Cherokee** *Fruit* Fruit eaten raw. (80:57) Fresh berries used for food. *Preserves* Berries used to

make jam. *Sauce & Relish* Berries used on shortcake. (126:56) **Cheyenne** *Fruit* Fruits formerly used for food. (83:34) **Chippewa** *Fruit* Berries eaten raw. (53:321) Strawberries considered an important part of the diet. (71:132) **Clallam** *Fruit* Berries eaten fresh. (57:202) **Cree, Woodlands** *Snack Food* Fresh fruit eaten on sight as a nibble. (109:38) **Dakota** *Fruit* Fruit used for food. (70:84) **Hesquiat** *Fruit* Berries used for food. (185:72) **Iroquois** *Bread & Cake* Fruit mashed, made into small cakes, and dried for future use. *Dried Food* Raw or cooked fruit sun or fire dried and stored for future use. (196:127) *Fruit* Fruits eaten raw. (124:96) Dried fruit taken as a hunting food. *Sauce & Relish* Dried fruit cakes soaked in warm water and cooked as a sauce or mixed with corn bread. (196:127) **Kitasoo** *Fruit* Fruit used for food. (43:342) **Klamath** *Fruit* Fresh fruit used for food. (45:98) **Menominee** *Fruit* Berries eaten fresh. (151:71) **Meskwaki** *Preserves* Berries cooked into a jam for winter use. (152:263) **Nitinaht** *Fruit* Berries eaten fresh. (186:117) **Ojibwa** *Fruit* Berries used fresh or preserved. (5:2220) Berries used in season. *Preserves* Berries used to make preserves for winter use. (153:409) *Winter Use Food* Berries used fresh or preserved. (5:2220) **Okanagan-Colville** *Fruit* Berries eaten fresh. *Winter Use Food* Berries canned for future use. (188:125) **Omaha** *Dried Food* Fruit dried for winter use. *Fruit* Fruit eaten fresh. (68:326) Fruit used for food. (70:84) **Oweekeno** *Fruit* Berries eaten fresh. *Preserves* Berries used to make jam. (43:108) **Pawnee** *Fruit* Fruit used for food. **Ponca** *Fruit* Fruit used for food. (70:84) **Salish, Coast** *Beverage* Leaves dried and used to make tea. *Fruit* Fruits eaten fresh. (182:86) **Shuswap** *Dried Food* Dried berries used for food. (123:66) **Thompson** *Dried Food* Berries, if plentiful, dried for future use. *Fruit* Berries eaten fresh. (187:259) **Winnebago** *Beverage* Young leaves used to make a tea-like beverage. *Fruit* Fruit used for food. (70:84)

Fragaria virginiana ssp. *platypetala*, Virginia Strawberry

Haisla & Hanaksiala *Fruit* Berries eaten

fresh. *Preserves* Berries used to make jam. (43:264) **Ojibwa** *Fruit* Fruit used for food. (135:235) **Sanpoil & Nespelem** *Fruit* Berries eaten fresh. (131:102)

Frangula californica ssp. *californica*, California Buckthorn
Costanoan *Fruit* Raw berries used for food. (as *Rhamnus californica* 21:250) **Paiute** *Dried Food* Fruit sun dried, stored in buckskin bags, and hung up for winter use. *Fruit* Fruit eaten fresh. (as *Rhamnus californica* 167:245)

Frangula californica ssp. *tomentella*, California Buckthorn

Kawaiisu *Fruit* Fruit eaten fresh. (as *Rhamnus californica* ssp. *tomentella* 206:58)

Frangula purshiana, Pursh's Buckthorn
Makah *Fruit* Berries eaten fresh in the summer. (as *Rhamnus purshiana* 79:40)

Frangula rubra ssp. *rubra*, Red Buckthorn
Atsugewi *Fruit* Fresh berries used for food. (as *Rhamnus rubra* 61:139)

Frasera speciosa, Showy Frasera
Apache *Unspecified* Roots used for food. (32:29) Root used for food. (121:49) **Arapaho** *Sweetener* Nectar used for honey. (118:17)

Fraxinus pennsylvanica, Green Ash
Ojibwa *Unspecified* Cambium layer scraped down in long, fluffy layers and cooked. They say it tastes like eggs. (153:407)

Fritillaria camschatcensis, Kamchatka Missionbells
Alaska Native *Dried Food* Bulbs dried and used in fish and meat stews. *Soup* Bulbs dried and used in fish and meat stews. *Staple* Bulbs pounded into a flour. (85:119) **Bella Coola** *Unspecified* Bulbs formerly boiled and eaten with sugar and grease. (184:199) **Haisla & Hanaksiala** *Unspecified* Bulbs eaten with west-

ern dock. (43:196) **Hesquiat** *Dried Food* Bulbs dried for winter use. *Forage* The first horse seen in the Hesquiat area was said to have eaten mission bells. *Vegetable* Boiled bulbs eaten with oil. (185:55) **Kitasoo** *Unspecified* Bulbs used for food. (43:320) **Kwakiutl, Southern** *Dried Food* Bulbs sun dried, steamed, covered with oil, and eaten at feasts. (183:273) **Oweekeno** *Unspecified* Bulbs boiled, mixed with oolichan (candlefish) grease and sugar, and eaten. (43:77) **Salish, Straits** *Unspecified* Roots formerly used for food. (186:85)

Fritillaria lanceolata, Rice Root
Okanagon *Staple* Roots used as a principal food. (178:238) *Unspecified* Cooked and used for food. (125:37) Roots used as an important food. (178:237) **Saanich** *Unspecified* Bulbs used for food. (182:75) **Salish, Coast** *Unspecified* Bulbs used for food. (183:300) **Shuswap** *Unspecified* Roasted roots and stems used for food. (123:54) **Thompson** *Dried Food* Washed bulbs dried for future use. *Spice* Bulbs used in flavoring soups. (187:125) *Unspecified* Cooked and used for food. (125:37) Thick, scaly bulbs cooked and eaten. (164:481) Roots used as an important food. (178:237) Roots steam cooked with a little water and put in puddings or pit cooked and used for food. (187:125)

Fritillaria pudica, Yellow Missionbells
Blackfoot *Soup* Bulbs eaten with soup. *Unspecified* Bulbs eaten fresh. (86:102) **Flathead** *Unspecified* Bulbous, underground corms boiled and used for food. (82:25) **Gosiute** *Unspecified* Bulbs formerly used for food. (39:370) **Montana Indian** *Forage* Bulbous, underground corms eaten by bears, gophers, and ground squirrels. Leafy tops eaten by deer. (82:25) *Unspecified* Bulb used for food. (19:12) **Okanagan-Colville** *Dried Food* Bulbs pit cooked, dried, and stored for future use. *Unspecified* Small bulbs eaten raw. (188:46) **Okanagon** *Staple* Roots used as a principal food. (178:238) *Unspecified* Small bulbs steamed and used for food. (125:37) **Paiute** *Unspecified* Bulb gathered, boiled, and eaten. (111:57) **Shuswap** *Unspecified* Root used for

food. (123:54) **Spokan** *Unspecified* Roots used for food. (178:343) **Thompson** *Unspecified* Small bulbs steamed and used for food. (125:37) Bulbs used for food. (164:482) Bulbs eaten when available. (187:125) **Ute** *Unspecified* Bulbs formerly used for food. (38:34)

Fritillaria recurva, Scarlet Mission-bells
Shasta *Unspecified* Bulbs boiled or roasted in ashes and eaten. (93:308)

Fucus gardneri, Sea Wrack
Haisla & Hanaksiala *Dried Food* Plant used to collect herring roe, dried and eaten with the roe. (43:125)

Gaillardia aristata, Common Gaillardia
Blackfoot *Soup* Flower heads used to absorb soups and broth. (86:113)

Gaillardia pinnatifida, Red Dome Blanketflower
Havasupai *Preserves* Seeds parched, ground, kneaded into seed butter, and eaten with fruit drinks or spread on bread. (197:67)

Gaultheria hispidula, Creeping Snowberry
Algonquin, Quebec *Fruit* Fruit used for food. (18:102) **Chippewa** *Beverage* Leaves used to make a beverage. (as *Chiogenes hispidula* 53:317)

Gaultheria ovatifolia, Western Teaberry
Hoh *Fruit* Fruits eaten fresh. *Preserves* Fruits stewed and made into jelly. *Sauce & Relish* Fruits stewed and made into a sauce. **Quileute** *Fruit* Fruits eaten fresh. *Preserves* Fruits stewed and made into jelly. *Sauce & Relish* Fruits stewed and made into a sauce. (137:67)

Gaultheria procumbens, Eastern Teaberry
Abnaki *Beverage* Used to make tea. (144:152)

Leaves used to make tea. (144:171) **Algonquin, Quebec** *Beverage* Used to make tea and medicinal tea. (18:116) *Snack Food* Berries used as a nibble food. (18:102) **Cherokee** *Beverage* Leaves used to make tea. *Fruit* Berries used for food. (126:38) *Unspecified* Species used for food. (80:61) **Chippewa** *Beverage* Leaves used to make a beverage. (53:317) Leaves used to make a pleasant, tea-like beverage. *Spice* Leaves used as a cooking flavor. (71:138) **Iroquois**

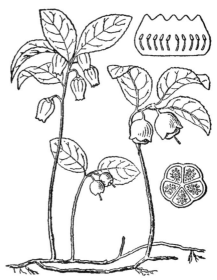

Gaultheria procumbens

Bread & Cake Fruit mashed, made into small cakes, and dried for future use. *Dried Food* Raw or cooked fruit sun or fire dried and stored for future use. *Fruit* Dried fruit taken as a hunting food. *Sauce & Relish* Dried fruit cakes soaked in warm water and cooked as a sauce or mixed with corn bread. (196:128) **Ojibwa** *Beverage* Leaves used to make tea. (96:17) Young, tender leaves used as a beverage tea and rheumatic medicine. (153:400) *Fruit* Fruit used for food. (135:239) Berries used for food. (153:400)

Gaultheria shallon, Salal

Alaska Native *Fruit* Berry-like fruits used for food. (85:83) **Bella Coola** *Bread & Cake* Berries dried in cakes and used as a winter food. (184:204) **Clallam** *Bread & Cake* Berries mashed, dried in cakes, soaked, dipped in oil, and eaten. (57:200) **Haisla & Hanaksiala** *Fruit* Berries used for food. (43:240) **Hesquiat** *Dried Food* Dried, caked berries rehydrated and eaten with oil. *Spice* Branches, with leaves attached, layered between fish heads and fish for flavoring. (185:65) **Karok** *Fruit* Berries used for food. (148:387) **Kitasoo** *Fruit* Fruit used for food. (43:333) **Klallam** *Bread & Cake* Berries mashed, dried, made into cakes, dipped in whale or seal oil, and eaten. (79:43) **Kwakiutl, Southern** *Dried Food* Berries mashed, dried over fire, and resulting cakes used as a winter food. (183:282) *Special Food* Berries mashed with stink currant berries and eaten by chiefs and their wives. (183:286) Ripe berries dipped into oil and eaten fresh at feasts. (183:282) **Makah** *Beverage* Leaves used as a remedy for thirst. *Bread & Cake* Berries mashed, formed into cakes, and sun or air dried for winter use. (67:299) Berries mashed, dried, made into cakes, dipped in whale or seal oil, and eaten. (79:43) *Dried Food* Berries dried for future use. *Fruit* Fruit used for food. Berries eaten fresh. *Pie & Pudding* Berries used to make pies. *Preserves* Berries used to make jellies. *Spice* Leaves used to flavor smoked fish. Leaves steamed with halibut heads for flavoring. **Nitinaht** *Dried Food* Berries dried for future use. (67:299) Berries mashed, dried into rectangular cakes, soaked, boiled, and eaten in winter.

Frozen Food Berries frozen and used for food. (186:104) *Fruit* Fruit used for food. (67:299) Berries eaten fresh. *Preserves* Berries made into jam and used for food. *Spice* Branches and leaves used in steam cooking pits to flavor the cooking food. *Starvation Food* Leaves chewed by those lost in the bushes to alleviate hunger. (186:104) **Okanagon** *Bread & Cake* Fruits pressed into cakes and used as a winter food. *Fruit* Fruits eaten fresh. (125:39) **Oweekeno** *Fruit* Berries eaten as fresh fruit. Berries mixed with stink currants, sugar, and oolichan (candlefish) grease and eaten. *Preserves* Berries used to make jam or jelly. (43:96) **Pomo** *Fruit* Raw or cooked berries used for food. (66:14) **Pomo, Kashaya** *Fruit* Berries eaten fresh from the vine. *Pie & Pudding* Berries used in pies. (72:101) **Quileute** *Bread & Cake* Berries mashed, dried, made into cakes, dipped in whale or seal oil, and eaten. *Fruit* Berries dipped in whale oil, and eaten fresh. **Quinault** *Bread & Cake* Berries mashed, dried, made into cakes, dipped in whale or seal oil and eaten. (79:43) **Salish, Coast** *Bread & Cake* Berries boiled, poured into frames, sun or fire dried into cakes, and used as a winter food. *Fruit* Berries eaten fresh. (182:83) **Samish** *Bread & Cake* Berries mashed, dried, made into cakes, dipped in whale or seal oil, and eaten. **Skagit** *Bread & Cake* Berries mashed, dried, made into cakes, dipped in whale or seal oil, and eaten. (79:43) **Skagit, Upper** *Dried Food* Fruit pulped and dried for winter use. *Fruit* Fruit eaten fresh. (179:38) **Skokomish** *Bread & Cake* Berries mashed, dried, made into cakes, dipped in whale or seal oil, and eaten. **Snohomish** *Bread & Cake* Berries mashed, dried, made into cakes, dipped in whale or seal oil, and eaten. **Swinomish** *Bread & Cake* Berries mashed, dried, made into cakes, dipped in whale or seal oil, and eaten. (79:43) **Thompson** *Bread & Cake* Fruits pressed into cakes and used as a winter food. (125:39) Berries picked with the stems attached, washed, destemmed, dried, and made into cakes for later use. (187:213) *Fruit* Fruits eaten fresh. (125:39) Berries picked with the stems attached, washed, destemmed, and eaten fresh with other berries. *Pie & Pudding*

Berries made into pies. *Preserves* Berries made into jams. (187:213) **Tolowa** *Fruit* Fresh fruit used for food. **Yurok** *Fruit* Fresh fruit used for food. (6:31)

Gaura parviflora, Velvetweed
Navajo, Kayenta *Unspecified* Roots stewed with meat or roasted and used for food. (205:33)

Gaylussacia baccata, Black Huckleberry
Cherokee *Bread & Cake* Berries mixed with flour or cornmeal, soda, and water and made into bread. *Frozen Food* Berries frozen for future use. *Fruit* Berries used for food. *Pie & Pudding* Berries used to make cobblers and pies. *Preserves* Berries used to make jam and canned for future use. (126:39) *Unspecified* Species used for food. (80:39) **Iroquois** *Bread & Cake* Fruits dried, soaked in water and used in bread. (124:96) Fruit mashed, made into small cakes, and dried for future use. *Dried Food* Raw or cooked fruit sun or fire dried and stored for future use. (196:128) *Fruit* Fruits eaten raw. (124:96) Dried fruit taken as hunting food. (196:128) *Pie & Pudding* Fruits dried, soaked in water and used in pudding. *Porridge* Berries dried, soaked in cold water, heated

Gaylussacia baccata

slowly, and mixed with bread meal or hominy in winter. *Sauce & Relish* Fruits dried, soaked in water, and used as a sauce. Berries dried, soaked in cold water, heated slowly, and used as a winter sauce. (124:96) Dried fruit cakes soaked in warm water and cooked as a sauce or mixed with corn bread. (196:128) *Soup* Fruits dried, soaked in water, and used in soups. (124:96) **Ojibwa** *Unspecified* Species used for food. (as *G. resinosa* 135:238)

Gaylussacia ursina, Bear Huckleberry
Cherokee *Preserves* Berries made into jelly or canned for future use. (126:39)

Gentiana douglasiana, Swamp Gentian
Hanaksiala *Candy* Flowers sucked by children for the sweet nectar. (43:252)

Geocaulon lividum, False Toadflax
Alaska Native *Fruit* Fruit used for food. (85:144)

Geranium caespitosum, Pineywoods Geranium
Keres, Western *Fodder* Considered good turkey food. (171:45)

Geranium viscosissimum, Sticky Geranium
Blackfoot *Spice* Leaves kept in food storage bags to mask the spoiling of the contents. (86:103)

Geum triflorum, Prairie Smoke
Thompson *Beverage* Roots boiled and drunk as tea. (164:493)

Gilia capitata ssp. *staminea*, Bluehead Gilia
Luiseño *Unspecified* Seeds used for food. (as *G. staminea* 155:230)

Gilia sinuata, Rosy Gilia
Havasupai *Preserves* Seeds parched, ground, kneaded into seed butter, and eaten with fruit drinks or spread on bread. (197:67)

Glaux maritima, Sea Milkwort
Kwakiutl, Southern *Unspecified* Fleshy roots boiled, dipped in oil, and used for food. (183:288) **Salish, Coast** *Unspecified* Roots eaten in spring. (182:86)

Gleditsia triacanthos, Honey Locust
Cherokee *Beverage* Seed pulp used to make a drink. (80:43) Pod juice, water, and sugar or pods soaked in water used as a beverage. *Unspecified* Ripe, raw pods used for food. (126:45)

Glyceria fluitans, Water Mannagrass
Crow *Unspecified* Seeds used for food. (19:12) **Klamath** *Unspecified* Seeds used for food. (as *Panicularia fluitans* 45:91)

Glycyrrhiza lepidota, American Licorice
Cheyenne *Unspecified* Shoots eaten raw. (76:178) Young shoots eaten raw in spring. (82:35) Tender, spring shoots eaten raw. (83:46) **Montana Indian** *Unspecified* Roots used for food. **Northwest Indian** *Unspecified* Roots used for food. (19:12)

Glyptopleura marginata, Carveseed
Paiute *Vegetable* Raw leaves eaten as greens. (118:23) **Paiute, Northern** *Vegetable* Leaves and stems eaten raw. (59:49)

Gnaphalium obtusifolium, Rabbit Tobacco
Rappahannock *Candy* Leaves chewed for "fun." (161:29)

Gossypium hirsutum, Upland Cotton
Pima, Gila River *Unspecified* Seeds used for food. (133:5)

Grindelia robusta, Great Valley Gumweed
Karok *Vegetable* Leaves eaten raw as greens. (148:389)

Gutierrezia sarothrae, Broom Snakeweed
Tewa *Forage* Plant eaten by livestock. (as *G. longifolia* 138:56)

Gymnocladus dioicus, Kentucky Coffee Tree
Meskwaki *Beverage* Roasted, ground seeds boiled to make coffee. *Unspecified* Roasted seeds eaten. (as *G. dioica* 152:260) **Pawnee** *Unspecified* Roasted seeds eaten like chestnuts. **Winnebago** *Unspecified* Seeds pounded in a mortar and used for food. (as *G. dioica* 70:89)

Hackelia diffusa, Spreading Stickseed
Thompson *Forage* Plant eaten by sheep. The plant was not used by people as it was considered a noxious weed because the burred fruits stuck to fur and clothing. (187:192)

Hamamelis virginiana, American Witchhazel
Cherokee *Beverage* Leaves and twigs used to make tea. (126:44)

Haplopappus sp.
Paiute *Unspecified* Species used for food. (as *Haploppapus* 167:243)

Hedeoma drummondii, Drummond's Falsepennyroyal
Lakota *Soup* Leaves used to make soup. (139:49)

Hedeoma nana, Falsepennyroyal
Apache, Chiricahua & Mescalero *Beverage* Leaves and young stems boiled to make a non-intoxicating beverage. (33:53) *Spice* Leaves used as flavoring. (33:47) **Isleta** *Spice* Leaves chewed for the mint flavor. (100:31) *Unspecified* Leaves chewed for their pleasing flavor. (32:30)

Hedophyllum sessile
Nitinaht *Unspecified* Plants eaten with herring spawn. (186:51)

Hedysarum alpinum, Alpine Sweetvetch
Alaska Native *Unspecified* Roots eaten raw, boiled, or roasted. (85:121) **Eskimo, Arctic** *Forage* Root tubers eaten by brown and black bears and meadow mice. *Vegetable* Tubers located in mice "caches" by specially trained dogs and eaten. (128:30) **Eskimo, Inupiat** *Frozen Food* Roots frozen for future use. *Vegetable* Roots, always with some kind of oil, eaten raw or cooked. *Winter Use Food* Roots stored in

buried sacks for winter use. Roots stored in seal oil, fish oil, or bear fat for winter use. (98:115) **Tanana, Upper** *Beverage* Fried roots, with or without grease, used to make tea. *Vegetable* Roots eaten raw, roasted over a fire, fried, or boiled. Roots dipped in or mixed with grease and eaten. *Winter Use Food* Used in the winter during times of food shortage. A large fire was set over an area where the Indians knew the roots to be abundant. By thawing the ground this way, they were able to dig them out. Roots stored, with or without grease, in a birch bark basket in an underground cache. (102:14)

Hedysarum boreale, Northern Sweetvetch
Eskimo, Arctic *Forage* Roots eaten by the brown bears, meadow mice, and lemmings. *Vegetable* Roots located in mice "caches" by dogs and eaten. (127:1)

Hedysarum boreale ssp. mackenziei, Mackenzie's Sweetvetch
Tanana, Upper *Unspecified* Roots used for food. (as *H. mackenzii* 77:28) Roots eaten fresh and boiled. *Winter Use Food* Fresh roots stored underground in brush-lined caches for future use. (as *H. mackenzii* 115:36)

Helenium puberulum, Rosilla
Mendocino Indian *Unspecified* Leaves and heads eaten raw. (41:394)

Helianthella californica, California Helianthella
Yana *Unspecified* Flowers cooked and eaten. (147:251)

Helianthus annuus, Common Sunflower
Apache, Chiricahua & Mescalero *Bread & Cake* Seeds ground, sifted, made into dough,

and baked on hot stones. *Sauce & Relish* Seeds ground into flour and used to make a thick gravy. (33:48) **Apache, White Mountain** *Staple* Seeds used to make flour. (136:158) **Cahuilla** *Staple* Dried seeds ground and mixed with flour from other seeds. (15:76) **Costanoan** *Unspecified* Seeds used for food, usually not in pinole. (21:254) **Gosiute** *Cooking Agent* Seeds a highly prized source of oil. *Unspecified* Seeds a highly prized source of food. (39:371) **Gros Ventre** *Staple* Powdered seed meal boiled or made into cakes with grease. *Unspecified* Seeds eaten raw. (19:12) **Havasupai** *Dried Food* Seeds sun dried and stored for winter use. (197:248) *Preserves* Seeds parched, ground, kneaded into seed butter, and eaten with fruit drinks or spread on bread. *Staple* Seeds ground and eaten as a ground or parched meal. (197:67) **Hopi** *Fodder* Used as an important food for summer birds. (200:96) **Kawaiisu** *Staple* Roasted seeds pounded, ground into a meal, and eaten dry. (206:34) **Kiowa** *Unspecified* Seeds ground into a paste-like consistency and eaten. (192:60) **Luiseño** *Unspecified* Seeds used for food. (155:228) **Mandan** *Staple* Powdered seed meal boiled or made into cakes with grease. *Unspecified* Seeds eaten raw. (19:12) **Mohave** *Staple* Seeds winnowed, parched,

ground, and eaten as pinole. *Winter Use Food* Seeds stored in gourds or ollas. (37:187) **Montana Indian** *Bread & Cake* Seeds dried, powdered, and grease added to make cakes. *Porridge* Seeds dried, powdered, and boiled to make gruel. (82:30) **Navajo** *Bread & Cake* Seeds mixed with corn, ground into a meal, and made into cakes. (55:87) Seeds ground and made into bread and dumplings. *Porridge* Seeds ground and made into gruel. (165:223) **Navajo, Ramah** *Fodder* Used for livestock feed. *Unspecified* Roasted, ground seeds made into cakes. (191:51) **Paiute** *Porridge* Roasted, ground seeds made into flour and used to make mush. (111:117) *Staple* Seeds parched, ground, and eaten as meal. (104:98) *Winter Use Food* Roasted, ground seeds made into flour and stored for winter use. (111:117) **Paiute, Northern** *Staple* Seeds ground into a meal and eaten. (59:47) **Pima** *Candy* Inner pulp of stalks used as chewing gum. Petals used by children as chewing gum. *Staple* Seeds ground into meal and used as food. *Unspecified* Seeds eaten raw or roasted. (47:103) **Pueblo** *Unspecified* Seeds used for food. (32:30) **Ree** *Staple* Powdered seed meal boiled or made into cakes with grease. *Unspecified* Seeds eaten raw. (19:12) **Sanpoil & Nespelem** *Dried Food* Dried roots stored for winter use. (131:100) *Unspecified* Stems eaten raw. (131:103) Seeds parched until brown, pulverized, and eaten. *Winter Use Food* Seeds parched until brown, pulverized, and stored in salmon skins. (131:104)

Helianthus anomalus, Western Sunflower
Hopi *Fodder* Used as an important food for summer birds. (200:96)

Helianthus bolanderi, Serpentine Sunflower
Paiute *Unspecified* Species used for food. (167:243)

Helianthus cusickii, Cusick's Sunflower
Paiute, Northern *Unspecified* Roots peeled and eaten raw. (59:43)

Helianthus annuus

Helianthus maximiliani, Maximilian
Sunflower
Sioux *Unspecified* Tubers were dug and eaten.
(19:13)

Helianthus petiolaris, Prairie
Sunflower
Havasupai *Dried Food* Seeds sun dried and
stored for winter use. (197:248) *Preserves* Seeds
parched, ground, kneaded into seed butter, and
eaten with fruit drinks or spread on bread. *Staple* Seeds ground and eaten as a ground or
parched meal. (197:67) **Hopi** *Fodder* Used as
an important food for summer birds. (200:96)

Helianthus tuberosus, Jerusalem
Artichoke
Cherokee *Vegetable* Root used as a vegetable
food. (126:34) **Cheyenne** *Unspecified* Species
used for food. (83:45) **Chippewa** *Unspecified*
Roots eaten raw like a radish. (53:319) **Dakota**
Unspecified Tubers boiled and sometimes fried
after boiling for food. Overuse of these tubers
was said to cause flatulence. (69:369) **Hopi**
Unspecified Tubers eaten in the spring. (200:97)
Huron *Starvation Food* Roots used with acorns
during famine. (3:63) **Iroquois** *Unspecified*
Roots used raw, boiled, or fried. (196:120)
Lakota *Starvation Food* Dried and eaten during famines. *Unspecified* Eaten fresh. (106:47)
Stalks and tubers used for food. (139:38)
Malecite *Unspecified* Species used for food.
(160:6) **Micmac** *Unspecified* Tubers eaten.
(159:258) **Omaha** *Fruit* Fruits eaten raw.
(58:341) *Unspecified* Tubers used as a common
food article. (68:325) Noncultivated tubers eaten raw, boiled, or roasted. **Pawnee** *Unspecified*
Noncultivated, raw tubers used for food. **Ponca**
Unspecified Noncultivated tubers eaten raw,
boiled, or roasted. (70:131) **Potawatomi** *Unspecified* Roots gathered for foodstuffs. (154:98)
Winnebago *Unspecified* Noncultivated tubers
eaten raw, boiled, or roasted. (70:131)

Heliomeris longifolia var. *annua*,
Longleaf Falsegoldeneye
Navajo, Ramah *Fodder* Used for sheep and
goat feed. (as *Viguiera annua* 191:54)

Heliomeris longifolia var. *longifolia*, Longleaf Falsegoldeneye
Navajo, Ramah *Fodder* Used for sheep feed.
(as *Viguiera longifolia* 191:54)

Heliomeris multiflora, Showy
Goldeneye
Gosiute *Unspecified* Seeds formerly used for
food. (as *Gymnolomia multiflora* 39:371)

Heliomeris multiflora var. *multiflora*, Showy Goldeneye
Navajo, Ramah *Fodder* Used for sheep and
deer feed. (as *Viguiera multiflora* 191:54)

Heliotropium convolvulaceum,
Phlox Heliotrope
Navajo, Kayenta *Porridge* Seeds made into
mush and used for food. (205:40)

Heliotropium curassavicum, Salt
Heliotrope
Tubatulabal *Unspecified* Seeds used extensively for food. (193:15)

Hemizonia clevelandii, Cleveland's
Tarweed
Pomo *Staple* Seeds used to make pinoles.
(11:86)

Hemizonia corymbosa, Coastal
Tarweed
Costanoan *Staple* Seeds eaten as a pinole.
(21:254)

Hemizonia fasciculata, Clustered
Tarweed
Cahuilla *Starvation Food* Whole plant, including the seeds, used as a famine plant. (15:77)

Hemizonia fitchii, Fitch's Tarweed
Miwok *Unspecified* Seeds used to make mush.
(as *Centromadia fitchii* 12:153)

Hemizonia luzulifolia, Hayfield
Tarweed
Mendocino Indian *Staple* Seeds used as an

important source of pinole. (41:394) **Pomo** *Staple* Seeds used to make pinoles. (11:86)

Heracleum maximum, Common Cow Parsnip

Alaska Native *Unspecified* Inner stem pulp eaten raw and often dipped in seal oil. (as *H. lanatum* 85:133) **Anticosti** *Forage* Whole plant eaten by cows. (as *H. lanatum* 143:67) **Bella Coola** *Unspecified* Young stems peeled and eaten with grease. (as *H. lanatum* 184:201) **Blackfoot** *Soup* Stem pieces dipped in blood, stored, and used to make soup and broths. (as *H. lanatum* 86:103) *Unspecified* Stalks roasted over hot coals and eaten. (as *H. lanatum* 114:277) *Vegetable* Young plant stems peeled and eaten like celery. (as *H. lanatum* 86:103) **California Indian** *Vegetable* Young, raw shoots eaten like celery. (as *H. lanatum* 19:13) **Carrier** *Unspecified* Young growth used for food. (as *H. lanatum* 31:82) **Coeur d'Alene** *Unspecified* Growing stalks used for food. (as *H. lanatum* 178:91) **Costanoan** *Unspecified* Boiled roots and foliage used for food. (as *H. spondylium* ssp. *montanum* 21:251) **Cree, Woodlands** *Unspecified* Leaf petiole peeled and eaten fresh. Pith scraped out of the roasted, main stem and eaten. (as *H. lanatum* 109:40)

Heracleum maximum

Gitksan *Unspecified* Stems used for food in spring. (as *H. lanatum* 73:154) Stalks eaten in spring. (as *H. lanatum* 74:25) **Haisla** *Unspecified* Stems used for food in spring. (as *H. lanatum* 73:154) **Haisla & Hanaksiala** *Unspecified* Petioles considered "the main food in spring." (as *H. lanatum* 43:214) **Hesquiat** *Forage* Young shoots eaten by cattle. *Unspecified* Raw stalks of young leaves and flower buds eaten with sugar or honey. (as *H. lanatum* 185:60) **Hoh** *Vegetable* Young shoots eaten raw as greens. (as *H. lanatum* 137:66) **Karok** *Unspecified* Fresh shoot used for food. (as *H. lanatum* 148:387) **Kitasoo** *Vegetable* Young stems and petioles eaten as a spring vegetable. (as *H. lanatum* 43:326) **Klamath** *Unspecified* Young shoots used for food. (as *H. lanatum* 45:102) **Kwakiutl, Southern** *Unspecified* Young stems and petioles peeled and eaten raw like celery. (as *H. lanatum* 183:276) **Makah** *Unspecified* Fresh petioles peeled, mixed with oil, and used for food. Stems considered a favored food. Plant eaten after peeling. (as *H. lanatum* 67:293) Young tops eaten raw in the spring. Stems used for food. (as *H. lanatum* 79:42) **Mendocino Indian** *Vegetable* Tender leaf and flower stalks eaten as green food in spring and early summer. (as *H. lanatum* 41:373) **Meskwaki** *Vegetable* Potatoes cooked like the rutabaga. (as *H. lanatum* 152:265) **Mewuk** *Unspecified* Young stems peeled and eaten raw. (as *H. lanatum* 117:366) **Montana Indian** *Vegetable* Young, raw shoots eaten like celery. (as *H. lanatum* 19:13) **Nitinaht** *Unspecified* Hollow and solid leafstalks peeled and used for food. (as *H. lanatum* 186:91) **Ojibwa** *Vegetable* Leaves used as greens. (as *H. lanatum* 135:237) **Okanagan-Colville** *Vegetable* Flower stalks and leaf stems peeled and eaten fresh. (as *H. lanatum* 188:62) **Okanagon** *Staple* Growing stalks used as a principal food. (as *H. lanatum* 178:239) *Unspecified* Young flower stalks peeled and eaten raw. (as *H. lanatum* 125:38) **Oweekeno** *Unspecified* Stems and petioles peeled and used for food. (as *H. lanatum* 43:84) **Pomo, Kashaya** *Unspecified* New shoots peeled and eaten raw. (as *H. lanatum* 72:87) **Quileute** *Unspecified* Stems dipped in seal oil and eaten. (as *H. lanatum* 79:42) *Vegetable* Young shoots eaten raw as greens. (as *H. lanatum* 137:66) **Quinault** *Unspecified* Stems dipped in seal oil and eaten. (as *H. lanatum* 79:42) **Salish, Coast** *Unspecified* Young stems and leaf stalks eaten raw or boiled. (as *H. lanatum* 182:89) **Shuswap** *Unspecified* Young stems eaten raw. (as *Meracleum lanatum* 123:56) **Spokan** *Unspecified* Stalks used for food. (as *H. lanatum* 178:344) **Thompson** *Dried Food* Plant formerly dried for storage. (as *H. lanatum* 187:152) *Forage* Stalks used as a common food for cattle. (as *H. lanatum* 164:482) *Frozen Food* Plant frozen for future use. (as *H. lanatum* 187:152) *Unspecified* Young flower stalks peeled and eaten raw. (as *H. lanatum* 125:38) Young stalks peeled and eaten raw. (as *H. lanatum* 164:482) *Vegetable* Peeled shoots eaten as vegetables with meat or fish. Peeled, raw, or cooked leaf stalks and flower stalks used for food. The stalks were ready to use around May and June, but after a while, they became tough, dry, or sticky and were no longer good to eat. The raw stalks would cause a burning like pepper if eaten in too great a quantity; it was better to eat cooked stalks. *Winter Use Food* Plant canned for future use. (as *H. lanatum* 187:152) **Tolowa** *Unspecified* Stem inner layers eaten raw. (as *H. lanatum* 6:32) **Wet'suwet'en** *Unspecified* Stems used for food in spring. (as *H. lanatum* 73:154) **Yuki** *Unspecified* Tender, young stems peeled and eaten raw. (as *H. lanatum* 49:87) **Yurok** *Unspecified* Stem inner layers eaten raw. (as *H. lanatum* 6:32)

Hericium coralloides, Coral Mushroom
Pomo, Kashaya *Vegetable* Baked on hot stones, in the oven, or fried. (72:129)

Hesperocallis undulata, Desert Lily
Cahuilla *Unspecified* Bulbs eaten raw or oven pit baked. (15:77) **Yuma** *Unspecified* Bulbs eaten raw, baked, or boiled. (37:207)

Heteromeles arbutifolia, Toyon
Cahuilla *Fruit* Berries eaten cooked and raw. (15:77) **Costanoan** *Fruit* Fruits eaten toasted or dried. (21:249) **Diegueño** *Fruit* Fruit used for food. (88:217) **Karok** *Fruit* Berries roasted over an open fire and eaten. (6:32) **Luiseño** *Dried Food* Parched berries used for food. (155:194) **Mahuna** *Fruit* Berries eaten mainly to quench the thirst. (140:70) **Mendocino Indian** *Fruit* Fruits eaten fresh. Fruits boiled or roasted and used for food. (41:355) **Pomo, Kashaya** *Fruit* Berries wilted in hot ashes and winnowed in a basket plate. (72:115) **Yurok** *Fruit* Berries roasted over an open fire and eaten by children. (6:32)

Heteromeles arbutifolia var. *arbutifolia*, Toyon
Karok *Fruit* Berries put on a basket plate in front of the fire, turned until wilted and eaten. (as *Photinia arbutifolia* 148:385) **Neeshenam** *Fruit* Bright, red berries used for food. (as *Photinea arbutifolia* 129:375) **Pomo** *Fruit* Wilted, winnowed berries used for food. (as *Photinia arbutifolia* 66:13)

Heterotheca villosa var. *villosa*, Hairy Goldenaster
Navajo, Ramah *Fodder* Used for sheep feed. (as *Chrysopsis villosa* 191:49)

Heuchera micrantha, Crevice Alumroot
Miwok *Dried Food* Steamed leaves dried and stored. *Vegetable* Boiled or steamed leaves eaten in spring. (12:159)

Hieracium sp., Hawkweed
Thompson *Unspecified* Chewed for pleasure. (164:492)

Hilaria jamesii, Galleta
Navajo, Ramah *Forage* Used as horse and sheep feed and able to withstand trampling and close grazing. (191:16)

Hippuris tetraphylla, Fourleaf Marestail
Eskimo, Alaska *Vegetable* Small, young leaves eaten as greens. (4:715)

Hippuris vulgaris, Common Marestail
Alaska Native *Soup* Whole plant used to make
soup. *Winter Use Food* Leaves piled on high
ground and stored for winter use. (85:135)
Eskimo, Alaska *Soup* Plant added to seal
blood soup and tom cod-liver soup. (1:37)
Eskimo, Inuktitut *Ice Cream* Used to make
"Eskimo ice cream." *Soup* Used as a condiment
for soups. *Unspecified* Eaten raw or with seal oil
and salmon eggs. (202:191)

Hirschfeldia incana, Shortpod
   Mustard
Cahuilla *Porridge* Seeds ground into a mush.
Vegetable Leaves eaten fresh or boiled. *Winter
Use Food* Leaves and seeds used as an important
winter food. (as *Brassica geniculata* 15:47)

Hoffmannseggia glauca, Indian
   Rushpea
Apache *Unspecified* Potatoes roasted and eaten
much more commonly in the past than currently.
(as *H. densiflora* 32:52) **Apache, Chiricahua
& Mescalero** *Unspecified* Roots eaten either
raw or cooked. (as *H. densiflora* 33:42) **Cocopa**
Unspecified Tuberous roots utilized as food. (as
H. densiflora 37:207) **Pima** *Unspecified* Bulbs
eaten raw or boiled. (as *H. stricta* 95:262) *Vegetable* Tubers boiled and eaten like potatoes.
(as *H. densiflora* 47:92) **Pima, Gila River**
Unspecified Roots boiled or roasted and eaten.
(as *H. densiflora* 133:7) Tubers eaten. (133:5)
Pueblo *Unspecified* Potatoes roasted and eaten
much more commonly in the past than currently.
(as *H. densiflora* 32:52)

Hoita orbicularis, Roundleaf
   Leatherroot
Luiseño *Vegetable* Plant used for greens. (as
Psoralea orbicularis 155:231)

Holodiscus dumosus, Rockspirea
Isleta *Beverage* Leaves steeped to make a beverage. (100:32)

Honckenya peploides, Seaside
   Sandplant
Eskimo, Inupiat *Vegetable* Sour leaves and

shoots eaten with seal oil and sugar. *Winter Use
Food* Leaves and shoots boiled many times and
stored in a large wooden barrel for winter use.
(98:42)

Honckenya peploides ssp.
   major, Seaside Sandplant
Eskimo, Alaska *Unspecified* Leaves and stems
boiled and eaten with seal oil. (1:35) Leaves
used for food. (as *Ammodenia peploides major*
4:715)

Honckenya peploides ssp. ***peploides***, Seaside Sandplant
Alaska Native *Dietary Aid* Fresh and raw
leaves eaten as a good source of vitamins A and
C. *Ice Cream* Leaves chopped, cooked in water,
soured, and mixed with reindeer fat and berries
into Eskimo ice cream. *Unspecified* Leaves eaten
with dried fish. *Vegetable* Leaves eaten raw or
mixed with other greens. Leaves mixed with
other greens and made into a kraut. (as *Arenaria peploides* 85:15) **Eskimo, Arctic** *Vegetable* Young stems and leaves pickled as "sauerkraut" or eaten as a potherb. (as *Arenaria
peploides* 128:29)

Hordeum jubatum, Foxtail Barley
Kawaiisu *Unspecified* Seeds pounded and
eaten dry. (206:34)

Hordeum marinum ssp. ***gusso-
nianum***, Mediterranean Barley
Mendocino Indian *Fodder* Green grass used
for fodder. (41:313)

Hordeum murinum, Mouse Barley
Mendocino Indian *Staple* Seeds used for
pinole. (41:313)

Hordeum murinum ssp. ***glaucum***, Smooth Barley
Cahuilla *Unspecified* Seeds eaten, when other
foods were scarce. (as *H. stebbinsi* 15:78)
Costanoan *Staple* Seeds used for pinole. (as *H.
glaucum* 21:255)

Hordeum vulgare, Common Barley
Cahuilla *Unspecified* Cultivated and used for
food. (15:78) **Papago** *Unspecified* Species used
for food. **Pima** *Unspecified* Species used for
food. (36:117) **Yuki** *Bread & Cake* Seeds
ground into flour and used to make bread. *Substitution Food* Seeds parched and used as a
substitute for coffee. (41:313)

Humulus lupulus, Common Hop
Algonquin, Quebec *Bread & Cake* Hops used
to make bread. (18:83) **Lakota** *Cooking Agent*
Used to make bread swell. (139:51) **Ojibwa**
Cooking Agent Hop fruit often used as a substi-
tute for baking soda. (153:411)

**Humulus lupulus var. neomexi-
canus**, Common Hop
Apache, Chiricahua & Mescalero *Spice* Hops
boiled and used to flavor wheat flour and potatoes. (33:47) Flower used to flavor drinks and
make them stronger. (33:51) **Navajo** *Unspecified* Hops used for cooking. (55:41)

Hydrangea arborescens, Wild
Hydrangea
Cherokee *Beverage* Peeled branches and twigs
boiled to make tea. (126:54) *Unspecified* New
growth of young twigs peeled, boiled thoroughly, fried, and eaten. (204:253) *Vegetable* Peeled
branches and twigs cooked in grease like green
beans. (126:54)

Hydrocotyle sp., Marsh Pennywort
Cahuilla *Vegetable* Plant used for greens.
(15:79)

**Hydrophyllum fendleri var. albi-
frons**, White Waterleaf
Okanagon *Forage* Thick roots eaten by cattle.
Unspecified Thick roots cooked and eaten.
Thompson *Forage* Thick roots eaten by cattle.
Unspecified Thick roots cooked and eaten. (as
H. albifrons 125:37)

Hydrophyllum occidentale, Western Waterleaf
Okanagon *Staple* Roots used as a principal

food. (178:238) **Thompson** *Forage* Roots eaten
by cattle. *Unspecified* Root cooked and eaten.
(164:480)

Hydrophyllum tenuipes, Pacific
Waterleaf
Cowlitz *Unspecified* Roots broken and eaten.
(79:45)

Hydrophyllum virginianum,
Shawnee Salad
Iroquois *Vegetable* Young plants or leaves
cooked and seasoned with salt, pepper, or butter. (196:117) **Menominee** *Vegetable* Leaves
wilted in maple sap vinegar, simmered, and
boiled in fresh water with pork and fine meal.
(151:68) **Ojibwa** *Fodder* Roots fed to ponies
to make them fatten rapidly. (153:405) Root
chopped and put into pony feed to make them
grow fat and have glossy hair. (153:419)

Hymenoclea monogyra, Singlewhorl
Burrobush
Seri *Unspecified* Seeds used for food. (50:136)

Hymenopappus filifolius, Fineleaf
Hymenopappus
Hopi *Bread & Cake* Leaves boiled, rubbed with

Hydrophyllum virginianum

cornmeal, and baked into bread. (32:29) **Zuni** *Candy* Root used as chewing gum. (166:68)

Hymenopappus filifolius var. *pauciflorus*, Fineleaf Hymenopappus
Hopi *Beverage* Used to make tea and coffee. (as *H. pauciflorus* 42:326)

Hymenoxys cooperi, Cooper's Hymenoxys
Hopi *Beverage* Used to make tea. (42:329)

Hymenoxys richardsonii, Pingue Hymenoxys
Navajo *Candy* Plant used as a chewing gum. (as *Actinella richardsoni* 55:80)

Hymenoxys richardsonii var. *floribunda*, Colorado Rubberweed
Isleta *Candy* Roots used as chewing gum. (as *H. floribunda* 100:32) **Keres, Western** *Candy* Root used as chewing gum. (as *H. floribunda* 171:48) **Spanish American** *Candy* Roots chewed as chewing gum. (as *H. floribunda* 32:30) **Tewa** *Candy* Root skins pounded and the gummy material chewed as gum. (as *H. floribunda* 138:56)

Hypericum scouleri ssp. *scouleri*, Scouler's St. John's Wort
Miwok *Dried Food* and *Staple* Eaten fresh, dried, or ground into flour and used like acorn meal. (as *H. formosum* var. *scouleri* 12:158)

Ilex sp., Holly
Comanche *Beverage* Leaves used to make a beverage. (29:522)

Ipomoea batatas, Sweet Potato
Cherokee *Vegetable* Potatoes used for food. (as *Impomoea batatas* 80:51) **Seminole** *Vegetable* Tubers eaten. (169:465)

Ipomoea cairica, Mile a Minute Vine
Hawaiian *Unspecified* Tubers grated, roasted, and eaten. (as *I. tuberculata* 112:69)

Ipomoea leptophylla, Bush Morningglory
Arapaho *Starvation Food* Root roasted for food when pressed by hunger. **Cheyenne** *Starvation Food* Root roasted for food when pressed by hunger. **Kiowa** *Starvation Food* Root roasted for food when pressed by hunger. (19:13)

Ipomoea pandurata, Man of the Earth
Cherokee *Unspecified* Roots used for food. (80:51) *Vegetable* Potatoes used for food. (as *Impomoea pandurata* 80:21)

Ipomopsis aggregata ssp. *aggregata*, Skyrocket Gilia
Hopi *Beverage* Boiled for a drink. (as *Gilia aggregata* 42:321) **Klamath** *Snack Food* Nectar sucked from flowers by children. (as *Gilia aggregata* 45:103)

Ipomopsis aggregata ssp. *attenuata*, Scarlet Skyrocket
Navajo *Forage* Used as a browse plant. (as *Gilia attenuata* 90:160)

Iris setosa, Beachhead Iris
Eskimo, Alaska *Beverage* Roasted, ground seeds used for coffee. (4:715)

Jacquemontia ovalifolia ssp. *sandwicensis*, Ovalleaf Clustervine
Hawaiian *Beverage* Dried leaves and stems used to make tea. *Unspecified* Dried leaves and stems eaten with coconut. (as *J. sandwicensis* 2:73)

Jacquinia pungens
Seri *Unspecified* Nuts used for food. (50:136)

Jamesia americana, Cliffbush
Apache, Chiricahua & Mescalero *Unspecified* Seeds occasionally eaten fresh. (33:45)

Juglans californica, California Walnut
Costanoan *Unspecified* Nuts used for food. (21:248)

Juglans cinerea, Butternut
Algonquin, Quebec *Unspecified* Nuts used for food. (18:78) **Cherokee** *Unspecified* Nuts used for food. (80:61) Raw nut used for food. (126:42) **Iroquois** *Baby Food* Fresh nutmeats crushed, boiled, and oil used as a baby food. *Beverage* Fresh nutmeats crushed, boiled, and liquid used as a drink. *Bread & Cake* Fresh nutmeats crushed and mixed with bread. (124:99) Nuts crushed, mixed with cornmeal and beans or berries, and made into bread. (196:123) *Pie & Pudding* Fresh nutmeats crushed and mixed with corn pudding. (124:99) *Sauce & Relish* Nuts pounded, boiled, resulting oil seasoned with salt and used as gravy. *Soup* Nutmeats crushed and added to corn soup. (196:123) *Special Food* Fresh nutmeats crushed, boiled, and oil used as a delicacy in corn bread and pudding. (124:99) Nutmeat oil added to the mush used by the False Face Societies. *Staple* Nutmeats crushed and added to hominy. *Unspecified* Nutmeats, after skimming off the oil, seasoned and mixed with mashed potatoes. (196:123) **Menominee** *Unspecified* Used in the

same way that the white man did. (151:68) **Meskwaki** *Winter Use Food* Nuts stored for winter use. (152:259) **Ojibwa** *Unspecified* Nuts used for food. (153:405) **Potawatomi** *Winter Use Food* Butternuts gathered for their edible quality and furnished a winter supply of food. (154:103)

Juglans hindsii, Hinds's Black Walnut
Pomo, Kashaya *Dried Food* Sweet nutmeat dried and stored for later use. *Unspecified* Sweet nutmeat eaten fresh. (72:117)

Juglans major, Arizona Walnut
Apache, Chiricahua & Mescalero *Unspecified* Nutmeats eaten raw. *Winter Use Food* Nutmeats mixed with mesquite gravy or ground with roasted mescal and stored. (33:42) **Apache, Mescalero** *Unspecified* Nutmeats mixed with mescal, datil, sotol, or mesquite and used for food. (14:46) **Hualapai** *Unspecified* Nuts used for food. (195:13) **Navajo** *Unspecified* Nuts gathered and eaten on a fairly large scale. (55:39) **Yavapai** *Beverage* Decoction of pulverized nut juice dipped up and sucked. (63:209) Meat pulverized in mescal syrup and used as a beverage. *Unspecified* Nutmeat used for food. *Winter Use Food* Nuts stored for later use. (65:256)

Juglans nigra, Black Walnut
Cherokee *Dried Food* Nuts dried in the rafters for future use. *Porridge* Nuts mixed with skinned hominy corn, water, and pinto beans. (126:43) *Unspecified* Nuts used for food. (80:61) **Comanche** *Unspecified* Nuts used for food. (29:522) *Winter Use Food* Nuts stored for winter use. (29:531) **Dakota** *Soup* Nuts used to make soup. *Unspecified* Nuts eaten plain or with honey. (70:74) **Iroquois** *Beverage* Fresh nutmeats crushed, boiled, and liquid used as a drink. *Bread & Cake* Fresh nutmeats crushed

and mixed with bread. (124:99) Nuts crushed, mixed with cornmeal and beans or berries, and made into bread. (196:123) *Pie & Pudding* Fresh nutmeats crushed and mixed with corn pudding. (124:99) *Sauce & Relish* Nuts pounded, boiled, resulting oil seasoned with salt and used as gravy. *Soup* Nutmeats crushed and added to corn soup. (196:123) *Special Food* Fresh nutmeats crushed, boiled, and oil used as a delicacy in corn bread and pudding. (124:99) Nutmeat oil added to the mush used by the False Face Societies. *Staple* Nutmeats crushed and added to hominy. *Unspecified* Nutmeats, after skimming off the oil, seasoned and mixed with mashed potatoes. (196:123) **Kiowa** *Unspecified* Nuts used for food. (192:20) **Lakota** *Unspecified* Nuts used for food. (139:49) **Meskwaki** *Unspecified* Nuts were relished. (152:259) **Omaha** *Soup* Nuts used to make soup. (70:74) *Unspecified* Nuts eaten plain or mixed with honey. (68:326) Nuts eaten plain or with honey. **Pawnee** *Soup* Nuts used to make soup. *Unspecified* Nuts eaten plain or with honey. **Ponca** *Soup* Nuts used to make soup. *Unspecified* Nuts eaten plain or with honey. **Winnebago** *Soup* Nuts used to make soup. *Unspecified* Nuts eaten plain or with honey. (70:74)

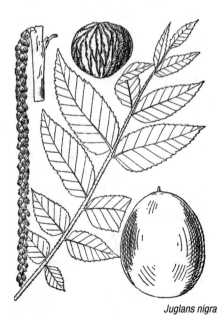

Juglans nigra

Juncus balticus, Baltic Rush
Paiute *Candy* Sugar, formed along tops of plants, gathered and eaten as candy. *Unspecified* Seeds used for food. (167:246) Species used for food. (167:243) **Paiute, Northern** *Beverage* Stems used to make a fermented drink. (59:53)

Juncus effusus, Common Rush
Mendocino Indian *Forage* Plants eaten by cows and horses in early spring. (41:318) **Okanagan-Colville** *Fodder* Plant used to feed horses. (188:38) **Snuqualmie** *Unspecified* Early sprouts eaten raw. (79:23)

Juncus ensifolius, Swordleaf Rush
Paiute *Fodder* Rushes used as food for livestock. (111:53) **Swinomish** *Unspecified* Bulbs used for food. (as *J. xiphioides* var. *triandrus* 79:23)

Juniperus californica, California Juniper
Cahuilla *Dried Food* Berries sun dried and preserved for future use. *Fruit* Berries eaten fresh. *Porridge* Dried berries ground into a flour and used to make mush or bread. (15:81) **Costanoan** *Fruit* Berries used for food. (21:248) **Diegueño** *Fruit* Fruit eaten, informally only. *Starvation Food* Fruit eaten in times of starvation. (88:216) **Kawaiisu** *Bread & Cake* Berries seeded, pounded into a meal, moistened, molded into cakes, and dried. *Dried Food* Unseeded berries dried and stored. *Fruit* Berries boiled fresh and eaten cold. *Staple* Berries seeded, pounded into a meal, and eaten. (206:35) **Mendocino Indian** *Dried Food* Dried fruits boiled and eaten. (41:306)

Juniperus communis, Common Juniper
Anticosti *Beverage* Fruits, branches, potatoes, yeast, and water boiled into a drink. (143:64) **Thompson** *Beverage* Small pieces of branches used to make a tea-like beverage. (187:92)

***Juniperus communis* var. *montana*, Common Juniper**
Jemez *Beverage* Leaves boiled into a beverage similar to coffee. (as *J. sibirica* 44:24)

***Juniperus deppeana*, Alligator Juniper**
Apache *Fruit* Berries boiled for food. (as *J. pachyphloea* 32:32) **Apache, Chiricahua & Mescalero** *Fruit* Raw fruit eaten fresh. *Preserves* Berries boiled and made into jelly or preserves. (as *J. pachyphloea* 33:45) **Isleta** *Fruit* Berries boiled for food. (as *J. pachyphloea* 32:32) Large fruit boiled and eaten as food. (as *J. pachyphloea* 100:33) **Navajo, Ramah** *Fruit* Fruit eaten raw or boiled and ground. *Winter Use Food* Fruit stored for winter use. (as *J. pachyphloea* 191:12) **San Felipe** *Fruit* Berries boiled for food. (as *J. pachyphloea* 32:32) **Yavapai** *Beverage* Pulverized berries soaked in water, put in mouth, and juice sucked, the solid matter spat out. (as *J. pachyphlaea* 63:212) Ground berries made into a meal, water added and used as a beverage. *Bread & Cake* Ground berries made into a meal, stored in baskets, and later made into a cake by dampening. *Staple* Ground berries made into a meal, water added and used as a beverage. (as *J. pachyphlaea* 65:257)

***Juniperus horizontalis*, Creeping Juniper**
Ojibwa *Beverage* Leaves used to make tea. (as *J. prostrata* 96:17)

***Juniperus monosperma*, Oneseed Juniper**
Acoma *Fruit* Fruits mixed with chopped meat, put into a clean deer stomach, and roasted. *Spice* Fruits used to season meats. *Starvation Food* Fruits eaten when other foods became scarce. (32:31) **Apache, Chiricahua & Mescalero** *Sauce & Relish* Fruit roasted, water added, and the mixture made into a gravy. (33:45) **Apache, White Mountain** *Fruit* Berries boiled and eaten. (136:158) **Cochiti** *Fruit* Fresh or cooked berries used for food. (32:31) **Hopi** *Fruit* Berries eaten with piki or cooked with stew. (42:330) **Jemez** *Fruit* Fresh or

cooked berries used for food. (32:31) **Keres, Western** *Spice* Berries used to season meat. *Starvation Food* Berries eaten in the fall or when food was scarce. (171:48) **Keresan** *Fruit* Berries used for food. (198:561) **Laguna** *Fruit* Fruits mixed with chopped meat, put into a clean deer stomach, and roasted. *Spice* Fruits used to season meats. *Starvation Food* Fruits eaten when other foods became scarce. (32:31) **Navajo** *Fodder* Branches cut off and given to the sheep to eat when the snow was deep. *Fruit* Berries eaten ripe. (55:19) *Starvation Food* Inner bark chewed in times of food shortage to obtain the juice. (32:31) Inner bark chewed in times of food shortage. (55:19) **Navajo, Ramah** *Unspecified* Berry-like cones eaten roasted or boiled. Pinyon nuts used for food. (191:11) **San Ildefonso** *Fruit* Berries eaten. (138:40) **Tewa** *Fruit* Fruits eaten fresh or heated. (32:31) Berries eaten with piki. (42:330) Berries eaten by children and young people. **Tewa of Hano** *Special Food* Gum chewed as a delicacy. (138:40)

***Juniperus occidentalis*, Western Juniper**
Apache, White Mountain *Fruit* Berries boiled and eaten. (136:158) **Atsugewi** *Dried Food* Berries dried, pounded into flour, and stored for later use. *Fruit* Fresh berries used for food. (61:139) **Miwok** *Unspecified* Ripe nuts used for food. (12:151) **Paiute** *Fruit* Berries and roasted, mashed deer liver combination used for food. *Winter Use Food* Berries stored without drying in a grass-lined hole in the ground for winter use. (111:47) **Paiute, Northern** *Fruit* Berries roasted, mixed with warm water, crushed, and eaten. (59:50)

***Juniperus osteosperma*, Utah Juniper**
Acoma *Soup* Berries cooked in a stew. (as *J. utahensis* 200:63) **Apache, White Mountain** *Fruit* Berries boiled and eaten. (as *J. californica* var. *utahensis* (*J. utahensis*) 136:158) **Gosiute** *Fruit* Berries eaten in the fall and winter after proper boiling. (as *J. californica* var. *utahensis* 39:372) **Havasupai** *Beverage* Dried berries used to make a drink. *Dried Food* Ber-

ries sun dried and stored for winter use. (197:206) **Hopi** *Fruit* Berries eaten with piki bread. (as *J. utahensis* 120:18) Berries used for food. (as *J. utahensis* 200:63) **Tubatulabal** *Fruit* Berries used extensively for food. Berries used extensively for food. (as *J. utaliensis* 193:15) **Yavapai** *Beverage* Ground berries made into a meal, water added, and used as a beverage. *Bread & Cake* Ground berries made into a meal, stored in baskets, and later made into a cake by dampening. *Staple* Ground berries made into a meal, water added, and used as a beverage. (as *J. utahensis* 65:257)

Juniperus scopulorum, Rocky Mountain Juniper
Apache, Chiricahua & Mescalero *Fruit* Berries mixed with mescal and eaten. (33:37)
Jemez *Fruit* Berries eaten raw or stewed.

(44:24) **Keresan** *Fruit* Berries eaten raw by hunters while out in the mountains, but better when cooked. (198:561) **Okanagan-Colville** *Beverage* Berries made into a drink and taken in the sweat house. This drink could only be taken with great caution, because the berries were believed to be poisonous. (188:19) **Tewa** *Fruit* Fruits eaten fresh or heated. (32:32)

Juniperus virginiana, Eastern Red Cedar
Comanche *Fruit* Fruits eaten for food. (29:522)
Lakota *Beverage* Berries eaten to relieve thirst. *Spice* Berries crushed and used to flavor soups, meats, and stews. (106:30)

Justicia californica, Beloperone
Diegueño *Sweetener* Flower sucked for the nectar. (as *Beloperone californica* 15:47)

Kalmia latifolia, Mountain Laurel
Mahuna *Forage* Plants eaten by deer. (140:52)

Kalmia microphylla, Alpine Laurel
Hanaksiala *Beverage* Leaves used to make tea. Leaves used to make tea. (43:241)

Kochia scoparia, Common Kochia
Navajo *Forage* Plant used as sheep forage, especially in the winter. (as *K. trichophylla* 90:152)

Koeleria macrantha, Prairie Junegrass
Havasupai *Bread & Cake* Seeds used to make bread. (as *K. cristata* 197:66) *Forage* Plant grazed by livestock. *Unspecified* Seeds used for food. *Winter Use Food* Seeds stored in blankets or bags of skin in caves. (as *K. cristata* 197:209) **Isleta** *Bread & Cake* Seeds made into

Koeleria macrantha

a meal and used to make bread. *Porridge* Seeds made into a meal and used to make mush. (as *K. cristata* 32:22) *Staple* Considered a very important source of food before the introduction of wheat. Seeds used to make flour for bread and mush. (as *K. cristata* 100:33) **Okanagan-Colville** *Fodder* Used as a good feed for cattle and horses. (as *K. cristata* 188:55)

Krascheninnikovia lanata,
Winter Fat
Havasupai *Fodder* Plant used for horse feed. (as *Ceratoides lanata* 197:218) **Keres, Western** *Forage* Considered a good forage plant. (as *Eurotia lanata* 171: 44) **Navajo** *Forage* Plant used as winter forage for the sheep. (as *Eurotia lanata* 55:44)

Lactuca canadensis, Canada Lettuce
Cherokee *Vegetable* Leaves cooked and eaten as greens. (80:42)

Lactuca ludoviciana, Biannual
Lettuce
Gosiute *Unspecified* Leaves used for food. (39:373)

Lactuca sativa, Garden Lettuce
Acoma *Vegetable* Young, tender plants eaten as greens. (as *L. integrata* 32:32) **Keres, Western** *Vegetable* Young, tender plants used as lettuce. (as *L. integrata* 171:51) **Laguna** *Vegetable* Young, tender plants eaten as greens. (as *L. integrata* 32:32)

Lactuca tatarica var. pulchella,
Blue Lettuce
Apache, White Mountain *Candy* Gummy substance from the root used for chewing gum. **Navajo** *Candy* Gummy substance from the root used for chewing gum. **Zuni** *Candy* Gummy substance from the root used for chewing gum. (as *L. pulchella* 136:158) Dried root gum used as chewing gum. (as *L. pulchella* 166:68)

Lagenaria siceraria, Bottle Gourd
Cherokee *Unspecified* Species used for food. (as *L. vulgaris* 80:37) **Ojibwa** *Vegetable* Gourds

eaten young, before the rind had hardened. (as *L. vulgaris* 153:400)

Laminaria groenlandica
Nitinaht *Unspecified* Plants eaten with herring spawn. (186:51)

Lappula occidentalis var. occidentalis, Desert Stickseed
Navajo, Ramah *Fodder* Used for sheep feed. (as *L. redowskii* 191:41)

Larix laricina, Tamarack
Anticosti *Beverage* Branches and needles used to make tea. (143:63) **Potawatomi** *Fodder* Shredded inner bark mixed with oats and fed to horses to make the hide of the animal loose. (154:122)

Larix occidentalis, Western Larch
Flathead *Candy* Solidified pitch chewed as gum. *Sauce & Relish* Sap used to make a sweet syrup. *Unspecified* Cambium layer eaten in spring. **Kutenai** *Sauce & Relish* Sap used to make a sweet syrup. (82:22) **Okanagan-Colville** *Candy* Sap hardened and eaten like candy. *Forage* Buds eaten by blue grouse. (188:25) **Paiute** *Candy* Syrup or "dark sugar" gathered as a confection. (111:43) **Sanpoil & Nespelem** *Unspecified* Gum collected on stump

of a burned or fallen larch and used for food. (131:105) **Thompson** *Candy* Gum from trunk and branches chewed for pleasure. (187:99) *Unspecified* Gum chewed for pleasure. (164:493)

Lasthenia californica, California Goldfields
Cahuilla *Porridge* Parched seeds ground into flour and used to make mush. (as *Baeria chrysostoma* 15:46)

Lasthenia glabrata, Yellowray Goldfields
Cahuilla *Dried Food* Parched seeds eaten dry. *Porridge* Parched seeds ground into flour and used to make mush. (15:84)

Lathyrus brachycalyx ssp. *brachycalyx*, Bonneville Peavine
Omaha *Unspecified* Roasted pods eaten by children in sport, but not considered of any importance. **Ponca** *Unspecified* Roasted seedpods eaten by children in sport, but not considered of any importance. (as *L. ornatus* 70:98)

Lathyrus graminifolius, Grassleaf Peavine
Karok *Vegetable* Tender plant eaten as greens in the spring. (148:385)

Lathyrus japonicus var. *maritimus*, Sea Peavine
Eskimo, Alaska *Beverage* Roasted seeds used to make coffee. (as *L. maritimus* 4:715) **Iroquois** *Vegetable* Stalks eaten as greens in spring. (as *L. maritimus* 124:93) **Makah** *Vegetable* Immature seeds eaten as peas. (67:281)

Lathyrus jepsonii ssp. *californicus*, California Peavine
Mendocino Indian *Fodder* Cut for hay and used as fodder for horses and cattle. **Yokia** *Vegetable* Cooked and eaten as greens when 3 inches high. (as *L. watsoni* 41:357)

Lathyrus lanszwertii var. *leucanthus*, Aspen Peavine
Apache, Chiricahua & Mescalero *Dried Food* Ripe pods dried, stored, and soaked and boiled when needed. *Unspecified* Ripe pods cooked and eaten. (as *L. leucanthus* 33:49)

Lathyrus nevadensis ssp. *lanceolatus* var. *nuttallii*, Nuttall's Peavine
Thompson *Forage* Used as a general forage for animals. (as *L. nuttallii* 164:516)

Lathyrus ochroleucus, Cream Peavine
Ojibwa *Fodder* Leaves and roots used to put spirit into a pony just before they expected to race him. (153:419) *Vegetable* Peas used for food. (135:235) Roots used as a sort of Indian potato and stored in deep garden pits, like regular potatoes. (153:406)

Lathyrus palustris, Slenderstem Peavine
Chippewa *Unspecified* Full grown peas shelled and cooked for food. (71:133) **Ojibwa** *Fodder* Foliage was specially fed to a pony to make it grow fat. (153:419) *Vegetable* Peas used for food. (135:235)

Lathyrus polymorphus ssp. *polymorphus* var. *polymorphus*, Manystem Peavine
Acoma *Unspecified* Whole pods used for food. **Cochiti** *Unspecified* Whole pods used for food. (as *L. decaphyllus* 32:32) **Keres, Western** *Vegetable* Peas used for food. (as *L. decaphyllus* 171:51) **Laguna** *Unspecified* Whole pods used for food. (as *L. decaphyllus* 32:32)

Lathyrus vestitus, Pacific Peavine
Miwok *Unspecified* Raw seeds used for food. *Vegetable* Greens used for food. (12:159)

Layia glandulosa, Whitedaisy Tidytips
Cahuilla *Porridge* Seeds ground into flour and used with other ground seeds in a mush. (15:84) **Luiseño** *Unspecified* Seeds used for food. (155:228)

Layia platyglossa, Coastal Tidytips
Cahuilla *Porridge* Seeds ground into flour and used with other ground seeds in a mush. (15:85) **Costanoan** *Staple* Seeds eaten in pinole. (21:254) **Mendocino Indian** *Staple* Seeds used to make a pinole. (as *Blepharipappus platyglossus* 41:393)

Ledum ×columbianum, Coast Labradortea
Pomo, Kashaya *Beverage* Leaves used to make a beverage tea. (as *L. glandulosum* ssp. *columbianum* 72:113)

Ledum glandulosum, Western Labradortea
Tolowa *Beverage* Leaves simmered to make tea. **Yurok** *Beverage* Leaves simmered to make a most prized tea. (6:34)

Ledum groenlandicum, Bog Labradortea
Alaska Native *Beverage* Strongly, aromatic leaves used to make tea. (as *L. palustre* ssp. *groenlandicum* 85:35) **Algonquin, Quebec** *Beverage* Leaves used to make tea and medicinal tea. (18:116) **Anticosti** *Beverage* Used to make tea. (143:68) **Bella Coola** *Beverage* Leaves boiled and used as a beverage. (184:205) **Chippewa** *Beverage* Leaves used to make a beverage. (53:317) **Cree** *Beverage* Used to make tea. (16:484) **Cree, Woodlands** *Beverage* Plant, with flower tops removed, used to make a tea. (109:42) **Eskimo, Arctic** *Beverage* Leaves dried and used as a substitute for tea. (128:31) **Haisla & Hanaksiala** *Beverage* Leaves used to make tea. (43:241) **Hesquiat** *Beverage* Toasted, dried leaves brewed or steeped to make tea. (185:65) **Kitasoo** *Beverage* Leaves used to make a beverage. (43:333) **Kwakiutl, Southern** *Beverage* Leaves used to make a hot, refreshing drink. (183:293) Leaves used to make tea. (183:283) **Makah** *Beverage* Leaves used to make a beverage tea. (67:301) Leaves steeped and drunk as a beverage tea. (79:43) **Malecite** *Beverage* Used to make tea. (160:6) **Micmac** *Beverage* Used to make a beverage. (159:258) **Nitinaht** *Beverage* Fresh or dried plant used to

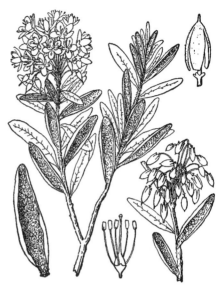

Ledum groenlandicum

make a hot tea beverage. (186:106) **Ojibwa** *Beverage* Leaves used to make tea. (96:17) Tender leaves used for beverage tea, a well-known tea, and sometimes eaten with the tea. (153:401) **Okanagan-Colville** *Beverage* Leaves and twigs used to make tea. (188:102) **Oweekeno** *Beverage* Leaves used to make tea. (43:96) **Potawatomi** *Beverage* Leaves used to make a beverage and also used as a brown dye material. (154:120) Leaves used to make a beverage. (154:99) **Saanich** *Beverage* Fresh or dried leaves made into tea. **Salish, Coast** *Beverage* Fresh or dried leaves made into tea. (182:83) **Shuswap** *Beverage* Dried leaves mixed with tea or mint. (123:62) **Thompson** *Beverage* Leaves made into a tea-like beverage. Leaves and twigs made into a tea-like beverage and used in place of coffee. (187:214)

Ledum palustre, Marsh Labradortea
Eskimo, Inupiat *Beverage* Young, dried, stored leaves used to make tea. (98:60) **Tanana, Upper** *Beverage* Leaves and stems used to make tea. *Spice* Leaves used as a spice for strong tasting meat. (102:16)

Ledum palustre ssp. decumbens,
Marsh Labradortea
Eskimo, Alaska *Beverage* Leaves used for tea.
(as *L. decumbens* 4:715) *Spice* Sprigs added
to tea to give it flavor. (1:37) **Eskimo, Arctic**
Beverage Leaves dried and used as a substitute
for tea. (as *L. decumbens* 128:31) **Eskimo,
Inupiat** *Beverage* Young, dried, stored leaves
used to make tea. (as *L. decumbens* 98:60)

Lens culinaris, Lentil
Papago *Dried Food* Threshed, dried on the
ground or roofs, stored, and used for food. (as
L. esculenta 34:33) *Unspecified* Species used
for food. **Pima** *Unspecified* Species used for
food. (as *L. esculenta* 36:120)

Lepidium campestre, Field
Pepperweed
Cherokee *Unspecified* Young plants boiled,
fried, and eaten. (204:252)

Lepidium fremontii, Desert
Pepperweed
Kawaiisu *Beverage* Seeds pounded, mixed
with water, and used as a beverage. (206:36)

Lepidium lasiocarpum, Shaggyfruit
Pepperweed
Havasupai *Bread & Cake* Seeds used to make
bread. (197:66) *Preserves* Seeds parched,
ground, kneaded into seed butter, and eaten
with fruit drinks or spread on bread. *Staple*
Seeds ground and eaten as a ground or parched
meal. (197:67) *Unspecified* Seeds used in a variety of ways. (197:220)

Lepidium montanum, Mountain
Pepperweed
Havasupai *Unspecified* Seeds used in a variety
of ways. (197:220) **Navajo, Ramah** *Fodder*
Used for sheep and horse feed. (191:29)

Lepidium nitidum, Shining Pepperweed
Diegueño *Vegetable* Plant tops and flowers
boiled and eaten as greens. (84:23) **Luiseño**
Unspecified Seeds used for food. *Vegetable*
Leaves used for greens. (155:232)

Lepidium thurberi, Thurber's
Pepperweed
Papago *Dried Food* Seeds basket winnowed,
parched, sun dried, cooked, stored, and used
for food. (34:24)

Lepidium virginicum, Virginia
Pepperweed
Cherokee *Unspecified* Species used for food.
(80:48) Young plants boiled, fried, and eaten.
(204:252)

**Lepidium virginicum var. men-
ziesii**, Menzies's Pepperweed
Hoh *Unspecified* Eaten raw. *Vegetable* Leaves
eaten as greens. **Quileute** *Unspecified* Eaten
raw. *Vegetable* Leaves eaten as greens. (as *L.
menziesii* 137:62)

Lespedeza capitata, Roundhead
Lespedeza
Comanche *Beverage* Leaves boiled for tea.
(29:522)

Lessoniopsis littoralis, Short Kelp
Hesquiat *Dried Food* Stipes and fronds with
attached herring eggs dried for later use.
(185:24)

Leucocrinum montanum, Common
Starlily
Crow *Unspecified* Roots used for food. (19:14)

Lewisia columbiana, Columbian
Bitterroot
Okanagon *Winter Use Food* Steamed or boiled
and used as a winter food. (125:36) **Thompson**
Unspecified Fleshy roots eaten. (164:480) *Winter Use Food* Steamed or boiled and used as a
winter food. (125:36) **Thompson, Upper
(Nicola Band)** *Unspecified* Fleshy roots eaten.
(164:480)

Lewisia pygmaea, Pigmy Bitterroot
Blackfoot *Dried Food* Roots dried for future
use. (97:34) **Thompson** *Unspecified* Roots
used for food. (164:479)

Lewisia rediviva, Oregon Bitterroot
Blackfoot *Unspecified* Plant boiled and eaten.
(114:278) **Coeur d'Alene** *Vegetable* Roots used
as a principal vegetable food. (178:88) **Kutenai**
Cooking Agent Roots steamed and used to
thicken gravy. *Dessert* Roots steamed, added
to camas bulbs, and eaten as a "sweet treat."
Dried Food Roots dried, stored, and used for
food. *Unspecified* Roots used for food as the
most important root crop. (82:46) **Montana
Indian** *Unspecified* Small pieces of bitterroot
steeped, boiled in water, and eaten. (19:14)
Roots boiled or steamed and eaten plain, mixed
with berries, or added to meat or bone marrow.
(82:46) **Okanagan-Colville** *Dried Food* Roots
peeled and dried for future use. *Unspecified*
Fresh or dried roots steamed or boiled and eat-
en. (188:114) **Okanagon** *Staple* Roots used as
a principal food. (178:238) *Unspecified* Roots
used as an important food. (178:237) *Winter
Use Food* Steamed or boiled and used as a winter food. (125:36) **Oregon Indian, Warm
Springs** *Unspecified* Roots used for food. **Paiute** *Dried Food* Roots dried and used for food.
Unspecified Roots boiled "like macaroni."
(104:102) *Winter Use Food* Roots peeled and
dried for winter use and boiled and eaten with
salmon. (111:70) **Paiute, Northern** *Unspecified* Roots peeled, boiled, or roasted and eaten
without grinding. *Vegetable* Leaves boiled like
spinach and eaten. (59:43) **Sanpoil & Nespelem** *Porridge* Roots mixed with serviceberries,
grease or fat added, and boiled into a congealed
mass. (131:100) **Shuswap** *Unspecified* Roots
cooked with serviceberries. (123:65) **Spokan**
Unspecified Roots used for food. (178:343)
Thompson *Bread & Cake* Roots used as an ingredient in fruit cake. *Dried Food* Peeled roots
dried loose or large roots stored on strings for
future use. The roots were dried on strings in
order to determine the market value or trade
worth. The dried roots were eaten with saskatoon berries and salmon eggs. *Pie & Pudding*
Roots cooked with black tree lichen, dough, and
fresh salmon and made into a pudding. Sometimes the roots were cooked with black tree lichen, fermented salmon eggs, yellow avalanche
lily corms, saskatoon berries, and deer fat to
make a similar kind of pudding. *Special Food*
Dried roots cooked in soups such as fish head
soup, but only served on special occasions. Because the roots were so valuable, they were only
served on special occasions. (187:243) *Unspecified* Used as an important food. (164:478)
Fleshy taproot eaten. (164:479) Roots used as
an important food. (178:237) Fresh roots pit
cooked or boiled in watertight baskets using
red-hot stones. (187:243) *Winter Use Food*
Steamed or boiled and used as a winter food.
(125:36)

Leymus cinereus, Basin Wildrye
Blackfoot *Forage* Used for grazing during the
winter. (as *Elymus cinereus* 97:20) **Okanagan-Colville** *Fodder* Leaves used as bedding
and horse feed. (as *Elymus cinereus* 188:55)

Leymus condensatus, Giant Wildrye
Klamath *Unspecified* Grains used for food. (as
Elymus condensatus 45:91) **Montana Indian**
Unspecified Seeds used for food. (as *Elymus
condensatus* 19:11) **Paiute** *Unspecified* Species
used for food. (as *Elymus condensatus*
167:244) **Paiute, Southern** *Unspecified* Species used for food. (as *Elymus condensatus*
15:69) **Shoshoni** *Starvation Food* Seeds stored
for times of famine. (as *Elymus condensatus*
118:17)

Leymus triticoides, Beardless Wildrye
Kawaiisu *Forage* Plant eaten by cows. *Porridge*
Seeds pounded in a bedrock mortar hole,
cooked into a thick mush and eaten. (as *Elymus
triticoides* 206:27) **Mendocino Indian** *Fodder*
Foliage used as fodder in late summer. *Staple*
Seeds used for pinole. (as *Elymus triticoides*
41:312)

Liatris punctata, Dotted Gayfeather
Blackfoot *Unspecified* Roots used for food.
(97:59) **Kiowa** *Unspecified* Springtime, sweet
roots baked over a fire and eaten. (192:61)
Lakota *Dietary Aid* Roots pulverized and eaten
to improve the appetite. (139:38)

Liatris punctata var. *punctata*,
Dotted Gayfeather
Blackfoot *Unspecified* Plant eaten raw. (as
Lacinaria punctata 114:274) **Kiowa** *Unspecified* Springtime, sweet roots baked over a fire
and eaten. (as *Lacinaria punctata* 192:61)
Tewa *Unspecified* Roots eaten as food. (as
Laciniaria punctata 138:57)

Licania michauxii, Gopher Apple
Seminole *Forage* Berries eaten by gophers.
(as *Chrysobalanus oblongifolius* 169:434)

Ligusticum californicum, California
Licoriceroot
Tolowa *Unspecified* Roots used for food. (6:34)

Ligusticum canadense, Canadian
Licoriceroot
Cherokee *Dried Food* Fresh greens gathered
into a bundle, dried, and hung until needed.
(126:58) *Unspecified* Young growth boiled,
fried with ramps (*Allium tricoccum?*) and eaten.
(204:252) *Vegetable* Leaves cooked and eaten
as greens. (80:61) Leaves and stalks boiled,
rinsed, and fried with grease and salt until soft
as a potherb. *Winter Use Food* Leaves and stalks
blanched, boiled in a can, and stored for future
use. (126:58)

Ligusticum canadense

Ligusticum grayi, Gray's Licoriceroot
Atsugewi *Substitution Food* Tender leaves
soaked in water, cooked, and used as a meat
substitute when acorns were eaten. *Vegetable*
Tender leaves soaked in water, cooked, and
used for food. *Winter Use Food* Tender leaves
soaked in water, cooked, and stored for later
use. (61:139)

Ligusticum porteri, Porter's
Licoriceroot
Apache, Chiricahua & Mescalero *Unspecified* Eaten without preparation or cooked with
green chile and meat or animal bones. (33:46)

Ligusticum scothicum, Scottish
Licoriceroot
Anticosti *Spice* Used to season fish or salads.
(143:67) **Eskimo, Inupiat** *Spice* Leaves used as
a spice for soups. *Vegetable* Leaves stored in oil
or cooked and eaten with dried meat or boiled
fish. Leaves used as greens in salads. (98:13)

Ligusticum scothicum ssp. hultenii, Hultén's Licoriceroot
Alaska Native *Dietary Aid* Fresh leaves used as
a good source for vitamins C and A. *Substitution Food* Leaves and stalks used as a substitute
for celery. *Unspecified* Leaves and stalks eaten
raw with seal oil. Leaves and stalks used in
cooking fish. *Vegetable* Leaves and stalks used
as a cooked vegetable. *Winter Use Food* Leaves
and stalks stored in seal oil for winter use. (as
L. hultenii 85:37) **Eskimo, Alaska** *Vegetable*
Young leaves and stems eaten raw or cooked
and often mixed with other wild greens. (1:37)
Winter Use Food Cut, mixed with fish, and
boiled for winter use. (as *L. hultenii* 4:715)

Lilium canadense, Canadian Lily
Cherokee *Starvation Food* Roots made into
flour and used to make bread for famine times.
(80:43) **Huron** *Starvation Food* Roots used
with acorns during famine. (3:63)

Lilium columbianum, Columbian Lily
Clallam *Unspecified* Bulbs steamed in pits and
used for food. (57:196) **Klallam** *Unspecified*

Corms steamed and eaten. **Lummi** *Unspecified* Corms steamed and eaten. (79:25) **Nitinaht** *Unspecified* Bulbs formerly steamed and eaten cold with oil. (186:85) **Okanagan-Colville** *Bread & Cake* Bulbs dried into cakes and stored for winter use. *Spice* Bulbs dried into cakes and used as seasoning in meat soups. *Unspecified* Bulbs eaten raw or boiled alone or with saskatoon berries. (188:46) **Okanogon** *Staple* Roots used as a principal food. (178:238) *Unspecified* Roots used as an important food. (178:237) Roots used extensively for food. (178:89) **Quileute** *Unspecified* Corms steamed and eaten. **Quinault** *Unspecified* Corms steamed and eaten. **Samish** *Unspecified* Corms steamed and eaten. (79:25) **Shuswap** *Unspecified* Roasted roots used for food. (123:54) Roots used extensively for food. (178:89) **Skagit** *Unspecified* Corms steamed and eaten. (79:25) **Skagit, Upper** *Unspecified* Bulbs baked or steamed in an earth oven and eaten. (179:40) **Skokomish** *Unspecified* Corms steamed and eaten. **Swinomish** *Unspecified* Corms steamed and eaten. (79:25) **Thompson** *Dried Food* Pit cooked bulbs dried for future use and usually cooked with meat. *Soup* Bulbs used to make a soup like clam chowder. A vegetable soup was made with salmon heads, bitterroot, tiger lily bulbs, water horehound roots, chocolate lily bulbs, the "dry" variety of saskatoon berries, dried powdered bracken fern rhizome, and chopped wild onions. *Spice* Thick, scaly bulbs eaten mainly as a condiment or cooked with food to add a pepper-like flavoring. (187:126) *Unspecified* Bulbs mixed with salmon roe and panther lily, boiled, and eaten as a favorite dish. Thick, scaly bulbs mixed with salmon roe, boiled, and eaten as a favorite dish. (as *L. parviflorum* 164:482) Roots used as an important food. (178:237) Roots used extensively for food. (178:89)

Lilium occidentale, Eureka Lily
Karok *Unspecified* Bulbs baked in the earth oven and eaten. (148:381)

Lilium pardalinum, Leopard Lily
Atsugewi *Unspecified* Bulbs cooked in earth oven and used for food. (61:138) **Karok** *Un-*

specified Bulbs baked in the earth oven and eaten. (148:381) **Yana** *Unspecified* Roots steamed and eaten. (147:251)

Lilium parvum, Sierran Tiger Lily
Paiute *Unspecified* Roots used for food. (167:244)

Lilium philadelphicum, Wood Lily
Blackfoot *Soup* Bulbs eaten with soup. *Unspecified* Bulbs eaten fresh. (86:103) **Meskwaki** *Vegetable* Straight roots gathered for potatoes. (152:262)

Lilium philadelphicum var. *andinum*, Wood Lily
Cree, Woodlands *Snack Food* Bulb segments eaten dried as a nibble. *Unspecified* Bulb segments eaten fresh. Seeds and underground bulbs used for food. (109:43)

Linanthus ciliatus, Whiskerbrush
Yuki *Substitution Food* Flowering heads used in the summer as a substitute for coffee. (41:381)

Lindera benzoin, Northern Spicebush
Cherokee *Beverage* Used to make a beverage. (80:56) Stems used to make tea. (126:44) *Spice* Used to flavor opossum or ground hog. (80:56)

Lindera benzoin var. *benzoin*, Northern Spicebush
Chippewa *Beverage* Leaves used to make a pleasant, tea-like beverage. *Spice* Leaves used as a flavor for masking or modifying the taste of naturally strong flavored meats. (as *Benzoin aestivale* 71:131)

Linnaea borealis, Twinflower
Carrier *Unspecified* Species used for food. (31:74)

Linum lewisii, Prairie Flax
Dakota *Fodder* Seeds used to flavor feed. (121:48) *Unspecified* Seeds used in cooking for the nutritive value and agreeable flavor. **Omaha**

Linum lewisii

Unspecified Seeds used in cooking for the nutritive value and agreeable flavor. **Pawnee** *Unspecified* Seeds used in cooking for the nutritive value and agreeable flavor. **Ponca** *Unspecified* Seeds used in cooking for the nutritive value and agreeable flavor. **Winnebago** *Unspecified* Seeds used in cooking for the nutritive value and agreeable flavor. (70:98)

Liquidambar styraciflua, Sweet Gum
Cherokee *Beverage* Bark, hearts-a-bustin-with-love (*Euonymus americana*), and summer grapes used to make tea. *Candy* Hardened gum used for chewing gum. (80:58)

Liriodendron tulipifera, Tuliptree
Cherokee *Sauce & Relish* Used to make honey. (80:50)

Lithocarpus densiflorus, Tan Oak
Costanoan *Unspecified* Acorns used for food. (21:248) **Hahwunkwut** *Bread & Cake* Acorns used to make bread. *Porridge* Acorns used to make mush. *Staple* Acorns used to make a meal. (117:187) **Hupa** *Bread & Cake* Acorns used to make bread, biscuits, pancakes, and cake. *Porridge* Acorns used to make mush. *Staple* Acorns used to make meal. *Unspecified* Acorns roasted and eaten. (117:200) **Karok**

Bread & Cake Acorn paste made into patties and baked in hot coals. *Porridge* Acorn flour used to make paste and gruel and flavored with venison and herbs. (6:35) Acorns shelled, dried, pounded into a meal, leached, and used to make gruel. (148:382) *Staple* Acorns considered the main staple. Acorns used to make flour. *Winter Use Food* Acorn flour stored in large storage baskets. (6:35) Acorns stored for winter use. (148:382) **Mendocino Indian** *Unspecified* Acorns leached and used for food. (as *Quercus densiflora* 41:342) **Poliklah** *Bread & Cake* Acorns used to make bread. (117:172) *Porridge* Acorns used to make mush. (117:170, 172) *Staple* Acorns form one of the principal foods. (117:168) **Pomo** *Bread & Cake* Acorns used to make black bread. (as *Quercus densiflora* 11:67) Acorns used to make bread. (117:290) *Porridge* Acorns used to make mush and gruel. (as *Quercus densiflora* 11:67) Moldy acorns mixed with whitened dried acorns and made into a mush. Leached acorns used for mush. (66:12) Acorns used to make mush. (117:290) *Soup* Acorns used to make soup. (as *Quercus densiflora* 11:67) Leached acorns used for soup. *Unspecified* Pulverized, leached acorns used for food. (66:12) **Pomo, Kashaya** *Dried Food* Acorns sun dried before storing. *Forage* Acorns collected by woodpeckers. *Porridge* Acorns used as flour for pancakes, bread, mush, or soup. (72:83) **Shasta** *Bread & Cake* Acorns pounded, winnowed, leached, and made into bread. *Porridge* Acorns pounded, winnowed, leached and made into mush. *Soup* Acorns pounded, winnowed, leached, and made into thin soup. *Staple* Acorns used as the basic staple. (as *Quercus densiflora* 93:308) **Tolowa** *Staple* Acorns considered the main staple. (6:35) **Yuki** *Bread & Cake* Acorns used to make pancakes. *Porridge* Acorns used to make mush. *Soup* Acorns used to make soup. (49:88) **Yurok** *Bread & Cake* Acorns used to make dough. *Soup* Acorns used to make soup. *Staple* Acorns considered the main staple. Acorns leached and ground into flour. (6:35) **Yurok, South Coast (Nererner)** *Staple* Acorns form one of the principal foods. (117:168)

Lithospermum canescens, Hoary
  Puccoon
Omaha *Cooking Agent* Root chewed with gum
by children, to color it red. Flowers chewed with
gum by children, to color it yellow. **Ponca**
Cooking Agent Root chewed with gum by children, to color it red. Flowers chewed with gum
by children, to color it yellow. (70:111)

Lithospermum incisum, Narrowleaf
  Gromwell
Blackfoot *Beverage* Roots used to make tea.
(as *L. angustifolium* 121:50) *Unspecified* Roots
eaten boiled or roasted. (as *L. linearifolium*
114:278) **Okanagon** *Unspecified* Plants boiled
and used for food. (as *Lithosperum angusto-
folium* 125:37) **Shoshoni** *Beverage* Roots used
to make tea. (as *Lithospermum angustifolium*
121:50) **Thompson** *Unspecified* Plants boiled
and used for food. (as *Lithosperum angusto-
folium* 125:37) Root cooked and eaten. (as
Lithospermum angustifolium 164:480)

Lithospermum multiflorum, Manyflowered Gromwell
Gosiute *Unspecified* Seeds formerly used for
food. (39:373)

Lithospermum ruderale, Western
  Gromwell
Gosiute *Unspecified* Seeds formerly used for
food. (as *L. pilosum* 39:373)

Lobularia maritima, Seaside
  Lobularia
Costanoan *Unspecified* Raw stems used for
food. (21:252)

Lolium temulentum, Darnel Ryegrass
Pomo *Staple* Seeds formerly used for pinole.
Yuki *Staple* Seeds formerly used for pinole.
(41:314)

Lomatium ambiguum, Wyeth
  Biscuitroot
Montana Indian *Staple* Spring roots reduced
to flour. *Unspecified* Spring roots eaten. (19:15)
Okanagan-Colville *Dried Food* Flowers and

upper leaves dried for future use. *Spice* Dried
flowers and upper leaves used to flavor meats,
stews, and salads. *Substitution Food* Flowers
and upper leaves sometimes used as a substitute
food. (188:70)

**Lomatium bicolor var. leptocar-
  pum**, Wasatch Desertparsley
Paiute *Dried Food* Roots dried and used for
food. *Unspecified* Roots eaten fresh. (as *L. lep-
tocarpum* 104:101)

Lomatium californicum, California
  Lomatium
Karok *Unspecified* Roots eaten raw. (as *Lepto-
taenia californica* 148:387) **Kawaiisu** *Vegeta-
ble* Spring leaves eaten raw as greens. (206:37)
Yuki *Unspecified* Young stems eaten raw.
Shoots cooked and used for food. (49:87)

Lomatium canbyi, Canby's Biscuitroot
Klamath *Dried Food* Dried roots used for food.
Porridge Mashed and boiled roots made into
mush. **Modoc** *Unspecified* Roots used for food.
(as *Peucedanum canbyi* 45:102) **Okanagan-
Colville** *Dried Food* Roots dried for future use.
Unspecified Roots eaten raw or pit cooked and
boiled. (188:64) **Paiute** *Bread & Cake* Peeled,
mashed roots formed into cakes and allowed to
dry, "Indian bread." (111:94) *Dried Food* Dried
roots cooked and used for food. *Unspecified*
Fresh roots cooked and used for food. (104:101)

Lomatium cous, Cous Biscuitroot
Montana Indian *Bread & Cake* Roots pulverized, moistened, partially baked, and made into
different sized cakes. *Dried Food* Whole roots
sun dried and stored for future food use. *Porridge* Roots pulverized and made into a gruel.
Soup Roots pulverized, moistened, partially
baked, mixed in water, and eaten as soup.
(82:26) *Staple* Spring roots eaten or reduced to
flour. *Unspecified* Spring roots eaten or reduced
to flour. (as *L. montanum* 19:15) Peeled roots
eaten raw or boiled. (82:26) **Okanagan-
Colville** *Dried Food* Roots dried for future use.
Unspecified Roots used for food. (188:65) **Oregon Indian** *Soup* Roots and fish used to make

stew. These roots were eaten at the first feast of the new year. This was called the Root Feast. (as *Cogswellia cous* 118:12)

Lomatium dissectum, Fernleaf Biscuitroot

Nez Perce *Unspecified* Roots pit baked and eaten. (82:26) **Okanagan-Colville** *Sauce & Relish* Young shoots eaten raw as a relish, alone or with meat. **Sanpoil** *Special Food* Shoots mixed with balsamroot and featured in the "first roots" ceremony. (188:66) **Shuswap** *Unspecified* Root of the young plant roasted and eaten. (123:56) **Thompson** *Unspecified* Roots dug in the early spring, pit cooked until soft, like balsamroots, and used for food. (187:154)

Lomatium dissectum var. *dissectum*, Fernleaf Biscuitroot

Okanagon *Dried Food* Thick, fleshy roots split, dried, and cooked for food. **Thompson** *Dried Food* Thick, fleshy roots split, dried, and cooked for food. (as *Leptotaenia dissecta* 125:37) Roots split, strung, dried, and cooked as needed. (as *Leptotaenia dissecta* 164:480)

Lomatium dissectum var. *multifidum*, Carrotleaf Biscuitroot

Gosiute *Unspecified* Young shoots, seeds used for food. (as *Ferula multifida* 39:369) **Great Basin Indian** *Beverage* Roots boiled to make a drink. *Vegetable* Long, young shoots cooked in the spring for greens. (as *Leptotaenia multifida* 121:49) **Montana Indian** *Unspecified* Young sprouts eaten, but poisonous to stock in early spring. (as *Leptotaenia multifida* 19:14)

Lomatium farinosum, Northern Biscuitroot

Okanagan-Colville *Unspecified* Roots boiled and eaten fresh. (188:68)

Lomatium geyeri, Geyer's Biscuitroot

Okanagan-Colville *Unspecified* Roots peeled, cooked, and eaten with bitterroot. (188:68)

Lomatium grayi, Gray's Biscuitroot

Paiute *Starvation Food* Roots eaten when hun-

gry in the winter. *Unspecified* Tender, young stems eaten raw. (111:95)

Lomatium macrocarpum, Bigseed Biscuitroot

Flathead *Dried Food* Roots dried and stored for future use. *Unspecified* Roots eaten raw. (82:26) **Okanagan-Colville** *Unspecified* Roots peeled and eaten raw or boiled. (188:69) **Okanagon** *Staple* Roots used as a principal food. (as *Peucedanum macrocarpum* 178:238) *Unspecified* Thick roots, tiger lily bulbs, and salmon roe boiled and eaten. (125:36) **Paiute** *Dried Food* Roots dried and used for food. *Unspecified* Roots eaten fresh. (104:101) Peeled roots eaten raw or baked. (111:95) **Paiute, Northern** *Unspecified* Roots roasted in the sand and eaten. (59:43) **Pomo, Kashaya** *Spice* Sweet seed used to flavor tea and pinole. *Unspecified* Young leaves used for food. (72:31) **Sanpoil** *Unspecified* Roots pit cooked and eaten. (188:69) **Shuswap** *Spice* Roots used to flavor dried salmon heated with dried bread over an open fire. *Unspecified* Roots roasted and eaten. (123:57) **Thompson** *Dried Food* Roots dug in the springtime, peeled, and dried for later use. *Pie & Pudding* Roots used in puddings. *Spice* Roots cooked with meat stews, saskatoon berries, or tiger lily bulbs as a flavoring. (187:155) *Unspecified* Thick roots, tiger lily bulbs, and salmon roe boiled and eaten. (125:36) Thick roots combined with salmon roe, boiled, and eaten. (as *Peucedanum macrocarpum* 164:479) Boiled roots used for food. (187:155)

Lomatium nevadense, Nevada Biscuitroot

Paiute, Northern *Unspecified* Roots eaten raw or cooked in the sand. (59:44)

Lomatium nevadense var. *parishii*, Parish's Biscuitroot

Paiute *Vegetable* Peeled roots eaten fresh like radishes. (111:95)

Lomatium nudicaule, Barestem Biscuitroot

Atsugewi *Unspecified* Raw leaves and tender

stems used for food. (61:139) **Okanagon** *Vegetable* Stalks used like celery. (125:38) **Paiute** *Vegetable* Stem eaten raw like celery. (111:96) **Thompson** *Beverage* Flowers, leaves, and stems dried, brought to a boil, and used as a drink. (as *Peucedanum leiocarpum* 164:494) Dried leaves used to make a tea-like beverage. Mature fruits, leaves and other plant parts preserved and used all year to make a tea-like beverage. Young, green fruits used to make tea. *Dried Food* Leaves frozen or canned for future use or dried and used to flavor stews or other dishes. *Frozen Food* Leaves frozen, canned, or dried for future use, and used to flavor stews or other dishes. *Fruit* Green, undeveloped fruits chewed raw. *Spice* Leaves used as a flavoring in soups and stews. Green, undeveloped fruits used as a flavoring. (187:156) *Unspecified* Stalks used for food. (as *Peucedanum leiocarpum* 164:484) Roots formerly used as food. (as *Peucedanum leiocarpum* 164:479) Stalks peeled and eaten as celery. (as *Peucedanum leiocarpum* 164:483) *Vegetable* Stalks used like celery. (125:38) Leaves eaten raw or cooked as a potherb. *Winter Use Food* Leaves frozen or canned for future use or dried and used to flavor stews and other dishes. (187:156)

Lomatium orientale, Northern Idaho Biscuitroot
Lakota *Unspecified* Roots used for food. (139:33) **Navajo** *Unspecified* Roots used for food. (55:68) Roots rubbed in hot ash to remove the strong taste and eaten raw or baked. (as *Cogswellia orientalis* 165:221)

Lomatium piperi, Indian Biscuitroot
Paiute *Unspecified* Roots used for food. (111:94)

Lomatium simplex, Narrowleaf Lomatium
Montana Indian *Vegetable* Fusiform root eaten baked, roasted, or raw. (19:15)

Lomatium simplex var. *leptophyllum*, Narrowleaf Lomatium
Blackfoot *Unspecified* Roots eaten raw or roasted. (97:48)

Lomatium simplex var. *simplex*, Great Basin Desertparsley
Montana Indian *Staple* Spring roots reduced to flour. *Unspecified* Spring roots eaten. (as *L. platycarpum* 19:15)

Lomatium triternatum, Nineleaf Biscuitroot
Atsugewi *Unspecified* Roots cooked in earth oven and used for food. (61:138) **Blackfoot** *Unspecified* Flowers used to make pemmican. (86:103) Roots eaten raw or roasted. (97:49) **Montana Indian** *Staple* Spring roots reduced to flour. *Unspecified* Spring roots eaten. (19:15) Roots eaten raw, roasted, or baked. (82:26) *Vegetable* Fusiform root eaten baked, roasted, or raw. (19:15) **Okanagan-Colville** *Dried Food* Flowers and upper leaves dried for future use. *Spice* Dried flowers and upper leaves used to flavor meats, stews, and salads. *Substitution Food* Flowers and upper leaves sometimes used as a substitute food. (188:70)

Lomatium utriculatum, Common Lomatium
Atsugewi *Unspecified* Raw leaves used for food. (61:139) **Kawaiisu** *Vegetable* Leaves, sometimes with flowers, cooked, fried in grease and salt, and eaten. (206:38) **Mendocino Indian** *Unspecified* Young leaves eaten raw in early summer. (41:373)

Lomatium watsonii, Watson's Desertparsley
Paiute *Winter Use Food* Peeled roots dried for winter use, ground, and boiled into a mush or used to flavor dried crickets. (111:94)

Lonicera ciliosa, Orange Honeysuckle
Nitinaht *Candy* Tubes formerly sucked by children for sweet nectar. (186:99) **Okanagan-Colville** *Forage* Flower nectar sucked by hummingbirds. (188:93) **Saanich** *Candy* Flower

nectar sucked by children. (182:79) **Thompson** *Candy* Nectar sucked from flowers by children. (187:196) *Forage* Flower nectar eaten by bees and hummingbirds. (164:516)

Lonicera conjugialis, Purpleflower Honeysuckle
Klamath *Fruit* Fresh berries used for food. (45:104)

Lonicera interrupta, Chaparral Honeysuckle
Mendocino Indian *Unspecified* Nectar sucked out of long, yellow flowers by children. (41:388)

Lonicera involucrata, Twinberry Honeysuckle
Bella Coola *Forage* Berries eaten by birds. (184:203) **Hesquiat** *Forage* Berries eaten by crows and other birds. (185:63) **Montana Indian** *Winter Use Food* Fruit dried and stored for winter use. (19:15) **Okanagan-Colville** *Forage* Berries eaten by bears. (188:94) **Okanagon** *Fruit* Fruits occasionally used for food. (125:39) **Oweekeno** *Fruit* Berries used for food. (43:89) **Thompson** *Forage* Berries eaten by grizzly bears. (187:197) *Fruit* Fruits occasionally used for food. (125:39) Berries eaten, but not commonly exploited as a food source. One informant ate the berries, but was told by her mother not to eat them. (187:197)

Lonicera involucrata

Lonicera utahensis, Utah Honeysuckle
Okanagan-Colville *Fruit* Berries used for food. (188:94)

Lotus mearnsii, Mearns's Birdsfoot Trefoil
Havasupai *Unspecified* Species used for food. (197:226)

Lotus procumbens, Silky Deerweed
Kawaiisu *Spice* Plant added to the dry pine needles spread as a layer in the pit roasting of the yucca. (206:38)

Lotus scoparius, Common Deerweed
Diegueño *Fodder* Leaves fed to domesticated animals. (88:218) **Tubatulabal** *Unspecified* Leaves used for food. (193:15)

Lotus strigosus, Bishop Lotus
Luiseño *Vegetable* Plant used for greens. (155:231)

Lotus unifoliolatus* var. *unifoliolatus, Prairie Trefoil
Kawaiisu *Spice* Plant used as a mat for the juniper cake which improves the taste of the cake. (as *L. purshianus* 206:39) **Miwok** *Cooking Agent* Green leaves pounded with oily acorns, to absorb some of the oil. (as *L. americanus* 12:144)

Lotus wrightii, Wright's Deervetch
Isleta *Forage* Considered an excellent grazing plant for sheep. (100:34)

Lupinus affinis, Fleshy Lupine
Mendocino Indian *Vegetable* Young leaves formerly roasted and eaten as greens. (as *L. carnosulus* 41:357)

Lupinus densiflorus, Whitewhorl Lupine
Miwok *Unspecified* Steamed leaves and flowers eaten with acorn soup. (12:159)

Lupinus latifolius, Broadleaf Lupine
Miwok *Sauce & Relish* Steamed, dried leaves

and flowers boiled and used as a relish with manzanita cider. *Winter Use Food* Steamed leaves and flowers dried and stored for winter use. (12:159)

Lupinus littoralis, Seashore Lupine
Haisla & Hanaksiala *Unspecified* Roots peeled and eaten raw. (43:249) **Kwakiutl, Southern** *Unspecified* Fleshy taproots eaten raw, boiled, or steamed in spring. If eaten raw, these roots caused dizziness. Therefore, they were usually eaten raw only before bedtime in the evening. (183:284)

Lupinus luteolus, Pale Yellow Lupine
Mendocino Indian *Forage* Succulent tops eaten sparingly by horses in early summer. *Vegetable* Plant tops eaten as greens. (41:358)

Lupinus nootkatensis, Nootka Lupine
Alaska Native *Unspecified* Roots peeled and inner portion eaten raw or boiled. (85:157)

Lupinus nootkatensis* var. *fruticosus, Nootka Lupine
Haisla & Hanaksiala *Unspecified* Roots peeled and eaten raw. (43:249) **Kimsquit** *Unspecified* Roots formerly roasted and used for food. (184:205)

Lupinus nootkatensis* var. *nootkatensis, Nootka Lupine
Haisla & Hanaksiala *Unspecified* Roots peeled and eaten raw. (43:249)

Lupinus polyphyllus, Bigleaf Lupine
Kwakiutl *Unspecified* Roots eaten fresh or steamed. (182:84)

Lupinus sericeus, Silky Lupine
Okanagan-Colville *Forage* Plant considered the marmot's favorite food. (188:105)

Lupinus sulphureus, Sulphur Lupine
Okanagan-Colville *Forage* Plant considered the marmot's favorite food. (188:105)

Lupinus wyethii, Wyeth's Lupine
Okanagan-Colville *Forage* Plant considered the marmot's favorite food. (188:105)

Lycium andersonii, Anderson's Wolfberry
Paiute, Northern *Dried Food* Berries dried in the sand for winter use. (59:50)

Lycium andersonii, Anderson's Wolfberry
Cahuilla *Dried Food* Dried berries boiled into mush or ground into flour and mixed with water. *Fruit* Berries eaten fresh. (15:87) **Kawaiisu** *Beverage* Fruit juice used as a beverage. *Dried Food* Fruit mashed, dried, soaked in warm water for an hour, and eaten. *Fruit* Fruit eaten fresh. (206:39) **Mohave** *Beverage* Berries crushed, strained, and used as a drink. *Dried Food* Berries dried like raisins. (37:205) **Paiute, Northern** *Fruit* Berries eaten fresh and crushed or mixed with water. *Porridge* Berries dried, mashed, and eaten like a mush. (59:50)

Lycium exsertum, Arizona Desertthorn
Yuma *Beverage* Berries gathered, washed, boiled, ground, mixed with water, and used as a beverage. *Dried Food* Berries sun dried, stored, and eaten without preparation. Berries washed, boiled, dried, and stored. *Porridge* Berries washed, boiled, strained, mashed, and wheat added to make mush. (37:204)

Lycium fremontii, Frémont's Desertthorn
Cahuilla *Dried Food* Dried berries boiled into mush or ground into flour and mixed with water. *Fruit* Berries eaten fresh. (15:87) **Maricopa** *Fruit* Black berries used for food. (95:265) **Papago** *Dried Food* Berries dried and eaten like raisins. (34:19) *Fruit* Berries used for food. (36:62) **Pima** *Beverage* Red berries boiled, mashed, and the liquid used as a beverage. (47:87) *Fruit* Red berries cooked and eaten warm or cold with sugar. (95:262) Red berries boiled and eaten. (146:75) **Yuma** *Beverage* Berries gathered, washed, boiled, ground,

mixed with water, and used as a beverage. *Dried Food* Berries sun dried, stored, and eaten without preparation. Berries washed, boiled, dried, and stored. *Porridge* Berries washed, boiled, strained, mashed, and wheat added to make mush. (37:204)

Lycium pallidum, Pale Wolfberry
Acoma *Sauce & Relish* Berries cooked into a syrup. (32:33) **Havasupai** *Beverage* Dried berries ground and mixed with water to make a drink. *Dried Food* Berries sun dried for future use. (197:239) **Hopi** *Fruit* Berries eaten fresh from the shrub. (56:19) Berries eaten. (138:47) *Porridge* Ground berries mixed with "potato clay" and eaten. (42:332) *Preserves* Berries cooked to make a jam-like food and served with fresh piki bread. (120:19) *Starvation Food* Berries boiled, ground, mixed with "potato clay," and eaten during past famines. (200:89) *Unspecified* Seeds eaten. (190:166) **Isleta** *Fruit* Fresh, summer berries eaten for food. (100:34) **Jemez** *Fruit* Ripe or cooked berries used for food. *Special Food* Unripe berries stewed, sweetened, and eaten as a delicacy. (32:33) **Keres, Western** *Sauce & Relish* Cooked berries made into a syrup. (171:52) **Laguna** *Sauce & Relish* Berries cooked into a syrup. (32:33) **Navajo** *Beverage* Berries mashed in water and used as a beverage. (110:32) *Dried Food* Fruits boiled, dried, stored for winter use, and eaten dry. (55:74) Sun dried berries used for food. (110:32) *Fruit* Fruits eaten fresh. (55:74) Berries used for food. (90:153) Berries eaten fresh off the bush. (110:32) Fresh, mashed berries mixed with powdered clay to counteract astringency and used for food. (165:222) *Soup* Fruits boiled, dried, stored for winter use, and made into a soup. (55:74) Berries used to make soup and stew. (110:32) *Special Food* Fruit sacrificed to the gods. (55:74) *Winter Use Food* Fresh berries soaked, boiled until tender, ground with clay, and stored for winter use. (165:222) **Navajo, Ramah** *Dried Food* Berries dried and boiled with clay, sugar, or wild potatoes. *Fruit* Berries eaten raw or boiled with clay. (191:42) **Zuni** *Fruit* Berries eaten raw when perfectly

ripe or boiled and sometimes sweetened. (166:68)

Lycium torreyi, Squawthorn
Navajo, Ramah *Dried Food* Berries dried and boiled with clay, sugar, or wild potatoes. *Fruit* Berries eaten raw or boiled with clay. (191:42) **Tubatulabal** *Fruit* Berries used extensively for food. (193:15)

Lycopersicon esculentum, Garden Tomato
Haisla & Hanaksiala *Fruit* Fruit used for food. (43:291) **Seminole** *Unspecified* Plant used for food. (169:508)

Lycopus asper, Rough Bugleweed
Chippewa *Dried Food* Dried, boiled, and used for food. (53:320)

Lycopus uniflorus, Northern Bugleweed
Okanagon *Staple* Roots used as a principal food. (as *Cycopus uniflorus* 178:238) **Thompson** *Dessert* Cooked tuberous root eaten for dessert. (187:232) *Unspecified* Roots eaten. (164:480) Tuberous root steamed or baked and used for food. (187:232)

Lygodesmia grandiflora, Large-flower Skeletonplant
Hopi *Spice* Boiled with a certain kind of mush for flavor. (190:168) *Unspecified* Leaves boiled with meats and eaten. (56:19) Leaves boiled with meat. (200:97) **Navajo, Kayenta** *Vegetable* Used for greens in foods. (205:48)

Lygodesmia juncea, Rush Skeletonplant
Lakota *Unspecified* Plant chewed. (139:38) **Navajo, Ramah** *Candy* Roots left in the sun until gum came out and hardened and used for chewing gum. (191:52) **Sioux** *Unspecified* Hardened juice chewed for the flavor. (82:27)

Lysichiton americanus, American Skunkcabbage
Cowlitz *Unspecified* Blossoms cooked over-

night and eaten no more than two or three at a time, otherwise one became sick. (79:22) **Haisla & Hanaksiala** *Forage* Roots eaten by black and grizzly bears after hibernation, to cleanse and strengthen their stomachs. (43:189) **Hesquiat** *Forage* Roots eaten by deer and bear. (185:48) **Hoh** *Forage* Plants eaten by bears in spring. *Spice* Leaves placed over roasting camas, wild onion, or garlic for flavoring. (as *L. camtschatcense* 137:59) **Okanagan-Colville** *Forage* Flower stalks sucked by grizzly and black bears. (188:35) **Oweekeno** *Forage* Roots eaten by bears after emerging from hibernation. (43:76) **Quileute** *Forage* Plants eaten by bears in spring. *Spice* Leaves placed over roasting camas, wild onion, or garlic for flavoring. (as *L. camtschatcense* 137:59) *Unspecified* Root cooked and eaten. **Skokomish** *Unspecified* Young leaves steamed and eaten. (79:22) **Tolowa** *Unspecified* Root centers eaten after boiling eight times. **Yurok** *Unspecified* Root centers eaten after boiling eight times. (6:38)

Machaeranthera gracilis, Slender Goldenweed
Navajo, Ramah *Dried Food* Dried seeds used for food. (as *Aplopappus gracilis* 191:47)

Machaerocereus eruca
Papago & Pima *Fruit* Fruit used for food. (35:42)

Machaerocereus gummosus, Pitahaya Agria
Papago & Pima Fruit used for food. (35:40)

Macrocystis integrifolia, Giant Kelp
Haisla & Hanaksiala *Unspecified* Plant used to collect herring roe, dried and eaten with the roe. (43:127) **Kitasoo** *Unspecified* Plant eaten with herring roe. (43:303) **Oweekeno** *Dried Food* Plant and herring eggs dried for future use. *Unspecified* Plant eaten with herring roe. *Winter Use Food* Plant and herring eggs preserved in brine for future use. (43:45)

Macrocystis luetkeana, Giant Kelp
Pomo *Unspecified* Plant chewed raw. (as *M. lütkeana* 11:94)

Madia capitata, Coast Tarweed
Pomo *Staple* Seeds used to make pinoles. (11:87)

Madia elegans, Common Madia
Hupa *Staple* Seeds parched and pounded into a flour. (148:390) **Mewuk** *Staple* Seeds roasted with hot coals, pounded or rolled into flour, and eaten dry. (117:338) **Miwok** *Staple* Pulverized seeds eaten as a dry meal. (12:154) **Neeshenam** *Bread & Cake* Seeds parched, ground into flour, and used to make bread. *Porridge* Seeds parched, ground into flour, and used to make mush. *Staple* Seeds parched, ground into flour, and used for food. (as *Madaria*, tarry smelling weed 129:377) **Pomo** *Staple* Seeds used to make pinoles. (11:87) **Pomo, Kashaya** *Staple* Seeds used to make pinole. (72:112) **Shoshoni** *Unspecified* Seeds roasted and eaten alone or mixed with manzanita berries, acorns, and pine nuts. (117:440)

Madia elegans ssp. *densifolia*, Showy Tarweed
Pomo *Staple* Seeds used to make pinoles. (as *M. densifolia* 11:87)

Madia glomerata, Mountain Tarweed
Crow *Unspecified* Seeds used for food. (19:15)
Klamath *Unspecified* Seeds used for food.
(45:106)

Madia gracilis ssp. gracilis, Grassy
  Tarweed
Mendocino Indian *Staple* Seeds used to make
pinole. (as *M. dissitiflora* 41:395) **Miwok** *Staple* Parched, pulverized seeds made into oily
meal and readily picked up in lumps. (as *M. dissitiflora* 12:154) **Pomo** *Staple* Seeds used to
make pinoles. (as *M. dissitiflora* 11:87)

Madia sativa, Coast Tarweed
Mendocino Indian *Cooking Agent* Oil from
seeds used for cooking. (41:395) **Miwok** *Unspecified* Seeds used for food. (12:154) **Pomo**
Porridge Parched, pulverized seeds eaten as
pinole and meal moistened to keep people from
choking on dry meal. (66:15) *Staple* Seeds used
to make pinoles. (11:87) *Winter Use Food* Raw
seeds stored for later use, parched, and pounded
when used for food. (66:15) **Pomo, Kashaya**
Staple Seeds used to make pinole. (72:111)

Mahonia aquifolium, Hollyleaved
  Barberry
Klallam *Fruit* Berries used for food. (as *Berberis aquifolium* 78:197) **Kwakiutl, Southern**

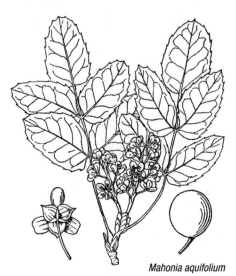
Mahonia aquifolium

Fruit Sour berries occasionally used for food.
(as *Berberis aquifolium* 183:279) **Makah** *Preserves* Fruit used to make preserves. (as *Berbaris aquifolium* 67:254) **Okanagan-Colville**
Fruit Berries eaten raw. (as *Berberis aquifolium* 188:85) **Salish, Coast** *Preserves* Berries
used to make jelly. (as *Berberis aquifolium*
182:78) **Samish** *Fruit* Berries eaten fresh. (as
Berberis aquifolium 79:30) **Sanpoil** *Fruit* Berries eaten fresh. *Preserves* Berries boiled into a
jam. (as *Berberis aquifolium* 188:85) **Sanpoil
& Nespelem** *Fruit* Berries eaten fresh. (as *Berberis aquifolium* 131:102) **Skagit, Upper**
Dried Food Berries pulped, dried, and stored in
cakes for winter use. (as *Berberis aquifolium*
179:37) *Fruit* Fruit eaten raw or mashed. (as
Berberis aquifolium 179:38) **Snohomish** *Fruit*
Berries eaten fresh. **Squaxin** *Fruit* Berries eaten. **Swinomish** *Fruit* Berries eaten fresh. (as
Berberis aquifolium 79:30) **Thompson** *Dried
Food* Fruit dried in the absence of any other
fruit. *Fruit* Fruit eaten fresh, a few at a time.
Preserves Fruit used to make jelly. (187:187)

Mahonia fremontii, Frémont's Mahonia
Hualapai *Beverage* Berries used to make a
beverage. *Fruit* Berries used for food. (as *Berberis fermontii* 195:5) **Yavapai** *Fruit* Raw
berries used for food. (65:257)

Mahonia haematocarpa, Red
  Barberry
Apache *Fruit* Berries eaten fresh. (as *Berberis
haematocarpa* 32:19) **Apache, Chiricahua &
Mescalero** *Preserves* Fruit cooked with a sweet
substance, strained, and eaten as jelly. (as *Berberis haematocarpa* 33:46) **Apache, Mescalero** *Fruit* Berries eaten fresh. (as *Berberis
haematocarpa* 14:49) **Pueblo** *Preserves* Berries used to make jelly. **Spanish American**
Preserves Berries used to make jelly. (as *Berberis haematocarpa* 32:19)

Mahonia nervosa, Cascade
  Oregongrape
Thompson *Preserves* Berries used to make
jelly. (187:187)

Mahonia nervosa var. *nervosa*,
Cascade Oregongrape

Clallam *Fruit* Sour berries used for food. (as *Berberis nervosa* 57:197) **Hoh** *Preserves* Berries used to make jelly. (as *Berberis nervosa* 137:61) **Klallam** *Fruit* Berries used for food. (as *Berberis nervosa* 78:197) **Kwakiutl, Southern** *Fruit* Sour berries occasionally used for food. (as *Berberis nervosa* 183:279) **Makah** *Preserves* Fruit used to make preserves. (as *Berbaris nervosa* 67:254) **Quileute** *Preserves* Berries used to make jelly. (as *Berberis nervosa* 137:61) **Salish, Coast** *Preserves* Berries used to make jelly. (as *Berberis nervosa* 182:78) **Skagit** *Fruit* Ripe berries formerly used for food. *Preserves* Ripe berries used to make jam. (as *Berberis nervosa* 79:30) **Skagit, Upper** *Dried Food* Berries pulped, dried, and stored in cakes for winter use. (as *Berberis nervosa* 179:37) *Fruit* Fruit eaten raw or mashed. (as *Berberis nervosa* 179:38)

Mahonia repens, Oregongrape

Blackfoot *Fruit* Berries eaten when nothing else was available. (as *Berberis repens* 86:101) Fruit used for food. (as *Berberis repens* 97:35) **Cheyenne** *Fruit* Fruits eaten for food. (as *Berberis repens* 83:15) **Flathead** *Dessert* Berries mashed, sugar and milk added, and eaten as a dessert. *Fruit* Berries roasted and used for food. **Kutenai** *Appetizer* Root tea taken as an appetizer. *Dessert* Berries mashed, sugar and milk added, and eaten as a dessert. (as *Berberis repens* 82:18) **Montana Indian** *Beverage* Fruit used to make wine and "lemonade." (as *Berberis repens* 19:8) Berries crushed, mixed with sugar and water, and made into a refreshing beverage. (as *Berberis repens* 82:18) *Fruit* Fruit eaten raw. *Preserves* Fruit used to make jelly. (as *Berberis repens* 19:8) Berries used to make jams and jellies. (as *Berberis repens* 82:18) **Shuswap** *Fruit* Ripe berries used for food. (as *Berberis repens* 123:59)

Maianthemum canadense, Canada Beadruby

Potawatomi *Fruit* Berries eaten, but the preparation as a food was not discovered. (154:105)

Maianthemum dilatatum, Twoleaf False Solomon's Seal

Bella Coola *Fruit* Ripe berries occasionally eaten by hunters and berry pickers. (184:199) **Haisla & Hanaksiala** *Fruit* Fruits eaten for food. (43:198) **Hesquiat** *Fruit* Raw fruit eaten with oil. (185:55) **Kitasoo** *Fruit* Berries eaten fresh. (43:321) **Kwakiutl, Southern** *Fruit* Berries occasionally eaten raw. (183:273) **Oweekeno** *Forage* Berries eaten by frogs. (43:78) **Salish, Coast** *Fruit* Berries occasionally eaten raw. (182:76)

Maianthemum racemosum ssp. *amplexicaule*, Western Solomon's Seal

Tewa *Fruit* Ripe berries eaten. (as *Vagnera amplexicaulis* 138:70)

Maianthemum racemosum ssp. *racemosum*, Feather Solomon's Seal

Costanoan *Fruit* Fruits eaten for food. (as *Smilacina racemosa* 21:255) **Hanaksiala** *Beverage* Juice mixed with Pacific crabapples and high-bush cranberries and drunk. (as *Smilacina racemosa* 43:200) **Ojibwa** *Fodder* Roots added to oats to make a pony grow fat. *Vegetable* Roots soaked in lye water, parboiled to get

Maianthemum racemosum ssp. *racemosum*

rid of the lye, and cooked like potatoes. (as *Smilacina racemosa* 153:407) **Okanagan-Colville** *Unspecified* Rhizomes dried, soaked, pit cooked with camas, and eaten. (as *Smilacina racemosa* 188:48) **Okanagon** *Fruit* Bright-colored berries used for food. (as *Vagnera racemosa* 125:38) **Skagit, Upper** *Fruit* Berries used for food. (as *Smilacina racemosa* 179:38) **Thompson** *Forage* Rhizomes eaten by bears. (as *Smilacina racemosa* 187:127) *Fruit* Bright-colored berries used for food. (as *Vagnera racemosa* 125:38) Berries eaten in large quantities. (as *Vagnera racemosa* 164:486) *Spice* Leafy shoots cooked as a flavoring for meat. *Unspecified* Roots used for food. *Vegetable* Young shoots cooked and eaten like asparagus. (as *Smilacina racemosa* 187:127)

Maianthemum stellatum, Starry False Solomon's Seal

Bella Coola *Fruit* Berries chewed and juice swallowed. (as *Smilacina stellata* 184:199) **Okanagon** *Fruit* Bright-colored berries used for food. **Thompson** *Fruit* Bright-colored berries used for food. (as *Vagnera stellata* 125:38) Berries eaten in large quantities. (as *Vagnera stellata* 164:486)

Malacothrix californica, California Desertdandelion

Luiseño *Unspecified* Seeds used for food. (155:228)

Malus angustifolia, Southern Crabapple

Cherokee *Dried Food* Sun dried, sliced fruit used for food. *Preserves* Fruit used to make clear jelly. (126:56)

Malus coronaria, Sweet Crabapple

Cherokee *Fruit* Fruit used for food. (80:31)

Malus coronaria var. *coronaria*, Sweet Crabapple

Iroquois *Bread & Cake* Fruit mashed, made into small cakes, and dried for future use. *Dried Food* Raw or cooked fruit sun or fire dried and stored for future use. *Fruit* Dried fruit taken as a hunting food. *Sauce & Relish* Dried fruit cakes soaked in warm water and cooked as a sauce or mixed with corn bread. (as *Pyrus coronaria* 196:129) **Ojibwa** *Fruit* Fruit used for food. (as *Pyrus coronaria* 135:236)

Malus fusca, Oregon Crabapple

Alaska Native *Cooking Agent* Used as a source of pectin for jelly making. (85:85) **Bella Coola** *Fruit* Berries used for food. (as *Pyrus fusca* 184:209) **Chinook, Lower** *Fruit* Fruits stored in baskets until soft and used for food. (as *Pyrus diversifolia* 79:38) **Clallam** *Fruit* Fruit softened in baskets and eaten. (as *Pyrus fusca* 57:202) **Cowlitz** *Fruit* Fruits cooked, stored in baskets until soft and used for food. (as *Pyrus diversifolia* 79:38) **Haisla & Hanaksiala** *Fruit* Fruit used for food. *Winter Use Food* Fruit boiled and stored in the cooking water or oil for winter use. (43:265) **Hesquiat** *Dried Food* Sour fruit dried for future use. (as *Pyrus fusca* 185:73) **Hoh** *Fruit* Fruits eaten for food. (as *Pyrus diversifolia* 137:64) **Kitasoo** *Special Food* Fruit used as a food item associated with ceremonial situations. *Winter Use Food* Fruit stored in water and topped with mammal or fish grease or oil. (43:342) **Kwakiutl, Southern** *Special Food* Fruits boiled until soft and eaten with oil at large feasts. (as *Pyrus fusca* 183:290) **Makah** *Fruit* Ripe fruit used for food. (as *Pyrus fusca* 67:268) Fruits stored in baskets until soft and used for food. (as *Pyrus diversifolia* 79:38) *Preserves* Ripe fruit used to make jelly. (as *Pyrus fusca* 67:268) **Nitinaht** *Forage* Fruits eaten by grouse. *Fruit* Fruits eaten for food. (as *Pyrus fusca* 186:121) **Oweekeno** *Fruit* Overripe fruit cooked with sugar and eaten. Fruit boiled and stored under grease in special boxes for future use. (43:109) **Quileute** *Fruit* Fruits eaten raw. (as *Pyrus diversifolia* 79:38) Fruits eaten for food. (as *Pyrus diversifolia* 137:64) **Quinault** *Fruit* Fruits stored in baskets until soft and used for food. (as *Pyrus diversifolia* 79:38) **Salish, Coast** *Fruit* Berries used for food. (as *Pyrus fusca* 182:87) **Samish** *Fruit* Fruits eaten raw. (as *Pyrus diversifolia* 79:38) **Skagit, Upper** *Fruit* Fruit ripened in storage and then eaten. (as *Pyrus diversifolia*

179:38) **Swinomish** *Fruit* Fruits eaten raw. (as *Pyrus diversifolia* 79:38) **Thompson** *Fruit* Fruit picked in fall when still green, allowed to ripen in a basket, and eaten with oulachen (candlefish) oil. (187:262)

Malus ioensis, Prairie Crabapple
Omaha *Fruit* Fruit used for food. **Ponca** *Fruit* Fruit used for food. (70:86)

Malus ioensis **var. *ioensis***, Prairie Crabapple
Meskwaki *Preserves* Fruit reduced to jelly. *Winter Use Food* Fruit dried for winter use. (as *Pyrus ioensis* 152:263)

Malus sylvestris, Apple
Haisla & Hanaksiala *Fruit* Fruit used for food. (43:270) **Hopi** *Unspecified* Species used for food. (200:79) **Iroquois** *Bread & Cake* Fruit mashed, made into small cakes, and dried for future use. *Dried Food* Raw or cooked fruit sun or fire dried and stored for future use. *Fruit* Dried fruit taken as a hunting food. *Sauce & Relish* Dried fruit cakes soaked in warm water and cooked as a sauce or mixed with corn bread. (as *Pyrus malus* 196:129) **Oweekeno** *Fruit* Fruit used for food. (43:110)

Malva nicaeensis, Bull Mallow
Pima *Unspecified* Leaves cooked, mixed with white flour, cooked again, and used for food. (as *M. borealis* 95:264)

Malva parviflora, Cheeseweed Mallow
Pima *Forage* Seeds eaten by hogs. (47:79)

Mammillaria dioica, Strawberry Cactus
Diegueño *Fruit* Small fruits eaten raw. (84:25)

Mammillaria grahamii, Graham's Nipple Cactus
Apache, Chiricahua & Mescalero *Dried Food* Dried fruit cooked and eaten. *Fruit* Raw fruit used for food. Raw fruit used for food. (as *Neomammillaria olivia* 33:41) **Apache, San Carlos** *Fruit* Fruits eaten for food. (95:257)

Mammillaria grahamii **var. *grahamii***, Graham's Nipple Cactus
Pima, Gila River *Baby Food* Raw pulp eaten primarily by children. (as *M. microcarpa* 133:7) *Snack Food* Pulp eaten, primarily by children, as a snack food. (as *M. microcarpa* 133:5)

Mammillaria mainiae, Counterclockwise Nipple Cactus
Apache, Chiricahua & Mescalero *Fruit* Raw fruit used for food. (as *Neomammillaria mainiae* 33:41)

Mammillaria wrightii, Wright's Nipple Cactus
Navajo, Ramah *Unspecified* Stems and ripe fruits used for food. (as *Neomammillaria wrightii* 191:37)

Mangifera indica, Mango
Seminole *Unspecified* Plant used for food. (169:491)

Manihot esculenta, Tapioca
Seminole *Unspecified* Plant used for food. (169:490)

Marah oreganus, Coastal Manroot
Yurok *Beverage* Young shoots and *Polypodium* rhizomes used to make tea. (6:39)

Marattia **sp.**, Pala Fern
Hawaiian *Unspecified* Leaf stem bases overcooked and eaten. (112:68)

Marrubium vulgare, Horehound
Diegueño *Candy* Infusion of leaves mixed with honey and made into candy. (84:25) **Navajo, Ramah** *Fodder* Used for sheep feed, made the meat bitter. (191:41)

Martynia **sp.**, Devil's Claw
Apache, Western *Beverage* Seeds cracked and chewed for the juice. *Winter Use Food* Seeds stored in pottery, gourd, or water-basket receptacles. (26:189)

Matelea producta, Texas Milkvine
Apache, Chiricahua & Mescalero *Unspecified* Seeds eaten fresh or boiled. (as *Vincetoxicum productum* 33:45)

Matricaria discoidea, Disc Mayweed
Eskimo, Alaska *Candy* Plant tops chewed by children for the pleasant flavor. (as *M. matricarioides* 1:38) **Flathead** *Preservative* Plants dried, pulverized, and used to preserve meat and berries. **Kutenai** *Unspecified* Small, yellowish green flower heads eaten occasionally. **Montana Indian** *Unspecified* Occasionally used for food. (as *M. matricarioides* 82:23) **Okanagan-Colville** *Unspecified* Flower heads eaten by children. (as *M. matricarioides* 188:84)

Medicago polymorpha, Bur Clover
Cahuilla *Porridge* Parched, ground seeds used to make mush. (as *M. hispida* 15:88) **Mendocino Indian** *Forage* Seeds and leaves used as a forage plant. Dried seedpods eaten by sheep in summer. (as *M. denticulata* 41:358)

Medicago sativa, Alfalfa
Navajo, Ramah *Fodder* Plant cultivated, harvested, dried, stacked, or stored in hogans, and fed to livestock in winter. (191:32) **Okanagan-Colville** *Spice* Plants placed above and below black tree lichen and camas in cooking pits for the sweet flavor. (188:105) **Shuswap** *Fodder* Used for horse feed. (123:64)

Melica bulbosa, Oniongrass
Pomo *Porridge* Raw roots pounded like pinole. *Unspecified* Raw roots used for food. (66:11)

Melica imperfecta, Smallflower
  Melicgrass
Kawaiisu *Porridge* Seeds winnowed, pounded in a bedrock mortar, and cooked into a mush. (206:40)

Melilotus officinalis, Yellow
  Sweetclover
Jemez *Forage* Plant very nutritious food for horses. (as *M. alba* 44:25)

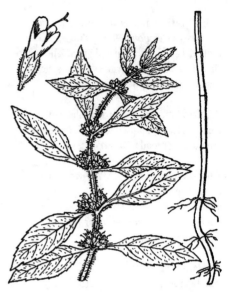

Mentha arvensis

Mentha arvensis, Wild Mint
Blackfoot *Beverage* Dried plant used to make tea. *Spice* Dried plant used to spice pemmican and soups. (86:103) **Cherokee** *Unspecified* Species used for food. (80:45) **Cheyenne** *Beverage* Leaves and stems made into a tea and used as a beverage. (83:27) **Kawaiisu** *Beverage* Green leaves brewed into an nonmedicinal beverage tea. (206:40) **Lakota** *Beverage* Used to make tea. (139:49) **Navajo, Kayenta** *Spice* Used as flavoring with meats or cornmeal mush. (205:40) **Okanagan-Colville** *Beverage* Stems used to make tea. (188:109) **Paiute** *Beverage* Dried leaves used to make a tea. (104:103) Leaves boiled into a refreshing drink. (167:245) **Saanich** *Spice* Leaves used for flavoring food. (182:84) **Sanpoil** *Beverage* Stems used to make tea. (188:109) **Shuswap** *Beverage* Leaves used in tea. (123:64) **Thompson** *Unspecified* Greens warmed over an open fire and eaten with dried fish. (187:233)

Mentha canadensis, Canadian Mint
Apache, Chiricahua & Mescalero *Spice* Leaves used as flavoring. (as *M. penardi* 33:47) **Blackfoot** *Beverage* Leaves used to make tea. *Spice* Leaves placed in parfleches to flavor dried meat. (114:278) **Chippewa** *Beverage* Leaves

used to make a pleasant, tea-like beverage. *Spice* Leaves used to add flavor to certain meats in cooking. (71:140) **Cree, Woodlands** *Beverage* Leaves added to store bought tea to improve the flavor. *Spice* Leaves added to sturgeon oil to sweeten the odor. (as *M. arvensis* var. *villosa* 109:45) **Dakota** *Beverage* Plant used to make a hot, tea-like beverage. (69:363) Plant used to make a tea-like beverage enjoyed for its pleasing, aromatic flavor. (70:112) *Spice* Plant used as a flavor for meat. (69:363) Plant used as a flavor in cooking meat. (70:112) *Unspecified* Plant laid in alternate layers with dried meat in the packing case. (69:363) Plant parts packed in alternate layers with dried meat for storage. (70:112) **Gosiute** *Beverage* Leaves formerly used to make tea. (39:374) **Hopi** *Sauce & Relish* Plant eaten as a relish. (56:19) *Spice* Boiled with mush for flavor. (190:165) **Klamath** *Beverage* Herbage used for tea. (45:104) **Malecite** *Spice* Plant used as a flavoring in soup. (116:250) **Ojibwa** *Beverage* Foliage used to make a beverage tea. (as *M. arvensis* var. *canadensis* 153:405) **Omaha** *Beverage* Leaves used to make a hot, aqueous, tea-like beverage. (68:329) Plant used to make a tea-like beverage enjoyed for its pleasing, aromatic flavor. (70:112) **Paiute** *Beverage* Fresh or dried leaves made into tea. (as *M. arvensis* var. *glabrata* 111:107) **Pawnee** *Beverage* Plant used to make a tea-like beverage enjoyed for its pleasing, aromatic flavor. **Ponca** *Beverage* Plant used to make a tea-like beverage enjoyed for its pleasing, aromatic flavor. (70:112) **Sanpoil & Nespelem** *Beverage* Leaves and stems boiled, liquid strained and drunk. (as *M. arvensis* var. *lanata* 131:104) **Winnebago** *Beverage* Plant used to make a tea-like beverage enjoyed for its pleasing, aromatic flavor. (70:112)

Mentha ×piperita
Cherokee *Spice* Used to flavor foods. *Unspecified* Species used for food. (water mint 80:48)

Mentha spicata, Spearmint
Cherokee *Spice* Used to flavor foods. *Unspecified* Species used for food. (80:48) **Kawaiisu** *Beverage* Leaves brewed into an nonmedicinal beverage tea. (206:41) **Miwok** *Beverage* Leaves

used for tea. (12:171) **Yuki** *Beverage* Used to make a beverage. (49:88)

Mentzelia affinis, Yellowcomet
Kawaiisu *Preserves* Seeds parched and ground into a "peanut butter"-like substance. *Winter Use Food* Seeds stored for future use. (206:41)

Mentzelia albicaulis, Whitestem Blazingstar
Cahuilla *Porridge* Parched seeds ground into flour and used to make mush. (15:88) **Havasupai** *Preserves* Seeds parched, ground, kneaded into seed butter, and eaten with fruit drinks or spread on bread. (197:67) *Soup* Seeds and Indian millet seeds ground and used to make soup or mush. (197:73) *Unspecified* Seeds formerly used for food. (197:232) **Hopi** *Staple* Seeds parched, ground into a fine, sweet meal, and eaten in pinches. (56:20) *Unspecified* Mashed seeds rolled into sticks and eaten. (190:164) **Kawaiisu** *Preserves* Seeds parched and ground into a "peanut butter"-like substance. *Winter Use Food* Seeds stored for future use. (206:41) **Klamath** *Unspecified* Seeds used for food. (45:100) **Montana Indian** *Unspecified* Seeds used for food. (19:15) **Paiute** *Sauce & Relish* Fried seeds and water used for gravy. (118:27) *Staple* Seeds parched, ground, and eaten as meal. (104:98) **Paiute, Northern** *Dried Food* Seeds dried and stored for winter use. *Porridge* Seeds dried, roasted, ground into a flour, and used to make mush. (59:46) **Tubatulabal** *Unspecified* Used extensively for food. (193:15)

Mentzelia albicaulis var. *veatchiana*, Whitestem Blazingstar
Cahuilla *Porridge* Parched seeds ground into flour and used to make mush. (as *M. veatchiana* 15:88) **Kawaiisu** *Preserves* Seeds parched and ground into a "peanut butter"-like substance. *Winter Use Food* Seeds stored for future use. (206:41)

Mentzelia congesta, United Blazingstar
Kawaiisu *Preserves* Seeds parched and ground into a "peanut butter"-like substance. *Winter Use Food* Seeds stored for future use. (206:41)

Mentzelia dispersa, Bushy Blazingstar
Kawaiisu *Preserves* Seeds parched and ground into a "peanut butter"-like substance. *Winter Use Food* Seeds stored for future use. (206:41)

Mentzelia gracilenta, Grass
  Blazingstar
Tubatulabal *Unspecified* Used extensively for food. (193:15)

Mentzelia involucrata, Whitebract
  Blazingstar
Cahuilla *Porridge* Parched seeds ground into flour and used to make mush. (15:88)

Mentzelia laevicaulis, Smoothstem
  Blazingstar
Paiute *Sauce & Relish* Fried seeds and water used for gravy. (118:27)

Mentzelia multiflora, Manyflowered
  Mentzelia
Navajo *Unspecified* Seeds used for food. (55:63)

Mentzelia multiflora var. *multi-flora*, Adonis Blazingstar
Navajo, Ramah *Staple* Seeds parched with hot coals in an old basket, ground lightly with a special rock. (as *M. pumila* var. *multiflora* 191:37)

Mentzelia puberula, Roughstem
  Blazingstar
Cahuilla *Porridge* Parched seeds ground into flour and used to make mush. (15:88)

Menyanthes trifoliata, Common
  Buckbean
Alaska Native *Bread & Cake* Rootstocks dried, ground, leached, dried, ground into flour, and used to make bread. *Dried Food* Rootstocks dried, ground, leached, dried, and used for food. *Starvation Food* Rootstocks used in the past as an emergency food. (85:145) **Hesquiat** *Forage* Deer put their heads under the surface of the water to get at the long, green rhizomes. (185:69)

Mertensia maritima, Oysterleaf
Eskimo, Alaska *Unspecified* Long, leafy stems boiled, cooked briefly, and eaten with seal oil. (1:38) Rootstock used for food. (4:715)

Microseris laciniata, Cutleaf
  Silverpuffs
Mendocino Indian *Substitution Food* Milky juice exposed to the sun and used by school children as a substitute for gum. *Unspecified* Roots formerly used for food. (as *Scorzonella maxima* 41:391)

Microseris nutans, Nodding Microseris
Montana Indian *Unspecified* Bitter, milky root juice eaten raw. (19:16)

Mimulus cardinalis, Crimson
  Monkeyflower
Kawaiisu *Unspecified* Tender stalks eaten raw. (206:41)

Mimulus eastwoodiae, Eastwood's
  Monkeyflower
Navajo, Kayenta *Fruit* Berries eaten raw. Berries stewed and used for food. (205:42)

Mimulus glabratus var. *jamesii*,
  James's Monkeyflower
Isleta *Vegetable* Tender shoots slit and eaten as a salad. (as *M. geyeri* 32:34) Salted, tender, young leaves used for salad. (as *M. geyeri* 100:35)

Mimulus guttatus, Seep Monkeyflower
Mendocino Indian *Substitution Food* Plants used as a substitute for lettuce. (41:387) **Miwok** *Vegetable* Boiled leaves used for food. (12:160)

Mimulus moschatus, Musk
  Monkeyflower
Miwok *Vegetable* Boiled, young plant used for food. (12:160)

Mimulus tilingii var. caespitosus, Subalpine Monkeyflower
Neeshenam *Vegetable* Leaves eaten as greens. (as *M. luteus* 129:377)

Mirabilis linearis, Narrowleaf Four o'Clock
Navajo, Kayenta *Fruit* Berries stewed and used for food. *Unspecified* Seeds roasted and used for food. (as *Oxybaphus linearis* 205:21)

Mirabilis multiflora, Colorado Four o'Clock
Navajo, Ramah *Beverage* Used to make tea. (191:26)

Mirabilis oxybaphoides, Smooth Spreading Four o'Clock
Navajo, Kayenta *Vegetable* Used for greens in foods. (205:21) **Navajo, Ramah** *Beverage* Used to make tea. (191:26)

Mitchella repens, Partridge Berry
Cherokee *Fruit* Fruit used for food. (80:47) **Iroquois** *Bread & Cake* Fruit mashed, made into small cakes, and dried for future use. *Dried Food* Raw or cooked fruit sun or fire dried and stored for future use. (196:128) *Fruit* Berries eaten by women. (124:96) Dried fruit taken as a hunting food. *Sauce & Relish* Dried

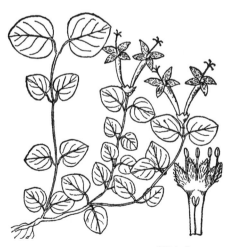

Mitchella repens

fruit cakes soaked in warm water and cooked as a sauce or mixed with corn bread. (196:128) **Micmac** *Beverage* Used to make a beverage. (159:258)

Monarda citriodora, Lemon Beebalm
Hopi *Unspecified* Plant boiled and eaten only with hares. (56:19)

Monarda didyma, Scarlet Beebalm
Cherokee *Unspecified* Species used for food. (80:39)

Monarda fistulosa, Wildbergamot Beebalm
Cherokee *Unspecified* Species used for food. (80:39) **Flathead** *Preservative* Leaves pulverized and sprinkled on meats as a preservative. (82:70) **Iroquois** *Beverage* Used to make a beverage. (196:149) **Lakota** *Special Food* Leaves chewed while people were singing and dancing. (139:50)

Monarda fistulosa ssp. fistulosa var. menthifolia, Mintleaf Beebalm
Acoma *Spice* Leaves ground and mixed with sausage for seasoning. (as *M. menthaefolia* 32:34) **Apache, Chiricahua & Mescalero** *Beverage* Leaves and young stems boiled to make a nonintoxicating beverage. (as *M. menthaefolia* 33:53) *Spice* Leaves used as flavoring. (as *M. menthaefolia* 33:47) **Hopi** *Dried Food* Dried in bundles for winter use. (as *M. menthaefolia* 200:91) **Isleta** *Spice* Leaves used for seasoning soups and stews. (as *M. menthaefolia* 100:35) **Laguna** *Spice* Leaves ground and mixed with sausage for seasoning. **Pueblo** *Dried Food* Dried and stored for winter use. *Spice* Cooked with meats and soups as a flavoring. (as *M. menthaefolia* 32:34) **San Ildefonso** *Spice* Used to flavor meat during cooking. (as *M. menthaefolia* 138:57) **Spanish American** *Dried Food* Dried and stored for winter use. *Spice* Cooked with meats and soups as a flavoring. (as *M. menthaefolia* 32:34) **Tewa of Hano** *Unspecified* Plant cooked and eaten. (as *M. menthaefolia* 138:57)

Monarda pectinata, Pony Beebalm
Acoma *Spice* Leaves ground and mixed with sausage for seasoning. (32:34) **Keres, Western** *Spice* Ground leaves mixed with sausage for seasoning. (171:54) **Laguna** *Spice* Leaves ground and mixed with sausage for seasoning. (32:34)

Monardella candicans, Sierran Mountainbalm
Tubatulabal *Beverage* Fresh or dried plants boiled, sugar added, and tea used as a beverage. (193:19) *Unspecified* Leaves and stalks used for food. (193:15)

Monardella lanceolata, Mustang Mountainbalm
Diegueño *Beverage* Infusion of plant used as a medicinal tea and beverage. (84:25) **Luiseño** *Beverage* Plant used to make a tea. (155:211)

Monardella linoides, Narrowleaf Monardella
Kawaiisu *Beverage* Leaves and flowers used to make a nonmedicinal tea. (206:42)

Monardella odoratissima, Pacific Monardella
Kawaiisu *Beverage* Leaves and flowers used to make a nonmedicinal tea. (206:42) **Miwok** *Beverage* Decoction of stems and flower heads used as a beverage. (12:171) **Okanagan-Colville** *Beverage* Leaves and stems used to make a hot or cold tea. (188:109) **Sanpoil & Nespelem** *Beverage* Leaves and stems boiled, liquid strained and used as a hot or cold beverage. (131:105)

Monardella villosa ssp. sheltonii, Shelton's Mountainbalm
Mendocino Indian *Substitution Food* Aromatic, sweet-scented leaves used dried or fresh as a substitute for tea. (as *M. sheltonii* 41:384)

Monardella viridis, Green Mountainbalm
Kawaiisu *Beverage* Leaves and flowers used to make a nonmedicinal tea. (206:42)

Moneses uniflora, Single Delight
Montana Indian *Fruit* Fruit used for food. (19:16)

Monolepis nuttalliana, Nuttall's Povertyweed
Hopi *Porridge* Ground seeds used to make mush. Ground seeds used to make mush. Ground seeds used to make mush. (190:161) **Navajo, Ramah** *Fodder* Used for sheep feed. (191:25) **Papago** *Dried Food* Seeds basket winnowed, parched, sun dried, cooked, stored, and used for food. (34:24) *Unspecified* Roots used for food. (36:60) **Pima** *Staple* Seeds boiled, partially dried, parched, ground, and eaten as pinole. *Unspecified* Roots boiled, cooled, mixed with fat or lard and salt, cooked, and eaten with tortillas. (as *M. chenopoides* 146:70) *Vegetable* Leaves boiled until tender, salted, fried in lard or fat, and eaten as greens. (47:70) **Pima, Gila River** *Vegetable* Leaves boiled or boiled, strained, refried, and eaten as greens. (133:5)

Moricandia arvensis, Purple Mistress
Hoh *Spice* Used for flavoring. *Vegetable* Plants eaten as greens. **Quileute** *Spice* Used for flavoring. *Vegetable* Plants eaten as greens. (as *Brassica arvensis* 137:61)

Morus alba, White Mulberry
Cherokee *Fruit* Fruit used for food. (80:45)

Morus microphylla, Texas Mulberry
Apache, Chiricahua & Mescalero *Bread & Cake* Fruit pressed into pulpy cakes, dried, and stored. *Fruit* Fruits eaten fresh. *Winter Use Food* Fruit pressed into pulpy cakes, dried, and stored for winter use. (33:44) **Apache, Mescalero** *Fruit* Berries eaten fresh. *Sauce & Relish* Berries dried and used as a spread on mescal. (14:47) **Yavapai** *Fruit* Raw berries used for food. (65:257)

Morus rubra, Red Mulberry
Cherokee *Beverage* Berries used to make juice. *Bread & Cake* Berries and pokeberries crushed, strained, mixed with sugar and cornmeal, and made into dumplings. (126:48) *Fruit*

Morus rubra

Fruit used for food. (as *M. ruba* 80:21) Fresh berries used for food. *Preserves* Berries used to make jam. *Winter Use Food* Berries canned for future use. (126:48) **Comanche** *Fruit* Fruits eaten for food. (29:523) **Iroquois** *Bread & Cake* Fruit mashed, made into small cakes, and dried for future use. *Dried Food* Raw or cooked fruit sun or fire dried and stored for future use. *Fruit* Dried fruit taken as a hunting food. *Sauce & Relish* Dried fruit cakes soaked in warm water and cooked as a sauce or mixed with corn bread. (196:128) **Omaha** *Dried Food* Fruit dried for winter use. *Fruit* Fruit eaten fresh. (68:326) **Seminole** *Unspecified* Plant used for food. (169:475)

Muhlenbergia filiformis, Pullup Muhly
Navajo, Ramah *Fodder* Used for sheep, horse, and cow feed. (191:16)

Muhlenbergia mexicana var. *mexicana*, Mexican Muhly
Navajo, Ramah *Fodder* Used for sheep and horse feed. (as *M. foliosa* 191:16)

Muhlenbergia richardsonis, Mat Muhly
Blackfoot *Forage* Plant eaten by horses. (97:22)

Muhlenbergia rigens, Deer Grass
Apache, Western *Porridge* Seeds ground, mixed with cornmeal and water, and made into a mush. (as *Epicompes rigens* 26:189) **Apache, White Mountain** *Bread & Cake* Seeds ground and used to make bread and pones. (as *Epicompes rigens* 136:149) *Fodder* Plant used for hay. (as *Epicampes rigens* 136:157) *Porridge* Seeds ground, mixed with meal and water, and eaten as mush. (as *Epicompes rigens* 136:149) *Unspecified* Seeds used for food. (as *Epicampes rigens* 136:157) **Hopi** *Bread & Cake* Ground seed meal used to make bread. Ground seed meal used to make bread. (190:158)

Musa sp., Banana
Seminole *Unspecified* Plant used for food. (169:509)

Musineon divaricatum var. *divaricatum*, Leafy Wildparsley
Blackfoot *Unspecified* Roots eaten raw. (114:278)

Musineon divaricatum var. *hookeri*, Hooker's Wildparsley
Crow *Unspecified* Fleshy root used for food. (as *Museneon hookeri* 19:16)

Myrica gale, Sweet Gale
Potawatomi *Preservative* Plant used to line the blueberry pail to keep the berries from spoiling. (154:121)

Myriophyllum spicatum, Spike Watermilfoil
Tanana, Upper *Frozen Food* Rhizomes frozen for future use. *Unspecified* Rhizomes eaten raw, fried in grease, or roasted. Rhizomes were sweet and crunchy and a much relished food. They were said to have been an important food during periods of low food supply as they were usually able to obtain them when needed. People give accounts of how they saved people's lives during such times. (102:14)

Myrtillocactus cochal, Cochal
Papago & Pima *Fruit* Fruit used for food. (35:42)

Nama demissum var. *demissum*,
Purplemat
Kawaiisu *Porridge* Seeds pounded in a bedrock mortar and boiled into a mush. (206:43)

Navarretia sp., Skunk Weed
Miwok *Unspecified* Dried, stored, parched, pulverized seeds used for food. (12:155)

Nelumbo lutea, American Lotus
Comanche *Unspecified* Boiled roots used for food. (29:523) **Dakota** *Soup* Hard, nut-like seeds cracked, freed from the shells, and used with meat to make soup. *Unspecified* Peeled tubers cooked with meat or hominy and used for food. (70:79) **Huron** *Starvation Food* Roots used with acorns during famine. Roots used with acorns during famine. (as *Nelumbium luteim* 3:63) **Meskwaki** *Unspecified* Seeds cooked with corn. *Winter Use Food* Terminal shoots cut crosswise, strung on string, and dried for winter use. (152:262) **Ojibwa** *Unspecified* Hard chestnut-like seeds roasted and made into a sweet meal. Shoots cooked with venison, corn, or beans. The terminal shoots are cut off at either end of the underground creeping rootstock and the remainder is their potato. These shoots are similar in shape and size to a banana, and form the starchy storage reservoirs for future growth. They have pores inside, but have more substance to them than the stems. They are cut crosswise and strung upon basswood strings, to hang from the rafters for winter use. (153:407) **Omaha** *Soup* Hard, nut-like seeds cracked, freed from the shells, and used with meat to make soup. *Unspecified* Peeled tubers cooked with meat or hominy and used for food. (70:79) *Vegetable* Roots boiled and eaten as vegetables. (as *Nelumbium luteum* 58:341) **Pawnee** *Soup* Hard, nut-like seeds cracked, freed from the shells, and used with meat to make soup. *Unspecified* Peeled tubers cooked with meat or hominy and used for food. **Ponca** *Soup* Hard, nut-like seeds cracked, freed from the shells, and used with meat to make soup. *Unspecified* Peeled tubers cooked with meat or hominy and used for food. (70:79) **Potawatomi** *Unspecified* Seeds gathered and roasted like chestnuts. *Winter Use Food* Roots gathered, cut, and strung for winter use. (154:105) **Winnebago** *Soup* Hard, nut-like seeds cracked, freed from the shells, and used with meat to make soup. *Unspecified* Peeled tubers cooked with meat or hominy and used for food. (70:79)

Nemopanthus mucronatus,
Catberry
Potawatomi *Sour* Berries edible, but quite bitter and kept for a food. (154:95)

Nemophila menziesii, Menzies's Baby
Blue Eyes
Kawaiisu *Forage* Plant eaten by the cows. (206:43)

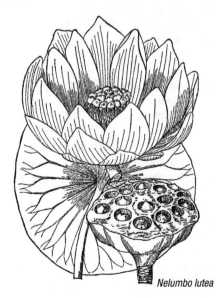

Nelumbo lutea

***Neomammillaria* sp.**, Fishhook Cactus
Navajo *Unspecified* Spines removed and used for food. (55:64)

Nepeta cataria, Catnip
Ojibwa *Beverage* Leaves used to make a beverage tea. (153:405) **Okanagan-Colville** *Forage* Plant eaten by skunks. (188:110)

Nephroma arcticum, Arctic Kidney Lichen
Eskimo, Inuktitut *Unspecified* Plant boiled and eaten with fish eggs. (202:187)

Nereocystis luetkeana
Oweekeno *Unspecified* Plant eaten with herring roe. *Winter Use Food* Plant and herring eggs salted for storage. (bull kelp 43:46) **Pomo, Kashaya** *Unspecified* Thick part of the stalk cooked in an oven or in hot ashes. *Winter Use Food* Stalks cut into lengthwise strips and dried for winter use. (bull kelp 72:124)

Nicotiana clevelandii, Cleveland's Tobacco
Cahuilla *Beverage* Leaves chewed, smoked, or used in a drinkable decoction. (15:90)

Nicotiana glauca, Tree Tobacco
Cahuilla *Beverage* Leaves chewed, smoked, or used in a drinkable decoction. (15:90)

Nicotiana trigonophylla, Desert Tobacco
Cahuilla *Beverage* Leaves chewed, smoked, or used in a drinkable decoction. (15:90)

Nolina bigelovii, Bigelow's Nolina
Cahuilla *Unspecified* Stalk baked in a rock-lined roasting pit and eaten. (15:94)

Nolina bigelovii* var. *parryi, Parry's Nolina
Hualapai *Fruit* Fruit used for food. (as *N. parryi* 195:26) **Tubatulabal** *Unspecified* Stalks used for food. (as *N. parryi* 193:15)

Nolina microcarpa, Sacahuista
Apache, Chiricahua & Mescalero *Unspecified* Stalks roasted, boiled, or eaten raw. *Vegetable* Stalks boiled, dried, and stored to be used as vegetables. (33:38) **Apache, Western** *Unspecified* Young stalks placed in fire, peeled, and eaten. (26:183) **Isleta** *Bread & Cake* Seeds made into a meal and used to make bread. (32:22) *Fruit* Fruit eaten fresh. (100:35) *Porridge* Seeds made into a meal and used to make mush. (32:22) *Preserves* Fruit eaten preserved. *Staple* Seeds used to make flour. (100:35)

Nuphar lutea, Yellow Pondlily
Lakota *Unspecified* Roots boiled and eaten. (as *N. luteum* 139:52)

Nuphar lutea* ssp. *advena, Yellow Pondlily
Comanche *Unspecified* Boiled roots used for food. (as *Nymphaea advena* 29:523) **Menominee** *Vegetable* Rhizomes cooked in the same manner as rutabagas. (as *Nymphaea advena* 151:69) **Montana Indian** *Snack Food* Parched seeds eaten like popcorn. *Soup* Seeds ground into meal used for thickening soups. *Unspecified* Thick, fleshy rhizomes boiled with fowl or other meat. Mucilaginous seedpods were well flavored and nutritious. (as *Nuphar advena* 19:17) **Pawnee** *Unspecified* Cooked seeds used for food. (as *Nymphaea advena* 70:79)

Nuphar lutea* ssp. *polysepala, Rocky Mountain Pondlily
Alaska Native *Vegetable* Rootstocks boiled or roasted and eaten as a vegetable. (as *Nuphar polysepalum* 85:145) **Cheyenne** *Unspecified* Roots eaten raw or boiled. (as *Nymphea polysepala* 76:173) Species used for food. (as *Nuphar polysepala* 83:45) **Klamath** *Bread & Cake* Ground seeds used for bread. *Dried Food* Seeds stored for later use. *Porridge* Ground seeds used for porridge. (as *Nymphaea polysepala* 45:96) *Special Food* Used as a delicacy. *Staple* Used as a staple food in primitive times. (as *Nymphaea polysepala* 46:728) Dried, roasted seeds used as cereal. (as *Nuphar polysepalum* 118:29) *Unspecified* Roasted seeds, tasted

like popcorn, used for food. (as *Nymphaea polysepala* 45:96) **Mendocino Indian** *Forage* Fleshy roots eaten as a favorite food by deer. *Unspecified* Seeds used for food. (as *Nymphaea polysepala* 41:347) **Thompson** *Dried Food* Rhizomes sliced and dried like apples. (187:235) **Tolowa** *Unspecified* Seeds used for food. (as *Nuphar polysepalum* 6:41)

Nuphar lutea ssp. variegata,
Variegated Yellow Pondlily
Algonquin, Tête-de-Boule *Beverage* Petiole sucked to relieve thirst. *Unspecified* Grains used for food. (as *N. variegatum* 132:129)

Cree, Woodlands *Dried Food* Sliced roots dried for food and eaten dried or cooked. (as *N. variegatum* 109:46) **Montana Indian** *Cooking Agent* Thin slices of rootstocks dried, ground, or pulverized into meal or gruel, and used to thicken soups. *Porridge* Seeds parched, ground into meal, and used for mush or gruel. *Unspecified* Root stocks eaten raw or boiled with meat. (as *N. variegatum* 82:33)

Nymphaea odorata, American White
Waterlily
Ojibwa *Unspecified* Buds eaten before opening. (as *Castalia odorata* 153:407)

Ochrosia compta, Ho-le-i
Hawaiian *Unspecified* Nuts used for food. (as *Ochorosia sandwicensis* 2:44)

Oemleria cerasiformis, Indian Plum
Cowlitz *Dried Food* Berries dried and eaten in the winter. *Fruit* Berries eaten fresh. (as *Osmaronia cerasiformis* 79:37) **Karok** *Forage* Berries eaten by ground squirrels. (as *Osmaronia cerasiformis* 148:384) **Kitasoo** *Fruit* Fruit used for food. (43:343) **Kwakiutl, Southern** *Fruit* Fruits eaten fresh with oil at family meals or large feasts. *Special Food* Fruits eaten fresh with oil at large feasts. (as *Osmaronia cerasiformis* 183:289) **Lummi** *Fruit* Berries eaten fresh. (as *Osmaronia cerasiformis* 79:37) **Nitinaht** *Fruit* Fruits formerly cooked and used for food. (as *Osmaronia cerasiformis* 186:118) **Quinault** *Fruit* Berries eaten fresh. (as *Osmaronia cerasiformis* 79:37) **Saanich** *Fruit* Berries eaten ripe. (as *Osmaronia cerasiformis* 182:86) **Samish** *Fruit* Berries eaten fresh. (as *Osmaronia cerasiformis* 79:37) **Shasta** *Fruit* Berries eaten raw with wild currants. (as *Osmaronia cerasiformis* 93:308) **Skagit**

Fruit Berries eaten fresh. (as *Osmaronia cerasiformis* 79:37) **Skagit, Upper** *Fruit* Fruit eaten fresh. (as *Osmaronia cerasiformis* 179:38) **Snohomish** *Fruit* Berries eaten fresh. **Squaxin** *Fruit* Berries eaten. **Swinomish** *Fruit* Berries eaten fresh. (as *Osmaronia cerasiformis* 79:37) **Thompson** *Bread & Cake* Smashed fruit made into bread. *Fruit* Fruit eaten fresh. It was cautioned that if too much fruit was eaten, one would get "bleeding lungs." (187:262) **Tolowa** *Fruit* Fruit used for food. This was called the "wood that lies" because it was the first to bloom in the spring and the last to set fruit. (6:41)

Oenanthe sarmentosa, Water Parsley
Costanoan *Unspecified* Raw or cooked stems used for food. (21:251) **Cowlitz** *Unspecified* Young, tender stems used for food. (79:42) **Hesquiat** *Unspecified* Stems formerly eaten. (185:61) **Skokomish** *Unspecified* Young, tender stems used for food. **Snuqualmie** *Unspecified* Young, tender stems used for food. (79:42)

Oenothera albicaulis

Oenothera albicaulis, Whitest Eveningprimrose
Apache *Fruit* Fruits eaten for food. (as *Anogra albicaulis* 32:17) **Apache, Chiricahua & Mescalero** *Sauce & Relish* Seeds ground and made into a gravy. *Soup* Seeds boiled in soups. *Special Food* Fruit chewed as a delicacy without preparation. (as *Anogra albicaulis* 33:45)

Oenothera biennis, Common Evening-primrose
Cherokee *Vegetable* Leaves cooked and eaten as greens. (80:33) Roots boiled like potatoes. (126:49) **Gosiute** *Unspecified* Seeds used for food. (39:375)

Oenothera elata ssp. hookeri, Hooker's Eveningprimrose
Paiute *Unspecified* Species used for food. (as *O. hookeri* 167:243)

Oenothera fruticosa, Narrowleaf Eveningprimrose
Cherokee *Vegetable* Leaves parboiled, rinsed, and cooked in hot grease as a potherb. (126:49)

Oenothera triloba, Stemless Evening-primrose
Zuni *Unspecified* Roots ground and used for food. (as *Lavauxia triloba* 136:158)

Olneya tesota, Desert Ironwood
Cahuilla *Staple* Roasted pods and seeds ground into flour. (15:94) **Cocopa** *Porridge* Seeds roasted, ground, and made into mush. **Mohave** *Bread & Cake* Seeds parched, ground lightly, roasted, and the meal made into thin loaves and baked. *Dried Food* Seeds parched, ground lightly, roasted, and eaten. (37:187) **Papago** *Dried Food* Seeds basket winnowed, parched, sun dried, cooked, stored and used for food. (34:24) Beans flailed, winnowed, parched, and used for food. (34:25) *Staple* Beans parched, sun dried, stored, ground into flour, and used as a staple food. (34:45) *Unspecified* Ground, leached seeds used for food. (36:60) **Pima** *Dried Food* Beans formerly pit roasted, parched, and eaten whole. (47:93) Seeds formerly dried, roasted, ground coarsely, and used for food. (95:263) Nuts parched and eaten. (146:70) *Staple* Beans formerly pit roasted, ground, mixed with water, and eaten as pinole. (47:93) **Pima, Gila River** *Unspecified* Seeds leached, roasted, and eaten. (133:5) Seeds parched and eaten. (133:7) **Seri** *Porridge* Beans ground into a meal, mixed with water or sea lion oil, and eaten. (50:136) **Yavapai** *Bread & Cake*, and *Staple* Dried, mashed, parched seeds ground into a meal and used to make greasy cakes. (63:211) **Yuma** *Bread & Cake* Seeds parched, ground lightly, roasted, and the meal made into thin loaves and baked. *Dried Food* Seeds parched, ground lightly, roasted, and eaten. (37:187)

Onoclea sensibilis, Sensitive Fern
Iroquois *Vegetable* Cooked and seasoned with salt, pepper, or butter. (196:118)

Oplopanax horridus, Devil's Club
Oweekeno *Unspecified* Young, spring buds boiled and eaten. (43:85)

Opuntia acanthocarpa, Buckhorn Cholla

Cahuilla *Dried Food* Fruit gathered in the spring and dried for storage. *Fruit* Fruit gathered in the spring and eaten fresh. (15:95) *Staple* Berries and stems were an important and dependable food source. (15:49) **Pima, Gila River** *Dried Food* Calyxes pit roasted with ink-weed and dried for future use. (133:4) *Staple* Flowers pit roasted and eaten as a staple. (133:7) *Unspecified* Calyxes pit roasted with inkweed and eaten fresh. (133:4)

Opuntia acanthocarpa var. *ramosa*, Cholla

Maricopa *Unspecified* Flower buds pit baked and used for food. (37:201)

Opuntia arbuscula, Arizona Pencil Cholla

Pima *Fruit* Green fruits boiled with saltbush and used for food. (47:59) **Pima, Gila River** *Dried Food* Calyxes pit roasted with inkweed and dried for future use. *Unspecified* Calyxes pit roasted with inkweed and eaten fresh. (133:4) Flowers pit roasted and eaten. (133:7)

Opuntia basilaris, Beavertail Pricklypear

Cahuilla *Dried Food* Buds cooked and dried for indefinite storage. *Porridge* Seeds ground into mush. *Unspecified* Buds cooked and eaten. *Vegetable* Joints boiled and mixed with other foods or eaten as greens. (15:95) **Diegueño** *Dried Food* Fruit cleaned of thorns, dried, and eaten. (84:27) **Kawaiisu** *Unspecified* Buds cooked and eaten. (206:46) **Tubatulabal** *Unspecified* Species used for food. (as *O. basilans* 193:16)

Opuntia bigelovii, Teddybear Cholla

Cahuilla *Dried Food* Buds cooked and dried for indefinite storage. (15:96) *Staple* Berries and stems were an important and dependable food source. (15:49) *Unspecified* Buds cooked and eaten. (15:96)

Opuntia caseyi var. *magenta*, Pursh

Tubatulabal *Unspecified* Species used for food. (193:16)

Opuntia chlorotica, Dollarjoint Pricklypear

Yavapai *Fruit* Raw fruit used for food. (65:257)

Opuntia clavata, Club Cholla

Acoma *Starvation Food* Stems and fruits roasted and eaten in times of food shortage. Joints roasted and eaten during famines. (32:35) **Keres, Western** *Starvation Food* Roasted joints used for food in times of famine. (171:56) **Laguna** *Starvation Food* Stems and fruits roasted and eaten in times of food shortage. Joints roasted and eaten during famines. (32:35)

Opuntia echinocarpa, Staghorn Cholla

Cocopa *Fruit* Fruits rolled on ground to remove spines and eaten raw. **Maricopa** *Fruit* Fruits rolled on ground to remove spines and eaten raw. **Mohave** *Fruit* Fruits rolled on ground to remove spines and eaten raw. (37:204) **Papago** *Staple* Buds and joints used as a staple crop. (34:15) Pit baked buds, fruits, and joints considered a staple food. (36:59) *Vegetable* Buds eaten as greens in May. (34:14) **Yavapai** *Fruit* Fruit boiled and eaten without mashing. (65:257)

Opuntia engelmannii, Cactus Apple

Acoma *Fruit* Ripe tunas eaten fresh. *Porridge* Tunas split, dried, ground, and the meal mixed with cornmeal to make a mush for winter use. (32:35) **Cocopa** *Fruit* Fruits rolled on ground to remove spines and eaten raw. (37:204) **Keres, Western** *Cooking Agent* Tunas used as a red dye for corn mush. *Fruit* Fresh tunas used for food. *Winter Use Food* Ground, dried tunas mixed in equal proportions with cornmeal and made into a mush for winter food. (171:56) **Laguna** *Fruit* Ripe tunas eaten fresh. *Porridge* Tunas split, dried, ground, and the meal mixed with cornmeal to make a mush for winter use. (32:35) **Maricopa** *Fruit* Fruits rolled on

ground to remove spines and eaten raw.
Mohave *Fruit* Fruits rolled on ground to remove spines and eaten raw. (37:204) **Papago**
Beverage Fruits formerly fermented and used
for a beverage. (34:26) *Sauce & Relish* Fruits
used to make syrup. (146:75) *Staple* Fruits and
joints used as a staple food. (36:60) *Vegetable*
Leaves with thorns scraped off sliced in strips
and eaten as greens in summer. (34:14) **Pima**
Fruit Fruits freed from thorns, peeled, and
eaten. (146:75) *Unspecified* Tender leaves
sliced, cooked, seasoned like string beans and
used for food. (47:60) **Pima, Gila River** *Fruit*
Fruits eaten raw. (133:7) **San Felipe** *Fruit* Ripe
tunas eaten fresh. *Porridge* Tunas split, dried,
ground, and the meal mixed with cornmeal to
make a mush for winter use. Seeds ground with
white corn and meal eaten as mush. (32:35)

Opuntia engelmannii var. *engel-mannii*, Cactus Apple

Cahuilla *Fruit* Fruit used for food. (as *O.
megacarpa* 15:97) *Staple* Berries and stems
were an important and dependable food source.
(as *O. occidentalis* var. *megacarpa* 15:49)
Unspecified Diced joints used for food. (as *O.
megacarpa* 15:97) **Diegueño** *Fruit* Fruit eaten
raw. *Vegetable* Pads boiled like cabbage or
string beans with tomatoes, onions, and peppers, like a stew. (as *O. phaeacantha* var. *dis-
cata* 84:27)

Opuntia engelmannii var. *lind-heimeri*, Texas Pricklypear

Keresan *Unspecified* Plant, with thorns burned
off, roasted in damp sand and eaten with chili.
(as *O. lindheimeri* 198:560) **Sia** *Unspecified*
Roasted in damp sand and eaten with chili. (as
O. lindheimeri 199:107)

Opuntia erinacea, Grizzlybear Pricklypear

Yavapai *Fruit* Raw fruit used for food. (65:257)

Opuntia erinacea var. *hystricina*, Grizzlybear Pricklypear

Hopi *Fruit* Fruits cooked, freed from thorns,
and served with cornmeal boiled bread. (as *O.*

hystricina 120:18) *Unspecified* Joints boiled,
dipped into syrup, and eaten after thorn removal. (as *O. hystricina* 200:85)

Opuntia ficus-indica, Tuna Cactus

Cahuilla *Dried Food* Diced pads dried and
stored for later use. Buds dried for future use.
Fruit Peeled, cool fruit eaten as a refreshing
early morning meal. (as *O. megacantha* 15:96)
Staple Berries and stems were an important and
dependable food source. (as *O. megacantha*
15:49) *Unspecified* Diced pads boiled and eaten.
Buds eaten fresh. (as *O. megacantha* 15:96)

Opuntia fragilis, Brittle Pricklypear

Okanagan-Colville *Soup* Flesh and fat boiled
into a soup. *Unspecified* Flesh pit cooked or
roasted and eaten. (188:92) **Shuswap** *Unspecified* Stems used for food. (123:60) **Thompson**
Dessert Stems roasted over a fire, peeled, and
eaten as dessert by children. *Starvation Food*
Stems used for food during times of famine. *Unspecified* Stems steam cooked in pits, the outer,
spiny skin peeled off, and the insides used for
food. *Winter Use Food* Stems mixed with berry
juice and canned for future use. (187:194)

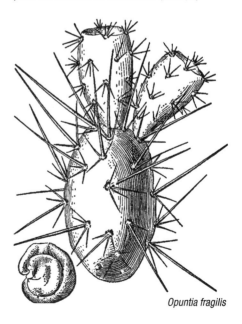

Opuntia fragilis

Opuntia fulgida, Jumping Cholla
Papago *Staple* Pit baked buds, fruits, and joints considered a staple food. (36:59) *Vegetable* Young shoots and buds eaten as greens in summer. (34:14)

Opuntia humifusa, Pricklypear
Dakota *Dried Food* Fruit dried for winter use. (69:366) Fruits, with bristles removed, dried for winter use. (70:104) *Fruit* Fruit eaten raw or stewed. (69:366) Fruits, with bristles removed, eaten fresh and raw or stewed. (70:104) *Starvation Food* Stems, cleared of spines, roasted, and used for food in times of scarcity. (69:366) Stems, with spines removed, roasted during food scarcities. (70:104) **Lakota** *Beverage* Fruit "insides" eaten for thirst. *Dried Food* Fruits dried and stored for winter use food. *Fruit* Fruits eaten fresh. Fruits stewed and used for food. (106:32) **Pawnee** *Dried Food* Fruits, with bristles removed, dried for winter use. *Fruit* Fruits, with bristles removed, eaten fresh and raw or stewed. *Starvation Food* Stems, with spines removed, roasted during food scarcities. (70:104)

Opuntia imbricata var. imbricata, Tree Cholla
Acoma *Dried Food* Young joints split lengthwise, dried, and stored for winter use. *Unspecified* Joints roasted and eaten. (as *O. arborescens* 32:35) **Apache, White Mountain** *Dried Food* Fruit dried for winter use. *Fruit* Fruit eaten raw or stewed. (as *O. arborescens* 136:159) **Keres, Western** *Starvation Food* Roasted joints used for food during times of famine. *Winter Use Food* Young, dried joints stored for winter food. (as *O. arborescens* 171:55) **Laguna** *Dried Food* Young joints split lengthwise, dried, and stored for winter use. *Unspecified* Joints roasted and eaten. (as *O. arborescens* 32:35) **Papago** *Vegetable* Eaten as greens in summer. (as *O. arborescens* 34:14) **Pima** *Dried Food* Fruits pit baked overnight, dried, and stored. (as *O. arborescens* 32:36) Fruits pit cooked, dried, boiled, salted, and eaten with pinole. (as *O. arborescens* 146:71) *Fruit* Fruits roasted in pits and eaten. (as *O. arborescens* 146:69)

Tewa of Hano *Fruit* Fruits boiled and eaten with sweetened cornmeal porridge. (as *O. arborescens* 138:62)

Opuntia ×kelvinensis, Kelvin's Pricklypear
Pima, Gila River *Unspecified* Flowers pit roasted and eaten. (133:7)

Opuntia leptocaulis, Christmas Cactus
Pima *Fruit* Fruits freed from thorns and eaten raw. (47:60) Small fruits eaten raw. (95:261) **Pima, Gila River** *Fruit* Fruits eaten raw. (133:7)

Opuntia macrorhiza var. macrorhiza, Twistspine Pricklypear
Navajo, Ramah *Dried Food* Fruit dried and boiled. *Fruit* Fruit eaten raw. *Winter Use Food* Fruit harvested for winter use. (as *O. plumbea* 191:37)

Opuntia ×occidentalis, Pricklypear
Cahuilla *Fruit* Fruit used for food. *Unspecified* Diced joints used for food. (15:97)

Opuntia parryi, Brownspined Pricklypear
Cahuilla *Staple* Berries and stems were an important and dependable food source. (15:49)

Opuntia phaeacantha, Tulip Pricklypear
Havasupai *Beverage* Plant used to make a drink. (197:66) *Bread & Cake* Dried fruit pounded into cakes for storage or pieces of cake eaten without further preparation. *Dried Food* Fruits sun dried for future use. *Fruit* Fruits eaten fresh. (197:233) **Navajo** *Beverage* Plant used to make fruit juice. *Bread & Cake* Pad pulp formed into cakes, dried, stored for later use, and fried or roasted. *Candy* Pads peeled, sliced, roasted, boiled in sugar water, dried, and eaten like candy. Pad strips peeled, parboiled, boiled, and used as chewing gum. *Cooking Agent* Seed flour used to thicken soups, puddings, or fruit dishes. *Dried Food* Plant eaten dried. *Fruit* Fruit eaten raw. *Preserves* Plant used to make jelly. Pads peeled, sliced, roasted,

boiled in sugar water until dissolved into a syrup, and eaten like jelly. *Staple* Dried seeds ground into flour. *Unspecified* Plant eaten fresh. Pads parboiled, peeled, sliced, boiled in salted water, and eaten. (110:14) **Pima** *Unspecified* Tender leaves sliced, cooked, seasoned like string beans, and used for food. (47:60)

Opuntia phaeacantha var. camanchica, Tulip Pricklypear

Keres, Western *Fruit* Mountain tunas used for food. (as *O. camanchica* 171:56) **Tewa** *Fruit* Fruits eaten for food. (as *O. camanchica* 138:62)

Opuntia polyacantha, Plains Pricklypear

Cheyenne *Cooking Agent* Pulp dried and used to thicken soups and stews. (82:39) *Dried Food* Fruits dried and used as a winter food. (83:16) *Fruit* Fruit eaten raw or dried for winter use. (76:180) Fruits eaten raw. (83:16) *Soup* Fruit stewed with meat and game into a soup. *Winter Use Food* Fruit dried for winter use. (76:180) **Gosiute** *Unspecified* Joints roasted in hot coals and eaten. (39:375) **Hopi** *Fruit* Fruits cooked, freed from thorns, and served with cornmeal boiled bread. (120:18) *Unspecified* Joints boiled, dipped into syrup, and eaten after thorn removal. (200:85) **Keres, Western** *Winter Use*

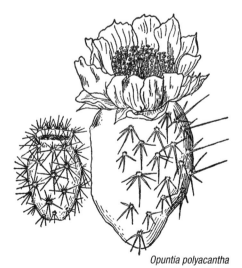

Opuntia polyacantha

Food Joints singed in hot coals, boiled with dried sweet corn, and used as a winter food. (171:57) **Montana Indian** *Dried Food* Fruits dried and stored for winter use. (82:39) *Fodder* In times of scarcity, spines were singed off and fed to stock. *Fruit* Ripe fruit eaten raw. (19:17) Fruits eaten raw. (82:39) *Preserves* Fruit made into preserves. *Unspecified* Young joint pulp boiled and fried. (19:17) Stems occasionally used for food. (82:39) **Okanagan-Colville** *Soup* Flesh and fat boiled into a soup. *Unspecified* Flesh pit cooked or roasted and eaten. (188:92) **Okanagon** *Unspecified* Insides of plants oven roasted and used for food. (125:36) **Paiute, Northern** *Unspecified* Flesh peeled and eaten roasted or uncooked and fresh. (59:49) **San Felipe** *Unspecified* Joints formerly roasted and eaten. *Winter Use Food* Joints singed in hot coals, boiled and dried with sweet corn to make a winter use food. (32:36) **Sanpoil & Nespelem** *Dried Food* Berry pits roasted, after spines burned off and removed, and used for food. (131:103) **Thompson** *Dessert* Stems roasted over a fire, peeled, and eaten as dessert by children. *Starvation Food* Stems used for food during times of famine. (187:194) *Unspecified* Insides of plants oven roasted and used for food. (125:36) Roots and little bulbs cooked, peeled, and the inside eaten. Stalks cooked, peeled, and the inside eaten. (164:480) Stems steam cooked in pits, the outer, spiny skin peeled off, and the insides used for food. *Winter Use Food* Stems mixed with berry juice and canned for future use. (187:194)

Opuntia polyacantha var. rufispina, Hairspine Pricklypear

Gosiute *Unspecified* Joints roasted in hot coals and eaten. (as *O. rutila* 39:375)

Opuntia ramosissima, Branched Pencil Cholla

Cahuilla *Dried Food* Fruit dried for later use. Stalks, with thorns removed, dried for future use. *Fruit* Fruit eaten fresh. *Soup* Stalks, with thorns removed, boiled into a soup. (15:97) *Staple* Berries and stems were an important and dependable food source. (15:49)

Opuntia spinosior, Walkingstick
  Cactus
Papago *Staple* Pit baked buds, fruits, and joints considered a staple food. (36:60)

Opuntia versicolor, Staghorn Cholla
Papago *Staple* Pit baked buds, fruits, and joints considered a staple food. (36:60) *Vegetable* Young shoots and buds eaten as greens in summer. (34:14) **Pima** *Fruit* Green fruits boiled with saltbush and used for food. (47:59) Fruits eaten raw. (146:78)

Opuntia whipplei, Whipple Cholla
Apache, White Mountain *Dried Food* Fruit dried for winter use. *Fruit* Fruit eaten raw or stewed. (136:159) **Hopi** *Unspecified* Buds boiled and eaten with cornmeal boiled bread. (120:19) **Zuni** *Dried Food* Fruit, with the spines rubbed off, dried for winter use. (166:69) *Fruit* Spineless fruits eaten raw or stewed. (32:36) Fruit, with the spines rubbed off, eaten raw or stewed. *Porridge* Dried fruit ground into a flour, mixed with parched cornmeal and made into a mush. (166:69)

Orobanche cooperi, Desert
  Broomrape
Pima, Gila River *Unspecified* Stalk, below the ground, eaten cooked or raw. (133:5) Roots eaten raw or roasted. (133:7)

Orobanche cooperi ssp. *cooperi*,
  Cooper's Broomrape
Cahuilla *Unspecified* Root peeled and eaten. (as *O. ludoviciana* var. *cooperi* 15:97)

Orobanche fasciculata, Clustered
  Broomrape
Gosiute *Unspecified* Entire plant sometimes eaten. (as *Aphyllon fasciculatum* 39:361) **Navajo, Ramah** *Unspecified* Roasted in ashes, the skin peeled off and eaten like a baked potato. (191:45) **Paiute, Northern** *Unspecified* Stems eaten raw or boiled. (59:49)

Orobanche ludoviciana, Louisiana
  Broomrape
Pima *Unspecified* Young sprouts covered with hot ashes, baked and the lower parts eaten. (47:49)

Orobanche ludoviciana ssp.
  multiflora, Manyflowered Broomrape
Pima *Unspecified* Plants cooked and used for food. (as *Orobranche multiflora* 95:264)

Orthocarpus attenuatus, Attenuate
  Indian Paintbrush
Miwok *Unspecified* Dried, parched, pulverized seeds used for food. (12:155)

Orthocarpus lithospermoides,
  Indian Paintbrush
Mendocino Indian *Forage* Plants eaten sparingly by horses. (41:387)

Oryza sativa, Rice
Haisla & Hanaksiala *Staple* Grains used for food. (43:207) **Kitasoo** *Unspecified* Grains used for food. (43:324) **Oweekeno** *Unspecified* Grains used for food. (43:81) **Seminole** *Unspecified* Seeds used for food. (169:470)

Oryzopsis hymenoides, Indian
  Ricegrass
Apache, Western *Porridge* Seeds ground, mixed with cornmeal and water, and made into a mush. (as *Eriocoma cuspidata* 26:189) **Apache, White Mountain** *Bread & Cake* Seeds ground and used to make bread and pones. (as *Eriocoma cuspidata* 136:149) *Fodder* Plant used for hay. (as *Eriocoma cuspidata* 136:157) *Porridge* Seeds ground, mixed with meal and water, and eaten as mush. (as *Eriocoma cuspidata* 136:149) *Unspecified* Seeds used for food. (as *Eriocoma cuspidata* 136:157) **Gosiute** *Unspecified* Seeds formerly used for food. (as *O. cuspidata* 39:375) **Havasupai** *Bread & Cake* Seeds parched, ground fine, boiled, thickened, made into balls, and eaten as dumplings. (197:66) *Soup* Seeds and Indian millet seeds ground and used to make soup or mush. (197:73) *Staple* Seeds ground and eaten as a ground or

parched meal. (197:67) **Hopi** *Bread & Cake* Seeds ground with corn into fine meal and used to make tortilla bread. (120:20) *Staple* Ground seeds used to make meal. (as *Stipa hymenoides* 190:158) *Starvation Food* Seeds eaten, especially in time of famine. (42:338) Plants formerly used for food during famines. (as *O. membranacea* 101:43) Seeds used during famines. (200:65) **Kawaiisu** *Staple* Seeds pounded into a meal and eaten dry. (206:46) **Montana Indian** *Unspecified* Seeds used for food. (as *Ericooma cuspidata* 19:11) **Navajo** *Bread & Cake* Ground seeds made into cakes. (55:26) Seeds ground and made into bread and dumplings. (165:223) *Fodder* Plant used as a fodder for both wild and domesticated animals. *Forage* Plant used as a forage for both wild and domesticated animals. (90:154) *Porridge* Seeds ground and made into gruel. (165:223) *Staple* Ground seeds used for food. (90:154) *Unspecified* Seeds used for food. (as *Eriocoma cuspidata* 32:27) **Navajo, Ramah** *Fodder* Young plants used as horse feed. *Porridge* Seeds finely ground and cooked into a mush with milk or water. (191:16) **Paiute** *Porridge* Seeds ground into a meal for mush. (118:26–27) *Sauce & Relish* Ground seeds used for sauce. *Staple* Ground

seeds used for flour. (118:32) Roasted and ground into flour. (167:244) **Paiute, Northern** *Porridge* Seeds dried, winnowed, ground into a flour, and used to make mush. *Soup* Seeds dried, winnowed, ground into a flour, and used to make soup. *Special Food* Seeds considered a good food to eat when suffering from stomachaches, colic, or aching bones. When a person was suffering from any of these sicknesses, Indian ricegrass seeds should have been the only food eaten. *Staple* Seeds used as a staple food. *Winter Use Food* Seeds stored for winter use. (59:46) **Zuni** *Staple* Ground seeds used as a staple before the availability of corn. After the introduction of corn, the ground seeds were mixed with cornmeal and made into steamed balls or pats. (as *Eriocoma cuspidata* 166:67) *Unspecified* Used especially in earlier times as an important source of food. (as *Eriocoma cuspidata* 32:27)

Osmorhiza berteroi, Sweetcicely
Karok *Vegetable* Young tops eaten raw as greens. (as *Osmorrhiza nuda* var. *brevipes* 148:386) **Miwok** *Vegetable* Boiled leaves used for food. (as *Osmorrhiza nuda* 12:160) **Okanagon** *Unspecified* Thick, aromatic roots used for food. (as *Washingtonia nuda* 125:36) **Thompson** *Unspecified* Thick, aromatic roots eaten. (as *Osmorrhiza nuda* 164:480) Thick, aromatic roots used for food. (as *Washingtonia nuda* 125:36)

Osmorhiza depauperata, Bluntseed Sweetroot
Isleta *Beverage* Roots and stems boiled to make a beverage. (as *Washingtonia obtusa* 100:45)

Osmorhiza longistylis, Longstyle Sweetroot
Omaha *Fodder* Root used to attract horses and catch them. **Ponca** *Fodder* Root used to attract horses and catch them. (as *Washingtonia longistylis* 70:107) **Potawatomi** *Fodder* Chopped roots added to oats or other seeds to fatten the ponies. (154:124)

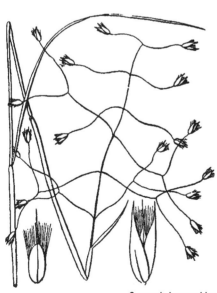

Oryzopsis hymenoides

Osmorhiza occidentalis, Western
  Sweetroot
Blackfoot *Candy* Root chewed, especially during the winter, as a confection. (86:103) **Shoshoni** *Spice* Steeped seeds added to dishes for flavoring. (118:29)

Osmunda cinnamomea, Cinnamon
  Fern
Abnaki *Snack Food* Used as a nibble. (144:152) *Unspecified* White base of plant eaten raw. (144:162) **Menominee** *Soup* Frond tips simmered to remove the ants, added to soup stock, and thickened with flour. (151:70)

Oxalis corniculata, Creeping
  Woodsorrel
Cherokee *Unspecified* Species used for food. (80:56) **Iroquois** *Vegetable* Eaten raw, sometimes with salt. (196:118)

Oxalis montana, Mountain Woodsorrel
Potawatomi *Dessert* Plant gathered, cooked, and sugar added to make a dessert. (as *O. acetosella* 154:106)

Oxalis oregana, Oregon Oxalis
Cowlitz *Unspecified* Leaves eaten fresh or cooked. (79:39) **Makah** *Unspecified* Leaves eaten fresh. (67:284) **Pomo, Kashaya** *Sour* Flowering plant leaves and stem chewed for the sour taste. (72:108) **Quileute** *Unspecified* Leaves eaten by hunters or by those traveling in the woods. **Quinault** *Unspecified* Leaves cooked with grease and used for food. (79:39) **Tolowa** *Unspecified* Plant eaten with dried fish. **Yurok** *Unspecified* Plant eaten with dried fish. (6:42)

Oxalis stricta, Common Yellow Oxalis
Cherokee *Vegetable* Leaves used for food. (126:49) **Meskwaki** *Sour* Eaten for its acidity. (152:271) **Omaha** *Fodder* Pounded bulbs fed to horses to make them fleet. *Unspecified* Leaves, flowers, scapes, and bulbs used for food by children. **Pawnee** *Fodder* Pounded bulbs fed to horses to make them fleet. *Forage* Plant much esteemed by buffalo. *Unspecified* Leaves, flowers,
scapes, and bulbs used for food by children. Plant considered to have a salty and sour taste. **Ponca** *Fodder* Pounded bulbs fed to horses to make them fleet. *Unspecified* Leaves, flowers, scapes, and bulbs used for food by children. (as *Xanthoxalis stricta* 70:98)

Oxalis violacea, Violet Woodsorrel
Apache, Chiricahua & Mescalero *Unspecified* Mixed with other leaves and cooked or eaten raw. Bulbs eaten raw or boiled. (33:47) **Cherokee** *Unspecified* Species used for food. (80:56) **Omaha** *Fodder* Pounded bulbs fed to horses to make them fleet. *Unspecified* Leaves, flowers, scapes, and bulbs used for food by children. **Pawnee** *Fodder* Pounded bulbs fed to horses to make them fleet. *Unspecified* Plant considered to have a salty and sour taste. Leaves, flowers, scapes, and bulbs used for food by children. **Ponca** *Fodder* Pounded bulbs fed to horses to make them fleet. *Unspecified* Leaves, flowers, scapes, and bulbs used for food by children. (as *Ionoxalis violacea* 70:98)

Oxydendrum arboreum, Sourwood
Cherokee *Sauce & Relish* Used to make honey. (80:56)

Oxypolis rigidior, Stiff Cowbane
Cherokee *Unspecified* Roots baked and eaten. (80:51)

Oxyria digyna, Alpine Mountainsorrel
Alaska Native *Dietary Aid* Leaves used as a good source of vitamin C. *Unspecified* Leaves eaten fresh and raw. (85:39) **Eskimo, Alaska** *Unspecified* Leaves and stems eaten raw or cooked with seal oil. (1:35) Leaves eaten fresh, soured, boiled or in oil, and root also utilized. (4:715) Fresh leaves mixed with seal blubber and eaten. **Eskimo, Arctic** *Unspecified* Leaves and young stems eaten raw and cooked. **Eskimo, Greenland** *Unspecified* Juice sweetened, thickened with a small amount of rice or potato flour and eaten. Fresh leaves mixed with seal blubber and eaten. (128:24) **Eskimo, Inuktitut** *Unspecified* Leaves eaten with seal oil. (202:190) **Eskimo, Inupiat** *Vegetable* Leaves eaten raw,

with seal oil, cooked, or fermented. (98:65)
Montana Indian *Vegetable* Acid-tasting leaves used as a salad. (19:17)

Oxytropis campestris, Cold Mountain Crazyweed
Thompson *Forage* Used as a common forage plant. (164:516)

Oxytropis lambertii, Lambert's Crazyweed
Lakota *Forage* Whole plant and roots eaten by horses. (139:47) **Navajo, Kayenta** *Porridge* Used to make a mush or parched and used for food. (205:28)

Oxytropis maydelliana, Maydell's Oxytrope
Eskimo, Inupiat *Frozen Food* Roots frozen for future use. *Vegetable* Roots, always with some kind of oil, eaten raw or cooked. *Winter Use Food* Roots stored in buried sacks for winter use. Roots stored in seal oil, fish oil, or bear fat for winter use. (98:122)

Oxytropis nigrescens, Blackish Oxytrope
Alaska Native *Unspecified* Roots used for food. (85:159)

Pachycereus pringlei
Papago & Pima *Cooking Agent* Pulp made into a flavoring substance and used for jellies. (cardon 35:37) **Seri** *Fruit* Fruits eaten for food. *Porridge* Seeds ground to a powder and made into a meal or paste. (giant cactus 50:134)

Paeonia californica, California Peony
Diegueño *Vegetable* Leaves cooked as greens. Young leaves were picked before the blossoms appeared in the spring. They were prepared by boiling, placing the boiled leaves in a cloth sack and weighting the sack down in the river with a stone, allowing the water to flow through the greens overnight to remove the bitterness in them. Alternatively, the boiled leaves could be soaked in a pan and the water changed until the bitterness was removed. The leaves were then cooked as greens, with onions, and eaten as a vegetable with acorn mush. The greens could also be prepared by boiling them twice, rather than letting them wash in the river. Buds cooked as vegetables. (84:28)

Panicum bulbosum, Bulb Panicgrass
Apache, Chiricahua & Mescalero *Bread & Cake* Seeds threshed, winnowed, ground, and the flour used to make bread. *Sauce & Relish* Seeds ground, made into gravy, and mixed with meat. (33:48)

Panicum capillare, Witch Grass
Hopi *Bread & Cake* Ground seed meal used to make bread. (190:159) *Staple* Seeds ground and mixed with cornmeal. (56:17) **Navajo** *Unspecified* Seeds used for food. (55:26) **Navajo, Ramah** *Fodder* Used for sheep and horse feed. (191:17)

Panicum hirticaule, Mexican Panicgrass
Cocopa *Bread & Cake* Seeds ground into a meal and used to make bread. *Sauce & Relish* Seeds ground into a meal and used to make gravy. *Winter Use Food* Seeds stored in ollas for future use. (37:175) **Yuma** *Staple* Seeds parched, winnowed, and ground into flour. (37:190)

Panicum obtusum, Obtuse Panicgrass
Apache, Chiricahua & Mescalero *Sauce & Relish* Seeds ground, made into gravy, and mixed with meat. (33:48) **Navajo, Ramah** *Fodder* Cut for hay. *Forage* Good forage. (191:17)

Panicum sonorum, Sauwi
Cocopa *Bread & Cake* Seeds ground, mixed with water, and dried to make cakes. *Winter Use Food* Seeds harvested, winnowed, and stored for winter use. **Warihio** *Beverage* Seeds ground into flour and mixed with milk to make a nourishing drink. *Staple* Seeds ground into flour and seasoned with salt and sugar. (37:170)

Panicum urvilleanum, Desert Panicgrass
Cahuilla *Porridge* Singed seeds boiled and made into a gruel. (15:98)

Parkinsonia aculeata, Jerusalem Thorn
Papago *Dried Food* Seeds basket winnowed, parched, sun dried, cooked, stored, and used for food. (34:24) Beans flailed, winnowed, parched, and used for food. (34:25) *Unspecified* Seeds used for food. (36:60)

Parkinsonia florida, Blue Paloverde
Cahuilla *Porridge* Dried beans ground into flour and used to make mush or cakes. (as *Cercidium floridum* 15:52) **Cocopa** *Porridge* Seeds roasted, ground, and made into mush. **Mohave** *Starvation Food* Seeds parched until almost burned and eaten as a famine food. (as *Cercidium floridum* 37:187) **Pima** *Unspecified* Green pods eaten raw in summer. (as *Cercidium floridum* 47:90) Beans formerly eaten fresh. (as *P. torreyana* 146:75) **Yuma** *Starvation Food* Seeds parched until almost burned and eaten as a famine food. (as *Cercidium floridum* 7:187)

Parkinsonia microphylla, Yellow Paloverde
Cocopa *Porridge* Seeds roasted, ground, and made into mush. **Mohave** *Starvation Food* Seeds parched until almost burned and eaten as

a famine food. (as *Cercidium microphyllum* 37:187) **Papago** *Dried Food* Seeds basket winnowed, parched, sun dried, cooked, stored, and used for food. (34:24) Beans flailed, winnowed, parched, and used for food. (34:25) *Staple* Beans parched, sun dried, stored, ground into flour, and used as a staple food. (34:45) *Unspecified* Seeds used for food. (as *Cercidium microphyllum* 36:60) **Pima** *Unspecified* Beans formerly eaten fresh. (146:75) **Pima, Gila River** *Unspecified* Peas eaten raw or cooked. (as *Cercidium microphyllum* 133:5) Seeds eaten raw and boiled. (as *Cercidium microphyllum* 133:7) **Yuma** *Starvation Food* Seeds parched until almost burned and eaten as a famine food. (as *Cercidium microphyllum* 37:187)

Parmelia physodes, Lichen
Potawatomi *Soup* and *Vegetable* Cooked into a soup, material swelled and afforded a pleasant flavor. (154:107)

Paronychia jamesii, James's Nailwort
Kiowa *Beverage* Used as a "tea" plant. (192:27)

Parrya nudicaulis, Nakedstem Wallflower
Alaska Native *Soup* Roots cooked and added to fish and meat stews. *Unspecified* Roots cooked and used for food. New, young leaves used for food. *Winter Use Food* Leaves stored raw in seal oil for winter use. (85:123)

Parthenium incanum, Mariola
Apache, Chiricahua & Mescalero *Beverage* Fresh leaves boiled and used similarly to coffee. (33:53)

Parthenocissus quinquefolia, Virginia Creeper
Chippewa *Unspecified* Stalks cut, boiled, peeled, and the sweetish substance between the bark and the wood used for food. (53:320)

Parthenocissus quinquefolia* var. *quinquefolia, Virginia Creeper
Montana Indian *Fruit* Ripe fruit collected and eaten like grapes. (as *Ampelopsis quinquefolia*

19:6) **Ojibwa** *Special Food* Root cooked and given as a special food by Winabojo. *Unspecified* Root cooked and eaten. (as *Psedera quinquefokia* 153:411)

Parthenocissus vitacea, Woodbine
Navajo, Ramah *Fruit* Berries used for food. (191:36)

Pascopyrum smithii, Western
  Wheatgrass
Lakota *Forage* Heads eaten by horses. (as *Agropyron smithii* 139:28) **Montana Indian** *Fodder* and *Forage* Most valuable forage grass and cultivated for hay, good keeping qualities, and high nutritional value. (as *Agropyron occidentale* 19:5)

Paspalum setaceum, Thin Paspalum
Kiowa *Fodder* Used as a valuable fodder plant. *Forage* Used as a valuable pasture plant. (as *P. stramineum* 192:16)

Passiflora incarnata, Purple
  Passionflower
Cherokee *Beverage* Used to make a social drink. (80:47) Crushed fruit strained into a juice, mixed with flour or cornmeal to thicken,

Passiflora incarnata

and used as a beverage. (126:50) *Fruit* Fruit used for food. (80:47) Fruit eaten raw. (126:50) *Unspecified* Young shoots and leaves boiled, fried, and often eaten with other greens. (204:253) *Vegetable* Leaves parboiled, rinsed, and cooked in hot grease with salt as a potherb. (126:50)

Paxistima myrsinites, Boxleaf Myrtle
Karok *Fruit* Berries used for food. (148:385) **Okanagan-Colville** *Forage* Plant used by deer as a good winter food. (188:95) **Thompson** *Forage* Long, narrow leaves eaten by cattle when other foods scarce. (164:515)

Pectis angustifolia, Narrowleaf Pectis
Acoma *Spice* Used as seasoning to counteract the taste of tainted meat. (32:38) **Havasupai** *Sauce & Relish* Plant used as a condiment. (197:74) **Hopi** *Dried Food* Plants dried and eaten with fresh roasted corn, dried parched corn, or corn dumplings. (120:20) Dried, stored, and used for food. *Spice* Used as a flavoring. *Unspecified* Eagerly eaten raw. (200:97) **Keres, Western** *Spice* Plant used as a seasoning for meat, to kill the tainted taste. (171:58) **Laguna** *Spice* Used as seasoning to counteract the taste of tainted meat. **Pueblo** *Spice* Used as seasoning. (32:38)

Pectis papposa, Cinchweed Fetid-
  marigold
Havasupai *Porridge* Seeds parched, ground, and used to make mush. (197:67) *Sauce & Relish* Fresh plant dipped in salted water and eaten with mush or cornmeal as a condiment. (197:249) *Soup* Seeds parched, ground, and used to make soup. (197:67) **Pueblo** *Spice* Used as seasoning. (32:38)

Pedicularis canadensis, Canadian
  Lousewort
Cherokee *Vegetable* Cooked leaves and stems used for food. (126:54) **Iroquois** *Vegetable* Cooked and seasoned with salt, pepper, or butter. (196:118) **Potawatomi** *Fodder* Roots mixed with oats to fatten the ponies. (154:123)

Pedicularis densiflora, Indian
  Warrior
Mendocino Indian *Forage* Flower nectar used
by yellowhammer birds. *Unspecified* Honey
sucked out of the flowers by children. (41:388)

Pedicularis lanata, Woolly Lousewort
Alaska Native *Unspecified* Flowers with water
added allowed to ferment. Roots boiled or
roasted. (85:125) **Eskimo, Arctic** *Unspecified*
Roots eaten either raw or cooked. Flowers
sucked by children for the sweet nectar. *Vegetable* Flowering stems boiled and eaten as a potherb. (128:23) **Eskimo, Inupiat** *Dessert* Fermented, frozen greens mashed, creamed, and
mixed with sugar and oil for a dessert. *Unspecified* Raw shoots and roots used for food. *Vegetable* Fermented young flower tops eaten with
oil and sugar, like sauerkraut. (98:56)

Pedicularis lanata ssp. lanata,
  Woolly Lousewort
Eskimo, Alaska *Unspecified* Raw roots eaten
with seal oil. (as *P. kanei* 1:38)

Pedicularis lanceolata, Swamp
  Lousewort
Iroquois *Vegetable* Cooked and seasoned with
salt, pepper, or butter. (196:118)

Pediomelum esculentum, Breadroot
  Scurfpea
Blackfoot *Dried Food* Peeled roots dried and
added to winter supplies. *Unspecified* Peeled
roots eaten fresh. (as *Psoralea esculenta*
86:104) **Cheyenne** *Cooking Agent* Dried plant
pieces powdered and used as a thickening for
soups, gravy, and dry meat. (as *Psoralea esculenta* 83:29) *Dried Food* Roots dried and eaten
as a winter food. (as *Psoralea esculenta* 83:30)
Roots formerly cut into thin, lengthwise slices
and dried for winter use. *Pie & Pudding* Dried
plant slices boiled, a sweetener added, and eat-
en as a sweet pudding. (as *Psoralea esculenta*
83:29) *Unspecified* Roots eaten fresh. (as *Psoralea esculenta* 83:30) Species used for food.
(as *Psoralea esculenta* 83:45) Roots formerly
eaten raw or cooked as one of the most impor-

tant foods. (as *Psoralea esculenta* 83:29)
Dakota *Dried Food* Roots dried for winter use.
The roots were peeled and braided into festoons
by their tapering roots or were split into halves
or quarters and after drying were stored in any
convenient container. (as *Psoralea esculenta*
69:365) Peeled roots braided and dried for winter use. (as *Psoralea esculenta* 70:92) *Unspecified* Roots eaten fresh. (as *Psoralea esculenta*
69:365) Peeled roots eaten fresh and uncooked
or cooked. (as *Psoralea esculenta* 70:92)
Lakota *Dried Food* Roots peeled, dried, and
used as a winter food. *Soup* Roots cooked in
soups and stews. *Unspecified* Roots peeled and
eaten raw. (as *Psoralea esculenta* 106:41)
Montana Indian *Bread & Cake* Roots dried,
mashed, and used to make cakes or breads.
Cooking Agent Roots dried, mashed, and used
to thicken soups. *Dried Food* Roots shredded,
dried, and stored for future use. *Porridge* Roots
dried, mashed, and used to make mush and
gruel. *Unspecified* Inner root core eaten raw,
roasted, or boiled. (as *Psoralea esculenta*
82:61) *Vegetable* Roots, similar to yams,
roasted in ashes. *Winter Use Food* Peeled, sliced
roots dried for winter use. (as *Psoralea esculenta* 19:20) **Omaha** *Dried Food* Thickened

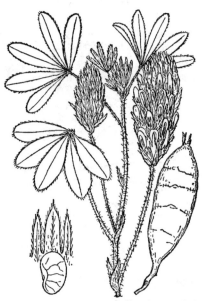

Pediomelum esculentum

root eaten dried. (as *Psoralea esculenta* 68:325) Peeled roots braided and dried for winter use. (as *Psoralea esculenta* 70:92) *Soup* Thickened root cooked with soup. *Unspecified* Thickened root eaten fresh and raw. (as *Psoralea esculenta* 68:325) Peeled roots eaten fresh and uncooked or cooked. **Pawnee** *Dried Food* Peeled roots braided and dried for winter use. *Unspecified* Peeled roots eaten fresh and uncooked or cooked. **Ponca** *Dried Food* Peeled roots braided and dried for winter use. *Unspecified* Peeled roots eaten fresh and uncooked or cooked. (as *Psoralea esculenta* 70:92) **Sioux** *Soup* Boiled or roasted roots eaten or dried and ground into meal and used in soups. *Winter Use Food* Plant gathered and hung up for winter use. (as *Psoralea esculenta* 118:13) **Winnebago** *Dried Food* Peeled roots braided and dried for winter use. *Unspecified* Peeled roots eaten fresh and uncooked or cooked. (as *Psoralea esculenta* 70:92)

Pediomelum hypogaeum var. *hypogaeum*, Scurfpea
Cheyenne *Dried Food* Roots dried and eaten as a winter food. (as *Psoralea hypogaea* 83:30) *Unspecified* Root eaten fresh. (as *Psoralea hypogeae* 76:178) Roots eaten fresh. (as *Psoralea hypogaea* 83:30) Species used for food. (as *Psoralea hypogea* 83:46) *Winter Use Food* Root dried for winter use. (as *Psoralea hypogeae* 76:178) **Comanche** *Unspecified* Raw roots used for food. (as *Psoralea hypogeae* 29:523)

Pellaea mucronata, Birdfoot Cliffbrake
Diegueño *Beverage* Used to make tea. (88:215) **Kawaiisu** *Beverage* Ferns brewed to make a nonmedicinal tea. (206:47) **Luiseño** *Beverage* Fronds used to make a beverage. (155:234)

Pellaea mucronata ssp. *californica*, California Cliffbrake
Tubatulabal *Unspecified* Leaves and stalks used for food. (as *P. compacta* 193:15)

Pellaea mucronata ssp. *mucronata*, Birdfoot Cliffbrake
Luiseño *Beverage* Plant used to make a tea. (as *P. ornithopus* 155:211)

Peltandra virginica, Green Arrow Arum
Seminole *Unspecified* Plant used for food. (169:494)

Peniocereus greggii var. *greggii*, Nightblooming Cereus
Apache, San Carlos *Unspecified* Red, doughnut-like fruits and flowers used for food. (as *Cereus greggii* 95:257) **Papago** *Beverage* Roots chewed for thirst. *Unspecified* Roots baked whole in ashes, peeled, and eaten. (as *Cereus greggii* 34:18) *Vegetable* Stalks eaten as greens. (as *Cereus greggii* 34:14) Shoots eaten as greens. (as *Cereus greggii* 34:16)

Peniocereus striatus, Gearstem Cactus
Papago & Pima *Fruit* Fruit used for food. (as *Wilcoxia striata* 35:42)

Penstemon centranthifolius, Scarlet Bugler
Diegueño *Unspecified* Flowers sucked for the good taste. (88:219)

Penstemon confertus, Yellow Penstemon
Thompson *Beverage* Dried stems and leaves boiled for a short time and drunk as a tea. (as *Pentstemon confertus* 164:493)

Penstemon fruticosus, Bush Penstemon
Thompson *Forage* Plant frequented by bees and hummingbirds for the nectar. *Spice* Plant used in pit cooking nodding onions. (187:286)

Pentaphylloides floribunda, Shrubby Cinquefoil
Blackfoot *Spice* Leaves mixed with dried meat as a deodorant and spice. (as *Potentilla fruticosa* 86:104) **Eskimo, Alaska** *Beverage* Dried

leaves used to make tea. (as *Potentilla frutico-sa* 4:715) **Eskimo, Arctic** *Beverage* Leaves dried and used as a substitute for tea. (as *Potentilla fruticosa* 128:31)

Penthorum sedoides, Ditch Stonecrop
Cherokee *Vegetable* Leaves used as a potherb. (126:50)

Perideridia bolanderi, Bolander's Yampah
Atsugewi *Bread & Cake* Stored, dried roots pounded and made into bread. *Dried Food* Dried roots stored for winter use. Stored, dried roots pounded and made into bread or dried and stored for later use. *Soup* Stored, dried roots pounded and made into soup. *Unspecified* Fresh, ground roots used for food. (as *Pteridendia bolanden* 61:138) **Miwok** *Substitution Food* Served as substitution food when acorn supply was reduced. *Unspecified* Eaten raw or cooked in baskets by stone boiling, becoming mealy like potatoes. (as *Eulophus bolanderi* 12:157)

Perideridia gairdneri, Gairdner's Yampah
Blackfoot *Snack Food* Roots eaten as snacks by children while playing on the prairie. *Soup* Roots stored for use in soups. *Staple* Root considered a staple. *Unspecified* Roots eaten fresh. (86:103) **Cheyenne** *Dried Food* Roots scraped, dried, and stored for winter use. *Porridge* Roots cooked, dried, pulverized, and eaten as mush. (82:65) *Unspecified* Species used for food. (83:45) **Flathead** *Bread & Cake* Roots smashed, formed into small, round cakes, sun dried, and stored for winter use. **Montana Indian** *Unspecified* Roots eaten raw or boiled. (82:65) **Okanagan-Colville** *Dried Food* Roots eaten raw, boiled, or cooked, sliced, dried, and mixed with dried, powdered deer meat. *Pie & Pudding* Roots mixed with flour or black tree lichen into a pudding. *Unspecified* Roots boiled alone or with saskatoon berries. *Winter Use Food* Roots stored in pits for future use. (188:71) **Paiute** *Dried Food* Dried, mashed corms used in a mush or gravy. *Unspecified* Corms eaten raw or

boiled. *Winter Use Food* Roots mixed with dirt and buried for winter use. (111:97) **Paiute, Northern** *Porridge* Roots dried, pounded, ground, and used to make mush. *Soup* Roots dried, pounded, ground, and used to make soup. *Staple* Roots ground into flour. *Unspecified* Roots peeled and eaten fresh, boiled, or roasted. (59:43) **Skagit, Upper** *Unspecified* Roots steamed in an earth oven and eaten. (179:40)

Perideridia gairdneri ssp. *gairdneri*, Gairdner's Yampah
Blackfoot *Spice* Used to flavor stews. *Vegetable* Eaten raw or boiled as a vegetable. (as *Carum gairdneri* 114:274) **Cheyenne** *Porridge* Dried roots cooked and used as a mush by pouring soup over them. *Unspecified* Roots eaten fresh. *Winter Use Food* Roots dried for winter use. (as *Carum gairdneri* 76:182) **Gosiute** *Unspecified* Roots roasted in a pit lined with hot stones and eaten. *Winter Use Food* Roots preserved in quantity for winter use. (as *Carum gairdneri* 39:365) **Great Basin Indian** *Unspecified* Root eaten raw or cooked. (as *Carum gairdneri* 121:49) **Karok** *Unspecified* Roots dried, peeled, cooked in an earth oven, and eaten. (as *Carum gairdneri* 148:387) **Klamath** *Unspecified* Roots used for food. (as *Carum gairdneri* 45:101) **Miwok** *Unspecified* Boiled and eaten like a potato. (as *Carum gairdneri* 12:157) **Montana Indian** *Vegetable* Roots boiled like potatoes. (as *Carum gairdneri* 19:9) **Nevada Indian** *Pie & Pudding* Roots ground into flour for puddings. *Unspecified* Boiled roots used for food. *Winter Use Food* Roots stored for winter use. (as *Carum gairdneri* 118:16) **Pomo** *Staple* Seeds used for pinole. Tubers eaten raw, cooked, or used for pinole. *Vegetable* Fresh tops eaten as greens. (as *Carum gairdneri* 11:89) **Umatilla** *Unspecified* Roots used for food. **Ute** *Unspecified* Roots used for food. (as *Carum gairdneri* 45:101) **Yana** *Unspecified* Roots roasted and eaten. Leaves eaten raw. (as *Carum gairdneri* 147:251)

Perideridia kelloggii, Kellogg's Yampah
Mendocino Indian *Spice* Seeds used to flavor

pinole. *Staple* Tubers and semifleshy roots eaten as pinole. *Unspecified* Leaves eaten raw. Tubers and semifleshy roots eaten raw or cooked like acorn bread. (as *Carum kelloggii* 11:86) **Pomo, Kashaya** *Unspecified* Young greens eaten raw. (72:89) **Yuki** *Unspecified* Young plants eaten raw. (as *Carum kelloggii* 49:88) 41:372) **Miwok** *Unspecified* Species used for food. (as *Carum kelloggii* 12:157) **Pomo** *Staple* Seeds used to make pinoles. (as *Carum kelloggii*

Perideridia oregana, Squaw Potato
Klamath *Dried Food* Dried roots eaten raw. (as *Carum oreganum* 45:101) **Paiute** *Dried Food* Roots sun dried and used for food. *Unspecified* Roots eaten raw or boiled. (as *Carum oreganum* 104:101)

Perideridia pringlei, Adobe Yampah
Kawaiisu *Vegetable* Peeled roots boiled like potatoes and eaten. (206:47) **Yana** *Unspecified* Roots roasted and eaten. (as *Eulophus pringlei* 147:251)

Petasites frigidus, Arctic Sweet Coltsfoot
Alaska Native *Vegetable* Leaves mixed with other greens. (85:41) **Eskimo, Alaska** *Vegetable* Leaves used for greens. (4:716) **Eskimo, Arctic** *Vegetable* Young leaves and flowering stems eaten raw as salad, cooked as a potherb, or made into a "sauerkraut." (128:26)

Petasites frigidus **var.** *palmatus*, Arctic Sweet Coltsfoot
Concow *Unspecified* Leaves and young stems used for food. (as *P. palmata* 41:395) **Nitinaht** *Forage* Plants eaten by elk. (186:98) **Sanpoil & Nespelem** *Unspecified* Petioles eaten raw after removal of integumental fibers. (as *Pedasites speciosa* 131:103)

Peucedanum **sp.**, Wild Celery
Coeur d'Alene *Unspecified* Growing stalks used for food. (178:91) **Okanagon** *Staple* Growing stalks used as a principal food. (178:239) **Thompson** *Unspecified* Roots and

stalks eaten. (164:482) **Thompson, Upper (Nicola Band)** *Unspecified* Roots and stems eaten. (164:479)

Peziza aurantia, Orange Peel Mushroom
Pomo, Kashaya *Vegetable* Cooked on hot stones, coals, or eaten fresh. (72:131)

Phacelia distans, Distant Phacelia
Kawaiisu *Vegetable* Leaves steam cooked and eaten as greens. (206:48)

Phacelia dubia, Smallflower Scorpionweed
Cherokee *Unspecified* Young growth boiled, fried, and eaten. (204:252) *Vegetable* Leaves cooked and eaten as greens. (80:49)

Phacelia heterophylla, Varileaf Phacelia
Navajo, Kayenta *Vegetable* Used for greens in foods. (205:39)

Phacelia ramosissima, Branching Phacelia
Kawaiisu *Vegetable* Leaves steam cooked and

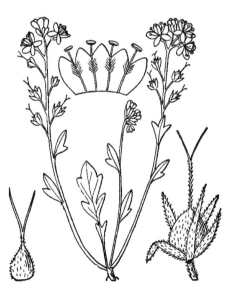

Phacelia dubia

eaten as greens. (206:48) **Luiseño** *Vegetable Plant* used for greens. (155:230)

Phalaris caroliniana, Carolina Canarygrass
Pima, Gila River *Unspecified* Seeds parched and eaten. (133:7)

Phalaris minor, Littleseed Canarygrass
Pima, Gila River *Unspecified* Seeds parched and eaten. (133:7)

Phaseolus acutifolius, Tepary Bean
Havasupai *Soup* Beans parched, ground, and added to hot water to make a soup. *Vegetable* Beans cooked with fresh corn, cooked in hot ashes under a fire, or boiled. *Winter Use Food* Beans stored in granaries or in frame houses for later use. (197:227) **Sia** *Vegetable* Cultivated beans used for food. (199:106)

Phaseolus acutifolius var. **latifolius**, Tepary Bean
Cocopa *Staple* Parched, ground, boiled beans and unparched maize made into a meal. *Winter Use Food* Beans stored in pots for later use. (64:264) **Kamia** *Unspecified* Species used for food. (62:21) **Papago** *Dried Food* Beans threshed, dried on the ground or roofs, stored, and used for food. *Staple* Used as a staple crop. (34:32)

Phaseolus coccineus, Scarlet Runner
Iroquois *Bread & Cake* Seeds cooked, mixed with corn bread paste, and again cooked in the making of the bread. *Dried Food* Seedpods boiled, dried in evaporating baskets or on flat boards, and stored away in bags or barrels. *Soup* Seedpods cooked and used to make soup. Beans boiled with green sweet corn, meat, and seasoned with salt, pepper, and butter or fat. Dried seedpods soaked, boiled, seasoning and butter added, and eaten as a soup. Seeds washed with hot water, cooked until soft, and sugar added to make a sweet soup. Ripe seeds boiled with beef or venison, mashed until thoroughly mixed, and eaten as soup. *Vegetable* Seedpods cooked and eaten whole or cooked with butter,

squash, or meat. Seeds boiled or fried in bear or sunflower oil, seasoned, and eaten. Seeds cooked "like potatoes" and mashed or pounded. (as *P. multiflorus* 196:103)

Phaseolus lunatus, Sieva Bean
Cherokee *Bread & Cake* Beans used to make bean bread. *Soup* Beans used to make hickory nut soup. *Vegetable* Beans used for food. (80:24) **Havasupai** *Soup* Beans parched, ground, and added to hot water to make a soup. *Vegetable* Beans cooked with fresh corn, cooked in hot ashes under a fire, or boiled. *Winter Use Food* Beans stored in granaries or in frame houses for later use. (197:227) **Iroquois** *Bread & Cake* Seeds cooked, mixed with corn bread paste, and again cooked in the making of the bread. *Dried Food* Seedpods boiled, dried in evaporating baskets or on flat boards, and stored away in bags or barrels. *Soup* Seedpods cooked and used to make soup. Beans boiled with green sweet corn, meat, and seasoned with salt, pepper, and butter or fat. Dried seedpods soaked, boiled, seasoning and butter added, and eaten as a soup. Seeds washed with hot water, cooked until soft, and sugar added to make a sweet soup. Ripe seeds boiled with beef or venison, mashed until thoroughly mixed, and eaten as soup. *Vegetable* Seedpods cooked and eaten whole or cooked with butter, squash, or meat. Seeds boiled or fried in bear or sunflower oil, seasoned, and eaten. Seeds cooked "like potatoes" and mashed or pounded. (196:103) **Navajo, Ramah** *Unspecified* Large, white bean cultivated for local use. Small, white lima bean cultivated for local use. (191:33) **Ojibwe** *Vegetable* The Ojibwe claim to have originally had the lima bean, but that is doubtful. (153:406)

Phaseolus vulgaris, Kidney Bean
Abnaki *Vegetable* Beans used for food. (144:169) **Apache, White Mountain** *Vegetable* Beans used for food. (136:159) **Cherokee** *Bread & Cake* Beans used to make bean bread. *Soup* Beans used to make hickory nut soup. (80:24) *Vegetable* Beans used for food. (80:21) **Havasupai** *Soup* Beans parched, ground, and added to hot water to make a soup. *Vegetable*

Beans cooked with fresh corn, cooked in hot ashes under a fire, or boiled. *Winter Use Food* Beans stored in granaries or in frame houses for later use. (197:227) **Iroquois** *Bread & Cake* Seeds cooked, mixed with corn bread paste, and again cooked in the making of the bread. *Dried Food* Seedpods boiled, dried in evaporating baskets or on flat boards, and stored away in bags or barrels. *Soup* Seedpods cooked and used to make soup. Beans boiled with green sweet corn, meat, and seasoned with salt, pepper, and butter or fat. Dried seedpods soaked, boiled, seasoning and butter added, and eaten as a soup. Seeds washed with hot water, cooked until soft, and sugar added to make a sweet soup. Ripe seeds boiled with beef or venison, mashed until thoroughly mixed, and eaten as soup. *Vegetable* Seedpods cooked and eaten whole or cooked with butter, squash, or meat. Seeds boiled or fried in bear or sunflower oil, seasoned, and eaten. Seeds cooked "like potatoes" and mashed or pounded. (196:103) **Menominee** *Staple* Berry used as a staple article of food. (151:69) **Navajo** *Soup* Beans boiled and used in stews. *Vegetable* Beans formed a large part of the vegetable diet. (165:221) **Navajo, Ramah** *Fodder* Plants, after harvesting the beans, used as stock feed. *Winter Use Food* Beans cultivated and stored for use during the winter. (191:33) **Ojibwa** *Vegetable* Similar to the white man's navy bean. Original source of all best commercial pole beans, used alone or in many peculiar combinations. (153:406) **Papago** *Dried Food* Beans threshed, dried on the ground or roofs, stored, and used for food. (34:32) *Unspecified* Beans grown for food. (36:99) **Potawatomi** *Vegetable* A great number of varieties of beans were used. (154:104) **Sia** *Vegetable* Cultivated beans used for food. (199:106) **Tewa** *Staple* Used as a staple food. (138:100) **Zuni** *Vegetable* Beans boiled and fried or crushed, boiled beans mixed with mush, baked in corn husks, and used for food. Boiled and fried beans used for food. (166:69)

***Phegopteris* sp.**, Ako-lea
Hawaiian *Unspecified* Roots cooked for food. (2:12)

Philadelphus microphyllus, Littleleaf Mockorange
Isleta *Fruit* Fruits formerly used for food. (32:30) Fruit formerly eaten as food. (100:36)

Phleum pratense, Timothy
Shuswap *Fodder* Plant used as feed for cows. (123:55)

Phlox stansburyi, Colddesert Phlox
Navajo, Kayenta *Vegetable* Eaten as greens with meat or as an emergency food. (205:38)

Pholisma arenarium, Desert Christmas Tree
Kawaiisu *Unspecified* Stems eaten raw, "roasted," or baked below the fire "like mushrooms." (206:48)

Pholisma sonorae, Sandfood
Cocopa *Dried Food* Roots baked, dried, boiled, and eaten. *Unspecified* Roots baked and eaten after stripping off the thin bark. (as *Ammobroma sonorae* 37:207) **Papago** *Dried Food* Surplus of roots sun dried on roofs and used for food. *Staple* Used as a staple root crop. (as *Ammobroma sonorae* 34:17) *Unspecified* Species used for food. (*Ammobroma sonorae* 32:7) Roots used for food. (as *Ammobroma sonorae* 36:60)

Pholistoma membranaceum, White Fiestaflower
Tubatulabal *Unspecified* Rolled in palm of hand with salt grass leaves and stems and eaten. (as *Ellisea membranacea* 193:19) Leaves used for food. (as *Ellisia membranacea* 193:15)

Phoradendron californicum, Mesquite Mistletoe
Maricopa *Porridge* Berries boiled to produce liquid and combined with wheat mush. (37:204) **Papago** *Dried Food* Berries sun dried, stored, and used for food. (34:19) **Pima** *Fruit* Berries boiled and eaten. (32:39) Berries boiled and eaten. (146:71) **Pima, Gila River** *Fruit* Berries eaten cooked or raw. (133:5) *Snack Food* Fruits eaten raw or boiled as a snack food. (133:7)

Phoradendron juniperinum, Juniper Mistletoe

Acoma *Starvation Food* Berries eaten when other foods became scarce. (32:39) **Havasupai** *Unspecified* Plant pounded and boiled for food. (197:216) **Keres, Western** *Fodder* Plant used as sheep and goat feed, to produce good milk. *Starvation Food* Berries eaten when other food was scarce. (171:59) **Laguna** *Starvation Food* Berries eaten when other foods became scarce. (32:39) **Navajo** *Beverage* Stems used to make tea. *Fruit* Berries used for food. (55:42)

Phragmites australis, Common Reed

Kawaiisu *Sweetener* Stems dried and beaten with sticks to remove the sugar crystals. (206:49) **Klamath** *Unspecified* Seeds used for food. (as *P. phragmites* 45:91) **Montana Indian** *Unspecified* Seeds used for food. (as *P. communis* 19:17) **Paiute** *Sweetener* Dried sap made into balls, softened by fire, and eaten like sugar. (as *P. communis* 167:245) **Paiute, Northern** *Candy* Sap crystallized, gathered, and eaten like candy. (as *P. communis* 59:53) **Thompson** *Forage* Used as a forage plant only in absence of other foods. (as *P. communis* 164:516) **Yuma** *Unspecified* Honeydew obtained from grass. (as *P. communis* 37:218)

Phyllospadix scouleri, Scouler's Surfgrass

Hesquiat *Unspecified* Leaves occasionally cooked and eaten when it had herring eggs on it. (185:58) **Makah** *Unspecified* Rhizomes chewed or eaten raw. (67:328) Roots eaten raw in the spring. (79:21)

Phyllospadix serrulatus, Toothed Surfgrass

Makah *Unspecified* Rhizomes chewed or eaten raw. (67:328)

Phyllospadix torreyi, Torrey's Surfgrass

Hesquiat *Dried Food* Leaves, with herring eggs on it, dried for later use. (185:58) **Makah** *Unspecified* Rhizomes chewed or eaten raw. (67:328)

Physalis acutifolia, Sharpleaf Groundcherry

Pima, Gila River *Baby Food* Fruits eaten raw, primarily by children. (133:7) *Snack Food* Fruit eaten primarily by children as a snack food. (133:5)

Physalis hederifolia* var. *fendleri, Fendler's Groundcherry

Apache, White Mountain *Fruit* Fruit eaten raw and cooked. (as *P. fendleri* 136:159) **Mohave** *Fruit* Fruits eaten fresh by children. **Yuma** *Fruit* Fruits eaten fresh by children. (as *P. fendleri* 37:207) **Zuni** *Sauce & Relish* Fruit boiled in small quantities of water, crushed, and used as a condiment. (as *P. fendleri* 166:70)

Physalis heterophylla, Clammy Groundcherry

Cherokee *Fruit* Fruit used for food. (80:37) **Cheyenne** *Fruit* Ripe fruits eaten in fall. (83:39) **Dakota** *Dried Food* Fruits, when in sufficient quantity, dried for winter use. (70:113) *Sauce & Relish* Fruit made into a sauce. (69:362) Fruits made into a sauce for food. (70:113) *Winter Use Food* Fruit dried and stored for winter use. (69:362) **Meskwaki** *Fruit* Berries eaten raw. (152:264) **Omaha** *Dried Food* Fruits, when in sufficient quantity, dried for winter use. *Sauce & Relish* Fruits made into a sauce for food.

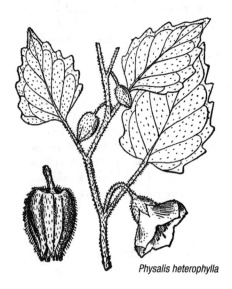

Physalis heterophylla

Pawnee *Dried Food* Fruits, when in sufficient quantity, dried for winter use. *Sauce & Relish* Fruits made into a sauce for food. **Ponca** *Dried Food* Fruits, when in sufficient quantity, dried for winter use. *Sauce & Relish* Fruits made into a sauce for food. (70:113)

Physalis lanceolata, Lanceleaf Groundcherry
Dakota *Unspecified* Bud clusters used in the spring for food. Firm, young, green seedpods boiled with meat in the spring. (69:363) **Navajo** *Fruit* Berries used for food. (90:154)

Physalis longifolia, Longleaf Groundcherry
Keres, Western *Fruit* Berries used for food. (171:59) **Pueblo** *Fruit* Berries eaten fresh or boiled. **San Felipe** *Fruit* Berries eaten fresh or boiled. (32:40) **Zuni** *Fruit* Berries boiled, ground in a mortar with raw onions, chile, and coriander seeds and used for food. (166:70)

Physalis pubescens, Husk Tomato
Mohave *Fruit* Fruits eaten fresh by children. (37:207) **Navajo** *Fruit* Sour berries mixed with honey and eaten. *Preserves* Sour berries used to make jam. *Staple* Berries dried, ground into a flour, and stored for winter use. (110:17) **Navajo, Ramah** *Fruit* Fruit eaten raw or boiled. (191:43) **Yuma** *Fruit* Fruits eaten fresh by children. (37:207)

Physalis subulata var. *neomexicana*, New Mexican Groundcherry
Apache, Chiricahua & Mescalero *Special Food* Fresh fruit eaten by children as a delicacy. (as *P. neomexicana* 33:45) **Keres, Western** *Fruit* Berries used for food. (as *P. neo-mexicana* 171:59) **Navajo** *Fruit* Raw fruit used for food. (as *P. neomexicana* 165:222) **Pueblo** *Fruit* Berries eaten fresh or boiled. (as *P. neomexicana* 32:39) **Tewa** *Fruit* Berries used for food. (as *P. neomexicana* 138:59)

Physalis virginiana, Virginia Groundcherry
Meskwaki *Fruit* Berries, touched by frost, eaten raw. (152:264)

Physocarpus capitatus, Pacific Ninebark
Miwok *Fruit* Raw berries used for food. (12:162)

Physocarpus malvaceus, Mallow Ninebark
Okanagan-Colville *Unspecified* Roots steam cooked and eaten. (188:126)

Phytolacca americana, American Pokeweed
Cherokee *Beverage* Crushed berries and sour grapes strained, mixed with sugar and cornmeal, and used as a beverage. (126:51) *Cooking Agent* Crushed berries used to add color to canned fruit. (80:50) Berries used to color canned fruit. *Dried Food* Leaves gathered into bundle and dried for future use. (126:51) *Unspecified* Young shoots cut, cooked, and eaten. (204:251) *Vegetable* Shoots, leaves, and stems parboiled, rinsed, and cooked alone or mixed with other greens and eggs. Peeled stalks cut lengthwise, parboiled, dipped in egg, rolled in cornmeal, and fried like fish. (126:51) **Iroquois** *Vegetable* Stalks eaten as greens in spring. (as *P. decandra* 124:93) **Malecite** *Unspecified* Shoots used for food. (160:6) **Mohegan** *Unspecified* Cooked and used for food. (as *P. decandra* 176:83)

Picea engelmannii, Engelmann's Spruce
Okanagan-Colville *Beverage* Branches used by mountain travelers to make a tea. (188:27) **Thompson** *Unspecified* Sap considered edible. (187:100)

Picea glauca, White Spruce
Algonquin, Quebec *Candy* Resin chewed like chewing gum. (18:73) **Cree, Woodlands** *Candy* Gum chewed for pleasure. Gum chewed as a confection. (109:48) **Eskimo, Alaska** *Candy* Resin chewed for pleasure. (as *P. canadensis*

4:716) **Eskimo, Inuktitut** *Unspecified* Cambium eaten in the spring. (202:188) **Gitksan** *Unspecified* Cambium eaten fresh. (as *P. glauca × engelmannii* 73:151) **Koyukon** *Candy* Pitch chewed like gum. (119:50) **Micmac** *Beverage* Bark used to make a beverage. (159:258) **Okanagan-Colville** *Beverage* Branches used by mountain travelers to make a tea. (188:27) **Tanana, Upper** *Candy* Hard pitch used for chewing gum. *Fodder* Rotten wood mixed with poque and fed to puppies. *Starvation Food* Cambium used as a food during periods of food shortage. *Unspecified* Fresh sap eaten as food during the summer. (102:2) **Wet'suwet'en** *Unspecified* Cambium eaten fresh. (as *P. glauca × engelmannii* 73:151)

Picea mariana, Black Spruce
Anticosti *Beverage* Branches used to make beer. (143:63) **Carrier** *Candy* Pitch used to chew. (31:69) **Cree, Woodlands** *Candy* Gum chewed for pleasure. (109:49) **Eskimo, Inuktitut** *Unspecified* Cambium eaten in the spring. (202:188) **Micmac** *Beverage* Bark used to make a beverage. (159:258)

Picea rubens, Red Spruce
Chippewa *Beverage* Leaves used to make a beverage. (as *P. rubra* 53:317)

Picea sitchensis, Sitka Spruce
Haisla & Hanaksiala *Candy* Pitch chewed like chewing gum. (43:175) **Hesquiat** *Candy* Cooled, rendered pitch chewed like gum. (185:41) **Kitasoo** *Dried Food* Inner bark cooked and dried for later use. (43:317) **Kwakiutl, Southern** *Candy* Pitch used as chewing gum. (183:293) **Makah** *Candy* Pitch used as chewing gum. (67:234) Pitch chewed as gum for pleasure. (79:17) *Unspecified* "Little cones" and buds used for food. (67:234) Young shoots eaten raw. (79:17) **Oweekeno** *Candy* Pitch boiled and used for chewing. (43:68) **Quinault** *Candy* Pitch chewed as gum for pleasure. (79:17)

Piloblephis rigida, Wild Pennyroyal
Seminole *Spice* Plant used for soup flavoring. (as *Pycnothymus rigidus* 169:482)

Pinus albicaulis, Whitebark Pine
Coeur d'Alene *Unspecified* Nutlets used for food. (178:90) Nutlets cooked in hot ashes and used for food. (178:93) **Montana Indian** *Unspecified* Inner bark used for food. Nuts were an important article of food. (19:18) **Okanagan-Colville** *Unspecified* Seeds used for food. *Winter Use Food* Seeds gathered and stored for winter use. (188:27) **Spokan** *Unspecified* Nutlets used for food. (178:344) **Thompson** *Dried Food* Dried nuts kept alone in sacks or mixed with dried serviceberries and stored for future use. *Porridge* Parched seeds pounded in a mortar to make a flour and mixed with water to form a mush. (187:101) *Unspecified* Seeds oven cooked or fire roasted. (164:492) Seeds eaten roasted or raw, but often considered bitter. If too many raw seeds were eaten, it would cause constipation. Roasted seeds were therefore preferred to raw seeds. (187:101) *Winter Use Food* Seeds cooked, crushed, mixed with dried serviceberries, and preserved for winter use. (164:492) Cooked, crushed seeds mixed with dried berries and preserved for winter use. (187:101)

Pinus banksiana, Jack Pine
Cree, Woodlands *Unspecified* Inner bark used for food. (109:50)

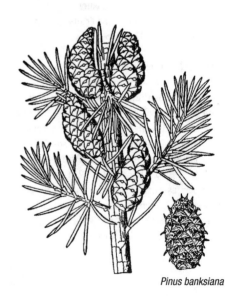

Pinus banksiana

Pinus contorta, Lodgepole Pine
Blackfoot *Candy* Pitch chewed like gum.
(86:104) **Coeur d'Alene** *Unspecified* Cambium
layer used for food. (178:91) **Flathead** *Candy*
Pitchy secretions chewed as gum. *Unspecified*
Inner bark used for food. Seeds used for food.
(82:52) **Gitksan** *Unspecified* Sap eaten fresh.
(73:151) **Hesquiat** *Candy* Pitch chewed like
gum. (185:44) **Kutenai** *Unspecified* Inner bark
used for food. (82:52) **Okanagan-Colville**
Forage Cambium layer eaten by grizzly bears.
Unspecified Cambium layer used for food.
(188:28) **Okanagon** *Staple* Cambium layer
used as a principal food. (178:239) *Unspecified*
Cambium layer and sap used for food. (125:38)
Salish, Coast *Bread & Cake* Juicy inner bark
dried in cakes and used for food. *Unspecified*
Juicy inner bark eaten fresh. (182:70) **Shuswap**
Unspecified Inner bark used for food. (123:51)
Spokan *Unspecified* Cambium used for food.
(178:344) **Thompson** *Beverage* Needles used
to make a tea-like beverage. Twigs with needles
attached used to make a tea-like beverage.
Candy Young shoots of branches chewed for
the honey. *Dried Food* Cambium and adjacent
phloem tissue dried for winter use. (187:102)
Unspecified Cambium layer and sap used for
food. (125:38) Cambium and adjacent phloem
tissue eaten fresh. (187:102) **Wet'suwet'en**
Dried Food Inner bark strips dried and stored
for future food use. *Unspecified* Sap eaten fresh.
(73:151)

Pinus contorta* var. *murrayana,
    Murray Lodgepole Pine
Montana Indian *Starvation Food* Inner cambium layer of the bark eaten in times of scarcity.
(as *P. murrayana* 19:18) **Okanagon** *Unspecified* Cambium layer and sap used for food.
Thompson *Unspecified* Cambium layer and sap
used for food. (125:38) Sap eaten especially in
the spring. (as *P. murrayana* 164:483)

Pinus edulis, Twoneedle Pinyon
Apache, Chiricahua & Mescalero *Pie & Pudding* Seeds mixed with yucca fruit pulp to make
a pudding. *Special Food* Seeds ground, rolled
into balls and eaten as a delicacy. (33:43) *Un-

specified Secretion from the trunk chewed.
(33:45) **Apache, Mescalero** *Dried Food* Nuts
parched, ground, mixed with datil fruit, mescal,
mesquite beans, or sotol and used for food.
Special Food Nuts used as an essential food
during girls' puberty ceremonies. (14:35)
Apache, Western *Candy* Pitch used as chewing
gum. *Porridge* Pinyon and corn flour mixed and
cooked into a mush. *Staple* Used as a staple
food. Nuts eaten raw, roasted, or ground into
flour. *Winter Use Food* Nuts stored in baskets or
pottery jars. (26:185) **Apache, White Mountain** *Unspecified* Nuts eaten raw. (136:159)
Gosiute *Unspecified* Nuts used for food.
(39:377) **Havasupai** *Preserves* Seeds parched,
ground, kneaded into seed butter, and eaten
with fruit drinks or spread on bread. (197:67)
Soup Nuts ground with the shells and used to
make soup. (197:73) *Spice* Sprigs placed in the
cooking pit with porcupine, bobcat, or badger
to improve the taste of the meat. *Unspecified*
Nuts formerly used as an important food source.
(197:205) **Hopi** *Special Food* Nuts roasted and
eaten as an after supper luxury. (120:18) *Unspecified* Nuts used for food. (42:347) Nuts
eaten for food. (200:63) **Hualapai** *Beverage*
Needles used to make a tea. *Bread & Cake* Nuts
formed into cakes. *Candy* Pitch chewed as a
gum. *Porridge* Nuts used to make a paste. *Soup*
Nuts used to make a soup. *Unspecified* Nuts eat-
en raw or roasted. (195:35) **Isleta** *Staple* Nuts
formerly used as a staple food. (100:37) *Unspecified* Seeds formerly considered an important food. (32:40) *Winter Use Food* Nuts gathered and stored for winter use. (100:37) **Jemez**
Unspecified Nuts gathered in large quantities to
save and sell. (44:26) **Keres, Western** *Unspecified* Raw or roasted nuts used for food.
(171:60) **Keresan** *Winter Use Food* Nuts gathered in large quantities, roasted, and eaten during the winter. (198:562) **Navajo** *Bread & Cake*
Ground nuts formed into cakes. (110:21) *Candy*
Sap used as a chewing gum. (55:21) *Porridge*
Nuts boiled into a gruel. (110:21) *Preserves*
Roasted nuts mashed into a butter. (55:21)
Nuts roasted, cracked and shelled on a metate,
ground fine, made into butter, and used with
bread. (165:222) *Special Food* Ground nuts

rolled into balls and eaten as a delicacy. (110:21) *Staple* Nuts hulled, parched, and ground with cornmeal to make a flour. (32:40) *Unspecified* Hardened resinous secretions chewed. (32:32) Nuts hulled, roasted, and eaten without further preparation. (32:40) Seeds used for food. (90:162) Nuts eaten raw or roasted directly from the shell. (110:21) **Navajo, Ramah** *Candy* Resin used for chewing gum. *Preserves* Roasted, ground nuts made into butter and spread on corn cakes or mixed with roasted, ground corn. *Starvation Food* Inside bark used as an emergency ration, when food was scarce. *Winter Use Food* Nuts gathered and stored for winter use. Roasted, ground nuts made into sun dried cakes and stored for winter. (191:12) **Pueblo** *Unspecified* Hardened resinous secretions chewed. (32:32) Seeds formerly considered an important food. (32:40) **Sia** *Unspecified* Nuts gathered in considerable quantities, roasted, and used for food. (199:107) **Tewa** *Unspecified* Fresh or roasted seeds formerly considered an important food. (32:40) Nuts used for food. (42:347) Nuts formerly roasted and used for food. (138:41) **Zuni** *Winter Use Food* Nuts gathered in great quantities, toasted, and stored for winter use. (166:70)

Pinus flexilis, Limber Pine
Apache, Chiricahua & Mescalero *Unspecified* Seeds roasted and hulled or sometimes the seeds ground, shell and all, and eaten. (33:43) **Montana Indian** *Unspecified* Nuts were an important article of food. (19:18)

Pinus jeffreyi, Jeffrey Pine
Paiute, Northern *Candy* Sap crystallized, gathered, and eaten like candy. *Winter Use Food* Sap crystallized, gathered, and stored for winter use. (59:53)

Pinus lambertiana, Sugar Pine
Karok *Unspecified* Roasted seeds used for food. (6:44) Coagulated sap gathered from hollow trees and eaten without preparation or mixing with other foods. Nuts roasted and used for food. (148:378) *Winter Use Food* Roasted seeds stored for winter use. (6:44) Nuts roasted and

stored for winter use. (148:378) **Kawaiisu** *Sweetener* Sap, drained through a hole cut into the tree, dried into a "powdered sugar" and eaten. *Unspecified* Seeds eaten raw, roasted, parched, boiled, or pounded and mixed with cold water. (206:50) **Klamath** *Unspecified* Seeds used for food. (45:88) **Mendocino Indian** *Unspecified* Nuts used for food. (41:306) **Miwok** *Sweetener* Sugar pine sugar eaten as a delicacy. (12:151) *Unspecified* Shelled nutmeats used for food. (12:150) Pulverized nutshells and meat made into peanut butter and used for feasts. (12:151) **Pomo** *Unspecified* Nuts rarely used for food. (11:79) Nuts used for food. Pitch used for food. (66:11) **Pomo, Kashaya** *Candy* Pitch chewed for gum. *Sweetener* Pitch tasted sweet like candy. *Unspecified* Nuts, inside the cone, eaten fresh. *Winter Use Food* Nuts, inside the cone, dried for winter use. (72:93) **Shasta** *Bread & Cake* Nuts dried, powdered, made into small cakes, and eaten with a very thin mush made of grass seeds. *Dried Food* Nuts dried and eaten. *Unspecified* Whole nuts mixed with powdered salmon and eaten. (93:308) **Yuki** *Candy* Sweet exudation chewed as gum. (49:88)

Pinus monophylla, Singleleaf Pinyon
Apache, Western *Candy* Pitch used as chewing gum. *Porridge* Pinyon and corn flour mixed and cooked into a mush. *Staple* Used as a staple food. Nuts eaten raw, roasted, or ground into flour. *Winter Use Food* Nuts stored in baskets or pottery jars. (26:185) **Cahuilla** *Baby Food* Nuts used as one of the few foods fed to babies instead of a natural milk diet. *Beverage* Ground nuts mixed with water and used as a drink. *Dried Food* Cooked, unshelled nuts stored for future use. *Porridge* Roasted, shelled nuts eaten whole or ground and made into mush. (15:102) **Cocopa** *Unspecified* Pinyons eaten in the mountains away from home. (37:188) **Diegueño** *Unspecified* Nuts used for food. (84:30) Seeds used for food. (88:215) **Gosiute** *Unspecified* Nuts used for food. (39:377) **Havasupai** *Spice* Sprigs placed in the cooking pit with porcupine, bobcat, or badger to improve the taste of the meat. *Unspecified* Nuts formerly used as an important food source. (197:205) **Hopi** *Unspeci-*

fied Nuts eaten for food. (200:63) **Kawaiisu** *Porridge* Roasted, steamed seeds pounded into a meal, mixed with cold water, and eaten. *Unspecified* Roasted, steamed seeds eaten hulled or unhulled. Roasted, steamed seeds hulled, the kernels boiled and eaten. *Winter Use Food* Unhulled seeds strung on cord, dried, and stored in sacks for winter use. (206:50) **Paiute** *Dried Food* Nuts sun dried or roasted and stored for future use. *Porridge* Roasted nuts ground into a flour and mixed with water into a paste or mush. *Soup* Roasted nuts ground into a flour and mixed with water into a soup. *Staple* Roasted nuts ground into flour. (167:241) *Unspecified* Nuts eaten and obtained from Nevada. Seeds used for food. (111:42) Nuts roasted and eaten whole. *Winter Use Food* Nuts gathered in great quantity and stored for future use. (167:241) **Paiute, Northern** *Bread & Cake* Nuts roasted, winnowed, dried, ground into a meal, made into a stiff flour dough, and eaten. (59:51) *Candy* Gum chewed as gum. (59:53) *Dried Food* Nuts dried and stored for future use. *Ice Cream* Nuts roasted, dried, ground into a meal, made into a stiff dough, frozen, and eaten like ice cream. *Soup* Nuts roasted, ground into a fine flour, and cooked into a thick soup. (59:51) **Shoshoni** *Unspecified* Nuts formed an important part of the diet. (117:443) **Tubatulabal** *Unspecified* Nuts used extensively for food. (193:15) **Washo** *Dried Food* Roasted nuts eaten fresh or stored for later use. (10:13) *Porridge* Nuts used to make mush. (10:14)

Pinus monticola, Western White Pine
Paiute *Unspecified* Nuts served as a minor source of subsistence. (111:40) **Salish, Coast** *Dried Food* Inner bark dried in cakes and used for food. *Unspecified* Inner bark eaten fresh. (182:71) **Shuswap** *Unspecified* Cones used for food. (123:51) **Thompson** *Unspecified* Gummy substance collected from trunk and branches and chewed. (164:493)

Pinus muricata, Bishop Pine
Pomo, Kashaya *Unspecified* Nuts eaten fresh. *Winter Use Food* Nuts dried for winter use. (72:92)

Pinus ponderosa, Ponderosa Pine
Blackfoot *Unspecified* Inner bark used for food. (97:18) **Cheyenne** *Candy* Pitch chewed as a gum. (82:50) *Unspecified* Seeds used for food. Young male cones chewed for the juice. (83:6) **Coeur d'Alene** *Unspecified* Nutlets used for food. (178:90) Cambium layer used for food. (178:91) **Havasupai** *Unspecified* Nuts roasted and eaten. (197:206) **Kawaiisu** *Unspecified* Kernels eaten raw. (206:51) **Klamath** *Sauce & Relish* Cambium layer scraped off and eaten as a relish. *Starvation Food* Cambium layer scraped off and eaten in time of famine. *Unspecified* Sweet layer between bark and sapwood scraped and used for food. (45:89) **Miwok** *Dried Food* Cones' extracted nuts gathered, dried in the sun, and eaten. (12:150) **Montana Indian** *Unspecified* Inner bark eaten in the spring. (19:18) Inner bark formerly used for food. (82:50) **Navajo, Ramah** *Unspecified* Bark eaten raw. (191:13) **Okanagan-Colville** *Candy* Pitch used as chewing gum. Green buds chewed and the juice sucked by children. *Frozen Food* Cambium frozen for future use. *Unspecified* Cambium used for food. Seeds eaten like nuts. *Winter Use Food* Seeds stored for winter use. (188:29) **Okanagon** *Staple* Nutlets or seeds used as a principal food. Cambium layer used as a principal food. (178:239) *Unspecified* Seeds used for food. (125:39) **Paiute** *Candy* Dried pitch used as chewing gum. *Dried Food* Inner bark sun dried and stored. *Unspecified* Inner bark eaten fresh and raw. Seeds used for food. (111:40) **Sanpoil & Nespelem** *Unspecified* Cambium layer eaten raw. This was an important food. The bark was removed in sections with the aid of wooden wedges. Sap scrapers were made from the rib of the deer by cutting it to an appropriate length, sharpening the edges, and rounding the working end. (as *P. poderosa* 131:103) Pine nuts eaten without special preparation. (131:104) **Shasta** *Bread & Cake* Nuts dried, powdered, made into small cakes, and eaten with a very thin mush made of grass seeds. *Dried Food* Nuts dried and eaten. *Unspecified* Whole nuts mixed with powdered salmon and eaten. (93:308) **Spokan** *Unspecified* Nutlets used for food. Cambium used for food. (178:344)

Thompson *Porridge* Seeds and whitebark pine seeds placed in a bag, pounded into a powder, mixed with water, and eaten. (187:104) *Unspecified* Seeds used for food. (125:39) Cambium of young twigs eaten. (164:484) Seeds eaten in small quantities. (164:491)

Pinus ponderosa var. *scopulorum*, Ponderosa Pine
Apache, Chiricahua & Mescalero *Bread & Cake* Inner bark scraped off and baked in the form of cakes. *Starvation Food* Seeds ground, rolled into balls, and eaten raw only in times of food scarcity. *Unspecified* Bark boiled or eaten raw. (as *P. scopulorum* 33:43)

Pinus quadrifolia h, Parry Pinyon
Cahuilla *Baby Food* Nuts used as one of the few foods fed to babies instead of a natural milk diet. *Beverage* Ground nuts mixed with water and used as a drink. *Dried Food* Cooked, unshelled nuts stored for future use. *Porridge* Roasted, shelled nuts eaten whole or ground and made into mush. (15:102) **Diegueño** *Unspecified* Nuts used for food. (84:30) Seeds used for food. (88:215)

Pinus sabiniana, California Foothill Pine
Costanoan *Unspecified* Pine nuts used for food. (21:248) **Kawaiisu** *Porridge* Seeds eaten fresh, roasted, boiled, or pounded, and mixed with cold water. *Unspecified* Seeds eaten fresh, roasted, boiled, or pounded, and mixed with cold water. (206:52) **Mendocino Indian** *Starvation Food* Fresh, inner bark formerly used for food during prolonged winters when other foods were scarce. (41:307) **Mewuk** *Unspecified* Nuts used for food. (117:333) **Miwok** *Unspecified* Nuts and cone pith eaten for food. (12:149) **Pomo** *Unspecified* Nuts rarely used for food. (11:79) **Pomo, Kashaya** *Staple* Dried nut eaten whole or pounded into a flour and mixed with pinole. *Unspecified* Nuts eaten fresh. *Winter Use Food* Nuts dried for winter use. (72:92) **Shasta** *Bread & Cake* Nuts dried, powdered, made into small cakes, and eaten with a very thin mush made of grass seeds. *Dried Food*

Nuts dried and eaten. *Unspecified* Whole nuts mixed with powdered salmon and eaten. (93:308) **Tubatulabal** *Unspecified* Nuts used extensively for food. (193:15) **Wailaki** *Candy* Gum chewed by children for pleasure. (41:307)

Pinus strobus, Eastern White Pine
Iroquois *Unspecified* Species used for food. (196:119) **Micmac** *Beverage* Bark used to make a beverage. (159:258) **Ojibwa** *Unspecified* Young staminate catkins of this pine cooked for food and stewed with meat. One might think this would taste rather like pitch, but they assured the writer that is was sweet and had no pitchy flavor. (153:407)

Piper nigrum, Black Pepper
Cherokee *Spice* Used to season food. (80:48) **Haisla & Hanaksiala** *Spice* Used for seasoning. (43:259)

Piperia elegans, Hillside Bogorchid
Pomo, Kashaya *Vegetable* Baked bulbs eaten like baked potatoes. (as *Habenaria elegans* 72:62)

Piperia unalascensis, Alaska Rein Orchid
Pomo, Kashaya *Vegetable* Baked bulbs eaten like baked potatoes. (as *Habenaria unalascensis* 72:62)

Piptatherum miliaceum, Smilograss
Paiute *Staple* Roasted and ground into flour. (as *Oryzopsis miliacea* 167:244)

Pisum sativum, Garden Pea
Cherokee *Vegetable* Peas used for food. (80:48) **Navajo, Ramah** *Vegetable* Used as a garden vegetable. (191:34) **Okanagan-Colville** *Unspecified* Seeds used for food. (188:106) **Papago** *Unspecified* Species used for food. **Pima** *Unspecified* Species used for food. (36:120)

Plagiobothrys fulvus var. *campestris*, Fulvous Popcornflower
Mendocino Indian *Staple* Seeds used to make

pinole. Seeds winnowed, parched, and flour eaten dry. *Unspecified* Crisp, tender shoots and flowers used as a sweet and aromatic food. (as *P. campestris* 41:382)

Plagiobothrys nothofulvus, Rusty Popcornflower
Yuki *Vegetable* Young leaves eaten as greens. (49:85)

Plantago lanceolata, Narrowleaf Plantain
Mendocino Indian *Fodder* Plant used as fodder for cattle. (41:388)

Plantago macrocarpa, Seashore Plantain
Alaska Native *Vegetable* Young, tender leaves used raw in salads or cooked as spinach. (85:43)

Plantago major, Common Plantain
Acoma *Unspecified* Young leaves used for food. (32:42) **Cherokee** *Vegetable* Leaves cooked and eaten as greens. (80:50) Cut leaves and stems cooked with fatback. (126:52) **Keres, Western** *Unspecified* Tender shoots used for food. (171:61) **Laguna** *Unspecified* Young leaves used for food. (32:42) **Mohegan** *Vegeta-*

ble Combined with pigweed, mustard, dock, and nettle and used as mixed greens. (176:83)

Plantago maritima, Goose Tongue
Alaska Native *Unspecified* Plant eaten fresh or cooked. *Winter Use Food* Plant canned for winter use. (85:45)

Plantago ovata, Desert Indianwheat
Pima *Fodder* Herbs used for fodder. (as *P. fastigiata* 47:96) **Pima, Gila River** *Unspecified* Seeds used for food. (as *P. insularis* 133:7)

Plantago patagonica, Woolly Plantain
Havasupai *Porridge* Seeds ground and made into mush. (as *P. purshii* 197:242) **Navajo, Kayenta** *Porridge* Seeds made into mush and used for food. (as *P. purshii* 205:43) **Pima, Gila River** *Unspecified* Seeds used for food. (as *P. purshii* 133:7)

Platanthera sparsiflora var. *sparsiflora*, Canyon Bog Orchid
San Felipe *Starvation Food* Plant used as food in times of food shortage. (as *Habenaria sparsiflora* 32:30)

Platanus racemosa, California Sycamore
Costanoan *Unspecified* Inner bark used for food. (21:249) **Kawaiisu** *Beverage* Small bark pieces boiled in water and drunk warm with sugar. (206:53)

Platystemon californicus, California Creamcups
Mendocino Indian *Vegetable* Green leaves eaten as greens. (41:351)

Pleurotus ostreatus, Oyster Mushroom
Pomo, Kashaya *Vegetable* Cooked on hot stones, baked in the oven, or fried. (72:131)

Pluchea sericea, Arrow Weed
Cahuilla *Unspecified* Roots roasted and eaten. (15:105) **Pima** *Forage* Plants browsed by deer, horses, and cattle. (47:105)

Plantago major

Poa arida, Plains Bluegrass
Gosiute *Unspecified* Seeds used for food. (as *P. californica* 39:377)

Poa fendleriana, Mutton Grass
Havasupai *Bread & Cake* Seeds parched, ground fine, boiled, thickened, made into balls, and eaten as dumplings. Seeds ground, kneaded into a thick paste, rolled into little balls, boiled, and eaten as marbles. (197:66) *Staple* Seeds ground and eaten as a ground or parched meal. (197:67) *Unspecified* Seeds used for food. (197:210)

Poa fendleriana ssp. fendleriana, Skyline Bluegrass
Navajo, Ramah *Fodder* Used for sheep and horse feed. (as *P. longiligula* 191:17)

Poa secunda, Sandberg Bluegrass
Gosiute *Unspecified* Seeds used for food. (as *P. tenuifolia* 39:377)

Podophyllum peltatum, May Apple
Cherokee *Fruit* Fruit used for food. (80:44) Ripe fruit used for food. (126:32) **Chippewa** *Fruit* Fruit considered very palatable. (71:130)

Podophyllum peltatum

Iroquois *Bread & Cake* Fruit mashed, made into small cakes, and dried for future use. *Dried Food* Raw or cooked fruit sun or fire dried and stored for future use. *Fruit* Dried fruit taken as a hunting food. *Sauce & Relish* Dried fruit cakes soaked in warm water and cooked as a sauce or mixed with corn bread. (196:129) **Menominee** *Fruit* Fresh, ripe fruits eaten. *Preserves* Fresh, ripe fruits preserved. (151:62) **Meskwaki** *Fruit* Fresh fruits eaten raw. *Preserves* Fruits cooked into a conserve. (152:256)

Pogogyne douglasii ssp. parviflora, Douglas's Mesamint
Concow *Substitution Food* Leaves used as a substitute for tea. **Numlaki** *Staple* Seeds used as a sweet, aromatic ingredient of wheat and barley pinole. **Yuki** *Staple* Seeds used as a sweet, aromatic ingredient of wheat and barley pinole. (as *P. parviflora* 41:384)

Polanisia dodecandra ssp. trachysperma, Sandyseed Clammyweed
Pueblo *Dried Food* Young plants boiled, pressed, rolled into balls, dried, and stored for winter use. *Soup* Plant made into a stew with wild onions, wild celery, tallow, or bits of meat. *Unspecified* Young plants boiled, pressed, rolled into balls, and eaten. *Vegetable* Young plants boiled with a pinch of salt and eaten as greens. (as *P. trachysperma* 32:25)

Poliomintha incana, Hoary Rosemarymint
Hopi *Dried Food* Dried plant stored for winter use. (42:351) Dried for winter use. (200:91) *Spice* Flowers boiled with a certain mush to give it a flavor. (190:165) Flowers used as flavoring. (200:91) *Unspecified* Plant eaten raw or boiled. (42:351) Plant dipped in salted water and eaten. (56:19) Flowers eaten. Flowers eaten and also boiled with a certain mush to give it a flavor. (190:165) Eaten raw or boiled. (200:91) **Tewa** *Dried Food* Dried plant stored for winter use. *Spice* Flowers used as flavoring. *Unspecified* Plant eaten raw or boiled. (42:351)

Polygonatum biflorum, King Solomon's Seal
Cherokee *Bread & Cake* Roots dried, beaten into flour, and used to make bread. (80:56) Roots used to make bread. (126:47) *Spice* Roots ground and used as salt. (80:56) *Unspecified* Young growth boiled, fried, and eaten. (204:252) *Vegetable* Leaves cooked and eaten as greens. (80:56) Stems and leaves parboiled, rinsed, fried with grease and salt until soft, and eaten as a potherb. *Winter Use Food* Stems and leaves mixed with bean salad and wanegedum (angelico, *Ligusticum canadense*), blanched, and boiled for 3 hours in a can. (126:47) Rhizomes boiled and eaten especially during winter. (204:252)

Polygonum alpinum, Alaska Wild Rhubarb
Alaska Native *Pie & Pudding* Chopped leaves and stems added to a thick pudding of flour and sugar and eaten. *Vegetable* Young stems cut into small pieces and used in the same manner as domesticated rhubarb. Young, tender leaves mixed with other greens and cooked in boiling water. (as *P. alaskanum* 85:47) **Eskimo, Arctic** *Beverage* Juice sweetened and used to make a beverage. *Pie & Pudding* Stems stewed and used as pie filling. *Unspecified* Stems stewed and eaten. (as *P. alaskanum* 128:26) **Eskimo, Inupiat** *Beverage* Stalks boiled, strained, and juice used as a beverage. *Dessert* Raw stalks eaten in a garden rhubarb dessert. Stored stalks boiled, mixed with cranberries, raisins, dried apples, or peaches and eaten as a dessert. *Sauce & Relish* Stalks boiled into a sauce and used on cooked fish. Stalks boiled, mixed with oil and sugar, and used as a sauce for dumplings, cake, or sweet breads. *Unspecified* Fresh, chopped stalks mixed with whitefish or pike eggs and livers, oil, and sugar and eaten. *Vegetable* Fresh stalks eaten raw with seal oil and meat or fish. Raw stalks eaten with peanut butter or cut up in a salad. Leaves boiled and eaten as hot greens. *Winter Use Food* Stalks boiled and stored in a barrel for winter use. (as *P. alaskanum* 98:45) **Koyukon** *Unspecified* Plant cooked and eaten. (as *P. alaskanum* 119:56)

Tanana, Upper *Frozen Food* Leaves and stems frozen for future use. *Vegetable* Stems and leaves boiled with sugar and flour or in whitefish broth, grease, and sugar and eaten. Stems and leaves eaten raw. (as *P. alaskanum* 102:15)

Polygonum amphibium var. **emersum**, Longroot Smartweed
Lakota *Unspecified* Species used for food. (as *P. coccineum* 139:54) **Sioux** *Sauce & Relish* Young shoots eaten in the spring as a relish. (as *P. emersum* 19:18)

Polygonum argyrocoleon, Silversheath Knotweed
Cocopa *Dried Food* Seeds parched, ground, and eaten. (37:187)

Polygonum bistorta, Meadow Bistort
Eskimo, Inupiat *Unspecified* Roots eaten raw and cooked. *Vegetable* Leaves preserved in seal oil and eaten with any meat or eaten raw in salads. (98:19)

Polygonum bistorta var. **plumosum**, Meadow Bistort
Alaska Native *Dietary Aid* Leaves rich in vitamin C and provitamin A. *Soup* Roots boiled and added to stews. *Unspecified* Roots boiled, mixed with seal oil, and eaten. *Vegetable* Leaves mixed with other greens, cooked, and eaten. (85:49)

Polygonum bistortoides, American Bistort
Blackfoot *Soup* Roots used in soups and stews. (97:33) Roots used in soups and stews. (114:278) **Cheyenne** *Unspecified* Fresh roots boiled with meat. (as *Bistorta bistortoides* 76:173) Species used for food. (83:46) Roots formerly used for food. (83:32)

Polygonum cuspidatum, Japanese Knotweed
Cherokee *Vegetable* Cooked leaves used for food. (126:53)

Polygonum douglasii, Douglas's
  Knotweed
Klamath *Porridge* Ground, parched seeds
used to make meal and eaten dry or mixed with
water and boiled. (45:95) **Montana Indian**
Staple Parched seeds made into meal. (19:18)

Polygonum hydropiper, Marsh-
  pepper Knotweed
Cherokee *Unspecified* Young growth boiled,
fried, and eaten. (as *P. hydopiper* 204:253)
Iroquois *Spice* Whole plant, except the roots,
used by older people as pepper. (141:40)

Polypodium glycyrrhiza, Licorice
  Fern
Hesquiat *Vegetable* Long, slender rhizomes
eaten raw as a food and to sweeten the mouth.
(185:30) **Kwakiutl, Southern** *Dietary Aid*
Roots kept in the mouth to prevent hunger and
thirst. *Starvation Food* Roots dried, steamed,
and eaten during famines. *Unspecified* Roots
scorched, pounded, cut in bite-size pieces,
dipped in oil, and chewed and sucked by old
people. (183:264) **Makah** *Dietary Aid* Rhizomes chewed, on hunting trips, to curb the appetite. *Unspecified* Rhizomes eaten raw, especially by children, because of the licorice flavor.
(67:220) **Thompson** *Candy* Rhizomes chewed
for the pleasant, sweet, licorice flavor. (187:91)

Polypodium hesperium, Western
  Polypody
Thompson *Candy* Rhizomes chewed for the
pleasant, sweet, licorice taste. (187:91)

Polypodium scouleri, Leathery
  Polypody
Hesquiat *Candy* Children chewed the thick
rhizomes. (185:30) **Makah** *Unspecified* Species
used for food. (67:221)

Polypodium virginianum, Rock
  Polypody
Salish, Coast *Dried Food* Rhizomes sun dried
and used as a winter food. *Substitution Food*
Rhizomes formerly used as a substitute for

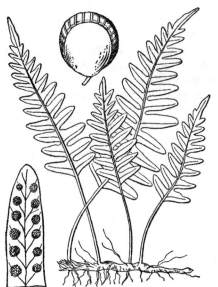

Polypodium virginianum

sugar. *Unspecified* Rhizomes eaten fresh. (as *P.
vulgare* 182:69)

Polypogon monspeliensis, Annual
  Rabbitsfoot Grass
Tubatulabal *Unspecified* Used extensively for
food. (193:15)

Polyporus harlowii, Bracket Fungus
Isleta *Unspecified* Fungi boiled or baked and
eaten. *Winter Use Food* Fungi stored for winter
use. **Pueblo** *Special Food* Fungi boiled and
eaten as a delicacy. (32:33)

Polystichum acrostichoides,
  Christmas Fern
Cherokee *Unspecified* Fiddle heads used for
food. (80:33)

Polystichum munitum, Western
  Swordfern
Klallam *Unspecified* Rhizomes boiled and
eaten. (79:13) **Kwakiutl, Southern** *Unspecified* Basal leaves and rhizomes steamed, peeled,
and used for food. (183:265) **Makah** *Spice*
Leaves used to steam salmonberry sprouts on
hot rocks, to give the sprouts flavor. *Unspecified*

Roots steamed or cooked in a pit. (67:221) Rhizomes boiled and eaten. (79:13) **Nitinaht** *Unspecified* Large rootstocks steam cooked and eaten in summer. (186:62) **Quileute** *Unspecified* Rhizomes peeled, pit baked, and eaten with fresh or dried salmon eggs. **Quinault** *Unspecified* Rhizomes pit baked on hot rocks and used for food. (79:13) **Thompson** *Unspecified* Rootstocks used for food. (187:89)

Polystichum munitum ssp. *munitum*, Western Swordfern
Costanoan *Unspecified* Rhizomes eaten, boiled or baked in coals. (21:247)

Populus ×acuminata, Lanceleaf Cottonwood
Lakota *Fodder* Boughs and bark fed to horses during winter. (106:33)

Populus angustifolia, Narrowleaf Cottonwood
Apache, White Mountain *Candy* Buds used as chewing gum. *Unspecified* Buds used for food. (136:159) **Montana Indian** *Fodder* Young twigs fed to horses when other food was not obtainable. *Unspecified* Inner bark considered a valuable mucilaginous food. (19:19) **Navajo** *Candy* Buds used as chewing gum. *Unspecified* Buds used for food. **Zuni** *Candy* Buds used as chewing gum. *Unspecified* Buds used for food. (136:159)

Populus balsamifera, Balsam Poplar
Montana Indian *Fodder* Young twigs fed to horses when other food was not obtainable. *Unspecified* Inner bark considered a valuable mucilaginous food. (19:19) **Tanana, Upper** *Unspecified* Sap used for food. (102:4)

Populus balsamifera ssp. *trichocarpa*, Black Cottonwood
Bella Coola *Dried Food* Inner cambium "slime" sun dried and eaten with grease. *Unspecified* Inner cambium "slime" eaten fresh. (as *P. trichocarpa* 184:210) **Blackfoot** *Unspecified* Inner bark and sap used for food. **Cheyenne** *Fodder* Twigs and bark fed to horses and

other livestock. (as *P. trichocarpa* 82:68) **Clallam** *Dried Food* Sap eaten dried. *Unspecified* Sap eaten fresh. (as *P. trichocarpa* 57:203) **Flathead** *Unspecified* Inner bark and sap used for food. (as *P. trichocarpa* 82:68) **Haisla** *Unspecified* Cambium eaten fresh in spring. (73:151) **Haisla & Hanaksiala** *Unspecified* Inner bark used for food. (43:284) **Kutenai** *Unspecified* Inner bark and sap used for food. (as *P. trichocarpa* 82:68) **Kwakiutl, Southern** *Unspecified* Cambium eaten in early spring. (as *P. trichocarpa* 183:292) **Oweekeno** *Unspecified* Cambium used for food. (43:116) **Thompson** *Forage* Leaves and twigs eaten by moose. (187:276)

Populus deltoides, Eastern Cottonwood
Blackfoot *Unspecified* Inner bark and sap used for food. **Cheyenne** *Fodder* Twigs and bark fed to horses and other livestock. (82:68) Bark and twigs formerly used to feed horses in winter. *Unspecified* Inner bark scraped and eaten in spring. (83:36) **Flathead** *Unspecified* Inner bark and sap used for food. **Kutenai** *Unspecified* Inner bark and sap used for food. (82:68) **Lakota** *Forage* Bark eaten by horses. (139:57) **Montana Indian** *Fodder* Young twigs fed to horses when other food was not obtainable. *Unspecified* Inner bark considered a valuable mucilaginous food. (19:19) **Pima** *Unspecified* Catkins eaten raw. (146:69)

Populus deltoides ssp. *monilifera*, Plains Cottonwood
Dakota *Candy* Fruit used as chewing gum by children. *Forage* Branches used as forage for horses. *Unspecified* Inner bark eaten for its pleasant, sweet taste and nutritive value. (as *P. sargentii* 70:72) **Ojibwa** *Unspecified* Buds and seed capsules used for food. (as *P. monilifera* 135:243) **Omaha** *Candy* Fruit used as chewing gum by children. **Pawnee** *Candy* Fruit used as chewing gum by children. **Ponca** *Candy* Cottony fruits used as chewing gum by children. (as *P. sargentii* 70:72)

Populus deltoides ssp. *wislizeni*,
Rio Grande Cottonwood

Acoma *Candy* Cotton from the pistillate catkins used as chewing gum. (as *P. wislizeni* 32:31) **Apache, Chiricahua & Mescalero** *Candy* Buds used as chewing gum. (as *P. wislizeni* 33:45) **Apache, White Mountain** *Candy* Buds used as chewing gum. *Unspecified* Buds used for food. (as *P. wislizeni* 136:159) **Isleta** *Candy* Fruit used by children for chewing gum. (as *P. wislizeni* 100:39) *Unspecified* Catkins eaten raw. **Jemez** *Unspecified* Catkins eaten raw. (as *P. wislizeni* 32:43) **Keres, Western** *Candy* Cotton used by children for chewing gum. (as *P. wislizenii* 171:62) **Laguna** *Candy* Cotton from the pistillate catkins used as chewing gum. (as *P. wislizeni* 32:31) **Navajo** *Candy* Sap or catkins, alone or mixed with animal fat, used for chewing gum. (as *P. wislizeni* 55:38) Buds used as chewing gum. *Unspecified* Buds used for food. (as *P. wislizeni* 136:159) **Pima** *Candy* Buds used for chewing gum in early spring. (as *P. fremontii wislizeni* 95:265) **Zuni** *Candy* Buds used as chewing gum. *Unspecified* Buds used for food. (as *P. wislizeni* 136:159)

Populus fremontii, Frémont's
Cottonwood

Havasupai *Candy* "Berries" eaten or chewed like gum. (197:213) **Pima** *Candy* Young, green pods chewed as gum. (47:109) **Pima, Gila River** *Snack Food* Catkins eaten as a snack food by all age groups. (133:5) Flowers eaten as a snack food. (133:7)

Populus grandidentata, Bigtooth
Aspen

Ojibwa *Unspecified* Cambium layer scraped, boiled, and eaten, something like eggs. (153:410)

Populus tremuloides, Quaking Aspen
Apache, Chiricahua & Mescalero *Bread & Cake* Inner bark scraped off and baked in the form of cakes. *Unspecified* Bark boiled or eaten raw. (33:43) **Apache, Mescalero** *Spice* Sap used as flavoring for wild strawberries. (14:50) **Blackfoot** *Fodder* Bark made an excellent win-

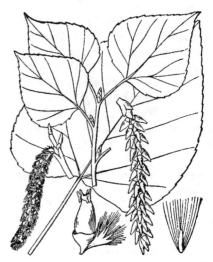

Populus tremuloides

ter food for horses. (86:89) Bark fed to horses during the winter. (97:28) *Snack Food* Cambium used as a snack food by children. *Special Food* Bark sucked by anyone observing a liquid taboo. *Unspecified* Cambium used for food. (86:104) Inner bark eaten in the spring. (97:28) **Cree, Woodlands** *Preservative* Dry, rotted wood used to make a fire to smoke cure whitefish and moose meat. *Unspecified* Cambium eaten fresh in early summer. Inner bark used for food in the spring. (109:52) **Montana Indian** *Fodder* Young twigs fed to horses when other food was not obtainable. *Unspecified* Inner bark considered a valuable mucilaginous food. (19:19) **Navajo, Ramah** *Starvation Food* Inner bark eaten raw as an emergency ration. (191:22) **Tanana, Upper** *Preservative* Wood used to smoke fish. *Unspecified* Sap and cambium used for food. (102:5) **Thompson** *Forage* Bark eaten by beavers. (187:277)

Porphyra abbottae, Edible Seaweed
Haisla & Hanaksiala *Dried Food* Plant gathered and dried for winter use. *Sauce & Relish* Plant dried, crushed, and sprinkled on various foods as a condiment. (43:131) **Kitasoo** *Bread & Cake* Plant pressed into boxes to form compressed cakes, dried, and stored for future use. *Unspecified* Plant eaten with salmon roe or but-

ter clams. (43:304) **Oweekeno** *Bread & Cake* Whole plant formed into flat sheets, pressed in boxes, dried, and made into cakes. *Dried Food* Whole plant dried for future use. *Unspecified* Whole plant cooked and eaten with salmon eggs, cooked salmon, clams, herring eggs, and other foods. (43:47)

Porphyra laciniata, Seaweed
Alaska Native *Dried Food* Leaves sun dried, chopped, dried, and stored in closed containers. *Snack Food* Leaves sun dried, chopped, dried, and eaten raw like popcorn. *Soup* Leaves used in fish stews and soups. (85:141)

Porphyra lanceolata
Pomo, Kashaya *Dried Food* Fresh seaweed dried for later use. *Unspecified* Fresh seaweed baked and eaten. (72:126) **Tolowa** *Unspecified* Species used for food. **Yurok** *Unspecified* Species used for food. (6:47)

Porphyra perforata
Hesquiat *Unspecified* Boiled with herring spawn and eaten with dogfish oil or eulachon (candlefish) oil. (edible seaweed 185:25) **Pomo** *Bread & Cake* Weeds stacked like cakes and dried until needed. *Dried Food* Seaweed sun dried and used for food. (11:94) *Winter Use Food* Plant made into a cake, cooked in earth oven, and stored for winter consumption. (66:10) **Pomo, Kashaya** *Dried Food* Fresh seaweed dried for later use. *Unspecified* Fresh seaweed baked and eaten. (72:125)

Portulaca oleracea, Little Hogweed
Acoma *Vegetable* Plants cooked with meat and eaten like spinach. (32:43) **Apache, Chiricahua & Mescalero** *Unspecified* Eaten without preparation or cooked with green chile and meat or animal bones. (33:46) **Hopi** *Unspecified* Cooked in a gravy. (200:75) **Iroquois** *Vegetable* Cooked and seasoned with salt, pepper, or butter. (196:118) **Isleta** *Vegetable* Plants oven dried, stored, and used as greens during the winter. (32:43) *Winter Use Food* Plants dried in ovens, stored, and used as greens in the winter. (100:39) **Keres, Western** *Vegetable* Plant

cooked with meat as greens. (171:62) **Laguna** *Vegetable* Plants cooked with meat and eaten like spinach. (32:43) **Luiseño** *Vegetable* Plant used for greens. (155:232) **Navajo** *Unspecified* Seeds used for food. (55:47) **Navajo, Ramah** *Spice* Leaves used as a potherb. *Vegetable* Leaves boiled as greens with meat. (191:26) **Pima, Gila River** *Unspecified* Leaves boiled and eaten. (133:7) **Tewa** *Unspecified* Fleshy plant tops boiled and eaten. (138:59)

Portulaca oleracea ssp. *oleracea*, Little Hogweed
Hopi *Unspecified* Plant boiled with meats and eaten. (as *P. retusa* 56:15) Plant formerly cut up fine and eaten in gravy. (as *P. retusa* 138:60) **Navajo** *Forage* Plant used as a good sheep forage. *Unspecified* Seeds used for food. (as *P. retusa* Engelm. 55:47) Plants used for food. (as *P. retusa* 90:154) **Pima, Gila River** *Unspecified* Leaves boiled and eaten. (as *P. retusa* 133:7) **San Felipe** *Unspecified* Young plants fried or boiled and mixed with young peas. *Vegetable* Young plants used as greens. (as *P. retusa* 32:43)

Postelsia palmaeformis, Sea Palm
Hesquiat *Dried Food* Stipes and fronds with attached herring eggs dried for later use. (185:24) **Pomo** *Unspecified* Cooked stalks used for food. Raw stalks chewed like sugar cane. (as *P. palmiformis* 66:10) Plant chewed raw. (11:95) **Pomo, Kashaya** *Dried Food* Stems cut into long strips and sun dried for winter use. *Unspecified* Fresh stem chewed raw or baked in an oven or hot ashes. (72:126)

Potamogeton sp., Pondweed
Hesquiat *Forage* Plant browsed by deer. (185:17) Deer wade into the water and put their heads under the surface to eat this plant. (185:56)

Prenanthes serpentaria, Cankerweed
Cherokee *Vegetable* Leaves eaten as cooked salad. (80:35)

Prenanthes trifoliolata, Gall of the
Earth
Cherokee *Vegetable* Leaves eaten as cooked
salad. (80:35)

Proboscidea althaeifolia, Devils-
horn
Cahuilla *Unspecified* Seeds used for food.
(15:107) **Papago** *Unspecified* Young pods used
for food. (as *Martynia arenaria* 47:107)

***Proboscidea louisianica* ssp.**
fragrans, Ram's Horn
Papago *Dried Food* Seeds basket winnowed,
parched, sun dried, cooked, stored, and used
for food. (as *Martynia fragrans* 34:24) *Unspecified* Seeds boiled and eaten. (as *Martynia fragrans* 34:25)

***Proboscidea louisianica* ssp.**
louisianica, Louisiana Ram's Horn
Apache, Chiricahua & Mescalero *Unspecified* Seeds eaten by prisoners of war in Oklahoma. (as *Martynia louisiana* 33:45)

Proboscidea parviflora, Doubleclaw
Havasupai *Dried Food* Fruit sun dried for future use. *Unspecified* Seeds used for food.
(197:241) **Hualapai** *Unspecified* Young pods
used for food. (195:38)

***Proboscidea parviflora* ssp.**
parviflora, Doubleclaw
Papago *Unspecified* Young pods used for food.
Pima *Unspecified* Seeds dried, cracked, and
eaten like pine nuts. (as *Martynia parviflora*
47:107)

Prosopis chilensis, Algarrobo
Kiowa *Fodder* Leaves used for fodder. *Vegeta-
ble* Pounded beans and pods used for food. (as
Ceratonia chilensis 192:33)

Prosopis glandulosa, Honey Mesquite
Acoma *Porridge* Beans formerly ground into
flour and prepared as mush. *Unspecified* Beans
eaten raw or cooked as string beans. (32:43)
Apache *Bread & Cake* Seeds ground into flour

and used in pancakes. *Preserves* Beans boiled,
pounded or ground, hand kneaded, and made
into a jam. (as *P. prosopis* 32:45) **Apache,
Chiricahua & Mescalero** *Beverage* Cooked
pods and seeds ground, water added, mixture
allowed to ferment, and used as a beverage.
(33:53) *Bread & Cake* Bean flour made into
pancakes and bread. Beans were gathered,
boiled, pounded on a hide or ground on a
metate, placed in a pan, and worked with the
hands until a thick consistency was attained.
Pie & Pudding Pods boiled in water, taken out,
mashed, boiled again, and eaten as pudding.
(33:41) *Spice* Root used to flavor drinks and
make them stronger. (33:51) *Substitution Food*
Flour used in the absence of sugar to sweeten
an intoxicating drink. (33:50) *Unspecified*
Beans cooked with meat and seed coats spit out
when eaten. (33:41) **Apache, Mescalero** *Beverage* Beans boiled, strained, and used as a
drink. *Staple* Beans ground into flour, mixed
with other plant foods, and eaten. (14:37)
Comanche *Staple* Pods made into a meal and
used for food. (29:523) **Isleta** *Bread & Cake*
Beans ground into a flour and used to make
bread. (100:39) *Candy* Beans toasted and eaten
as a confection by sucking out the juice. (32:43)
Roasted beans eaten as a confection. (100:39)
Keres, Western *Porridge* Beans ground into a

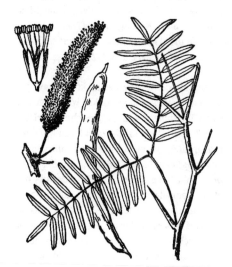

Prosopis glandulosa

flour, made into a mush, and used for food. *Vegetable* Beans eaten raw for the sweet taste or cooked like string beans. (171:63) **Kiowa** *Fodder* Leaves used for fodder. *Vegetable* Pounded beans and pods used for food. (192:33) **Laguna** *Porridge* Beans formerly ground into flour and prepared as mush. *Unspecified* Beans eaten raw or cooked as string beans. (32:43) **Pima** *Candy* White resinous secretions used to make candy. (as *P. prosopis* 32:45) **Yavapai** *Staple* Pods pulverized and made into a meal for transporting. (65:257)

Prosopis glandulosa var. *glandulosa*, Honey Mesquite

Apache, Western *Beverage* Pounded bean pulp squeezed for the juice and drunk just like milk. *Bread & Cake* Dried seeds pounded into flour, moistened, allowed to harden into cakes, and stored. *Candy* Dried beans pounded into flour and eaten as candy. *Dried Food* Pods dried and stored. *Porridge* Dried beans pounded into flour and mixed into a mush. *Staple* Fresh pods pounded into a flour. *Substitution Food* Pitch chewed as a substitute for gum. (as *P. chilensis* 26:176) **Havasupai** *Beverage* Plant used to make a drink. (as *P. juliflora* 197:66) *Candy* Pods eaten raw like a stick of candy. (as *P. juliflora* 197:228) **Kamia** *Unspecified* Pod used for food. (as *P. juliflora* 62:23) **Kiowa** *Fodder* Leaves used for fodder. Leaves used for fodder. Leaves used for fodder. *Vegetable* Pounded beans and pods used for food. Pounded beans and pods used for food. Pounded beans and pods used for food. (as *P. juliflora glandulosa* 192:33) **Luiseño** *Staple* Ground beans made into a flour and used for food in some places. (as *P. juliflora* 155:231) **Mahuna** *Bread & Cake* Bean pods ground into flour and used to make cakes and tarts. *Dried Food* Dried bean pods eaten raw. *Porridge* Bean pods ground into flour, mixed with hot or cold water, and eaten as porridge. (as *P. juliflora* 140:57) **Maricopa** *Beverage* Unripe beans pounded and mixed with water to make a drink. (as *P. juliflora* 37:181) **Mohave** *Bread & Cake* Dried bean pods ground into a meal and used to make cakes. *Dried Food* Beans dried and stored in

giant basket granaries for winter use. *Vegetable* Beans eaten raw or roasted. (as *P. juliflora* 168:46) **Paiute** *Unspecified* Pounded beans used for food. (as *P. juliflora* 118:27) **Papago** *Staple* Fruits and seeds used for food. (as *P. chilensis* 36:60) **Seri** *Porridge* Beans ground into a meal, mixed with water or sea lion oil, and eaten. (as *P. juliflora* 50:136) **Southwest Indians** *Unspecified* Seeds used for food. (as *P. chilensis* 17:15) **Yuma** *Beverage* Dried pods boiled to make a beverage. Pods crushed and steeped in water to make a beverage. *Bread & Cake* Meal molded into cakes for storage. *Dried Food* Pods dried on roof tops and stored. *Staple* Pods crushed or ground into a meal. (as *P. juliflora* 37:181)

Prosopis glandulosa var. *torreyana*, Western Honey Mesquite

Cahuilla *Beverage* Blossoms used to make tea. Pods crushed into a pulpy juice and used to make a beverage. Pod meal and water used to make a beverage. *Bread & Cake* Pod meal and water used to make cakes. *Porridge* Pod meal and water used to make mush. *Staple* Pods dried and ground into a meal. *Unspecified* Roasted blossoms stored in pottery vessels and cooked in boiling water when needed. Pods eaten fresh. (as *P. juliflora* var. *torreyana* 15:107) **Cocopa** *Unspecified* Pods used for food. *Winter Use Food* Pods stored for later use. (as *P. odorata* 64:267) **Diegueño** *Bread & Cake* Beans ground into a meal and used to make cakes. (84:32) **Kawaiisu** *Bread & Cake* Seeds pounded and molded into a cake without cooking. Pods crushed into a meal, molded into a dry cake, and stored and eaten at a later time. *Porridge* Pods crushed into a meal and eaten with water. (206:54) **Pima** *Beverage* Beans sun dried, pounded into meal, mixed with cold water, and used as a drink. (as *P. odorata* 95:261) **Yavapai** *Unspecified* Seeds used for food. (as *Cercidium torreyana* 63:211) Parched, ground seeds dampened, sometimes mixed with ground saguaro seed, and used for food. (as *Cercidium torreyanum* 65:256) **Yuma** *Beverage* Pods crushed and steeped in water to make a beverage. *Dried Food* Pit cooked pods dried and stored in baskets. Pods dried on roof tops and stored. *Staple* Beans dried thoroughly and pounded into meal. *Unspecified* Pit cooked pods pounded in a mortar and prepared as food. (as *P. odorata* 37:181)

Prosopis pubescens, Screwbean Mesquite

Apache, Chiricahua & Mescalero *Beverage* Fruit ground and sugar added to make a thick drink. (as *Strombocarpa pubescens* 33:53) *Bread & Cake* Pods dried, washed, ground into flour, and made into bread. *Dried Food* Fruits gathered, dried, and stored in sacks. *Special Food* Raw pods chewed and eaten as a delicacy. (as *Strombocarpa pubescens* 33:41) **Cahuilla** *Beverage* Pods crushed into a pulpy juice and used to make a beverage. Pod meal and water used to make a beverage. *Bread & Cake* Pod meal and water used to make cakes. *Dried Food* Ripe pods allowed to dry or picked after fully dried and ground into meal. *Staple* Pods used as one of the important food staples. Ripe pods allowed to dry or picked after fully dried and ground into meal. Pod meal and water used to make mush. (15:118) **Hualapai** *Dried Food* Pods dried and stored for later use. *Unspecified* Pods used for food. (195:45) **Isleta** *Unspecified* Pods chewed for the starch content and agreeable taste. (as *Strombocarpa pubescens* 100:43) **Kamia** *Unspecified* Coiled pod used for food. (62:23) **Mohave** *Beverage* Bean pods rotted in a pit for a month, dried, ground into a flour, and used to make a drink. *Vegetable* Bean pods used for food. (168:46) **Paiute** *Unspecified* Pounded beans used for food. (118:27) **Pima** *Beverage* Beans ground, mixed with water, and made into a nourishing and sweet beverage. (as *Strombocarpa pubescens* 47:96) Beans sun dried, pounded into meal, mixed with cold water, and used as a drink. (95:261) *Candy* Fresh, sugary pods chewed by children. *Forage* Pods and foliage eaten by grazing animals. (as *Strombocarpa pubescens* 47:96) *Staple* Beans pit roasted for several days, dried, and ground into a pinole. (as *Strombocarpa pubescens* 32:45) Beans pit cooked, dried, pounded, and eaten as pinole. (146:75) **Pima,**

Gila River *Snack Food* Sap eaten as a snack food by all age groups. Catkins eaten as a snack food by all age groups. *Staple* Beans used to make flour. (133:5) Fruit used as a staple food. (133:7)

Prosopis velutina, Velvet Mesquite

Cocopa *Unspecified* Pods used for food. *Winter Use Food* Pods stored for later use. (64:267) **Maricopa** *Unspecified* Beans formerly eaten as an important food. (32:44) **Papago** *Candy* Gum-like secretions found on branches and chewed. Gum-like secretions found on branches, dried, ground, boiled in gruel, cooled, and eaten like candy. (34:28) *Dried Food* Seeds basket winnowed, parched, sun dried, cooked, stored, and used for food. (34:24) *Preserves* Gum-like secretions found on branches, dried, ground, mixed with saguaro syrup, and eaten like jam. (34:28) *Staple* Beans ground into flour and used for food. (34:25) Beans pounded in mortars and used as a staple food. (34:45) *Unspecified* Pods eaten fresh. Beans and pods pounded into a pulpy mass, boiled, and used for food. (34:25) **Pima** *Beverage* Beans pounded, added to cold water, strained, and used as a sweet drink. (47:93) *Bread & Cake* Seeds ground into flour and used to make bread. (32:44) Beans boiled, cooled, pressed out into dumplings, and eaten. *Candy* Gum formerly eaten raw as a sweet. (47:93) White gum used to make candy. (146:74) *Porridge* Beans used to make mush. (47:93) *Staple* Seeds ground into flour and eaten as a pinole. (32:44) Beans parched, ground, and eaten as pinole. *Substitution Food* Inner bark used as a substitute for rennet. (146:74) *Sweetener* Seeds ground into flour and used to sweeten pinole. (32:44) *Unspecified* Sugary bean pods relished as food. Catkins sucked for their sweet taste. (47:93) Beans and pods pounded, ground, and used for food. Catkins eaten raw. (146:74) **Pima, Gila River** *Beverage* Pods crushed in a wooden mortar, soaked in water, and used to make vau (a drink). *Bread & Cake* Pods made into flour and used to make an uncooked cake or loaf. (133:4) *Snack Food* Sap eaten as a snack food by all age groups. Catkins eaten as a snack food by all age groups.

Staple Beans used to make flour. (133:5) Fruit used as a staple food. (133:7) *Winter Use Food* Pods stored in great quantities in large arrow-weed baskets or bins. (133:4)

Prunella vulgaris, Common Selfheal
Cherokee *Vegetable* Leaves cooked and eaten as greens. (80:54) Small leaves used as a pot-herb. (as *Frunella vulgaris* 126:44) Leaves cooked with sochan (*Rudbeckia laciniata*), creaseys (probably *Lepidium virginicum*), and other potherbs and eaten. (204:253) **Thompson** *Beverage* Plant soaked in cold water and used as one of the most common drinks. (164:494)

Prunus americana, American Plum
Apache, Mescalero *Dried Food* Fruits dried and stored for future food use. (14:50) **Cherokee** *Beverage* Fruit used to make juice. *Fruit* Fruit used for food. *Preserves* Fruit used to make jelly. (80:50) **Cheyenne** *Pie & Pudding* Fruits, sugar, and flour used to make a pudding. *Special Food* Fruits pulverized, sun dried, boiled, and eaten as a delicacy. (83:35) *Winter Use Food* Sun dried plums stored for winter use. (76:177) **Chippewa** *Bread & Cake* Berries cooked, spread on birch bark into little cakes, dried, and stored for winter use. *Fruit* Berries eaten raw. (53:321) **Crow** *Fruit* Ripe plums used fresh. *Winter Use Food* Ripe plums dried for winter use. (19:19) **Dakota** *Dried Food* Fruit boiled, pitted, and dried for winter use. (69:364) Highly valued fruit pitted and dried for winter use. (70:87) *Fruit* Fruit eaten fresh. (69:364) Highly valued fruit eaten fresh and raw. (70:87) *Sauce & Relish* Fruit made into a sauce. (69:364) Highly valued fruit cooked as a sauce. (70:87) **Iroquois** *Beverage* Fruit sun dried and boiled in water to make coffee. (196:145) *Bread & Cake* Fruit mashed, made into small cakes, and dried for future use. *Dried Food* Raw or cooked fruit sun or fire dried and stored for future use. *Fruit* Dried fruit taken as a hunting food. *Sauce & Relish* Dried fruit cakes soaked in warm water and cooked as a sauce or mixed with corn bread. (196:128) **Isleta** *Fruit* Fruits eaten for food.

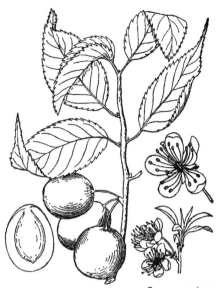

Prunus americana

Fruits eaten fresh. (32:46) Fruit eaten for food. (100:40) **Kiowa** *Fruit* Fruit gathered in great quantities and used immediately. *Winter Use Food* Fruit gathered in great quantities, dried, and stored for winter use. (192:29) **Lakota** *Fruit* Fruits eaten fresh. (106:37) Fruits eaten for food. (139:56) *Starvation Food* Fruits dried and eaten during famines. (106:37) **Meskwaki** *Fruit* Plums eaten fresh. *Preserves* Plums made into plum butter for winter use. (152:263) **Ojibwa** *Dried Food* Fruit dried for winter use. *Fruit* Fruit eaten fresh. *Soup* Dried fruit ground into a flour and used to make soup. (135:235) **Omaha** *Dried Food* Fruit pitted and dried for winter use. (68:326) Highly valued fruit pitted and dried for winter use. (70:87) *Fruit* Fruit eaten fresh in season. (68:326) Highly valued fruit eaten fresh and raw. *Sauce & Relish* Highly valued fruit cooked as a sauce. **Pawnee** *Dried Food* Highly valued fruit eaten fresh and raw, cooked as a sauce, or dried with the pits for winter use. *Fruit* Highly valued fruit eaten fresh and raw. *Sauce & Relish* Highly valued fruit cooked as a sauce. **Ponca** *Dried Food* Highly valued fruit pitted and dried for winter use. *Fruit* Highly valued fruit eaten fresh and raw. *Sauce & Relish* Highly valued fruit cooked as a sauce.

Winnebago *Dried Food* Highly valued fruit pitted and dried for winter use. *Fruit* Highly valued fruit eaten fresh and raw. *Sauce & Relish* Highly valued fruit cooked as a sauce. (70:87)

Prunus andersonii, Desert Peach
Cahuilla *Fruit* Fruit considered a great delicacy, important food and a highly prized food source. *Preserves* Fruit boiled, sweetened with sugar, and used to make jelly. (15:119)

Prunus angustifolia, Chickasaw Plum
Comanche *Fruit* Fresh fruits used for food. *Winter Use Food* Stored fruits used for food. (29:523)

Prunus armeniaca, Apricot
Hopi *Unspecified* Species used for food. (200:79) **Keresan** *Dried Food* Fruit dried for winter use. *Fruit* Fruit eaten fresh. (198:558)

Prunus cerasus, Sour Cherry
Cherokee *Fruit* Fruit used for food. (80:28)

Prunus dulcis, Sweet Almond
Hopi *Unspecified* Species used for food. (as *P. amygdalus* 200:79)

Prunus emarginata, Bitter Cherry
Cahuilla *Fruit* Fruit considered a great delicacy, important food and a highly prized food source. (15:119) **Coeur d'Alene** *Fruit* Berries occasionally eaten fresh. (178:90) **Hoh** *Preserves* Fruits used to make jelly. (137:64) **Klamath** *Fruit* Fruit used for food. (45:98–99) **Quileute** *Preserves* Fruits used to make jelly. (137:64) **Shuswap** *Fruit* Cherries used for food. (123:67) **Thompson** *Dessert* Fruits sometimes eaten as a dessert. *Fruit* Fruits eaten occasionally because of the bitter taste. (187:263)

Prunus fasciculata, Desert Almond
Cahuilla *Fruit* Fruit considered a great delicacy, important food and a highly prized food source. (15:119)

Prunus fremontii, Desert Apricot
Cahuilla *Fruit* Fruit considered a great delicacy,

important food and a highly prized food source. (15:119)

Prunus gracilis, Oklahoma Plum
Kiowa *Candy* Dried fruit used as an ingredient in making candy. *Winter Use Food* Dried fruit stored for winter use, eaten uncooked, or pounded and made into cakes. (192:30)

Prunus ilicifolia, Holly Leaf Cherry
Cahuilla *Fruit* Fruit considered a great delicacy, important food and a highly prized food source. (15:119) **Costanoan** *Fruit* Fruits eaten for food. *Unspecified* Soaked, roasted inner kernels used for food. (21:249) **Diegueño** *Bread & Cake* Large seed cracked, the kernel extracted, pounded into a meal, and made into patties and roasted. *Fruit* Fruit eaten fresh. (84:32) Fruit used for food. *Porridge* Seeds ground, leached, and used to make atole. (88:217) **Luiseño** *Fruit* Fruit used for food. (as *Cerasus ilicifolia* 155:232) Fruit, similar to plums or cherries, formerly used to some extent as food. *Porridge* Sun dried fruit kernels made into a flour and cooked in an earthen vessel. The sun dried fruit kernels were extracted from the shells, made into a flour, and then leached to remove the bitterness. The flour was either leached with hot water, placed in a rush basket, and warm water poured over it, or placed in a sand hole and warm water poured over it to remove the bitterness. (155:194) *Staple* Kernels ground into a flour and used for food. (as *Cerasus ilicifolia* 155:232) *Unspecified* Pulp eaten for food. (155:194) **Mahuna** *Fruit* Berries eaten mainly to quench the thirst. (140:70)

Prunus nigra, Canadian Plum
Algonquin, Quebec *Fruit* Fruit eaten. *Preserves* Fruit made into preserves. (18:95) **Iroquois** *Bread & Cake* Fruit mashed, made into small cakes and dried for future use. *Dried Food* Raw or cooked fruit sun or fire dried and stored for future use. *Fruit* Dried fruit taken as a hunting food. *Sauce & Relish* Dried fruit cakes soaked in warm water and cooked as a sauce or mixed with corn bread. (196:128) **Meskwaki** *Fruit* Plums eaten fresh. *Preserves* Plums made

into plum butter for winter use. (152:263) **Ojibwa** *Fruit* Large quantities of plums found in thickets and gathered for food. *Preserves* Large quantities of plums found in thickets and gathered for preserves. (153:409)

Prunus pensylvanica, Pin Cherry

Algonquin, Quebec *Fruit* Fruit eaten fresh. *Preserves* Fruit made into jelly. (18:95) **Cherokee** *Fruit* Fruit used for food. (80:28) *Pie & Pudding* Fruit used to make pies. *Preserves* Fruit used to make jam. (126:58) **Cree, Woodlands** *Preserves* Juice used to make jelly. (109:53) **Iroquois** *Bread & Cake* Fruit mashed, made into small cakes, and dried for future use. *Dried Food* Raw or cooked fruit sun or fire dried and stored for future use. (196:128) *Fruit* Fruit used for food. (141:46) Dried fruit taken as a hunting food. *Sauce & Relish* Dried fruit cakes soaked in warm water and cooked as a sauce or mixed with corn bread. (196:128) **Ojibwa** *Dried Food* Fruit dried for winter use. *Fruit* Fruit eaten fresh. (135:235) Berries used for food. The pin cherry was abundant around the Flambeau Reservation and the Ojibwe were fond of it. It was an education in itself to see a group of Ojibwe women working on mats with a supply of fruit laden branches beside them.

Prunus pensylvanica

With one hand they would start a stream of berries into the mouth and the stream of cherry stones ejected from the other corner of the mouth seemed ceaseless. The Pillager Ojibwe also had the tree and used it is the same manner. (153:409) *Soup* Dried fruit ground into a flour and used to make soup. (135:235) **Potawatomi** *Fruit* Cherries eaten as the women worked making baskets. (154:108)

Prunus persica, Peach

Cherokee *Fruit* Fruit used for food. (80:47) **Havasupai** *Beverage* Dried fruits pounded, stewed, and the water drunk. *Dried Food* Fruit split open, pitted, and sun dried for later consumption. (197:224) **Hopi** *Dried Food* Fruits split open and dried for winter use. *Fruit* Fruits eaten fresh. (200:79) **Iroquois** *Bread & Cake* Fruit mashed, made into small cakes, and dried for future use. *Dried Food* Raw or cooked fruit sun or fire dried and stored for future use. *Fruit* Dried fruit taken as a hunting food. *Sauce & Relish* Dried fruit cakes soaked in warm water and cooked as a sauce or mixed with corn bread. (196:129) **Keres, Western** *Fruit* Fresh peaches eaten for food. *Winter Use Food* Peaches dried for winter use. (171:63) **Keresan** *Dried Food* Fruit dried for winter use. *Fruit* Fruit eaten fresh. (198:562) **Navajo, Ramah** *Fruit* Favorite fruit used for food. (191:31) **Seminole** *Unspecified* Plant used for food. (169:507)

Prunus pumila, Sandcherry

Menominee *Fruit* Berries eaten fresh. *Preserves* Berries sometimes gathered and preserved. (151:71) **Ojibwa** *Dried Food* Fruit used dried. *Fruit* Fruit used fresh. (5:2221) This species was plentiful on sandy openings in the forest and the fruit gathered for food. (153:409)

Prunus pumila var. *besseyi*, Western Sandcherry

Dakota *Dried Food* Pitted fruit dried for winter use. (as *P. besseyi* 69:364) Fruit dried for winter use. (as *P. besseyi* 70:88) *Fruit* Pitted fruit eaten fresh. (as *P. besseyi* 69:364) *Sauce & Relish* Fruit used to make a sauce during the fruiting season. (as *P. besseyi* 70:88) **Lakota** *Fruit*

Fruits eaten for food. (as *P. besseyi* 139:56) **Omaha** *Dried Food* Fruit dried for winter use. (as *P. besseyi* 70:88) *Fruit* Fruit eaten fresh. (as *P. besseyi* 68:326) *Sauce & Relish* Fruit used to make a sauce during the fruiting season. **Pawnee** *Dried Food* Fruit dried for winter use. *Sauce & Relish* Fruit used to make a sauce during the fruiting season. **Ponca** *Dried Food* Fruit dried for winter use. *Sauce & Relish* Fruit used to make a sauce during the fruiting season. (as *P. besseyi* 70:88)

Prunus pumila var. *susquehanae*, Sesquehana Sandcherry
Potawatomi *Beverage* Cherries used to improve the flavor of whisky. (as *P. cuneata* 154:107)

Prunus serotina, Black Cherry
Cherokee *Fruit* Fruit used for food. (80:28) **Chippewa** *Beverage* Twigs used to make a beverage. (53:317) *Bread & Cake* Berries cooked, spread on birch bark into little cakes, dried, and stored for winter use. *Fruit* Berries eaten raw. (53:321) **Iroquois** *Bread & Cake* Fruit mashed, made into small cakes, and dried for future use. *Dried Food* Raw or cooked fruit sun or fire dried and stored for future use. *Fruit* Dried fruit taken as a hunting food. *Sauce & Relish* Dried fruit cakes soaked in warm water and cooked as a sauce or mixed with corn bread. (196:128) **Mahuna** *Fruit* Berries eaten mainly to quench the thirst. (140:70) **Menominee** *Fruit* Cherries, if eaten when picked and allowed to stand some time, said to make the Indian drunk. Cherries eaten fresh. (151:71) **Ojibwa** *Beverage* Ripe cherries used to make whisky. (153:409) *Dried Food* Fruit dried for winter use. (135:235) This cherry was preferred to all other wild cherries and dried for winter use. (153:409) *Fruit* Fruit eaten fresh. *Soup* Dried fruit ground into a flour and used to make soup. (135:235) **Potawatomi** *Beverage* Cherries mostly used in wine or whisky. *Fruit* Cherries used for food. (154:108)

Prunus subcordata, Klamath Plum
Atsugewi *Bread & Cake* Seeds removed, pulp

pounded, and stored for winter in small cakes. (61:139) **Klamath** *Dried Food* Fresh or dried fruit used for food. *Fruit* Dried or fresh fruit used for food. (45:99) **Mendocino Indian** *Dried Food* Fruits dried and eaten. *Fruit* Fruits eaten for food. (41:356) **Modesse** *Fruit* Fruit used for food. (117:223) **Wintoon** *Fruit* Fruit used for food. (117:264)

Prunus subcordata var. *oregana*, Oregon Klamath Plum
Wintoon *Fruit* Fruit used for food. (as *P. oregana* 117:264)

Prunus virginiana, Common Chokecherry
Abnaki *Fruit* Fruits eaten for food. (144:168) **Algonquin, Quebec** *Beverage* Fruits used to make a wine. (18:113) Cherries used to make wine. *Fruit* Cherries eaten fresh. *Preserves* Cherries made into preserves. (18:96) **Apache, Western** *Fruit* Berries eaten raw. (26:190) **Blackfoot** *Beverage* Juice given as a special drink to husbands or the favorite child. *Dried Food* Berries greased, sun dried, and stored for future use. *Fruit* Crushed berries mixed with back fat, and used to make pemmican. *Soup* Crushed berries mixed with back fat, and used to make soup. (86:104) *Special Food* Berry soup used for most ceremonial events. (86:26) *Spice* Peeled sticks inserted into roasting meat as a spice. *Staple* Berries considered a staple. (86:104) **Cherokee** *Fruit* Fruit used for food. (80:28) **Cheyenne** *Bread & Cake* Fruits pounded, formed into flat cakes, sun dried, and used as a winter food. *Pie & Pudding* Berries boiled, sugar and flour added, and eaten as a pudding. (83:35) **Chippewa** *Beverage* Twigs used to make a beverage. (53:317) *Dried Food* Fruits pounded, dried, and used for food. (53:321) **Cree, Woodlands** *Fruit* Fruit and pits, sometimes with fish eggs, crushed, mixed with grease, and eaten. *Sauce & Relish* Fruit used to make pancake syrup. (109:53) **Iroquois** *Bread & Cake* Fruit mashed, made into small cakes, and dried for future use. (196:128) *Dried Food* Fruits dried and used as a winter food. (124:95) Raw or cooked fruit sun or fire

dried and stored for future use. *Fruit* Dried
fruit taken as a hunting food. *Sauce & Relish*
Dried fruit cakes soaked in warm water and
cooked as a sauce or mixed with corn bread.
(196:128) *Soup* Fruits pulverized, mixed with
dried meat flour, and eaten as soup. (124:95)
Lakota *Beverage* Leaves used to make a tea
during the Sun Dance. *Fruit* Berries eaten fresh.
(106:38) Fruits eaten for food. (139:57) *Pie &
Pudding* Berries mixed with cornstarch and
sugar to make a pudding. *Special Food* Small
branches sucked or chewed for thirst during the
Sun Dance. (106:38) **Menominee** *Beverage*
Bark boiled into regular tea and drunk with
meals. *Fruit* Cherries eaten fresh. (151:71)
Meskwaki *Beverage* Bark made into a beverage. *Fruit* Cherries eaten raw. (152:263) **Montana Indian** *Bread & Cake* Berries pulverized,
shaped into round cakes, sun dried, and stored
for winter use. *Fruit* Berries eaten raw. Berries
pulverized, shaped into round cakes, sun dried,
and used to make pemmican. *Pie & Pudding*
Berries mixed with sugar and flour and used
to make a pudding. *Soup* Berries pulverized,
shaped into round cakes, sun dried, and used
in soups and stews. (82:42) **Ojibwa** *Dried Food*
Berries used dried. (5:2222) Fruit dried for
winter use. (135:235) *Fruit* Berries used fresh.
(5:2222) Fruit eaten fresh. (135:235) Fruit of
this cherry was liked, especially after the fruit
had been frosted. (153:409) *Soup* Dried berry
powder mixed with dried meat flour for soup.
(5:2222) Dried fruit ground into a flour and
used to make soup. (135:235) **Okanagan-
Colville** *Bread & Cake* Berries mashed, seeds
and all, and sun dried into thin cakes. *Fruit*
Berries eaten fresh. *Winter Use Food* Berries
stored for winter use. (188:127) **Omaha** *Dried
Food* Fruit pounded with the pits, made into
thin cakes, and dried for winter use. *Fruit* Fruit
eaten fresh. (68:326) **Potawatomi** *Fruit* Cherry
used for food and for seasoning or flavoring
wine. (154:108) **Thompson** *Beverage* Fruit
used to make wine and juice. *Dried Food* Fruit,
with the pit, dried for future use. *Fruit* Fruit
used for food. *Sauce & Relish* Fruit used to make
syrup. *Winter Use Food* Fruit, with the pit,
canned for future use. (187:264)

Prunus virginiana var. *demissa*,
Western Chokecherry

Atsugewi *Porridge* Ripe, mashed fruit added to
water to form a paste and eaten without cooking. (as *P. demissa* 61:139) **Blackfoot** *Fruit*
Berries eaten raw. Berries pounded, mixed with
meat, and eaten. *Soup* Berries used for soups.
(as *P. demissa* 114:277) **Cahuilla** *Dried Food*
Fruit sun dried for future use. *Fruit* Fruit considered a great delicacy, important food and a
highly prized food source. Fruit eaten fresh.
Staple Ground pit used as a meal. (15:119)
Coeur d'Alene *Dried Food* Berries dried and
used for food. *Fruit* Berries eaten fresh. Berries
mashed and eaten. *Soup* Berries dried, boiled
with roots, and eaten as soup. (as *P. demissa*
178:89) **Costanoan** *Fruit* Fruits used for food,
late in season only. (21:249) **Gosiute** *Dried
Food* Fruit mashed, sun dried, and stored for
winter use. *Fruit* Fruit used for food. *Porridge*
Fruit mashed, sun dried, stored for winter, and
used to make a mush. (as *P. demissa* 39:378)
Haisla & Hanaksiala *Forage* Fruit eaten by
bears. *Fruit* Fruit used for food. (43:273)
Karok *Fruit* Berries used for food. (as *P. demissa* 148:384) **Kawaiisu** *Fruit* Berries eaten
fresh. *Preserves* Berries used to make jelly. (as
P. demissa 206:54) **Kiowa** *Fruit* Fruit eaten
fresh. *Winter Use Food* Fruit dried in large
quantities for winter use. (as *Cerasus demissa*
192:30) **Klamath** *Dried Food* Fruit dried for
later use. (as *P. demissa* 45:98) **Luiseño** *Fruit*
Fruit used for food. (as *P. demissa* 155:232)
Mendocino Indian *Preserves* Fruits made into
a jelly and used for food. (as *Cerasus demissa*
41:356) **Modesse** *Fruit* Fruit used for food. (as
Cerasus demissa 117:223) **Montana Indian**
Beverage Ripe fruit collected each fall and
made into wine. *Fruit* Fruit eaten fresh. *Preserves* Ripe fruit collected each fall and made
into marmalade. *Staple* Fruit used as an important ingredient in the preparation of "pemmican." *Winter Use Food* Crushed, dried fruit
strips stored for winter use. (as *P. demissa*
19:19) **Ojibwa** *Dried Food* Fruit dried for winter use. *Fruit* Fruit eaten fresh. *Soup* Dried fruit
ground into a flour and used to make soup. (as
P. demissa 135:235) **Okanagon** *Staple* Berries

used as a principal food. (as *P. demissa* 178:238) **Paiute** *Beverage* Fruits added to hot water and used as a beverage. Stems used to make tea. (as *P. demissa* 104:99) Bark and twigs made into a tea and taken with meals. (as *P. demissa* 111:84) *Dried Food* Fruits broken, molded into cakes, hardened, ground, boiled, dried, and used for food. *Fruit* Fruits eaten fresh. (as *P. demissa* 104:99) Chokecherry cakes ground and boiled with flour, sugar, and occasionally roasted deer liver. *Winter Use Food* Chokecherries made into cakes for winter use. (as *P. demissa* 111:84) **Paiute, Northern** *Bread & Cake* Berries mashed, made into round cakes, and eaten dry. *Dried Food* Berries dried, cooked, and eaten. *Fruit* Berries eaten ripe. *Porridge* Berries dried, ground, and boiled into a mush. *Winter Use Food* Berries dried and stored for winter use. (as *P. demissa* 59:49) **Round Valley Indian** *Dried Food* Fruits dried and used for food. *Fruit* Fruits eaten. (as *Cerasus demissa* 41:356) **Shuswap** *Beverage* Boiled roots used to make beer. Dried berries used to make wine. *Winter Use Food* Berries dried for winter use. (123:67) **Spokan** *Fruit* Berries used for food. (as *P. demissa* 178:343) **Thompson** *Unspecified* Dark purple drupe used as part of the diet. (as *P. demissa* 164:490) **Wintoon** *Fruit* Fruit used for food. (as *P. demissa* 117:264) **Yuki** *Fruit* Berries eaten raw. Ripe berries cooked and eaten. (as *P. demissa* 49:87) **Yurok** *Fruit* Fruit used for food. (6:48)

Prunus virginiana var. *melanocarpa*, Black Chokecherry

Acoma *Dried Food* Fruits dried for winter use. *Fruit* Fruits eaten fresh. (as *P. melanocarpa* 32:46) **Apache** *Bread & Cake* Berries ground and meal made into sweet, blackish cakes. (as *Padus melanocarpa* 138:47) **Apache, Chiricahua & Mescalero** *Fruit* Fruit eaten fresh. *Preserves* Fruit cooked to make a preserve. *Winter Use Food* Fruits ground, pressed, and saved for winter. (as *Prunus melanocarpa* 33:46) **Cheyenne** *Fruit* Fresh or pounded, dried berries and pits used to make berry pemmican. *Winter Use Food* Pounded berries and pits made into flat cakes and sun dried for win-

ter use. (as *P. melanocarpa* 76:177) **Cochiti** *Dried Food* Fruits dried for winter use. *Fruit* Fruits eaten fresh. (as *P. melanocarpa* 32:46) **Dakota** *Fruit* Fresh fruit used for food. *Winter Use Food* Fruit pounded to a pulp, made into small cakes, dried in the sun, and stored for winter use. (as *P. melanocarpa* 69:364) **Great Basin Indian** *Dried Food* Mashed berries dried for winter use. (as *P. melanocarpa* 121:48) **Keres, Western** *Fruit* Fruit used for food. *Winter Use Food* Fruit dried for winter use. (as *P. melanocarpa* 171:63) **Kiowa** *Fruit* and *Winter Use Food* Fruit eaten fresh and dried in large quantities for winter use. (192:30) **Laguna** *Dried Food* Fruits dried for winter use. *Fruit* Fruits eaten fresh. **Navajo** *Porridge* Fruits cooked into a gruel with cornmeal. (as *P. melanocarpa* 32:46) **Navajo, Ramah** *Bread & Cake* Fruit ground and made into small cakes. *Fruit* Fruit eaten fresh. *Winter Use Food* Fruit dried for winter use. (191:31) **Pueblo** *Fruit* Fruits eaten fresh or cooked. **San Felipe** *Dried Food* Fruits dried for winter use. *Fruit* Fruits eaten fresh. (as *P. melanocarpa* 32:46) **Sanpoil & Nespelem** *Beverage* Branches used to make a beverage. (131:104) *Bread & Cake* Berries mashed, mixed with dried salmon into a pemmican, formed into cakes, dried, and stored. *Fruit* Fruit eaten fresh or dried. (131:101) **Spanish American** *Preserves* Fruits made into jelly and jam. (as *P. melanocarpa* 32:46) **Tewa** *Fruit* Berries boiled and eaten. Berries eaten raw. (as *Padus melanocarpa* 138:47)

Prunus virginiana var. *virginiana*, Chokecherry

Dakota *Bread & Cake* Fruit and pits pounded to a pulp, formed into small cakes, sun dried, and stored for winter use. *Dried Food* Fruit dried for winter use. *Fruit* Fruit eaten fresh. **Omaha** *Bread & Cake* Fruit and pits pounded to a pulp, formed into small cakes, sun dried, and stored for winter use. *Dried Food* Fruit dried for winter use. *Fruit* Fruit eaten fresh. **Pawnee** *Bread & Cake* Fruit and pits pounded to a pulp, formed into small cakes, sun dried, and stored for winter use. *Dried Food* Fruit dried for winter use. *Fruit* Fruit eaten fresh.

Ponca *Bread & Cake* Fruit and pits pounded to a pulp, formed into small cakes, sun dried, and stored for winter use. *Dried Food* Fruit dried for winter use. *Fruit* Fruit eaten fresh. (as *Padus nana* 70:88)

Pseudocymopterus montanus,
Alpine False Springparsley
Hopi *Vegetable* Plant used for greens. (42:352) **Navajo, Ramah** *Unspecified* Ground root cooked with meat. Leaves boiled with cornmeal. (191:38)

Pseudoroegneria spicata ssp.
spicata, Bluebunch Wheatgrass
Okanagan-Colville *Forage* Plant used as grazing grass for livestock and deer. (as *Agropyron spicatum* 188:53)

Pseudotsuga menziesii, Douglas Fir
Apache, White Mountain *Candy* Pitch used as gum. (as *P. mucronata* 136:159) **Gosiute** *Candy* Gum used for chewing gum. (as *P. douglasii* 39:378) **Karok** *Beverage* Young sprouts used to make tea. (6:48) **Montana Indian** *Substitution Food* Leaves sometimes used as a substitute for coffee. (as *P. mucronata* 19:20) **Paiute** *Spice* Boughs or branches used for flavoring barbecued bear meat. (as *P. mucronata* 111:44) **Round Valley Indian** *Substitution Food* Fresh leaves used as a substitute for coffee. (as *P. mucronata* 41:309) **Shuswap** *Sweetener* Sap used as a sugar-like food. (123:52) **Thompson** *Sweetener* Wild sugar gathered and eaten whenever possible. (187:107) **Yuki** *Substitution Food* Fresh leaves used as a substitute for coffee. (as *P. mucronata* 41:309) **Yurok** *Beverage* Young sprouts used to make tea. *Candy* Young sprouts used to chew. (6:48)

Pseudotsuga menziesii var.
glauca, Rocky Mountain Douglas Fir
Okanagan-Colville *Unspecified* White, crystalline sugar exuded from branches and eaten alone or with balsamroot seeds. *Winter Use Food* White, crystalline sugar exuded from branches and stored for future use. (188:34)

Pseudotsuga menziesii var. menziesii, Douglas Fir
Apache, White Mountain *Candy* Pitch used as gum. (as *P. taxifolia* 136:159) **Cowlitz** *Candy* Pitch chewed as a gum. (as *P. taxifolia* 79:19) **Karok** *Spice* Boughs used as "seasoning" for barbecued elk or deer meat. (as *P. taxifolia* 148:379) **Klallam** *Candy* Pitch chewed as a gum. **Quinault** *Candy* Pitch chewed as a gum. (as *P. taxifolia* 79:19)

Psidium guajava, Guava
Seminole *Unspecified* Plant used for food. (169:464)

Psoralidium tenuiflorum, Slimflower Scurfpea
Yavapai *Beverage* Used as ingredient of modern intoxicant made from mescal. (65:257)

Ptelea trifoliata ssp. trifoliata var. mollis, Common Hoptree
San Felipe *Fruit* Fruits commonly eaten by children. (as *P. tomentosa* 32:47)

Pteridium aquilinum, Western Brackenfern
Alaska Native *Substitution Food* Young fiddlenecks peeled, boiled, or steamed and eaten as a substitute for asparagus. *Winter Use Food* Young fiddlenecks canned for winter use. (85:51) **Atsugewi** *Unspecified* Raw leaves and tender stems used for food. (61:139) **Bella Coola** *Unspecified* Rhizomes toasted and eaten in summer. (184:197) **Clallam** *Staple* Rhizomes roasted, pounded into a flour, and eaten. (57:194) **Costanoan** *Unspecified* Young fronds eaten raw or cooked. (21:247) **Hahwunkwut** *Unspecified* Roots cooked in ground ovens. (as *Pteris aquilina* 117:185) **Hesquiat** *Vegetable* Long, mashed rhizomes eaten boiled or steamed. (185:32) **Kwakiutl, Southern** *Unspecified* Rhizomes roasted, beaten until soft, broken into pieces, and used for food. (183:265) **Mahuna** *Unspecified* Young shoots cut, cooked, and eaten like asparagus. (as *Pteris aquilina* 140:58) **Montana Indian** *Unspecified* Peeled root roasted for food. (as *Pteris aquilina*

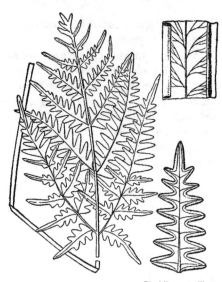

Pteridium aquilinum

19:20) **Nitinaht** *Unspecified* Rhizomes roasted, pounded, and inner portions used for food. *Vegetable* Long, thick rhizomes formerly steamed, dried, and used as a vegetable food in winter. (186:63) **Ojibwa** *Soup* Young fern sprouts used as a soup material. The tips were thrown into hot water for an hour to rid them of ants, then put into soup stock and thickened with flour. The flavor resembles wild rice. Hunters were very careful to live wholly upon this when stalking does in the spring. The doe feeds upon the fronds and the hunter does also, so that his breath does not betray his presence. He claims to be able to approach within 20 feet without disturbing the deer, from which distance he can easily make a fatal shot with his bow and arrow. After killing the deer, the hunter will eat whatever strikes his fancy. *Unspecified* Young fern tips, with coiled fronds, were like asparagus tips, only not stringy like asparagus. (as *Pteris aquilina* 153:408) **Okanagon** *Unspecified* Rootstocks boiled or roasted and used for food. (125:38) **Salish, Coast** *Bread & Cake* Rhizomes pounded into flour and baked to make bread. *Unspecified* Rhizomes eaten fresh in late fall or winter. Young shoots used for food. (182:69) **Sierra** *Staple* Roots used as a staple food. (41:304) **Skagit, Upper**

Unspecified Roots roasted in ashes, peeled, and eaten. (179:40) **Thompson** *Staple* Cooked, inner rhizome pounded into a flour and used for food. (187:90) *Unspecified* Rootstocks boiled or roasted and used for food. (125:38) Rootstocks cooked and eaten. Rootstocks used as a nutritious food. (164:482) Dried, toasted rhizomes beaten with a stick to remove the bark and the white insides used for food. The rhizomes were usually eaten with fish and were said to be very sweet, but one informant's father said it would give her worms. Fiddleheads broken off and the stem portion of the shoot used for food, often with fish. (187:90)

Pteridium aquilinum var. *pubescens*, Hairy Brackenfern

Chehalis *Unspecified* Rhizomes roasted, peeled, and the starchy centers eaten. **Cowlitz** *Unspecified* Rhizomes roasted, peeled, and the starchy centers eaten. Young plant tops eaten raw. **Green River Group** *Unspecified* Rhizomes roasted, peeled, and the starchy centers eaten. **Klallam** *Unspecified* Rhizomes roasted, peeled and the starchy centers eaten. **Lummi** *Unspecified* Rhizomes roasted, peeled, and the starchy centers eaten. (79:14) **Makah** *Unspecified* Steamed rhizomes used for food. (67:224) Rhizomes roasted, peeled, and the starchy centers eaten. (79:14) **Nitinaht** *Unspecified* Steamed rhizomes used for food. (67:224) **Quileute** *Unspecified* Rhizomes roasted, peeled, and the starchy centers eaten. **Quinault** *Unspecified* Rhizomes roasted, peeled, and the starchy centers eaten. **Skagit** *Unspecified* Rhizomes roasted, peeled, and the starchy centers eaten. **Skokomish** *Unspecified* Rhizomes roasted, peeled, and the starchy centers eaten. **Snohomish** *Unspecified* Rhizomes roasted, peeled, and the starchy centers eaten. **Squaxin** *Unspecified* Rhizomes roasted, peeled, and the starchy centers eaten. **Swinomish** *Unspecified* Rhizomes roasted, peeled, and the starchy centers eaten. (79:14)

Pterospora andromedea, Woodland Pinedrops

Kawaiisu *Unspecified* Stems eaten raw,

"roasted," or baked below the fire "like mushrooms." (206:55)

Puccinellia distans, Weeping
Alkaligrass
Gosiute *Unspecified* Seeds formerly used for food. (as *Glyceria distans* 39:370)

Purshia stansburiana, Stansbury
Cliffrose
Navajo *Forage* Plant used for deer and livestock forage. (as *Cowania stansburiana* 90:159)

Purshia tridentata, Antelope Bitterbrush
Navajo *Forage* Considered an important browse plant. (90:154) **Okanagan-Colville** *Forage* Plant eaten by deer. (188:128)

Pycnanthemum flexuosum, Appalachian Mountainmint
Cherokee *Unspecified* Species used for food. (80:45)

Pycnanthemum incanum, Hoary
Mountainmint
Cherokee *Unspecified* Species used for food. (80:45)

Pycnanthemum virginianum,
Virginia Mountainmint
Chippewa *Spice* Buds and flowers used to season meat or broth. (as *Koellia virginiana* 53:318)

Pyrola sp., Wintergreen
Malecite *Beverage* Used to make tea. (160:6)

Pyrrhopappus carolinianus, Carolina Desertchicory
Kiowa *Unspecified* Autumn, sweet roots used for food. (as *Sitilias caroliniana* 192:61)

Pyrus communis, Common Pear
Cherokee *Fruit* Fruit used for food. (80:48)
Hopi *Unspecified* Species used for food. (200:79) **Iroquois** *Bread & Cake* Fruit mashed, made into small cakes and dried for future use. *Dried Food* Raw or cooked fruit sun or fire dried and stored for future use. *Fruit* Dried fruit taken as a hunting food. *Sauce & Relish* Dried fruit cakes soaked in warm water and cooked as a sauce or mixed with corn bread. (196:129) **Seminole** *Unspecified* Plant used for food. (169:496)

Quercus agrifolia, California Live Oak
Cahuilla *Bread & Cake* Acorns ground into a fine meal and used to make bread. *Dried Food* Dried acorns stored for a year or more in granaries. *Porridge* Cooked acorns used to make mush. *Special Food* Acorn meat considered a delicacy and favored at social and ceremonial occasions. (15:121) **Costanoan** *Unspecified* Acorns used for food. (21:248) **Luiseño** *Porridge* Acorns leached, ground into a meal, cooked in an earthen vessel, and eaten. (155:194) *Staple* Acorns eaten as a staple food. (155:193) Acorns from storage granaries pounded in a mortar and pestle to make a flour. *Winter Use Food* Acorns formerly gathered for storage in acorn granaries. (155:194) **Pomo** *Unspecified* Acorns used for food. (66:12) **Pomo, Kashaya** *Dried Food* Acorns sun dried before storing. *Porridge* Acorns used as flour for pancakes, bread, mush, or soup. (72:80)

Quercus agrifolia var. agrifolia,
　California Live Oak
Diegueño *Porridge* Acorns shelled, pounded, leached, and cooked into a mush or gruel. (84:33)

Quercus alba, White Oak
Iroquois *Unspecified* Acorns used for food. (196:123) **Menominee** *Pie & Pudding* Acorns boiled, simmered to remove lye, ground, sifted, and made into pie. *Porridge* Acorns boiled, simmered to remove lye, ground, sifted, and made into mush with bear oil seasoning. *Staple* Acorns boiled, simmered to remove lye, ground, sifted, cooked in soup stock to flavor, and eaten. (151:66) **Meskwaki** *Beverage* Ground, scorched acorns made into a drink similar to coffee. *Porridge* Dried acorns made into mush. (152:257) **Ojibwa** *Soup* Acorns soaked in lye water to remove bitter tannin taste, dried for storage, and used to make soup. Lye for leach-

ing acorns was obtained by soaking wood ashes in water. Acorns were put in a net bag and then soaked in the lye, then rinsed several times in warm water. The acorns were then dried for storage, and when wanted, pounded into a coarse flour which was used to thicken soups or form a sort of mush. (153:401)

Quercus bicolor, Swamp White Oak
Iroquois *Unspecified* Acorns used for food. (196:123)

Quercus chrysolepis, Canyon Live Oak
Cahuilla *Bread & Cake* Acorns ground into a fine meal and used to make bread. *Dried Food* Dried acorns stored for a year or more in granaries. *Porridge* Cooked acorns used to make mush. *Special Food* Acorn meat considered a delicacy and favored at social and ceremonial occasions. (15:121) **Diegueño** *Porridge* Acorns shelled, pounded, leached, and cooked into a mush or gruel. (84:33) **Karok** *Fruit* Fruit bur-

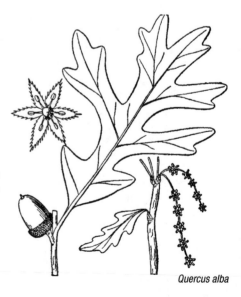

Quercus alba

ied from 1 to 4 years to kill the bugs and worms and used for food. (6:49) *Unspecified* Acorns used for food. (148:382) **Kawaiisu** *Bread & Cake* Acorns made into a fine meal, cooked into a mush, and allowed to stand and harden into a "cake." *Staple* Acorns dried, pounded, sifted into a fine meal, and leached. *Winter Use Food* Acorns stored for future use. (206:56) **Luiseño** *Porridge* Acorns leached, ground into a meal, cooked in an earthen vessel, and eaten. *Staple* Acorns from storage granaries pounded in a mortar and pestle to make a flour. (155:194) *Substitution Food* Acorns used as a substitution during a scarcity of common live oak or black oak. (155:193) *Winter Use Food* Acorns formerly stored in acorn granaries. (155:194) **Pomo** *Bread & Cake* Acorns used to make bread. *Porridge* Acorns used to make mush. (117:290) **Shasta** *Bread & Cake* Acorns pounded, winnowed, leached, and made into bread. *Porridge* Acorns pounded, winnowed, leached, and made into mush. *Soup* Acorns pounded, winnowed, leached, and made into thin soup. *Staple* Acorns used as the basic staple. (93:308) **Tubatulabal** *Unspecified* Acorns used extensively for food. (193:15) **Wintoon** *Dried Food* Acorns dried and preserved for future use. *Unspecified* Acorns leached all winter in cold, wet, swampy ground, boiled or roasted, and eaten in the spring. (117:265)

Quercus douglasii, Blue Oak
Kawaiisu *Bread & Cake* Acorns made into a fine meal, cooked into a mush, and allowed to stand and harden into a "cake." *Staple* Acorns dried, pounded, sifted into a fine meal, and leached. *Winter Use Food* Acorns stored for future use. (206:56) **Mendocino Indian** *Bread & Cake* Thick acorns used to make bread. *Soup* Thick acorns used to make soup. (41:342) **Miwok** *Bread & Cake* Acorns ground into a meal and used to make bread and biscuits. *Porridge* Acorns considered a staple food and used to make mush. *Soup* Acorns ground into a meal and used to make soup. *Winter Use Food* Whole acorns stored for winter use. (12:142) **Tubatulabal** *Unspecified* Acorns used extensively for food. (193:14) **Yana** *Bread & Cake*

Acorn flour used to make bread. *Dried Food* Acorns dried for winter use. *Porridge* Acorn flour used to make mush. *Staple* Dried acorns ground into flour. (147:249) **Yokut** *Unspecified* Acorns used for food. (117:420)

Quercus dumosa, California Scrub Oak
Cahuilla *Bread & Cake* Acorns ground into a fine meal and used to make bread. *Dried Food* Dried acorns stored for a year or more in granaries. *Porridge* Cooked acorns used to make mush. *Special Food* Acorn meat considered a delicacy and favored at social and ceremonial occasions. (15:121) **Diegueño** *Porridge* Acorns shelled, pounded, leached, and cooked into a mush or gruel. (84:33) **Kawaiisu** *Bread & Cake* Acorns made into a fine meal, cooked into a mush, and allowed to stand and harden into a "cake." *Staple* Acorns dried, pounded, sifted into a fine meal, and leached. *Winter Use Food* Acorns stored for future use. (206:56) **Luiseño** *Porridge* Acorns leached, ground into a meal, cooked in an earthen vessel, and eaten. *Staple* Stored acorns pounded in a mortar and pestle to make a flour. (155:194) *Substitution Food* Acorns used only when more preferred species could not be obtained. (155:193) *Winter Use Food* Acorns formerly stored in acorn granaries. (155:194) **Pomo, Kashaya** *Forage* Acorns not used by people but eaten as a favorite food by deer, squirrels, chipmunks, quail, and jays. (72:82) **Tubatulabal** *Unspecified* Acorns used extensively for food. (193:15)

Quercus dunnii, Palmer Oak
Diegueño *Fruit* Fruit formerly used for food. (as *Q. palmeri* 88:216) **Paiute** *Porridge* Acorns boiled into mush. *Winter Use Food* Acorns stored for future use in pits lined and covered with sage bark. (as *Q. palmeri* 167:246)

Quercus ellipsoidalis, Northern Pin Oak
Menominee *Beverage* Roasted acorn ground for coffee. (151:66)

Quercus emoryi, Emory's Oak
Apache, Western *Unspecified* Acorns eaten

whole and raw, ground on a metate, or boiled. (26:174) **Papago** *Candy* Acorns chewed as a confection. (34:47) *Unspecified* Acorns eaten fresh from the shell. (34:19) Acorns used for food. (36:61) **Yavapai** *Cooking Agent* Ground meat used as thickening for venison stew. *Winter Use Food* Nuts stored for later use. (65:257)

Quercus engelmannii, Engelmann's Oak

Diegueño *Candy* Bark gum pounded, washed, and chewed like chewing gum. *Porridge* Acorns shelled, pounded, leached, and cooked into a mush or gruel. (84:33) **Luiseño** *Porridge* Acorns leached, ground into a meal, cooked in an earthen vessel, and eaten. *Staple* Stored acorns pounded in a mortar and pestle to make a flour. (155:194) *Substitution Food* Acorns used only when more preferred species could not be obtained. (155:193) *Winter Use Food* Acorns formerly stored in acorn granaries. (155:194)

Quercus gambelii, Gambel's Oak

Acoma *Staple* Acorns ground into meal. *Unspecified* Acorns boiled and eaten. (32:47) **Apache, Chiricahua & Mescalero** *Fruit* Raw fruit used for food. *Winter Use Food* Acorns roasted slightly, pounded, mixed with dried meat, and stored away in hide containers. (33:42) **Apache, Western** *Unspecified* Acorns eaten whole and raw, ground on a metate, or boiled. (26:174) **Apache, White Mountain** *Unspecified* Acorns used for food. (136:160) **Cochiti** *Staple* Acorns ground into meal. *Unspecified* Acorns boiled and eaten. (32:47) **Havasupai** *Porridge* Acorns parched, ground, and used to make mush. *Soup* Acorns parched, ground, and used to make soup. (197:67) *Spice* Acorns ground and added to flavor beef or deer soups. (197:74, 215) *Unspecified* Acorns parched on a tray or eaten raw. (197:215) **Hualapai** *Soup* Acorns used to make soup. *Unspecified* Acorns roasted and used for food. (195:12) **Isleta** *Staple* Acorns formerly used as a staple food. (100:41) **Laguna** *Staple* Acorns ground into meal. *Unspecified* Acorns boiled and eaten. (32:47) **Navajo, Ramah** *Staple* Acorns eaten

raw, boiled, roasted in ashes, or dried, ground, and cooked like cornmeal. (191:22) **Neeshenam** *Bread & Cake* Acorns ground into flour, soaked in water, and baked to make a bread. *Porridge* Acorns ground into flour, soaked in water, and cooked to make mush. (129:374) **Pueblo** *Unspecified* Acorns formerly used extensively for food. **San Felipe** *Staple* Acorns ground into meal. *Unspecified* Acorns boiled and eaten. (32:47) **Yavapai** *Cooking Agent* Acorns sometimes added as thickening to venison stews. *Unspecified* Uncooked acorns used for food. (65:257)

Quercus gambelii var. *gambelii*, Gambel's Oak

Acoma *Staple* Acorns ground into meal. *Unspecified* Acorns boiled and eaten. **Cochiti** *Staple* Acorns ground into meal. *Unspecified* Acorns boiled and eaten. (as *Q. utahensis* 32:47) **Keres, Western** *Staple* Acorns ground into flour. *Unspecified* Acorns boiled and eaten. (as *Q. utahensis* 171:64) **Laguna** *Staple* Acorns ground into meal. *Unspecified* Acorns boiled and eaten. (as *Q. utahensis* 32:47) **Navajo** *Unspecified* Acorns seldom used for food. (as *Q. utahensis* 165:222) **Pueblo** *Unspecified* Acorns formerly used extensively for food. **San Felipe** *Staple* Acorns ground into meal. *Unspecified* Acorns boiled and eaten. (as *Q. utahensis* 32:47) **Tewa** *Unspecified* Acorns used for food. (as *Q. utahensis* 138:44)

Quercus garryana, Oregon White Oak

Chehalis *Unspecified* Acorns roasted and eaten. **Cowlitz** *Unspecified* Acorns buried in the mud for leaching and used for food. (79:27) **Karok** *Unspecified* Acorns used for food. (148:382) **Mendocino Indian** *Bread & Cake* Acorns used to make bread. *Soup* Acorns used to make soup. (41:343) **Nisqually** *Unspecified* Acorns used for food. (79:27) **Paiute** *Unspecified* Autumn acorns buried in mud to ripen and eaten. (111:65) **Pomo** *Bread & Cake* Acorns used to make bread. *Porridge* Acorns used to make mush. (117:290) *Unspecified* Acorns used for food. (66:12) **Pomo, Kashaya** *Dried Food* Acorns sun dried before storing. *Porridge* Acorns used as flour for pancakes, bread, mush, or soup. (72:81) **Salish, Coast** *Unspecified* Acorns steamed, roasted, or boiled and used for food. (182:84) **Shasta** *Bread & Cake* Acorns pounded, winnowed, leached, and made into bread. *Porridge* Acorns pounded, winnowed, leached, and made into mush. *Soup* Acorns pounded, winnowed, leached, and made into thin soup. *Staple* Acorns used as the basic staple. (93:308) **Squaxin** *Unspecified* Acorns roasted on hot rocks and eaten. (79:27)

Quercus garryana var. *semota*, Oregon White Oak

Kawaiisu *Bread & Cake* Acorns made into a fine meal, cooked into a mush, and allowed to stand and harden into a "cake." *Staple* Acorns dried, pounded, sifted into a fine meal, and leached. *Winter Use Food* Acorns stored for future use. (206:56)

Quercus grisea, Gray Oak

Apache, Chiricahua & Mescalero *Fruit* Raw fruit used for food. (33:42) *Spice* Shaved root chips used to flavor drinks. (33:51) *Winter Use Food* Ripe acorns roasted slightly, pounded, and mixed with dried meat and stored. (33:42) **Navajo, Ramah** *Unspecified* Acorns used for food. (191:22)

Quercus kelloggii, California Black Oak

Cahuilla *Bread & Cake* Acorns ground into a fine meal and used to make bread. *Dried Food* Dried acorns stored for a year or more in granaries. *Porridge* Cooked acorns used to make mush. *Special Food* Acorn meat considered a delicacy and favored at social and ceremonial occasions. (15:121) **Diegueño** *Porridge* Acorns shelled, pounded, leached, and cooked into a mush or gruel. (84:33) **Karok** *Fruit* Fruit soaked in mud for a year and used for food. (6:49) *Unspecified* Acorns made into "houm" and eaten. (148:382) **Kawaiisu** *Bread & Cake* Acorns made into a fine meal, cooked into a mush, and allowed to stand and harden into a "cake." *Staple* Acorns dried, pounded, sifted into a fine meal, and leached. *Winter Use Food*

Acorns stored for future use. (206:56) **Luiseño** *Porridge* Acorns leached, ground into a meal, cooked in an earthen vessel, and eaten. (as *Q. californica* 155:194) *Staple* Acorns eaten as a staple food. (as *Q. californica* 155:193) Acorns from storage granaries pounded in a mortar and pestle to make a flour. *Winter Use Food* Acorns formerly gathered for storage in acorn granaries. (as *Q. californica* 155:194) **Mendocino Indian** *Bread & Cake* Acorns used to make bread. *Soup* Acorns used to make soup. (as *Q. californicum* 41:342) **Mewuk** *Bread & Cake* Acorns used to make bread. *Porridge* Acorns used to make mush. (as *Q. californicus* 117:327) *Unspecified* Acorns used for food. (as *Q. californicus* 117:333) **Miwok** *Bread & Cake* Acorns ground into a meal and used to make bread and biscuits. *Porridge* Acorns considered a staple food and used to make mush. *Soup* Acorns ground into a meal and used to make soup. *Winter Use Food* Whole acorns stored for winter use. (12:142) **Modesse** *Staple* Acorns used as the principal vegetable food. (as *Q. californica* 117:223) **Neeshenam** *Unspecified* Acorns occasionally used for food. (as *Q. sonomensis* 129:374) **Paiute** *Porridge* Acorns boiled into mush. *Winter Use Food* Acorns stored for future use in pits lined and covered with sage bark. (167:246) **Paiute, Northern** *Staple* Acorns ground into flour, leached, and eaten. (59:52) **Pomo** *Bread & Cake* Acorns used to make white bread. (as *Q. californica* 11:67) Acorns used to make bread. (as *Q. californica* 117:290) *Porridge* Acorns used to make gruel and mush. (as *Q. californica* 11:67) Acorns used to make mush. (as *Q. californica* 117:290) *Soup* Acorns used to make soups. (as *Q. californica* 11:67) *Unspecified* Acorns used for food. (66:12) **Pomo, Kashaya** *Dried Food* Acorns sun dried before storing. *Porridge* Acorns used as flour for pancakes, bread, mush, or soup. (72:79) **Shasta** *Bread & Cake* Acorns pounded, winnowed, leached, and made into bread. *Porridge* Acorns pounded, winnowed, leached, and made into mush. *Soup* Acorns pounded, winnowed, leached, and made into thin soup. *Staple* Acorns used as the basic staple. (as *Q. californica* 93:308) **Tolowa** *Fruit*

Fruit used for food. (6:49) **Tubatulabal** *Unspecified* Acorns used extensively for food. (as *Q. californica* 193:15) **Yokut** *Unspecified* Acorns used for food. (as *Q. californica* 117:420) **Yuki** *Bread & Cake* Nutmeats pounded into fine meal, winnowed, and made into bread. *Porridge* Nutmeats pounded into fine meal, winnowed, boiled, and eaten as mush. (49:89) **Yurok** *Fruit* Fruit used for food. (6:49)

Quercus lobata Née, California White Oak

Kawaiisu *Bread & Cake* Acorns made into a fine meal, cooked into a mush, and allowed to stand and harden into a "cake." *Staple* Acorns dried, pounded, sifted into a fine meal, and leached. *Winter Use Food* Acorns stored for future use. (206:56) **Mendocino Indian** *Bread & Cake* Large acorns used to make bread. (41:343) **Miwok** *Bread & Cake* Acorns ground into a meal and used to make bread and biscuits. *Soup* Acorns ground into a meal and used to make soup. *Staple* Acorns considered a staple food and used to make mush. *Winter Use Food* Whole acorns stored for winter use. (12:142) **Pomo** *Bread & Cake* Acorns used to make white and black bread. (11:67) Acorns used to make bread. (117:290) *Porridge* Acorns used to make gruel and mush. (11:67) Acorns used to make mush. (117:290) *Soup* Acorns used to make soup. (11:67) **Pomo, Kashaya** *Porridge* Acorns used to make mush or soup rather than bread. (72:84) **Tubatulabal** *Unspecified* Acorns used extensively for food. (193:15) **Wintoon** *Unspecified* Roasted seeds used for food. (117:274) **Yokut** *Unspecified* Acorns used for food. (117:420) **Yuki** *Bread & Cake* Nutmeats pounded into fine meal, winnowed, and made into bread. *Porridge* Nutmeats pounded into fine meal, winnowed, boiled, and eaten as mush. (49:89)

Quercus macrocarpa, Bur Oak

Cheyenne *Unspecified* Acorns formerly used for food. (83:26) **Chippewa** *Unspecified* Acorns roasted in ashes or boiled, mashed, and eaten with grease or duck broth. *Vegetable* Acorns boiled, split open, and eaten like a vege-

Quercus macrocarpa

table. (53:320) **Dakota** *Unspecified* Acorns leached with basswood ashes to remove the bitter taste and used for food. (70:75) **Lakota** *Soup* Acorns chopped and cooked in soups and meats. *Unspecified* Acorns chopped, cooked over fire, and eaten. (106:31) **Ojibwa** *Unspecified* Acorns treated with lye to remove bitterness and eaten. (153:402) **Omaha** *Unspecified* Acorns leached with basswood ashes to remove the bitter taste and used for food. **Pawnee** *Unspecified* Acorns leached with basswood ashes to remove the bitter taste and used for food. **Ponca** *Unspecified* Acorns leached with basswood ashes to remove the bitter taste and used for food. **Winnebago** *Unspecified* Acorns leached with basswood ashes to remove the bitter taste and used for food. (70:75)

Quercus marilandica, Blackjack Oak

Comanche *Starvation Food* Boiled acorns used for food in times of scarcity. (29:524)

Quercus nigra, Water Oak

Choctaw *Staple* Pounded acorns boiled and made into a meal. Pounded acorns used as cornmeal. (as *Q. aquatica* 25:8) **Kiowa** *Beverage* Acorns used to make a beverage. *Unspecified* Acorns used for food. (192:21)

***Quercus oblongifolia*, Mexican Blue Oak**
Papago *Unspecified* Acorns used for food. (36:61) **Pima** *Staple* Hulls removed, acorns parched, ground into meal, and used for food. (146:78)

***Quercus ×pauciloba*, Wavyleaf Oak**
Apache, Western *Unspecified* Acorns eaten whole and raw, ground on a metate, or boiled. (as *Q. undulata* 26:174) **Apache, White Mountain** *Beverage* Acorns used to make "coffee." *Bread & Cake* Acorns ground into flour and used to make bread. *Unspecified* Acorns eaten raw. (as *Q. undulata* 136:148) **Gosiute** *Unspecified* Acorns used only in season for food. (as *Q. undulata* 39:378) **Navajo, Ramah** *Unspecified* Acorns used for food. (as *Q. undulata* 191:22)

***Quercus peninsularis*, Peninsula Oak**
Diegueño *Staple* Acorns pounded, sun dried, ground, and leached. (88:216)

***Quercus phellos*, Willow Oak**
Seminole *Unspecified* Plant used for food. (169:471)

***Quercus prinus*, Chestnut Oak**
Iroquois *Unspecified* Acorns used for food. (196:123)

***Quercus pumila*, Running Oak**
Seminole *Unspecified* Plant used for food. (169:493)

***Quercus pungens*, Pungent Oak**
Navajo *Candy* Gum used for chewing gum. (55:41)

***Quercus rubra*, Northern Red Oak**
Dakota *Unspecified* Acorns leached with basswood ashes to remove the bitter taste and used for food. (70:75) **Iroquois** *Unspecified* Acorns used for food. (196:123) **Ojibwa** *Staple* Acorns leached with lye and used as of the most important starchy foods. (153:402) **Omaha** *Unspecified* Acorns freed from tannic acid by boiling

with wood ashes and used for food. (68:327) Acorns leached with basswood ashes to remove the bitter taste and used for food. **Pawnee** *Unspecified* Acorns leached with basswood ashes to remove the bitter taste and used for food. **Ponca** *Unspecified* Acorns leached with basswood ashes to remove the bitter taste and used for food. (70:75) **Potawatomi** *Porridge* Dried, ground acorns used as a flour to make gruel. Hardwood ashes and water furnished the lye for soaking the acorns, to swell them and remove the tannic acid. A bark bag or reticule served to hold the acorns while they were washed through a series of hot and cold water to remove the lye. Then they were dried in the sun and became perfectly sweet and palatable. They were ground on depressions of rocks which served as a mortar with a stone pestle, to a flour, which was cooked as a gruel, sometimes called samp. (154:100)

***Quercus sadleriana*, Deer Oak**
Karok *Unspecified* Acorns shelled, parched, and eaten. (148:382)

***Quercus stellata*, Post Oak**
Kiowa *Beverage* Acorns used to make a drink similar to coffee. *Dried Food* Dried, pounded acorns used for food. (192:22)

***Quercus turbinella*, Shrub Live Oak**
Hualapai *Bread & Cake* Acorns used to make bread. *Soup* Acorns used to make stew. *Unspecified* Acorns roasted like pinyons. (195:11) **Mohave** *Porridge* Acorns used to make mush. (37:187) **Pima, Gila River** *Snack Food* Fruits eaten raw as a snack food. (133:7)

***Quercus velutina*, Black Oak**
Lakota *Staple* Acorns used to make flour. (139:49) **Ojibwa** *Unspecified* Acorns, with tannic acid extracted, equally as good as other acorns. (153:402)

***Quercus virginiana*, Live Oak**
Mahuna *Dessert* Acorns ground into a fine meal, sun dried, made into porridge, cooked, and eaten as a dessert. *Unspecified* Acorns ground into

a fine meal, sun dried, made into porridge, and eaten with deer meat. (140:55) **Seminole** *Fodder* Acorns used as hog food. (169:493)

Quercus wislizeni, Interior Live Oak
Luiseño *Porridge* Acorns leached, ground into a meal, cooked in an earthen vessel, and eaten. (155:194) *Staple* Stored acorns pounded in a mortar and pestle to make a flour. *Substitution Food* Acorns used only when more preferred species could not be obtained. (155:193) *Winter Use Food* Acorns formerly stored in acorn granaries. (155:194) **Miwok** *Bread & Cake* Acorns ground into a meal and used to make bread and biscuits. *Porridge* Acorns considered a staple food and used to make mush. *Soup* Acorns ground into a meal and used to make soup. *Winter Use Food* Whole acorns stored for winter use. (12:142) **Neeshenam** *Unspecified* Acorns

occasionally used for food. (129:374) **Tubatulabal** *Unspecified* Acorns used extensively for food. (193:15)

Quercus wislizeni var. *frutescens*, Interior Live Oak
Diegueño *Porridge* Acorns shelled, pounded, leached, and cooked into a mush or gruel. (84:33) **Kawaiisu** *Bread & Cake* Acorns made into a fine meal, cooked into a mush, and allowed to stand and harden into a "cake." *Staple* Acorns dried, pounded, sifted into a fine meal, and leached. *Winter Use Food* Acorns stored for future use. (206:56)

Quincula lobata, Chinese Lantern
Kiowa *Preserves* Berries gathered to make jelly. Berries gathered to make jelly. (192:50)

Ranunculus abortivus, Littleleaf Buttercup
Cherokee *Vegetable* Leaves cooked and eaten as greens. (80:31)

Ranunculus acris, Tall Buttercup
Cherokee *Vegetable* Leaves cooked and eaten as greens. (80:31)

Ranunculus aquatilis, Whitewater Crowfoot
Gosiute *Unspecified* Entire plant boiled and eaten. (39:379)

Ranunculus californicus, California Buttercup
Miwok *Unspecified* Dried, stored, parched, pulverized seeds used for food. (12:155)
Neeshenam *Bread & Cake* Seeds parched,

Ranunculus acris

ground into flour and used to make bread. *Porridge* Seeds parched, ground into flour, and used to make mush. *Staple* Seeds parched, ground into flour, and used for food. (129:377)

Ranunculus cymbalaria, Alkali Buttercup
Iroquois *Unspecified* Mature leaves used for food. (142:87)

Ranunculus inamoenus, Graceful Buttercup
Acoma *Unspecified* Roots used for food. (32:48) **Keres, Western** *Unspecified* Roots considered good to eat. (171:65) **Laguna** *Unspecified* Roots used for food. (32:48)

Ranunculus lapponicus, Lapland Buttercup
Eskimo, Inuktitut *Soup* Leaves and stems stewed with duck and fresh fish. (202:183)

Ranunculus occidentalis var. *eisenii*, Western Buttercup
Mendocino Indian *Staple* Smooth, flat, and orbicular seeds used alone or mixed with other seeds to make pinole. (as *R. eisenii* 41:347) **Pomo** *Staple* Seeds used to make pinoles. (11:87)

Ranunculus occidentalis var. *rattanii*, Western Buttercup
Pomo *Staple* Seeds used to make pinoles. (11:87)

Ranunculus pallasii, Pallas's Buttercup
Alaska Native *Unspecified* Young, tender shoots cooked and eaten. (85:53) **Eskimo, Alaska** *Unspecified* Shoots and stems boiled until tender and eaten with seal oil. (1:35) Rootstocks used as food, but became bitter after leaves developed. (4:715)

Ranunculus recurvatus, Blisterwort
Cherokee *Vegetable* Leaves cooked and eaten as greens. (80:31)

Ranunculus repens, Creeping Buttercup
Hesquiat *Forage* Eaten by cows and deer. (185:71)

Ranunculus reptans, Buttercup
Makah *Unspecified* Roots cooked on hot rocks, dipped in whale or seal oil, and eaten with dried salmon eggs. **Quileute** *Unspecified* Roots cooked on hot rocks, dipped in whale or seal oil, and eaten with dried salmon eggs. (79:29)

Raphanus sativus, Wild Radish
Costanoan *Unspecified* Raw stems used for food. (as *R. sativum* 21:252)

Ratibida columnifera, Upright Prairie Coneflower
Dakota *Beverage* Leaves used to make a hot, tea-like beverage. (as *R. columnaris* 69:368) **Oglala** *Beverage* Leaves and cylindrical heads used to make a tea-like beverage. (as *R. columnaris* 70:131)

Rhamnus crocea, Redberry Buckthorn
Cahuilla *Fruit* Berries used for food. (15:131)

Rheum rhabarbarum, Garden Rhubarb
Haisla & Hanaksiala *Unspecified* Petioles used for food. (43:259) **Kitasoo** *Pie & Pudding* Stalks used to make pie. *Preserves* Stalks used to make jam. (43:340)

Rheum rhaponticum, False Rhubarb
Cherokee *Unspecified* Species used for food. (80:52)

Rhexia virginica, Handsome Harry
Montagnais *Beverage* Leaves and stems used to make a sour drink. (156:314)

Rhododendron albiflorum, Cascade Azalea
Okanagan-Colville *Beverage* Leaves used to make tea. (188:102) **Thompson** *Preservative* Branches used in bottoms of berry baskets and

on top of the berries to keep them fresh. (187:216)

Rhododendron calendulaceum,
Flame Azalea
Cherokee *Unspecified* Fungus "apple" formed on the stem eaten to appease thirst. (80:24)

Rhodymenia palmata, Dulse
Alaska Native *Dried Food* Leaves air dried and stored for winter use. *Soup* Leaves air dried and added to soups and fish head stews. *Unspecified* Leaves eaten fresh or singed on a hot stove or griddle. (85:143)

Rhus aromatica, Fragrant Sumac
Midoo *Fruit* Berries pounded and eaten. (117:312)

Rhus copallinum, Flameleaf Sumac
Cherokee *Fruit* Berries used for food. (80:57)

Rhus glabra, Smooth Sumac
Apache, Chiricahua & Mescalero *Special Food* Bark eaten by children as a delicacy. (as *R. cismontana* 33:44) **Cherokee** *Fruit* Berries used for food. (80:57) **Comanche** *Fruit* Fruits eaten by children. (29:524) **Gosiute** *Fruit*

Rhus glabra

Berries used for food. (39:379) **Iroquois** *Beverage* Bobs boiled and used as a drink in winter. (124:96) *Unspecified* Sprouts eaten raw. (124:93) Fresh shoots peeled and eaten raw. (196:119) **Meskwaki** *Beverage* Berries and sugar used to make a cooling drink in the summertime and stored for winter use. (152:255) **Ojibwa** *Beverage* Fresh or dried berries sweetened with maple sugar and made into a hot or cool beverage like lemonade. (153:397) **Okanagan-Colville** *Beverage* Seed heads used to make tea. (188:59)

Rhus hirta, Staghorn Sumac
Algonquin, Quebec *Beverage* Berries steeped in water, sweetened with sugar, and drunk like lemonade. (as *R. typhina* 18:114) **Cherokee** *Fruit* Berries used for food. (as *R. typhina* 80:57) **Menominee** *Beverage* Infusion of dried berries used as a beverage very similar to lemonade. *Winter Use Food* Berries dried for winter use. (as *R. typhina* 151:62) **Ojibwa** *Beverage* Fresh or dried berries sweetened with maple sugar and made into a hot or cool beverage like lemonade. *Winter Use Food* Seed heads dried for winter use. (as *R. typhina* 153:397) **Potawatomi** *Sour* Berries eaten to satisfy a natural craving for something acid or tart. (as *R. typhina* 154:95)

Rhus integrifolia, Lemonade Sumac
Cahuilla *Beverage* Berries soaked in water and used as a beverage. (15:131) **Diegueño** *Beverage* Leaf wad kept in the mouth to assuage thirst on long journeys by foot. (84:37) **Mahuna** *Fruit* Berries eaten mainly to quench the thirst. (140:70)

Rhus microphylla, Littleleaf Sumac
Apache *Fruit* Fruits eaten for food. (32:49) **Apache, Chiricahua & Mescalero** *Preserves* Dried fruits ground, pulp mixed with water and sugar and cooked to make jam. (33:46)

Rhus ovata, Sugar Sumac
Cahuilla *Dried Food* Berries dried. *Fruit* Berries eaten fresh. *Porridge* Berries ground into a flour for mush. *Sweetener* Fruit sap used as a

sweetener. (15:131) **Yavapai** *Fruit* Mashed, raw berries used for food. (63:212)

Rhus trilobata, Skunkbush Sumac

Acoma *Appetizer* Fruits eaten fresh as appetizers. *Spice* Fruits mixed with various foods as seasoning. **Apache** *Fruit* Fruits eaten fresh. *Staple* Fruits ground into meal. (32:48) **Apache, Chiricahua & Mescalero** *Dried Food* Fruits ground with mescal, dried, and stored. (33:37) *Preserves* Dried fruits ground, pulp mixed with water, and sugar and cooked to make jam. (33:46) Fruits formerly used to make jam. (33:49) **Apache, Western** *Beverage* Berries stirred in warm water to make a nonintoxicating drink. *Fruit* Berries ground or chewed raw for the juice. (26:190) **Apache, White Mountain** *Fruit* Berries used for food. (136:160) **Atsugewi** *Beverage* Berries pounded into flour, mixed with manzanita flour and water, and used as a beverage. *Dried Food* Berries washed, dried, and stored for later use. *Preserves* Berries mixed with sugar and made into jam. (61:139) **Cahuilla** *Beverage* Berries soaked in water and used as a beverage. *Fruit* Berries eaten fresh. *Soup* Berries ground into a flour and used to make soup. (15:131) **Gosiute** *Fruit* Berries used for food. (39:379) **Great Basin Indian** *Beverage* Berries used to make an acid drink. (121:48) **Havasupai** *Beverage* Berries crushed, soaked in water, ground, more water added, and used as a drink. *Dried Food* Berries sun dried and kept in sacks for future use. (197:229) **Hopi** *Beverage* Berries used to make "lemonade." (42:356) Berries pounded, soaked in water, and used to make a refreshing drink. (120:20) Berries made into lemonade. (200:84) *Fruit* Berries eaten by young people. (56:16) **Hualapai** *Beverage* Berries used to make a drink. *Fruit* Berries used for food. (195:15) **Isleta** *Sauce & Relish* Sour, acid flavored fruits eaten as an appetizer or relish. (100:41) **Jemez** *Fruit* Berries used for food. (44:27) **Keres, Western** *Beverage* Berries used to make a beverage. *Fruit* Raw berries eaten as an appetizer. *Spice* Berries used as a lemon flavored seasoning for food. (171:66) **Keresan** *Fruit* Berries used for food. (198:563) **Kiowa** *Beverage* Ber-

ries boiled into a "tea." *Fruit* Berries mixed with cornmeal and eaten. Berries mixed with cornmeal and eaten. (as *Schmaltzia bakeri* 192:39) **Laguna** *Appetizer* Fruits eaten fresh as appetizers. *Spice* Fruits mixed with various foods as seasoning. (32:48) **Luiseño** *Porridge* Berries ground into a meal and used for food. (155:195) **Mahuna** *Fruit* Berries eaten mainly to quench the thirst. (140:70) **Montana Indian** *Fruit* Berries used for food. (19:21) **Navajo** *Beverage* Berries used to make juice. (110:26) Berries ground, washed, mixed with water, and used as a beverage. *Bread & Cake* Berries used to make cakes. (165:222) *Dried Food* Berries dried for future use. (110:26) *Fruit* Fruits eaten fresh. (32:48) Fruits eaten as they come off the bush. Fruits ground with sugar in a little water and eaten. (55:60) Berries boiled with meat. (165:222) *Porridge* Fruits cooked into a gruel with cornmeal. (32:48) Fruits ground into a meal, cooked with cornmeal, and eaten as a gruel. (55:60) Berries ground, mixed with flour and sugar, and made into a mush. (165:222) *Staple* Fruits ground into a meal and eaten. (55:60) Berries ground into a flour. (110:26) **Navajo, Ramah** *Dried Food* Fruit dried for later use, ground, and soaked before using. *Fruit* Fruit eaten raw, with sugar, sometimes ground, and used with other foods, especially roasted corn. *Unspecified* Inner bark used for food. (191:35) **Shoshoni** *Beverage* Berries used to make a cooling drink. *Winter Use Food* Berries kept in large quantities for future use. (117:440) **Tewa** *Fruit* Fruits eaten whole or ground. (as *Schmaltzia bakeri* 138:49) **Wintoon** *Fruit* Berries used for food. (117:264) **Yokut** *Fruit* Sour berries gathered and used for food. (117:420)

Rhus trilobata var. *pilosissima*, Pubescent Squawbush

Yavapai *Beverage* Mashed berries mixed with water or mescal syrup and used as a beverage. *Unspecified* Seeds used for food. (as *R. emoryi* 65:257)

Rhus trilobata var. *trilobata*, Skunkbush Sumac

Kiowa *Beverage* Berries boiled into a "tea."

Fruit Berries mixed with cornmeal and eaten. (as *Schmaltzia trilobata* 192:39) **Ute** *Fruit* Berries used for food. (as *R. aromatica* var. *trilobata* 38:36)

Ribes amarum, Bitter Gooseberry
Mahuna *Fruit* Berries eaten mainly to quench the thirst. (140:70)

Ribes americanum, American Black Currant
Chippewa *Dried Food* Dried fruit used for food. *Fruit* Fresh fruit used for food. (as *R. floridum* 71:131) **Iroquois** *Bread & Cake* Fruit mashed, made into small cakes, and dried for future use. *Dried Food* Raw or cooked fruit sun or fire dried and stored for future use. *Fruit* Dried fruit taken as a hunting food. *Sauce & Relish* Dried fruit cakes soaked in warm water and cooked as a sauce or mixed with corn bread. (as *R. floridum* 196:128) **Lakota** *Fruit* Fruits eaten fresh. (106:35) Fruits eaten for food. (139:58) *Starvation Food* Berries dried and eaten during famines. (106:35) **Meskwaki** *Fruit* Currants used for food. (as *R. floridum* 152:264) **Montana Indian** *Fruit* Fruit highly esteemed as an article of diet. (as *R. floridum* 19:21) **Ojibwa** *Dried Food* Fruit dried for future use. (as *R. floridum* 135:236) Berries dried for

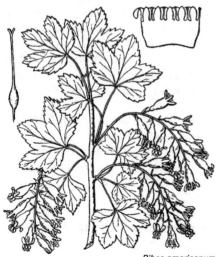

Ribes americanum

winter use. (153:410) *Fruit* Fruit eaten fresh. (as *R. floridum* 135:236) Berries eaten fresh. In the winter, a favorite dish was wild currants cooked with sweet corn. *Preserves* Berries used to make jams and preserves. (153:410)

Ribes aureum, Golden Currant
Blackfoot *Fruit* Berries used for food. (86:119) **Cheyenne** *Winter Use Food* Pounded, dried berries formed into cakes for winter use. (76:175) **Gosiute** *Dried Food* Berries dried and stored for winter use. *Fruit* Berries used for food. (39:379) **Klamath** *Fruit* Berries used for food. (45:97) **Montana Indian** *Fruit* Fruit highly esteemed as an article of diet. (19:21) **Okanagan-Colville** *Bread & Cake* Dried berries mixed with other berries and made into cakes. *Dried Food* Berries dried and stored for future use. *Fruit* Berries eaten fresh. (188:106) **Paiute** *Dried Food* Berries dried for later use. (111:78) Fruit sun dried, stored in buckskin bags, and hung up for winter use. (167:245) *Fruit* Ripe, crushed berries eaten with sugar. (111:78) Fruit eaten fresh. (167:245) **Paiute, Northern** *Dried Food* Berries eaten dried. *Fruit* Berries eaten fresh. *Porridge* Berries dried, ground, mixed with seed flour, and used to make mush. (59:50) **Ute** *Fruit* Berries used for food. (38:36) **Yavapai** *Fruit* Raw berries used for food. (65:258)

Ribes aureum var. *villosum*, Golden Currant
Comanche *Fruit* Fruits eaten for food. (as *R. odoratum* 29:524) **Kiowa** *Fruit* Fruit eaten raw. *Preserves* Fruit made into jelly. (as *Chrysobotrya odorata* 192:29) **Lakota** *Fruit* Fruits eaten fresh. (as *R. odoratum* 106:36) Fruits eaten for food. (as *R. odoratum* 139:58) *Starvation Food* Fruits dried and eaten during famines. (as *R. odoratum* 106:36)

Ribes bracteosum, Stink Currant
Bella Coola *Fruit* Berries used for food. (184:206) **Hanaksiala** *Winter Use Food* Fruit cooked and stored underground in barrels with elderberries and cooked western dock for winter use. (43:253) **Hesquiat** *Fruit* Berries eaten

with oil and could cause stomachache, if too many were eaten. *Preserves* Berries made excellent jam. (185:68) **Kitasoo** *Fruit* Fruit used for food. (43:338) **Kwakiutl, Southern** *Fruit* Fruits eaten raw with large quantities of oil. *Winter Use Food* Fruits boiled, mixed with powdered skunk cabbage leaves, dried, and eaten with oil in winter. (183:286) **Makah** *Fruit* Fruit used for food. (67:257) Berries eaten fresh. (79:32) **Nitinaht** *Dessert* Berries boiled, mixed in molasses, and eaten as dessert. (186:113) **Oweekeno** *Fruit* Berries mixed with salal berries, oolichan (candlefish) grease, and sugar, and eaten. (43:103) **Paiute** *Forage* Berries eaten only by bears. (111:78) **Salish, Coast** *Bread & Cake* Berries boiled, dried into rectangular cakes, and used as a winter food. (182:84)

Ribes californicum, Hillside Gooseberry

Kawaiisu *Dried Food* Berries dried in the shade for about a week and stored. *Fruit* Berries eaten fresh. *Preserves* Fresh berries boiled into a jelly. (206:59) **Mendocino Indian** *Fruit* Fruits eaten directly from the bushes by children. (41:353) **Pomo, Kashaya** *Fruit* Singed berries eaten whole. (72:51)

Ribes cereum, Wax Currant

Hopi *Fruit* Berries used for food. (56:16) **Keres, Western** *Fruit* Berries used for food. (171:66) **Klamath** *Fruit* Berries used for food. (45:97) **Montana Indian** *Fruit* Fruit highly esteemed as an article of diet. (19:21) **Okanagan-Colville** *Forage* Berries eaten by grouse and pheasant. *Fruit* Berries eaten fresh. (188:107) **Okanagon** *Fruit* Insipid, bright orange-red fruits used for food. (125:38) *Staple* Berries used as a principal food. (178:239) **Paiute** *Fruit* Fruits eaten fresh. (104:100) **Sanpoil & Nespelem** *Fruit* Berries eaten raw. Only currants from the bushes growing along the Columbia River were eaten. Berries from bushes growing in the hills were not eaten because it was thought that they caused headaches, nosebleeds, and sore eyes. (131:102) **Thompson** *Fruit* Insipid, bright orange-red fruits used for

food. (125:38) Insipid, rubbery berries used for food. (187:226)

Ribes cereum var. *pedicellare*, Whisky Currant

Acoma *Fruit* Fruits eaten fresh. *Preserves* Fruits preserved and eaten. (as *R. inebrians* 32:49) **Apache, White Mountain** *Fruit* Fruit eaten raw and cooked. (as *R. inebrians* 136:160) **Cheyenne** *Dried Food* Pounded berries formed into cakes, dried, and stewed with buffalo hide chips. (as *R. inebrians* 76:175) **Hopi** *Fruit* Berries eaten with fresh piki bread. (as *R. inebrians* 120:18) **Isleta** *Fruit* Fruit eaten fresh. *Preserves* Fruit eaten preserved. (as *R. inebrians* 100:42) **Laguna** *Fruit* Fruits eaten fresh. *Preserves* Fruits preserved and eaten. (as *R. inebrians* 32:49) **Navajo** *Fruit* Fruits eaten for food. (as *R. inebrians* 55:52) **Navajo, Ramah** *Fruit* Berries eaten raw. (as *R. inebrians* 191:30) **Tewa** *Fruit* Fruits eaten for food. (as *R. inebrians* 138:48) **Zuni** *Fruit* Highly relished berries used for food. (as *R. inebrians* 166:70) *Unspecified* Leaves eaten with uncooked mutton fat or deer fat. (as *R. inebrians* 32:49) Fresh leaves eaten with uncooked mutton fat or with deer fat. (as *R. inebrians* 166:70)

Ribes cruentum, Shinyleaf Currant

Karok *Fruit* Fresh fruits used for food. (6:50)

Ribes cruentum var. *cruentum*, Shinyleaf Currant

Karok Berries eaten raw. (as *R. roezlii* var. *cruentum* 148:384)

Ribes cynosbati, Eastern Prickly Gooseberry

Algonquin, Quebec *Fruit* Fruit used fresh. *Preserves* Fruit preserved. (18:87) **Cherokee** *Winter Use Food* Berries canned for future use. (126:54) **Chippewa** *Fruit* Berries used for food. (71:131) **Menominee** *Fruit* Berries used in favorite aboriginal Menomini dish. *Preserves* Berries preserved. *Winter Use Food* Berries stored for winter use. (151:71) **Meskwaki** *Dessert* Berries cooked with sugar as a dessert. (152:264) **Ojibwa** *Fruit* Berries relished when ripe. *Preserves* Berries made into preserves for winter use. (153:410) **Potawatomi** *Fruit* Berries used for food. *Preserves* Berries made into jams and jellies. (154:109)

Ribes divaricatum, Spreading Gooseberry

Bella Coola *Fruit* Ripe, black berries used for food. *Sauce & Relish* Green berries boiled into a thick sauce and used for food. (184:206) **Clallam** *Fruit* Berries eaten fresh. (57:200) **Cowlitz** *Dried Food* Green berries dried and stored for winter use. *Fruit* Green berries eaten fresh. (79:32) **Gosiute** *Dried Food* Berries dried and stored for winter use. *Fruit* Berries used for food. (39:379) **Haisla & Hanaksiala** *Fruit* Fruit used for food. (43:254) **Hesquiat** *Fruit* Raw, fresh berries eaten with oil. (185:69) **Karok** *Fruit* Berries eaten raw. (148:384) **Makah** *Fruit* Fruit eaten fresh. (67:258) **Mendocino Indian** *Fruit* Black, juicy berries used for food. (41:353) **Nitinaht** *Fruit* Fruit used for food. (67:258) Berries formerly eaten fresh. (186:114) **Oweekeno** *Fruit* Berries used for food. (43:104) **Quinault** *Preservative* Berries mixed with elderberries and buried with them for preservation. (79:32) **Salish, Coast** *Bread & Cake* Berries boiled, dried into rectangular cakes, and used as a winter food. (182:84) **Skagit, Upper** *Fruit* Berries eaten fresh and never stored. (179:38) **Swinomish** *Fruit* Berries eaten fresh. (79:32) **Thompson** *Beverage* Berries made into juice. *Fruit* Berries eaten fresh or cooked. *Pie & Pudding* Berries made into pies. (187:227)

Ribes glandulosum, Skunk Currant

Algonquin, Quebec *Fruit* Fruit used for food. (18:88) **Cree, Woodlands** *Beverage* Stem used to make a bitter tea. *Fruit* Fresh berries eaten in considerable quantity. (109:54)

Ribes hirtellum, Hairystem Gooseberry

Klamath *Dried Food* Dried berries used for food. *Fruit* Fresh berries used for food. (as *R. oxyacanthoides saxosum* 45:97)

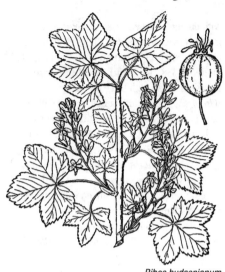

Ribes hudsonianum

Ribes hudsonianum, Northern Black Currant

Cree, Woodlands *Preserves* Berries used to make jam and eaten with fish, meat, or bannock. (109:55) **Ojibwa** *Dried Food* Fruit dried for future use. *Fruit* Fruit eaten fresh. (135:236) **Salish, Coast** *Bread & Cake* Berries boiled, dried into rectangular cakes, and used as a winter food. (182:84) **Shuswap** *Fruit* Berries used for food. (123:63) **Tanana, Upper** *Fruit* Currants mixed with moose grease and dried whitefish eggs and eaten. *Preserves* Currants used to make jam. (102:11) **Thompson** *Forage* Berries eaten by bears. (164:514) *Fruit* Berries eaten, sparingly by some. (164:489) Fresh berries used for food. (187:227)

Ribes hudsonianum var. *petiolare*, Western Black Currant

Montana Indian *Fruit* Fruit highly esteemed as an article of diet. (as *R. petiolare* 19:21)

Ribes inerme, Whitestem Gooseberry

Apache *Fruit* Berries used for food. (32:49) **Keres, Western** *Fruit* Berries used for food. (as *R. inverme* 171:66) **Navajo** *Fruit* Berries eaten during the winter. (90:155) **Pueblo** *Fruit* Berries used for food. (32:49) **Thompson** *Beverage* Berries used to make juice. *Fruit* Berries eaten fresh or cooked. *Pie & Pudding* Berries used to make pies. (187:227)

Ribes lacustre, Prickly Currant
Bella Coola *Fruit* Berries used for food. (184:206) **Cheyenne** *Dried Food* Berries dried for future use. *Fruit* Berries eaten fresh. (76:175) **Gosiute** *Dried Food* Berries dried and stored for winter use. *Fruit* Berries used for food. (39:379) **Haisla & Hanaksiala** *Fruit* Berries used for food. (43:254) **Montana Indian** *Fruit* Fruit highly esteemed as an article of diet. (19:21) **Okanagon** *Staple* Berries used as a principal food. (178:239) **Paiute** *Sauce & Relish* Fruit eaten raw or boiled into a sauce. (111:77) **Salish, Coast** *Bread & Cake* Berries boiled, dried into rectangular cakes, and used as a winter food. (182:84) **Shuswap** *Fruit* Berries used for food. (123:63) **Skagit, Upper** *Fruit* Berries eaten fresh. (179:38) **Thompson** *Dried Food* Berries dried or sometimes buried fresh in the ground for future use. *Frozen Food* Berries stored in the freezer for future use. *Preserves* Berries used to make jam. (187:229)

Ribes laxiflorum, Trailing Black Currant
Bella Coola *Fruit* Berries used for food. (184:206) **Haisla & Hanaksiala** *Fruit* Berries used for food. (43:255) **Hesquiat** *Fruit* Raw or cooked berries eaten with oil or sugar. (185:69) **Kwakiutl, Southern** *Fruit* Fruits eaten for food. (183:286) **Lummi** *Fruit* Berries eaten fresh. (79:32) **Makah** *Fruit* Fruit eaten fresh. (67:260) Berries eaten fresh. (79:32) *Preserves* Fruit used to make jelly. (67:260) **Oweekeno** *Fruit* Berries used for food. (43:105) **Skagit** *Fruit* Berries eaten fresh. (79:32) **Skagit, Upper** *Fruit* Berries eaten fresh. (179:38) **Tanana, Upper** *Fruit* Fruit used for food. (77:28)

Ribes leptanthum, Trumpet Gooseberry
Apache, Chiricahua & Mescalero *Bread & Cake* Fruit made into cakes for use during winter. *Fruit* Raw fruit eaten fresh. (33:44) **Isleta** *Fruit* Berries eaten fresh. **Jemez** *Fruit* Berries eaten fresh. (32:49) Berries eaten fresh. (as *Grossularia leptantha* 44:23) **Spanish Ameri-**can *Beverage* Fruits used to make wine. *Preserves* Fruits used to make jelly. (32:49)

Ribes lobbii, Gummy Gooseberry
Klallam *Fruit* Berries used for food. (78:197) **Kwakiutl, Southern** *Fruit* Green berries occasionally eaten raw. *Special Food* Berries boiled, cooled, and eaten with oulachen (candlefish) oil at feasts. (183:286) **Salish, Coast** *Bread & Cake* Berries boiled, dried into rectangular cakes, and used as a winter food. (182:84) **Tolowa** *Fruit* Fresh fruits used for food. (6:50)

Ribes malvaceum var. *viridifolium*, Chaparral Currant
Cahuilla *Fruit* Berries eaten fresh. (15:133)

Ribes mescalerium, Mescalero Currant
Apache, Chiricahua & Mescalero *Fruit* Raw fruit eaten without preparation. (33:44)

Ribes missouriense, Missouri Gooseberry
Chippewa *Fruit* Berries used for food. (as *R. gracile* 71:131) **Dakota** *Fruit* Berries used for food in season. (as *Grossularia missouriensis* 70:84) **Lakota** *Fruit* Fruits eaten fresh. *Starvation Food* Fruits dried and eaten during famines. (106:35) **Ojibwa** *Dried Food* Fruit dried for future use. *Fruit* Fruit eaten fresh. (as *R. gracile* 135:236) **Omaha** *Dried Food* Fruit dried for winter use. *Fruit* Fruit eaten fresh. (68:326) Berries used for food in season. **Ponca** *Fruit* Berries used for food in season. **Winnebago** *Fruit* Berries used for food in season. (as *Grossularia missouriensis* 70:84)

Ribes montigenum, Gooseberry Currant
Cahuilla *Fruit* Berries eaten fresh. (15:133)

Ribes nevadense, Sierran Currant
Miwok *Fruit* Raw berries used for food. (12:162) **Tolowa** *Spice* Leaves placed between seaweed patties to keep them from sticking and flavors the patties. (6:50)

Ribes oxyacanthoides, Canadian
Gooseberry
Blackfoot *Fruit* Berries eaten fresh. *Soup* Berries added to soups. (86:104) **Cree, Woodlands** *Fruit* Berries eaten fresh. (109:55) **Gosiute** *Dried Food* Berries dried and stored for winter use. *Fruit* Berries used for food. (39:379) **Ojibwa** *Dried Food* Fruit dried for future use. *Fruit* Fruit eaten fresh. (135:236) Berries gathered for fresh food. Berries often cooked with sweet corn. *Preserves* Berries used to make preserves for winter use. (153:410)

Ribes oxyacanthoides* ssp. *irriguum, Idaho Gooseberry
Okanagan-Colville *Bread & Cake* Berries, alone or mixed with other berries, used to make cakes. *Forage* Berries eaten by bears. *Fruit* Berries eaten green. *Winter Use Food* Berries canned for future use. (as *R. irriguum* 188:107) **Sanpoil & Nespelem** *Fruit* Berries eaten fresh. (as *R. irriguum* 131:102) **Thompson** *Beverage* Berries used to make juice. (as *R. irriguum* 187:227) *Fruit* Berries mainly eaten fresh. (as *Grossularia irrigua* 164:489) Berries eaten fresh or cooked. *Pie & Pudding* Berries used to make pies. (as *R. irriguum* 187:227)

Ribes oxyacanthoides* ssp. *setosum, Inland Gooseberry
Cheyenne *Fruit* Fruit eaten raw or cooked. *Winter Use Food* Dried fruit formed into little cakes and used for winter food. (as *Grossularia setosa* 76:175) **Montana Indian** *Fruit* Fruit highly esteemed as an article of diet. (as *R. setosum* 19:21)

Ribes pinetorum, Orange Gooseberry
Apache, Chiricahua & Mescalero *Bread & Cake* Fruit ground and compressed into cakes for winter use. (33:44) **Navajo, Ramah** *Fruit* Berries used for food. (191:30)

Ribes quercetorum, Rock Gooseberry
Kawaiisu *Dried Food* Berries dried in the shade for about a week and stored. *Fruit* Berries eaten fresh. *Preserves* Fresh berries boiled

into a jelly. (206:59) **Tubatulabal** *Fruit* Berries used extensively for food. (193:15)

Ribes roezlii, Sierran Gooseberry
Atsugewi *Fruit* Fresh berries used for food. (61:139) **Karok** *Fruit* Fresh berries used for food. (6:50) **Kawaiisu** *Dried Food* Berries dried in the shade for about a week and stored. *Fruit* Berries eaten fresh. *Preserves* Fresh berries boiled into a jelly. (206:59) **Miwok** *Fruit* Pulverized, raw berries used for food. (12:162) **Yurok** *Fruit* Fresh berries used for food. (6:50)

Ribes rotundifolium, Appalachian
Gooseberry
Cherokee *Winter Use Food* Berries canned for future use. (126:54)

Ribes rubrum, Cultivated Currant
Chippewa *Fruit* Fresh or dried fruit used for food. (71:131)

Ribes rubrum* var. *subglandulosum, Cultivated Currant
Ojibwa *Dried Food* Fruit dried for future use. *Fruit* Fruit eaten fresh. (135:236)

Ribes sanguineum, Redflower Currant
Chehalis *Fruit* Berries eaten by children. (79:32) **Hoh** *Fruit* Fruits eaten raw. Fruits stewed and used for food. *Winter Use Food* Fruits canned and saved for future food use. (137:62) **Klallam** *Fruit* Berries used for food. Fruits eaten fresh. (78:197) **Paiute** *Fruit* Berries used for food. (111:78) **Quileute** *Fruit* Fruits eaten raw. Fruits stewed and used for food. *Winter Use Food* Fruits canned and saved for future food use. (137:62) **Salish, Coast** *Bread & Cake* Berries boiled, dried into rectangular cakes, and used as a winter food. (182:84) **Skagit, Upper** *Fruit* Fruit eaten fresh. (179:38) **Squaxin** *Fruit* Berries eaten by children. (79:32) **Thompson** *Dried Food* Berries sometimes dried and used in soups as flavoring. *Fruit* Berries eaten fresh. *Spice* Berries sometimes dried and used in soups as flavoring. (187:229) **Thompson, Upper (Lytton Band)** *Fruit* Grayish black berries eaten. (164:487)

Ribes sanguineum var. *glutinosum*, Blood Currant
Mahuna *Fruit* Berries eaten mainly to quench the thirst. (as *R. glutinosum* 140:70)

Ribes triste, Red Currant
Alaska Native *Fruit* Berries used raw. *Preserves* Berries made into jams and jellies. (85:87) **Chippewa** *Bread & Cake* Berries cooked, spread on birch bark into little cakes, dried, and stored for winter use. *Fruit* Berries eaten raw. (53:321) **Eskimo, Alaska** *Unspecified* Species used for food. (4:715) **Eskimo, Inupiat** *Dessert* Berries mixed with other berries and used to make traditional dessert. *Fruit* Berries eaten raw or cooked. *Sauce & Relish* Berries mixed with rose hips and high-bush cranberries and boiled into a catsup or syrup. (98:105) **Iroquois** *Bread & Cake* Fruit mashed, made into small cakes, and dried for future use. *Dried Food* Raw or cooked fruit sun or fire dried and stored for future use. *Fruit* Dried fruit taken as a hunting food. *Sauce & Relish* Dried fruit cakes soaked in warm water and cooked as a sauce or mixed with corn bread. (196:128) **Ojibwa** *Dried Food* Berries dried for winter use. *Fruit* In the winter, a favorite dish was wild currants cooked with sweet corn. Berries eaten fresh. *Preserves* Berries used to make jams and preserves. (153:410) **Tanana, Upper** *Fruit* Berries used for food. (102:11)

Ribes velutinum, Desert Gooseberry
Gosiute *Dried Food* Berries dried and stored for winter use. *Fruit* Berries used for food. (as *R. leptanthum* var. *brachyanthum* 39:379)

Ribes velutinum var. *velutinum*, Desert Gooseberry
Kawaiisu *Dried Food* Berries dried in the shade for about a week and stored. *Fruit* Berries eaten fresh. *Preserves* Fresh berries boiled into a jelly. (206:59)

Ribes viscosissimum, Sticky Currant
Montana Indian *Fruit* Fruit highly esteemed as an article of diet. (19:21)

Ribes wolfii, Wolf's Currant
Apache, Chiricahua & Mescalero *Bread & Cake* Fruit ground, dried, and pressed into cakes for storage. *Fruit* Raw fruit eaten without preparation. *Preserves* Fruit used to make jelly. (33:44)

Robinia neomexicana, New Mexico Locust
Apache, Chiricahua & Mescalero *Vegetable* Raw pods eaten as food. *Winter Use Food* Pods cooked and stored. (33:42) **Apache, Mescalero** *Dried Food* Flowers boiled, dried, and stored for winter food use. *Unspecified* Fresh flowers cooked with meat or bones and used for food. (14:47) **Apache, White Mountain** *Vegetable* Beans and pods used for food. (136:160) **Jemez** *Unspecified* Large clusters of flowers eaten without preparation. (32:49) Flowers eaten as food. (44:27)

Robinia pseudoacacia, Black Locust
Cherokee *Beverage* Bark steeped into tea. (126:46) **Mendocino Indian** *Forage* Leaves eaten by horses as forage. **Wailaki** *Forage* Seeds eaten by chickens as forage. (41:359)

Romneya coulteri, Coulter's Matilija Poppy
Cahuilla *Beverage* Watery substance in the stalk used as a beverage. (15:133)

Rorippa curvisiliqua var. *curvisiliqua*, Curvepod Yellowcress
Paiute *Unspecified* Species used for food. (as *Radicula curvisiliqua* 167:242)

Rorippa islandica, Northern Marsh Yellowcress
Eskimo, Inuktitut *Spice* Used as a condiment in fish soup. (202:185)

Rorippa nasturtium-aquaticum, Water Cress
Algonquin, Quebec *Vegetable* Used as a salad plant. (as *Nasturtium officinale* 18:86) **Cahuilla** *Vegetable* Eaten fresh in the spring, cooked like spinach, or mixed with less flavor-

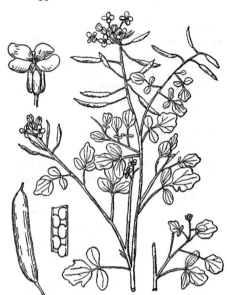

Rorippa nasturtium-aquaticum

ful greens into a salad. (as *Nasturtium officinale* 15:90) **Cherokee** *Vegetable* Leaves eaten
cooked or raw as greens. (as *Nasturtium officinale* 80:61) Leaves boiled and eaten with bacon
grease as potherbs. Leaves used in salads. (as
Nasturtium officinale 126:37) **Diegueño** *Vegetable* Leaves boiled and eaten as greens. (84:37)
Gosiute *Unspecified* Species used for food. (as
Nasturtium palustre 39:375) **Havasupai** *Unspecified* Species used for food. (197:220)
Iroquois *Vegetable* Eaten raw, sometimes with
salt. (as *Radicula nasturtium-aquaticum*
196:118) **Karok** *Unspecified* Young plants
boiled and eaten. (6:51) **Kawaiisu** *Unspecified*
Leaves eaten raw, usually with salt, or boiled
and fried in grease and salt. (206:60) **Luiseño**
Vegetable Plant used for greens. (as *Nasturtium
officinale* 155:232) **Mendocino Indian** *Sauce
& Relish* Leaves eaten as a relish. (as *Roripa
nasturtium* 41:352) **Okanagan-Colville** *Starvation Food* Leaves used as a good emergency
food. *Vegetable* Leaves eaten raw as salad
greens. (188:92) **Saanich** *Unspecified* Young
leaves eaten raw. (182:82) **Tubatulabal** *Vegetable* Leaves and stems boiled as greens. (as
Radicula nasturtium-aquaticum 193:16)

Rorippa teres, Southern Marsh
  Yellowcress
Navajo, Ramah *Fodder* Used for sheep feed.
(as *R. obtusa* 191:29)

Rosa acicularis, Prickly Rose
Alaska Native *Beverage* Rose hips cooked,
juice extracted, pasteurized, and mixed with
other fruit juices. Leaves used to make tea.
Dietary Aid Rose hips used as one of the richest
known food sources of vitamin C. *Preserves*
Rose hip juice used to make jellies. Rose hip
pulp, with seeds and skins removed, used to
make jams and marmalades. *Sauce & Relish*
Rose hip juice used to make syrups. Rose hip
pulp, with seeds and skins removed, used to
make ketchups. (85:89) **Cree, Woodlands**
Snack Food Ripe hips eaten as a nibble. (109:55)
Eskimo, Inupiat *Beverage* Used to make juice.
Frozen Food Frozen and stored for future use.
Ice Cream Used with oil and water to make ice
cream. *Preserves* Used to make jam or jelly.
Sauce & Relish Used to make syrup. *Unspecified*
Eaten fresh or cooked. (98:101) **Koyukon**
Fruit Berries used for food. (119:55) **Montana
Indian** *Fruit* Fruit and hips used for food.
(19:21) **Okanagan-Colville** *Forage* Hips eaten
by coyotes. *Spice* Leaves placed under and over
food while pit cooking to add flavor and prevent
burning. *Unspecified* Orange, outer rind of the
hips used for food. (188:131) **Tanana, Upper**
Beverage Leaves boiled into tea. (102:12) *Fruit*
Rose hips used for food. (as *R. acidularis*
77:28) Rose hips eaten raw or cooked with
grease and sugar. *Preserves* Rose hips used to
make jelly. *Unspecified* Raw petals used for
food. *Winter Use Food* Leaves dried and saved
for later use. (102:12) **Thompson** *Beverage*
Shoots or hips or leaves and young twigs used to
make a tea-like beverage. *Forage* Hips eaten by
bears before hibernation. *Preserves* Hips used
to make jelly. *Sauce & Relish* Hips used to make
syrup. *Unspecified* Hips used only sparingly for
food because of the seeds and the insipid taste.
Young, tender shoots peeled and eaten in the
spring. (187:267)

Rosa acicularis ssp. *sayi*, Prickly Rose

Blackfoot *Fruit* Berries eaten raw. (as *R. sayi* 114:275) **Montana Indian** *Fruit* Fruit used for food. (as *R. sayi* 19:21) **Ojibwa** *Unspecified* Buds used for food. (as *R. sayi* 135:236)

Rosa arkansana, Prairie Rose

Lakota *Beverage* Petals used to make tea. Roots used to make a strong tea. *Dried Food* Hips dried and used for food. *Preserves* Petals used to make jam. *Soup* Hips dried, added to soups or stews, and used for food. *Starvation Food* Hips eaten during famines. (106:39)

Rosa arkansana var. *suffulta*, Prairie Rose

Dakota *Starvation Food* Fruit sometimes eaten in times of food scarcity. **Omaha** *Starvation Food* Fruit sometimes eaten in times of food scarcity. **Pawnee** *Starvation Food* Fruit sometimes eaten in times of food scarcity. **Ponca** *Starvation Food* Fruit sometimes eaten in times of food scarcity. (as *R. pratincola* 70:85)

Rosa californica, California Wild Rose

Cahuilla *Beverage* Blossoms soaked in water to make a beverage. *Unspecified* Buds eaten fresh. (15:133) **Gosiute** *Fruit* Berries used for food. (39:379) **Kawaiisu** *Fruit* Fruit, a "fleshy hip," eaten ripe. (206:60) **Pomo, Kashaya** *Fruit* Fresh fruit used for food. (72:99)

Rosa gymnocarpa, Dwarf Rose

Okanagan-Colville *Forage* Hips eaten by coyotes. *Spice* Leaves placed under and over food while pit cooking to add flavor and prevent burning. *Unspecified* Orange, outer rind of the hips used for food. (188:131) **Pomo, Kashaya** *Fruit* Fresh fruit used for food. (72:99) **Thompson** *Beverage* Young leaves and stalks boiled and drunk as a tea. (164:493) Shoots used to make a tea-like beverage. (187:267) *Fruit* Small fruits occasionally eaten. (164:488) Fruits eaten, but not in large quantities. (164:489)

Rosa nutkana, Nootka Rose

Bella Coola *Fruit* Fruits used for food in late fall. (184:209) **Blackfoot** *Fruit* Raw berries used for food. *Preserves* Berries used to make jelly. (118:22) **Carrier** *Preserves* Berries used to make jam. (31:86) **Cowichan** *Fruit* Hips eaten raw in fall. (182:87) **Hesquiat** *Forage* Eaten by deer. *Fruit* Outside of the fruit, or hip, eaten with oil. (185:74) **Lummi** *Beverage* Twigs peeled, boiled, and used as a beverage. *Dried Food* Hips dried and used for food. (79:34) **Montana Indian** *Fruit* Fruit and hips used for food. (19:21) **Nitinaht** *Fruit* Hips eaten raw in fall. (186:123) **Okanagan-Colville** *Forage* Hips eaten by coyotes. *Spice* Leaves placed under and over food while pit cooking to add flavor and prevent burning. *Unspecified* Orange, outer rind of the hips used for food. (188:131) **Quinault** *Unspecified* Hips used for food. (79:34) **Rocky Boy** *Fruit* Raw berries used for food. *Preserves* Berries used to make jelly. (118:22) **Saanich** *Fruit* Hips eaten raw in fall. (182:87) **Salish** *Unspecified* Hips used for food. (183:290) **Salish, Coast** *Unspecified* Young shoots used for food. (182:87) **Shuswap** *Beverage* Stems and flowers used to make tea. (123:67) **Skagit** *Beverage* Leaves used to make tea. *Unspecified* Hips mixed with dried salmon eggs and used for food. (79:34) **Skagit, Upper** *Beverage* Leaves used to make tea. *Spice* Hips mixed with dried salmon eggs to enhance the flavor. (179:42) **Skokomish** *Unspecified* Hips eaten in the fall. **Snohomish** *Unspecified* Hips used for food. **Swinomish** *Unspecified* Hips used for food. (79:34) **Thompson** *Beverage* Shoots used to make a tea-like beverage. Leaves and young twigs used to make a tea-like beverage. *Unspecified* Young, tender shoots peeled and eaten in the spring. (187:267) **Washo** *Fruit* Raw berries used for food. (118:22)

Rosa nutkana var. *hispida*, Bristly Nootka Rose

Blackfoot *Fruit* Raw berries used for food. *Preserves* Berries used to make jelly. **Rocky Boy** *Fruit* Raw berries used for food. *Preserves* Berries used to make jelly. **Washo** *Fruit* Raw berries used for food. (as *R. spaldingii* 118:22)

Rosa nutkana* var. *nutkana, Nootka
  Rose
Haisla & Hanaksiala *Beverage* Leaves dried
and mixed with American red raspberry leaves
to make tea. *Unspecified* Hips mixed with oolichan (candlefish) grease and sugar and eaten.
(43:273) **Makah** *Beverage* Leaves used to make
tea. *Unspecified* Hips used for food. **Nitinaht**
Unspecified Hips and petals used for food.
(67:270)

Rosa pisocarpa, Cluster Rose
Hoh *Fruit* Fruits eaten fresh. *Winter Use Food*
Fruits eaten in winter. (137:63) **Paiute** *Unspecified* Haws pounded with deer tallow and eaten.
(104:103) Species used for food. (167:244)
Quileute *Fruit* Fruits eaten fresh. *Winter Use
Food* Fruits eaten in winter. (137:63) **Squaxin**
Unspecified Hips eaten fresh. (79:34) **Thompson** *Beverage* Shoots used to make a tea-like
beverage. Leaves and young twigs used to make
a tea-like beverage. *Unspecified* Young, tender
shoots peeled and eaten in the spring. (187:267)

Rosa virginiana, Virginia Rose
Ojibwa *Unspecified* Buds used for food. (as *R.
lucida* 135:236)

Rosa woodsii, Woods's Rose
Arapaho *Beverage* Bark used to make tea.

Rosa woodsii

(121:48) **Lakota** *Fruit* Rose hips used for food.
(139:57) **Montana Indian** *Fruit* Fruit used for
food. (19:21) **Okanagan-Colville** *Forage* Hips
eaten by coyotes. *Spice* Leaves placed under and
over food while pit cooking to add flavor and
prevent burning. *Unspecified* Orange, outer
rind of the hips used for food. (188:131)
Thompson *Beverage* Shoots or hips or leaves
and young twigs used to make a tea-like beverage. *Forage* Hips eaten by bears before hibernation. *Preserves* Hips used to make jelly. *Sauce &
Relish* Hips used to make syrup. *Unspecified*
Hips eaten only sparingly because of the seeds
and the insipid taste. Young, tender shoots
peeled and eaten in the spring. (187:267)

Rosa woodsii* var. *ultramontana,
  Woods's Rose
Hopi *Fruit* Fruits occasionally eaten by children. (as *R. arizonica* 200:78) **Kawaiisu** *Fruit*
Fruit, a "fleshy hip," eaten ripe. (206:60) **Sanpoil & Nespelem** *Starvation Food* Pips eaten
in times of famine. (as *R. californica* var. *ultramontana* 131:108)

Rosa woodsii* var. *woodsii, Woods's
  Rose
Apache, Chiricahua & Mescalero *Fruit* Rose
hips eaten fresh. *Preserves* Rose pulps squeezed
into water and boiled to make jelly. (as *R.
fendleri* 33:46) **Cheyenne** *Fruit* Berries not
to be eaten too freely. (as *R. fendleri* 76:177)
Gosiute *Fruit* Berries used for food. (as *R.
fendleri* 39:379) **Klamath** *Fruit* Fruit used for
food. (as *R. fendleri* 45:99) **Navajo** *Fruit* Fruits
eaten for food. (as *R. fendleri* 55:55) **Navajo,
Ramah** *Fruit* Fruit eaten raw. Fruit eaten raw.
(as *R. neomexicana* 191:31) **Ute** *Fruit* Berries
used for food. (as *R. fendleri* 38:36)

Rubus aculeatissimus, Red Raspberry
Iroquois *Unspecified* Fresh shoots peeled and
eaten. (196:119)

Rubus allegheniensis, Allegheny
  Blackberry
Cherokee *Beverage* Fruit used to make juice.
Fruit Fruit used for food. (80:26) **Chippewa**

Dried Food Fruit dried for winter use. *Fruit* Fruit eaten fresh. (71:133) **Menominee** *Fruit* Berries eaten fresh. *Pie & Pudding* Berries made into pies. *Winter Use Food* Berries dried for winter use. (151:71) **Meskwaki** *Fruit* Berries eaten fresh. *Pie & Pudding* Berries made into pies. *Preserves* Berries made into jams. *Winter Use Food* Berries sun dried for winter use. (152:264) **Ojibwa** *Preserves* Berries used to make jam for winter use. (153:409) **Potawatomi** *Fruit* Blackberries only used for food. (154:108)

Rubus arcticus, Arctic Blackberry

Alaska Native *Preserves* Fruit used to make a superior jelly. (85:91) **Eskimo, Alaska** *Fruit* Berries sometimes used for food, but not considered a significant food source. (1:36) **Eskimo, Inuktitut** *Winter Use Food* Berries added to stored salmonberries. (202:189) **Eskimo, Inupiat** *Dessert* Berries used to make traditional dessert. *Fruit* Berries eaten fresh. *Winter Use Food* Berries mixed with salmonberries and stored in a barrel for future use. (98:103) **Koyukon** *Fruit* Berries used for food. (119:55) **Tanana, Upper** *Frozen Food* Berries frozen for future use. *Fruit* Berries eaten raw, plain, or mixed raw with sugar, grease, or the combination of the two. Berries fried in grease with sugar or dried fish eggs. Berries boiled with sugar and flour to thicken. *Pie & Pudding* Berries used to make pies. *Preserves* Berries used to make jam and jelly. *Winter Use Food* Berries preserved alone or in grease and stored in a birch bark basket in an underground cache. (102:12)

Rubus arcticus ssp. acaulis, Dwarf Raspberry

Cree, Woodlands *Fruit* Fruit eaten fresh. (109:56)

Rubus argutus, Sawtooth Blackberry

Cherokee *Beverage* Fruit used to make juice. *Fruit* Fruit used for food. (80:26)

Rubus arizonensis, Arizona Dewberry

Apache, Chiricahua & Mescalero *Bread & Cake* Fruit pressed into pulpy cakes, dried, and stored. *Fruit* Fruits eaten fresh. *Winter Use Food* Fruit pressed into pulpy cakes, dried, and stored for winter use. (33:44) **Navajo** *Fruit* Fruits eaten for food. (as *R. arizonicus* 55:55)

Rubus canadensis, Smooth Blackberry

Chippewa *Fruit* Fruit used for food. (71:133) **Iroquois** *Beverage* Berries, water, and maple sugar used to make a drink for home consumption and longhouse ceremonies. *Bread & Cake* Fruit mashed, made into small cakes, and dried for future use. *Dried Food* Raw or cooked fruit sun or fire dried and stored for future use. *Fruit* Dried fruit taken as a hunting food. *Sauce & Relish* Dried fruit cakes soaked in warm water and cooked as a sauce or mixed with corn bread. (196:127) **Ojibwa** *Fruit* Berries used fresh. *Winter Use Food* Berries used preserved. (5:2223)

Rubus chamaemorus, Cloudberry

Alaska Native *Dietary Aid* Berries used as a very rich source of vitamin C. *Frozen Food* Fruit stored in seal pokes, kegs, or barrels and buried in the frozen tundra for future use. *Fruit* Berries eaten raw with sugar, seal oil, or both. *Pie & Pudding* Berries used to make berry

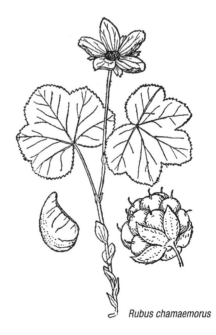

Rubus chamaemorus

shortcakes and pies. *Winter Use Food* Fruit stored in large quantities for winter use. (85:93) **Anticosti** *Preserves* Fruits used to make jelly. *Winter Use Food* Fruits stored for winter use. (143:67) **Cree, Woodlands** *Fruit* Fruit eaten fresh. (109:56) **Eskimo** *Fruit* Fruits eaten for food. (181:233) **Eskimo, Alaska** *Winter Use Food* Berries stored with seal oil in barrels or sealskin pokes for winter use. (1:36) **Eskimo, Arctic** *Ice Cream* Berries mixed with seal oil and chewed caribou tallow, beaten, and eaten as "Eskimo ice cream." (128:21) **Eskimo, Inuktitut** *Frozen Food* Berries frozen for future use. *Fruit* Berries eaten fresh or mixed with oil or fat. (202:183) **Eskimo, Inupiat** *Dessert* Berries mixed with sugar and seal oil and eaten as a dessert. *Frozen Food* Berries mixed with blueberries and frozen for future use. *Fruit* Berries eaten fresh. Berries mixed with blueberries and eaten fresh. *Ice Cream* Berries added to fluffy fat and eaten as ice cream. *Winter Use Food* Berries mixed with blackberries, preserved in a poke or barrel, and stored for winter use. (98:73) **Koyukon** *Fruit* Berries used for food. (119:55) **Tanana, Upper** *Frozen Food* Berries frozen for future use. *Fruit* Berries eaten raw, plain, or mixed raw with sugar, grease, or the combination of the two. Berries fried in grease with sugar or dried fish eggs. Berries boiled with sugar and flour to thicken. *Pie & Pudding* Berries used to make pies. *Preserves* Berries used to make jam and jelly. *Winter Use Food* Berries preserved alone or in grease and stored in a birch bark basket in an underground cache. (102:12)

Rubus discolor, Himalayan Blackberry
Haisla & Hanaksiala *Fruit* Fruit used for food. (43:278) **Kitasoo** *Fruit* Fruit used for food. (43:348) **Makah** *Fruit* Fruit used for food. (67:272)

Rubus flagellaris, Northern Dewberry
Cherokee *Beverage* Fruit used to make juice. *Fruit* Fruit used for food. (80:26)

Rubus frondosus, Yankee Blackberry
Chippewa *Bread & Cake* Berries cooked,

spread on birch bark into little cakes, dried, and stored for winter use. *Fruit* Berries eaten raw. (53:321)

Rubus idaeus, American Red Raspberry
Abnaki *Fruit* Fruits eaten for food. (144:169) **Alaska Native** *Fruit* Berries eaten raw. *Preserves* Berries made into jams and jellies. (85:93) **Algonquin, Quebec** *Fruit* Fruit eaten fresh. *Preserves* Fruit preserved. (18:92) **Algonquin, Tête-de-Boule** *Fruit* Fruits eaten for food. (132:130) **Bella Coola** *Fruit* Berries eaten fresh. *Preserves* Berries cooked into jam. (184:209) **Cherokee** *Fruit* Fruit used for food. (80:52) **Cree, Woodlands** *Fruit* Fruit eaten with dried fish flesh and fish oil. *Unspecified* Young, leafy shoots peeled and the tender inner part eaten. (109:57) **Eskimo, Inupiat** *Dessert* Berries used to make traditional dessert. (98:107) **Koyukon** *Fruit* Berries used for food. (119:55) **Okanagan-Colville** *Dried Food* Berries dried for future use. *Frozen Food* Berries frozen for future use. *Fruit* Berries eaten fresh. *Winter Use Food* Berries canned for future use. (188:131) **Tanana, Upper** *Frozen Food* Berries frozen for future use. (102:12) *Fruit* Berries used for food. (77:28) Berries eaten raw, plain, or mixed raw with sugar, grease, or the combination of the two. Berries fried in grease with sugar or dried fish eggs. Berries boiled with sugar and flour to thicken. *Pie & Pudding* Berries used to make pies. *Preserves* Berries used to make jam and jelly. *Winter Use Food* Berries preserved alone or in grease and stored in a birch bark basket in an underground cache. (102:12) **Thompson** *Bread & Cake* Fruit steamed, dried, and made into a cake. *Dried Food* Fruit sun dried loose on mats. *Frozen Food* Fruit frozen or made into a jam. *Fruit* Fruit eaten fresh. *Preserves* Fruit frozen or made into jam. (187:269)

Rubus idaeus ssp. *strigosus*,
Grayleaf Red Raspberry
Cheyenne *Fruit* Berries always eaten fresh. (as *R. melanolasius* 76:177) **Chippewa** *Beverage* Twigs used to make a beverage. (as *R. strigosus* 53:317) *Bread & Cake* Berries cooked, spread

on birch bark into little cakes, dried, and stored for winter use. (as *R. strigosus* 53:321) *Dried Food* Fruit dried for winter use. (as *R. strigosus* 71:132) *Fruit* Berries eaten raw. (as *R. strigosus* 53:321) Fruit eaten fresh. (as *R. strigosus* 71:132) **Dakota** *Beverage* Young leaves steeped to make a tea-like beverage. *Dried Food* Fruit dried for winter use. *Fruit* Fruit eaten fresh. (as *R. strigosus* 70:84) **Haisla & Hanaksiala** *Beverage* Leaves mixed with young Nootka rose leaves to make tea. *Fruit* Fruit used for food. (43:274) **Hoh** *Fruit* Fruits eaten raw. Fruits stewed and used for food. *Winter Use Food* Fruits canned and saved for future food use. (as *R. strigosus* 137:63) **Iroquois** *Bread & Cake* Fruit mashed, made into small cakes, and dried for future use. *Dried Food* Raw or cooked fruit sun or fire dried and stored for future use. *Fruit* Dried fruit taken as a hunting food. *Sauce & Relish* Dried fruit cakes soaked in warm water and cooked as a sauce or mixed with corn bread. (196:127) **Kitasoo** *Fruit* Fruit used for food. (43:345) **Menominee** *Fruit* Berries eaten fresh. (as *R. idaeus aculeatissimus* 151:71) **Montana Indian** *Fruit* Fruit was highly esteemed. (as *R. strigosus* 19:22) **Ojibwa** *Dried Food* Berries used dried. (5:2223) Fruit dried for winter use. (as *R. strigosus* 135:235) *Fruit* Berries used fresh. (5:2223) Fruit eaten fresh. (as *R. strigosus* 135:235) This was a favorite fresh fruit. *Preserves* Berries used to make jam for winter use. (153:410) **Omaha** *Beverage* Young leaves steeped to make a tea-like beverage. *Dried Food* Fruit dried for winter use. *Fruit* Fruit eaten fresh. (as *R. strigosus* 70:84) **Oweekeno** *Fruit* Fruit used for food. (43:111) **Pawnee** *Beverage* Young leaves steeped to make a tea-like beverage. *Dried Food* Fruit dried for winter use. *Fruit* Fruit eaten fresh. **Ponca** *Beverage* Young leaves steeped to make a tea-like beverage. *Dried Food* Fruit dried for winter use. *Fruit* Fruit eaten fresh. (as *R. strigosus* 70:84) **Potawatomi** *Fruit* Berries, a favorite article of food, eaten fresh. *Preserves* Berries, a favorite article of food, made into jams and jellies. (154:109) **Quileute** *Fruit* Fruits eaten raw. Fruits stewed and used for food. *Winter Use Food* Fruits canned and saved for future

food use. (as *R. strigosus* 137:63) **Shuswap** *Fruit* Berries used for food. (123:67)

Rubus laciniatus, Cutleaf Blackberry

Hoh *Fruit* Fruits stewed and used for food. Fruits eaten raw. *Winter Use Food* Fruits canned and saved for future food use. (137:63) **Makah** *Fruit* Fresh fruit used for food. *Pie & Pudding* Fruit used to make pies. *Preserves* Fruit used to make jam. (67:272) **Quileute** *Fruit* Fruits stewed and used for food. Fruits eaten raw. *Winter Use Food* Fruits canned and saved for future food use. (137:63)

Rubus lasiococcus, Roughfruit Berry

Hoh *Fruit* Fruits eaten raw. Fruits stewed and used for food. *Winter Use Food* Fruits canned and saved for future food use. **Quileute** *Fruit* Fruits eaten raw. Fruits stewed and used for food. *Winter Use Food* Fruits canned and saved for future food use. (137:62)

Rubus leucodermis, Whitebark Raspberry

Bella Coola *Bread & Cake* Berries formerly dried in cakes and used for food. *Fruit* Berries eaten fresh. *Preserves* Berries cooked into jam. (184:209) **Cahuilla** *Beverage* Berries soaked in water to make a beverage. *Dried Food* Berries dried for later use. *Fruit* Berries eaten fresh. (15:134) **Coeur d'Alene** *Fruit* Berries eaten fresh. Berries mashed and eaten. (178:90) **Costanoan** *Fruit* Raw fruits used for food. (21:250) **Cowlitz** *Dried Food* Berries sun or fire dried and stored for winter use. *Fruit* Berries eaten fresh. (79:35) **Gosiute** *Fruit* Berries used for food. (39:380) **Green River Group** *Fruit* Berries eaten fresh. (79:35) **Hesquiat** *Fruit* Berries eaten with oil. (185:74) **Hoh** *Fruit* Fruits eaten raw. Fruits stewed and used for food. *Winter Use Food* Fruits canned and saved for future food use. (137:63) **Karok** *Fruit* Fruit eaten fresh. (6:51) Berries used for food. (148:384) **Klallam** *Dried Food* Berries dried and used for food. *Fruit* Fruits eaten fresh. (78:197) Berries eaten fresh. (79:35) *Unspecified* Leaves and sprouts used for food. (78:197) Sprouts and young leaves eaten. (79:35) **Klam-**

ath *Dried Food* Berries dried for later use. *Fruit* Berries used for food. (45:99) **Makah** *Fruit* Fruit eaten fresh. *Pie & Pudding* Fruit used to make pies. *Preserves* Fruit used to make jam. (67:273) **Mendocino Indian** *Dried Food* Fruits dried or canned for winter use. *Fruit* Fruits eaten fresh. *Winter Use Food* Fruits dried or canned for winter use. (41:355) **Montana Indian** *Fruit* Fruit was highly esteemed. (19:22) **Nisqually** *Fruit* Berries eaten fresh. (79:35) **Nitinaht** *Fruit* Fruits eaten fresh and raw. (186:123) **Okanagan-Colville** *Dessert* Dried berries soaked in water or boiled and eaten as a dessert. *Dried Food* Berries dried and stored for winter use. *Fruit* Dried berries eaten with dried meat or fish. (188:132) **Okanagon** *Staple* Berries used as a principal food. (178:238) *Unspecified* Used commonly for food. (125:38) **Pomo** *Fruit* Raw berries used for food. *Winter Use Food* Berries cooked, bottled, and stored for later use. (66:13) **Pomo, Kashaya** *Fruit* Berries eaten fresh. *Winter Use Food* Berries canned. (72:96) **Puyallup** *Fruit* Berries eaten fresh. (79:35) **Quileute** *Fruit* Fruits eaten raw. Fruits stewed and used for food. *Winter Use Food* Fruits canned and saved for future food use. (137:63) **Salish, Coast** *Bread & Cake* Berries mashed, dried in rectangular frames, and cakes used as a winter food. *Fruit* Berries eaten fresh. (182:87) **Shuswap** *Fruit* Berries used for food. (123:67) **Skagit, Upper** *Dried Food* Berries pulped and dried for winter use. *Fruit* Berries eaten fresh. (179:38) **Spokan** *Fruit* Berries used for food. (178:343) **Thompson** *Dried Food* Fruit dried for winter use. (187:269) *Fruit* Reddish purple berries eaten. (164:487) Fruit used for food. (187:269) *Unspecified* Used commonly for food. (125:38) Young shoots peeled, cooked over a fire, and eaten alone or with fish. (187:269) **Yuki** *Dried Food* Berries dried and cooked as a winter food. *Fruit* Berries eaten fresh. (49:87) **Yurok** *Fruit* Fruit eaten fresh. (6:51)

Rubus leucodermis var. *leuco-dermis*, Whitebark Raspberry
Haisla & Hanaksiala *Fruit* Fruit used for food. (43:275) **Kitasoo** *Fruit* Fruit used for

food. (43:348) **Oweekeno** *Fruit* Fruit used for food. (43:112)

Rubus nivalis, Snow Raspberry
Hoh *Fruit* Fruits eaten raw. Fruits stewed and used for food. *Winter Use Food* Fruits canned and saved for future food use. **Quileute** *Fruit* Fruits eaten raw. Fruits stewed and used for food. *Winter Use Food* Fruits canned and saved for future food use. (137:63)

Rubus occidentalis, Black Raspberry
Cherokee *Fruit* Fruit used for food. (80:52) Fresh fruit used for food. *Pie & Pudding* Fruit used to make pies. *Preserves* Fruit used to make jelly. *Winter Use Food* Fruit canned for future use. (126:57) **Chippewa** *Dried Food* Fruit dried for winter use. *Fruit* Fruit eaten fresh. (71:133) **Dakota** *Beverage* Young leaves steeped to make a tea-like beverage. *Dried Food* Fruit dried for winter use. *Fruit* Fruit eaten fresh. (70:84) **Iroquois** *Bread & Cake* Fruits dried, soaked in water, and used in bread. (124:95) Fruit mashed, made into small cakes, and dried for future use. *Dried Food* Raw or cooked fruit sun or fire dried and stored for future use. *Fruit* Dried fruit taken as a hunting food. (196:127) *Pie & Pudding* Fruits dried, soaked in water, and used

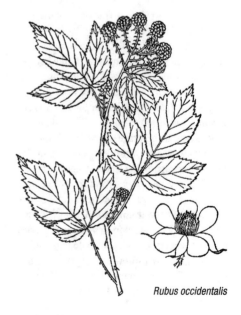

Rubus occidentalis

in pudding. *Porridge* Berries dried, soaked in cold water, heated slowly, and mixed with bread meal or hominy in winter. *Sauce & Relish* Fruits dried, soaked in water, and used as a sauce. Berries dried, soaked in cold water, heated slowly, and used as a winter sauce. (124:95) Dried fruit cakes soaked in warm water and cooked as a sauce or mixed with corn bread. (196:127) *Soup* Fruits dried, soaked in water, and used in soups. (124:95) **Lakota** *Fruit* Fruits eaten for food. (139:57) **Menominee** *Fruit* Berries eaten fresh, not important as a fresh fruit. (151:71) **Meskwaki** *Beverage* Root bark used to make tea. *Fruit* Berries eaten fresh. *Winter Use Food* Berries sun dried for winter use. (152:264) **Ojibwa** *Fruit* Berries used fresh. *Winter Use Food* Berries used preserved. (5:2224) **Omaha** *Beverage* Leaves used to make a hot, aqueous, tea-like beverage. (68:329) Young leaves steeped to make a tea-like beverage. (70:84) *Dried Food* Fruit dried for winter use. *Fruit* Fruit eaten fresh. (68:326) **Pawnee** *Beverage* Young leaves steeped to make a tea-like beverage. *Dried Food* Fruit dried for winter use. *Fruit* Fruit eaten fresh. **Ponca** *Beverage* Young leaves steeped to make a tea-like beverage. *Dried Food* Fruit dried for winter use. *Fruit* Fruit eaten fresh. (70:84) **Thompson** *Unspecified* Sprouts or young shoots eaten like rhubarb. (164:484)

Rubus odoratus, Purpleflowering Raspberry

Algonquin, Quebec *Fruit* Fruit used for food. (18:92) **Cherokee** *Fruit* Fruit used for food. (80:52) Fresh fruit used for food. *Pie & Pudding* Fruit used to make pies. *Preserves* Fruit used to make jelly. *Winter Use Food* Fruit canned for future use. (126:57) **Chippewa** *Dried Food* Fruit dried for winter use. *Fruit* Fruit eaten fresh. (71:133) **Iroquois** *Bread & Cake* Fruit mashed, made into small cakes, and dried for future use. *Dried Food* Raw or cooked fruit sun or fire dried and stored for future use. *Fruit* Dried fruit taken as a hunting food. *Sauce & Relish* Dried fruit cakes soaked in warm water and cooked as a sauce or mixed with corn bread. (196:127)

Rubus parviflorus, Thimbleberry

Alaska Native *Fruit* Berries used for food. (85:97) **Bella Coola** *Preserves* Berries cooked with wild raspberries and other fruits into a thick jam, dried, and used for food. *Unspecified* Young sprouts peeled and eaten in spring. (184:209) **Blackfoot** *Fruit* Ripe fruit used for food. (86:105) **Cahuilla** *Beverage* Berries soaked in water to make a beverage. *Dried Food* Berries dried for later use. *Fruit* Berries eaten fresh. (15:134) **Chehalis** *Fruit* Berries eaten fresh. (79:34) **Clallam** *Fruit* Berries eaten fresh. (57:203) **Cowlitz** *Fruit* Berries eaten fresh. (79:34) **Gosiute** *Fruit* Berries used for food. (as *R. nutkanus* 39:380) **Hesquiat** *Dried Food* Berries dried for future use. *Fruit* Berries eaten fresh. *Preserves* Berries made into jam. *Spice* Fish boiled with leaves as flavoring and kept the fish from sticking to the pot. (185:74) **Hoh** *Fruit* Fruits eaten raw. Fruits stewed and used for food. *Winter Use Food* Fruits canned and saved for future food use. (137:63) **Isleta** *Fruit* Berries grown in the mountains, considered a strawberry and used for food. (as *Bossekia parvifolia* 100:25) *Special Food* Fruits eaten as a delicacy. (as *Bossekia parviflora* 32:19) **Karok** *Fruit* Berries used for food. (148:384) **Klallam** *Dried Food* Berries dried and used for food. *Unspecified* Sprouts used for food. (78:197) Sprouts eaten in early spring. (79:34) **Kwakiutl, Southern** *Dried Food* Berries dried in cakes and used as a winter food. *Fruit* Berries eaten fresh. (183:291) **Luiseño** *Fruit* Fruit used for food. (155:232) **Makah** *Fruit* Fruit eaten fresh. *Preservative* Fruit used to make jam and jelly. *Unspecified* Raw sprouts used for food. (67:273) Sprouts eaten in early spring. (79:34) **Montana Indian** *Unspecified* Young sprouts eaten raw or tied into bundles and steamed. (as *R. nutkanus* 19:21) **Nitinaht** *Fruit* Berries eaten raw. *Unspecified* Young, tender sprouts peeled and eaten raw in spring. (186:124) **Okanagan-Colville** *Fruit* Berries eaten fresh. (188:132) **Paiute** *Fruit* Berries eaten ripe and fresh. (111:83) **Pomo** *Fruit* Raw berries used for food. (66:13) **Pomo, Kashaya** *Fruit* Berries eaten fresh. (72:113) **Quileute** *Fruit* Berries eaten fresh. (79:34) Fruits eaten raw. Fruits stewed and used for food. *Winter Use Food* Fruits canned and saved for future food use. (137:63) **Quinault** *Fruit* Berries eaten fresh. (79:34) **Salish, Coast** *Bread & Cake* Berries dried into cakes and used for food. *Fruit* Berries eaten fresh or boiled. *Unspecified* Young, tender shoots eaten in spring. (182:87) **Samish** *Fruit* Berries eaten fresh. *Unspecified* Sprouts eaten in early spring with half-dried salmon eggs. (79:34) **Sanpoil & Nespelem** *Fruit* Berries eaten fresh. (131:102) **Shuswap** *Fruit* Berries used for food. (123:67) **Skagit** *Fruit* Berries eaten fresh. *Unspecified* Sprouts eaten in early spring. (79:34) **Skagit, Upper** *Fruit* Berries eaten fresh. *Unspecified* Tender shoots peeled and eaten in spring and early summer. (179:38) **Snohomish** *Fruit* Berries eaten fresh. **Squaxin** *Dried Food* Berries dried, stored in soft or hard baskets, and used for food. *Fruit* Berries mixed with blackberries and eaten fresh. **Swinomish** *Fruit* Berries eaten fresh. *Unspecified* Sprouts eaten in early spring with half-dried salmon eggs. (79:34) **Thompson** *Fruit* Berries eaten fresh, often with fish. *Sweetener* Roots used for sugar. *Unspecified* Toasted shoots eaten alone or with meat and fish. (187:270) **Tsimshian** *Fruit* Berries used for food. (43:346) **Wintoon** *Fruit* Berries used for food. (117:264) **Yurok** *Fruit* Fruit eaten fresh. (6:51)

Rubus parviflorus ssp. *parviflorus*, Thimbleberry

Haisla *Bread & Cake* Berries used to make dried berry cakes for winter use. (43:276) **Oweekeno** *Beverage* Fall, brown leaves used to make tea. *Fruit* Fruit eaten fresh. *Preserves* Fruit used to make jelly. *Unspecified* Sprouts used for food. (43:112)

Rubus parviflorus var. *velutinus*, Western Thimbleberry

Mendocino Indian *Fruit* Berries eaten fresh. (41:354)

Rubus pedatus, Strawberryleaf Raspberry

Alaska Native *Preserves* Fruit used to make an excellent jelly. (85:99) **Haisla & Hanaksiala**

Forage Berries eaten by porcupines and groundhogs. *Fruit* Berries eaten in small quantities. (43:278) **Kitasoo** *Fruit* Berries eaten fresh. (43:346) **Thompson** *Fruit* Small fruits rarely eaten. (187:272)

Rubus procumbens, Wild Blackberry

Mahuna *Fruit* Berries eaten mainly to quench the thirst. (as *R. villosus* 140:70)

Rubus pubescens, Dwarf Red Blackberry

Cree, Woodlands *Fruit* Fruit eaten fresh. (109:57) **Iroquois** *Fruit* Fruit used for food. (142:92)

Rubus pubescens var. *pubescens*, Dwarf Red Blackberry

Chippewa *Fruit* Delicate, delicious fruit used for food. (as *R. triflorus* 71:133) **Iroquois** *Bread & Cake* Fruit mashed, made into small cakes, and dried for future use. *Dried Food* Raw or cooked fruit sun or fire dried and stored for future use. *Fruit* Dried fruit taken as a hunting food. *Sauce & Relish* Dried fruit cakes soaked in warm water and cooked as a sauce or mixed with corn bread. (as *R. triflorus* 196:127)

Rubus spectabilis, Salmon Berry

Alaska Native *Fruit* Fruit eaten raw. *Preserves* Fruit made into jams and jellies. (85:101) **Bella Coola** *Bread & Cake* Berries cooked, dried in cakes, and used for food. *Fruit* Berries eaten raw. *Unspecified* Sprouts peeled and eaten in spring. (184:209) **Carrier** *Fruit* Berries used for food. (31:77) **Chehalis** *Fruit* Berries eaten fresh. *Unspecified* Sprouts cooked in a pit and eaten with dried salmon. **Chinook, Lower** *Fruit* Berries eaten fresh. *Unspecified* Sprouts cooked in a pit and eaten with dried salmon. (79:35) **Clallam** *Fruit* Berries eaten fresh. (57:203) **Cowlitz** *Fruit* Berries eaten fresh. *Unspecified* Sprouts cooked in a pit and eaten with dried salmon. **Green River Group** *Fruit* Berries eaten fresh. *Unspecified* Sprouts cooked in a pit and eaten with dried salmon. (79:35) **Haisla & Hanaksiala** *Beverage* Berries used to make homemade wine. *Dried Food* Berries dried for winter use. *Fruit* Berries eaten fresh. *Special Food* Young sprouts peeled and served as a featured item at salmonberry sprout feasts. (43:279) **Hesquiat** *Unspecified* Young, fresh shoots eaten with oil. (185:74) **Hoh** *Fruit* Fruits stewed and used for food. Fruits eaten raw. *Winter Use Food* Fruits canned and saved for future food use. (137:63) **Kitasoo** *Fruit* Berries eaten fresh. *Unspecified* Sprouts peeled and eaten fresh or steamed with oolichan (candlefish) grease, salmon, or salmon roe. (43:347) **Kwakiutl, Southern** *Dried Food* Fruits boiled, mashed, dried, and used as a winter food. *Fruit* Fruits eaten fresh. *Unspecified* Young shoots eaten in spring. (183:291) **Lummi** *Fruit* Berries eaten fresh. *Unspecified* Sprouts cooked in a pit and eaten with dried salmon. (79:35) **Makah** *Fruit* Fruit eaten fresh. (67:275) Berries eaten fresh. (79:35) *Special Food* Sprouts available in large amounts often the occasion for sprout parties. Makah women would collect canoe loads of sprouts and pit steam them on the beach. People would sing and dance while waiting for the steaming sprouts to finish cooking. *Unspecified* Sprouts peeled and eaten raw, boiled, or steamed on hot rocks. (67:275) Sprouts cooked in a pit and eaten with dried salmon. (79:35) *Winter Use Food* Fruit canned for winter use. Sprouts eaten with fermented salmon eggs collected during the previous autumn. (67:275) **Nitinaht** *Dessert* Sprouts eaten raw or steam cooked like a dessert. *Fruit* Berries eaten fresh. (186:124) **Okanagon** *Fruit* Yellow fruits used for food. *Unspecified* Young, sweet shoots used for food. (125:38) **Oweekeno** *Fruit* Berries eaten fresh. *Preserves* Berries used to make jam. *Unspecified* Sprouts used for food. *Winter Use Food* Berries preserved for winter use. (43:113) **Paiute** *Fruit* Berries eaten ripe and fresh. (111:82) **Pomo** *Fruit* Raw berries used for food. (66:13) **Pomo, Kashaya** *Fruit* Berries eaten fresh. (72:102) **Quileute** *Fruit* Berries eaten fresh. (79:35) Fruits stewed and used for food. Fruits eaten raw. (137:63) *Unspecified* Sprouts cooked in a pit and eaten with dried salmon. (79:35) *Winter Use Food* Fruits canned and saved for future food use. (137:63) **Quinault** *Fruit* Berries eaten fresh.

Unspecified Sprouts cooked in a pit and eaten with dried salmon. (79:35) **Salish, Coast** *Fruit* Berries eaten fresh in summer. *Unspecified* Sprouts peeled and eaten raw in early spring. (182:88) **Skagit, Upper** *Fruit* Berries eaten fresh. *Unspecified* Green sprouts peeled and eaten or cooked in an earth oven. (179:38) **Squaxin** *Fruit* Berries eaten fresh. *Unspecified* Sprouts cooked in a pit and eaten with dried salmon. **Swinomish** *Fruit* Berries eaten fresh. *Unspecified* Sprouts cooked in a pit and eaten with dried salmon. (79:35) **Thompson** *Dried Food* Fruit eaten dried. (187:272) *Fruit* Yellow fruits used for food. (125:38) Fruits eaten for food. (164:486) Fruit eaten fresh. (187:272) *Unspecified* Young, sweet shoots used for food. (125:38) Young shoots eaten. (164:482) **Tolowa** *Fruit* Berries eaten fresh. *Unspecified* Young sprouts eaten with seaweed and dried eels. **Yurok** *Fruit* Berries eaten fresh. (6:51)

Rubus trivialis, Southern Dewberry
Cherokee *Beverage* Fruit used to make juice. *Fruit* Fruit used for food. (80:26)

Rubus ursinus, California Blackberry
Clallam *Fruit* Berries used for food. (57:203) **Diegueño** *Dried Food* Fruit dried and cooked. *Fruit* Fruit eaten fresh. (84:39) **Hesquiat** *Fruit* Berries eaten and well liked. (185:75) **Makah** *Fruit* Fruit eaten fresh. *Pie & Pudding* Fruits used to make pies. *Preserves* Fruits used to make jam. (67:278) **Pomo, Kashaya** *Fruit* Fresh berries eaten whole or mashed with bread. *Pie & Pudding* Berries cooked as pie filling. *Sauce & Relish* Fresh berries mashed as topping for ice cream. Berries cooked as sauce for dumplings. (72:22) **Saanich** *Beverage* Old, dry leaves used to make tea. **Salish, Coast** *Bread & Cake* Berries mashed, dried in cakes, placed in hot water, and used for food. *Fruit* Berries eaten fresh. (182:88) **Thompson** *Dried Food* Berries sun dried on mats. (187:272)

Rubus ursinus* ssp. *macropetalus, California Blackberry
Cowlitz *Dried Food* Berries dried and eaten. *Fruit* Berries eaten fresh. (as *R. macropetalus*

79:35) **Haisla & Hanaksiala** *Fruit* Berries used for food. (43:282) **Hoh** *Fruit* Fruits stewed and used for food. Fruits eaten raw. *Winter Use Food* Fruits canned and saved for future food use. (as *R. macropetalus* 137:63) **Nitinaht** *Fruit* Berries used for food. (186:125) **Okana-gon** *Unspecified* Used commonly for food. Used commonly for food. (as *R. macropetalus* 125:38) **Quileute** *Beverage* Fresh or dried vines and leaves used to make a beverage tea. *Dried Food* Berries dried and eaten. *Fruit* Berries eaten fresh. (as *R. macropetalus* 79:35) Fruits stewed and used for food. Fruits eaten raw. *Winter Use Food* Fruits canned and saved for future food use. (as *R. macropetalus* 137:63) **Skagit** *Dried Food* Berries dried and eaten. *Fruit* Berries eaten fresh. (as *R. macropetalus* 79:35) **Skagit, Upper** *Dried Food* Berries pulped and dried for winter use. *Fruit* Berries eaten fresh. (as *R. macropetalus* 179:38) **Thompson** *Fruit* Berries eaten. (as *R. macropetalus* 164:487) *Unspecified* Used commonly for food. (as *R. macropetalus* 125:38)

Rubus vitifolius, Pacific Dewberry
Cahuilla *Beverage* Berries soaked in water to make a beverage. *Dried Food* Berries dried for later use. *Fruit* Berries eaten fresh. (15:134) **Costanoan** *Fruit* Fruits eaten for food. (21:250) **Karok** *Fruit* Fruit eaten fresh. (6:52) Berries used for food. (148:384) **Klamath** *Unspecified* Species used for food. (45:99) **Luiseño** *Fruit* Fruit used for food. (155:232) **Mendocino Indian** *Dried Food* Black, juicy berries dried for winter use. *Fruit* Black, juicy berries eaten fresh. (41:355) **Wintoon** *Fruit* Berries used for food. (117:264) **Yurok** *Beverage* Young shoots boiled with other vine shoots into a tea. *Fruit* Berries eaten fresh. (6:52)

Rudbeckia laciniata, Cutleaf Coneflower
Cherokee *Dried Food* Leaves and stems tied together and hung up to dry or sun dried and stored for future use. *Frozen Food* Tender leaves and stems frozen in early spring. (126:34) *Unspecified* Young shoots and leaves boiled, fried with fat, and eaten. (204:251) *Vegetable* Leaves

used as cooked spring salad to keep well. (80:30) Leaves and stems parboiled, rinsed, and boiled in hot grease until soft. Leaves and stems cooked alone or with poke, eggs, dock, cornfield creasy (probably *Barbarea verna*), or any other greens. *Winter Use Food* Leaves and stems preserved by blanching, then boiling in a can, with or without salt. (126:34) **San Felipe** *Vegetable* Young stems eaten like celery. (32:50)

Rumex acetosa, Garden Sorrel
Cherokee *Vegetable* Leaves used for food. (126:53)

Rumex acetosella, Common Sheep Sorrel
Anticosti *Unspecified* Leaves eaten fresh by children. (143:65) **Bella Coola** *Unspecified* Leaves eaten raw. (184:207) **Chehalis** *Unspecified* Leaves eaten raw or boiled. (79:29) **Cherokee** *Unspecified* Species used for food. (80:56) *Vegetable* Leaves used for food. (126:53) **Delaware** *Unspecified* Plant used as filling for pies. (176:59) **Hanaksiala** *Unspecified* Leaves eaten by children. (43:260) **Hesquiat** *Sour* Tart, tangy leaves chewed by children. (185:71) **Iroquois** *Spice* Used with salt in a brine for cucumbers. (196:113) *Vegetable* Eaten raw, sometimes with salt. (196:118) **Miwok** *Vegetable*

Rumex acetosella

Moistened, pulverized leaves eaten with salt, tasted sour like vinegar. (12:160) **Okanagan-Colville** *Vegetable* Leaves eaten raw. (188:113) **Saanich** *Vegetable* Acid-tasting leaves eaten like lettuce. (182:85) **Thompson** *Unspecified* Leaves chewed by children for the tangy, sour taste. (187:239)

Rumex aquaticus var. *fenestratus*, Western Dock

Apache, Chiricahua & Mescalero *Unspecified* Leaves eaten without preparation or cooked with green chile and meat or animal bones. (as *R. occidentalis* 33:46) **Bella Coola** *Vegetable* Young leaves mashed, cooked, mixed with grease, and eaten like spinach. (as *R. occidentalis* 184:207) **Haisla & Hanaksiala** *Vegetable* Leaves and stems eaten with oolichan (candlefish) grease and sugar. **Hanaksiala** *Beverage* Plant formerly used to make a type of home-brew or wine. *Winter Use Food* Plant cooked and stored underground in barrels with stink currants and red elderberries for winter use. (as *R. occidentalis* var. *procerus* 43:260) **Heiltzuk** *Unspecified* Stems, leaves, sprouts, and shoots eaten with sugar and grease. (as *R. occidentalis* var. *procerus* 43:107) **Kitasoo** *Vegetable* Leaves cooked and eaten. (as *R. occidentalis* 43:340) **Klallam** *Unspecified* Plants used for food. (as *R. occidentalis* 78:197) **Montana Indian** *Unspecified* Seeds used for food. *Vegetable* Spring leaves used for "greens." (as *R. occidentalis* 19:22) **Oweekeno** *Unspecified* Stems, leaves, sprouts, and shoots used for food. (as *R. occidentalis* var. *procerus* 43:107) **Tanana, Upper** *Frozen Food* Leaves and stems frozen for future use. *Vegetable* Leaves and stems eaten raw or boiled with sugar. (as *R. fenestratus* 102:15)

Rumex arcticus, Arctic Dock

Alaska Native *Dietary Aid* Fresh, green leaves used as a source for vitamins A and C. *Vegetable* Leaves used as salad greens and cooked as vegetables. *Winter Use Food* Leaves cooked, chopped, mixed with other greens, and stored in kegs or barrels for winter use. (85:55) **Eskimo, Alaska** *Unspecified* Young, tender leaves boiled and eaten either hot or cold with

seal oil and sometimes with sugar. The cooked leaves were sometimes served with a sauce-like coating of imported milk. (1:35) Leaves eaten fresh, soured, boiled or in oil. Root also utilized. (4:715) *Winter Use Food* Boiled leaves mixed with seal oil and preserved for months. (1:35) **Eskimo, Arctic** *Vegetable* Leaves from young stems eaten raw as a salad or cooked like spinach. (128:26) **Eskimo, Inuktitut** *Ice Cream* Leaves and stems boiled, cooled, and added to "Eskimo ice cream." *Unspecified* Leaves used for food. (202:186) **Eskimo, Inupiat** *Dessert* Leaves eaten cold with seal oil and sugar, like a rhubarb dessert. *Vegetable* Leaves eaten raw in a salad or boiled and eaten hot with seal oil, blubber, or butter. *Winter Use Food* Leaves chopped, cooked with blubber, and stored in a 10- to 30-gallon wooden barrel for winter use. (98:35) **Koyukon** *Unspecified* Plant cooked and eaten. (119:56) **Tanana, Upper** *Frozen Food* Leaves and stems frozen for future use. *Vegetable* Leaves and stems eaten raw or boiled with sugar. (102:15)

Rumex conglomeratus, Clustered Dock

Miwok *Vegetable* Cooked leaves eaten as greens. (12:160)

Rumex crispus, Curly Dock

Cherokee *Vegetable* Leaves and stems mixed with other greens, parboiled, rinsed, and cooked in hot grease as a potherb. (126:53) Young leaves cooked with sochan (*Rudbeckia laciniata*), creaseys (probably *Lepidium virginicum*), and other greens and eaten. (204:253) **Cheyenne** *Unspecified* Stems peeled and inner portions eaten raw. (83:32) **Cocopa** *Unspecified* Seeds gathered and eaten. (37:188) **Costanoan** *Staple* Seeds used for pinole. *Vegetable* Leaves used for greens. (21:249) **Havasupai** *Vegetable* Leaves boiled and eaten. (197:217) Young, fresh, tender leaves boiled, drained, balled into individual portions, and served. (197:66) **Iroquois** *Vegetable* Stalks eaten as greens in spring. (124:93) Young leaves, before the stem appeared, cooked and seasoned with salt, pepper, or butter. (196:117) **Isleta** *Vegetable* Leaves eaten as greens. (100:42) **Kawaiisu** *Porridge* Seeds parched with hot coals, pounded, and cooked to the consistency of "thick gravy." *Unspecified* Stems boiled with sugar or roasted, inner pulp pushed out of the burned skin, and eaten hot or cold. (206:60) **Mendocino Indian** *Porridge* Seeds used to make mush. *Vegetable* Leaves used as greens in food. (41:345) **Mohave** *Vegetable* Leaves boiled and eaten as greens. (37:201) **Mohegan** *Vegetable* Combined with pigweed, mustard, plantain, and nettle and used as mixed greens. (176:83) **Montana Indian** *Unspecified* Seeds used for food. *Vegetable* Spring leaves used for "greens." (19:22) **Omaha** *Unspecified* Boiled leaves used for food. (70:77) **Paiute, Northern** *Bread & Cake* Seeds soaked in water, ground into a doughy flour, and baked in the sand. *Starvation Food* Roots pit baked in the winter when food was scarce. (59:48) **Pima** *Vegetable* Leaves eaten as greens. (47:51) **Pima, Gila River** *Unspecified* Leaves boiled and eaten. (133:7) **Yavapai** *Starvation Food* Upper stalk roasted during food shortage. (65:258)

Rumex hymenosepalus, Canaigre Dock

Cahuilla *Vegetable* Crisp, juicy stalks eaten as greens. (15:134) **Hualapai** *Beverage* Stems, before the buds bloom, boiled into a drink. (195:53) **Kawaiisu** *Porridge* Seeds parched with hot coals, pounded, and cooked to the consistency of "thick gravy." *Unspecified* Stems boiled with sugar, or roasted, inner pulp pushed out of the burned skin and eaten hot or cold. (206:60) **Navajo** *Porridge* Seeds used to make mush. *Unspecified* Leaves roasted in ashes or boiled and served with butter or chopped and fried with mutton grease. (110:30) *Vegetable* Stems baked and eaten. (55:43) **Papago** *Vegetable* Leaves eaten as greens in spring. (34:14) Roasted in ashes and eaten as greens. (34:46) Greens used for food. (36:61) **Pima** *Bread & Cake* Seeds formerly roasted, ground, added to water to form flat cakes, baked, and eaten. (47:51) *Candy* Roots used for chewing gum by school girls. (95:265) *Pie & Pudding* Stems boiled, strained, flour added, combined with sugar, filled into pie crusts, baked, and eaten.

(47:51) *Unspecified* Stalks formerly cooked or roasted, peeled, and insides eaten. (95:264) Stems roasted or stewed and used for food. Roots eaten raw by children in early spring. (146:77) *Vegetable* Young, succulent leaves boiled or roasted and eaten as greens in spring. (47:51)

Rumex maritimus, Golden Dock

Navajo, Kayenta *Porridge* Seeds made into a mush and used for food. (as *R. fueginus* 205:20)

Rumex obtusifolius, Bitter Dock

Saanich *Unspecified* Young stems cooked and used for food. (182:85)

Rumex paucifolius, Fewleaved Dock

Klamath *Unspecified* Leaves and stems eaten fresh. Ripe seeds used for food. (as *R. geyeri* 45:95) **Montana Indian** *Vegetable* Herbage eaten raw. (as *R. geyeri* 19:22)

Rumex salicifolius, Willow Dock

Kawaiisu *Porridge* Seeds parched with hot coals, pounded, and cooked to the consistency of "thick gravy." *Unspecified* Stems boiled with sugar, or roasted, inner pulp pushed out of the burned skin and eaten hot or cold. (206:60) **Klamath** *Unspecified* Seeds used for food. (45:95) **Montana Indian** *Unspecified* Seeds used for food. *Vegetable* Spring leaves used for "greens." (19:22)

Rumex salicifolius var. *mexicanus*, Mexican Dock

Cochiti *Vegetable* Leaves used as greens. (as *R. mexicanus* 32:50)

Rumex venosus, Veiny Dock

San Felipe *Unspecified* Young stems eaten like rhubarb. (32:50)

Rumex violascens, Violet Dock

Pima, Gila River *Unspecified* Leaves boiled and eaten. (133:7)

Ruppia sp., Sea Grass

Seri *Staple* Seeds made into a meal. (50:134)

Sabal minor, Dwarf Palmetto
Houma *Bread & Cake* Fresh root slices baked
and eaten as bread. (as *S. adansonii* 158:55)

Sabal palmetto, Cabbage Palmetto
Seminole *Unspecified* Plant used for food.
(169:506)

Saccharum officinarum, Sugarcane
Seminole *Unspecified* Plant used for food.
(169:471)

Sadleria cyatheoides, Amaumau Fern
Hawaiian *Beverage* Plant powdered and used
to make a beverage similar to coffee or tea.
(2:16)

Sagittaria cuneata, Arumleaf
    Arrowhead
Klamath *Unspecified* Rootstocks used for food.
(as *S. arifolia* 45:90) **Menominee** *Winter Use
Food* Boiled, sliced potatoes strung on a string
for winter use. (as *S. arifolia* 151:61) **Montana
Indian** *Unspecified* Tubers eaten raw or boiled.
(as *S. arifolia* 19:22) **Ojibwa** *Forage* Recognized as a favorite food of ducks and geese.
Staple Corms, a most valued food, boiled fresh,
dried, or candied with maple sugar. Muskrat
and beavers store them in large caches, which
the Indians learned to recognize and appropriate. (as *S. arifolia* 153:396) **Paiute, Northern**
Unspecified Roots used for food. (59:44)

Sagittaria latifolia, Broadleaf
    Arrowhead
Chippewa *Dried Food* "Potatoes" at the end of
the roots dried, boiled, and used for food.
(53:319) **Cocopa** *Unspecified* Tubers baked,
peeled, and eaten whole or mashed. (37:207)
Dakota *Unspecified* Roasted or boiled tubers
used for food. (70:65) **Klamath** *Unspecified*
Species used for food. (45:90) **Lakota** *Unspeci-*

fied Roots used for food and eaten as medicine.
(139:26) **Meskwaki** *Forage* Muskrats gathered
these corms for winter store of food and found
to save the trouble of digging. *Winter Use Food*
Boiled, sliced potatoes strung on a piece of
basswood string and hung for winter supply.
(152:254) **Omaha** *Unspecified* Tubers cooked
as a farinaceous food. (68:325) Roasted or
boiled tubers used for food. **Pawnee** *Unspeci-*
fied Roasted or boiled tubers used for food.
(70:65) **Pomo** *Unspecified* Potato-like tubers
eaten. (11:89) **Potawatomi** *Unspecified* Plant,
growing along the streams and lakes, used as
food by many tribes. Several days were required
to cook the potatoes properly. The potatoes
were cooked in a hole 6 feet deep. Thus, an article, unfit to eat raw, was made very nutritious
and very palatable. (154:94) *Vegetable* Potatoes,
deer meat, and maple sugar made a very tasty
dish. *Winter Use Food* Boiled, sliced potatoes
strung on a string and hung for storage and
winter use. (154:95) **Thompson** *Dried Food*
Cooked root, dried, soaked, and used with fish

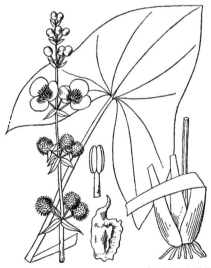

Sagittaria latifolia

for food. *Unspecified* Cooked roots used for food. (187:112) **Winnebago** *Unspecified* Roasted or boiled tubers used for food. (70:65)

Sagittaria latifolia var. *latifolia*,
Broadleaf Arrowhead
Omaha *Vegetable* Bulbs boiled and eaten as vegetables. (as *S. variabilis* 58:341)

Salicornia maritima, Slender
Glasswort
Gosiute *Bread & Cake* Seeds ground into a meal and used to make a "sweet bread." (as *S. herbacea* 39:380)

Salicornia virginica, Virginia
Glasswort
Salish, Coast *Unspecified* Fleshy stems used for food. (182:80)

Salix alaxensis, Feltleaf Willow
Alaska Native *Dietary Aid* Young, tender leaves and shoots used as sources for vitamin C. *Snack Food* Inner bark eaten raw with seal oil and sugar as a winter tidbit. *Unspecified* Leaves used for food. Young, new shoots eaten raw or dipped in seal oil. (85:59) **Eskimo, Alaska** *Unspecified* Leaf tips eaten raw with seal oil in early spring. (1:34) **Eskimo, Inupiat** *Sweetener* Flowers sucked by children for the sweet nectar. *Unspecified* Leaf buds used for food. Tender, new shoots peeled and eaten. Juice sucked from the stem. Juicy cambium, tasted like watermelon or cucumber, used for food. Tiny, green leaves used for food. (98:7)

Salix bonplandiana, Red Willow
Kawaiisu *Candy* Sticky, sweet substance relished like candy and honey. (as *S. laevigata* 206:61)

Salix exigua, Sandbar Willow
Navajo *Beverage* Leaves used to make a drink "like orange juice." *Fodder* and *Forage* Leaves and bark used as food for both wild and domesticated animals. (90:155)

Salix gooddingii, Goodding's Willow
Cocopa & Yuma *Unspecified* Honeydew obtained from cut branches. (37:218) **Mohave** *Beverage* Young shoots used to make tea. (37:201) **Pima** *Unspecified* Catkins eaten raw. (47:108) **Yuma** *Beverage* Leaves and twig bark steeped to make tea. *Unspecified* Bark eaten raw or cooked in hot ashes. (37:201)

Salix hindsiana, Hinds's Willow
Kawaiisu *Candy* Sticky, sweet substance relished like candy and honey. (206:61)

Salix hookeriana, Dune Willow
Quileute *Spice* Leaves put in cooking baskets and used as a food flavoring. (as *S. piperi* 79:26)

Salix planifolia ssp. *pulchra*,
Tealeaf Willow
Alaska Native *Dietary Aid* Shoots probably the first spring source of vitamin C. Leaves used as one of the richest sources of vitamin C. *Unspecified* Shoots peeled and eaten raw. Young, tender leaves mixed with seal oil and eaten raw. *Winter Use Food* Leaves mixed with seal oil and stored in barrels, kegs, or seal pokes for winter use. (as *S. pulchra* 85:61) **Eskimo, Alaska** *Unspecified* Young leaves gathered in the spring and eaten raw with seal oil. (1:34) Cambium layer scraped off and eaten. *Vegetable* Young shoots and catkins used fresh or in seal oil. (as *S. pulchra* 4:715) *Winter Use Food* Leaves soaked in seal oil and saved for future use. (1:34) Young shoots and catkins stored in oil for winter use. (as *S. pulchra* 4:715) **Eskimo, Arctic** *Unspecified* Leaves used for food. (as *S. pulchra* 128:29) **Eskimo, Inupiat** *Beverage* Dried leaves used to make tea. *Soup* Dried leaves used in soups. *Vegetable* Leaves used as greens in fresh salads. *Winter Use Food* Leaves preserved in seal or fish oil or canned for winter use and eaten with meat or fish. (as *S. pulchra* 98:10)

Salix scouleriana, Scouler's Willow
Shuswap *Preservative* Wood used to smoke salmon. (123:68)

Salsola australis, Prickly Russian Thistle

Havasupai *Forage* Young plants eaten by horses. (as *S. kali* 197:218) **Navajo** *Unspecified* Roasted seeds used for food. (as *S. kali* var. *tenuifolia* 90:155) Sprouts boiled and eaten with butter or small pieces of mutton fat. *Vegetable* Very young, raw sprouts chopped into salads. (as *S. kali* 110:27) **Navajo, Ramah** *Fodder* Young plants used for sheep and horse feed. (as *S. pestifer* 191:25)

Salvia apiana, White Sage

Cahuilla *Spice* Leaves used as flavoring for mush. *Staple* Parched seeds ground into a flour and used to make mush. (15:136) **Diegueño** *Porridge* Seeds mixed with wheat or wild oats, toasted, ground fine, and eaten as a dry cereal. *Unspecified* Young stalks eaten raw. (84:39) **Luiseño** *Unspecified* Ripe stem tops peeled and eaten uncooked. Seeds eaten for food. (as *Ramona polystachya* 155:229)

Salvia carduacea, Thistle Sage

Cahuilla *Porridge* Parched seeds ground into flour, mixed with other seeds, and used to make mush. (15:136) **Diegueño** *Spice* Seeds added to wheat to improve the flavor. (84:41) **Luiseño** *Unspecified* Seeds used for food. (155:229) **Tubatulabal** *Unspecified* Seeds used extensively for food. (193:15)

Salvia columbariae, Chia

Cahuilla *Beverage* Seeds used to make a beverage. *Dietary Aid* Seeds used to render water palatable by removing the alkalies. *Staple* Parched seeds ground into flour and used to make cakes or mush. (15:136) **Costanoan** *Staple* Seeds used for pinole. (21:253) **Diegueño** *Spice* Seeds added to wheat to improve the flavor. (84:41) **Kawaiisu** *Beverage* Seeds parched, pounded, mixed with water, and used as a beverage. (206:62) **Luiseño** *Unspecified* Seeds used for food. (155:229) **Mahuna** *Porridge* Seeds winnowed, ground into a fine meal, and made into porridge. (140:54) **Mohave** *Beverage* Seeds ground and mixed with water. *Staple* Seeds used to make pinole. (37:187) **Paiute**

Porridge Seeds used to make mush. (167:243) **Papago** *Beverage* Seeds steeped and used as tea-like drinks for refreshment. (34:27) **Pima** *Beverage* Seeds made into a popular, mucilaginous beverage. (146:77) **Pima, Gila River** *Beverage* Seeds used to make a mucilaginous drink. *Porridge* Seeds used to make a mucilaginous mass and eaten. (133:5) *Unspecified* Seeds eaten raw and parched. (133:7) **Pomo** *Staple* Seeds used to make pinoles. (11:87) Ground seeds used for pinole. (118:28) **Tubatulabal** *Unspecified* Seeds used extensively for food. (193:15) **Yavapai** *Unspecified* Species used for food. (65:258)

Salvia mellifera, Black Sage

Cahuilla *Spice* Leaves and stalks used as a food flavoring. *Staple* Parched seeds ground into a meal. (15:136) **Luiseño** *Unspecified* Seeds used for food. (as *Ramona stachyoides* 155:229)

Sambucus canadensis, American Elder

Cherokee *Beverage* Berries used to make wine. (126:32) *Fruit* Fruit used for food. (80:33) *Pie & Pudding* Berries used to make pie. (126:32) *Preserves* Berries used to make jellies. (80:33) Berries used to make jelly.

Sambucus canadensis

(126:32) **Chippewa** *Dried Food* Fruit dried for winter use. *Fruit* Fruit eaten fresh. (71:142) **Dakota** *Beverage* Blossoms dipped in hot water to make a pleasant drink. *Fruit* Fresh fruit used for food. (70:115) **Iroquois** *Bread & Cake* Fruit mashed, made into small cakes, and dried for future use. *Dried Food* Raw or cooked fruit sun or fire dried and stored for future use. (196:128) *Fruit* Fruits eaten raw. (124:96) Dried fruit taken as a hunting food. (196:128) *Porridge* Berries dried, soaked in cold water, heated slowly, and mixed with bread meal or hominy in winter. *Sauce & Relish* Berries used as a sauce. Berries dried, soaked in cold water, heated slowly, and used as a winter sauce. (124:96) Dried fruit cakes soaked in warm water and cooked as a sauce or mixed with corn bread. (196:128) **Meskwaki** *Fruit* Berries eaten raw. *Preserves* Berries cooked without sugar into a conserve. (152:256) **Omaha** *Beverage* Blossoms dipped in hot water to make a pleasant drink. *Fruit* Fresh fruit used for food. **Pawnee** *Beverage* Blossoms dipped in hot water to make a pleasant drink. *Fruit* Fresh fruit used for food. **Ponca** *Beverage* Blossoms dipped in hot water to make a pleasant drink. *Fruit* Fresh fruit used for food. (70:115) **Seminole** *Starvation Food* Plant used as a scarcity food. (as *S. simpsoni* 169:505)

Sambucus cerulea, Blue Elderberry

Costanoan *Fruit* Fruits eaten for food. (21:254) **Kawaiisu** *Preserves* Dried or fresh berries used to make jelly. (206:62) **Okanagan-Colville** *Frozen Food* Berries frozen for future use. *Fruit* Berries used for food. (188:94) **Pomo, Kashaya** *Fruit* Tart berries eaten fresh in small quantities, canned, or cooked for pie filling. (72:42) **Salish, Coast** *Fruit* Berries cooked and used for food. (182:80) **Sanpoil & Nespelem** *Fruit* Berries eaten fresh. (131:102) **Thompson** *Dried Food* Fruits dried for future use. (164:490) Dried fruit used for food. (187:199) *Fruit* Fruits eaten fresh in large quantities. (164:490) Fresh fruit used for food. *Preserves* Berries cooked to make jam. *Spice* Berry juice used for marinating fish. (187:199) **Yuki** *Dried Food* Berries dried and used as a

winter food. *Fruit* Berries eaten raw. *Soup* Berries formerly made into soup. (as *S. coerules* 49:86) **Yurok** *Fruit* Fresh berries used for food. (6:53)

Sambucus cerulea var. *cerulea*, Blue Elderberry

Chehalis *Winter Use Food* Berries steamed on rocks, cooled, and eaten in the winter. **Green River Group** *Winter Use Food* Berries steamed on rocks, cooled, and eaten in the winter. (as *S. glauca* 79:47) **Karok** *Fruit* Mashed berries used for food. (as *S. glauca* 148:389) **Klallam** *Fruit* Berries used for food. (as *S. glauca* 78:197) *Winter Use Food* Berries steamed on rocks, cooled, and eaten in the winter. (as *S. glauca* 79:47) **Klamath** *Fruit* Berries used for food. (as *S. glauca* 45:104) **Luiseño** *Dried Food* Fruit eaten dried. *Fruit* Fruit eaten fresh. (as *S. glauca* 155:229) **Lummi** *Winter Use Food* Berries steamed on rocks, cooled, and eaten in the winter. (as *S. glauca* 79:47) **Mendocino Indian** *Dried Food* Berries formerly dried for winter use. *Fruit* Berries formerly eaten raw. *Pie & Pudding* Berries made into pies and used for food. *Preserves* Berries made into jelly and used for food. (as *S. glauca* 41:388) **Montana Indian** *Beverage* Fruit used to make. *Fruit* Fruit eaten raw or cooked. *Pie & Pudding* Fruit used to make pies. *Preserves* Fruit used to make jelly. (as *S. glauca* 19:23) **Paiute** *Dried Food* Fruits dried and eaten. *Fruit* Fruits eaten fresh. (as *S. glauca* 104:100) Berries eaten fresh or boiled. (as *S. glauca* 111:111) **Quinault** *Winter Use Food* Berries steamed on rocks, cooled, and eaten in the winter. **Skagit** *Winter Use Food* Berries steamed on rocks, cooled, and eaten in the winter. (as *S. glauca* 79:47) **Skagit, Upper** *Dried Food* Berries steamed, pulped, and dried for winter use. (as *S. glauca* 179:38) *Fruit* Fruit eaten fresh. (as *S. glauca* 179:37) **Skokomish** *Fruit* Berries eaten fresh. **Squaxin** *Winter Use Food* Berries steamed on rocks, cooled, and eaten in the winter. **Swinomish** *Winter Use Food* Berries steamed on rocks, cooled, and eaten in the winter. (as *S. glauca* 79:47) **Wintoon** *Fruit* Berries used for food. (as *S. glauca* 117:264) **Yokut** *Dried Food* Berries eaten dried. *Winter Use Food* Berries stored for winter use and cooked. (as *S. glauca* 117:436)

Sambucus cerulea var. mexicana, Blue Elder

Cahuilla *Dried Food* Berries dried for future use. *Fruit* Berries eaten fresh. *Preserves* Berries used to make jams and jellies. *Sauce & Relish* Berries cooked into a rich sauce. (as *S. mexicana* 15:138) **Diegueño** *Fruit* Berries eaten fresh. *Winter Use Food* Berries dried for winter use and boiled like raisins. (as *S. mexicana* 84:41) **Paiute** *Dried Food* Fruit sun dried, stored in buckskin bags, and hung up for winter use. *Fruit* Fruit eaten fresh. (as *S. mexicana* 167:245) **Pima** *Preserves* Berries used to make jams and jellies. (as *S. mexicana* 47:75) **Pima, Gila River** *Beverage* Fruits brewed into a wine. *Fruit* Fruits eaten for food. (as *S. mexicana* 133:5) *Snack Food* Fruits eaten raw as a snack food. (as *S. mexicana* 133:7)

Sambucus cerulea var. velutina, Blue Elderberry

Atsugewi *Bread & Cake* Mashed berries mixed with manzanita flour and stored in dried cakes. (as *S. velutinus* 61:139) **Tubatulabal** *Fruit* Berries used for food. (as *S. velutina* 193:15)

Sambucus nigra, European Black Elder

Cherokee *Fruit* Fruit used for food. *Preserves* Berries used to make jellies. (80:33)

Sambucus racemosa, Scarlet Elderberry

Apache, White Mountain *Fruit* Berries used for food. (136:160) **Bella Coola** *Beverage* Berries used to make wine. *Dried Food* Berries formerly boiled into a thick sauce, dried, and used for food. *Preserves* Berries used to make jelly. (184:203) **Gosiute** *Fruit* Fruit used in season for food. (39:380) **Hesquiat** *Fruit* Fruit cooked with sugar and eaten. Berries should always be eaten cooked, as they are potentially poisonous when raw. *Preserves* Cooked fruit made excellent jelly and jam. (185:63) **Kitasoo** *Bread & Cake* Fruit cooked, dried into cakes, stored, reconstituted, and eaten. (43:329) **Kwakiutl,**

Southern *Bread & Cake* Berries pit steamed, dried over fire into cakes, and eaten at noon. (183:280) **Makah** *Dried Food* Fruit steamed, sun dried, and placed in bentwood cedar boxes for storage. *Fruit* Fruit eaten fresh. Fruit mixed with sugar, steamed, and eaten. *Winter Use Food* Fruit canned for winter use. Berry clusters placed in alder bark cones and submerged in cold creeks for storage. **Nitinaht** *Fruit* Fruit used for food. (67:318) **Ojibwa** *Unspecified* Species used for food. (135:237) **Okanagon** *Fruit* Fruits eaten for food. (125:39) **Quileute** *Fruit* Fruit eaten fresh. *Winter Use Food* Fruit canned for winter use. (67:318) **Thompson** *Fruit* Fruits eaten for food. (125:39) Berries stewed or eaten fresh with salmon egg "cheese." *Soup* Mashed berries dried in cakes, broken off, and added to salmon head soup and other dishes. *Spice* Berry juice used to marinate salmon. (187:199)

Sambucus racemosa ssp. pubens, Red Elderberry

Paiute, Northern *Dried Food* Berries dried for future use. *Fruit* Berries used for food. *Soup* Berries dried and boiled into a soup. (59:50)

Sambucus racemosa ssp. pubens var. arborescens, Pacific Red Elder

Chehalis *Winter Use Food* Berries steamed on rocks, cooled, and eaten in the winter. **Cowlitz** *Winter Use Food* Berries steamed on rocks, cooled, and eaten in the winter. **Green River Group** *Winter Use Food* Berries steamed on rocks, cooled, and eaten in the winter. (as *S. callicarpa* 79:47) **Haisla** *Fruit* Berries used extensively, especially to mix with and extend other berries. **Haisla & Hanaksiala** *Beverage* Berries used to make wine. *Dried Food* Berries dried for future use. *Winter Use Food* Berries formerly an important winter food. **Hanaksiala** *Fruit* Berries mixed with blueberries, Pacific crabapples, and oolichan (candlefish) grease and eaten. (43:229) **Hoh** *Fruit* Berries pit baked and used for food. *Sauce & Relish* Fruits used to make a sauce. *Winter Use Food* Berries cooked, wrapped in skunk cabbage leaves, and preserved for winter use. (as *S. calliocarpa*

137:69) **Klallam** *Fruit* Berries used for food. (as *S. callicarpa* 78:197) *Winter Use Food* Berries steamed on rocks, cooled, and eaten in the winter. **Makah** *Winter Use Food* Berries steamed on rocks, cooled, and eaten in the winter. (as *S. callicarpa* 79:47) **Nitinaht** *Fruit* Berries formerly used for food. *Preserves* Berries pounded, dried, soaked in water until jam-like, mixed with sugar, and used for food. (186:100) **Oweekeno** *Dried Food* Berries dried for storage. *Preserves* Berries used to make jam. (43:90) **Quileute** *Fruit* Berries pit baked and used for food. *Sauce & Relish* Fruits used to make a sauce. (as *S. calliocarpa* 137:69) *Winter Use Food* Berries steamed on rocks, cooled, and eaten in the winter. (as *S. callicarpa* 79:47) Berries cooked, wrapped in skunk cabbage leaves, and preserved for winter use. (as *S. calliocarpa* 137:69) **Quinault** *Winter Use Food* Berries steamed on rocks, cooled, and eaten in the winter. **Skagit** *Winter Use Food* Berries steamed on rocks, cooled, and eaten in the winter. (as *S. callicarpa* 79:47) **Skagit, Upper** *Dried Food* Berries steamed, pulped, and dried for winter use. (as *S. callicarpa* 179:38) *Fruit* Fruit eaten fresh. (as *S. callicarpa* 179:37) **Skokomish** *Winter Use Food* Berries steamed on rocks, cooled, and eaten in the winter. **Snohomish** *Winter Use Food* Berries steamed on rocks, cooled, and eaten in the winter. **Squaxin** *Winter Use Food* Berries steamed on rocks, cooled, and eaten in the winter. **Swinomish** *Winter Use Food* Berries steamed on rocks, cooled, and eaten in the winter. (as *S. callicarpa* 79:47) **Yurok** *Fruit* Fresh berries used for food. (as *S. callicarpa* 6:53)

Sambucus racemosa ssp. *pubens* var. *leucocarpa*, European Red Elderberry

Mahuna *Fruit* Berries eaten mainly to quench the thirst. (as *S. pubens* 140:70)

Sambucus racemosa ssp. *pubens* var. *microbotrys*, European Red Elderberry

Apache *Fruit* Fruits eaten fresh or cooked. (as *S. microbotrys* 32:50) **Apache, Chiricahua &**

Mescalero *Preserves* Fruit cooked with a sweet substance, strained, and eaten as jelly. (as *S. microbotrys* 33:46)

Sanicula bipinnata, Poison Sanicle

Karok *Vegetable* Leaves eaten as greens. (148:386)

Sanicula tuberosa, Turkey Pea

Mendocino Indian *Unspecified* Bulbs eaten raw. (41:374) **Neeshenam** *Unspecified* Eaten raw, roasted, or boiled. (as *S. luberosa* 129:377) **Pomo** *Unspecified* Tuberous roots eaten raw. (11:89)

Sarcobatus vermiculatus, Greasewood

Keres, Western *Forage* Shrub used as winter pasture for sheep. (171:68) **Montana Indian** *Vegetable* Young twigs used for greens. (19:23) **Navajo** *Forage* Used as forage by sheep and eaten for the salt. (55:44) *Fruit* "Seeds" (actually fruits) used for food. (90:155) **Navajo, Ramah** *Fodder* Used for sheep and horse feed in the spring. (191:25) **Pima** *Forage* Succulent, young leaves and branches eaten by cattle and sheep. *Starvation Food* Seeds roasted and eaten during "hard times." (47:71)

Sarcobatus vermiculatus

Sarcocornia pacifica, Pacific
Swampfire
Alaska Native *Vegetable* Young plants used in
salads or for pickles. (as *Salicornia pacifica*
85:57)

Sarcostemma cynanchoides ssp.
hartwegii, Hartweg's Twinevine
Luiseño *Unspecified* Plant eaten raw with salt.
(as *Philibertia heterophylla* 155:230) **Papago**
Candy Gum-like secretions heated over coals
and chewed by children. (as *Philibertella heterophylla* 34:28) **Pima** *Candy* Milk extracted
from main stem, baked or boiled, and used as
chewing gum. (as *Funastrum heterophyllum*
47:82) **Pima, Gila River** *Baby Food* Sap
roasted on coals and eaten primarily by children. (133:7)

Sassafras albidum, Sassafras
Cherokee *Beverage* Roots and barks used to
make a beverage tea. (80:54) Red and white
roots, red roots preferred, used to make tea.
(126:44) **Chippewa** *Beverage* Root bark used
to make a pleasant, tea-like beverage. *Spice*
Leaves used in meat soups for the bay leaf-like
flavor. (as *S. variifolium* 71:130) **Choctaw**
Spice Pounded, dry leaves added to soup for flavor. (as *Laurus sassafras* 25:8)

Satureja douglasii, Yerba Buena
Diegueño *Beverage* Leaves used to make mint
tea. (84:41) **Luiseño** *Beverage* Plant used to
make a tea. (as *Micromeria douglasii* 155:211)
Mendocino Indian *Substitution Food* Slender,
leafy vines made into rolls, dried, and used as a
substitute for tea. (as *Micromeria douglasii*
41:383) **Pomo, Kashaya** *Beverage* Decoction
of crawling stems and leaves used as a beverage
tea. (72:121) **Saanich** *Beverage* Leaves used to
make a refreshing tea. (182:84) **Tolowa** *Beverage* Fresh leaves used to make a refreshing tea.
(6:54)

Saxifraga micranthidifolia,
Lettuceleaf Saxifrage
Cherokee *Unspecified* Young growth boiled,
fried with ramps (*Allium tricoccum*?), and

eaten. (204:252) *Vegetable* Leaves used in salads or wilted in boiling water with bacon grease
dripped on the top. (126:54)

Saxifraga nelsoniana ssp. *nelsoniana*, Brook Saxifrage
Alaska Native *Dietary Aid* Leaves prepared
and eaten soon after picking as a good source
of vitamin C and provitamin A. *Unspecified*
Leaves mixed with seal or walrus oil and eaten
raw. (as *S. punctata* 85:63) **Eskimo, Alaska**
Unspecified Leaves and stalks eaten raw with
seal oil and fish. (as *S. punctata* ssp. *nelsoniana* 1:36) Leaves eaten fresh or in oil. Leaves
preserved for long periods in oil. (as *Saxifrage
punctata* 4:715) *Winter Use Food* Leaves preserved in seal oil for later use. (as *Saxifraga
punctata* ssp. *nelsoniana* 1:36) **Eskimo,
Arctic** *Vegetable* Leaves eaten raw with seal
blubber or as "sauerkraut." (as *S. punctata*
128:29) **Eskimo, Inupiat** *Vegetable* Leaves
preserved in seal oil and eaten with fish or meat
or used fresh in salads. (as *S. punctata* 98:21)

Saxifraga pensylvanica, Eastern
Swamp Saxifrage
Cherokee *Vegetable* Leaves eaten raw as
greens. (80:26)

Saxifraga spicata, Spiked Saxifrage
Alaska Native *Dietary Aid* Leaves used as a
fair source of vitamin C. *Vegetable* Young, tender
leaves used as a salad green. (85:65) **Eskimo,
Alaska** *Unspecified* Young, tender leaves eaten
raw with seal oil and often with fish. Young
stems eaten raw. (1:36)

Saxifraga tricuspidata, Three
Toothed Saxifrage
Eskimo, Inuktitut *Unspecified* Flowers eaten
as food. (202:186)

Scirpus acutus, Hardstem Bulrush
Cheyenne *Unspecified* Inner part of stems eaten
raw. (83:8) **Cree, Woodlands** *Unspecified*
Stem base and tender leaf bases eaten fresh as
collected by boat. Stem base and roots used for
food. (109:59) **Dakota** *Unspecified* Tender,

white stem base eaten fresh and uncooked. (as
S. lacustris 69:359) **Gosiute** *Unspecified* Lower,
tender stem portions formerly used for food. (as
S. lacustris var. *occidentalis* 39:381) **Hesquiat**
Forage Cows were said to eat it. (185:53) **Hopi**
Unspecified Lower end of the stalk eaten raw.
(as *S. lacustris* 190:159) **Klamath** *Unspecified*
Seeds used for food. (as *S. lacustris occidentalis* 45:92) **Montana Indian** *Sauce & Relish*
Roots boiled with water and made into a syrup.
Staple Roots made into flour and used to make
bread. *Unspecified* Roots eaten raw. Seeds used
for food. (as *S. lacustris occidentalis* 19:23)
Paiute, Northern *Unspecified* Roots peeled
and eaten raw, boiled, or roasted. (59:49)
Shoots eaten raw. Rhizomes peeled and chewed
to extract the juices. Basal lengths of stalks eaten
fresh. (60:72) **Pomo** *Unspecified* New sprouts
eaten in the spring. (as *S. lacustris* 117:284)
Vegetable Roots eaten as greens. Young shoots
eaten as greens. (as *S. lacustris* var. *occidentalis* 11:92) **Sioux** *Unspecified* Young, spring
shoots used for food. (as *S. lacustris occidentalis* 19:23) **Tubatulabal** *Unspecified* Roots
used for food. (193:15)

Scirpus americanus, American Bulrush
Keres, Western *Unspecified* Roots and tender
shoots used for food. (as *S. alneyi* 171:68)

Scirpus maritimus, Saltmarsh Bulrush
Paiute, Northern *Porridge* Seeds parched,
ground into flour, and made into mush. (60:74)
Unspecified Seeds used for food. (59:48) *Winter Use Food* Seeds parched and stored for later
use. (60:74) **Pima, Gila River** *Unspecified*
Roots eaten raw. (133:7)

Scirpus nevadensis, Nevada Bulrush
Cheyenne *Unspecified* Peeled roots eaten raw.
(76:170)

Scirpus pungens, Threesquare Bulrush
Paiute, Northern *Porridge* Seeds ground lightly into a flour and boiled into a mush. (59:49)
Seeds parched, ground into flour, and made into mush. (60:74)

Scirpus robustus, Alkali Bulrush
Montana Indian *Unspecified* Autumn tubers
used for food. (as *S. campestris* 19:23) **Pomo**
Vegetable Young shoots eaten as greens. Roots
eaten as greens. (11:92)

Scirpus tabernaemontani, Softstem Bulrush
Chippewa *Unspecified* Sweet bulbs eaten raw
in midsummer. (as *S. validus* 53:320) **Cree,
Woodlands** *Unspecified* Stem base and roots
used for food. Stem base and tender leaf bases
eaten fresh as collected by boat. (as *S. validus*
109:60) **Dakota** *Unspecified* Fresh, raw stems
used for food. (as *S. validus* 70:69) **Hopi** *Unspecified* Lower end of the stalk eaten raw. (as
S. validus 190:159) **Kawaiisu** *Unspecified* Tender, lower portions of the plant eaten raw. (as *S.
validus* 206:63) **Lakota** *Unspecified* Species
used for food. (as *S. validus* 139:26) **Ute** *Unspecified* Lower, tender portions of the plant
used for food. (as *S. validus* 38:36)

Scorzonella sp.
Paiute *Unspecified* Roots roasted and used for
food. (104:103)

Scrophularia sp.
Yavapai *Vegetable* Boiled leaves used for
greens. (65:258)

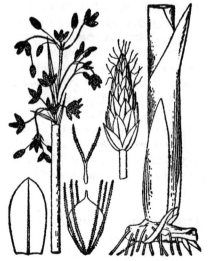

Scirpus tabernaemontani

Sedum divergens, Pacific Stonecrop
Gitksan *Unspecified* Leaves used for food.
Haisla *Unspecified* Leaves used for food.
Wet'suwet'en *Unspecified* Leaves used for food.
(73:154)

**Sedum integrifolium ssp. integri-
folium**, Entireleaf Stonecrop
Eskimo, Alaska *Beverage* Red plant tops used
to make a tea-like beverage. (as *S. rosea* ssp.
integrifolium 1:36) *Unspecified* Plant eaten
fresh, soured, or in oil. Root used for food. (as
Rhodiola integrifolia 4:715)

Sedum laxum, Roseflower Stonecrop
Tubatulabal *Unspecified* Rolled in palm of
hand with salt grass leaves and stems and eaten.
(as *Cotyledon laxa* 193:19) Leaves used for
food. (as *Cotyledon laxa* 193:15)

Sedum rosea, Roseroot Stonecrop
Alaska Native *Unspecified* Roots used for food.
Vegetable Leaves and succulent, fleshy stems
used raw in mixed salads or cooked as a green
vegetable. (as *S. roseum* 85:67) **Eskimo, Arctic** *Vegetable* Young leaves and flowering stems
eaten raw as salad, cooked as a potherb, or
made into a "sauerkraut." (as *Rhodiola rosea*
128:28) **Eskimo, Inupiat** *Frozen Food* Fermented stems, leaves, and young flower buds
frozen through the winter. *Staple* Roots stored
buried in the sand and grass and used in hard
times when short of food. *Unspecified* Roots
eaten with oil. *Vegetable* Fermented stems,
leaves, and young flower buds eaten with walrus
blubber, any kind of blubber, or oil. Stems,
leaves, and young flower buds were preserved
by fermenting in water. A barrel was filled with
clean, unchopped roseroot plants which were
covered with water. Plants were pressed under
the water with a plate and stored in a medium
warm to cool place to ferment. If it was too
cold, the roseroot would not ferment. If it was
too warm, it might spoil first. In 2 to 3 weeks,
or, when the plants were squashed together, the
lids were taken off and another batch of roseroot was added and covered again. More water
was added, when necessary, to cover the plants.

Roseroot was continuously added and let to ferment down until the barrel was full. When the
taste was just right, the batches were taken out
and put into plastic bags, plants and juice together, and frozen. (as *S. roseum* 98:54)

Selaginella densa, Lesser Spikemoss
Blackfoot *Spice* Dried plant used to spice meat.
Starvation Food Very bitter berries eaten only
through necessity and never stored. (86:105)

Senecio congestus, Marsh Fleabane
Eskimo, Arctic *Vegetable* Young leaves and
flowering stems eaten raw as salad, cooked as a
potherb, or made into a "sauerkraut." (128:27)

Senecio multicapitatus, Ragwort
Groundsel
Navajo, Ramah *Candy* Root bark used for
chewing gum. *Starvation Food* Roasted, ground
seeds, cornmeal, and goat's milk made into flat
cakes or mush in times of famine. (191:53)

Senecio pseudoarnica, Seaside
Ragwort
Eskimo, Alaska *Unspecified* Fleshy stems and
boiled leaves used for food. The leaves were edible only when boiled. The plant was eaten only
when young and tender. (1:38)

Senna occidentalis, Septicweed
Kiowa *Beverage* Ground seeds boiled to make
a coffee-like beverage. (as *Ditremexa occidentalis* 192:31)

Serenoa repens, Saw Palmetto
Seminole *Fruit* Fruit and trunk used for food.
(169:504)

Shepherdia argentea, Silver Buffalo
Berry
Arapaho *Preserves* Berries used to make jelly.
Winter Use Food Berries dried for winter use.
(121:49) **Blackfoot** *Forage* Berries eaten by
buffalo. (97:48) **Cheyenne** *Pie & Pudding* Berries boiled, flour and sugar added, and eaten as
a pudding. (83:24) **Dakota** *Dried Food* Fruit
dried for winter use. *Fruit* Fruit eaten fresh in

season. (as *Lepargyrea argentea* 70:106)
Gosiute *Fruit* Berries used for food. (39:381)
Lakota *Dried Food* Berries dried and used for
food. *Fruit* Berries eaten fresh. (106:43) Fruits
eaten for food. (139:44) **Montana Indian**
Dried Food Fruits dried and stored for winter
use. (82:57) *Fruit* Fruit eaten fresh. (19:23)
Fruits eaten fresh. (82:57) *Preserves* Fruit used
to make jelly. (19:23) *Sauce & Relish* Fruits
used to make a meat flavoring sauce. (82:57)
Winter Use Food Fruit dried for winter use.
(19:23) **Navajo** *Dried Food* Dried fruit used for
food. *Fruit* Fresh fruit used for food. (90:156)
Omaha *Dried Food* Fruit dried for winter use.
(as *Lepargyraea argentea* 68:326) Fruit dried
for winter use. (as *Lepargyrea argentea*
70:106) *Fruit* Fruit eaten fresh. (as *Lepargyraea argentea* 68:326) Fruit eaten fresh in season. (as *Lepargyrea argentea* 70:106) **Paiute**
Dried Food Berries cooked, dried, boiled,
drained, crushed, and used for food. *Fruit*
Fruits eaten fresh. *Pie & Pudding* Berries, flour,
and sugar mixed and eaten as a pudding.
(104:100) **Paiute, Northern** *Dried Food* Berries dried for winter use. *Porridge* Berries
dried, mashed, and eaten like a mush. (59:50)
Pawnee *Dried Food* Fruit dried for winter use.
Fruit Fruit eaten fresh in season. **Ponca** *Dried*

Shepherdia argentea

Food Fruit dried for winter use. *Fruit* Fruit eat-
en fresh in season. (as *Lepargyrea argentea*
70:106) **Thompson** *Fruit* Scarlet, sour fruits
eaten fresh. *Winter Use Food* Scarlet, sour fruits
preserved for winter use. (as *Lepargyrea argentea* 164:489) **Ute** *Fruit* Berries formerly used
for food. (38:36) **Winnebago** *Dried Food* Fruit
dried for winter use. *Fruit* Fruit eaten fresh in
season. (as *Lepargyrea argentea* 70:106)

Shepherdia canadensis, Russet
Buffalo Berry

Alaska Native *Dessert* Berries mixed with sugar and water, beaten with hands into foam, and
used on desserts like whipped cream. (85:146)
Bella Coola *Ice Cream* Berries mixed with water, whipped, and eaten as "Indian ice-cream."
(184:204) **Blackfoot** *Starvation Food* Bitter
berries eaten in lean times. (86:105) **Carrier**
Dried Food Berries dried for future use. (31:76)
Fruit Berries used for food. (89:12) *Ice Cream*
Berries beaten by hand in a birch basket into
Indian ice cream. (31:76) Berries used to make
a froth similar to ice cream. The berries were
macerated. In this process, it was most essential
that all grease be kept away and the utensils be
kept perfectly clean. A smooth froth, almost like
ice cream of light consistency, was formed,
which was edible and to those accustomed to it
of good taste. Sugar was added to sweeten. This
froth appeared to be formed from the saponins
which were admixed with the other components
of the fruit. (89:12) *Preserves* Berries used to
make jam. (31:76) Berries used to make jelly.
(89:12) **Cheyenne** *Preserves* Fruit used to
make excellent preserves. (as *Lepargyraea canadensis* 76:181) **Clallam** *Ice Cream* Berries
whipped until foamy and eaten as "Indian ice
cream." (57:199) **Coeur d'Alene** *Fruit* Berries
eaten fresh. (178:90) *Ice Cream* Berries used
to make a froth similar to ice cream. (89:12)
Eskimo, Inupiat *Dessert* Berries, water, and
sugar whipped into a foamy dessert. (98:111)
Flathead *Beverage* Berries, water, sugar, and
lemon or vanilla used to make a drink. (19:24)
Ice Cream Berries used to make a froth similar
to ice cream. (89:12) **Haisla & Hanaksiala**
Dried Food Berries dried for future use. *Ice*

Cream Berries whipped into a froth and eaten as "Indian ice cream." *Special Food* Berries served at large gatherings, special occasions, and feasts. (43:236) **Kitasoo** *Ice Cream* Berries whipped into "Indian ice cream." *Winter Use Food* Berries canned for future use. (43:331) **Kwakiutl, Southern** *Fruit* Berries whipped until white and frothy and used for food. (183:282) **Lillooet** *Ice Cream* Berries used to make a froth similar to ice cream. (89:12) **Makah** *Dessert* Berries used to make a frothy dessert. (67:288) Berries whipped into a froth and used as dessert at feasts. (79:41) *Dried Food* Purchased berries dried or canned for storage. *Winter Use Food* Purchased berries dried or canned for storage. (67:288) **Montana Indian** *Dried Food* Berries sun dried and stored for future use. *Fruit* Berries eaten fresh. *Ice Cream* Berries used to make a frothy or foamy "Indian Ice Cream." (82:53) **Nanaimo** *Dessert* Berries crushed in water, beaten to make a froth, and eaten as a favorite dessert. (182:82) **Nitinaht** *Ice Cream* Berries whipped in small amounts of water and eaten as "Indian ice cream" at large feasts. (186:103) **Northwest Indian** *Beverage* Berries made into a foaming drink. (as *Lepargyrea canadensis* 118:17) **Okanagan-Colville** *Ice Cream* Berries used to make "Indian ice cream." (188:99) **Okanagon** *Beverage* Fruits fermented to make an alcoholic drink. *Fruit* Fruits eaten fresh by children. (125:39) *Staple* Berries used as a principal food. (178:239) **Oregon Indian** *Beverage* Berries used to make a foaming drink. (as *Lepargyrea canadensis* 118:20) **Oweekeno** *Fruit* Berries whipped, mixed with sugar, and eaten. *Winter Use Food* Berries canned for future use. (43:93) **Salish, Coast** *Dessert* Berries crushed in water, beaten to make a froth, and eaten as a favorite dessert. (182:82) **Sanpoil** *Ice Cream* Berries used to make a froth similar to ice cream. (89:12) **Shuswap** *Beverage* Canned berry juice used as a beverage during haying time. *Dessert* Berries canned with sugar, mixed with equal amount of water, and whipped into a foam; whipped cream. *Fruit* Berries mixed with timber grass, dried, water added, and beaten to a foam. (123:61) *Ice*

Cream Berries used to make a froth similar to ice cream. (89:12) **Spokan** *Fruit* Berries used for food. (178:343) **Tanana, Upper** *Fruit* Raw berries whipped with sugar until frothy. Berries mixed with sugar, fried, and eaten. (102:13) **Thompson** *Beverage* Fruits fermented to make an alcoholic drink. (125:39) Berries squeezed through a rice bag or some other straining cloth and made into juice. *Bread & Cake* Soapberries dried on mats and formed into cakes. The berries were gathered in the summer, but were not hand picked because they were too soft. A clean mat was placed underneath the bush, then a branch laden with fruit was held and hit with a stick until the fruit fell off. The ripe berries were then placed in a basket, heated with hot rocks, and spread out on mats or on a layer of "timbergrass" set on a scaffolding and allowed to dry. A small fire was lit beneath so that the smoke would drive away the flies. The dried soapberry cakes were then broken off, placed in a birch bark basket with water, and "swished" with a whisk of maple bark tied to a stick. The mixture was originally sweetened with the "white" variety of saskatoon berries that were dried and soaked in water to reconstitute them. More recently, sugar was added to the whip to sweeten it. The sweetened froth was served in small containers, first to the men and then to the women, as a sort of dessert or confection. It was said that the soapberries must never come into contact with grease or oil or the berries would not whip. One informant said that special containers were used for the preparation of soapberries, not for cooking or any other purpose, so that the berries could be kept free of grease. It was said that pregnant women should never eat the soapberry whip. *Candy* Berries made into juice and used to make a frothy confection. *Forage* Berries eaten by bears. (187:209) *Fruit* Fruits eaten fresh by children. (125:39) *Preserves* Berries made into jam. (187:209) **Thompson, Lower** *Ice Cream* Berries used to make a froth similar to ice cream. (89:12)

Sidalcea malviflora, Dwarf Checkermallow
Luiseño *Vegetable* Plant used as greens.

(155:231) **Yana** *Spice* Dried, mashed leaves used to flavor black manzanita berries. (147:251)

Sideroxylon foetidissimum, False Mastic
Seminole *Unspecified* Plant used for food. (169:494)

Sideroxylon lanuginosum, Gum Bully
Kiowa *Candy* Outer bark yields a mucilaginous substance used as chewing gum. (192:46)

Sideroxylon lanuginosum ssp. *lanuginosum*, Gum Bumelia
Kiowa *Candy* Outer bark yields a mucilaginous substance used as chewing gum. (as *Bumelia lanuginosa* 192:46)

Silene acaulis var. *exscapa*, Moss Campion
Eskimo, Inuktitut *Unspecified* Raw root skins used for food. (202:182)

Silphium laciniatum, Compass Plant
Dakota *Candy* Gum from upper part of stem used as chewing gum by children. **Omaha** *Candy* Gum from upper part of stem used as chewing gum by children. **Pawnee** *Candy* Gum from upper part of stem used as chewing gum by children. **Ponca** *Candy* Gum from upper part of stem used as chewing gum by children. **Winnebago** *Candy* Gum from upper part of stem used as chewing gum by children. (70:132)

Simmondsia chinensis, Jojoba
Cahuilla *Beverage* Seeds eaten fresh or ground into powder and used to make a coffee-like beverage. (15:139) **Coahuilla** *Beverage* Ground nut meal boiled into a "coffee." (as *S. californica* 13:74) **Cocopa** *Bread & Cake* Kernels molded into oily cake, boiled, and eaten. *Unspecified* Nuts cleaned, winnowed, shelled, and eaten. (37:188) **Papago** *Unspecified* Nuts eaten fresh from the shell. (as *S. californica* 34:19) **Yavapai** *Preserves* Berries parched and ground to consistency of peanut butter. (as *S. californica* 65:258)

Sinapis alba, White Mustard
Hoh *Spice* Used for flavoring. *Vegetable* Plants eaten as greens. **Quileute** *Spice* Used for flavoring. *Vegetable* Plants eaten as greens. (as *Brassica alba* 137:62)

Sisymbrium altissimum, Tall Tumblemustard
Navajo *Porridge* Seeds used, with goat's milk, to make a mush. (55:50)

Sisymbrium irio, London Rocket
Cahuilla *Vegetable* Immature leaves boiled or fried and used for greens. (15:140) **Mohave** *Starvation Food* Young shoots roasted and eaten as a famine food. (37:201) **Pima** *Porridge* Seeds formerly parched, ground, water added, and eaten as a gruel. *Winter Use Food* Seeds stored and used as a winter food. (47:84) **Pima, Gila River** *Beverage* Seeds mixed with water to make a drink. *Porridge* Seeds used to make a mucilaginous mass and eaten. *Staple* Seeds ground, parched, and used to make pinole. (133:5) *Unspecified* Seeds mixed with water and eaten. (133:7)

Sisymbrium officinale, Hedge Mustard
Cherokee *Vegetable* Leaves cooked and eaten as salad greens. (80:46) **Navajo** *Forage* Plant used by horses for forage. (55:50) *Porridge* Seeds ground and eaten as a mush or gruel. (165:223) *Soup* Seeds parched, ground into meal, and made into soup or stew. (32:22) Parched, ground seeds used to make soup or stew. (55:50) **Tubatulabal** *Unspecified* Leaves fried in grease and eaten. (193:16)

Sisyrinchium angustifolium, Narrowleaf Blueeyed Grass
Cherokee *Vegetable* Mixed into other greens and eaten. (as *S. augustifolium* 204:252)

Sium suave, Hemlock Waterparsnip
Algonquin, Quebec *Unspecified* Root used for food. (18:101) **Bella Coola** *Unspecified* Tubers eaten. **Carrier** *Unspecified* Tubers eaten. (184:200) **Cree, Woodlands** *Unspecified*

Sium suave

Roots collected in early spring or late fall, roasted, fried, or eaten raw. (109:61) **Klamath** *Sauce & Relish* Herbage eaten as a relish. (as *S. cicutaefolium* 45:102) **Montana Indian** *Sauce & Relish* Herbage has an aromatic flavor and eaten as a relish. (as *S. cicutaefolium* 19:24) **Okanagan-Colville** *Unspecified* Roots eaten raw in the early spring. (188:71) **Okanagon** *Staple* Roots used as a principal food. (as *S. lineare* 178:238) **Shuswap** *Unspecified* Crispy, delicious roots eaten raw or steamed. (123:57) **Thompson** *Dried Food* Roots dug in the spring and fall, washed, pit cooked, and dried for later use. (187:159) *Forage* Rootstocks or rhizomes eaten by cattle. *Unspecified* Rootstocks or rhizomes eaten. (as *S. laeve* 164:482) Roots sometimes eaten raw. (187:159)

Smilax bona-nox, Saw Greenbrier
Choctaw *Bread & Cake* Tuberous roots dried, ground into flour, and used to make bread. **Houma** *Bread & Cake* Tuberous roots dried, ground into flour, and used to make bread. (158:58)

Smilax glauca, Cat Greenbrier
Cherokee *Unspecified* Roots used for food. (80:37)

Smilax herbacea, Smooth Carrionflower
Cherokee *Unspecified* Roots used for food.

(80:37) **Meskwaki** *Fruit* Fruit of the carrion flower used as food. (152:262) **Omaha** *Fruit* Fruits eaten for their pleasant taste. (70:71)

Smilax laurifolia, Laurel Greenbrier
Choctaw *Bread & Cake* Pounded roots made into cakes and fried in grease. (25:8) Tuberous roots dried, ground into flour, and used to make bread. **Houma** *Bread & Cake* Tuberous roots dried, ground into flour, and used to make bread. (158:58)

Smilax pseudochina, Bamboovine
Cherokee *Unspecified* Roots used for food. (as *S. tamnifolia* 80:37)

Smilax rotundifolia, Roundleaf
  Greenbrier
Cherokee *Unspecified* Roots used for food. (80:37)

Solanum douglasii, Greenspot
  Nightshade
Luiseño *Vegetable* Leaves used for greens. (155:229)

Solanum elaeagnifolium, Silverleaf
  Nightshade
Cochiti *Substitution Food* Fruits used as a substitute for rennet in curdling milk. (32:51) **Navajo** *Cooking Agent* Dried or fresh berries added to goat's milk to make it curdle for cheese. (165:222) **Pima** *Fruit* Berries powdered, placed in milk, a piece of rabbit or cow stomach added, and liquid eaten as cheese. (47:88) *Substitution Food* Berries used as a substitute for rennet. (146:78) **Spanish American** *Substitution Food* Fruits used as a substitute for rennet in curdling milk. (32:51) **Zuni** *Beverage* Berries mixed with curdled goat milk and considered a delicious beverage. (166:70)

Solanum fendleri, Fendler's Horsenettle
Apache, Chiricahua & Mescalero *Bread & Cake* Plant dried, stored, ground into flour, and used to make bread. (33:42) **Keresan** *Starvation Food* Raw potatoes mixed with clay or boiled with clay and eaten only in times of ex-

treme scarcity. (198:562) **Pueblo** *Unspecified* Tubers eaten. (32:51) **Sia** *Vegetable* Potatoes eaten raw or cooked with clay to counteract the astringency. (199:107) **Zuni** *Unspecified* Raw tubers used for food. After every mouthful of potato, a bite of white clay was taken to counteract the unpleasant astringent effect of the potato in the mouth. (166:71)

Solanum jamesii, Wild Potato
Apache, Chiricahua & Mescalero *Vegetable* Unpeeled potatoes boiled and eaten. (33:42) **Hopi** *Cooking Agent* Small potatoes used to make yeast. (190:166) *Unspecified* Plant boiled and eaten. (56:19) Tubers boiled and eaten with magnesia clay. (120:20) **Isleta** *Vegetable* Small tubers cooked as potatoes. (100:43) **Keres, Western** *Vegetable* Small tubers used for food. (171:70) **Keresan** *Starvation Food* Raw potatoes mixed with clay or boiled with clay and eaten only in times of extreme scarcity. (198:562) **Navajo** *Vegetable* Tubers eaten raw, boiled, or baked. (55:75) Potatoes mixed with white clay to remove the astringent effect on the mouth and eaten like mush. (165:221) **Navajo, Ramah** *Vegetable* Potato boiled with clay. *Winter Use Food* Potato dug with a stick, halved, sun dried, and stored in a pit for winter. (191:43) **Sia** *Vegetable* Potatoes eaten raw or cooked with clay to counteract the astringency. (199:107) **Tewa** *Vegetable* Tubers eaten. (138:73)

Solanum nigrum, Black Nightshade
Cherokee *Vegetable* Young leaves used as a potherb. (80:51) Used as the most relished potherb. (203:74) **Mendocino Indian** *Fruit* Fully ripe berries used for food. (41:387) **Tubatulabal** *Fruit* Berries used for food. (193:15)

Solanum triflorum, Cutleaf Nightshade
Acoma *Starvation Food* Berries eaten in times of food shortages. (32:52) **Keres, Western** *Starvation Food* Berries eaten in times of famine. (171:70) **Laguna** *Starvation Food* Berries eaten in times of food shortages. (32:52) **Zuni** *Sauce & Relish* Ripe fruit boiled, ground, mixed with ground chile and salt, and eaten as a condiment with mush or bread. (166:71)

Solanum tuberosum, Irish Potato
Abnaki *Vegetable* Tubers eaten. (144:171) **Cherokee** *Vegetable* Roots used for food. (80:51) **Haisla & Hanaksiala** *Vegetable* Tubers eaten. (43:293) **Iroquois** *Unspecified* Tubers eaten. (196:120) **Kitasoo** *Vegetable* Tubers eaten. (43:350) **Makah** *Vegetable* Potatoes dipped in oil and eaten with smoked fish. (67:314) **Menominee** *Vegetable* Deep purple potatoes used for food. (151:72) **Meskwaki** *Vegetable* Potatoes used for food. (152:264) **Navajo, Ramah** *Pie & Pudding* Cut, dried potatoes boiled into a pudding, in the winter months. *Winter Use Food* Potatoes cultivated, harvested, and stored in a root cellar for winter use. (191:43) **Ojibwa** *Soup* Potato cultivated and prized for use in soups. *Vegetable* Potato cultivated and always firm and crisp when cooked. (153:410) **Oweekeno** *Vegetable* Tubers eaten. (43:119) **Seminole** *Vegetable* Tubers eaten. (169:466) **Sia** *Vegetable* Cultivated potatoes used for food. (199:106)

Solanum umbelliferum, Bluewitch Nightshade
Costanoan *Fruit* Fruits eaten for food. (21:253)

Solanum xantii, Purple Nightshade
Miwok *Fruit* Raw berries used for food. (12:162)

Solidago canadensis, Canada Goldenrod
Gosiute *Unspecified* Seeds used for food. (39:382) **Navajo, Kayenta** *Unspecified* Roots steeped or eaten. (205:50)

Solidago nemoralis, Dyersweed Goldenrod
Gosiute *Unspecified* Seeds used for food. (39:382)

Solidago spectabilis, Nevada Goldenrod
Gosiute *Unspecified* Seeds used for food. (39:382)

Sonchus asper

Sonchus asper, Spiny Sowthistle
Luiseño *Vegetable* Plant used for greens.
(155:228) **Mohave** *Starvation Food* Young
shoots roasted and eaten as a famine food.
(37:201) **Pima** *Unspecified* Tender leaves
rubbed between the palms and eaten raw.
Stalks peeled and eaten raw like celery. *Vegetable* Tender leaves cooked as greens. (47:106)
Pima, Gila River *Unspecified* Leaves eaten
raw. (133:7)

Sonchus oleraceus, Common Sowthistle
Houma *Fodder* Plants used for hog feed.
(158:64) **Kamia** *Vegetable* Boiled leaves used
for food as greens. (62:24) **Pima** *Unspecified*
Leaves and stems rubbed between the palms of
the hands and eaten raw. (47:106) **Pima, Gila
River** *Unspecified* Leaves eaten raw and boiled.
(133:7) **Yaqui** *Vegetable* Tender, young leaves
boiled in salted water with chile and eaten as
greens. (47:106)

Sophora nuttalliana, Silky Sophora
Acoma *Special Food* Sweet roots chewed as a
delicacy. (as *S. serecia* 32:33) **Keres, Western**
Sweetener Roots chewed for the sweet taste. (as
S. sericea 171:71) **Laguna** *Special Food* Sweet

roots chewed as a delicacy. (as *S. serecia* 32:33)
Navajo *Forage* Plant used by sheep for forage.
(as *S. sericea* 55:58) **San Felipe** *Special Food*
Sweet roots chewed as a delicacy. (as *S. serecia*
32:33)

Sorbus americana, American
Mountainash
Algonquin, Quebec *Fruit* Fruit used for food.
(as *Pyrus americana* 18:90) **Montagnais** *Forage* Berries eaten by bears. *Fruit* Berries used
for food. (156:313) **Ojibwa** *Fruit* Fruit used for
food. (as *Pyrus sambucifolia* 135:236)

Sorbus sitchensis, Western
Mountainash
Thompson *Dried Food* Berries sometimes
dried for storage. *Fruit* Berries boiled and eaten
alone. *Soup* Berries boiled and eaten in soups
such as salmon head soup. *Spice* Berries cooked
with marmot to flavor meat, and a cluster of
berries was added to the top of a jar of blueberries as a flavor when canning. *Winter Use
Food* Berries usually buried and kept fresh.
(187:273)

Sorbus sitchensis var. grayi, Gray's
Mountainash
Heiltzuk *Forage* Considered a food for black
bears. (43:116)

Sorbus sitchensis var. sitchensis,
Sitka Mountainash
Okanagon *Fruit* Fruits occasionally used for
food. **Thompson** *Fruit* Fruits occasionally used
for food. (as *Pyrus sitchensis* 125:38) Fruits
eaten except by some of the Upper Thompsons.
(as *Pyrus sitchensis* 164:488)

Sorghum bicolor ssp. bicolor,
Broomcorn
Hopi *Sauce & Relish* Used as a sweet syrup. (as
S. vulgare 200:66)

Sorghum halepense, Johnson Grass
Kiowa *Fodder* Used as a fodder for horses.
(192:16)

Sparganium eurycarpum, Broad-
fruit Burreed
Klamath *Unspecified* Rootstocks used for food.
Bulb at base of stem used for food. (45:90)
Okanagan-Colville *Fodder* Used as hay for
cattle. (188:57)

Spartina alterniflora, Smooth
Cordgrass
Iroquois *Forage* Used as forage. (142:106)

***Sphaeralcea angustifolia* ssp.
*lobata***, Copper Globemallow
Navajo *Unspecified* Seeds used for food. (as *S.
lobata* 55:63)

Sphaeralcea coccinea, Scarlet
Globemallow
Navajo, Kayenta *Beverage* Used to make a
beverage. (205:31)

***Sphaeralcea coccinea* ssp. *coc-
cinea***, Scarlet Globemallow
Navajo *Starvation Food* Roots chewed during
food shortages. (as *Malvastrum coccineum*
55:62)

***Sphagnum* sp.**
Carrier *Beverage* Leaves used to make tea.
(diaper moss 31:87) **Haisla & Hanaksiala**
Forage Plant eaten by grizzly bears. (sphagnum
moss 43:148)

Spiraea alba* var. *latifolia, White
Meadowsweet
Abnaki *Beverage* Used to make tea. (as *S. latifolia* 144:152) Leaves used to make tea. (as *S.
latifolia* 144:168)

Spiraea betulifolia, White Spirea
Thompson *Beverage* Plant used to make a tea-
like beverage. (187:274)

Spiraea douglasii, Douglas's Spirea
Thompson *Forage* Dried flower spikes eaten by
grouse. (187:274)

Spiraea ×pyramidata, Pyramid
Spirea
Thompson *Beverage* Flowers, stems, and
leaves boiled and drunk as a tea. (164:494)

Spiraea stevenii, Beauverd Spirea
Tanana, Upper *Beverage* Fresh or dried leaves
made into tea. (as *S. beauverdiana* 102:8)

***Spiranthes* sp.**, Spiral Orchid
Paiute *Unspecified* Roots used for food.
(167:244)

Sporobolus airoides, Alkali Sacaton
Hopi *Starvation Food* Grain occasionally used
for food during famines. (200:66)

Sporobolus contractus, Spike
Dropseed
Apache, Western *Porridge* Seeds ground,
mixed with cornmeal and water, and made into
a mush. (as *S. strictus* 26:189) **Apache, White
Mountain** *Bread & Cake* Seeds ground and
used to make bread and pones. *Porridge* Seeds
ground, mixed with meal and water, and eaten
as mush. (as *S. strictus* 136:149) **Navajo** *Bread
& Cake* Seeds used to make bread. (165:223)

Sporobolus cryptandrus, Sand
Dropseed
Apache, Chiricahua & Mescalero *Bread &
Cake* Seeds threshed, winnowed, ground, and
the flour used to make bread. *Porridge* Seeds
boiled and eaten as porridge. (33:48) **Hopi**
Bread & Cake Plant used to make bread. *Pie &
Pudding* Plant used to make pudding. (42:364)
Keres, Western *Fodder* Grass considered good
pony feed. (171:72) **Kiowa** *Fodder* Foliage was
a valuable fodder. (as *Vilfa cryptandra* 192:17)
Navajo *Bread & Cake* Seeds ground to make
dumplings, rolls, griddle cakes, and tortillas.
(55:26) *Forage* Used as forage by animals.
(90:163) **Navajo, Ramah** *Porridge* Ground
seeds alone or with corn made into mush or
bread. (191:17)

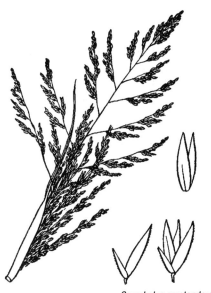

Sporobolus cryptandrus

Sporobolus flexuosus, Mesa
Dropseed
Hopi *Starvation Food* Grain occasionally used
for food during famines. (200:66)

Sporobolus giganteus, Giant
Dropseed
Hopi *Porridge* Seeds threshed, ground with
corn into fine meal and used to make a mush.
(120:20) *Spice* Seeds used as flavoring for
cornmeal. (42:365)

Sporobolus wrightii, Giant Sacaton
Navajo, Ramah *Porridge* Ground seeds alone
or with corn made into mush or bread. (191:17)
Papago *Dried Food* Seeds basket winnowed,
parched, sun dried, cooked, stored, and used
for food. (34:24)

Stachys albens, Whitestem Hedgenettle
Kawaiisu *Spice* Bunched leaves used as "cork"
for the basketry water bottle, "it gives a good
taste to the water." (206:65)

Stachys ciliata, Great Hedgenettle
Saanich *Forage* Roots eaten by wounded deer.
(as *S. cooleyae* 182:84)

Stachys mexicana, Emerson Betony
Quinault *Unspecified* Honey sucked out of the
blossoms and used for food. (as *S. ciliata* 79:45)

Stachys palustris, Marsh Hedgenettle
Gosiute *Unspecified* Seeds used for food.
(39:383)

Stanleya albescens, White Princesplume
Hopi *Unspecified* Leaves boiled and eaten.
(56:15) Boiled and eaten. (190:163) *Vegetable*
Eaten as greens in the spring. (200:77)

Stanleya pinnata, Desert Princesplume
Havasupai *Vegetable* Leaves boiled two or
three times to remove poisons and eaten.
(197:220) Young, fresh, tender leaves boiled,
drained, balled into individual portions, and
served. (197:66) **Hopi** *Vegetable* Boiled plant
used for greens in the spring. (42:366) Eaten as
greens in the spring. (200:77) **Kawaiisu** *Vege-table* Leaves and stems boiled, squeezed out in
cold water to remove the bitterness, fried in
grease, and eaten. (206:65) **Tewa** *Vegetable*
Boiled plant used for greens in the spring.
(42:366)

Stellaria media, Common Chickweed
Iroquois *Forage* Plant eaten by chickens.
(142:86)

Stenocereus thurberi, Organ Pipe
Cactus
Apache, Chiricahua & Mescalero *Fruit* Fruit
used for food. (as *Lemaireocereus thurberi*
33:40) **Papago** *Beverage* Juice used as a cere-monial drink. (as *Lemaireocereus thurberi*
34:26) *Bread & Cake* Seeds parched, stored,
and used to make meal cakes. *Cooking Agent*
Seeds parched, ground, water added, and oil
extracted. (as *Lemaireocereus thurberi* 34:22)
Dried Food Fruits dried, stored in jars, and
used as sweets. (as *Lemaireocereus thurberi*
34:46) *Fodder* Seeds parched and used as a
chicken feed. *Preserves* Pulp boiled to a sweet,
sticky mass and used like raspberry jam. Juice
made into cactus jam and used as the most im-portant sweet in the diet. (as *Lemaireocereus*

thurberi 34:22) Fruits made into jam. *Sauce & Relish* Fruits made into a syrup. (as *Lemaireocereus thurberi* 34:46) *Staple* Seeds made into flour and used for food. *Unspecified* Pulp eaten fresh. (as *Lemaireocereus thurberi* 34:22) Fruits and seeds used for food. (as *Lemaireocereus thurberi* 36:59) **Papago & Pima** *Beverage* Fruit used to make wine. (as *Lemaireocereus thurberi* 35:10) Juice used to make wine. (as *Lemaireocereus thurberi* 35:34) *Candy* Used to make candy. (as *Lemaireocereus thurberi* 35:17) *Fruit* Fruit used for food. (as *Lemaireocereus thurberi* 35:11) *Porridge* Seeds mixed with the pulp, formed into a paste, and eaten. (as *Lemaireocereus thurberi* 35:7) *Preserves* Fruit boiled, without sugar, to make preserves. (as *Lemaireocereus thurberi* 35:17) *Sauce & Relish* Fruit used to make syrup. (as *Lemaireocereus thurberi* 35:11) **Seri** *Fruit* Fruits eaten for food. *Porridge* Seeds ground to a powder and made into a meal or paste. (as *Lemaireocereus thurberi* 50:134)

Stephanomeria pauciflora, Brownplume Wirelettuce
Kawaiisu *Candy* Thick liquid used as chewing gum. (206:65) **Navajo, Kayenta** *Candy* Used as chewing gum. (205:50) **Navajo, Ramah** *Candy* Root used for chewing gum. (191:53)

Sticta glomulifera, Tree Lichen
Ojibwa *Unspecified* Boiled until the lichens coagulate like scrambled eggs. (153:406)

Stipa robusta, Sleepygrass
Navajo, Ramah *Fodder* Used for sheep and horse feed. (191:17)

Stipa speciosa, Desert Needlegrass
Kawaiisu *Unspecified* Seeds used for food. When ripe in June, the grass was cut off in bunches, tied together with stems of the grass, and thrown over the shoulder into the carrying basket suspended on one's back. Two procedures were used in preparing the seeds for food. First, the grass was spread out on a flat rock, where it was allowed to dry a half day and then threshed by burning. If the fire burned too

quickly, green spear grass was added to slow it down. The burned stalks were stirred and lifted with a green stick so that the seeds would fall out. The seeds were gathered and winnowed by being poured from one basket to another. Boiled, the seeds swelled "like rice." A cupful would fill a pot. Second, the grass was dried for a day or two and the seeds beaten out. They would be boiled whole or first pounded to a meal and then cooked. (206:66) **Paiute** *Porridge* Seeds used to make mush. (167:243)

Streptanthus cordatus, Heartleaf Twistflower
Navajo, Kayenta *Vegetable* Used for greens in foods. (205:25)

Streptopus amplexifolius, Claspleaf Twistedstalk
Alaska Native *Fruit* Berries used for food. *Vegetable* Young, tender shoots used in salads. (85:69) **Cherokee** *Vegetable* Leaves cooked and eaten as greens. (80:59) **Hesquiat** *Forage* Eaten by deer. (185:55) **Montagnais** *Forage* Berries and roots eaten by snakes. (156:314) **Nitinaht** *Forage* Berries eaten by wolves. (186:86) **Okanagon** *Fruit* Bright-colored berries used for food. (125:38) **Oweekeno** *Forage*

Streptopus amplexifolius

Berries eaten by frogs. (43:79) **Thompson** *Fruit* Bright-colored berries used for food. (125:38) Berries eaten in large quantities. (164:486)

Streptopus roseus, Rosy Twistedstalk
Cherokee *Unspecified* Young growth boiled, fried, and eaten. (204:251) *Vegetable* Leaves cooked and eaten as greens. (80:59) Leaves and stalks mixed with wanegedum (angelico) and sweet salad and cooked as greens. *Winter Use Food* Leaves and stalks mixed with wanegedum (angelico) and sweet salad and canned for future use. (as *S. roseus* 126:48)

Strophostyles helvula, Trailing Fuzzybean
Choctaw *Unspecified* Boiled, mashed roots used for food. (as *Phaseolus diversifolius* 25:8)

Suaeda arborescens
Pima *Spice* Added as flavoring to greens or cactus fruits. (146:78)

Suaeda calceoliformis, Pursh Seepweed
Gosiute *Unspecified* Seeds used for food. (as *S. depressa* 39:383) **Paiute** *Staple* Seeds parched, ground, and eaten as meal. (as *S. depressa* var. *erecta* 104:98) **Paiute, Northern** *Unspecified* Seeds used for food. (as *S. depressa* 59:47)

Suaeda moquinii, Mojave Seablite
Navajo *Porridge* Seeds boiled into a gruel. (as *S. torreyana* 55:45) **Pima, Gila River** *Unspecified* Leaves pit roasted and eaten. (133:7)

Suaeda suffrutescens, Desert Seepweed
Papago *Spice* Leaves and stalks lined inside cooking holes to give cactus fruits a salty flavor. **Pima** *Spice* Leaves and stalks lined inside cooking holes to give cactus fruits a salty flavor. (as *Dondia suffrutescens* 95:264) Added as flavoring to greens or cactus fruits. (146:78)

Symphoricarpos albus, Common Snowberry
Okanagan-Colville *Forage* Berries eaten by ruffed grouse and other birds. (188:95) **Squaxin** *Dried Food* Berries dried and used for food. (79:47)

Symphoricarpos albus var. *laevigatus*, Common Snowberry
Haisla & Hanaksiala *Forage* Berries eaten by crows and bears. (43:231)

Symphoricarpos occidentalis, Western Snowberry
Blackfoot *Starvation Food* Fruits eaten in times of scarcity. (97:55) **Sioux** *Fruit* Fruit used for food. (19:24)

Symplocarpus foetidus, Skunk Cabbage
Iroquois *Vegetable* Young leaves and shoots cooked and seasoned with salt, pepper, or butter. (196:118)

Tacca leontopetaloides, Batflower
Hawaiian *Unspecified* Tubers grated, roasted, and eaten. (as *T. pinnatifida* 112:68)

Taraxacum californicum, California
  Dandelion
Cahuilla *Vegetable* Stems and leaves gathered and eaten in spring and early summer. (15:141)

Taraxacum officinale, Common
  Dandelion
Apache, Chiricahua & Mescalero *Spice* Flower used to flavor drinks and make them stronger. (33:51) **Cherokee** *Vegetable* Leaves and stems used for potherbs and salads. (126:35) **Iroquois** *Beverage* Used to make wine. (142:99) *Vegetable* Young plants boiled and eaten as greens. (124:93) Cooked and seasoned with salt, pepper, or butter. (196:118) **Kiowa** *Vegetable* Young leaves used as greens. (192:62) **Malecite** *Unspecified* Species used for food. (160:6) **Menominee** *Vegetable* Leaves cooked with maple sap vinegar for a dish of greens. (151:65) **Meskwaki** *Vegetable* Spring leaves used as greens and cooked with pork. (152:257) **Micmac** *Vegetable* Leaves used as greens in food. (159:258) **Mohegan** *Unspecified* Cooked and used for food. (176:83) **Ojibwa** *Vegetable* Young leaves gathered in spring and cooked as greens with pork or venison and maple sap vinegar. (153:399) **Okanagan-Colville** *Vegetable* Leaves eaten as greens. (188:85) **Papago** *Vegetable* Cooked or uncooked leaves eaten as greens. (34:14) **Potawatomi** *Unspecified* Leaves cooked with maple sap vinegar and often combined with pork or deer meat. (154:98) **Ute** *Unspecified* Leaves formerly used as food. (38:36)

**Taraxacum officinale ssp. vul-
  gare**, Common Dandelion
Tewa *Vegetable* Young plants eaten as greens. (as *T. taraxacum* 138:61)

Taxus brevifolia, Pacific Yew
Karok *Fruit* Berries eaten one at a time. (6:57)
Mendocino Indian *Fruit* Red, fleshy berries used for food. (41:305)

Taxus canadensis, Canada Yew
Iroquois *Beverage* Fruits, leaves, cold water, and maple water fermented into a "little beer." (141:34) **Penobscot** *Beverage* Twigs used to make a beverage. (as *T. minor* 156:309)

Thalia geniculata, Bent Alligatorflag
Seminole *Unspecified* Plant used for food. (169:505)

Thalictrum occidentale, Western
  Meadowrue
Blackfoot *Spice* Fruit used to spice pemmican, dried meat, and broths. (86:105)

Thalictrum pubescens, King of the
  Meadow
Montagnais *Spice* Leaves used to flavor salmon. (as *T. polygamum* 156:315)

**Thelesperma filifolium var. fili-
  folium**, Stiff Greenthread
Keres, Western *Beverage* Infusion of plant used as a beverage. (as *Theleosperma trifidum* 171:72) **Tewa** *Beverage* Leaves steeped and the tea drunk as a beverage. (as *Thelesperma trifidum* 138:61)

Thelesperma longipes, Longstalk
  Greenthread
Isleta *Beverage* Young plant leaves boiled to make a beverage resembling commercial tea. *Winter Use Food* Plants stored well for future use. (100:43) **Navajo** *Substitution Food* Leaves and stems used as a substitute for tea. (55:89)

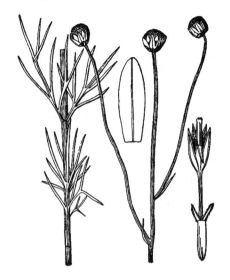

Thelesperma megapotamicum

Thelesperma megapotamicum, Hopi Tea Greenthread

Apache, Chiricahua & Mescalero *Beverage* Leaves and young stems boiled to make a non-intoxicating beverage. Fresh or stored portions boiled in water and liquid consumed with or without sugar. (as *T. gracile* 33:53) **Hopi** *Beverage* Flowers used to make a beverage. (as *T. gracile* 56:15) Used to make coffee. (as *T. gracile* 190:168) Flowers and tips of young leaves dried, boiled, and used to make tea. (as *T. gracile* 200:98) **Keres, Western** *Beverage* Infusion of plant used as a beverage. (as *Theleosperma gracile* 171:72) **Keresan** *Beverage* Leaves and roots boiled to make tea. (as *Thelesperma gracile* 198:563) **Navajo** *Substitution Food* Leaves and stems used as a substitute for tea. (as *T. gracile* 55:89) **Navajo, Ramah** *Beverage* Decoction of leaves and flowers, with lots of sugar, used as a tea. (191:53) **Tewa** *Beverage* Leaves steeped and the tea drunk as a beverage. (as *T. gracile* 138:61)

Thelesperma subnudum, Sand Fringedpod

Hopi *Beverage* Flowers and tips of young leaves dried, boiled, and used to make tea. (200:98)

Thelypodium integrifolium ssp. *integrifolium*, Entireleaved Thelypody

Mohave *Starvation Food* Young shoots roasted and eaten as a famine food. (as *T. lilacinum* 37:201)

Thelypodium wrightii ssp. *wrightii*, Wright's Thelypody

Pueblo *Dried Food* Young plants boiled, pressed, rolled into balls, dried, and stored for winter use. *Soup* Plant made into a stew with wild onions, wild celery, tallow, or bits of meat. *Unspecified* Young plants boiled, pressed, rolled into balls, and eaten. *Vegetable* Young plants boiled with a pinch of salt and eaten as greens. (as *Stanleyella wrightii* 32:25) **Tewa** *Unspecified* Species used for food. (as *Stanleyella wrightii* 138:61)

Theobroma cacao, Cacao

Haisla & Hanaksiala *Beverage* Used to make a beverage. (43:294)

Thlaspi arvense, Field Pennycress

Cherokee *Vegetable* Leaves used for food. (126:37) **Havasupai** *Unspecified* Seeds used in a variety of ways. (197:221)

Thlaspi montanum, Alpine Pennycress

Havasupai *Unspecified* Seeds used in a variety of ways. (197:221)

Thuja occidentalis, Eastern Arborvitae

Chippewa *Beverage* Leaves used to make a hot, tea-like beverage. (71:123) **Ojibwa** *Beverage* Leaves steeped for tea. (as *Thuga canadensis* 5:2234)

Thuja plicata, Western Red Cedar

Hesquiat *Starvation Food* Branches used to make fish traps became "fish flavored" and the sticks were boiled for broth. (185:35) **Kwakiutl, Southern** *Candy* Pitch used as chewing gum. (183:293) **Montana Indian** *Dried Food* Spring cambium pressed into cakes and dried for storage. *Unspecified* Spring cambium eaten fresh. (19:25) **Salish, Coast** *Dried Food* Cambium dried and eaten in spring. *Unspecified* Cambium eaten fresh in spring. (182:71)

Thysanocarpus curvipes, Sand
    Fringepod
Mendocino Indian *Staple* Seeds used in pinole mixtures. (as *T. elegans* 41:352)

Tilia americana, American Basswood
Chippewa *Vegetable* Young twigs and buds cooked as greens or eaten raw. (71:136)

Tolmiea menziesii, Youth on Age
Makah *Unspecified* Sprouts eaten raw in early spring. (79:31)

Torreya californica, California Nutmeg
Mendocino Indian *Unspecified* Whole nuts roasted and used for food. (as *Tumion californicum* 41:305)

Toxicodendron diversilobum,
    Pacific Poison Oak
Karok *Candy* Plant chewed like tobacco, "just to raise heck." (6:58) **Mendocino Indian** *Forage* Fruits eaten by yellowhammers and squirrels as forage. Fruits and leaves eaten by hogs as forage. (as *Rhus diversiloba* 41:364)

Tradescantia occidentalis, Prairie
    Spiderwort
Acoma *Unspecified* Tender shoots eaten without preparation. (32:53) **Hopi** *Vegetable* Plant used for greens. (42:369) **Keres, Western** *Unspecified* Tender shoots eaten for food. (171:73) **Laguna** *Unspecified* Tender shoots eaten without preparation. (32:53)

Tradescantia virginiana, Virginia
    Spiderwort
Cherokee *Unspecified* Young growth parboiled, fried, frequently mixed with other greens, and eaten. (204:252) *Vegetable* Leaves and stems mixed with other greens or grease and parboiled until tender. (126:33)

Tragopogon porrifolius, Salsify
Navajo *Beverage* Latex used as milk. (90:156)

Okanagon *Unspecified* Stems broken at the base and hardened juice chewed for food. **Thompson** *Unspecified* Stems broken at the base and hardened juice chewed for food. (125:38) **Thompson, Upper (Nicola Band)** *Unspecified* Latex exposed to air, chewed, and swallowed. **Thompson, Upper (Spences Bridge)** *Unspecified* Latex exposed to air, chewed, and swallowed. (164:484)

Tragopogon pratensis, Meadow
    Salsify
Okanagan-Colville *Forage* Plant eaten by deer, horses, and cattle. (188:85)

Trianthema portulacastrum,
    Desert Horsepurslane
Pima *Vegetable* Plants cooked and eaten as greens in summer. (47:64)

Trichostema lanceolatum, Vinegar
    Weed
Kawaiisu *Beverage* Leaves used to make a nonmedicinal beverage. (206:67)

Tridens muticus var. muticus,
    Rough Tridens
Navajo, Ramah *Fodder* Used for sheep and horse feed. (as *Triodia mutica* 191:17)

Trifolium albopurpureum, Rancheria Clover
Pomo, Kashaya *Unspecified* Leaves eaten alone or with salt or peppernut cakes. (72:36)

Trifolium bifidum, Notchleaf Clover
Mendocino Indian *Staple* Seeds eaten as a pinole. *Unspecified* Eaten sparingly when young. (41:360)

Trifolium ciliolatum, Foothill Clover
Luiseño *Unspecified* Plant eaten both cooked and raw. Seeds used for food. (155:231) **Miwok** *Dried Food* Steamed clover dried for later use. Dried clover stored for later use. *Unspecified* Raw or steamed clover used for food. (12:160) **Wailaki** *Forage* Eaten by horses with impunity.

Unspecified Species used for food. **Yokia** *Unspecified* Species used for food. (41:360)

Trifolium cyathiferum, Cup Clover
Mendocino Indian *Unspecified* Flowers eaten as food. (41:361)

Trifolium dichotomum, Branched
    Indian Clover
Mendocino Indian *Staple* Seeds eaten as a pinole. *Unspecified* Young leaves sparingly eaten. (41:361)

Trifolium fucatum, Bull Clover
Mendocino Indian *Unspecified* Herbage used for food. Flowers and seedpods used for food. Seeds eaten raw. (as *T. virescens* 41:361) **Pomo, Kashaya** *Unspecified* Sweet flowers and leaves eaten alone, with salt or peppernut cakes. (72:35)

Trifolium gracilentum, Pinpoint
    Clover
Luiseño *Unspecified* Plant eaten both cooked and raw. (155:231)

Trifolium microcephalum, Small-
    head Clover
Luiseño *Unspecified* Plant cooked and eaten. (155:231)

Trifolium obtusiflorum, Clammy
    Clover
Luiseño *Unspecified* Plant cooked and eaten. (155:231) **Mendocino Indian** *Unspecified* Leaves eaten after acid exudation washed away. (41:361)

Trifolium pratense, Red Clover
Shuswap *Fodder* Used with timothy as a good feed for cows. (123:64) **Thompson** *Fodder* Plant used as food for livestock. (187:224)

Trifolium variegatum, Whitetip Clover
Mendocino Indian *Vegetable* Eaten considerably as greens. (41:361) **Pomo, Kashaya** *Unspecified* Sweet flowers and leaves eaten alone, with salt or peppernut cakes. (72:36)

Trifolium willdenowii, Tomcat Clover
Luiseño *Unspecified* Plant eaten cooked or raw. Seeds used for food. (as *T. tridentatum* 155:231) **Miwok** *Unspecified* Raw or steamed leaves eaten before plant bloomed. Raw or steamed buds eaten before plant bloomed. (as *T. tridentatum* 12:160) *Winter Use Food* Steamed, dried leaves soaked in water or boiled before eating in winter. (as *T. tridentatum* 12:161) **Paiute** *Unspecified* Seeds used for food. *Vegetable* Whole plant used, without cooking, as greens. (as *T. tridentatum* 167:243) Young, tender plants eaten uncooked as greens. (as *T. tridentatum* 167:244)

Trifolium wormskioldii, Cow Clover
Bella Coola *Unspecified* White, brittle roots formerly pit steamed or boiled and eaten with eulachon (candlefish) grease and stink salmon. (184:205) **Haisla & Hanaksiala** *Unspecified* Rhizomes used for food. (43:251) **Hesquiat** *Unspecified* Steamed or boiled rhizomes eaten with oil or stink salmon eggs. Stink salmon eggs made by placing salmon roe in a codfish stomach, plugging it with a cedarwood cork, and allowing the eggs to ferment. (185:68) **Kawaiisu** *Vegetable* Green leaves eaten raw with salt. (206:68) **Kitasoo** *Unspecified* Rhizomes used for food. (43:337) **Kwakiutl, Southern** *Vegetable* Thin, wiry roots dried, steamed, or boiled, dipped in oil, and eaten as vegetables. (183:285) **Makah** *Unspecified* Roots steamed and eaten. (as *T. fimbriatum* 79:38) **Mendocino Indian** *Unspecified* Flowers and leaves used for food. (41:362) **Miwok** *Beverage* Wilted, dry leaves soaked and stirred in cold water to make a sour drink. *Unspecified* Leaves and flowers, never cooked or dried, eaten raw. (as *T. involucratum* 12:160) **Nitinaht** *Dried Food* Rhizomes steam cooked, dried, resteamed, dipped in oil, and eaten in winter. (186:110) *Unspecified* Roots eaten raw or cooked with fermented salmon eggs. (67:281) Rhizomes eaten as accompaniments to cooked duck. (186:131) Rhizomes steam cooked, cooled, and eaten immediately. (186:110) *Vegetable* Rhizomes formerly steamed, dried, and used as a vegetable food in winter. (186:63) **Nuxalkmc** *Unspecified*

Rhizomes used for food. (43:251) **Oweekeno** *Unspecified* Rhizomes cooked with riceroot and eaten. (43:102) **Paiute** *Vegetable* Leaves eaten uncooked as greens. (as *T. involucratum* var. *fendlari* 167:244) **Pomo, Kashaya** *Unspecified* Flowers and leaves eaten alone or with salt or peppernut cakes. (72:38) **Tubatulabal** *Unspecified* Leaves and stems used extensively for food. (as *T. involucratum* 193:15)

Triglochin maritimum, Seaside Arrowgrass
Gosiute *Unspecified* Seeds used for food. (39:383) **Klamath** *Beverage* Roasted and used as a substitute for coffee. *Unspecified* Parched plant used for food. (45:90) **Montana Indian** *Unspecified* Seeds used for food. (19:25) **Salish** *Vegetable* Grass-like plant eaten as a vegetable. (185:54)

Trillium petiolatum, Idaho Trillium
Okanagan-Colville *Appetizer* Roots used to make a tea and taken as an appetizer. (188:50)

Trisetum spicatum, Spike Trisetum
Gosiute *Unspecified* Seeds used for food. (as *T. subspicatum* 39:383)

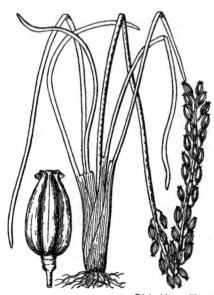
Triglochin maritimum

Triteleia grandiflora, Wild Hyacinth
Okanagan-Colville *Unspecified* Corms used for food. (as *Brodiaea douglasii* 188:41) **Okanagon** *Unspecified* Bulbs formerly steamed and used for food. (as *Hookera douglasii* 125:37) **Pomo** *Vegetable* Potatoes used for food. (as *Brodiaea grandiflora* 117:284) **Thompson** *Unspecified* Bulbs formerly steamed and used for food. (as *Hookera douglasii* 125:37) Bulbs eaten with yellowbell bulbs. (187:131) **Thompson, Upper (Lytton Band)** *Unspecified* Large bulbs eaten. **Thompson, Upper (Spences Bridge)** *Unspecified* Large bulbs eaten. (164:481) **Yana** *Unspecified* Roots roasted and eaten. (as *Brodiaea grandiflora* 147:251)

Triteleia hyacinthina, Hyacinth Brodiaea
Pomo *Unspecified* Bulbs eaten for food. (as *Hookera nyocintlima* var. *lactea* 11:90)

Triteleia hyacinthina var. **hyacinthina**, Fool's Onion
Atsugewi *Unspecified* Cooked in earth oven and used for food. (as *Brodiaea hyacinthina* 61:138) **Mendocino Indian** *Unspecified* Bulbs eaten raw or cooked. (as *Hesperoscordum lacteum* 41:326) **Miwok** *Unspecified* Bulbs steamed in earth oven and used as food. (as *Brodiaea hyacinthina* 12:156) **Neeshenam** *Unspecified* Eaten raw, roasted, or boiled. (as *Hesperoscordium lacteum* 129:377) **Paiute** *Unspecified* Bulbs roasted and used for food. (as *Brodiaea hyacinthina* 104:102) *Vegetable* Root eaten boiled and mashed, like potatoes. (as *Brodiaea hyacinthina* 111:55)

Triteleia ixioides, Prettyface
Miwok *Unspecified* Bulbs used for food. (as *Brodiaea ixioides* 12:156)

Triteleia ixioides ssp. **scabra**, Prettyface
Neeshenam *Unspecified* Eaten raw, roasted, or boiled. (as *Calliproa lutea* 129:377)

Triteleia laxa, Grass Nut
Karok *Unspecified* Bulbs roasted and eaten.

(as *Brodiaea laxa* 148:380) **Pomo** *Unspecified* Bulbs eaten for food. Bulbs eaten for food. Bulbs eaten as potatoes. (11:90) Corms cooked in hot ashes or boiled for food. (as *Brodiaea laxa* 66:12) **Pomo, Kashaya** *Vegetable* Baked or boiled corms eaten like baked or boiled potatoes. (as *Brodiaea laxa* 72:25) **Yuki** *Unspecified* Bulbs used for food. (41:327) Bulbs cooked and used for food. (as *Brodiaea laxa* 49:86)

Triteleia peduncularis, Longray Tripletlily

Mendocino Indian *Unspecified* Bulbs used for food. (41:329) **Pomo** *Unspecified* Bulbs eaten for food. (11:90)

Triticum aestivum, Common Wheat

Apache, White Mountain *Bread & Cake* Seeds used to make bread. (as *T. vulgare* 136:161) **Cahuilla** *Porridge* Parched seeds ground into flour and used to make mush. (15:142) **Haisla & Hanaksiala** *Bread & Cake* Grains used to make bread. *Staple* Grains used for food. (43:208) **Navajo, Ramah** *Fodder* Used for horse feed. *Unspecified* Species used for food. (191:17) **Okanagan-Colville** *Unspecified* Kernels boiled until opened and eaten. (188:57) **Papago** *Bread & Cake* Used for making native breads. (34:38) *Staple* Grains trampled, winnowed, softened with water, pounded, dried, and ground into flour. (34:37) **Pima** *Bread & Cake* Seeds ground into meal, water and salt added, and dough used to make tortillas and cakes. (as *T. sativum* 47:73) Ground into flour and used to make bread. *Porridge* Parched, ground, and eaten as a thin gruel. (as *T. sativum* 146:76) **Pomo, Kashaya** *Porridge* Seed used in mush and to make flour for bread. (72:54) **Sia** *Staple* Corn and wheat, the most important foods, used for food. (as *T. vulgare* 199:106) **Zuni** *Beverage* Dried, ground wheat mixed with water to make a beverage. *Bread & Cake* Wheat made into flour and used to make doughnuts. (as *T. vulgare* 166:71)

Triticum durum, Durum Wheat

Pima *Unspecified* Species used for food. (36:116)

Triticum polonicum, Polish Wheat

Pima *Unspecified* Species used for food. (36:116)

Tsuga canadensis, Eastern Hemlock

Chippewa *Beverage* Leaves used to make a beverage. (53:317) **Iroquois** *Beverage* Branches and maple water used to make tea. (141:36) **Micmac** *Beverage* Bark used to make a beverage. (159:258) **Ojibwa** *Beverage* Leaves made into a tea and used as a beverage and to disguise medicine. (153:408)

Tsuga heterophylla, Western Hemlock

Alaska Native *Bread & Cake* Inner bark roasted in a pit oven, sometimes mixed with dried berries, and pressed into cakes. (85:146) **Bella Coola** *Dried Food* Inner bark steamed overnight, pounded, formed into balls, sun dried, and eaten in winter. (184:198) **Cowlitz** *Spice* Branch tips used to flavor cooking bear meat. (79:17) **Gitksan** *Staple* Cambium pit cooked, pounded, formed into cakes, dried, stored, and eaten as a staple food. *Sweetener* Cambium used as a sweetener for other foods. *Winter Use Food* Inner bark used as a survival food in winter. (73:150) **Haisla** *Dried Food* Cambium cooked in skunk cabbage leaves, pounded, dried, and stored for winter use. (43:180) *Staple* Cambium pit cooked, pounded, formed into cakes, dried, stored, and eaten as a staple food. *Sweetener* Cambium used as a sweetener for other foods. *Winter Use Food* Inner bark used as a survival food in winter. (73:150) **Haisla & Hanaksiala** *Winter Use Food* Cambium dried, pounded, served with oolichan (candlefish) grease and Pacific crabapples, and used as winter food. **Hanaksiala** *Bread & Cake* Cambium formed into cakes, cooked, dried, powdered, mixed with water, grease, and fruit, and eaten. (43:180) **Hesquiat** *Candy* Pitch, from the outside of a crevice, chewed like gum. (185:44) **Kitasoo** *Dried Food* Inner bark boiled and dried for storage. *Unspecified* Inner bark soaked in oolichan (candlefish) grease, drained, cooked, and eaten with sugar. (43:318) **Montana Indian** *Bread & Cake* Cambium made into a coarse bread.

(19:25) **Nitinaht** *Starvation Food* Old leaves eaten sparingly to keep alive when hungry in the woods. (67:238) Light, green branch tips eaten to relieve hunger when lost in the woods. (186:74) *Unspecified* Young growth used for food. (67:238) **Oweekeno** *Dried Food* Inner bark dried for future use. *Unspecified* Inner bark used for food. (43:71) **Salish, Coast** *Dried Food* Cambium dried in sheets and used as a winter food. (182:72) **Wet'suwet'en** *Sweetener* Cambium used as a sweetener for other foods. *Unspecified* Cambium used for food. *Winter Use Food* Inner bark used as a survival food in winter. (73:150)

Typha angustifolia, Narrowleaf Cattail
Hopi *Candy* Mature heads chewed with tallow as gum. (200:64) **Pima** *Bread & Cake* Pollen baked into brownish biscuits and used for food. *Porridge* Pollen mixed with ground wheat, stirred into boiling water, and eaten as a gruel. *Unspecified* Tender, white stalks eaten raw. (47:64)

Typha domingensis, Southern Cattail
Havasupai *Fruit* Ripe, fruiting heads eaten "like corn." (197:208) **Kawaiisu** *Unspecified* White stem bases and brown flowers eaten raw. Green seeds used for food. (206:68) **Paiute, Northern** *Bread & Cake* Seeds gathered into a dough, kneaded, made into flat cakes, and roasted under hot coals. Seeds roasted, winnowed, ground into fine flour, boiled, made into round cakes, and sun dried. (59:48) Dried rhizomes ground into flour, made into mush, and the mush used to make cakes. Pollen mixed with water, kneaded, formed into cakes, and baked. (60:69) *Dried Food* Roots dried for future use. (59:49) Rhizomes peeled and dried for future use. (60:69) *Porridge* Roots dried, ground into flour, and made into a sweet mush. (59:49) Dried rhizomes ground into flour and made into mush. Seeds roasted, ground into a meal, and stone boiled into a mush. (60:69) *Soup* Seeds ground into meal and made into soup. (59:48) *Staple* Seeds roasted, ground into a meal, and eaten with a little water without boiling. (60:69) *Unspecified* Seeds eaten fresh

and raw or cooked. Roots peeled, chewed, juice swallowed, and the stringy pulp spat out. Seeds roasted, ground, and eaten in powder form. (59:48) Roots peeled and eaten fresh. (59:49) Stalks used for food. Rhizomes peeled and eaten fresh. Green spikes eaten fresh. Seeds roasted and eaten. (60:69) **Pima, Gila River** *Unspecified* Roots eaten raw. (133:7)

Typha latifolia, Broadleaf Cattail
Acoma *Unspecified* Roots and tender shoots salted and eaten as food. (32:53) **Alaska Native** *Unspecified* Shoots eaten boiled or roasted. Green flower spikes boiled in salted water and eaten. (85:137) **Apache** *Unspecified* Roots used for food. (32:53) **Apache, Chiricahua & Mescalero** *Unspecified* Rootstocks cooked with meat. (33:47) **Apache, Mescalero** *Unspecified* Species used for food. Stem bases eaten raw or cooked with other foods in early spring. (14:46) **Blackfoot** *Unspecified* Rootstocks used for food. (97:19) **Cahuilla** *Porridge* Pollen used to make cakes and mush. *Staple* Dried roots ground into a meal. (15:142) **Carrier** *Unspecified* Stems peeled and eaten. (31:85) **Chehalis** *Unspecified* Roots and inner stalks baked in ashes and eaten. (79:21) **Clallam** *Unspecified* Fleshy interior eaten raw or pit cooked. (57:197) **Costanoan** *Unspecified*

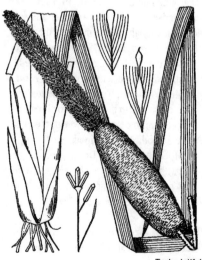

Typha latifolia

Roots used for food. Shoots used for food. Pollen used for food. (21:255) **Cree, Woodlands** *Dried Food* Peeled roots dried over a fire for winter storage. *Unspecified* Fresh stem bases and young shoots eaten in July. Raw roots used for food. Roots taken just before the plant bloomed and eaten raw or dipped in boiling water. (109:62) **Gosiute** *Unspecified* Seeds roasted and used for food. (39:383) **Keres, Western** *Unspecified* Roots and tender shoots eaten with salt for food. (171:73) **Klamath** *Unspecified* Rootstocks used for food. (45:90) **Laguna** *Unspecified* Roots and tender shoots salted and eaten as food. (32:53) **Lakota** *Staple* Pollen used as flour. (106:50) **Mendocino Indian** *Unspecified* Roots and stem bases used for food. (41:310) **Montana Indian** *Unspecified* Young roots and shoots eaten raw. (19:25) **Navajo, Ramah** *Unspecified* Rhizomes eaten raw in summer. Young stalks just appearing above the ground used for food. (191:14) **Ojibwa** *Dried Food* Green flower dried and used for food. *Staple* Pollen used for flour. *Unspecified* Green flower boiled and used for food. (5:2226) **Okanagan-Colville** *Fruit* Young, fruiting heads boiled or roasted and eaten. *Unspecified* Young sprouts used for food. Roots pit cooked and eaten. (188:57) **Paiute** *Unspecified* Seeds used for food. (32:53) **Paiute, Northern** *Bread & Cake* Seeds gathered into a dough, kneaded, made into flat cakes, and roasted under hot coals. Seeds roasted, winnowed, ground into fine flour, boiled, made into round cakes, and sun dried. (59:48) Dried rhizomes ground into flour, made into mush, and the mush used to make cakes. Pollen mixed with water, kneaded, formed into cakes, and baked.

(60:69) *Dried Food* Roots dried for future use. (59:49) Rhizomes peeled and dried for future use. (60:69) *Porridge* Roots dried, ground into flour, and made into a sweet mush. (59:49) Dried rhizomes ground into flour and made into mush. Seeds roasted, ground into a meal and stone boiled into a mush. (60:69) *Soup* Seeds ground into meal and made into soup. (59:48) *Staple* Seeds roasted, ground into a meal, and eaten with a little water without boiling. (60:69) *Unspecified* Seeds eaten fresh and raw or cooked. Roots peeled, chewed, juice swallowed, and the stringy pulp spat out. Seeds roasted, ground and eaten in powder form. (59:48) Roots peeled and eaten fresh. (59:49) Stalks used for food. Rhizomes peeled and eaten fresh. Green spikes eaten fresh. Seeds roasted and eaten. (60:69) **Pomo** *Vegetable* Roots eaten as greens. Young shoots eaten as greens. (11:92) **San Felipe** *Unspecified* Shoots ground, mixed with cornmeal, and used as food. (32:53) **Sioux** *Unspecified* Young roots and shoots eaten raw. (19:25) **Tanana, Upper** *Unspecified* Lower part of stem used for food. (102:9) **Thompson** *Unspecified* Rootstocks used as an important food. (164:482) **Tubatulabal** *Unspecified* Roots used extensively for food. (193:15) **Yuma** *Bread & Cake* Pollen shaped into flat cakes and baked. *Dried Food* Rhizomes dried, stored temporarily, pounded, and boiled with fish. Pollen dried and stored for future use. *Porridge* Young shoots used in combination with corn or tepary meal to make mush. Pollen boiled in water into a thin gruel. *Spice* Pollen used as flavoring. *Unspecified* Fleshy rhizomes eaten without preparation. Young shoots eaten raw. Pollen gathered, sifted, and eaten raw. (37:207)

Ulmus americana, American Elm
Cheyenne *Beverage* Red, inner bark used like coffee. (83:39)

Ulmus rubra, Slippery Elm
Kiowa *Beverage* Inner bark used to brew a "tea." *Winter Use Food* Dried, stored inner bark used to brew a "tea" during the winter. (as *U. fulva* 192:23) **Omaha** *Preservative* Bark cooked with rendering fat as a preservative. (as *U. fulva* 68:325) Inner bark cooked with buffalo fat as a preservative, to prevent it from becoming rancid. (as *U. fulva* 70:76) *Snack Food* Bark cooked with rendering fat and prized by children as special tidbits. *Spice* Bark cooked with rendering fat as a flavoring. (as *U. fulva* 68:325) Inner bark cooked with buffalo fat for its desirable flavor when rendering out the tallow. *Unspecified* Inner bark cooked with buffalo fat and prized by children as tidbits. (as *U. fulva* 70:76)

Ulva lactuca, Sea Lettuce
Pomo, Kashaya *Spice* Peppery seaweed used as flavoring with other seaweeds. (72:127)

Umbellularia californica, California Laurel
Concow *Beverage* Root bark used to make a drink. (41:349) **Costanoan** *Bread & Cake* Kernels roasted or ground into flour for cakes. *Fruit* Fruits eaten raw or boiled. (21:249) **Karok** *Unspecified* Seeds shelled, roasted, and eaten. (6:59) Nuts hulled, stored, parched in ashes, cracked open, and eaten. *Winter Use Food* Nuts hulled and stored in big baskets for winter use. (148:383) **Mendocino Indian** *Bread & Cake* Nuts roasted, shelled, pounded into a small mass, and molded into "bread." *Sauce & Relish* Nuts eaten as a relish. Nuts used as a condiment. *Unspecified* Nuts roasted and eaten. (41:349) **Pomo, Kashaya** *Dried Food* Fruit sun dried. *Fruit* Fleshy end of the husk

eaten raw and the kernel roasted and eaten whole. *Unspecified* Roasted kernels or kernel meal cakes eaten with greens, buckeye meal, acorn meal, mush, or seaweed. *Winter Use Food* Pounded kernel meal used to make sun dried, flat cakes and stored for winter use. (72:90) **Tolowa** *Fruit* Fruit shelled, roasted, and eaten. (6:59) **Yuki** *Unspecified* Species used for food. (48:47) Nuts roasted in hot ashes, cracked, and eaten. (49:87) **Yurok** *Fruit* Fruit used for food. *Unspecified* Seeds baked in the sand under a fire and used for food. (6:59)

Urtica dioica, Stinging Nettle
Iroquois *Vegetable* Cooked and seasoned with salt, pepper, or butter. (196:118) **Makah** *Unspecified* Plant tops used for food. (67:246) **Mohegan** *Vegetable* Combined with pigweed, mustard, plantain, and dock and used as mixed greens. (176:83) **Okanagan-Colville** *Vegetable* New growths dipped in boiling water and eaten as greens. (188:140) **Shuswap** *Beverage* Used for bathing and drinking. (123:70) **Thompson** *Vegetable* Greens cooked as green vegetables. (187:288) Plant tops eaten as a potherb after the arrival of the Chinese. (187:289)

Urtica dioica ssp. gracilis, California Nettle
Alaska Native *Dietary Aid* Fresh, green leaves used as a good source of provitamin A, vitamin C, and some of the minerals. *Substitution Food* Leaves used as a good substitute for spinach. *Unspecified* Leaves boiled and eaten. (as *U. lyalli* 85:73) **Cowichan** *Vegetable* Young stems and leaves boiled and eaten like spinach. (182:90) **Haisla & Hanaksiala** *Preserves* Plant boiled with sugar to make jam. *Unspecified* Young shoots steamed and eaten with bear meat. (43:294) **Hoh** *Vegetable* Plant tops eaten as greens. (as *U. lyallii* 137:61) **Montana Indian** *Vegetable* Young shoots used as a potherb.

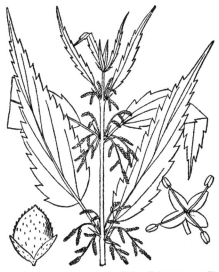

Urtica dioica ssp. *gracilis*

(as *U. gracilis* 19:25) **Oweekeno** *Unspecified* Plant fried and eaten. (as *U. dioca* ssp. *gracilis* var. *lyallii* 43:119) **Quileute** *Vegetable* Plant tops eaten as greens. (as *U. lyallii* 137:61) **Saanich** *Vegetable* Young stems and leaves boiled and eaten like spinach. (182:90) **Skagit, Upper** *Unspecified* Tender shoots cooked and eaten. (as *U. lyallii* 179:42)

Urtica dioica ssp. *holosericea*,
Stinging Nettle
Cahuilla *Vegetable* Leaves eaten raw or boiled as greens. (as *U. holosericea* 15:143)

Urtica urens, Dwarf Nettle
Shuswap *Beverage* Used for bathing and drinking. (123:70)

Usnea sp., Tree Lichen
Hesquiat *Forage* Plant browsed by deer. (185:17)

Ustilago zeae, Corn Smut
Apache, White Mountain *Unspecified* Smut boiled and eaten. (136:161) **Hopi** *Unspecified* Used with sweet corn as food. (200:100)

Uvularia perfoliata, Perfoliate
Bellwort
Cherokee *Unspecified* Plants boiled, fried, and eaten with fat. (204:252)

Uvularia sessilifolia, Sessileleaf
Bellwort
Cherokee *Vegetable* Leaves eaten as cooked greens. (80:25)

Vaccinium alpinum, Blueberry
Eskimo, Alaska *Fruit* Fruit used for food. (4:715)

Vaccinium angustifolium, Lowbush
Blueberry
Abnaki *Fruit* Fruits eaten for food. (144:171) Fruit used for food. (as *V. augustifolium* 144:152) **Algonquin, Quebec** *Fruit* Berries used fresh. Berries canned or used to make fruit pemmican and pâté. *Pie & Pudding* Berries used to make pies, cobblers, and upside-down cakes. *Preserves* Berries made into preserves and butter. (18:104) **Chippewa** *Fruit* Berries boiled, seasoned, combined with moose fat and deer tallow, and used for food. (53:321) **Iroquois** *Bread & Cake* Fruit mashed, made into small cakes, and dried for future use. *Dried Food* Raw or cooked fruit sun or fire dried and stored for future use. *Fruit* Dried fruit taken as a hunting food. (as *V. pennsylvanicum* 196:128) *Preserves* Flowers used to make preserves. (142:96) *Sauce & Relish* Dried fruit cakes soaked in warm water and cooked

as a sauce or mixed with corn bread. (as *V. pennsylvanicum* 196:128) *Unspecified* Flowers eaten fresh. (142:96) **Menominee** *Winter Use Food* Sun dried berries and dried sweet corn sweetened with maple sugar and stored for winter use. (as *V. pennsylvanicum* 151:66) **Ojibwa** *Dried Food* Berries sun dried for winter use. (as *V. pennsylvanicum* 135:238) Berries dried like currants and cooked in winter with corn, rice, and venison. (as *V. pennsylvanicum* 153:401) *Fruit* Berries eaten fresh. *Winter Use Food* Berries canned for future use. (as *V. pennsylvanicum* 135:238)

Vaccinium cespitosum, Dwarf Blueberry

Alaska Native *Bread & Cake* Berries cooked in muffins. Berries eaten raw or cooked in pies, puddings, and muffins. *Dietary Aid* Berries used as a fair source of vitamin C. *Frozen Food* Berries frozen or canned for winter use. *Fruit* Berries eaten raw or cooked in pies, puddings, and muffins. *Pie & Pudding* Berries eaten raw or cooked in pies, puddings, and muffins. *Winter Use Food* Berries frozen or canned for winter use. (as *V. paludicola* 85:107) **Bella Coola** *Fruit* Berries formerly used for food. (184:205) **Okanagan-Colville** *Dried Food* Berries dried for future use. *Forage* Berries eaten by domestic sheep. *Fruit* Berries eaten fresh. *Winter Use Food* Berries canned for future use. (188:102) **Paiute** *Fruit* Berries eaten fresh. *Winter Use Food* Berries sometimes canned. (111:102) **Shuswap** *Fruit* Berries used for food. (123:63) **Thompson** *Dried Food* Berries dried loose like raisins or canned and used for food. *Pie & Pudding* Berries used in pies. *Preserves* Berries used in jams. *Winter Use Food* Berries dried loose like raisins or canned and used for food in winter. (187:217)

Vaccinium cespitosum var. *cespitosum*, Tall Bilberry

Hanaksiala *Bread & Cake* Berries dried in the form of cakes and reconstituted during the winter. (43:244) **Kitasoo** *Bread & Cake* Berries dried into cakes and eaten. *Fruit* Berries eaten fresh. (43:335) **Oweekeno** *Fruit* Berries used

for food. (43:98) *Special Food* Berries picked for feasts. (43:99)

Vaccinium cespitosum var. *paludicola*, Dwarf Blueberry

Hanaksiala *Bread & Cake* Berries dried in the form of cakes and reconstituted during the winter. (43:244) **Kitasoo** *Bread & Cake* Berries dried into cakes and eaten. *Fruit* Berries eaten fresh. (43:335) **Oweekeno** *Fruit* Berries used for food. (43:98) *Special Food* Berries picked for feasts. (43:99)

Vaccinium corymbosum, Highbush Blueberry

Algonquin, Quebec *Fruit* Berries canned or used to make fruit pemmican and pâté. Berries used fresh. *Pie & Pudding* Berries used to make pies, cobblers, and upside-down cakes. *Preserves* Berries made into preserves and butter. (18:104) **Iroquois** *Bread & Cake* Fruit mashed, made into small cakes, and dried for future use. *Dried Food* Raw or cooked fruit sun or fire dried and stored for future use. *Fruit* Dried fruit taken as hunting food. *Sauce & Relish* Dried fruit cakes soaked in warm water and cooked as a sauce or mixed with corn bread. (196:128)

Vaccinium deliciosum, Blueleaved Huckleberry

Hoh *Fruit* Berries eaten raw. *Sauce & Relish* Berries stewed and made into a sauce. *Winter Use Food* Berries canned and used as a winter food. **Quileute** *Fruit* Berries eaten raw. *Sauce & Relish* Berries stewed and made into a sauce. *Winter Use Food* Berries canned and used as a winter food. (137:67) **Thompson** *Dried Food* Berries dried loose like raisins. *Pie & Pudding* Berries used in pies. *Preserves* Berries used in jams. *Winter Use Food* Berries canned and used for food. (187:217)

Vaccinium macrocarpon, Cranberry

Algonquin, Quebec *Fruit* Berries used for food. (18:105) **Algonquin, Tête-de-Boule** *Fruit* Fruits eaten for food. (132:134) **Anticosti** *Winter Use Food* Fruits stored for winter use. (143:68) **Chippewa** *Fruit* Berries cooked and used for food. (as *Oxycoccus macrocarpus* 53:321) **Iroquois** *Bread & Cake* Fruit mashed, made into small cakes, and dried for future use. *Dried Food* Raw or cooked fruit sun or fire dried and stored for future use. *Fruit* Dried fruit taken as a hunting food. *Sauce & Relish* Dried fruit cakes soaked in warm water and cooked as a sauce or mixed with corn bread. (196:128) **Ojibwa** *Fruit* Fruit used for food. (135:238)

Vaccinium membranaceum, Blue Huckleberry

Alaska Native *Bread & Cake* Berries cooked in muffins. *Dietary Aid* Berries used as a fair source of vitamin C. *Frozen Food* Berries frozen for winter use. *Fruit* Berries eaten raw. *Pie & Pudding* Berries cooked in pies and puddings. *Winter Use Food* Berries frozen or canned for winter use. (85:107) **Bella Coola** *Fruit* Berries used for food. (184:205) **Coeur d'Alene** *Dried Food* Berries dried and used for food. *Fruit* Berries eaten fresh, boiled and eaten, or mashed and eaten. *Soup* Berries dried, boiled with roots, and eaten as soup. (178:90) **Hanaksiala** *Bread & Cake* Berries dried in the form of cakes and reconstituted during the winter. (43:244) **Kitasoo** *Dried Food* Berries dried for future use. *Fruit* Berries eaten fresh.

Vaccinium membranaceum

(43:335) **Klamath** *Winter Use Food* Dried berries stored for winter use. (45:103) **Montana Indian** *Bread & Cake* Berries used to make pancakes and muffins. *Dried Food* Fruits sun dried and stored for winter use. (as *V. globulare* 82:63) *Fruit* Fruit eaten fresh. (19:25) Berries eaten fresh. (as *V. globulare* 82:63) *Pie & Pudding* Fruit used for making pies. *Preserves* Fruit used for making jelly. (19:25) Berries used to make jams and jellies. (as *V. globulare* 82:63) *Winter Use Food* Fruit dried for winter. (19:25) **Okanagan-Colville** *Dried Food* Berries dried, boiled, and eaten. *Fruit* Berries eaten fresh. *Winter Use Food* Berries canned for future use. (188:103) **Okanagon** *Staple* Berries used as a principal food. (178:239) **Oweekeno** *Special Food* Berries picked for feasts. (43:99) **Paiute** *Dried Food* Berries eaten dried. *Fruit* Berries eaten fresh. *Preserves* Berries canned or refrigerated for future use. (111:102) **Shuswap** *Fruit* Berries used for food. (123:63) **Skagit, Upper** *Dried Food* Berries pulped, dried, and stored for winter use. *Fruit* Berries eaten fresh. (179:38) **Spokan** *Fruit* Berries used for food. (178:343) **Thompson** *Dried Food* Berries dried or canned for future use. *Frozen Food* Berries frozen for future use. (187:218) *Fruit* Sweet berries eaten as a favorite food. (164:490) Berries eaten fresh. *Preserves* Berries made into jam. (187:218)

Vaccinium myrsinites, Shiny Blueberry

Seminole *Unspecified* Plant used for food. (169:494)

Vaccinium myrtilloides, Velvetleaf Huckleberry

Abnaki *Fruit* Fruit used for food. (*Vaccinium canadense* 144:152) Fruits eaten for food. (as *V. canadense* 144:171) **Algonquin, Quebec** *Fruit* Fruit gathered to eat and sell. (18:103) **Algonquin, Tête-de-Boule** *Unspecified* Flowers eaten as food. (as *V. canadense* 132:133) **Cree, Woodlands** *Fruit* Berries eaten raw. Sun dried berries boiled or pounded into pemmican and eaten. *Preserves* Berries made into jam and eaten with fish and bannock. (109:63) **Hesquiat** *Pie & Pudding* Berries ordered and used to make pies. *Preserves* Berries ordered and used to make preserves. (185:67) **Hoh** *Fruit* Berries eaten raw. *Sauce & Relish* Berries stewed and made into a sauce. *Winter Use Food* Berries canned and used as a winter food. (as *V. macrophyllum* 137:67) **Iroquois** *Preserves* Flowers used to make preserves. *Unspecified* Flowers eaten fresh. (as *V. canadense* 142:96) **Ojibwa** *Dried Food* Berries sun dried for winter use. *Fruit* Berries eaten fresh. *Winter Use Food* Berries canned for future use. (as *V. canadense* 135:238) **Potawatomi** *Dried Food* Berries and low sweet blueberry were important items of food and used dried. *Fruit* Berries and low sweet blueberry were important items of food and used fresh or canned. (as *V. canadense* 154:99) **Quileute** *Fruit* Berries eaten raw. *Sauce & Relish* Berries stewed and made into a sauce. *Winter Use Food* Berries canned and used as a winter food. (as *V. macrophyllum* 137:67) **Thompson** *Pie & Pudding* Berries made into pies. (187:218)

Vaccinium myrtillus, Whortleberry
Okanagon *Staple* Berries used as a principal food. (178:239)

Vaccinium myrtillus var. *oreophilum*, Whortleberry
Thompson *Fruit* Small, black berries eaten. (as *V. oreophilum* 164:486)

Vaccinium ovalifolium, Ovalleaf Blueberry
Alaska Native *Bread & Cake* Berries eaten raw or cooked in pies, puddings, and muffins. *Dietary Aid* Berries used as a fair source of vitamin C. *Frozen Food* Berries frozen or canned for winter use. *Fruit* Berries eaten raw or cooked in pies, puddings, and muffins. *Pie & Pudding* Berries eaten raw or cooked in pies, puddings, and muffins. *Winter Use Food* Berries frozen or canned for winter use. (85:107) **Bella Coola** *Bread & Cake* Berries formerly dried in cakes and used for food. *Fruit* Berries used for food. (as *V. alaskense* 184:205) **Chinook, Lower** *Dried Food* Berries dried and eaten. *Fruit* Berries eaten fresh. (79:44) **Clallam** *Dried Food*

Berries eaten dried. *Fruit* Berries eaten fresh. (57:200) **Haisla & Hanaksiala** *Fruit* Berries used for food. (43:245) **Hanaksiala** *Dried Food* Berries dried for winter use. *Fruit* Berries eaten fresh. (as *V. alaskaense* 43:243) **Hesquiat** *Fruit* Berries eaten with oil of whale, dogfish, hair seal, or sea lion. (as *V. alaskaense* 185:65) Berries eaten with oil. *Preserves* Berries preserved or made into jam. (185:67) **Hoh** *Fruit* Berries eaten raw. *Sauce & Relish* Berries stewed and made into a sauce. *Winter Use Food* Berries canned and used as a winter food. (137:68) **Kitasoo** *Bread & Cake* Berries dried into cakes and eaten. (as *V. alaskaense* 43:334) Berries dried into cakes and eaten. (43:335) *Fruit* Berries eaten fresh. (as *V. alaskaense* 43:334) Berries eaten fresh. (43:335) **Klallam** *Dried Food* Berries dried and eaten. *Fruit* Berries eaten fresh. (79:44) **Kwakiutl, Southern** *Fruit* Berries used for food. (as *V. alaskaense* 183:283) Berries used for food. (183:284) **Makah** *Bread & Cake* Fruit formed into cakes, dried, and stored for future use. (as *V. alaskaense* 67:304) Fruit dried into cakes and stored for future use. (67:305) *Dried Food* Berries dried and eaten. (79:44) *Fruit* Fruit eaten fresh. (as *V. alaskaense* 67:304) Fruit eaten fresh. (67:305) Berries eaten fresh. (79:44) *Winter Use Food* Fruit canned for future use. (as *V. alaskaense* 67:304) Fruit canned for winter use. (67:305) **Nitinaht** *Dried Food* Fruits mashed, poured into rectangular frames to dry, soaked, boiled, and eaten in winter. (as *V. alaskaense* 186:107) Fruits formerly mashed, poured into rectangular frames to dry, soaked, boiled, and eaten in winter. (186:108) *Fruit* Fruits eaten fresh. (as *V. alaskaense* 186:107) Fruits eaten fresh. (186:108) *Special Food* Fruits eaten at impromptu village feasts. Fruits eaten at impromptu village feasts. (186:107) **Oweekeno** *Fruit* Berries used for food. *Winter Use Food* Berries preserved for future use. (as *V. alaskaense* 43:97) Berries preserved for winter use. (43:99) **Paiute** *Dried Food* Berries eaten dried. *Fruit* Berries eaten fresh. *Preserves* Berries canned or refrigerated for future use. (111:102) **Quileute** *Dried Food* Berries dried and eaten. *Fruit* Berries eaten fresh. (79:44) Berries eaten raw. *Sauce & Relish* Berries stewed and made into a sauce. *Winter Use Food* Berries canned and used as a winter food. (137:68) **Quinault** *Dried Food* Berries dried and eaten. *Fruit* Berries eaten fresh. (79:44) **Salish, Coast** *Dried Food* Berries dried and used for food. *Fruit* Berries eaten fresh. (182:83) **Shuswap** *Fruit* Berries used for food. (123:63) **Tanana, Upper** *Fruit* Berries used for food. (115:36) **Thompson** *Bread & Cake* Berries scattered thinly on a mat and dried over a fire or mashed up and dried into a thin cake. (187:220) *Dried Food* Berries soaked, mashed, and dried for winter use. The berries were soaked, mashed, and then placed on drying racks with a small fire lit beneath them to keep away the flies. (as *V. alaskaense* 187:217) *Fruit* Sweet berries eaten as a favorite food. (164:490) Berries eaten fresh. (as *V. alaskaense* 187:217)

Vaccinium ovatum, Evergreen Huckleberry

Costanoan *Fruit* Raw fruit used for food. (21:252) **Hesquiat** *Fruit* Berries eaten with oil. *Preserves* Berries cooked and made into jam or jelly. Berries stored with water in jars. (185:67) **Hoh** *Fruit* Berries eaten raw. *Sauce & Relish* Berries stewed and made into a sauce. *Winter Use Food* Berries canned and used as a winter food. (137:67) **Karok** *Fruit* Fresh berries used for food. (6:60) *Winter Use Food* Berries stored in baskets for future use. (148:388) **Makah** *Bread & Cake* Fruit dried into cakes and stored for future use. *Fruit* Fruit used for food. (67:306) **Nitinaht** *Fruit* Ripe berries used for food. *Pie & Pudding* Berries used in pies. (186:108) **Poliklah** *Fruit* Berries used extensively for food. (117:173) **Pomo** *Dried Food* Dried berries stored in large coiled baskets, boiled, and eaten. (66:15) *Fruit* Berries eaten fresh. (41:377) Raw or stone boiled berries used for food. (66:15) *Pie & Pudding* Berries made into pies and eaten. (41:377) **Pomo, Kashaya** *Dried Food* Berries eaten dried. *Fruit* Berries eaten fresh. *Pie & Pudding* Berries used for dumplings, pies, puddings, and toppings. (72:60) **Quileute** *Fruit* Berries eaten raw. *Sauce & Relish* Berries stewed and made into a sauce. *Winter Use Food* Berries

canned and used as a winter food. (137:67) **Quinault** *Fruit* Berries eaten fresh. (79:44) **Salish** *Fruit* Berries used for food. (182:83) **Thompson** *Fruit* Fruit used for food. (187:220) **Tolowa** *Dried Food* Berries dried and stored. *Fruit* Fresh berries used for food. (6:60)

Vaccinium oxycoccos, Small Cranberry

Alaska Native *Fruit* Fruit eaten raw. Fruit cooked and used for food. (85:103) **Algonquin, Quebec** *Fruit* Berries used for food. (18:105) **Algonquin, Tête-de-Boule** *Fruit* Fruits eaten for food. (132:134) **Anticosti** *Winter Use Food* Fruits stored for winter use. (143:68) **Clallam** *Beverage* Leaves used to make tea. (57:200) **Cree, Woodlands** *Fruit* Fresh berries used for food. Berries stewed and eaten with smoked fish. *Winter Use Food* Berries picked in the fall and stored outside in birch bark containers for winter use. (as *Oxycoccus quadripetalus* 109:47) **Eskimo, Alaska** *Fruit* Berries eaten occasionally, but not considered an important food source. (as *Oxycoccus microcarpus* 1:37) **Eskimo, Inupiat** *Dessert* Berries whipped with frozen fish eggs and eaten as a frozen dessert. Raw berries mashed with canned milk and seal oil into a dessert. *Fruit* Berries cooked with fish

Vaccinium oxycoccos

eggs, fish (whitefish, sheefish, or pike), blubber, and eaten. *Pie & Pudding* Berries boiled with sugar, water, and flour into a pudding. *Sauce & Relish* Berries boiled with dried fruit and eaten with meat or used as topping for ice cream, yogurt, or cake. Whole or mashed berries used cooked or raw, whipped with fat, and made into a sauce. Berries boiled with sugar, water, and flour into a topping for hot cakes or bread. Berries boiled with sugar, water, and flour and eaten with meats. *Winter Use Food* Berries boiled, cooled, blackberries or blueberries added, and stored for winter use. (98:104) **Haisla & Hanaksiala** *Winter Use Food* Berries boiled and stored in barrels of oolichan (candlefish) grease for winter use. (43:247) **Hesquiat** *Forage* Berries eaten by geese. *Fruit* Raw berries, without sugar, eaten with oil. *Preserves* Berries stored with water in jars. Berries made into jam. (185:67) **Iroquois** *Bread & Cake* Fruit mashed, made into small cakes, and dried for future use. *Dried Food* Raw or cooked fruit sun or fire dried and stored for future use. *Fruit* Dried fruit taken as a hunting food. *Sauce & Relish* Dried fruit cakes soaked in warm water and cooked as a sauce or mixed with corn bread. (196:128) **Kitasoo** *Fruit* Berries used for food. (43:336) **Klallam** *Fruit* Berries stored in boxes or baskets until soft and brown and used for food. (79:45) **Makah** *Fruit* Fruit eaten fresh. (67:307) Berries stored in boxes or baskets until soft and brown and used for food. (79:45) *Pie & Pudding* Fruit used to make pies. *Preserves* Fruit used to make jam and jellies. *Winter Use Food* Fruit canned for future use. (67:307) **Menominee** *Fruit* Berries sweetened with maple sugar and eaten. (151:65) **Nitinaht** *Fruit* Berries formerly eaten in fall. (186:109) **Ojibwa** *Fruit* Fruit used for food. (135:238) This was an important wild food. (153:401) **Oweekeno** *Fruit* Berries used for food. (43:100) **Potawatomi** *Fruit* Berries sweetened with maple sugar and always used as an article of food. (154:99) **Quinault** *Fruit* Berries stored in boxes or baskets until soft and brown and used for food. (79:45) **Salish, Coast** *Dried Food* Fruits dried and used for food. *Fruit* Berries eaten fresh. (182:83) **Tanana, Upper** *Fro-*

zen Food Berries frozen for future use. Berries eaten raw, plain, or mixed raw with sugar, grease, or the combination of the two. Berries fried in grease with sugar or dried fish eggs. Berries boiled with sugar and flour to thicken. *Pie & Pudding* Berries used to make pies. *Preserves* Berries used to make jam and jelly. *Winter Use Food* Berries preserved alone or in grease and stored in a birch bark basket in an underground cache. (as *Oxycoccus microcarpus* 102:10) **Thompson** *Fruit* Fresh fruit used for food. This fruit was not dried because it remained fresh for a long time and could be picked any time until winter. (187:221)

Vaccinium parvifolium, Red Huckleberry

Alaska Native *Preserves* Fruit used to make a very superior jelly. (85:105) **Bella Coola** *Bread & Cake* Berries formerly dried in cakes and used for food. *Frozen Food* Berries frozen and used for food. *Fruit* Berries used for food. (184:205) **Clallam** *Fruit* Berries eaten fresh. (57:200) **Haisla & Hanaksiala** *Fruit* Fruit eaten, sometimes at feasts. *Special Food* Fruit eaten, sometimes at feasts. (43:248) **Hesquiat** *Beverage* Berries made excellent wine. *Fruit* Raw berries eaten with oil. *Preserves* Berries used for jam. (185:67) **Hoh** *Fruit* Berries eaten raw. *Sauce & Relish* Berries stewed and made into a sauce. *Winter Use Food* Berries canned and used as a winter food. (137:68) **Karok** *Fruit* Berries eaten raw. (148:388) **Kitasoo** *Fruit* Berries used for food. (43:337) **Klallam** *Fruit* Berries used for food. (79:44) **Kwakiutl, Southern** *Special Food* Berries boiled, mixed with red salmon spawn and oil and eaten at feasts in winter ceremonies. (183:284) **Lummi** *Fruit* Berries used for food. (79:44) **Makah** *Frozen Food* Fruit frozen for future use. *Fruit* Fruit eaten fresh. (67:308) Berries used for food. (79:44) *Winter Use Food* Fruit canned for winter use. (67:308) **Nitinaht** *Dried Food* Berries mashed, poured into frames, dried into cakes, soaked, boiled, and eaten with oil or syrup. *Frozen Food* Berries frozen and used for food. *Fruit* Berries eaten fresh. (186:109) *Special Food* Fruits eaten at impromptu village feasts. (186:107) **Oweekeno** *Winter Use Food* Berries preserved for future use. (43:101) **Paiute** *Dried Food* Berries eaten dried. *Fruit* Berries eaten fresh. (111:103) **Poliklah** *Fruit* Berries used extensively for food. (117:173) **Pomo, Kashaya** *Fruit* Berries eaten fresh. (72:61) **Quileute** *Fruit* Berries used for food. (79:44) Berries eaten raw. *Sauce & Relish* Berries stewed and made into a sauce. *Winter Use Food* Berries canned and used as a winter food. (137:68) **Quinault** *Beverage* Leaves used to make tea. *Fruit* Berries used for food. (79:44) **Salish, Coast** *Dried Food* Fruits dried and used for food. *Fruit* Berries eaten fresh or cooked. (182:83) **Skagit** *Fruit* Berries used for food. (79:44) **Skagit, Upper** *Fruit* Berries eaten fresh. (179:38) **Skokomish** *Fruit* Berries used for food. **Snohomish** *Fruit* Berries used for food. **Swinomish** *Fruit* Berries used for food. (79:44) **Thompson** *Bread & Cake* Berries used in pancakes and muffins. (187:221) *Fruit* Bright red, acidic berries eaten in large quantities. (164:490) *Preserves* Berries used to make jam. (187:221) **Tolowa** *Dried Food* Berries dried and stored. *Fruit* Fresh berries used for food. **Yurok** *Fruit* Fresh berries used for food. (6:61)

Vaccinium scoparium, Grouse Whortleberry

Klamath *Dried Food* Dried berries used for food. *Fruit* Fresh berries used for food. (45:103) **Okanagan-Colville** *Fruit* Berries used for food. (188:105) **Thompson** *Dried Food* Berries dried loose like raisins. *Pie & Pudding* Berries used in pies. *Preserves* Berries used in jams. *Winter Use Food* Berries canned and used for food. (187:217) **Yurok** *Fruit* Fresh berries used for food. (6:61)

Vaccinium uliginosum, Bog Blueberry

Alaska Native *Bread & Cake* Berries cooked in muffins. *Dietary Aid* Berries used as a fair source of vitamin C. *Frozen Food* Berries frozen for winter use. *Fruit* Berries eaten raw. *Pie & Pudding* Berries cooked in pies and puddings. *Winter Use Food* Berries frozen or canned for winter use. (85:107) **Eskimo, Alaska** *Fruit* Fresh berries used for food. (1:37) Fruit used

for food. (4:715) **Eskimo, Inuktitut** *Fruit* Berries used for food. (202:184) Berries used for food. (202:186) **Eskimo, Inupiat** *Cooking Agent* Berry juice made into a vinegar and used to pickle meats and greens. *Dessert* Fresh or frozen berries mixed with sugar and seal oil and eaten as a dessert. *Frozen Food* Berries frozen for future use. *Fruit* Berries eaten fresh. Berries mixed with raw, fresh fish eggs and eaten with seal oil and sugar. Berries mixed with sourdough and fermented. Berries mixed with potatoes, cabbage, or lettuce and pickled. Berries mixed with blubber and blackberries and eaten with or without sugar. *Ice Cream* Fresh or frozen berries used to make ice cream or yogurt. *Pie & Pudding* Stored berries used to make traditional desserts and pies. Berries and water boiled, flour paste, sugar, or honey added, and eaten hot or cold as a pudding. *Sauce & Relish* Berry pudding used as a topping for hot cakes, bread, or desserts. *Winter Use Food* Berries boiled with water, mixed with blackberries, and stored in a poke or barrel for winter use. (98:78) **Haisla & Hanaksiala** *Fruit* Fruit used for food. (43:249) **Kitasoo** *Bread & Cake* Berries dried into cakes and eaten. *Fruit* Berries eaten fresh. (43:335) **Koyukon** *Frozen Food* Berries frozen for winter use. (119:54) **Kwakiutl, Southern** *Fruit* Berries used for food. (183:284) **Oweekeno** *Winter Use Food* Berries preserved for winter use. (43:99) **Salish, Coast** *Dried Food* Berries dried and used for food. *Fruit* Berries eaten fresh. (182:83) **Tanana, Upper** *Fruit* Berries used for food. (77:28) Berries used for food. (as *V. uglinosum* 115:36) *Preserves* Berries gathered and preserved in quantity. (102:9) *Winter Use Food* Berries mixed with grease and preserved in caches. (77:28)

Vaccinium vitis-idaea, Lingonberry

Alaska Native *Preserves* Berries mixed with rose hip pulp and sugar to make jam. *Sauce & Relish* Berries cooked as a sauce. *Winter Use Food* Berries stored for future use. (85:109) **Carrier** *Preserves* Berries used to make jam. (31:76) **Eskimo, Arctic** *Beverage* Juice diluted and sweetened to make a refreshing beverage.

Frozen Food Berries frozen and stored until the next spring. *Preserves* Berries used to make jams and jellies. (128:22) **Eskimo, Inupiat** *Dessert* Berries whipped with frozen fish eggs and eaten as a frozen dessert. Raw berries mashed with canned milk and seal oil into a dessert. *Fruit* Berries cooked with fish eggs, fish (whitefish, sheefish, or pike), blubber, and eaten. *Pie & Pudding* Berries boiled with sugar, water, and flour into a pudding. *Sauce & Relish* Berries boiled with dried fruit and eaten with meat or used as topping for ice cream, yogurt, or cake. Whole or mashed berries used cooked or raw, whipped with fat, and made into a sauce. Berries boiled with sugar, water, and flour into a topping for hot cakes or bread. Berries boiled with sugar, water, and flour and eaten with meats. *Winter Use Food* Berries boiled, cooled, blackberries or blueberries added, and stored for winter use. (98:86) **Koyukon** *Frozen Food* Berries frozen for winter use. (as *V. vitis* 119:55) **Tanana, Upper** *Frozen Food* Berries frozen for future use. (102:9) *Fruit* Berries used for food. (77:28) Berries eaten raw, plain, or mixed raw with sugar, grease, or the combination of the two. Berries fried in grease with sugar or dried fish eggs. Berries boiled with sugar and flour to thicken. (102:9) Berries used for food. (115:36) *Pie & Pudding* Berries used to make pies. *Preserves* Berries used to make jam and jelly. (102:9) *Winter Use Food* Berries preserved in caches. (77:28) Berries preserved alone or in grease and stored in a birch bark basket in an underground cache. (102:9)

Vaccinium vitis-idaea ssp. *minus*, Northern Mountain Cranberry
Anticosti *Preserves* Fruit used to make jams and jellies. (143:68) **Cree, Woodlands** *Frozen Food* Berries stored during the winter by freezing outside. *Fruit* Berries mixed with boiled fish eggs, livers, air bladders, and fat, and eaten. *Snack Food* Berries eaten raw as a nibble. *Soup* Berries stewed and served with fish or meat. (109:64) **Eskimo, Alaska** *Fruit* Berries eaten occasionally, but not considered an important food source. (1:37) Fruit used for food. (4:715) **Eskimo, Inuktitut** *Fruit* Berries used for food.

(202:183) **Haida** *Fruit* Berries used for food. **Hesquiat** *Fruit* Berries used for food. **Oweekeno** *Fruit* Berries used for food. **Tsimshian** *Fruit* Berries used for food. (43:101)

Valeriana dioica var. *sylvatica*, Woods Valerian
Thompson *Forage* Leaves eaten by deer. (187:290)

Valeriana edulis, Edible Valerian
Klamath *Unspecified* Steamed, cooked roots used for food. (45:104) **Montana Indian** *Unspecified* Large quantities of roots cooked in a kiln until black and very sticky. (19:26) **Okanagan-Colville** *Winter Use Food* Roots stored in underground pits for about a year. (188:142) **Paiute** *Unspecified* Roots cooked overnight and eaten. (104:103) Boiled root used for food. (118:16) **Sanpoil & Nespelem** *Unspecified* Roots used for food. (188:142)

Valeriana sitchensis, Sitka Valerian
Thompson *Forage* Leaves eaten by deer. (187:290)

Valerianella locusta, Lewiston Cornsalad
Cherokee *Vegetable* Leaves cooked and eaten as greens. (as *V. olitoria* 80:30) Leaves used as a potherb. (as *V. olitoria* 126:59)

Veratrum californicum, California False Hellebore
Miwok *Unspecified* Roasted in hot ashes, peeled, and eaten. (12:158)

Veratrum viride, American False Hellebore
Blackfoot *Soup* Leaves used to make soups. (86:105)

Verbena hastata, Swamp Verbena
Concow *Staple* Seeds used to make pinole. (41:383) **Omaha** *Beverage* Leaves steeped to make a tea-like beverage. (70:111)

Verbena stricta, Hoary Verbena
Omaha *Beverage* Leaves used to make a hot, aqueous, tea-like beverage. (68:329)

Verbesina encelioides* ssp. *exauriculata, Golden Crownbeard
Navajo *Unspecified* Seeds used for food. (55:90)

Vernonia missurica, Missouri Ironweed
Kiowa *Candy* Pressed blossoms made into small wads for a short, sweet chew. (192:62)

Viburnum edule, Mooseberry Viburnum
Alaska Native *Preserves* Berries used to make jelly. (85:111) **Bella Coola** *Winter Use Food* Berries mixed with grease and other berries and used as a winter food. (184:203) **Carrier** *Preserves* Berries used to make jelly. (31:77) **Cree, Woodlands** *Frozen Food* Fruit collected in the fall and frozen or left to freeze on the bush and eaten as a nibble. *Preserves* Fruit used to make jam or jelly. *Snack Food* Fruit eaten raw as a nibble. Fruit left to freeze on the bush and eaten as a nibble. (109:65) **Eskimo, Inuktitut** *Fruit* Berries used for food. (202:188) **Eskimo, Inupiat** *Beverage* Berries used to make juice. *Dessert* Berries mixed with other berries and used to make traditional dessert. *Frozen Food* Berries frozen and stored for future use. *Fruit* Berries eaten fresh or cooked. *Ice Cream* Berries, oil, and water used to make ice cream. *Preserves* Berries used to make jam or jelly. *Sauce & Relish* Berries used to make catsup, syrup, juice, jam, or jelly. (98:106) **Haisla & Hanaksiala** *Fruit* Berries used for food. *Winter Use Food* Berries stored with oolichan (candlefish) grease in barrels for winter use. (43:232) **Hesquiat** *Fruit* Raw berries gathered to eat with oil "on the spot." (185:63) **Kitasoo** *Winter Use Food* Berries stored for future use. (43:329) **Koyukon** *Frozen Food* Berries frozen for winter use. (119:55) **Kwakiutl, Southern** *Preserves* Berries steamed, covered with oil, preserved, and used for food. *Special Food* Fresh, ripe berries eaten at feasts only. *Winter Use Food* Green berries steamed, covered with

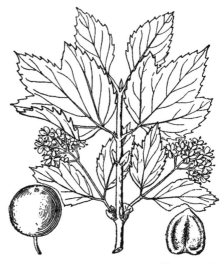
Viburnum edule

water, and used as a winter food. (183:281) **Okanagan-Colville** *Fruit* Berries used for food. (188:95) **Oweekeno** *Preserves* Berries used to make jam. (43:91) **Salish, Coast** *Fruit* Berries cooked and eaten with oil. Berries eaten raw. (182:80) **Tanana, Upper** *Frozen Food* Berries frozen for future use. (102:11) *Fruit* Fruit used for food. (77:28) Berries eaten raw, plain, or mixed raw with sugar, grease, or the combination of the two. Berries boiled with sugar and flour to thicken. (102:11) Berries mixed with fat and used for food. (as *V. pauciflorum* 115:37) *Pie & Pudding* Berries used to make pies. *Preserves* Berries used to make jam and jelly. *Winter Use Food* Berries preserved alone or in grease and stored in a birch bark basket in an underground cache. (102:11) **Thompson** *Dried Food* Fruit eaten dried. *Fruit* Fruit eaten fresh. *Preserves* Fruit made into jelly. *Sauce & Relish* Fruit made into a sauce with the seeds strained and cornstarch added. *Soup* Fruit cooked in soups. (187:201) *Unspecified* Small, acidic drupes eaten. (as *V. pauciflorum* 164:487)

Viburnum lentago, Nannyberry
Dakota *Fruit* Fruit eaten from the hand, but not gathered in quantity. (70:115) **Iroquois** *Bread & Cake* Fruit mashed, made into small cakes, and dried for future use. *Dried Food* Raw or

cooked fruit sun or fire dried and stored for future use. *Fruit* Dried fruit taken as a hunting food. *Sauce & Relish* Dried fruit cakes soaked in warm water and cooked as a sauce or mixed with corn bread. (196:128) **Menominee** *Fruit* Berries used for food. (151:63) **Ojibwa** *Fruit* Berries eaten fresh from the bush. *Preserves* Berries used in jam with wild grapes. (153:398) **Omaha** *Fruit* Fruit eaten from the hand, but not gathered in quantity. **Pawnee** *Fruit* Fruit eaten from the hand, but not gathered in quantity. **Ponca** *Fruit* Fruit eaten from the hand, but not gathered in quantity. **Winnebago** *Fruit* Fruit eaten from the hand, but not gathered in quantity. (70:115)

Viburnum nudum var. *cassinoides*, Possumhaw
Abnaki *Fruit* Fruit used for food. (as *Viburnum cassinoides* 144:152) *Unspecified* Grains used for food. (as *V. cassinoides* 144:173) **Algonquin, Quebec** *Fruit* Berries used for food. (as *V. cassinoides* 18:107)

Viburnum opulus, European Cranberrybush Viburnum
Iroquois *Fruit* Berries used as a favorite autumn food. (124:96) **Ojibwa** *Fruit* Fruit used for food. (135:237) **Shuswap** *Fruit* Berries eaten raw. *Preserves* Berries made into jelly. (123:61)

Viburnum opulus var. *americanum*, American Cranberry Viburnum
Algonquin, Quebec *Fruit* Berries eaten fresh. *Preserves* Berries made into preserves. (as *V. trilobum* 18:107) **Chippewa** *Sauce & Relish* Fresh and dried fruits used as an acid sauce. (as *V. americanum* 71:141) **Iroquois** *Bread & Cake* Fruit mashed, made into small cakes, and dried for future use. *Dried Food* Raw or cooked fruit sun or fire dried and stored for future use. *Fruit* Dried fruit taken as a hunting food. *Sauce & Relish* Dried fruit cakes soaked in warm water and cooked as a sauce or mixed with corn bread. (196:128) **Menominee** *Fruit* Berries used for food. (151:63) **Okanagon** *Fruit* Fruits occasionally used for food. **Thompson** *Fruit* Fruits occasionally used for food. (125:38)

Viburnum prunifolium, Black Haw
Meskwaki *Fruit* Berries eaten raw. *Preserves* Berries cooked into a jam. (152:256)

Vicia americana, American Vetch
Acoma *Unspecified* Seeds used for food. (32:32) **Keres, Western** *Vegetable* Black peas used for food. (171:74) **Laguna** *Unspecified* Seeds used for food. Whole pods used for food. (32:32) **Mendocino Indian** *Fodder* Used for fodder. *Vegetable* Stems baked or boiled and eaten as greens. (41:362) **Montana Indian** *Unspecified* Cooked and eaten for greens. (19:26) **Thompson** *Fodder* Plant used as fodder for horses and cattle. (164:515)

Vicia faba, Horsebean
Sia *Vegetable* Cultivated beans used for food. (199:106)

Vicia melilotoides, Vetch
Apache, Chiricahua & Mescalero *Dried Food* Ripe pods dried, stored, and soaked and boiled when needed. *Unspecified* Ripe pods cooked and eaten. (33:49)

Vicia nigricans ssp. *gigantea*, Giant Vetch
Kwakiutl, Southern *Fruit* Pea-like fruits roasted and used for food. (as *Vicea gigantea* 183:285)

Vigna unguiculata, Blackeyed Pea
Cocopa *Unspecified* Whole pods boiled, strings removed, and used for food; very hungry people ate strings. (as *V. sinensis* 64:264) **Cocopa, Maricopa, Mohave & Yuma** *Porridge* Ripe seeds parched, ground into flour, and boiled with corn to make mush. (as *V. sinensis* 37:129) **Kamia** *Unspecified* Species used for food. (as *V. sinensis* 62:21) **Mohave** *Dried Food* Ripe pods trampled, winnowed, and dried thoroughly. *Unspecified* Unripe seeds cooked in salted water and eaten. (as *V. sinensis* 37:129) **Papago** *Unspecified* Species used for food. **Pima** *Unspecified* Species used for food. (as *V. sinensis* 36:120)

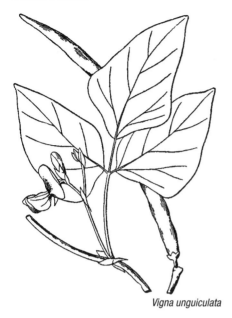

Vigna unguiculata

Viola blanda, Sweet White Violet
Cherokee *Vegetable* Leaves and stems mixed with other greens, parboiled, rinsed, and fried with grease and salt until soft. (126:60)

Viola pedunculata, California Golden
 Violet
Diegueño *Vegetable* Young leaves, picked before the flowers appear in the spring, boiled once and eaten as greens. (84:43) **Luiseño** *Vegetable* Leaves used as greens. (155:230)

Viola pubescens var. pubescens,
 Smooth Yellow Violet
Cherokee *Vegetable* Leaves and stems mixed with other greens, parboiled, rinsed, and fried with grease and salt until soft. (as *V. pensylvanica* 126:60)

Vitex trifolia var. unifoliolata,
 Simpleleaf Chastetree
Hawaiian *Unspecified* Leaves eaten with dried coconut. (2:72)

Vitis aestivalis, Summer Grape
Cherokee *Beverage* Fruit mixed with sour grape, pokeberry juice, sugar, and cornmeal

used as a juice. *Bread & Cake* Fruit used to make juice and dumplings. (126:60) *Fruit* Fruit used for food. (80:37) Raw fruit used for food. (126:60)

Vitis aestivalis var. aestivalis,
 Summer Grape
Seminole *Unspecified* Plant used for food. (as *V. rufotomentosa* 169:475)

Vitis arizonica, Canyon Grape
Apache, Chiricahua & Mescalero *Dried Food* Fruit dried and eaten like raisins. *Fruit* Raw fruit eaten fresh. (33:44) **Apache, Mescalero** *Fruit* Fruits eaten fresh. (14:50) **Apache, Western** *Beverage* Juice boiled to make wine. *Dried Food* Berries pounded, dried, and stored in sacks. *Fruit* Ripe berries eaten raw. (26:190) **Havasupai** *Fruit* Fruit used for food. (197:231) **Isleta** *Fruit* Fruit considered an important part of the diet. (100:44) **Jemez** *Fruit* Grapes used for food. (44:28)

Vitis californica, California Wild Grape
Costanoan *Fruit* Raw fruits used for food. (21:251) **Karok** *Fruit* Fruit used for food. (148:386) **Mendocino Indian** *Preserves* Fruits used to make jelly. (41:369) **Pomo** *Fruit* Raw berries used for food. (66:14) **Pomo, Kashaya** *Fruit* Berries eaten fresh. (72:51) **Tubatulabal** *Fruit* Berries used for food. (193:15) **Wintoon** *Fruit* Fruit used for food. (117:264) **Yurok** *Fruit* Fresh berries used for food. (6:62)

Vitis cinerea, Graybark Grape
Dakota *Dried Food* Fruit dried for winter use. *Fruit* Fruit eaten fresh. (70:102) **Kiowa** *Dried Food* Grapes gathered in large quantities and dried for later use. *Fruit* Grapes gathered in large quantities and eaten raw. *Preserves* Grapes gathered in large quantities and made into jams and jellies. (192:42) **Omaha** *Dried Food* Fruit dried for winter use. *Fruit* Fruit eaten fresh. **Pawnee** *Beverage* Fresh sap used as grape juice. *Dried Food* Fruit dried for winter use. *Fruit* Fruit eaten fresh. **Ponca** *Dried Food* Fruit dried for winter use. *Fruit* Fruit eaten

fresh. **Winnebago** *Dried Food* Fruit dried for winter use. *Fruit* Fruit eaten fresh. (70:102)

Vitis cinerea var. *baileyana*, Graybark Grape

Cherokee *Beverage* Fruit mixed with sour grape, pokeberry juice, sugar, and cornmeal used as a juice. *Bread & Cake* Fruit used to make juice and dumplings. *Fruit* Raw fruit used for food. (as *V. baileyana* 126:60)

Vitis girdiana, Valley Grape

Cahuilla *Beverage* Fruit used to make wine. *Dried Food* Fruit dried into raisins. *Fruit* Fruit eaten fresh and cooked in stews. *Porridge* Fruit used to make mush. (15:144) **Diegueño** *Dried Food* Fruit dried into raisins and cooked. *Fruit* Fruit eaten fresh. (84:43) **Luiseño** *Fruit* Cooked fruit used for food. (155:231)

Vitis labrusca, Fox Grape

Cherokee *Beverage* Fruit mixed with sour grape, pokeberry juice, sugar, and cornmeal used as a juice. *Bread & Cake* Fruit used to make juice and dumplings. (126:60) *Fruit* Fruit used for food. (80:37) Raw fruit used for food. (126:60)

Vitis munsoniana, Munson's Grape

Seminole *Unspecified* Plant used for food. (169:479)

Vitis riparia, Riverbank Grape

Omaha *Dried Food* Fruit dried for winter use. *Fruit* Fruit eaten fresh in season. (68:326)

Vitis rotundifolia, Muscadine

Cherokee *Beverage* Fruit mixed with sour grape, pokeberry juice, sugar, and cornmeal used as a juice. *Bread & Cake* Fruit used to make juice and dumplings. *Fruit* Raw fruit used for food. (126:60)

Vitis vinifera, Domestic Grape

Haisla & Hanaksiala *Fruit* Fruit used for food. (43:296)

Vitis vulpina, Frost Grape

Cherokee *Fruit* Fruit used for food. (80:37) **Cheyenne** *Fruit* Fruit eaten fresh and never dried. (76:180) **Chippewa** *Fruit* Fruits eaten raw. (as *V. cordifolia* 53:321) **Crow** *Dried Food* Fruit eaten dried. *Fruit* Fruit eaten fresh. (19:26) **Dakota** *Dried Food* Fruit dried for winter use. *Fruit* Fruit eaten fresh. (70:102) **Iroquois** *Bread & Cake* Fruit mashed, made into small cakes, and dried for future use. *Dried Food* Raw or cooked fruit sun or fire dried and stored for future use. *Fruit* Dried fruit taken as a hunting food. *Sauce & Relish* Dried fruit cakes soaked in warm water and cooked as a sauce or mixed with corn bread. (196:128) *Unspecified* Fresh shoots eaten without peeling. (196:119) **Keres, Western** *Fruit* Fruit considered an important food. (171:74) **Lakota** *Fruit* Fruits eaten for food. (139:61) *Special Food* Vine pieces sucked or chewed for thirst during the Sun Dance. (106:44) **Mahuna** *Fruit* Berries eaten mainly to quench the thirst. (140:70) **Menominee** *Dried Food* Berries eaten dried. *Fruit* Berries eaten fresh. *Preserves* Berries eaten preserved or jellied. (as *V. cordifolia* 151:72) **Meskwaki** *Dessert* Grapes, touched by frost, prized as a dessert fruit. (as *V. cordifolia* 152:265) **Ojibwa**

Vitis vulpina

Preserves Frosted grapes made into jelly for winter use. (153:411) **Omaha** *Dried Food* Fruit dried for winter use. (68:326) Fruit dried for winter use. (70:102) *Fruit* Fruit eaten fresh in season. (68:326) Fruit eaten fresh. **Pawnee** *Beverage* Fresh sap used as grape juice. *Dried Food* Fruit dried for winter use. *Fruit* Fruit eaten fresh. **Ponca** *Dried Food* Fruit dried for winter use. *Fruit* Fruit eaten fresh. (70:102) **Sioux** *Dried Food* Fruit eaten dried. *Fruit* Fruit eaten fresh. (19:26) **Winnebago** *Dried Food* Fruit dried for winter use. *Fruit* Fruit eaten fresh. (70:102)

Vulpia octoflora* var. *glauca, Sixweeks Fescue
Gosiute *Unspecified* Seeds used for food. (as *Festuca tenella* 39:369)

Vulpia octoflora* var. *octoflora, Sixweeks Fescue
Navajo, Kayenta *Unspecified* Seeds roasted and used for food. (as *Festuca octoflora* 205:16)

Washingtonia filifera, California Fan Palm
Cahuilla *Beverage* Fruit soaked in water to make a beverage. *Dried Food* Fruit sun dried for future use. *Fruit* Fruit eaten fresh. *Porridge* Fruit and seed ground into a flour and used to make mush. *Preserves* Fruit used to make jelly. (15:145) **Cocopa** *Beverage* Juice squeezed out of fruits, added to water, and used as a beverage. (37:204) **Pima, Gila River** *Baby Food* Fruits eaten raw primarily by children. (133:7) *Snack Food* Fruit eaten primarily by children as a snack food. (133:5)

Wislizenia refracta* ssp. *refracta, Spectacle Fruit
Hopi *Unspecified* Young plants boiled for food. (as *W. melilotoides* 200:78)

Wyethia amplexicaulis, Mulesears Wyethia
Gosiute *Unspecified* Seeds used for food. (39:384) **Montana Indian** *Unspecified* Root heated, fermented, and eaten. (19:26)

Wyethia angustifolia, California Compassplant
Costanoan *Staple* Seeds eaten in pinole. *Unspecified* Raw stems used for food. (21:255) **Pomo** *Staple* Seeds used to make pinoles. (11:87) **Pomo, Kashaya** *Staple* Seeds ground to mix with pinole. *Winter Use Food* Seeds dried for winter use. (72:111) **Yuki** *Spice* Seeds used to flavor pinole. (49:85)

Wyethia glabra, Coast Range Mulesears
Pomo, Kashaya *Unspecified* Seeds used in pinole or eaten fresh. (72:74)

Wyethia helianthoides, Sunflower Wyethia
Montana Indian *Unspecified* Plant heated, fermented, and eaten. (19:26)

Wyethia longicaulis, Humboldt Mulesears
Mendocino Indian *Staple* Seeds used with parched wheat for pinole. *Unspecified* Leaves and young stems used for food. (41:396) **Pomo** *Staple* Seeds used to make pinoles. (11:87)

Wyethia mollis, Woolly Wyethia
Paiute *Staple* Seeds parched, ground, and
eaten as meal. *Unspecified* Stems and seeds
eaten raw. (104:98) **Paiute, Northern** *Porridge* Seeds parched, winnowed, ground, and
used to make mush. *Unspecified* Seeds roasted,
ground, sometimes mixed with other seeds, and
eaten. *Winter Use Food* Seeds stored for winter
use. (59:47)

Wyethia ovata, Southern Mulesears
Paiute *Unspecified* Species used for food.
(167:242)

***Xanthium strumarium* var.
 *canadense***, Canada Cockleburr
Apache, White Mountain *Bread & Cake* Seeds
ground and used to make bread. (as *X. commune* 136:161) **Costanoan** *Staple* Seeds eaten
in pinole. (21:255) **Zuni** *Bread & Cake* Seeds
ground, mixed with cornmeal, made into pats,
and steamed. (as *X. commune* 32:54) Seeds
ground with cornmeal, made into cakes or
balls, steamed, and used for food. (as *X. commune* 166:71)

Xanthosoma atrovirens, Yautia
 Amarilla
Seminole *Unspecified* Plant used for food.
(169:465)

Ximenia americana, Tallow Wood
Seminole *Unspecified* Plant used for food.
(169:488)

Yucca angustissima, Narrowleaf Yucca
Hopi *Fruit* Fruit sometimes used for food.
(17:64) Fruits pit baked with lamb's-quarter
leaves and eaten with corn dumplings in salted
water. (120:18) **Southwest Indians** *Starvation
Food* Used when agricultural reserves dwindled.
(17:10)

Yucca baccata, Banana Yucca
Acoma *Beverage* Dried fruits dissolved in water
to make a drink. *Bread & Cake* Fruits baked,
boiled, dried, rolled into loaves, and stored for
winter use. (32:54) *Dried Food* Fruits sun dried
and stored for winter use. *Fruit* Fruits eaten
raw, boiled, or baked. (32:55) *Preserves* Dried
fruits eaten as a paste. *Sauce & Relish* Dried
fruits dissolved in water and used as a dip.
(32:54) *Starvation Food* Tender crowns roasted
and eaten in times of food shortages. (32:55)
Apache *Beverage* Baked fruit pounded to a
pulp, drained, and juice drunk. *Bread & Cake*
Fruit roasted, pulp made into cakes, and stored.
Sauce & Relish Baked fruit pounded to a pulp,
drained, and juice poured over cakes. (17:18)

Soup Young leaves cooked in soups or with meat. *Unspecified* Flowers eaten as food only if obtained at the proper time. (32:56) *Vegetable* Flowers eaten as a vegetable only if obtained before the summer rains. (17:19) **Apache, Chiricahua & Mescalero** *Bread & Cake* Fruit roasted, split, seeds removed, and pulp ground into large cakes. Fruit pulp ground, made into large cakes, and stored indefinitely. *Soup* Leaves cooked in soups. *Unspecified* Leaves boiled with meat. *Vegetable* Flowers eaten if obtained before the summer rain, otherwise they taste bitter. (33:39) **Apache, Mescalero** *Beverage* Fruits used to make a drink. *Dried Food* Ripe fruits cooked, split, cleaned of seeds, dried, and used for food. *Sauce & Relish* Fruits made into a syrup and placed on fruits before drying. (14:33) **Apache, Western** *Dried Food* Fruit roasted, dried, wrapped, and stored indefinitely. (26:181) *Sauce & Relish* Fruit pounded together to make gravy. (26:182) **Apache, White Mountain** *Dried Food* Pods dried for future use. *Unspecified* Pods roasted and used for food. (136:147) **Cochiti** *Unspecified* Used as a source of food. (32:14) **Havasupai** *Beverage* Plant used to make a drink. (197:66) *Dried Food* Sheet of fruit flesh dried and the bits eaten dry when needed. (17:17) Fruits split, sun dried, and prepared for storage in the shape of a mat. (197:212) **Hopi** *Fruit* Baked fruits used for food. (42:371) Fruit used for food. (56:17) Fruits eaten for food. (138:51) Large fruits oven baked. (200:71) *Preserves* Fruits sun dried, boiled into jam, and eaten with corn dumplings or boiled bread. (120:18) **Hualapai** *Beverage* Fruit used to make a fermented beverage. *Dried Food* Fruit baked, prepared, and dried for winter use. *Fruit* Fruit eaten raw. *Staple* Fruit cooked and ground into a meal. (195:39) **Isleta** *Forage* Fruit often eaten by deer which left few for the Isletans. *Fruit* Fruit baked, seasoned, and used for food. (100:45) *Unspecified* Used as a source of food. (32:14) *Winter Use Food* Sun dried fruit used for winter storage. (100:45) **Jemez** *Unspecified* Used as a source of food. (32:14) **Keres, Western** *Fruit* Fruit eaten when thoroughly ripe. *Sauce & Relish* Soaked, cooked fruit made into a syrup and used as hot chocolate. *Winter Use*

Food Cooked, dried fruit stored for winter use. (171:74) **Keresan** *Fruit* Fruit used for food. (198:564) **Laguna** *Beverage* Dried fruits dissolved in water to make a drink. *Bread & Cake* Fruits baked, boiled, dried, rolled into loaves, and stored for winter use. (32:54) *Dried Food* Fruits sun dried and stored for winter use. *Fruit* Fruits eaten raw, boiled, or baked. (32:55) *Preserves* Dried fruits eaten as a paste. *Sauce & Relish* Dried fruits dissolved in water and used as a dip. (32:54) *Starvation Food* Tender crowns roasted and eaten in times of food shortages. (32:55) **Navajo** *Bread & Cake* Pulp made into cakes, dried, and stored for winter use. (17:20) Ripe fruits dried, ground, kneaded into small cakes, and slightly roasted. (32:54) Baked or dried fruits ground, made into small cakes, and roasted again. (55:32) *Dessert* Fruit boiled in water with or without sugar and eaten as a dessert. (165:221) *Dried Food* Fruits dried and stored for winter use. (32:54) Fruit dried and carried, when at war, with grass seeds and jerked venison. (55:32) Fruit dried for winter use. (110:31) Ripe fruit, with seeds removed, boiled down like jam, made into rolls, and dried for winter use. (165:221) *Fruit* Fruits eaten ripe or cooked. (17:20) Fruit eaten raw or cooked. (32:54) Fruit eaten when picked or cooked.

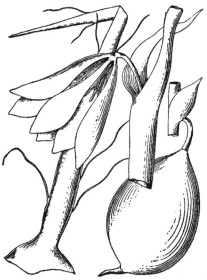

Yucca baccata

(55:32) Fruit eaten raw or baked in hot coals. (110:31) Dried fruit rolls soaked in hot water and eaten with corn mush. (165:221) *Porridge* Ripe fruits dried, ground, kneaded into small cakes, and boiled with cornmeal into a mush. (32:54) Baked or dried fruits ground, made into cakes, roasted again, mixed with cornmeal, and made into gruel. (55:32) Dried fruit cakes boiled with cornmeal into a gruel. (110:31) *Preserves* Fruit used to make jelly. (55:32) *Sauce & Relish* Fruit pulp made into cakes and mixed with water to make a syrup eaten with meat or bread. (17:20) Dried fruit cakes mixed with water to make a syrup and eaten with meat and bread. (110:31) *Special Food* Dried fruit eaten by warriors at war. (17:20) *Winter Use Food* Fruit cut in half, dried, and stored for winter use. Baked or dried fruits ground, made into small cakes, roasted again, and stored for winter use. (55:32) **Navajo, Ramah** *Bread & Cake* Fruit molded into foot-long rolls. *Preserves* Fruit used to make preserves. (191:21) **Papago** *Dried Food* Seeds dried and used for food. *Fruit* Fruits eaten fresh. *Porridge* Fresh fruits made into a gruel and used for food. *Staple* Fruits used as an important staple crop. *Unspecified* Pulp ground, cooked, and used for food. (34:23) Species used for food. (36:61) **Pima** *Beverage* Dried fruit made into cakes, cooked in water, and liquid drunk. *Bread & Cake* Dried fruit made into cakes. (17:16) *Dried Food* Fruits boiled, dried, ground, boiled with flour, and used for food. (146:72) *Porridge* Dried fruit made into cakes, ground, and cooked with cornmeal to make gruel. (17:16) **Pima, Gila River** *Candy* Plant dried and used as sweets. (133:6) *Fruit* Fruits eaten raw and pit roasted. (133:7) **Pueblo** *Dried Food* Fruits sun dried and stored for winter use. *Fruit* Fruits eaten raw, boiled, or baked. (32:55) **San Felipe** *Dried Food* Partly matured fruits cooked to form a semiliquid substance, dried, and stored for winter use. *Fruit* Ripe fruits eaten without preparation. (32:54) *Unspecified* Used as a source of food. (32:14) **Sia** *Fruit* Fruit used for food. (199:107) **Southwest Indians** *Beverage* Dried fruit pulp boiled in water and drunk. *Bread & Cake* Pulp mixed with chokecherries and made into cake. (17:11)

Pulp patted into cakes and dried thoroughly. (17:15) *Dessert* Preserved fruit soaked in water, cooked to a thick syrup, and eaten as a sauce-like dessert. (17:12) *Dried Food* Pulp cooked to a paste, dried, and stored for winter use. (17:10) Rind dried and eaten without cooking. Partially ripened fruits gathered, cooked, the pulp dried and stored for winter use. Pulp cooked to a paste and dried for winter use. (17:11) Fruits dried between beds of grass, split into halves, dried further in the sun, and stored. (17:15) *Fruit* Fruit eaten raw. (17:10) Fruits eaten for food. (17:9) *Preserves* Fruit pared, pulp chewed, cooked, dried, and eaten as a conserve. (17:12) *Staple* Seeds dried, stored in baskets and ground into meal when needed. (17:15) *Sweetener* Fruit pared, pulp chewed, cooked, dried, and conserve dissolved in water to sweeten beverages. (17:12) *Unspecified* Greatly sought after and utilized as food. (17:10) Green pods gathered and allowed to mature in sun or dwellings. (17:9) **Tewa** *Fruit* Fruits formerly eaten. (138:50) **Walapai** *Beverage* Fruits mixed with water and liquid drunk. *Dried Food* Fruit dried, folded, and stored for winter use. (17:17) **Yavapai** *Beverage* Dried fruit soaked in water until pulp dissolved and liquid drunk. (17:16) Sun dried fruit boiled and used as a beverage. *Dried Food* Sun dried fruit boiled and used for food. *Fruit* Fruit cooked in coals and used for food. (65:258) *Unspecified* Flower stalks gathered before blossoming, roasted in fire, and prepared for use. (17:16) **Zuni** *Fruit* Fruits pared and eaten raw or boiled and skinned. (32:54) Fruit eaten fresh or boiled, cooled, and the skin peeled off with a knife. (166:72) *Preserves* Flesh cooked, made into pats, sun dried, and eaten as a conserve. (32:54) Fruit made into conserves and used for food. (166:72) *Sauce & Relish* Flesh cooked, made into pats, sun dried, and mixed with water to form a syrup. (32:54) *Sweetener* Fruit made into conserves and used as a sweetener before the introduction of coffee and sugar. (166:72)

Yucca brevifolia, Joshua Tree

Cahuilla *Unspecified* Blossoms used for food. (15:150) **Kawaiisu** *Dried Food* Fruit pit roasted, mashed, dried, and stored for future use. *Fruit*

Fruit pit roasted and eaten. (206:69) **Southwest Indians** *Fruit* Fruits eaten for food. (17:63) **Tubatulabal** *Unspecified* Immature pods used for food. (193:16)

Yucca elata, Soaptree Yucca
Apache *Unspecified* Species used for food. (17:64) *Vegetable* Flowers boiled and eaten as a vegetable. (17:19) **Apache, Chiricahua & Mescalero** *Dried Food* Stems baked overnight, dried, broken into pieces, softened, and eaten. (33:38) *Vegetable* Flowers boiled and eaten as a vegetable. (33:39) **Apache, Mescalero** *Dried Food* Trunks pit cooked, dried, and stored for future food use. Flowers boiled, dried, and stored for future food use. *Soup* Flowers used as fresh vegetables in soups. *Staple* Trunks pit cooked, pounded, and made into flour. *Unspecified* Young stalks cooked, peeled, and eaten hot. (14:40) **Apache, Western** *Dried Food* Boiled blossoms dried and stored in a dry place. *Unspecified* Blossoms boiled with seeds, fat, or bones. Stalk charred and eaten like sugar cane. (26:182) Blossoms used for food. (26:193) **Papago** *Unspecified* Species used for food. (17:64) **Southwest Indians** *Dried Food* Stems baked, dried, softened in water, and eaten. (17:19)

Yucca glauca, Small Soapweed
Acoma *Dried Food* Fruits sun dried and stored for winter use. *Fruit* Fruits eaten raw, boiled, or baked. (32:55) **Apache** *Unspecified* Stalks roasted, boiled, or eaten raw. (17:19) Flowers eaten as food. (32:56) **Apache, Chiricahua & Mescalero** *Unspecified* Stalks roasted, boiled, or eaten raw. *Vegetable* Stalks boiled, dried, and stored to be used as vegetables. (33:38) **Apache, White Mountain** *Dried Food* Pods dried for future use. *Unspecified* Pods roasted and used for food. (136:147) **Cochiti** *Unspecified* Used as a source of food. (32:14) **Isleta** *Forage* Fruit often eaten by deer, which left few for the Isletans. *Fruit* Fruit baked, seasoned, and used for food. (100:45) *Unspecified* Used as a source of food. (32:14) *Winter Use Food* Sun dried fruit stored for winter use. (100:45) **Jemez** *Unspecified* Used as a source of food. (32:14) **Keres, Western** *Beverage* Dried, fruit

cakes used to make a beverage. *Bread & Cake* Boiled, dried fruit made into cakes. (171:76) *Fruit* Fruit eaten when thoroughly ripe. *Sauce & Relish* Soaked, cooked fruit make into a syrup and used as hot chocolate. (171:74) Dried, fruit cakes made into a syrup. *Starvation Food* Roasted hearts used for food in times of famine. *Unspecified* Tender heart shoots eaten for food. (171:76) *Winter Use Food* Cooked, dried fruit stored for winter use. (171:74) **Laguna** *Dried Food* Fruits sun dried and stored for winter use. *Fruit* Fruits eaten raw, boiled, or baked. (32:55) **Lakota** *Unspecified* Flowers and buds eaten fresh or cooked. (106:51) **Navajo** *Fruit* Fruit eaten raw or baked in ashes. *Winter Use Food* Fruit sliced and dried for winter use. (55:33) **Navajo, Ramah** *Fruit* Fruit roasted in ashes and eaten. *Unspecified* Flower buds roasted in ashes and leaves boiled with salt and used for food. (191:21) **Pueblo** *Dried Food* Fruits sun dried and stored for winter use. *Fruit* Fruits eaten raw, boiled, or baked. (32:55) **San Felipe** *Unspecified* Used as a source of food. (32:14) **Southwest Indians** *Sauce & Relish* Pods boiled in water and made into pickles. *Starvation Food* Crowns roasted and used in times of food shortage. (17:14) Used when agricultural reserves dwindled. (17:9) *Unspecified* Tender stalks boiled or baked. Seeds eaten with the pods. (17:14) **Tewa** *Fruit* Fruits eaten for food. (138:52) **Zuni** *Unspecified* Seedpods boiled and used for food. (166:73)

Yucca harrimaniae, Spanish Bayonet
Southwest Indians *Starvation Food* Used when agricultural reserves dwindled. (17:9)

Yucca schidigera, Mojave Yucca
Cahuilla *Unspecified* Fruit pods eaten raw or roasted. (15:150) **Hualapai** *Dried Food* Fruits baked, prepared, and dried for winter use. *Fruit* Fruit eaten raw. *Staple* Fruits cooked and ground into a meal. (as *Y. mohavensis* 195:40) **Luiseño** *Unspecified* Blossoms cooked in water and used for food. (as *Y. mohavensis* 155:195) Pods roasted on coals and used for food. (as *Y. mohavensis* 155:196) **Mohave** *Fruit* Fruit peeled and eaten without preparation. (37:204)

Southwest Indians *Beverage* Fruit cooked and made into a drink. *Dried Food* Dried fruit used for food. (as *Y. mohavensis* 17:18) *Fruit* Fruit used for food. (17:22) Fruits eaten for food. (17:63)

Yucca schottii, Schott's Yucca
Apache, San Carlos *Dried Food* Fruits dried and used for food. *Fruit* Fruits cooked, skins peeled off, and pulp used for food. (95:258) **Papago** *Fruit* Fruits cooked and eaten with white flour. Fruits eaten raw. **Pima** *Fruit* Fruits cooked and eaten with white flour. Fruits eaten raw. (95:262)

Yucca torreyi, Torrey's Yucca
Apache *Beverage* Baked fruit pounded to a pulp, drained, and juice drunk. *Bread & Cake* Fruit roasted, pulp made into cakes, and stored. *Sauce & Relish* Baked fruit pounded to a pulp, drained and juice poured over cakes. (17:18) **Apache, Chiricahua & Mescalero** *Bread & Cake* Fruit roasted, split, seeds removed, and pulp ground into large cakes. Fruit pulp ground, made into large cakes, and stored indefinitely. (as *Y. macrocarpa* 33:39) **Southwest Indians** *Fruit* Fruits eaten occasionally. (17:63)

Yucca whipplei, Chaparral Yucca
Cahuilla *Bread & Cake* Roasted stalks dried,

ground, and mixed with water to make cakes. *Dried Food* Flowers and stalks sun dried and preserved. *Unspecified* Less mature flowers parboiled and very mature flowers boiled three times with salt and eaten. *Vegetable* Sliced stalks parboiled and cooked like squash. (15:150) **Luiseño** *Unspecified* Roasted stalks used for food. Plant head roasted in an earth oven and formerly used for food. Blossoms cooked in water and used for food. (155:195) **Mahuna** *Sauce & Relish* Stalks pit roasted and used to make a syrup. *Unspecified* Flowers eaten as food. (140:58) **Tubatulabal** *Unspecified* Stalks used for food in late winter and early spring. (193:11) Stalks used extensively for food. (193:15)

Yucca whipplei* var. *caespitosa, Chaparral Yucca
Kawaiisu *Dried Food* Apical meristems pit roasted, mashed, dried, and stored for future use. *Unspecified* Apical meristems pit roasted and eaten. Stalks roasted, peeled, and eaten. (206:69)

Yucca whipplei* ssp. *whipplei, Chaparral Yucca
Diegueño *Unspecified* Young stalk peeled, roasted, and eaten in the spring. Blossoms picked before opening in the spring, boiled twice, and eaten. (84:45)

Zamia pumila, Coontie
Seminole *Unspecified* Plant used for food. (as *Z. floridana* 169:489)

Zea mays, Corn
Abnaki *Soup* Seeds used to make soup. (144:175) **Cahuilla** *Porridge* Ground into a meal, boiled, and eaten. (15:153) **Cherokee** *Vegetable* Corn used for food. (80:30) **Chippewa** *Porridge* Used to make a "hominy." *Soup* Kernels pounded into a meal and used to make "parched corn soup." *Vegetable* Fresh ears roasted in the husks and used for food. (53:319) **Choctaw** *Vegetable* Seeds parched and mixed with water or boiled with or without meat. (25:8–9) **Dakota** *Staple* Ripe, parched corn ground into a meal and used for food. Ripe corn hulled with lye from ashes and used to make hominy. *Sweetener* Sun dried corn silks ground with parched corn for sweetness. *Winter Use Food* Sun dried corn silks stored for future use. (70:67) **Delaware** *Bread & Cake* Dry, unparched corn made into flour and used to make bread. *Dried Food* Ears boiled, cooled, the grains dried and used for food. *Porridge* Ears sun dried, grains pounded into hominy grits and used for food. *Soup* Dried corn boiled in alkaline liquid and hulls combined with fresh or dried meat for stew. *Staple* Used as the staple vegetable food to provide nourishment for the soul and the body. *Unspecified* Ears roasted and used for food. Dried corn boiled in alkaline liquid and hulls eaten with milk and sugar or fried with potatoes. (176:55) **Havasupai** *Bread & Cake* Seeds used to make wafer bread. (as *Z. arnylacea* 162:103) Seeds used to make bread. Seeds parched, ground fine, mixed with salt water into thin gruel, and cooked in thin layer into piki. Seeds ground, added to boiling water, kneaded, rolled in corn husks, boiled, and eaten as tamales. Seeds parched, ground fine, boiled, thickened, made into balls, and eaten as

dumplings. Seeds ground, kneaded into a thick paste, rolled into little balls, boiled, and eaten as marbles. (197:66) *Porridge* Seeds parched, ground, and used to make mush. *Soup* Seeds parched, ground, and used to make soup. *Staple* Seeds ground and eaten as a ground or parched meal. (197:67) *Vegetable* Seeds eaten fresh, baked on the cob, roasted, or boiled. *Winter Use Food* Seeds pit baked and stored for winter use. (197:66) **Hopi** *Bread & Cake* Seeds ground into meal and used to make wafer bread. (200:67) *Dried Food* Pit baked, husked, strung, and sun dried. (as *Z. mays saccharata* 200:69) *Porridge* Grains soaked in water with juniper ash, boiled, and washed to make hominy. Made into hominy and other dishes, plant constituted the main food supply. *Staple* Ground into meal. (as *Z. mays amylacea* 200:67) *Sweetener* Ears pit baked, husked, strung, sun dried, and used as a sweetener in the winter. *Unspecified* Pit baked and eaten immediately. (as *Z. mays saccharata* 200:69) **Iroquois** *Baby Food* Seeds boiled into a liquor and used in the preparation of food for infants. Seeds used to make a meal gruel for babies. (196:71) *Beverage* Stalks cut between the joints and chewed to quench the thirst. (196:119) Dried, roasted seeds boiled in water to make coffee. (196:145) Seeds boiled into a liquor and used as a beverage or made into soup. *Bread & Cake* Seeds ground into a meal or flour and used to make boiled bread. Seeds ground, mixed with hot water, molded, dropped into boiling water, and eaten as dumplings. *Pie & Pudding* Seeds, pumpkin mush, and maple sugar used to make pudding. *Porridge* Seeds used to make hominy. *Sauce & Relish* Seeds used to make succotash. *Snack Food* Seeds used to make popcorn. *Soup* Seeds used with beans, squash, and meats to make soups and broths. *Special Food* Seeds used to make wedding bread or bread placed in the coffin with the corpse. Seeds used for ceremonial occasions, such as False-Face Society functions. *Vegetable* Seeds eaten raw or cooked while traveling or hunting. Corn on the cob roasted and eaten. (196:71) **Isleta** *Beverage* Ground corn used to make a slightly intoxicating beverage. *Bread & Cake* Cornmeal used to make various breads. *Candy* Parched corn eaten as a confection. *Porridge* Cornmeal used to make a mush. *Staple* Parched corn eaten as a staple. *Sweetener* Evaporated liquid from crushed, soaked stalks used to make sugar. *Unspecified* Corn husks used to wrap tamales. *Winter Use Food* Cornmeal used to make mush, dried, and stored for winter use. (100:46) **Kamia** *Unspecified* Species used for food. (62:21) **Keres, Western** *Staple* Cornmeal used as one of the main foods. (171:76) *Vegetable* Roasted corn ears eaten warm for food. *Winter Use Food* Roasted corn ears dried and stored for winter use. (171:77) **Kiowa** *Fodder* Valued as a fodder for livestock. *Unspecified* Valued as a food. (192:17) **Menominee** *Beverage* Scorched or parched corn often used as a substitute for coffee. *Special Food* Parched, ground corn mixed with bear oil and used as trail ration. *Staple* Roasted popcorn pounded into a meal added to dried venison, maple sugar, or wild rice or all three. *Substitution Food* Scorched or parched corn often used as a substitute for coffee. *Vegetable* Ears roasted and made into hominy. *Winter Use Food* Ears parboiled and the kernels sun dried for winter use. (151:66) **Meskwaki** *Unspecified* Boiled or parched corn eaten or made into corn hominy grits. *Winter Use Food* Boiled or parched corn stored for winter use. (152:257) **Navajo** *Beverage* Cornmeal and juniper ash water used to make a beverage. *Bread & Cake* Corn and juniper ash used to make bread and dumplings. *Porridge* Corn and meat boiled all night into hominy. Cornmeal and juniper ash water used to make mush. *Special Food* Cornmeal porridge, served in wedding baskets, used as a nuptial dish. *Staple* Green corn roasted, shelled, ground, dried, and wrapped in corn husks, like tamales, for journeys. *Unspecified* Immature corn pounded, mixed with pumpkin, wrapped in a corn husk, and baked in ashes. *Vegetable*

Leaves eaten like lettuce. (55:27) **Navajo, Ramah** *Fodder* Used as horse feed. *Special Food* Cornmeal used to make ceremonial cakes. *Vegetable* Young corn and cob eaten. *Winter Use Food* Roasted, dried corn on the cob stored for winter use. (191:18) **Ojibwa** *Dried Food* Kernels dried for winter use. *Vegetable* Several sorts of corn were grown, modern and ancient. Ears were roasted and made into hominy. (153:402) **Omaha** *Staple* Ripe, parched corn ground into a meal and used for food. Ripe corn hulled with lye from ashes and used to make hominy. (70:67) *Sweetener* Sun dried corn silks ground with parched corn for sweetness. *Winter Use Food* Sun dried corn silks stored for future use. (70:68) **Papago** *Dried Food* Grains parched, dried on mats on the roofs, and used for food. *Special Food* Cornmeal used ceremonially. *Staple* Whole ears roasted in open pits, dried, grains removed, winnowed, and ground into meal. *Unspecified* Whole ears roasted in open pits, dried, grains removed, winnowed, and cooked whole with meat. (34:34) **Pawnee** *Staple* Ripe, parched corn ground into a meal and used for food. Ripe corn hulled with lye from ashes and used to make hominy. *Sweetener* Sun dried corn silks ground with parched corn for sweetness. *Winter Use Food* Sun dried corn silks stored for future use. (70:67) **Pima** *Bread & Cake* Ground, baked in large cakes, and used for food. *Porridge* Boiled with ashes, dried, hulls washed off, dried, parched with coals, and made into gruel. (146:72) **Ponca** *Staple* Ripe, parched corn ground into a meal and used for food. Ripe corn hulled with lye from ashes and used to make hominy. *Sweetener* Sun dried corn silks ground with parched corn for sweetness. *Winter Use Food* Sun dried corn silks stored for future use. (70:67) **Potawatomi** *Winter Use Food* Elm bark bags, filled with corn or beans and peas, buried in the ground to keep for the winter. (154:101) **Pueblo** *Special Food* Cornmeal used ceremonially. (34:34) **Seminole** *Unspecified* Seeds used for food. (169:473) **Sia** *Staple* Corn and wheat, the most important foods, used for food. (199:106) **Tewa** *Beverage* Corn ground and sifted into boiling water to make a gruel formerly drunk in the morning. Cornmeal mixed with cold water and drunk as a nourishing drink. *Bread & Cake* Corn ground on a metate, formed into cakes, rolled, and baked. *Forage* Husks, stalks, and leaves used for stock winter forage. *Staple* Used as a staple food. (138:78) **Zuni** *Beverage* Popped corn ground as fine as possible, mixed with cold water, strained, and used as a beverage. *Bread & Cake* Toasted or untoasted corn ground into a flour and used to make bread. *Porridge* Corn used to make gruel. *Snack Food* Corn used to make popcorn. *Staple* Toasted or untoasted corn ground into a flour and used to make bread eaten as a staple on journeys. (166:73)

Zea mays var. *rugosa*, Corn
Navajo *Bread & Cake* Sweet cornmeal and herb roots made into cakes and baked in a pit. (55:30)

Zigadenus paniculatus, Foothill Deathcamas
Navajo, Kayenta *Unspecified* Bulbs cooked with meat and corn and used for food. *Vegetable* Plants used as greens. (205:17)

Zigadenus venenosus, Meadow Deathcamas
Karok *Unspecified* Bulbs used for food. (6:64)

Zizania aquatica, Annual Wildrice
Dakota *Staple* Grain used as an important and prized food item. (69:360) Rice considered an important dietary element. (70:67) **Menominee** *Staple* Rice cooked with deer broth, pork, or butter and seasoned with maple sugar. (151:67) **Meskwaki** *Unspecified* Rice used for food. (152:259) **Ojibwa** *Bread & Cake* Seeds used to make gem cakes, duck stuffing, and fowl stuffing. *Breakfast Food* Seeds steamed into puffed rice and eaten for breakfast with sugar and cream. *Special Food* Seeds boiled with rabbit excrements, eaten and esteemed as a luxury. (135:246) **Omaha** *Staple* Grains used as a staple food. (68:328) Rice considered an important dietary element. **Ponca** *Staple* Rice considered an important dietary element. (70:67)

Zizania aquatica

Thompson *Unspecified* Rice cooked with meat. (187:144) **Winnebago** *Staple* Rice considered an important dietary element. (70:67)

Zizania palustris, Northern Wildrice
Chippewa *Unspecified* Cooked alone or with meat and used as the principal cereal food. (53:318) **Ojibwa** *Staple* Formed an important staple in the diet, cooked with deer broth and maple sugar and eaten. (153:403) **Potawatomi** *Dried Food* Rice gathered and dried for a winter supply of food. *Pie & Pudding* Wild rice sweetened with maple sugar and used to make pudding. *Staple* Rice valuable for cooking with wild fowl or game and maple sugar used to season the mixture. (154:101)

Ziziphus obtusifolia, Lote Bush
Papago *Beverage* Fruits formerly fermented and used for a beverage. (as *Zizyphus lycioides* 34:26) *Sauce & Relish* Fruits boiled to a syrup and used for food. (as *Zizyphus lycioides* 34:19) **Pima** *Fruit* Black berries beaten with sticks and eaten raw. (as *Zizyphus lycioides* 146:76) **Yavapai** *Beverage* Mashed berries added to water and use as a drink. (as *Zizyphus cycioides* 65:258)

Ziziphus obtusifolia var. *canescens*, Lote Bush

Maricopa *Dried Food* Berries dried and stored, to be soaked in hot water and used later. *Fruit* Fruits mashed into a concoction and eaten. **Mohave** *Dried Food* Berries dried and stored, to be soaked in hot water and used later. **Maricopa & Mohave** *Fruit* Fruits mashed into a concoction and eaten. (as *Condalia lycioides* var. *canescens* 37:204) **Pima** *Fodder* Seeds squeezed out from boiled berries and fed to chickens. *Fruit* Ripe, black berries eaten raw. *Sauce & Relish* Berries boiled and used to make a syrup. (as *Condalia lycioides* var. *canescens* 47:50) **Pima, Gila River** *Fruit* Fruits eaten raw and boiled. (133:7)

Ziziphus parryi, Parry's Jujube

Cahuilla *Fruit* Drupes eaten fresh. *Porridge* Drupes dried and ground into flour for mush. *Staple* Leached nutlet of the drupe ground into a flour. (as *Condalia parryi* 15:56)

Zostera marina, Seawrack

Bellabella *Unspecified* Plants eaten raw with eulachon (candlefish) grease. (184:200) **Cowichan** *Spice* Fleshy roots and leaf bases used to flavor seal, porpoise, and deer meat. (182:77) **Hesquiat** *Forage* Brownish "roots" (actually rhizomes) eaten by black brants, Canada geese, mallard ducks, and cattle. *Unspecified* Brownish "roots" (actually rhizomes) cleaned, washed, and eaten raw. Greenish "root" eaten raw. (185:59) **Kwakiutl, Southern** *Special Food* Stems and roots dipped in oil and eaten during feasts. (183:274) *Unspecified* Plants eaten raw with eulachon (candlefish) grease. (184:200) **Nitinaht** *Unspecified* Fleshy, whitish rhizomes formerly eaten raw. (186:89) **Oweekeno** *Unspecified* Leaves picked with attached herring spawn and eaten. (43:82) **Saanich** *Spice* Fleshy roots and leaf bases used to flavor seal, porpoise, and deer meat. (182:77)

Bibliography

1. Ager, Thomas A., and Lynn Price Ager. 1980. Ethnobotany of the Eskimos of Nelson Island, Alaska. Arctic Anthropology 27: 26–48.
2. Akana, Akaiko. 1922. Hawaiian Herbs of Medicinal Value. Honolulu: Pacific Book House.
3. Aller, Wilma F. 1954. Aboriginal Food Utilization of Vegetation by the Indians of the Great Lake Region as Recorded in the Jesuit Relations. Wisconsin Archeologist 35: 59–73.
4. Anderson, J. P. 1939. Plants Used by the Eskimo of the Northern Bering Sea and Arctic Regions of Alaska. American Journal of Botany 26: 714–716.
5. Arnason, Thor, Richard J. Hebda and Timothy Johns. 1981. Use of Plants for Food and Medicine by Native Peoples of Eastern Canada. Canadian Journal of Botany 59(11): 2189–2325.
6. Baker, Marc A. 1981. The Ethnobotany of the Yurok, Tolowa and Karok Indians of Northwest California. M.A. Thesis, Humboldt State University, Arcata, California.
7. Bank, Theodore P., II. 1951. Botanical and Ethnobotanical Studies in the Aleutian Islands I. Aleutian Vegetation and Aleut Culture. Botanical and Ethnobotanical Studies Papers, Michigan Academy of Science, Arts and Letters, 37: 13–30.
8. Bank, Theodore P., II. 1953. Botanical and Ethnobotanical Studies in the Aleutian Islands II. Health and Medical Lore of the Aleuts. Botanical and Ethnobotanical Studies Papers, Michigan Academy of Science, Arts and Letters, 38: 415–431.
9. Barrett, S. A. 1908. Pomo Indian Basketry. University of California Publications in American Archaeology and Ethnology 7: 134–308.
10. Barrett, S. A. 1917. The Washoe Indians. Bulletin of the Public Museum of the City of Milwaukee 2(1): 1–52.
11. Barrett, S. A. 1952. Material Aspects of Pomo Culture. Bulletin of the Public Museum of the City of Milwaukee, Number 20.
12. Barrett, S. A., and E. W. Gifford. 1933. Miwok Material Culture. Bulletin of the Public Museum of the City of Milwaukee 2(4): 11.
13. Barrows, David Prescott. 1967. The Ethno-Botany of the Coahuilla Indians of Southern California. Banning, California: Malki Museum Press. Originally published in 1900.
14. Basehart, Harry W. 1974. Apache Indians XII. Mescalero Apache Subsistence Patterns and Socio-Political Organization. New York: Garland Publishing.
15. Bean, Lowell John, and Katherine Siva Saubel. 1972. Temalpakh (From the Earth); Cahuilla Indian Knowledge and Usage of Plants. Banning, California: Malki Museum Press.
16. Beardsley, Gretchen 1941. Notes on Cree Medicines, Based on Collections Made by I. Cowie in 1892. Papers of the Michigan Academy of Science, Arts and Letters 28: 483–496.
17. Bell, Willis H., and Edward F. Castetter. 1941. Ethnobiological Studies in the Southwest VII. The Utilization of Yucca, Sotol and Beargrass by the Aborigines in the

American Southwest. University of New Mexico Bulletin 5(5): 1–74.

18. Black, Meredith Jean. 1980. Algonquin Ethnobotany: An Interpretation of Aboriginal Adaptation in South Western Quebec. Ottawa: National Museums of Canada. Mercury Series, Number 65.

19. Blankinship, J. W. 1905. Native Economic Plants of Montana. Bozeman: Montana Agricultural College Experimental Station, Bulletin 56.

20. Boas, Franz 1966. Kwakiutl Ethnography. Chicago: University of Chicago Press.

21. Bocek, Barbara R. 1984. Ethnobotany of Costanoan Indians, California, Based on Collections by John P. Harrington. Economic Botany 38(2): 240–255.

22. Bradley, Will T. 1936. Medical Practices of the New England Aborigines. Journal of the American Pharmaceutical Association 25(2): 138–147.

23. Brugge, David M. 1965. Navajo Use of *Agave*. Kiva 31(2): 88–98.

24. Burgesse, J. Allen 1944. The Woman and the Child among the Lac-St.-Jean Montagnais. Primitive Man 17: 1–18.

25. Bushnell, David I., Jr. 1909. The Choctaw of Bayou Lacomb, St. Tammany Parish, Louisiana. Smithsonian Institution, Bureau of American Ethnology Bulletin, Number 48.

26. Buskirk, Winfred. 1986. The Western Apache: Living with the Land before 1950. Norman: University of Oklahoma Press.

27. Camazine, Scott, and Robert A. Bye 1980. A Study of the Medical Ethnobotany of the Zuni Indians of New Mexico. Journal of Ethnopharmacology 2: 365–388.

28. Campbell, T. N. 1951. Medicinal Plants Used by Choctaw, Chickasaw, and Creek Indians in the Early Nineteenth Century. Journal of the Washington Academy of Sciences 41(9): 285–290.

29. Carlson, Gustav G., and Volney H. Jones. 1940. Some Notes on Uses of Plants by the Comanche Indians. Papers of the Michigan Academy of Science, Arts and Letters 25: 517–542.

30. Carr, Lloyd G., and Carlos Westey. 1945. Surviving Folktales and Herbal Lore among the Shinnecock Indians. Journal of American Folklore 58: 113–123.

31. Carrier Linguistic Committee. 1973. Plants of Carrier Country. Fort St. James, British Columbia: Carrier Linguistic Committee.

32. Castetter, Edward F. 1935. Ethnobiological Studies in the American Southwest I. Uncultivated Native Plants Used as Sources of Food. University of New Mexico Bulletin 4(1): 1–44.

33. Castetter, Edward F., and M. E. Opler. 1936. Ethnobiological Studies in the American Southwest III. The Ethnobiology of the Chiricahua and Mescalero Apache. University of New Mexico Bulletin 4(5): 1–63.

34. Castetter, Edward F., and Ruth M. Underhill. 1935. Ethnobiological Studies in the American Southwest II. The Ethnobiology of the Papago Indians. University of New Mexico Bulletin 4(3): 1–84.

35. Castetter, Edward F., and Willis H. Bell. 1937. Ethnobiological Studies in the American Southwest IV. The Aboriginal Utilization of the Tall Cacti in the American South. University of New Mexico Bulletin 5: 1–48.

36. Castetter, Edward F., and Willis H. Bell. 1942. Pima and Papago Indian Agriculture. Albuquerque: University of New Mexico Press.

37. Castetter, Edward F., and Willis H. Bell. 1951. Yuman Indian Agriculture. Albuquerque: University of New Mexico Press.

38. Chamberlin, Ralph V. 1909. Some Plant Names of the Ute Indians. American Anthropologist 11: 27–40.

39. Chamberlin, Ralph V. 1911. The Ethno-Botany of the Gosiute Indians of Utah. Memoirs of the American Anthropological Association 2(5): 331–405.

40. Chandler, R. Frank, Lois Freeman, and Shirley N. Hooper. 1979. Herbal Remedies of the Maritime Indians. Journal of Ethnopharmacology 1: 49–68.

41. Chesnut, V. K. 1902. Plants Used by the Indians of Mendocino County, California.

Contributions from the U.S. National Herbarium 7: 295–408.

42. Colton, Harold S. 1974. Hopi History and Ethnobotany. Pages 279–373 in D. A. Horr (editor), Hopi Indians. New York: Garland Publishing.

43. Compton, Brian Douglas. 1993. Upper North Wakashan and Southern Tsimshian Ethnobotany: The Knowledge and Usage of Plants . . . Ph.D. Dissertation, University of British Columbia, Vancouver.

44. Cook, Sarah Louise. 1930. The Ethnobotany of Jemez Indians. M.A. Thesis, University of New Mexico, Albuquerque.

45. Coville, Frederick V. 1897. Notes on the Plants Used by the Klamath Indians of Oregon. Contributions from the U.S. National Herbarium 5(2): 87–110.

46. Coville, Frederick V. 1904. Wokas, a Primitive Food of the Klamath Indians. Washington, D.C.: Smithsonian Institution, U.S. National Museum.

47. Curtin, L. S. M. 1949. By the Prophet of the Earth. Sante Fe, New Mexico: San Vicente Foundation.

48. Curtin, L. S. M. 1957. Some Plants Used by the Yuki Indians . . . I. Historical Review and Medicinal Plants. Masterkey 31: 40–48.

49. Curtin, L. S. M. 1957. Some Plants Used by the Yuki Indians . . . II. Food Plants. Masterkey 31: 85–94.

50. Dawson, E. Yale. 1944. Some Ethnobotanical Notes on the Seri Indians. Desert Plant Life 9: 133–138.

51. Densmore, Frances. 1913. Chippewa Music—II. Smithsonian Institution, Bureau of American Ethnology Bulletin, Number 53.

52. Densmore, Frances. 1918. Teton Sioux Music. Smithsonian Institution, Bureau of American Ethnology Bulletin, Number 61.

53. Densmore, Frances. 1928. Uses of Plants by the Chippewa Indians. Smithsonian Institution, Bureau of American Ethnology Annual Report 44: 273–379.

54. Densmore, Francis. 1932. Menominee Music. Smithsonian Institution, Bureau of American Ethnology Bulletin, Number 102.

55. Elmore, Francis H. 1944. Ethnobotany of the Navajo. Sante Fe, New Mexico: School of American Research.

56. Fewkes, J. Walter. 1896. A Contribution to Ethnobotany. American Anthropologist 9: 14–21.

57. Fleisher, Mark S. 1980. The Ethnobotany of the Clallam Indians of Western Washington. Northwest Anthropological Research Notes 14(2): 192–210.

58. Fletcher, Alice C., and Francis la Flesche. 1911. The Omaha Tribe. Smithsonian Institution, Bureau of American Ethnology Annual Report, Number 27.

59. Fowler, Catherine S. 1989. Willard Z. Park's Ethnographic Notes on the Northern Paiute of Western Nevada 1933–1940. Salt Lake City: University of Utah Press.

60. Fowler, Catherine S. 1990. Tule Technology: Northern Paiute Uses of Marsh Resources in Western Nevada. Washington, D.C.: Smithsonian Institution Press.

61. Garth, Thomas R. 1953. Atsugewi Ethnography. Anthropological Records 14(2): 140–141.

62. Gifford, E. W. 1931. The Kamia of Imperial Valley. Washington, D.C.: U.S. Government Printing Office.

63. Gifford, E. W. 1932. The Southeastern Yavapai. University of California Publications in American Archaeology and Ethnology 29: 177–252.

64. Gifford, E. W. 1933. The Cocopa. University of California Publications in American Archaeology and Ethnology 31: 263–270.

65. Gifford, E. W. 1936. Northeastern and Western Yavapai. University of California Publications in American Archaeology and Ethnology 34: 247–345.

66. Gifford, E. W. 1967. Ethnographic Notes on the Southwestern Pomo. Anthropological Records 25: 10–15.

67. Gill, Steven J. 1983. Ethnobotany of the Makah and Ozette People, Olympic Peninsula, Washington (USA). Ph.D. Thesis, Washington State University, Pullman.

68. Gilmore, Melvin R. 1913. A Study in the Ethnobotany of the Omaha Indians. Nebraska State Historical Society Collections 17: 314–357.

69. Gilmore, Melvin R. 1913. Some Native Nebraska Plants with Their Uses by the Dakota. Collections of the Nebraska State Historical Society 17: 358–370.

70. Gilmore, Melvin R. 1919. Uses of Plants by the Indians of the Missouri River Region. Smithsonian Institution, Bureau of American Ethnology Annual Report, Number 33.

71. Gilmore, Melvin R. 1933. Some Chippewa Uses of Plants. Ann Arbor: University of Michigan Press.

72. Goodrich, Jennie, and Claudia Lawson. 1980. Kashaya Pomo Plants. Los Angeles: American Indian Studies Center, University of California, Los Angeles.

73. Gottesfeld, Leslie M. J. 1992. The Importance of Bark Products in the Aboriginal Economies of Northwestern British Columbia, Canada. Economic Botany 46(2): 148–157.

74. Gottesfeld, Leslie M. J., and Beverley Anderson. 1988. Gitksan Traditional Medicine: Herbs And Healing. Journal of Ethnobiology 8(1): 13–33.

75. Grinnell, George Bird. 1905. Some Cheyenne Plant Medicines. American Anthropologist 7: 37–43.

76. Grinnell, George Bird. 1972. The Cheyenne Indians—Their History and Ways of Life, Volume 2. Lincoln: University of Nebraska Press.

77. Guédon, Marie-Francoise. 1974. People of Tetlin, Why Are You Singing? Ottawa: National Museums of Canada. Mercury Series, Number 9.

78. Gunther, Erna. 1927. Klallam Ethnography. Seattle: University of Washington Press.

79. Gunther, Erna. 1973. Ethnobotany of Western Washington. Revised edition. Seattle: University of Washington Press.

80. Hamel, Paul B., and Mary U. Chiltoskey. 1975. Cherokee Plants and Their Uses—A 400 Year History. Sylva, North Carolina: Herald Publishing.

81. Hann, John H. 1986. The Use and Processing of Plants by Indians of Spanish Florida. Southeastern Archaeology 5(2): 1–102.

82. Hart, Jeff. 1992. Montana Native Plants and Early Peoples. Helena: Montana Historical Society Press.

83. Hart, Jeffrey A. 1981. The Ethnobotany of the Northern Cheyenne Indians of Montana. Journal of Ethnopharmacology 4: 1–55.

84. Hedges, Ken. 1986. Santa Ysabel Ethnobotany. San Diego Museum of Man Ethnic Technology Notes, Number 20.

85. Heller, Christine A. 1953. Edible and Poisonous Plants of Alaska. College, Alaska: Cooperative Agricultural Extension Service.

86. Hellson, John C. 1974. Ethnobotany of the Blackfoot Indians. Ottawa: National Museums of Canada. Mercury Series, Number 19.

87. Herrick, James William. 1977. Iroquois Medical Botany. Ph.D. Thesis, State University of New York, Albany.

88. Hinton, Leanne. 1975. Notes on La Huerta Diegueno Ethnobotany. Journal of California Anthropology 2: 214–222.

89. Hocking, George M. 1949. From Pokeroot to Penicillin. Rocky Mountain Druggist, November 1949, pages 12, 38.

90. Hocking, George M. 1956. Some Plant Materials Used Medicinally and Otherwise by the Navaho Indians in the Chaco Canyon, New Mexico. Palacio 56: 146–165.

91. Hoffman, W. J. 1891. The Midewiwin or "Grand Medicine Society" of the Ojibwa. Smithsonian Institution, Bureau of American Ethnology Annual Report, Number 7.

92. Holmes, E. M. 1884. Medicinal Plants Used by Cree Indians, Hudson's Bay Territory. Pharmaceutical Journal and Transactions 15: 302–304.

93. Holt, Catharine. 1946. Shasta Ethnography. Anthropological Records 3(4): 308.

94. Howard, James. 1965. The Ponca Tribe. Smithsonian Institution, Bureau of American Ethnology Bulletin, Number 195.

95. Hrdlicka, Ales. 1908. Physiological and Medical Observations among the Indians of Southwestern United States and North-

ern Mexico. Smithsonian Institution, Bureau of American Ethnology Bulletin 34: 1–427.

96. Jenness, Diamond. 1935. The Ojibwa Indians of Parry Island, Their Social and Religious Life. National Museums of Canada Bulletin, Number 78, Anthropological Series, Number 17.

97. Johnston, Alex. 1987. Plants and the Blackfoot. Lethbridge, Alberta: Lethbridge Historical Society.

98. Jones, Anore. 1983. Nauriat Niginaqtuat = Plants That We Eat. Kotzebue, Alaska: Maniilaq Association Traditional Nutrition Program.

99. Jones, David E. 1968. Comanche Plant Medicine. Papers in Anthropology 9: 1–13.

100. Jones, Volney H. 1931. The Ethnobotany of the Isleta Indians. M.A. Thesis, University of New Mexico, Albuquerque.

101. Jones, Volney H. 1938. An Ancient Food Plant of the Southwest and Plateau Regions. Palacio 44: 41–53.

102. Kari, Priscilla Russe. 1985. Upper Tanana Ethnobotany. Anchorage: Alaska Historical Commission.

103. Kelly, Isabel T. 1930. Yuki Basketry. University of California Publications in American Archaeology and Ethnology 24: 421–444.

104. Kelly, Isabel T. 1932. Ethnography of the Surprise Valley Paiute. University of California Publications in American Archaeology and Ethnology 31(3): 67–210.

105. Kirk, Ruth E. 1952. Panamint Basketry: A Dying Art. Masterkey 26: 76–86.

106. Kraft, Shelly Katherene. 1990. Recent Changes in the Ethnobotany of Standing Rock Indian Reservation. M.A. Thesis, University of North Dakota, Grand Forks.

107. Krause, Aurel. 1956. The Tlingit Indians. Translated by Erna Gunther. Seattle: University of Washington Press.

108. Lantis, Margaret. 1959. Folk Medicine and Hygiene. Anthropological Papers of the University of Alaska 8: 1–75.

109. Leighton, Anna L. 1985. Wild Plant Use by the Woods Cree (Nihithawak) of East-
Central Saskatchewan. Ottawa. National Museums of Canada. Mercury Series, Number 101.

110. Lynch, Regina H. 1986. Cookbook. Chinle, Arizona: Navajo Curriculum Center, Rough Rock Demonstration School.

111. Mahar, James Michael. 1953. Ethnobotany of the Oregon Paiutes of the Warm Springs Indian Reservation. B.A. Thesis, Reed College, Portland, Oregon.

112. Malo, David. 1903. Hawaiian Antiquities. Honolulu: Hawaiian Gazette Co., Ltd.

113. Mandelbaum, David G. 1940. The Plains Cree. Anthropological Papers of the American Museum of Natural History 37: 202–203.

114. McClintock, Walter. 1909. Medizinal- und Nutzpflanzen der Schwarzfuss Indianer. Zeitschrift für Ethnologie 41: 273–279.

115. McKennan, Robert A. 1959. The Upper Tanana Indians. Yale University Publications in Anthropology, Number 55.

116. Mechling, W. H. 1959. The Malecite Indians with Notes on the Micmacs. Anthropologica 8: 239–263.

117. Merriam, C. Hart. 1966. Ethnographic Notes on California Indian Tribes. Berkeley: University of California Archaeological Research Facility.

118. Murphey, Edith Van Allen. 1990. Indian Uses of Native Plants. Glenwood, Illinois: Meyerbooks. Originally published in 1959.

119. Nelson, Richard K. 1983. Make Prayers to the Raven—A Koyukon View of the Northern Forest. Chicago: University of Chicago Press.

120. Nequatewa, Edmund. 1943. Some Hopi Recipes for the Preparation of Wild Plant Foods. Plateau 18: 18–20.

121. Nickerson, Gifford S. 1966. Some Data on Plains and Great Basin Indian Uses of Certain Native Plants. Tebiwa 9(1): 45–51.

122. Oswalt, W. H. 1957. A Western Eskimo Ethnobotany. Anthropological Papers of the University of Alaska 6: 17–36.

123. Palmer, Gary. 1975. Shuswap Indian Ethnobotany. Syesis 8: 29–51.

124. Parker, Arthur Caswell. 1910. Iroquois Uses of Maize and Other Food Plants. Albany, New York: University of the State of New York.

125. Perry, F. 1952. Ethno-Botany of the Indians in the Interior of British Columbia. Museum and Art Notes 2(2): 36–43.

126. Perry, Myra Jean. 1975. Food Use of "Wild" Plants by Cherokee Indians. M.S. Thesis, University of Tennessee, Knoxville.

127. Porsild, A. E. 1937. Edible Roots and Berries of Northern Canada. Toronto: Canada Department of Mines and Resources, National Museum of Canada.

128. Porsild, A. E. 1953. Edible Plants of the Arctic. Arctic 6: 15–34.

129. Powers, Stephen. 1874. Aboriginal Botany. Proceedings of the California Academy of Science 5: 373–379.

130. Radin, Paul. 1923. The Winnebago Tribe. Smithsonian Institution, Bureau of American Ethnology Annual Report, Number 37.

131. Ray, Verne F. 1932. The Sanpoil and Nespelem: Salishan Peoples of Northeastern Washington. University of Washington Publications in Anthropology, Volume 5.

132. Raymond, Marcel. 1945. Notes Ethnobotaniques sur les Tête-de-Boule de Manouan. Contributions de l'Institut Botanique de l'Université de Montréal 55: 113–134.

133. Rea, Amadeo M. 1991. Gila River Pima Dietary Reconstruction. Arid Lands Newsletter 31: 3–10.

134. Reagan, Albert. 1934. Various Uses of Plants by West Coast Indians. Washington Historical Quarterly 25: 133–137.

135. Reagan, Albert B. 1928. Plants Used by the Bois Fort Chippewa (Ojibwa) Indians of Minnesota. Wisconsin Archeologist 7(4): 230–248.

136. Reagan, Albert B. 1929. Plants Used by the White Mountain Apache Indians of Arizona. Wisconsin Archeologist 8: 143–161.

137. Reagan, Albert B. 1936. Plants Used by the Hoh and Quileute Indians. Kansas Academy of Science 37: 55–70.

138. Robbins, W. W., J. P. Harrington, and B. Freire-Marreco 1916. Ethnobotany of the Tewa Indians. Smithsonian Institution, Bureau of American Ethnology Bulletin, Number 55.

139. Rogers, Dilwyn J. 1980. Lakota Names and Traditional Uses of Native Plants by Sicangu (Brule) People in the Rosebud Area, South Dakota. St. Francis, South Dakota: Rosebud Educational Society.

140. Romero, John Bruno. 1954. The Botanical Lore of the California Indians. New York: Vantage Press.

141. Rousseau, Jacques. 1945. Le Folklore Botanique de Caughnawaga. Contributions de l'Institut Botanique de l'Université de Montréal 55: 7–72.

142. Rousseau, Jacques. 1945. Le Folklore Botanique de l'Ile aux Coudres. Contributions de l'Institut Botanique de l'Université de Montréal 55: 75–111.

143. Rousseau, Jacques. 1946. Notes Sur l'Ethnobotanique d'Anticosti. Archives de Folklore 1: 60–71.

144. Rousseau, Jacques. 1947. Ethnobotanique Abénakise. Archives de Folklore 11: 145–182.

145. Rousseau, Jacques. 1948. Ethnobotanique et Ethnozoologie Gaspésiennes. Archives de Folklore 3: 51–64.

146. Russell, Frank. 1908. The Pima Indians. Smithsonian Institution, Bureau of American Ethnology Annual Report 26: 1–390.

147. Sapir, Edward, and Leslie Spier. 1943. Notes on the Culture of the Yana. Anthropological Records 3(3): 252–253.

148. Schenck, Sara M., and E. W. Gifford. 1952. Karok Ethnobotany. Anthropological Records 13(6): 377–392.

149. Smith, G. Warren. 1973. Arctic Pharmacognosia. Arctic 26: 324–333.

150. Smith, Harlan I. 1929. Materia Medica of the Bella Coola and Neighboring Tribes of British Columbia. National Museum of Canada Bulletin 56: 47–68.

151. Smith, Huron H. 1923. Ethnobotany of the Menomini Indians. Bulletin of the Public Museum of the City of Milwaukee 4: 1–174.

152. Smith, Huron H. 1928. Ethnobotany of the Meskwaki Indians. Bulletin of the Public

Museum of the City of Milwaukee 4: 175–326.

153. Smith, Huron H. 1932. Ethnobotany of the Ojibwe Indians. Bulletin of the Public Museum of Milwaukee 4: 327–525.

154. Smith, Huron H. 1933. Ethnobotany of the Forest Potawatomi Indians. Bulletin of the Public Museum of the City of Milwaukee 7: 1–230.

155. Sparkman, Philip S. 1908. The Culture of the Luiseno Indians. University of California Publications in American Archaeology and Ethnology 8(4): 187–234.

156. Speck, Frank G. 1917. Medicine Practices of the Northeastern Algonquians. Proceedings of the 19th International Congress of Americanists, pages 303–321.

157. Speck, Frank G. 1937. Catawba Medicines and Curative Practices. Publications of the Philadelphia Anthropological Society 1: 179–197.

158. Speck, Frank G. 1941. A List of Plant Curatives Obtained from the Houma Indians of Louisiana. Primitive Man 14: 49–75.

159. Speck, Frank G., and R. W. Dexter. 1951. Utilization of Animals and Plants by the Micmac Indians of New Brunswick. Journal of the Washington Academy of Sciences 41: 250–259.

160. Speck, Frank G., and R. W. Dexter. 1952. Utilization of Animals and Plants by the Malecite Indians of New Brunswick. Journal of the Washington Academy of Sciences 42: 1–7.

161. Speck, Frank G., R. B. Hassrick, and E. S. Carpenter. 1942. Rappahannock Herbals, Folk-Lore and Science of Cures. Proceedings of the Delaware County Institute of Science 10: 7–55.

162. Spier, Leslie. 1928. Havasupai Ethnography. Anthropological Papers of the American Museum of Natural History 29(3): 101–123, 284–285.

163. Spier, Leslie. 1930. Klamath Ethnography. University of California Publications in American Archaeology and Ethnology 30: 1–338.

164. Steedman, E. V. 1928. The Ethnobotany of the Thompson Indians of British Columbia. Smithsonian Institution, Bureau of American Ethnology Annual Report 45: 441–522.

165. Steggerda, Morris. 1941. Navajo Foods and Their Preparation. Journal of the American Dietetic Association 17(3): 217–225.

166. Stevenson, Matilda Coxe. 1915. Ethnobotany of the Zuni Indians. Smithsonian Institution, Bureau of American Ethnology Annual Report, Number 30.

167. Steward, Julian H. 1933. Ethnography of the Owens Valley Paiute. University of California Publications in American Archaeology and Ethnology 33(3): 233–250.

168. Stewart, Kenneth M. 1965. Mohave Indian Gathering of Wild Plants. Kiva 31(1): 46–53.

169. Sturtevant, William Curtis. 1955. The Mikasuki Seminole: Medical Beliefs and Practices. Ph.D. Thesis, Yale University, New Haven, Connecticut. Ann Arbor: University Microfilms.

170. Swan, James Gilchrist. 1869. The Indians of Cape Flattery . . . Washington Territory. Washington, D.C.: Smithsonian Institution.

171. Swank, George R. 1932. The Ethnobotany of the Acoma and Laguna Indians. M.A. Thesis, University of New Mexico, Albuquerque.

172. Swanton, John R. 1928. Religious Beliefs and Medical Practices of the Creek Indians. Smithsonian Institution, Bureau of American Ethnology Annual Report 42: 473–672.

173. Swartz, B. K., Jr. 1958. A Study of Material Aspects of Northeastern Maidu Basketry. Kroeber Anthropological Society Publications 19: 67–84.

174. Tantaquidgeon, Gladys. 1928. Mohegan Medicinal Practices, Weather-Lore and Superstitions. Smithsonian Institution, Bureau of American Ethnology Annual Report 43: 264–270.

175. Tantaquidgeon, Gladys. 1942. A Study of Delaware Indian Medicine Practice and Folk Beliefs. Harrisburg: Pennsylvania Historical Commission.

176. Tantaquidgeon, Gladys. 1972. Folk Medicine of the Delaware and Related Algonkian Indians. Harrisburg: Pennsylvania Historical Commission Anthropological Papers, Number 3.

177. Taylor, Linda Averill. 1940. Plants Used as Curatives by Certain Southeastern Tribes. Cambridge, Massachusetts: Botanical Museum of Harvard University.

178. Teit, James A. 1928. The Salishan Tribes of the Western Plateaus. Smithsonian Institution, Bureau of American Ethnology Annual Report, Number 45.

179. Theodoratus, Robert J. 1989. Loss, Transfer, and Reintroduction in the Use of Wild Plant Foods in the Upper Skagit Valley. Northwest Anthropological Research Notes 23(1): 35–52.

180. Train, Percy, James R. Henrichs, and W. Andrew Archer. 1941. Medicinal Uses of Plants by Indian Tribes of Nevada. Washington, D.C.: U.S. Department of Agriculture.

181. Turner, Lucien M. 1890. Ethnology of the Ungava District, Hudson Bay Territory. Smithsonian Institution, Bureau of American Ethnology Annual Report 11: 159–350.

182. Turner, Nancy Chapman, and Marcus A. M. Bell. 1971. The Ethnobotany of the Coast Salish Indians of Vancouver Island, I and II. Economic Botany 25(1): 63–104, 335–339.

183. Turner, Nancy Chapman, and Marcus A. M. Bell. 1973. The Ethnobotany of the Southern Kwakiutl Indians of British Columbia. Economic Botany 27: 257–310.

184. Turner, Nancy J. 1973. The Ethnobotany of the Bella Coola Indians of British Columbia. Syesis 6: 193–220.

185. Turner, Nancy J., and Barbara S. Efrat 1982. Ethnobotany of the Hesquiat Indians of Vancouver Island. Victoria: British Columbia Provincial Museum.

186. Turner, Nancy J., John Thomas, Barry F. Carlson, and Robert T. Ogilvie. 1983. Ethnobotany of the Nitinaht Indians of Vancouver Island. Victoria: British Columbia Provincial Museum.

187. Turner, Nancy J., Laurence C. Thompson, M. Terry Thompson, and Annie Z. York. 1990. Thompson Ethnobotany: Knowledge and Usage of Plants by the Thompson Indians of British Columbia. Victoria: Royal British Columbia Museum.

188. Turner, Nancy J., R. Bouchard, and Dorothy I. D. Kennedy. 1980. Ethnobotany of the Okanagan-Colville Indians of British Columbia and Washington. Victoria: British Columbia Provincial Museum.

189. Veniamenov, I. 1840. Notes on the Islands in the Unalaska District. Translated by Human Relations Area Files, New Haven, Connecticut.

190. Vestal, Paul A. 1940. Notes on a Collection of Plants from the Hopi Indian Region of Arizona Made by J. G. Owens in 1891. Botanical Museum Leaflets (Harvard University) 8(8): 153–168.

191. Vestal, Paul A. 1952. The Ethnobotany of the Ramah Navaho. Papers of the Peabody Museum of American Archaeology and Ethnology 40(4): 1–94.

192. Vestal, Paul A., and Richard Evans Schultes. 1939. The Economic Botany of the Kiowa Indians. Cambridge, Massachusetts: Botanical Museum of Harvard University.

193. Voegelin, Ermine W. 1938. Tubatulabal Ethnography. Anthropological Records 2(1): 1–84.

194. Wallis, Wilson D. 1922. Medicines Used by the Micmac Indians. American Anthropologist 24: 24–30.

195. Watahomigie, Lucille J. 1982. Hualapai Ethnobotany. Peach Springs, Arizona: Hualapai Bilingual Program, Peach Springs School District Number 8.

196. Waugh, F. W. 1916. Iroquis Foods and Food Preparation. Ottawa: Canada Department of Mines.

197. Weber, Steven A., and P. David Seaman. 1985. Havasupai Habitat: A. F. Whiting's Ethnography of a Traditional Indian Culture. Tucson: University of Arizona Press.

198. White, Leslie A. 1945. Notes on the Ethnobotany of the Keres. Papers of the Michi-

gan Academy of Arts, Sciences and Letters 30: 557-568.

199. White, Leslie A. 1962. The Pueblo of Sia, New Mexico. Smithsonian Institution, Bureau of American Ethnology Bulletin, Number 184.

200. Whiting, Alfred F. 1939. Ethnobotany of the Hopi. Museum of Northern Arizona Bulletin, Number 15.

201. Willoughby, C. 1889. Indians of the Quinaielt Agency, Washington Territory. Smithsonian Institution Annual Report for 1886.

202. Wilson, Michael R. 1978. Notes on Ethnobotany in Inuktitut. Western Canadian Journal of Anthropology 8: 180–196.

203. Witthoft, John. 1947. An Early Cherokee Ethnobotanical Note. Journal of the Washington Academy of Sciences 37(3): 73–75.

204. Witthoft, John. 1977. Cherokee Indian Use of Potherbs. Journal of Cherokee Studies 2(2): 250–255.

205. Wyman, Leland C., and Stuart K. Harris. 1951. The Ethnobotany of the Kayenta Navaho. Albuquerque: University of New Mexico Press.

206. Zigmond, Maurice L. 1981. Kawaiisu Ethnobotany. Salt Lake City: University of Utah Press.

Index of Tribes

Plant usages are listed under the names of Native American groups, which are arranged alphabetically. Particular food usages are listed alphabetically. Plants are identified below to the level of species. If subspecies or varieties appear in the Catalog of Plants, check under those names, too, for all usages given below. For example, one may find Thompson below and under Candy see that *Agoseris glauca* was used. The specific ethnobotanical information and the sources from which the information was obtained may be found by turning to *Agoseris glauca* and *Agoseris glauca* var. *dasycephala* in the Catalog of Plants. Repeated genera are abbreviated to the first letter, so under Abnaki fruit, you can find two species of *Vaccinium*, indicated as "*Vaccinium angustifolium, V. myrtilloides.*"

Abnaki

Beverage: *Gaultheria procumbens, Spiraea alba*
Forage: *Cladonia rangiferina*
Fruit: *Aronia melanocarpa, Cornus canadensis, Fragaria virginiana, Prunus virginiana, Rubus idaeus, Vaccinium angustifolium, V. myrtilloides, Viburnum nudum*
Sauce & Relish: *Cardamine diphylla*
Snack Food: *Osmunda cinnamomea*
Soup: *Zea mays*
Sweetener: *Acer rubrum*
Unspecified: *Acorus calamus, Aronia melanocarpa, Caltha palustris, Cardamine diphylla, Osmunda cinnamomea, Viburnum nudum*
Vegetable: *Caltha palustris, Phaseolus vulgaris, Solanum tuberosum*

Acoma

Appetizer: *Rhus trilobata*
Beverage: *Yucca baccata*
Bread & Cake: *Yucca baccata*
Candy: *Asclepias speciosa, Populus deltoides*
Dried Food: *Amaranthus blitoides, A. hybridus, A. retroflexus, Opuntia imbricata, Prunus virginiana, Yucca baccata, Y. glauca*
Fruit: *Atriplex argentea, Ceanothus fendleri, Celtis laevigata, Juniperus monosperma, Opuntia engelmannii, Prunus virginiana, Ribes cereum, Yucca baccata, Y. glauca*
Porridge: *Cleome serrulata, Opuntia engelmannii, Prosopis glandulosa*
Preserves: *Ribes cereum, Yucca baccata*
Sauce & Relish: *Lycium pallidum, Yucca baccata*
Soup: *Juniperus osteosperma*
Special Food: *Sophora nuttalliana*
Spice: *Agastache pallidiflora, Berlandiera lyrata, Juniperus monosperma, Monarda fistulosa, M. pectinata, Pectis angustifolia, Rhus trilobata*
Staple: *Amaranthus blitoides, Dalea candida, Quercus gambelii*
Starvation Food: *Juniperus monosperma, Opuntia clavata, Phoradendron juniperinum, Solanum triflorum, Yucca baccata*
Unspecified: *Abronia fragrans, Allium cernuum, Astragalus lentiginosus, Cyperus squarrosus, Lathyrus polymorphus, Opuntia imbricata, Plantago major, Prosopis glandulosa, Quercus gambelii, Ranunculus inamoenus, Tradescantia occidentalis, Typha latifolia, Vicia americana*
Vegetable: *Amaranthus blitoides, A. hybridus, A. retroflexus, Cymopterus bulbosus, Lactuca sativa, Portulaca oleracea*

Alaska Native

Beverage: *Ledum groenlandicum, Rosa acicularis*

Bread & Cake: *Amelanchier alnifolia, Menyanthes trifoliata, Tsuga heterophylla, Vaccinium cespitosum, V. membranaceum, V. ovalifolium, V. uliginosum*

Cooking Agent: *Malus fusca*

Dessert: *Shepherdia canadensis*

Dietary Aid: *Chenopodium album, C. capitatum, Claytonia sibirica, C. tuberosa, Epilobium angustifolium, Fragaria chiloensis, Honckenya peploides, Ligusticum scothicum, Oxyria digyna, Polygonum bistorta, Rosa acicularis, Rubus chamaemorus, Rumex arcticus, Salix alaxensis, S. planifolia, Saxifraga nelsoniana, S. spicata, Urtica dioica, Vaccinium cespitosum, V. membranaceum, V. ovalifolium, V. uliginosum*

Dried Food: *Amelanchier alnifolia, Fritillaria camschatcensis, Menyanthes trifoliata, Porphyra laciniata, Rhodymenia palmata*

Frozen Food: *Rubus chamaemorus, Vaccinium cespitosum, V. membranaceum, V. ovalifolium, V. uliginosum*

Fruit: *Amelanchier alnifolia, Arctostaphylos alpina, Elaeagnus commutata, Fragaria chiloensis, Gaultheria shallon, Geocaulon lividum, Ribes triste, Rubus chamaemorus, R. idaeus, R. parviflorus, R. spectabilis, Streptopus amplexifolius, Vaccinium cespitosum, V. membranaceum, V. ovalifolium, V. oxycoccos, V. uliginosum*

Ice Cream: *Honckenya peploides*

Pie & Pudding: *Amelanchier alnifolia, Empetrum nigrum, Polygonum alpinum, Rubus chamaemorus, Vaccinium cespitosum, V. membranaceum, V. ovalifolium, V. uliginosum*

Preserves: *Empetrum nigrum, Fragaria chiloensis, Ribes triste, Rosa acicularis, Rubus arcticus, R. idaeus, R. pedatus, R. spectabilis, Vaccinium parvifolium, V. vitis-idaea, Viburnum edule*

Sauce & Relish: *Rosa acicularis, Vaccinium vitis-idaea*

Snack Food: *Porphyra laciniata, Salix alaxensis*

Soup: *Claytonia tuberosa, Fritillaria camschatcensis, Hippuris vulgaris, Parrya nudicaulis, Polygonum bistorta, Porphyra laciniata, Rhodymenia palmata*

Staple: *Fritillaria camschatcensis*

Starvation Food: *Menyanthes trifoliata*

Substitution Food: *Chenopodium album, Ligusticum scothicum, Pteridium aquilinum, Urtica dioica*

Unspecified: *Allium schoenoprasum, Anemone narcissiflora, Angelica lucida, Caltha palustris, Carex aquatilis, Claytonia acutifolia, Dryopteris carthusiana, Epilobium angustifolium, Eriophorum angustifolium, Hedysarum alpinum, Heracleum maximum, Honckenya peploides, Ligusticum scothicum, Lupinus nootkatensis, Oxyria digyna, Oxytropis nigrescens, Parrya nudicaulis, Pedicularis lanata, Plantago maritima, Polygonum bistorta, Ranunculus pallasii, Rhodymenia palmata, Salix alaxensis, S. planifolia, Saxifraga nelsoniana, Sedum rosea, Typha latifolia, Urtica dioica*

Vegetable: *Angelica lucida, Arabis lyrata, Argentina egedii, Barbarea orthoceras, Chenopodium album, C. capitatum, Claytonia sibirica, C. tuberosa, Cochlearia officinalis, Dryopteris carthusiana, Epilobium angustifolium, E. latifolium, Honckenya peploides, Ligusticum scothicum, Nuphar lutea, Petasites frigidus, Plantago macrocarpa, Polygonum alpinum, P. bistorta, Rumex arcticus, Sarcocornia pacifica, Saxifraga spicata, Sedum rosea, Streptopus amplexifolius*

Winter Use Food: *Hippuris vulgaris, Ligusticum scothicum, Parrya nudicaulis, Plantago maritima, Pteridium aquilinum, Rubus chamaemorus, Rumex arcticus, Salix planifolia, Vaccinium cespitosum, V. membranaceum, V. ovalifolium, V. uliginosum, V. vitis-idaea*

Algonquin, Quebec

Beverage: *Aralia nudicaulis, Gaultheria procumbens, Ledum groenlandicum, Prunus virginiana, Rhus hirta*

Bread & Cake: *Humulus lupulus*

Candy: *Picea glauca*

Fruit: *Fragaria virginiana, Gaultheria hispi-
dula, Prunus nigra, P. pensylvanica, P. vir-
giniana, Ribes cynosbati, R. glandulosum,
Rubus idaeus, R. odoratus, Sorbus ameri-
cana, Vaccinium angustifolium, V. corym-
bosum, V. macrocarpon, V. myrtilloides,
V. oxycoccos, Viburnum nudum, V. opulus*
Pie & Pudding: *Vaccinium angustifolium,
V. corymbosum*
Preserves: *Fragaria virginiana, Prunus nigra,
P. pensylvanica, P. virginiana, Ribes cynos-
bati, Rubus idaeus, Vaccinium angustifoli-
um, V. corymbosum, Viburnum opulus*
Sauce & Relish: *Acer rubrum, A. saccharum,
Betula papyrifera, Cardamine diphylla*
Snack Food: *Cornus canadensis, Gaultheria
procumbens*
Substitution Food: *Betula alleghaniensis*
Sweetener: *Acer rubrum, A. saccharum*
Unspecified: *Corylus cornuta, Fagus grandi-
folia, Juglans cinerea, Sium suave*
Vegetable: *Aster macrophyllus, Claytonia virgi-
nica, Rorippa nasturtium-aquaticum*

Algonquin, Tête-de-Boule
Beverage: *Nuphar lutea*
Fruit: *Fragaria virginiana, Rubus idaeus,
Vaccinium macrocarpon, V. oxycoccos*
Spice: *Allium sativum*
Unspecified: *Nuphar lutea, Vaccinium
myrtilloides*

Anticosti
Beverage: *Anaphalis margaritacea, Beta vul-
garis, Juniperus communis, Larix laricina,
Ledum groenlandicum, Picea mariana*
Forage: *Heracleum maximum*
Preserves: *Rubus chamaemorus, Vaccinium
vitis-idaea*
Soup: *Allium schoenoprasum*
Spice: *Ligusticum scothicum*
Unspecified: *Rumex acetosella*
Winter Use Food: *Rubus chamaemorus, Vac-
cinium macrocarpon, V. oxycoccos*

Apache
Beverage: *Yucca baccata, Y. torreyi*

Bread & Cake: *Prosopis glandulosa, Prunus
virginiana, Yucca baccata, Y. torreyi*
Dried Food: *Agave americana, A. parryi*
Fruit: *Juniperus deppeana, Mahonia haemato-
carpa, Oenothera albicaulis, Rhus micro-
phylla, R. trilobata, Ribes inerme, Sambucus
racemosa*
Preserves: *Prosopis glandulosa*
Sauce & Relish: *Yucca baccata, Y. torreyi*
Soup: *Yucca baccata*
Special Food: *Fragaria vesca*
Staple: *Agastache pallidiflora, Agave ameri-
cana, A. parryi, Rhus trilobata*
Unspecified: *Agave parryi, Allium geyeri, Fra-
sera speciosa, Hoffmannseggia glauca,
Typha latifolia, Yucca baccata, Y. elata,
Y. glauca*
Vegetable: *Chenopodium album, C. leptophyl-
lum, Yucca baccata, Y. elata*

Apache, Chiricahua & Mescalero
Beverage: *Artemisia dracunculus, Cheilanthes
fendleri, Dasylirion wheeleri, Hedeoma
nana, Monarda fistulosa, Parthenium inca-
num, Prosopis glandulosa, P. pubescens,
Thelesperma megapotamicum*
Bread & Cake: *Amaranthus albus, A. retroflexus,
Camelina microcarpa, Capsella bursa-
pastoris, Celtis laevigata, Cirsium pallidum,
Crataegus erythropoda, Dasylirion wheeleri,
Descurainia incana, Dyssodia papposa,
Helianthus annuus, Morus microphylla,
Panicum bulbosum, Pinus ponderosa, Pop-
ulus tremuloides, Prosopis glandulosa, P.
pubescens, Ribes leptanthum, R. pinetorum,
R. wolfii, Rubus arizonensis, Solanum fend-
leri, Sporobolus cryptandrus, Yucca baccata,
Y. torreyi*
Candy: *Asclepias speciosa, Populus deltoides*
Dried Food: *Acer negundo, Lathyrus lansz-
wertii, Mammillaria grahamii, Prosopis pu-
bescens, Rhus trilobata, Vicia melilotoides,
Vitis arizonica, Yucca elata*
Fodder: *Cyperus fendlerianus*
Fruit: *Carnegia gigantea, Celtis laevigata,
Crataegus erythropoda, Echinocereus
coccineus, E. engelmannii, E. fendleri, E.
polyacanthus, E. rigidissimus, Forestiera*

*pubescens, Fragaria vesca, Juniperus dep-
peana, J. scopulorum, Mammillaria grahamii, M. mainiae, Morus microphylla, Prunus
virginiana, Quercus gambelii, Q. grisea, Ribes leptanthum, R. mescalerium, R. wolfii,
Rosa woodsii, Rubus arizonensis, Stenocereus thurberi, Vitis arizonica*

Pie & Pudding: *Pinus edulis, Prosopis
glandulosa*

Porridge: *Sporobolus cryptandrus*

Preserves: *Celtis laevigata, Juniperus deppeana, Mahonia haematocarpa, Prunus
virginiana, Rhus microphylla, R. trilobata,
Ribes wolfii, Rosa woodsii, Sambucus
racemosa*

Sauce & Relish: *Helianthus annuus, Juniperus
monosperma, Oenothera albicaulis, Panicum bulbosum, P. obtusum*

Soup: *Oenothera albicaulis, Yucca baccata*

Special Food: *Oenothera albicaulis, Physalis
subulata, Pinus edulis, Prosopis pubescens,
Rhus glabra*

Spice: *Allium cernuum, A. geyeri, Artemisia
ludoviciana, Cymopterus acaulis, Draco-
cephalum parviflorum, Hedeoma nana,
Humulus lupulus, Mentha canadensis,
Monarda fistulosa, Prosopis glandulosa,
Quercus grisea, Taraxacum officinale*

Starvation Food: *Pinus ponderosa*

Substitution Food: *Carnegia gigantea, Prosopis
glandulosa*

Sweetener: *Acer glabrum, A. negundo*

Unspecified: *Agave parryi, Amaranthus albus,
A. retroflexus, Calylophus lavandulifolius,
Camelina microcarpa, Capsella bursa-
pastoris, Chenopodium album, Cirsium pallidum, Cymopterus acaulis, Cyperus fendlerianus, Dasylirion wheeleri, Descurainia
incana, Dyssodia papposa, Epixiphium wislizeni, Hoffmannseggia glauca, Jamesia
americana, Juglans major, Lathyrus lansz-
wertii, Ligusticum porteri, Matelea producta,
Nolina microcarpa, Oxalis violacea, Pinus
edulis, P. flexilis, P. ponderosa, Populus
tremuloides, Portulaca oleracea, Proboscidea louisianica, Prosopis glandulosa,
Rumex aquaticus, Typha latifolia, Vicia
melilotoides, Yucca baccata, Y. glauca*

Vegetable: *Agave parryi, Allium cernuum, A.
geyeri, Capsella bursa-pastoris, Dasylirion
wheeleri, Dyssodia papposa, Nolina microcarpa, Robinia neomexicana, Solanum
jamesii, Yucca baccata, Y. elata, Y. glauca*

Winter Use Food: *Crataegus erythropoda,
Juglans major, Morus microphylla, Prunus
virginiana, Quercus gambelii, Q. grisea,
Robinia neomexicana, Rubus arizonensis*

Apache, Mescalero

Beverage: *Dasylirion wheeleri, Prosopis glandulosa, Yucca baccata*

Bread & Cake: *Agave parryi, Dasylirion
wheeleri*

Dried Food: *Dasylirion wheeleri, Pinus edulis,
Prunus americana, Robinia neomexicana,
Yucca baccata, Y. elata*

Fruit: *Mahonia haematocarpa, Morus microphylla, Vitis arizonica*

Sauce & Relish: *Morus microphylla, Yucca
baccata*

Soup: *Dasylirion wheeleri, Yucca elata*

Special Food: *Pinus edulis*

Spice: *Populus tremuloides*

Staple: *Prosopis glandulosa, Yucca elata*

Unspecified: *Dasylirion wheeleri, Juglans major, Robinia neomexicana, Typha latifolia,
Yucca elata*

Apache, San Carlos

Beverage: *Ferocactus wislizeni*

Bread & Cake: *Carnegia gigantea*

Dried Food: *Yucca schottii*

Fruit: *Canotia holacantha, Carnegia gigantea,
Mammillaria grahamii, Yucca schottii*

Porridge: *Ferocactus wislizeni*

Unspecified: *Dichelostemma pulchellum,
Peniocereus greggii*

Apache, Western

Beverage: *Agave palmeri, A. parryi, Carnegia
gigantea, Martynia sp., Prosopis glandulosa,
Rhus trilobata, Vitis arizonica*

Bread & Cake: *Carnegia gigantea, Prosopis
glandulosa*

Candy: *Agave palmeri, A. parryi, Pinus edulis,
P. monophylla, Prosopis glandulosa*

Dried Food: *Agave palmeri, A. parryi, Carnegia gigantea, Prosopis glandulosa, Vitis arizonica, Yucca baccata, Y. elata*

Fruit: *Canotia holacantha, Carnegia gigantea, Prunus virginiana, Rhus trilobata, Vitis arizonica*

Pie & Pudding: *Carnegia gigantea*

Porridge: *Bouteloua gracilis, Carnegia gigantea, Muhlenbergia rigens, Oryzopsis hymenoides, Pinus edulis, P. monophylla, Prosopis glandulosa, Sporobolus contractus*

Sauce & Relish: *Yucca baccata*

Staple: *Pinus edulis, P. monophylla, Prosopis glandulosa*

Substitution Food: *Agave palmeri, A. parryi, Prosopis glandulosa*

Unspecified: *Agave palmeri, A. parryi, Chenopodium incanum, C. leptophyllum, Nolina microcarpa, Quercus emoryi, Q. gambelii, Q. ×pauciloba, Yucca elata*

Vegetable: *Cleome serrulata*

Winter Use Food: *Martynia* sp., *Pinus edulis, P. monophylla*

Apache, White Mountain

Beverage: *Agave americana, A. decipiens, Artemisia tridentata, Chamaesyce serpyllifolia, Datura wrightii, Ephedra nevadensis, Quercus ×pauciloba*

Bread & Cake: *Bouteloua gracilis, Cucurbita pepo, Muhlenbergia rigens, Oryzopsis hymenoides, Quercus ×pauciloba, Sporobolus contractus, Triticum aestivum, Xanthium strumarium*

Candy: *Lactuca tatarica, Populus angustifolia, P. deltoides, Pseudotsuga menziesii*

Cooking Agent: *Chamaesyce serpyllifolia*

Dried Food: *Chamaesyce serpyllifolia, Opuntia imbricata, O. whipplei, Yucca baccata, Y. glauca*

Fodder: *Elytrigia repens, Muhlenbergia rigens, Oryzopsis hymenoides*

Fruit: *Astragalus lentiginosus, Carnegia gigantea, Cereus* sp., *Juniperus monosperma, J. occidentalis, J. osteosperma, Opuntia imbricata, O. whipplei, Physalis hederifolia, Rhus trilobata, Ribes cereum, Sambucus racemosa*

Porridge: *Bouteloua gracilis, Muhlenbergia rigens, Oryzopsis hymenoides, Sporobolus contractus*

Preserves: *Carnegia gigantea, Cereus* sp.

Spice: *Artemisia tridentata*

Staple: *Cycloloma atriplicifolium, Helianthus annuus*

Unspecified: *Agave americana, A. decipiens, Allium bisceptrum, Amaranthus albus, A. blitoides, Artemisia carruthii, Asclepias subverticillata, Berula erecta, Chenopodium incanum, C. leptophyllum, Chrysothamnus nauseosus, Cucurbita pepo, Elytrigia repens, Muhlenbergia rigens, Oryzopsis hymenoides, Pinus edulis, Populus angustifolia, P. deltoides, Quercus gambelii, Q. ×pauciloba, Ustilago zeae, Yucca baccata, Y. glauca*

Vegetable: *Phaseolus vulgaris, Robinia neomexicana*

Winter Use Food: *Agave americana*

Apalachee

Fruit: *Citrullus lanatus*

Arapaho

Beverage: *Rosa woodsii*

Preserves: *Shepherdia argentea*

Starvation Food: *Ipomoea leptophylla*

Sweetener: *Frasera speciosa*

Winter Use Food: *Shepherdia argentea*

Atsugewi

Beverage: *Arctostaphylos patula, Rhus trilobata*

Bread & Cake: *Amsinckia lycopsoides, Arctostaphylos patula, Balsamorhiza deltoidea, B. hookeri, B. sagittata, Chenopodium carinatum, Descurainia pinnata, Perideridia bolanderi, Prunus subcordata, Sambucus cerulea*

Dried Food: *Amelanchier alnifolia, Juniperus occidentalis, Perideridia bolanderi, Rhus trilobata*

Fruit: *Frangula rubra, Juniperus occidentalis, Ribes roezlii*

Porridge: *Amelanchier alnifolia, Prunus virginiana*

Preserves: *Rhus trilobata*

Soup: *Perideridia bolanderi*
Substitution Food: *Ligusticum grayi*
Unspecified: *Brodiaea coronaria, Cirsium drummondii, Dichelostemma multiflorum, Lilium pardalinum, Lomatium nudicaule, L. triternatum, L. utriculatum, Perideridia bolanderi, Pteridium aquilinum, Triteleia hyacinthina*
Vegetable: *Ligusticum grayi*
Winter Use Food: *Arctostaphylos patula, Ligusticum grayi*

Bellabella

Unspecified: *Zostera marina*

Bella Coola

Beverage: *Aralia nudicaulis, Ledum groenlandicum, Sambucus racemosa*
Bread & Cake: *Gaultheria shallon, Rubus leucodermis, R. spectabilis, Vaccinium ovalifolium, V. parvifolium*
Dietary Aid: *Dryopteris filix-mas*
Dried Food: *Egregia menziesii, Populus balsamifera, Sambucus racemosa, Tsuga heterophylla*
Forage: *Clintonia uniflora, Lonicera involucrata*
Frozen Food: *Vaccinium parvifolium*
Fruit: *Amelanchier alnifolia, Cornus unalaschkensis, Crataegus douglasii, Fragaria vesca, F. virginiana, Maianthemum dilatatum, M. stellatum, Malus fusca, Ribes bracteosum, R. divaricatum, R. lacustre, R. laxiflorum, Rosa nutkana, Rubus idaeus, R. leucodermis, R. spectabilis, Vaccinium cespitosum, V. membranaceum, V. ovalifolium, V. parvifolium*
Ice Cream: *Shepherdia canadensis*
Preserves: *Rubus idaeus, R. leucodermis, R. parviflorus, Sambucus racemosa*
Sauce & Relish: *Ribes divaricatum*
Special Food: *Arctostaphylos uva-ursi*
Unspecified: *Allium cernuum, Angelica lucida, Argentina egedii, Dryopteris filix-mas, Egregia menziesii, Fritillaria camschatcensis, Heracleum maximum, Populus balsamifera, Pteridium aquilinum, Rubus parviflorus, R. spectabilis, Rumex acetosella, Sium suave, Trifolium wormskioldii*

Vegetable: *Epilobium angustifolium, Rumex aquaticus*
Winter Use Food: *Viburnum edule*

Blackfoot

Beverage: *Achillea millefolium, Arctostaphylos uva-ursi, Equisetum hyemale, Eriogonum umbellatum, Fragaria virginiana, Lithospermum incisum, Mentha arvensis, M. canadensis, Prunus virginiana*
Bread & Cake: *Camassia quamash*
Candy: *Abies lasiocarpa, Antennaria rosea, Artemisia ludoviciana, Elaeagnus commutata, Escobaria vivipara, Osmorhiza occidentalis, Pinus contorta*
Dessert: *Amelanchier alnifolia*
Dried Food: *Amelanchier alnifolia, A. arborea, Arctostaphylos uva-ursi, Lewisia pygmaea, Pediomelum esculentum, Prunus virginiana*
Fodder: *Populus tremuloides*
Forage: *Artemisia cana, Buchloe dactyloides, Carex nebrascensis, Chrysothamnus nauseosus, Leymus cinereus, Muhlenbergia richardsonis, Shepherdia argentea*
Fruit: *Amelanchier alnifolia, Arctostaphylos uva-ursi, Cornus sericea, Crataegus chrysocarpa, Disporum trachycarpum, Elaeagnus commutata, Escobaria vivipara, Fragaria virginiana, Mahonia repens, Prunus virginiana, Ribes aureum, R. oxyacanthoides, Rosa acicularis, R. nutkana, Rubus parviflorus*
Preserves: *Amelanchier alnifolia, Rosa nutkana*
Snack Food: *Amelanchier alnifolia, Cornus sericea, Perideridia gairdneri, Populus tremuloides*
Soup: *Amelanchier alnifolia, A. arborea, Asclepias viridiflora, Elaeagnus commutata, Erythronium grandiflorum, Fritillaria pudica, Gaillardia aristata, Heracleum maximum, Lilium philadelphicum, Perideridia gairdneri, Polygonum bistortoides, Prunus virginiana, Ribes oxyacanthoides, Veratrum viride*
Special Food: *Amelanchier alnifolia, Camassia quamash, Populus tremuloides, Prunus virginiana*

Spice: *Acer glabrum, Allium cernuum, Artemisia frigida, Asclepias viridiflora, Geranium viscosissimum, Mentha arvensis, M. canadensis, Pentaphylloides floribunda, Perideridia gairdneri, Prunus virginiana, Selaginella densa, Thalictrum occidentale*

Staple: *Amelanchier alnifolia, Astragalus canadensis, Perideridia gairdneri, Prunus virginiana*

Starvation Food: *Selaginella densa, Shepherdia canadensis, Symphoricarpos occidentalis*

Unspecified: *Amelanchier arborea, Asclepias viridiflora, Astragalus canadensis, Camassia quamash, C. scilloides, Epilobium angustifolium, Eriogonum flavum, Erythronium grandiflorum, Fritillaria pudica, Heracleum maximum, Lewisia rediviva, Liatris punctata, Lilium philadelphicum, Lithospermum incisum, Lomatium simplex, L. triternatum, Musineon divaricatum, Pediomelum esculentum, Perideridia gairdneri, Pinus ponderosa, Populus balsamifera, P. deltoides, P. tremuloides, Typha latifolia*

Vegetable: *Allium cernuum, Claytonia lanceolata, Heracleum maximum, Perideridia gairdneri*

Winter Use Food: *Amelanchier alnifolia, Arctostaphylos uva-ursi, Camassia quamash*

Cahuilla

Baby Food: *Pinus monophylla, P. quadrifolia*

Beverage: *Allenrolfea occidentalis, Arctostaphylos glandulosa, A. glauca, A. pungens, Ephedra nevadensis, Eriodictyon trichocalyx, Ferocactus cylindraceus, Fouquieria splendens, Nicotiana clevelandii, N. glauca, N. trigonophylla, Pinus monophylla, P. quadrifolia, Prosopis glandulosa, P. pubescens, Rhus integrifolia, R. trilobata, Romneya coulteri, Rosa californica, Rubus leucodermis, R. parviflorus, R. vitifolius, Salvia columbariae, Simmondsia chinensis, Vitis girdiana, Washingtonia filifera*

Bread & Cake: *Allenrolfea occidentalis, Prosopis glandulosa, P. pubescens, Quercus agrifolia, Q. chrysolepis, Q. dumosa, Q. kelloggii, Yucca whipplei*

Candy: *Chenopodium californicum*

Dietary Aid: *Salvia columbariae*

Dried Food: *Agave deserti, Amelanchier pallida, Arctostaphylos glandulosa, A. glauca, A. pungens, Cucurbita moschata, Ferocactus cylindraceus, Juniperus californica, Lasthenia glabrata, Lycium andersonii, L. fremontii, Opuntia acanthocarpa, O. basilaris, O. bigelovii, O. ficus-indica, O. ramosissima, Pinus monophylla, P. quadrifolia, Prosopis pubescens, Prunus virginiana, Quercus agrifolia, Q. chrysolepis, Q. dumosa, Q. kelloggii, Rhus ovata, Rubus leucodermis, R. parviflorus, R. vitifolius, Sambucus cerulea, Vitis girdiana, Washingtonia filifera, Yucca whipplei*

Fruit: *Amelanchier pallida, Arctostaphylos glandulosa, A. pungens, Atriplex semibaccata, Citrullus lanatus, Fragaria vesca, Heteromeles arbutifolia, Juniperus californica, Lycium andersonii, L. fremontii, Opuntia acanthocarpa, O. engelmannii, O. ficus-indica, O. ×occidentalis, O. ramosissima, Prunus andersonii, P. emarginata, P. fasciculata, P. fremontii, P. ilicifolia, P. virginiana, Rhamnus crocea, Rhus ovata, R. trilobata, Ribes malvaceum, R. montigenum, Rubus leucodermis, R. parviflorus, R. vitifolius, Sambucus cerulea, Vitis girdiana, Washingtonia filifera, Ziziphus parryi*

Porridge: *Acacia greggii, Allenrolfea occidentalis, Amaranthus fimbriatus, Arctostaphylos glandulosa, A. glauca, A. pungens, Atriplex lentiformis, Avena fatua, Chaenactis glabriuscula, Cucurbita foetidissima, Fouquieria splendens, Hirschfeldia incana, Juniperus californica, Lasthenia californica, L. glabrata, Layia glandulosa, L. platyglossa, Medicago polymorpha, Mentzelia albicaulis, M. involucrata, M. puberula, Opuntia basilaris, Panicum urvilleanum, Parkinsonia florida, Pinus monophylla, P. quadrifolia, Prosopis glandulosa, Quercus agrifolia, Q. chrysolepis, Q. dumosa, Q. kelloggii, Rhus ovata, Salvia carduacea, Triticum aestivum, Typha latifolia, Vitis girdiana, Washingtonia filifera, Zea mays, Ziziphus parryi*

Preserves: *Prunus andersonii, Sambucus cerulea, Washingtonia filifera*

Sauce & Relish: *Arctostaphylos glandulosa, A. glauca, A. pungens, Sambucus cerulea*

Soup: *Opuntia ramosissima, Rhus trilobata*

Special Food: *Quercus agrifolia, Q. chrysolepis, Q. dumosa, Q. kelloggii*

Spice: *Allium validum, Descurainia pinnata, Distichlis spicata, Salvia apiana, S. mellifera*

Staple: *Arctostaphylos glandulosa, A. glauca, A. pungens, Arthrocnemum subterminale, Chenopodium californicum, Echinocactus polycephalus, Eriophyllum confertiflorum, Ferocactus cylindraceus, Helianthus annuus, Olneya tesota, Opuntia acanthocarpa, O. bigelovii, O. engelmannii, O. ficus-indica, O. parryi, O. ramosissima, Prosopis glandulosa, P. pubescens, Prunus virginiana, Salvia apiana, S. columbariae, S. mellifera, Typha latifolia, Ziziphus parryi*

Starvation Food: *Bromus tectorum, Hemizonia fasciculata*

Sweetener: *Castilleja foliolosa, Rhus ovata*

Unspecified: *Adenostoma sparsifolium, Agave deserti, Apiastrum angustifolium, Avena barbata, Bloomeria crocea, Calochortus catalinae, C. concolor, C. flexuosus, C. palmeri, Capsella bursa-pastoris, Chilopsis linearis, Cirsium drummondii, Cucurbita moschata, Dichelostemma pulchellum, Ferocactus cylindraceus, Fouquieria splendens, Hesperocallis undulata, Hordeum murinum, H. vulgare, Nolina bigelovii, Opuntia basilaris, O. bigelovii, O. engelmannii, O. ficus-indica, O. ×occidentalis, Orobanche cooperi, Pluchea sericea, Proboscidea althaeifolia, Prosopis glandulosa, Rosa californica, Yucca brevifolia, Y. schidigera, Y. whipplei*

Vegetable: *Acacia greggii, Allium validum, Amaranthus fimbriatus, Apium graveolens, Camissonia claviformis, Capsella bursa-pastoris, Chenopodium californicum, C. fremontii, C. humile, C. murale, Chlorogalum pomeridianum, Claytonia perfoliata, C spathulata, Descurainia pinnata, Hirschfeldia incana, Hydrocotyle sp., Opuntia basilaris, Rorippa nasturtium-aquaticum, Rumex hymenosepalus, Sisymbrium irio,*
Taraxacum californicum, Urtica dioica, Yucca whipplei

Winter Use Food: *Citrullus lanatus, Hirschfeldia incana*

California Indian

Vegetable: *Heracleum maximum*

Canadian Indian

Unspecified: *Astragalus australis*

Carrier

Beverage: *Sphagnum* sp.

Candy: *Picea mariana*

Dried Food: *Shepherdia canadensis*

Fruit: *Arctostaphylos uva-ursi, Rubus spectabilis, Shepherdia canadensis*

Ice Cream: *Shepherdia canadensis*

Preserves: *Rosa nutkana, Shepherdia canadensis, Vaccinium vitis-idaea, Viburnum edule*

Soup: *Arctostaphylos uva-ursi*

Unspecified: *Heracleum maximum, Linnaea borealis, Sium suave, Typha latifolia*

Chehalis

Fruit: *Amelanchier alnifolia, Fragaria ×ananassa, Ribes sanguineum, Rubus parviflorus, R. spectabilis*

Soup: *Camassia quamash*

Spice: *Amelanchier alnifolia*

Unspecified: *Corylus cornuta, Pteridium aquilinum, Quercus garryana, Rubus spectabilis, Rumex acetosella, Typha latifolia*

Winter Use Food: *Corylus cornuta, Sambucus cerulea, S. racemosa*

Cherokee

Beverage: *Gaultheria procumbens, Gleditsia triacanthos, Hamamelis virginiana, Hydrangea arborescens, Lindera benzoin, Liquidambar styraciflua, Morus rubra, Passiflora incarnata, Phytolacca americana, Prunus americana, Robinia pseudoacacia, Rubus allegheniensis, R. argutus, R. flagellaris, R. trivialis, Sambucus canadensis, Sassafras albidum, Vitis aestivalis, V. cinerea, V. labrusca, V. rotundifolia*

Bread & Cake: *Amphicarpaea bracteata, Castanea dentata, Coix lacryma-jobi, Gaylussacia baccata, Morus rubra, Phaseolus lunatus, P. vulgaris, Polygonatum biflorum, Vitis aestivalis, V. cinerea, V. labrusca, V. rotundifolia*

Candy: *Liquidambar styraciflua*

Cooking Agent: *Phytolacca americana*

Dried Food: *Juglans nigra, Ligusticum canadense, Malus angustifolia, Phytolacca americana, Rudbeckia laciniata*

Fodder: *Aplectrum hyemale*

Frozen Food: *Gaylussacia baccata, Rudbeckia laciniata*

Fruit: *Amelanchier arborea, A. laevis, Arctostaphylos uva-ursi, Asimina triloba, Crataegus macrosperma, Diospyros virginiana, Fragaria virginiana, Gaultheria procumbens, Gaylussacia baccata, Malus coronaria, Mitchella repens, Morus alba, M. rubra, Passiflora incarnata, Physalis heterophylla, Podophyllum peltatum, Prunus americana, P. cerasus, P. pensylvanica, P. persica, P. serotina, P. virginiana, Pyrus communis, Rhus copallinum, R. glabra, R. hirta, Rubus allegheniensis, R. argutus, R. flagellaris, R. idaeus, R. occidentalis, R. odoratus, R. trivialis, Sambucus canadensis, S. nigra, Vitis aestivalis, V. cinerea, V. labrusca, V. rotundifolia, V. vulpina*

Pie & Pudding: *Diospyros virginiana, Gaylussacia baccata, Prunus pensylvanica, Rubus occidentalis, R. odoratus, Sambucus canadensis*

Porridge: *Juglans nigra*

Preserves: *Fragaria virginiana, Gaylussacia baccata, G. ursina, Malus angustifolia, Morus rubra, Prunus americana, P. pensylvanica, Rubus occidentalis, R. odoratus, Sambucus canadensis, S. nigra*

Sauce & Relish: *Armoracia rusticana, Fragaria virginiana, Liriodendron tulipifera, Oxydendrum arboreum*

Snack Food: *Chimaphila maculata*

Soup: *Phaseolus lunatus, P. vulgaris*

Spice: *Arnoglossum atriplicifolium, Capsella bursa-pastoris, Chenopodium album, Eupatorium purpureum, Lindera benzoin, Mentha ×piperita, M. spicata, Piper nigrum, Polygonatum biflorum*

Starvation Food: *Lilium canadense*

Substitution Food: *Apios americana, Castanea dentata*

Sweetener: *Acer saccharum*

Unspecified: *Allium cernuum, A. tricoccum, Amphicarpaea bracteata, Barbarea verna, B. vulgaris, Beta vulgaris, Carya alba, C. laciniosa, C. pallida, Castanea dentata, Cercis canadensis, Chelone glabra, Chenopodium album, Citrullus lanatus, Corylus americana, Cucurbita pepo, Dentaria sp., Gaultheria procumbens, Gaylussacia baccata, Gleditsia triacanthos, Hydrangea arborescens, Ipomoea pandurata, Juglans cinerea, J. nigra, Lagenaria siceraria, Lepidium campestre, L. virginicum, Ligusticum canadense, Mentha arvensis, M. ×piperita, M. spicata, Monarda didyma, M. fistulosa, Oxalis corniculata, O. violacea, Oxypolis rigidior, Passiflora incarnata, Phacelia dubia, Phytolacca americana, Polygonatum biflorum, Polygonum hydropiper, Polystichum acrostichoides, Pycnanthemum flexuosum, P. incanum, Rheum rhaponticum, Rhododendron calendulaceum, Rudbeckia laciniata, Rumex acetosella, Saxifraga micranthidifolia, Smilax glauca, S. herbacea, S. pseudochina, S. rotundifolia, Streptopus roseus, Tradescantia virginiana, Uvularia perfoliata*

Vegetable: *Allium canadense, A. tricoccum, Amphicarpaea bracteata, Apios americana, Asparagus officinalis, Barbarea verna, B. vulgaris, Brassica napus, B. oleracea, B. rapa, Capsella bursa-pastoris, Cardamine diphylla, Chenopodium album, Cucurbita pepo, Helianthus tuberosus, Hydrangea arborescens, Ipomoea batatas, I. pandurata, Lactuca canadensis, Ligusticum canadense, Oenothera biennis, O. fruticosa, Oxalis stricta, Passiflora incarnata, Pedicularis canadensis, Penthorum sedoides, Phacelia dubia, Phaseolus lunatus, P. vulgaris, Phytolacca americana, Pisum sativum, Plantago major, Polygonatum biflorum, Polygonum cuspidatum, Prenanthes serpentaria, P. tri-*

foliolata, Prunella vulgaris, Ranunculus abortivus, R. acris, R. recurvatus, Rorippa nasturtium-aquaticum, Rudbeckia laciniata, Rumex acetosa, R. acetosella, R. crispus, Saxifraga micranthidifolia, S. pensylvanica, Sisymbrium officinale, Sisyrinchium angustifolium, Solanum nigrum, S. tuberosum, Streptopus amplexifolius, S. roseus, Taraxacum officinale, Thlaspi arvense, Tradescantia virginiana, Uvularia sessilifolia, Valerianella locusta, Viola blanda, V. pubescens, Zea mays

Winter Use Food: *Ligusticum canadense, Morus rubra, Polygonatum biflorum, Ribes cynosbati, R. rotundifolium, Rubus occidentalis, R. odoratus, Rudbeckia laciniata, Streptopus roseus*

Cheyenne

Beverage: *Agastache foeniculum, Amelanchier alnifolia, Arabis glabra, Mentha arvensis, Ulmus americana*

Bread & Cake: *Prunus virginiana*

Candy: *Acer negundo, Asclepias speciosa, Pinus ponderosa*

Cooking Agent: *Opuntia polyacantha, Pediomelum esculentum*

Dried Food: *Calochortus gunnisonii, Crataegus douglasii, Escobaria vivipara, Opuntia polyacantha, Pediomelum esculentum, P. hypogaeum, Perideridia gairdneri, Ribes cereum, R. lacustre*

Fodder: *Populus balsamifera, P. deltoides*

Fruit: *Asclepias speciosa, Crataegus douglasii, Escobaria vivipara, Fragaria virginiana, Mahonia repens, Opuntia polyacantha, Physalis heterophylla, Prunus virginiana, Ribes lacustre, R. oxyacanthoides, Rosa woodsii, Rubus idaeus, Vitis vulpina*

Pie & Pudding: *Amelanchier alnifolia, Pediomelum esculentum, Prunus americana, P. virginiana, Shepherdia argentea*

Porridge: *Calochortus gunnisonii, Perideridia gairdneri*

Preserves: *Shepherdia canadensis*

Sauce & Relish: *Asclepias speciosa*

Soup: *Asclepias speciosa, Opuntia polyacantha*

Special Food: *Amelanchier alnifolia, Cirsium edule, Prunus americana*

Spice: *Allium drummondii, A. schoenoprasum*

Starvation Food: *Ipomoea leptophylla*

Unspecified: *Allium drummondii, A. schoenoprasum, Apios tuberosum, Asclepias speciosa, Calochortus gunnisonii, Castilleja sessiliflora, Cirsium edule, Glycyrrhiza lepidota, Helianthus tuberosus, Nuphar lutea, Pediomelum esculentum, P. hypogaeum, Perideridia gairdneri, Pinus ponderosa, Polygonum bistortoides, Populus deltoides, Quercus macrocarpa, Rumex crispus, Scirpus acutus, S. nevadensis*

Vegetable: *Apios tuberosum*

Winter Use Food: *Amelanchier alnifolia, Calochortus gunnisonii, Crataegus douglasii, Opuntia polyacantha, Pediomelum hypogaeum, Perideridia gairdneri, Prunus americana, P. virginiana, Ribes aureum, R. oxyacanthoides*

Chinook, Lower

Dried Food: *Arctostaphylos uva-ursi, Vaccinium ovalifolium*

Fruit: *Arctostaphylos uva-ursi, Malus fusca, Rubus spectabilis, Vaccinium ovalifolium*

Unspecified: *Equisetum arvense, Rubus spectabilis*

Chippewa

Appetizer: *Asclepias syriaca*

Beverage: *Comptonia peregrina, Gaultheria hispidula, G. procumbens, Ledum groenlandicum, Lindera benzoin, Mentha canadensis, Picea rubens, Prunus serotina, P. virginiana, Rubus idaeus, Sassafras albidum, Thuja occidentalis, Tsuga canadensis*

Bread & Cake: *Prunus americana, P. serotina, Ribes triste, Rubus frondosus, R. idaeus*

Dried Food: *Amelanchier canadensis, Lycopus asper, Prunus virginiana, Ribes americanum, Rubus allegheniensis, R. idaeus, R. occidentalis, R. odoratus, Sagittaria latifolia, Sambucus canadensis*

Fruit: *Amelanchier canadensis, Amphicarpaea bracteata, Cornus canadensis, Fragaria vesca, F. virginiana, Podophyllum peltatum,*

Prunus americana, P. serotina, Ribes americanum, R. cynosbati, R. missouriense, R. rubrum, R. triste, Rubus alleghaniensis, R. canadensis, R. frondosus, R. idaeus, R. occidentalis, R. odoratus, R. pubescens, Sambucus canadensis, Vaccinium angustifolium, V. macrocarpon, Vitis vulpina
Porridge: *Zea mays*
Preserves: *Asclepias syriaca*
Sauce & Relish: *Viburnum opulus*
Soup: *Zea mays*
Spice: *Arctostaphylos uva-ursi, Asarum canadense, Gaultheria procumbens, Lindera benzoin, Mentha canadensis, Pycnanthemum virginianum, Sassafras albidum*
Sweetener: *Acer saccharinum*
Unspecified: *Amphicarpaea bracteata, Corylus americana, Fagus grandifolia, Helianthus tuberosus, Lathyrus palustris, Parthenocissus quinquefolia, Quercus macrocarpa, Scirpus tabernaemontani, Zizania palustris*
Vegetable: *Apios americana, Asclepias syriaca, Caltha palustris, Quercus macrocarpa, Tilia americana, Zea mays*
Winter Use Food: *Corylus americana*

Choctaw
Bread & Cake: *Smilax bona-nox, S. laurifolia*
Soup: *Carya alba*
Spice: *Sassafras albidum*
Staple: *Quercus nigra*
Unspecified: *Strophostyles helvula*
Vegetable: *Zea mays*

Clallam
Beverage: *Epilobium angustifolium, Vaccinium oxycoccos*
Bread & Cake: *Gaultheria shallon*
Dried Food: *Acer circinatum, A. macrophyllum, Populus balsamifera, Vaccinium ovalifolium*
Fruit: *Fragaria chiloensis, F. vesca, F. virginiana, Mahonia nervosa, Malus fusca, Ribes divaricatum, Rubus parviflorus, R. spectabilis, R. ursinus, Vaccinium ovalifolium, V. parvifolium*
Ice Cream: *Shepherdia canadensis*
Staple: *Pteridium aquilinum*

Sweetener: *Alnus rubra*
Unspecified: *Abronia latifolia, Acer circinatum, A. macrophyllum, Allium cernuum, Camassia quamash, Daucus pusillus, Dryopteris expansa, Equisetum telmateia, Lilium columbianum, Populus balsamifera, Typha latifolia*

Coahuilla
Beverage: *Ephedra nevadensis, Simmondsia chinensis*
Candy: *Asclepias erosa*
Unspecified: *Adenostoma sparsifolium*

Cochiti
Dried Food: *Prunus virginiana*
Fruit: *Juniperus monosperma, Prunus virginiana*
Special Food: *Fragaria vesca*
Staple: *Quercus gambelii*
Substitution Food: *Solanum elaeagnifolium*
Unspecified: *Echinocereus fendleri, E. triglochidiatus, Lathyrus polymorphus, Quercus gambelii, Yucca baccata, Y. glauca*
Vegetable: *Amaranthus albus, A. retroflexus, Atriplex powellii, Cymopterus bulbosus, Rumex salicifolius*

Cocopa
Beverage: *Washingtonia filifera*
Bread & Cake: *Panicum hirticaule, P. sonorum, Simmondsia chinensis*
Dried Food: *Citrullus lanatus, Cucurbita pepo, Pholisma sonorae, Polygonum argyrocoleon*
Fruit: *Citrullus lanatus, Opuntia echinocarpa, O. engelmannii*
Porridge: *Chasmanthium latifolium, Echinochloa colona, Eragrostis mexicana, Eriochloa aristata, Olneya tesota, Parkinsonia florida, P. microphylla*
Sauce & Relish: *Panicum hirticaule*
Staple: *Descurainia pinnata, Echinochloa colona, Eragrostis mexicana, Eriochloa aristata, Phaseolus acutifolius*
Unspecified: *Agave deserti, Amaranthus caudatus, A. palmeri, Chasmanthium latifolium, Cucurbita pepo, Cyperus odoratus, Echinochloa crus-galli, Hoffmannseggia glauca,*

Pholisma sonorae, Pinus monophylla, Prosopis glandulosa, P. velutina, Rumex crispus, Sagittaria latifolia, Simmondsia chinensis, Vigna unguiculata
Vegetable: *Amaranthus caudatus, A. palmeri, Chenopodium fremontii, Cucurbita pepo, Descurainia obtusa*
Winter Use Food: *Amaranthus caudatus, A. palmeri, Chasmanthium latifolium, Citrullus lanatus, Echinochloa crus-galli, Panicum hirticaule, P. sonorum, Phaseolus acutifolius, Prosopis glandulosa, P. velutina*

Cocopa & Yuma
Unspecified: *Salix gooddingii*

Cocopa, Maricopa, Mohave & Yuma
Porridge: *Vigna unguiculata*

Coeur d'Alene
Dried Food: *Arctostaphylos uva-ursi, Prunus virginiana, Vaccinium membranaceum*
Fruit: *Arctostaphylos uva-ursi, Fragaria vesca, Prunus emarginata, P. virginiana, Rubus leucodermis, Shepherdia canadensis, Vaccinium membranaceum*
Ice Cream: *Shepherdia canadensis*
Soup: *Arctostaphylos uva-ursi, Prunus virginiana, Vaccinium membranaceum*
Unspecified: *Alectoria jubata, Heracleum maximum, Peucedanum sp., Pinus albicaulis, P. contorta, P. ponderosa*
Vegetable: *Camassia scilloides, Lewisia rediviva*

Comanche
Beverage: *Ilex sp., Lespedeza capitata*
Candy: *Dalea purpurea*
Fruit: *Celtis laevigata, Diospyros texana, D. virginiana, Juniperus virginiana, Morus rubra, Prunus angustifolia, Rhus glabra, Ribes aureum*
Staple: *Agastache pallidiflora, Agave americana, A. parryi, Prosopis glandulosa*
Starvation Food: *Quercus marilandica*
Unspecified: *Caesalpinia jamesii, Camassia scilloides, Carya illinoinensis, Cirsium*

undulatum, Cymopterus acaulis, Juglans nigra, Nelumbo lutea, Nuphar lutea, Pediomelum hypogaeum
Winter Use Food: *Carya illinoinensis, Juglans nigra, Prunus angustifolia*

Concow
Beverage: *Umbellularia californica*
Staple: *Ceanothus integerrimus, Verbena hastata*
Substitution Food: *Pogogyne douglasii*
Unspecified: *Petasites frigidus*

Costanoan
Bread & Cake: *Umbellularia californica*
Dried Food: *Heteromeles arbutifolia*
Fruit: *Aesculus californica, Amelanchier pallida, Arbutus menziesii, Frangula californica, Heteromeles arbutifolia, Juniperus californica, Maianthemum racemosum, Prunus ilicifolia, P. virginiana, Rubus leucodermis, R. vitifolius, Sambucus cerulea, Solanum umbelliferum, Umbellularia californica, Vaccinium ovatum, Vitis californica*
Staple: *Calandrinia ciliata, Elymus glaucus, Hemizonia corymbosa, Hordeum murinum, Layia platyglossa, Rumex crispus, Salvia columbariae, Wyethia angustifolia, Xanthium strumarium*
Unspecified: *Acer macrophyllum, Alnus rhombifolia, Calandrinia ciliata, Camissonia ovata, Chlorogalum pomeridianum, Claytonia perfoliata, Corylus cornuta, Cyperus esculentus, Dryopteris arguta, Erodium cicutarium, Helianthus annuus, Heracleum maximum, Juglans californica, Lithocarpus densiflorus, Lobularia maritima, Oenanthe sarmentosa, Pinus sabiniana, Platanus racemosa, Polystichum munitum, Prunus ilicifolia, Pteridium aquilinum, Quercus agrifolia, Raphanus sativus, Typha latifolia, Wyethia angustifolia*
Vegetable: *Rumex crispus*
Winter Use Food: *Asyneuma prenanthoides*

Costanoan (Olhonean)
Beverage: *Arctostaphylos pumila*

Cowichan

Fruit: *Rosa nutkana*
Special Food: *Camassia leichtlinii, C. quamash*
Spice: *Acer macrophyllum, Zostera marina*
Unspecified: *Cirsium brevistylum, Daucus pusillus*
Vegetable: *Urtica dioica*

Cowlitz

Beverage: *Fragaria vesca*
Candy: *Pseudotsuga menziesii*
Dried Food: *Equisetum hyemale, Fragaria vesca, Oemleria cerasiformis, Ribes divaricatum, Rubus leucodermis, R. ursinus*
Fruit: *Fragaria vesca, Malus fusca, Oemleria cerasiformis, Ribes divaricatum, Rubus leucodermis, R. parviflorus, R. spectabilis, R. ursinus*
Spice: *Tsuga heterophylla*
Unspecified: *Dryopteris expansa, Equisetum telmateia, Hydrophyllum tenuipes, Lysichiton americanus, Oenanthe sarmentosa, Oxalis oregana, Pteridium aquilinum, Quercus garryana, Rubus spectabilis*
Winter Use Food: *Corylus cornuta, Sambucus racemosa*

Cree

Beverage: *Elaeagnus commutata, Ledum groenlandicum*
Fruit: *Elaeagnus commutata*
Sweetener: *Acer negundo*
Vegetable: *Allium cernuum*

Cree, Plains

Dried Food: *Amelanchier alnifolia*

Cree, Woodlands

Beverage: *Agastache foeniculum, Ledum groenlandicum, Mentha canadensis, Ribes glandulosum*
Candy: *Picea glauca, P. mariana*
Dried Food: *Amelanchier alnifolia, Nuphar lutea, Typha latifolia*
Frozen Food: *Vaccinium vitis-idaea, Viburnum edule*
Fruit: *Amelanchier alnifolia, Arctostaphylos uva-ursi, Empetrum nigrum, Prunus virgin-iana, Ribes glandulosum, R. oxyacanthoides, Rubus arcticus, R. chamaemorus, R. idaeus, R. pubescens, Vaccinium myrtilloides, V. oxycoccos, V. vitis-idaea*
Preservative: *Amelanchier alnifolia, Betula papyrifera, Populus tremuloides*
Preserves: *Prunus pensylvanica, Ribes hudsonianum, Vaccinium myrtilloides, Viburnum edule*
Sauce & Relish: *Betula papyrifera, Prunus virginiana*
Snack Food: *Amelanchier alnifolia, Cornus canadensis, Fragaria virginiana, Lilium philadelphicum, Rosa acicularis, Vaccinium vitis-idaea, Viburnum edule*
Soup: *Vaccinium vitis-idaea*
Spice: *Allium schoenoprasum, Carum carvi, Mentha canadensis*
Staple: *Carum carvi*
Substitution Food: *Betula papyrifera*
Unspecified: *Allium schoenoprasum, Betula papyrifera, Corylus cornuta, Heracleum maximum, Lilium philadelphicum, Pinus banksiana, Populus tremuloides, Rubus idaeus, Scirpus acutus, S. tabernaemontani, Sium suave, Typha latifolia*
Winter Use Food: *Corylus cornuta, Vaccinium oxycoccos*

Crow

Dried Food: *Vitis vulpina*
Fruit: *Escobaria missouriensis, Prunus americana, Vitis vulpina*
Sauce & Relish: *Asclepias speciosa*
Unspecified: *Asclepias speciosa, Catabrosa aquatica, Glyceria fluitans, Leucocrinum montanum, Madia glomerata, Musineon divaricatum*
Winter Use Food: *Prunus americana*

Dakota

Beverage: *Agastache foeniculum, Ceanothus americanus, Mentha canadensis, Ratibida columnifera, Rubus idaeus, R. occidentalis, Sambucus canadensis*
Bread & Cake: *Prunus virginiana*
Candy: *Populus deltoides, Silphium laciniatum*
Dried Food: *Opuntia humifusa, Pediomelum*

esculentum, Physalis heterophylla, Prunus americana, P. pumila, P. virginiana, Rubus idaeus, R. occidentalis, Shepherdia argentea, Vitis cinerea, V. vulpina

Fodder: *Linum lewisii*

Forage: *Dyssodia papposa, Populus deltoides*

Fruit: *Amelanchier alnifolia, Fragaria vesca, F. virginiana, Opuntia humifusa, Prunus americana, P. pumila, P. virginiana, Ribes missouriense, Rubus idaeus, R. occidentalis, Sambucus canadensis, Shepherdia argentea, Viburnum lentago, Vitis cinerea, V. vulpina*

Sauce & Relish: *Allium canadense, Physalis heterophylla, Prunus americana, P. pumila*

Soup: *Carya ovata, Chenopodium album, Corylus americana, Juglans nigra, Nelumbo lutea*

Spice: *Allium canadense, Celtis occidentalis, Mentha canadensis*

Staple: *Zea mays, Zizania aquatica*

Starvation Food: *Opuntia humifusa, Rosa arkansana*

Sweetener: *Acer negundo, A. saccharinum, A. saccharum, Agastache foeniculum, Carya ovata, Zea mays*

Unspecified: *Acorus calamus, Allium canadense, Amphicarpaea bracteata, Apios americana, Asclepias syriaca, Astragalus crassicarpus, Carya ovata, Chenopodium album, Corylus americana, Helianthus tuberosus, Juglans nigra, Linum lewisii, Mentha canadensis, Nelumbo lutea, Pediomelum esculentum, Physalis lanceolata, Populus deltoides, Quercus macrocarpa, Q. rubra, Sagittaria latifolia, Scirpus acutus, S. tabernaemontani*

Winter Use Food: *Physalis heterophylla, Prunus virginiana, Zea mays*

Delaware

Bread & Cake: *Apios americana, Zea mays*

Dried Food: *Zea mays*

Porridge: *Zea mays*

Soup: *Zea mays*

Staple: *Zea mays*

Unspecified: *Agaricus campestris, Apios americana, Rumex acetosella, Zea mays*

Winter Use Food: *Apios americana*

Diegueño

Beverage: *Monardella lanceolata, Pellaea mucronata, Rhus integrifolia, Satureja douglasii*

Bread & Cake: *Prosopis glandulosa, Prunus ilicifolia*

Candy: *Eriodictyon lanatum, Marrubium vulgare, Quercus engelmannii*

Dried Food: *Eriodictyon lanatum, Opuntia basilaris, Rubus ursinus, Vitis girdiana*

Fodder: *Acacia greggii, Lotus scoparius*

Fruit: *Arctostaphylos glauca, Fragaria vesca, Heteromeles arbutifolia, Juniperus californica, Mammillaria dioica, Opuntia engelmannii, Prunus ilicifolia, Quercus dunnii, Rubus ursinus, Sambucus cerulea, Vitis girdiana*

Porridge: *Avena fatua, Prunus ilicifolia, Quercus agrifolia, Q. chrysolepis, Q. dumosa, Q. engelmannii, Q. kelloggii, Q. wislizeni, Salvia apiana*

Spice: *Salvia carduacea, S. columbariae*

Staple: *Quercus peninsularis*

Starvation Food: *Juniperus californica*

Sweetener: *Justicia californica*

Unspecified: *Agave deserti, Cleome isomeris, Dudleya pulverulenta, Penstemon centranthifolius, Pinus monophylla, P. quadrifolia, Salvia apiana, Yucca whipplei*

Vegetable: *Brassica nigra, Chenopodium album, Claytonia perfoliata, Erodium cicutarium, Lepidium nitidum, Opuntia engelmannii, Paeonia californica, Rorippa nasturtium-aquaticum, Viola pedunculata*

Winter Use Food: *Sambucus cerulea*

Eskimo

Fruit: *Rubus chamaemorus*

Eskimo, Alaska

Beverage: *Comarum palustre, Iris setosa, Lathyrus japonicus, Ledum palustre, Pentaphylloides floribunda, Sedum integrifolium*

Candy: *Matricaria discoidea, Picea glauca*

Fruit: *Arctostaphylos alpina, Cornus canadensis, C. suecica, Empetrum nigrum, Rubus arcticus, Vaccinium alpinum, V. oxycoccos, V. uliginosum, V. vitis-idaea*

Ice Cream: *Anemone narcissiflora, Empetrum nigrum*

Soup: *Dryopteris expansa, Hippuris vulgaris*

Spice: *Ledum palustre*

Unspecified: *Anemone narcissiflora, Angelica lucida, Artemisia tilesii, Astragalus polaris, Caltha palustris, Claytonia acutifolia, Dryopteris expansa, Epilobium angustifolium, Equisetum arvense, Honckenya peploides, Mertensia maritima, Oxyria digyna, Pedicularis lanata, Ranunculus pallasii, Ribes triste, Rumex arcticus, Salix alaxensis, S. planifolia, Saxifraga nelsoniana, S. spicata, Sedum integrifolium, Senecio pseudoarnica*

Vegetable: *Angelica lucida, Hippuris tetraphylla, Ligusticum scothicum, Petasites frigidus, Salix planifolia*

Winter Use Food: *Empetrum nigrum, Ligusticum scothicum, Rubus chamaemorus, Rumex arcticus, Salix planifolia, Saxifraga nelsoniana*

Eskimo, Arctic

Beverage: *Ledum groenlandicum, L. palustre, Pentaphylloides floribunda, Polygonum alpinum, Vaccinium vitis-idaea*

Forage: *Arctostaphylos alpina, A. rubra, Hedysarum alpinum, H. boreale*

Frozen Food: *Empetrum nigrum, Vaccinium vitis-idaea*

Fruit: *Arctostaphylos uva-ursi, Empetrum nigrum*

Ice Cream: *Rubus chamaemorus*

Pie & Pudding: *Polygonum alpinum*

Preserves: *Vaccinium vitis-idaea*

Unspecified: *Oxyria digyna, Pedicularis lanata, Polygonum alpinum, Salix planifolia*

Vegetable: *Claytonia tuberosa, Epilobium latifolium, Hedysarum alpinum, H. boreale, Honckenya peploides, Pedicularis lanata, Petasites frigidus, Rumex arcticus, Saxifraga nelsoniana, Sedum rosea, Senecio congestus*

Eskimo, Greenland

Unspecified: *Oxyria digyna*

Vegetable: *Angelica archangelica, Epilobium latifolium*

Eskimo, Inuktitut

Fodder: *Alectoria nigricans, A. nitidula, A. ochroleuca, Cornicularia divergens*

Frozen Food: *Rubus chamaemorus*

Fruit: *Rubus chamaemorus, Vaccinium uliginosum, V. vitis-idaea, Viburnum edule*

Ice Cream: *Dryopteris campyloptera, Hippuris vulgaris, Rumex arcticus*

Sauce & Relish: *Cetraria cucullata*

Soup: *Hippuris vulgaris, Ranunculus lapponicus*

Spice: *Allium schoenoprasum, Cetraria crispa, Rorippa islandica*

Unspecified: *Angelica lucida, Cicuta virosa, Epilobium angustifolium, E. latifolium, Eriophorum angustifolium, Hippuris vulgaris, Nephroma arcticum, Oxyria digyna, Picea glauca, P. mariana, Rumex arcticus, Saxifraga tricuspidata, Silene acaulis*

Winter Use Food: *Rubus arcticus*

Eskimo, Inupiat

Beverage: *Ledum palustre, Polygonum alpinum, Rosa acicularis, Salix planifolia, Viburnum edule*

Cooking Agent: *Vaccinium uliginosum*

Dessert: *Empetrum nigrum, Pedicularis lanata, Polygonum alpinum, Ribes triste, Rubus arcticus, R. chamaemorus, R. idaeus, Rumex arcticus, Shepherdia canadensis, Vaccinium oxycoccos, V. uliginosum, V. vitis-idaea, Viburnum edule*

Dried Food: *Chenopodium album*

Frozen Food: *Arctostaphylos uva-ursi, Chenopodium album, Hedysarum alpinum, Oxytropis maydelliana, Rosa acicularis, Rubus chamaemorus, Sedum rosea, Vaccinium uliginosum, Viburnum edule*

Fruit: *Arctostaphylos alpina, A. uva-ursi, Empetrum nigrum, Ribes triste, Rubus arcticus, R. chamaemorus, Vaccinium oxycoccos, V. uliginosum, V. vitis-idaea, Viburnum edule*

Ice Cream: *Arctostaphylos uva-ursi, Rosa acicularis, Rubus chamaemorus, Vaccinium uliginosum, Viburnum edule*

Pie & Pudding: *Empetrum nigrum, Vaccinium oxycoccos, V. uliginosum, V. vitis-idaea*

Preserves: *Rosa acicularis, Viburnum edule*

Sauce & Relish: *Polygonum alpinum, Ribes triste, Rosa acicularis, Vaccinium oxycoccos, V. uliginosum, V. vitis-idaea, Viburnum edule*

Soup: *Allium schoenoprasum, Salix planifolia*

Spice: *Ligusticum scothicum*

Staple: *Sedum rosea*

Sweetener: *Epilobium angustifolium, Salix alaxensis*

Unspecified: *Angelica lucida, Epilobium latifolium, Equisetum pratense, Eriophorum angustifolium, Pedicularis lanata, Polygonum alpinum, P. bistorta, Rosa acicularis, Salix alaxensis, Sedum rosea*

Vegetable: *Allium schoenoprasum, Chenopodium album, Epilobium angustifolium, Hedysarum alpinum, Honckenya peploides, Ligusticum scothicum, Oxyria digyna, Oxytropis maydelliana, Pedicularis lanata, Polygonum alpinum, P. bistorta, Rumex arcticus, Salix planifolia, Saxifraga nelsoniana, Sedum rosea*

Winter Use Food: *Arctostaphylos rubra, A. uvaursi, Empetrum nigrum, Epilobium angustifolium, Equisetum pratense, Eriophorum angustifolium, Hedysarum alpinum, Honckenya peploides, Oxytropis maydelliana, Polygonum alpinum, Rubus arcticus, R. chamaemorus, Rumex arcticus, Salix planifolia, Vaccinium oxycoccos, V. uliginosum, V. vitis-idaea*

Flathead

Beverage: *Camassia quamash, Shepherdia canadensis*

Bread & Cake: *Perideridia gairdneri*

Candy: *Larix occidentalis, Pinus contorta*

Dessert: *Mahonia repens*

Dried Food: *Lomatium macrocarpum*

Fruit: *Cornus sericea, Mahonia repens*

Ice Cream: *Shepherdia canadensis*

Pie & Pudding: *Amelanchier alnifolia*

Preservative: *Matricaria discoidea, Monarda fistulosa*

Sauce & Relish: *Allium cernuum, Arctostaphylos uva-ursi, Camassia quamash, Larix occidentalis*

Soup: *Camassia quamash*

Staple: *Allium cernuum*

Unspecified: *Balsamorhiza sagittata, Camassia quamash, Cirsium scariosum, Fritillaria pudica, Larix occidentalis, Lomatium macrocarpum, Pinus contorta, Populus balsamifera, P. deltoides*

Gitksan

Staple: *Tsuga heterophylla*

Sweetener: *Tsuga heterophylla*

Unspecified: *Epilobium angustifolium, Heracleum maximum, Picea glauca, Pinus contorta, Sedum divergens*

Winter Use Food: *Tsuga heterophylla*

Gosiute

Beverage: *Mentha canadensis*

Bread & Cake: *Salicornia maritima*

Candy: *Asclepias asperula, Chrysothamnus viscidiflorus, Pseudotsuga menziesii*

Cooking Agent: *Balsamorhiza sagittata, Brickellia grandiflora, Helianthus annuus*

Dried Food: *Amelanchier alnifolia, Calochortus nuttallii, Prunus virginiana, Ribes aureum, R. divaricatum, R. lacustre, R. oxyacanthoides, R. velutinum*

Fruit: *Amelanchier alnifolia, Fragaria vesca, Juniperus osteosperma, Prunus virginiana, Rhus glabra, R. trilobata, Ribes aureum, R. divaricatum, R. lacustre, R. oxyacanthoides, R. velutinum, Rosa californica, R. woodsii, Rubus leucodermis, R. parviflorus, Sambucus racemosa, Shepherdia argentea*

Porridge: *Descurainia pinnata, Prunus virginiana*

Unspecified: *Agastache urticifolia, Agoseris aurantiaca, Allium acuminatum, A. bisceptrum, Amsinckia tessellata, Artemisia biennis, A. dracunculus, A. ludoviciana, A. tripartita, Atriplex canescens, A. confertifolia, A. truncata, Balsamorhiza hookeri, B. sagittata, Bromus marginatus, Calochortus nuttallii, Camassia scilloides, Carex utriculata, Catabrosa aquatica, Chenopodium capitatum, C. leptophyllum, C. rubrum, Cinna arundinacea, Cirsium drummondii, C. eatonii, C. undulatum, Claytonia caroliniana, Crepis runcinata, Cymopterus*

*longipes, C. montanus, Deschampsia cespi-
tosa, Dracocephalum parviflorum, Elymus
canadensis, E. sibiricus, Elytrigia repens,
Festuca brachyphylla, Fritillaria pudica,
Helianthus annuus, Heliomeris multiflora,
Lactuca ludoviciana, Lithospermum multi-
florum, L. ruderale, Lomatium dissectum,
Oenothera biennis, Opuntia polyacantha,
Orobanche fasciculata, Oryzopsis hymenoi-
des, Perideridia gairdneri, Pinus edulis,
P. monophylla, Poa arida, P. secunda,
Puccinellia distans, Quercus ×pauciloba,
Ranunculus aquatilis, Rorippa nasturtium-
aquaticum, Scirpus acutus, Solidago
canadensis, S. nemoralis, S. spectabilis,
Stachys palustris, Suaeda calceoliformis,
Triglochin maritimum, Trisetum spicatum,
Typha latifolia, Vulpia octoflora, Wyethia
amplexicaulis*
Winter Use Food: *Camassia scilloides, Peride-
ridia gairdneri*

Great Basin Indian

Beverage: *Lomatium dissectum, Rhus trilobata*
Dried Food: *Amelanchier alnifolia, Prunus
virginiana*
Fruit: *Amelanchier alnifolia*
Unspecified: *Allium schoenoprasum, Peride-
ridia gairdneri*
Vegetable: *Lomatium dissectum*
Winter Use Food: *Calochortus nuttallii*

Green River Group

Fruit: *Rubus leucodermis, R. spectabilis*
Unspecified: *Pteridium aquilinum, Rubus
spectabilis*
Winter Use Food: *Sambucus cerulea, S.
racemosa*

Gros Ventre

Staple: *Helianthus annuus*
Unspecified: *Helianthus annuus*

Hahwunkwut

Bread & Cake: *Lithocarpus densiflorus*
Porridge: *Lithocarpus densiflorus*
Staple: *Lithocarpus densiflorus*
Unspecified: *Pteridium aquilinum*

Haida

Fruit: *Vaccinium vitis-idaea*

Haihais

Unspecified: *Conioselinum gmelinii*

Haisla

Bread & Cake: *Rubus parviflorus*
Dried Food: *Tsuga heterophylla*
Fruit: *Amelanchier alnifolia, Sambucus
racemosa*
Staple: *Tsuga heterophylla*
Sweetener: *Tsuga heterophylla*
Unspecified: *Abies amabilis, Conioselinum
gmelinii, Epilobium angustifolium, Herac-
leum maximum, Populus balsamifera,
Sedum divergens*
Winter Use Food: *Tsuga heterophylla*

Haisla & Hanaksiala

Beverage: *Camellia sinensis, Ledum groen-
landicum, Rosa nutkana, Rubus idaeus,
R. spectabilis, Sambucus racemosa, Theo-
broma cacao*
Bread & Cake: *Triticum aestivum*
Candy: *Picea sitchensis*
Dessert: *Cornus canadensis, C.
unalaschkensis*
Dried Food: *Cornus canadensis, C. unalasch-
kensis, Egregia menziesii, Fucus gardneri,
Porphyra abbottae, Rubus spectabilis, Sam-
bucus racemosa, Shepherdia canadensis*
Forage: *Achillea millefolium, Blechnum spi-
cant, Cornus sericea, Equisetum arvense,
E. scirpoides, Lysichiton americanus,
Prunus virginiana, Rubus pedatus, Sphag-
num sp., Symphoricarpos albus*
Fruit: *Citrus limon, C. sinensis, Crataegus
douglasii, Fragaria chiloensis, F. vesca,
F. virginiana, Gaultheria shallon, Lycopersi-
con esculentum, Maianthemum dilatatum,
Malus fusca, M. sylvestris, Prunus virgini-
ana, Ribes divaricatum, R. lacustre, R.
laxiflorum, Rubus discolor, R. idaeus,
R. leucodermis, R. pedatus, R. spectabilis,
R. ursinus, Vaccinium ovalifolium, V. parvi-
folium, V. uliginosum, Viburnum edule,
Vitis vinifera*

Ice Cream: *Shepherdia canadensis*
Preservative: *Alnus rubra*
Preserves: *Fragaria chiloensis, F. vesca, F. virginiana, Urtica dioica*
Sauce & Relish: *Porphyra abbottae*
Special Food: *Rubus spectabilis, Shepherdia canadensis, Vaccinium parvifolium*
Spice: *Piper nigrum*
Staple: *Oryza sativa, Triticum aestivum*
Unspecified: *Argentina egedii, Avena sativa, Conioselinum gmelinii, Epilobium angustifolium, Exobasidium* sp., *Fritillaria camschatcensis, Heracleum maximum, Lupinus littoralis, L. nootkatensis, Macrocystis integrifolia, Populus balsamifera, Rheum rhabarbarum, Rosa nutkana, Trifolium wormskioldii, Urtica dioica*
Vegetable: *Allium cepa, A. cernuum, Brassica oleracea, B. rapa, Daucus carota, Rumex aquaticus, Solanum tuberosum*
Winter Use Food: *Malus fusca, Sambucus racemosa, Tsuga heterophylla, Vaccinium oxycoccos, Viburnum edule*

Hanaksiala

Beverage: *Kalmia microphylla, Maianthemum racemosum, Rumex aquaticus*
Bread & Cake: *Tsuga heterophylla, Vaccinium cespitosum, V. membranaceum*
Candy: *Aquilegia formosa, Gentiana douglasiana*
Dried Food: *Amelanchier alnifolia, Vaccinium ovalifolium*
Fruit: *Arctostaphylos uva-ursi, Sambucus racemosa, Vaccinium ovalifolium*
Special Food: *Arctostaphylos uva-ursi*
Unspecified: *Angelica genuflexa, Conioselinum gmelinii, Rumex acetosella*
Winter Use Food: *Ribes bracteosum, Rumex aquaticus*

Havasupai

Beverage: *Agave utahensis, Aloysia wrightii, Ephedra fasciculata, E. nevadensis, E. torreyana, E. viridis, Eriogonum microthecum, Ficus carica, Juniperus osteosperma, Lycium pallidum, Opuntia phaeacantha, Proso-*

pis glandulosa, Prunus persica, Rhus trilobata, Yucca baccata*
Bread & Cake: *Acacia greggii, Amaranthus hybridus, Chenopodium fremontii, Koeleria macrantha, Lepidium lasiocarpum, Opuntia phaeacantha, Oryzopsis hymenoides, Poa fendleriana, Zea mays*
Candy: *Populus fremontii, Prosopis glandulosa*
Dried Food: *Cucurbita moschata, Ficus carica, Helianthus annuus, H. petiolaris, Juniperus osteosperma, Lycium pallidum, Opuntia phaeacantha, Proboscidea parviflora, Prunus persica, Rhus trilobata, Yucca baccata*
Fodder: *Coleogyne ramosissima, Krascheninnikovia lanata*
Forage: *Amelanchier utahensis, Koeleria macrantha, Salsola australis*
Fruit: *Citrullus lanatus, Ficus carica, Opuntia phaeacantha, Typha domingensis, Vitis arizonica*
Porridge: *Amaranthus hybridus, Citrullus lanatus, Cucurbita moschata, Pectis papposa, Plantago patagonica, Quercus gambelii, Zea mays*
Preserves: *Gaillardia pinnatifida, Gilia sinuata, Helianthus annuus, H. petiolaris, Lepidium lasiocarpum, Mentzelia albicaulis, Pinus edulis*
Sauce & Relish: *Pectis angustifolia, P. papposa*
Soup: *Amaranthus hybridus, Cucurbita moschata, Mentzelia albicaulis, Oryzopsis hymenoides, Pectis papposa, Phaseolus acutifolius, P. lunatus, P. vulgaris, Pinus edulis, Quercus gambelii, Zea mays*
Spice: *Pinus edulis, P. monophylla, Quercus gambelii*
Staple: *Helianthus annuus, H. petiolaris, Lepidium lasiocarpum, Oryzopsis hymenoides, Poa fendleriana, Zea mays*
Starvation Food: *Allium bisceptrum*
Unspecified: *Allium cepa, Amaranthus hybridus, Calochortus nuttallii, Cleome serrulata, Koeleria macrantha, Lepidium lasiocarpum, L. montanum, Lotus mearnsii, Mentzelia albicaulis, Phoradendron juniperinum, Pinus edulis, P. monophylla, P. ponderosa, Poa fendleriana, Proboscidea parviflora,*

Quercus gambelii, Rorippa nasturtium-
aquaticum, Thlaspi arvense, T. montanum
Vegetable: *Amaranthus hybridus, Cucurbita*
moschata, Eriogonum inflatum, Phaseolus
acutifolius, P. lunatus, P. vulgaris, Rumex
crispus, Stanleya pinnata, Zea mays
Winter Use Food: *Ficus carica, Koeleria mac-*
rantha, Phaseolus acutifolius, P. lunatus,
P. vulgaris, Zea mays

Hawaiian

Beverage: *Cordyline fruticosa, Jacquemontia*
ovalifolia, Sadleria cyatheoides
Fruit: *Artocarpus altilis, Carica papaya, Cler-*
montia arborescens, Dioscorea bulbifera
Unspecified: *Colocasia esculenta, Cordyline*
fruticosa, Dioscorea pentaphylla, Diplazium
meyenianum, Ipomoea cairica, Jacque-
montia ovalifolia, Marattia sp., Ochrosia
compta, Phegopteris sp., Tacca leontopetal-
oides, Vitex trifolia
Vegetable: *Colocasia esculenta*

Heiltzuk

Forage: *Sorbus sitchensis*
Unspecified: *Conioselinum gmelinii, Rumex*
aquaticus

Hesquiat

Beverage: *Ledum groenlandicum, Vaccinium*
parvifolium
Candy: *Picea sitchensis, Pinus contorta, Poly-*
podium scouleri, Tsuga heterophylla
Dessert: *Cornus sericea*
Dried Food: *Alaria marginata, Costaria costata,*
Fritillaria camschatcensis, Gaultheria shal-
lon, Lessoniopsis littoralis, Malus fusca,
Phyllospadix torreyi, Postelsia palmaefor-
mis, Rubus parviflorus
Forage: *Amelanchier alnifolia, Anthoxanthum*
odoratum, Enteromorpha intestinalis, Frit-
illaria camschatcensis, Heracleum maxi-
mum, Lonicera involucrata, Lysichiton
americanus, Menyanthes trifoliata, Potamo-
geton sp., Ranunculus repens, Rosa nutka-
na, Scirpus acutus, Streptopus amplexi-
folius, Usnea sp., Vaccinium oxycoccos,
Zostera marina

Fruit: *Amelanchier alnifolia, Fragaria chiloen-*
sis, F. vesca, F. virginiana, Maianthemum
dilatatum, Ribes bracteosum, R. divarica-
tum, R. laxiflorum, Rosa nutkana, Rubus
leucodermis, R. parviflorus, R. ursinus,
Sambucus racemosa, Vaccinium ovalifoli-
um, V. ovatum, V. oxycoccos, V. parvifolium,
V. vitis-idaea, Viburnum edule
Pie & Pudding: *Vaccinium myrtilloides*
Preserves: *Ribes bracteosum, Rubus parvi-*
florus, Sambucus racemosa, Vaccinium
myrtilloides, V. ovalifolium, V. ovatum,
V. oxycoccos, V. parvifolium
Sour: *Rumex acetosella*
Special Food: *Cornus canadensis*
Spice: *Gaultheria shallon, Rubus parviflorus*
Starvation Food: *Blechnum spicant, Thuja*
plicata
Unspecified: *Argentina egedii, Boschniakia*
hookeri, Cirsium brevistylum, C. vulgare,
Heracleum maximum, Oenanthe sarmen-
tosa, Phyllospadix scouleri, Porphyra per-
forata, Rubus spectabilis, Trifolium worm-
skioldii, Zostera marina
Vegetable: *Camassia quamash, Equisetum*
arvense, Fritillaria camschatcensis, Poly-
podium glycyrrhiza, Pteridium aquilinum

Hoh

Dried Food: *Equisetum hyemale, E. laevigatum*
Forage: *Lysichiton americanus*
Fruit: *Amelanchier alnifolia, Fragaria chiloen-*
sis, Gaultheria ovatifolia, Malus fusca, Ribes
sanguineum, Rosa pisocarpa, Rubus idaeus,
R. laciniatus, R. lasiococcus, R. leucoder-
mis, R. nivalis, R. parviflorus, R. spectabilis,
R. ursinus, Sambucus racemosa, Vaccinium
deliciosum, V. myrtilloides, V. ovalifolium,
V. ovatum, V. parvifolium
Preserves: *Gaultheria ovatifolia, Mahonia ner-*
vosa, Prunus emarginata
Sauce & Relish: *Gaultheria ovatifolia, Sambu-*
cus racemosa, Vaccinium deliciosum,
V. myrtilloides, V. ovalifolium, V. ovatum,
V. parvifolium
Special Food: *Equisetum hyemale, E.*
laevigatum

Spice: *Brassica nigra, Lysichiton americanus, Moricandia arvensis, Sinapis alba*

Unspecified: *Allium acuminatum, A. cernuum, Camassia quamash, Equisetum hyemale, Lepidium virginicum*

Vegetable: *Brassica nigra, Cirsium edule, Heracleum maximum, Lepidium virginicum, Moricandia arvensis, Sinapis alba, Urtica dioica*

Winter Use Food: *Ribes sanguineum, Rosa pisocarpa, Rubus idaeus, R. laciniatus, R. lasiococcus, R. leucodermis, R. nivalis, R. parviflorus, R. spectabilis, R. ursinus, Sambucus racemosa, Vaccinium deliciosum, V. myrtilloides, V. ovalifolium, V. ovatum, V. parvifolium*

Hopi

Beverage: *Bidens amplectens, Hymenopappus filifolius, Hymenoxys cooperi, Ipomopsis aggregata, Rhus trilobata, Thelesperma megapotamicum, T. subnudum*

Bread & Cake: *Chenopodium graveolens, Eriogonum corymbosum, Hymenopappus filifolius, Muhlenbergia rigens, Oryzopsis hymenoides, Panicum capillare, Sporobolus cryptandrus, Zea mays*

Candy: *Astragalus ceramicus, Calochortus nuttallii, Dalea lanata, Erodium cicutarium, Typha angustifolia*

Cooking Agent: *Amaranthus cruentus, Carthamus tinctorius, Citrullus lanatus, Cucurbita moschata, Solanum jamesii*

Dried Food: *Capsicum annuum, Cucumis melo, Cucurbita moschata, Eriogonum corymbosum, Monarda fistulosa, Pectis angustifolia, Poliomintha incana, Prunus persica, Zea mays*

Fodder: *Croton texensis, Helianthus annuus, H. anomalus, H. petiolaris*

Forage: *Bouteloua gracilis*

Fruit: *Juniperus monosperma, J. osteosperma, Lycium pallidum, Opuntia erinacea, O. polyacantha, Prunus persica, Rhus trilobata, Ribes cereum, Rosa woodsii, Yucca angustissima, Y. baccata*

Pie & Pudding: *Atriplex confertifolia, Sporobolus cryptandrus*

Porridge: *Amaranthus blitoides, Chenopodium album, C. fremontii, C. leptophyllum, Cycloloma atriplicifolium, Lycium pallidum, Monolepis nuttalliana, Sporobolus giganteus, Zea mays*

Preserves: *Lycium pallidum, Yucca baccata*

Sauce & Relish: *Coriandrum sativum, Mentha canadensis, Sorghum bicolor*

Special Food: *Cucurbita moschata, Pinus edulis*

Spice: *Allium cernuum, A. geyeri, Artemisia frigida, Atriplex confertifolia, A. obovata, Capsicum annuum, Chenopodium fremontii, Chrysothamnus viscidiflorus, Coriandrum sativum, Descurainia pinnata, Eriogonum hookeri, Lygodesmia grandiflora, Mentha canadensis, Pectis angustifolia, Poliomintha incana, Sporobolus giganteus*

Staple: *Citrullus lanatus, Digitaria cognata, Mentzelia albicaulis, Oryzopsis hymenoides, Panicum capillare, Zea mays*

Starvation Food: *Amaranthus acanthochiton, Lycium pallidum, Oryzopsis hymenoides, Sporobolus airoides, S. flexuosus*

Substitution Food: *Atriplex canescens*

Sweetener: *Dalea lanata, Echinocereus fendleri, Zea mays*

Unspecified: *Allium cernuum, A. geyeri, A. vineale, Amaranthus arenicola, A. blitoides, A. powellii, Artemisia dracunculus, Asclepias speciosa, A. verticillata, Astragalus ceramicus, Atriplex argentea, A. confertifolia, A. powellii, Calochortus aureus, C. nuttallii, Castilleja linariifolia, Chenopodium album, Citrullus lanatus, Cleome serrulata, Coriandrum sativum, Cucumis melo, Cucurbita maxima, C. moschata, Cycloloma cornutum, Cymopterus multinervatus, C. newberryi, Descurainia pinnata, Helianthus tuberosus, Lycium pallidum, Lygodesmia grandiflora, Malus sylvestris, Mentzelia albicaulis, Monarda citriodora, Opuntia erinacea, O. polyacantha, O. whipplei, Pectis angustifolia, Pinus edulis, P. monophylla, Poliomintha incana, Portulaca oleracea, Prunus armeniaca, P. dulcis, Pyrus communis, Scirpus acutus, S. tabernaemontani,*

Solanum jamesii, Stanleya albescens, Usti-
lago zeae, Wislizenia refracta, Zea mays
Vegetable: *Amaranthus acanthochiton, A.*
blitoides, A. powellii, Atriplex argentea, A.
confertifolia, A. obovata, A. powellii, A. sac-
caria, Chenopodium fremontii, C. incanum,
Cleome serrulata, Descurainia obtusa, D.
pinnata, Pseudocymopterus montanus,
Stanleya albescens, S. pinnata, Tradescan-
tia occidentalis

Houma

Bread & Cake: *Sabal minor, Smilax bona-nox,*
S. laurifolia
Fodder: *Sonchus oleraceus*
Unspecified: *Cirsium horridulum*

Hualapai

Beverage: *Mahonia fremontii, Pinus edulis,*
Rhus trilobata, Rumex hymenosepalus,
Yucca baccata
Bread & Cake: *Pinus edulis, Quercus*
turbinella
Candy: *Pinus edulis*
Dried Food: *Celtis laevigata, Prosopis pubes-*
cens, Yucca baccata, Y. schidigera
Fruit: *Celtis laevigata, Mahonia fremontii,*
Nolina bigelovii, Rhus trilobata, Yucca bac-
cata, Y. schidigera
Porridge: *Pinus edulis*
Soup: *Pinus edulis, Quercus gambelii, Q.*
turbinella
Staple: *Yucca baccata, Y. schidigera*
Unspecified: *Juglans major, Pinus edulis, Pro-*
boscidea parviflora, Prosopis pubescens,
Quercus gambelii, Q. turbinella

Hupa

Bread & Cake: *Lithocarpus densiflorus*
Porridge: *Lithocarpus densiflorus*
Staple: *Lithocarpus densiflorus, Madia elegans*
Unspecified: *Lithocarpus densiflorus*

Huron

Starvation Food: *Apios americana, Arachis*
hypogaea, Helianthus tuberosus, Lilium
canadense, Nelumbo lutea

Iroquois

Baby Food: *Carya ovata, Juglans cinerea, Zea*
mays
Beverage: *Acer saccharinum, A. saccharum,*
Alisma plantago-aquatica, Aralia nudicau-
lis, Betula lenta, Carya cordiformis, C. ovata,
Castanea dentata, Corylus americana,
Fagus grandifolia, Juglans cinerea, J. nigra,
Monarda fistulosa, Prunus americana, Rhus
glabra, Rubus canadensis, Taraxacum offi-
cinale, Taxus canadensis, Tsuga canaden-
sis, Zea mays
Bread & Cake: *Acer rubrum, A. saccharinum,*
A. saccharum, Amelanchier canadensis,
Asimina triloba, Carya cordiformis, C.
ovata, Castanea dentata, Citrullus lanatus,
Corylus americana, Crataegus pruinosa,
C. submollis, Cucumis melo, C. sativus,
Cucurbita maxima, C. moschata, C. pepo,
Fagus grandifolia, Fragaria vesca, F. virgin-
iana, Gaultheria procumbens, Gaylussacia
baccata, Juglans cinerea, J. nigra, Malus
coronaria, M. sylvestris, Mitchella repens,
Morus rubra, Phaseolus coccineus, P. luna-
tus, P. vulgaris, Podophyllum peltatum,
Prunus americana, P. nigra, P. pensylvanica,
P. persica, P. serotina, P. virginiana, Pyrus
communis, Ribes americanum, R. triste,
Rubus canadensis, R. idaeus, R. occidenta-
lis, R. odoratus, R. pubescens, Sambucus
canadensis, Vaccinium angustifolium, V.
corymbosum, V. macrocarpon, V. oxycoccos,
Viburnum lentago, V. opulus, Vitis vulpina,
Zea mays
Dried Food: *Amelanchier canadensis, Arctium*
lappa, Asimina triloba, Citrullus lanatus,
Crataegus pruinosa, C. submollis, Cucumis
melo, C. sativus, Cucurbita maxima, C.
moschata, C. pepo, Fragaria vesca, F. virgin-
iana, Gaultheria procumbens, Gaylussacia
baccata, Malus coronaria, M. sylvestris,
Mitchella repens, Morus rubra, Phaseolus
coccineus, P. lunatus, P. vulgaris, Podophyl-
lum peltatum, Prunus americana, P. nigra,
P. pensylvanica, P. persica, P. serotina, P.
virginiana, Pyrus communis, Ribes ameri-
canum, R. triste, Rubus canadensis, R.
idaeus, R. occidentalis, R. odoratus,

R. pubescens, Sambucus canadensis, Vaccinium angustifolium, V. corymbosum, V. macrocarpon, V. oxycoccos, Viburnum lentago, V. opulus, Vitis vulpina

Forage: *Artemisia biennis, Spartina alterniflora, Stellaria media*

Fruit: *Amelanchier canadensis, Asimina triloba, Corylus cornuta, Crataegus pruinosa, C. submollis, Fragaria vesca, F. virginiana, Gaultheria procumbens, Gaylussacia baccata, Malus coronaria, M. sylvestris, Mitchella repens, Morus rubra, Podophyllum peltatum, Prunus americana, P. nigra, P. pensylvanica, P. persica, P. serotina, P. virginiana, Pyrus communis, Ribes americanum, R. triste, Rubus canadensis, R. idaeus, R. occidentalis, R. odoratus, R. pubescens, Sambucus canadensis, Vaccinium angustifolium, V. corymbosum, V. macrocarpon, V. oxycoccos, Viburnum lentago, V. opulus, Vitis vulpina*

Pie & Pudding: *Carya cordiformis, C. ovata, Castanea dentata, Corylus americana, Cucurbita pepo, Fagus grandifolia, Gaylussacia baccata, Juglans cinerea, J. nigra, Rubus occidentalis, Zea mays*

Porridge: *Gaylussacia baccata, Rubus occidentalis, Sambucus canadensis, Zea mays*

Preserves: *Vaccinium angustifolium, V. myrtilloides*

Sauce & Relish: *Amelanchier canadensis, Asimina triloba, Carya cordiformis, C. ovata, Castanea dentata, Corylus americana, Crataegus pruinosa, C. submollis, Cucurbita pepo, Fagus grandifolia, Fragaria vesca, F. virginiana, Gaultheria procumbens, Gaylussacia baccata, Juglans cinerea, J. nigra, Malus coronaria, M. sylvestris, Mitchella repens, Morus rubra, Podophyllum peltatum, Prunus americana, P. nigra, P. pensylvanica, P. persica, P. serotina, P. virginiana, Pyrus communis, Ribes americanum, R. triste, Rubus canadensis, R. idaeus, R. occidentalis, R. odoratus, R. pubescens, Sambucus canadensis, Vaccinium angustifolium, V. corymbosum, V. macrocarpon, V. oxycoccos, Viburnum lentago, V. opulus, Vitis vulpina, Zea mays*

Snack Food: *Zea mays*

Soup: *Arctium lappa, Carya cordiformis, C. ovata, Castanea dentata, Corylus americana, Fagus grandifolia, Gaylussacia baccata, Juglans cinerea, J. nigra, Phaseolus coccineus, P. lunatus, P. vulgaris, Prunus virginiana, Rubus occidentalis, Zea mays*

Special Food: *Carya cordiformis, C. ovata, Castanea dentata, Citrullus lanatus, Corylus americana, Cucumis melo, C. sativus, Cucurbita maxima, C. moschata, C. pepo, Fagus grandifolia, Juglans cinerea, J. nigra, Zea mays*

Spice: *Castanea dentata, Polygonum hydropiper, Rumex acetosella*

Staple: *Carya cordiformis, C. ovata, Castanea dentata, Corylus americana, Fagus grandifolia, Juglans cinerea, J. nigra*

Sweetener: *Acer saccharinum, A. saccharum*

Unspecified: *Apios americana, Cardamine concatenata, C. diphylla, Carya cordiformis, C. ovata, Castanea dentata, Claytonia virginica, Corylus americana, Fagus grandifolia, Helianthus tuberosus, Juglans cinerea, J. nigra, Pinus strobus, Quercus alba, Q. bicolor, Q. prinus, Q. rubra, Ranunculus cymbalaria, Rhus glabra, Rubus aculeatissimus, Solanum tuberosum, Vaccinium angustifolium, V. myrtilloides, Vitis vulpina*

Vegetable: *Allium canadense, A. tricoccum, Amaranthus retroflexus, Arctium lappa, Asclepias syriaca, Asparagus officinalis, Brassica nigra, Caltha palustris, Chenopodium album, Citrullus lanatus, Cucumis melo, C. sativus, Cucurbita maxima, C. moschata, C. pepo, Hydrophyllum virginianum, Lathyrus japonicus, Onoclea sensibilis, Oxalis corniculata, Pedicularis canadensis, P. lanceolata, Phaseolus coccineus, P. lunatus, P. vulgaris, Phytolacca americana, Portulaca oleracea, Rorippa nasturtium-aquaticum, Rumex acetosella, R. crispus, Symplocarpus foetidus, Taraxacum officinale, Urtica dioica, Zea mays*

Isleta

Beverage: *Androsace sp., Echinocereus triglochidiatus, Holodiscus dumosus, Osmorhiza*

*depauperata, Thelesperma longipes, Zea
mays*
Bread & Cake: *Cleome serrulata, Echinocereus
triglochidiatus, Koeleria macrantha, Nolina
microcarpa, Prosopis glandulosa, Zea mays*
Candy: *Apocynum cannabinum, Echinocereus
triglochidiatus, Hymenoxys richardsonii,
Populus deltoides, Prosopis glandulosa, Zea
mays*
Fodder: *Equisetum laevigatum*
Forage: *Artemisia frigida, Erodium cicutarium,
Lotus wrightii, Yucca baccata, Y. glauca*
Fruit: *Amelanchier utahensis, Cucurbita foe-
tidissima, Echinocereus triglochidiatus,
Fragaria vesca, Juniperus deppeana, Lycium
pallidum, Nolina microcarpa, Philadelphus
microphyllus, Prunus americana, Ribes
cereum, R. leptanthum, Rubus parviflorus,
Vitis arizonica, Yucca baccata, Y. glauca*
Porridge: *Koeleria macrantha, Nolina micro-
carpa, Zea mays*
Preserves: *Echinocereus triglochidiatus, Nolina
microcarpa, Ribes cereum*
Sauce & Relish: *Aletes anisatus, Echinocereus
triglochidiatus, Rhus trilobata*
Special Food: *Fragaria vesca, Rubus
parviflorus*
Spice: *Hedeoma nana, Monarda fistulosa*
Staple: *Koeleria macrantha, Nolina micro-
carpa, Pinus edulis, Quercus gambelii, Zea
mays*
Sweetener: *Zea mays*
Unspecified: *Allium cernuum, Asparagus offi-
cinalis, Echinocereus triglochidiatus, Hede-
oma nana, Pinus edulis, Polyporus barlowii,
Populus deltoides, Prosopis pubescens,
Yucca baccata, Y. glauca, Zea mays*
Vegetable: *Aletes anisatus, Allium cernuum,
Amaranthus retroflexus, Asparagus offici-
nalis, Atriplex argentea, Cleome serrulata,
Echinocereus triglochidiatus, Mimulus gla-
bratus, Portulaca oleracea, Rumex crispus,
Solanum jamesii*
Winter Use Food: *Allium cernuum, Pinus edu-
lis, Polyporus barlowii, Portulaca oleracea,
Thelesperma longipes, Yucca baccata,
Y. glauca, Zea mays*

Jemez
Beverage: *Juniperus communis*
Bread & Cake: *Cleome serrulata*
Forage: *Melilotus officinalis*
Fruit: *Berberis fendleri, Juniperus monosper-
ma, J. scopulorum, Lycium pallidum, Rhus
trilobata, Ribes leptanthum, Vitis arizonica*
Special Food: *Lycium pallidum*
Unspecified: *Amaranthus retroflexus, Asclepias
subverticillata, Astragalus lentiginosus,
Pinus edulis, Populus deltoides, Robinia
neomexicana, Yucca baccata, Y. glauca*
Vegetable: *Cleome serrulata*

Kamia
Bread & Cake: *Anemopsis californica*
Porridge: *Anemopsis californica, Cyperus
erythrorhizos*
Staple: *Atriplex torreyi*
Unspecified: *Citrullus lanatus, Cucurbita pepo,
Phaseolus acutifolius, Prosopis glandulosa,
P. pubescens, Vigna unguiculata, Zea mays*
Vegetable: *Sonchus oleraceus*

Karok
Beverage: *Arctostaphylos canescens, A. manzanita, A. nevadensis, Eriodictyon californicum, Pseudotsuga menziesii*
Bread & Cake: *Lithocarpus densiflorus*
Candy: *Agoseris aurantiaca, Asclepias cordifolia, A. eriocarpa, Toxicodendron
diversilobum*
Dried Food: *Amelanchier alnifolia, Arbutus
menziesii, Arctostaphylos canescens, A.
manzanita, A. nevadensis, A. patula*
Forage: *Ceanothus integerrimus, Disporum
smithii, Oemleria cerasiformis*
Frozen Food: *Arbutus menziesii*
Fruit: *Amelanchier alnifolia, Arbutus menziesii, Arctostaphylos canescens, A. manzanita, A. nevadensis, Fragaria vesca, Gaultheria shallon, Heteromeles arbutifolia,
Paxistima myrsinites, Prunus virginiana,
Quercus chrysolepis, Q. kelloggii, Ribes
cruentum, R. divaricatum, R. roezlii, Rubus
leucodermis, R. parviflorus, R. vitifolius,
Sambucus cerulea, Taxus brevifolia,*

Vaccinium ovatum, V. parvifolium, Vitis californica

Porridge: *Bromus diandrus, B. hordeaceus, Elymus glaucus, Lithocarpus densiflorus*

Preservative: *Alnus rhombifolia*

Spice: *Pseudotsuga menziesii*

Staple: *Lithocarpus densiflorus*

Unspecified: *Allium acuminatum, A. bolanderi, Apocynum cannabinum, Armillaria ponderosa, Avena sativa, Balsamorhiza deltoidea, Boschniakia strobilacea, Calochortus pulchellus, Castanopsis chrysophylla, Chlorogalum pomeridianum, Corylus cornuta, Dichelostemma multiflorum, D. pulchellum, Epilobium canum, Eriogonum nudum, Heracleum maximum, Lilium occidentale, L. pardalinum, Lomatium californicum, Perideridia gairdneri, Pinus lambertiana, Quercus chrysolepis, Q. garryana, Q. kelloggii, Q. sadleriana, Rorippa nasturtium-aquaticum, Triteleia laxa, Umbellularia californica, Zigadenus venenosus*

Vegetable: *Angelica tomentosa, Camassia quamash, Crepis acuminata, Darmera peltata, Eriogonum nudum, Grindelia robusta, Lathyrus graminifolius, Osmorhiza berteroi, Sanicula bipinnata*

Winter Use Food: *Castanopsis chrysophylla, Corylus cornuta, Lithocarpus densiflorus, Pinus lambertiana, Umbellularia californica, Vaccinium ovatum*

Kawaiisu

Beverage: *Arctostaphylos glauca, Cheilanthes covillei, Descurainia pinnata, D. sophia, Distichlis spicata, Ephedra californica, E. nevadensis, E. viridis, Eriogonum baileyi, E. roseum, E. wrightii, Lepidium fremontii, Lycium andersonii, Mentha arvensis, M. spicata, Monardella linoides, M. odoratissima, M. viridis, Pellaea mucronata, Platanus racemosa, Salvia columbariae, Trichostema lanceolatum*

Bread & Cake: *Aesculus californica, Juniperus californica, Prosopis glandulosa, Quercus chrysolepis, Q. douglasii, Q. dumosa, Q. garryana, Q. kelloggii, Q. lobata, Q. wislizeni*

Candy: *Asclepias californica, Salix bonplandi-*

ana, S. hindsiana, Stephanomeria pauciflora

Dried Food: *Eriophyllum ambiguum, Juniperus californica, Lycium andersonii, Ribes californicum, R. quercetorum, R. roezlii, R. velutinum, Yucca brevifolia, Y. whipplei*

Forage: *Erodium cicutarium, Leymus triticoides, Nemophila menziesii*

Fruit: *Amelanchier pallida, Arctostaphylos glauca, Frangula californica, Juniperus californica, Lycium andersonii, Prunus virginiana, Ribes californicum, R. quercetorum, R. roezlii, R. velutinum, Rosa californica, R. woodsii, Yucca brevifolia*

Porridge: *Deschampsia danthonioides, Elymus multisetus, Eriogonum inflatum, E. plumatella, Leymus triticoides, Melica imperfecta, Nama demissum, Pinus monophylla, P. sabiniana, Prosopis glandulosa, Rumex crispus, R. hymenosepalus, R. salicifolius*

Preserves: *Mentzelia affinis, M. albicaulis, M. congesta, M. dispersa, Prunus virginiana, Ribes californicum, R. quercetorum, R. roezlii, R. velutinum, Sambucus cerulea*

Spice: *Chrysothamnus nauseosus, Lotus procumbens, L. unifoliolatus, Stachys albens*

Staple: *Eriogonum baileyi, E. davidsonii, E. inflatum, E. pusillum, E. roseum, E. wrightii, Helianthus annuus, Juniperus californica, Oryzopsis hymenoides, Quercus chrysolepis, Q. douglasii, Q. dumosa, Q. garryana, Q. kelloggii, Q. lobata, Q. wislizeni*

Sweetener: *Coreopsis bigelovii, Phragmites australis, Pinus lambertiana*

Unspecified: *Avena fatua, Carex douglasii, Castanopsis sempervirens, Caulanthus inflatus, Cirsium californicum, C. congdonii, C. occidentale, Cistanthe monandra, Cleome isomeris, Dendromecon rigida, Ephedra californica, E. nevadensis, E. viridis, Eriogonum angulosum, E. nudum, E. pusillum, Hordeum jubatum, Mimulus cardinalis, Opuntia basilaris, Pholisma arenarium, Pinus lambertiana, P. monophylla, P. ponderosa, P. sabiniana, Pterospora andromedea, Rorippa nasturtium-aquaticum, Rumex crispus, R. hymenosepalus, R. salici-*

folius, Scirpus tabernaemontani, Stipa speciosa, Typha domingensis, Yucca whipplei
Vegetable: *Agoseris retrorsa, Amsinckia tessellata, Atriplex serenana, Caulanthus coulteri, Chenopodium album, Claytonia perfoliata, Coreopsis bigelovii, Lomatium californicum, L. utriculatum, Perideridia pringlei, Phacelia distans, P. ramosissima, Stanleya pinnata, Trifolium wormskioldii*
Winter Use Food: *Descurainia pinnata, D. sophia, Mentzelia affinis, M. albicaulis, M. congesta, M. dispersa, Pinus monophylla, Quercus chrysolepis, Q. douglasii, Q. dumosa, Q. garryana, Q. kelloggii, Q. lobata, Q. wislizeni*

Keresan

Beverage: *Thelesperma megapotamicum*
Dried Food: *Prunus armeniaca, P. persica*
Fruit: *Juniperus monosperma, J. scopulorum, Prunus armeniaca, P. persica, Rhus trilobata, Yucca baccata*
Soup: *Capsicum annuum*
Spice: *Coriandrum sativum, Cucumis melo*
Starvation Food: *Solanum fendleri, S. jamesii*
Unspecified: *Cleome serrulata, Dalea candida, Opuntia engelmannii*
Vegetable: *Amaranthus cruentus, Cleome serrulata*
Winter Use Food: *Pinus edulis*

Keres, Western

Beverage: *Rhus trilobata, Thelesperma filifolium, T. megapotamicum, Yucca glauca*
Bread & Cake: *Yucca glauca*
Candy: *Asclepias speciosa, A. subverticillata, Hymenoxys richardsonii, Populus deltoides*
Cooking Agent: *Opuntia engelmannii*
Fodder: *Geranium caespitosum, Phoradendron juniperinum, Sporobolus cryptandrus*
Forage: *Atriplex argentea, Bouteloua gracilis, Krascheninnikovia lanata, Sarcobatus vermiculatus*
Fruit: *Ceanothus fendleri, Celtis occidentalis, Echinocereus triglochidiatus, Opuntia engelmannii, O. phaeacantha, Physalis longifolia, P. subulata, Prunus persica, P. virginiana, Rhus trilobata, Ribes cereum,*

R. inerme, Vitis vulpina, Yucca baccata, Y. glauca
Porridge: *Cleome serrulata, Prosopis glandulosa*
Sauce & Relish: *Lycium pallidum, Yucca baccata, Y. glauca*
Spice: *Agastache pallidiflora, Allium geyeri, Berlandiera lyrata, Juniperus monosperma, Monarda pectinata, Pectis angustifolia, Rhus trilobata*
Staple: *Dalea candida, Quercus gambelii, Zea mays*
Starvation Food: *Juniperus monosperma, Opuntia clavata, O. imbricata, Phoradendron juniperinum, Solanum triflorum, Yucca glauca*
Sweetener: *Dalea candida, Sophora nuttalliana*
Unspecified: *Amaranthus hybridus, A. retroflexus, Aster laevis, Astragalus cyaneus, Atriplex argentea, Pinus edulis, Plantago major, Quercus gambelii, Ranunculus inamoenus, Scirpus americanus, Tradescantia occidentalis, Typha latifolia, Yucca glauca*
Vegetable: *Allium cernuum, Amaranthus hybridus, A. retroflexus, Atriplex powellii, Cleome serrulata, Cymopterus acaulis, Cyperus squarrosus, Lactuca sativa, Lathyrus polymorphus, Portulaca oleracea, Prosopis glandulosa, Solanum jamesii, Vicia americana, Zea mays*
Winter Use Food: *Amaranthus hybridus, A. retroflexus, Opuntia engelmannii, O. imbricata, O. polyacantha, Prunus persica, P. virginiana, Yucca baccata, Y. glauca, Zea mays*

Kimsquit

Dried Food: *Arctostaphylos uva-ursi*
Unspecified: *Lupinus nootkatensis*

Kiowa

Beverage: *Paronychia jamesii, Quercus nigra, Q. stellata, Rhus trilobata, Senna occidentalis, Ulmus rubra*
Candy: *Apocynum cannabinum, Euphorbia marginata, Prunus gracilis, Sideroxylon lanuginosum, Vernonia missurica*

Dried Food: *Quercus stellata, Vitis cinerea*
Fodder: *Bouteloua curtipendula, B. hirsuta,
Bromus catharticus, Cyperus schweinitzii,
Dichanthelium oligosanthes, Elymus cana-
densis, Paspalum setaceum, Prosopis chil-
ensis, P. glandulosa, Sorghum halepense,
Sporobolus cryptandrus, Zea mays*
Forage: *Paspalum setaceum*
Fruit: *Celtis occidentalis, Prunus americana,
P. virginiana, Ribes aureum, Rhus trilobata,
Ribes aureum, Vitis cinerea*
Preserves: *Quincula lobata, Ribes aureum,
Vitis cinerea*
Starvation Food: *Ipomoea leptophylla*
Unspecified: *Cirsium ochrocentrum, Dalea
candida, Eriogonum longifolium, Helian-
thus annuus, Juglans nigra, Liatris punc-
tata, Pyrrhopappus carolinianus, Quercus
nigra, Zea mays*
Vegetable: *Prosopis chilensis, P. glandulosa,
Taraxacum officinale*
Winter Use Food: *Prunus americana, P. graci-
lis, P. virginiana, Ulmus rubra*

Kitasoo

Beverage: *Ledum groenlandicum*
Bread & Cake: *Porphyra abbottae, Sambucus
racemosa, Vaccinium cespitosum, V. ovali-
folium, V. uliginosum*
Dried Food: *Picea sitchensis, Tsuga hetero-
phylla, Vaccinium membranaceum*
Fruit: *Amelanchier alnifolia, Cornus unalasch-
kensis, Fragaria chiloensis, F. vesca, F. vir-
giniana, Gaultheria shallon, Maianthemum
dilatatum, Oemleria cerasiformis, Ribes
bracteosum, Rubus discolor, R. idaeus,
R. leucodermis, R. pedatus, R. spectabilis,
Vaccinium cespitosum, V. membranaceum,
V. ovalifolium, V. oxycoccos, V. parvifolium,
V. uliginosum*
Ice Cream: *Shepherdia canadensis*
Pie & Pudding: *Rheum rhabarbarum*
Preserves: *Rheum rhabarbarum*
Special Food: *Malus fusca*
Unspecified: *Abies amabilis, Argentina egedii,
Egregia menziesii, Fritillaria camschatcen-
sis, Macrocystis integrifolia, Oryza sativa,*

*Porphyra abbottae, Rubus spectabilis, Tri-
folium wormskioldii, Tsuga heterophylla*
Vegetable: *Brassica oleracea, B. rapa, Conioselinum gmelinii, Daucus carota, Heracleum
maximum, Rumex aquaticus, Solanum
tuberosum*
Winter Use Food: *Malus fusca, Shepherdia
canadensis, Viburnum edule*

Klallam

Bread & Cake: *Gaultheria shallon*
Candy: *Pseudotsuga menziesii*
Dried Food: *Rubus leucodermis, R. parviflorus,
Vaccinium ovalifolium*
Fruit: *Fragaria ×ananassa, Mahonia aquifolium, M. nervosa, Ribes lobbii, R. sanguineum, Rubus leucodermis, Sambucus cerulea,
S. racemosa, Vaccinium ovalifolium, V. oxycoccos, V. parvifolium*
Unspecified: *Abronia latifolia, Allium cernuum, Equisetum telmateia, Lilium columbianum, Polystichum munitum, Pteridium
aquilinum, Rubus leucodermis, R. parviflorus, Rumex aquaticus*
Winter Use Food: *Sambucus cerulea, S.
racemosa*

Klamath

Beverage: *Mentha canadensis, Triglochin
maritimum*
Bread & Cake: *Nuphar lutea*
Dried Food: *Camassia quamash, Lomatium
canbyi, Nuphar lutea, Perideridia oregana,
Prunus subcordata, P. virginiana, Ribes
hirtellum, Rubus leucodermis, Vaccinium
scoparium*
Fruit: *Amelanchier alnifolia, Arctostaphylos
patula, Fragaria virginiana, Lonicera con-
jugialis, Prunus emarginata, P. subcordata,
Ribes aureum, R. cereum, R. hirtellum, Rosa
woodsii, Rubus leucodermis, Sambucus
cerulea, Vaccinium scoparium*
Pie & Pudding: *Camassia leichtlinii*
Porridge: *Lomatium canbyi, Nuphar lutea,
Polygonum douglasii*
Preservative: *Achillea millefolium*
Sauce & Relish: *Pinus ponderosa, Sium suave*
Snack Food: *Ipomopsis aggregata*

Special Food: *Nuphar lutea*
Staple: *Nuphar lutea*
Starvation Food: *Pinus ponderosa*
Unspecified: *Agrostis perennans, Amaranthus blitoides, Amelanchier alnifolia, Balsamorhiza deltoidea, B. sagittata, Beckmannia syzigachne, Calochortus macrocarpus, Camassia quamash, Castanopsis chrysophylla, Chenopodium fremontii, Corylus cornuta, Descurainia incana, Glyceria fluitans, Heracleum maximum, Leymus condensatus, Madia glomerata, Mentzelia albicaulis, Nuphar lutea, Perideridia gairdneri, Phragmites australis, Pinus lambertiana, P. ponderosa, Rubus vitifolius, Rumex paucifolius, R. salicifolius, Sagittaria cuneata, S. latifolia, Scirpus acutus, Sparganium eurycarpum, Triglochin maritimum, Typha latifolia, Valeriana edulis*
Winter Use Food: *Amelanchier alnifolia, Vaccinium membranaceum*

Koyukon
Beverage: *Empetrum nigrum*
Candy: *Picea glauca*
Frozen Food: *Vaccinium uliginosum, V. vitis-idaea, Viburnum edule*
Fruit: *Rosa acicularis, Rubus arcticus, R. chamaemorus, R. idaeus*
Unspecified: *Allium schoenoprasum, Polygonum alpinum, Rumex arcticus*
Winter Use Food: *Arctostaphylos alpina, A. uva-ursi*

Kutenai
Appetizer: *Mahonia repens*
Cooking Agent: *Lewisia rediviva*
Dessert: *Lewisia rediviva, Mahonia repens*
Dried Food: *Lewisia rediviva*
Fruit: *Cornus sericea*
Sauce & Relish: *Allium cernuum, Larix occidentalis*
Staple: *Allium cernuum*
Unspecified: *Balsamorhiza sagittata, Camassia quamash, Cirsium scariosum, Lewisia rediviva, Matricaria discoidea, Pinus contorta, Populus balsamifera, P. deltoides*

Kwakiutl
Dried Food: *Erythronium oregonum*
Unspecified: *Erythronium oregonum, Lupinus polyphyllus*

Kwakiutl, Southern
Beverage: *Ledum groenlandicum*
Bread & Cake: *Sambucus racemosa*
Candy: *Picea sitchensis, Thuja plicata*
Dietary Aid: *Polypodium glycyrrhiza*
Dried Food: *Argentina egedii, Erythronium revolutum, Fritillaria camschatcensis, Gaultheria shallon, Rubus parviflorus, R. spectabilis*
Fruit: *Amelanchier alnifolia, Arctostaphylos uva-ursi, Cornus canadensis, Crataegus douglasii, Mahonia aquifolium, M. nervosa, Maianthemum dilatatum, Oemleria cerasiformis, Ribes bracteosum, R. laxiflorum, R. lobbii, Rubus parviflorus, R. spectabilis, Shepherdia canadensis, Vaccinium ovalifolium, V. uliginosum, Vicia nigricans*
Preserves: *Viburnum edule*
Special Food: *Argentina egedii, Gaultheria shallon, Malus fusca, Oemleria cerasiformis, Ribes lobbii, Vaccinium parvifolium, Viburnum edule, Zostera marina*
Starvation Food: *Polypodium glycyrrhiza*
Unspecified: *Allium cernuum, Aralia nudicaulis, Camassia leichtlinii, C. quamash, Castilleja miniata, Dryopteris campyloptera, Erythronium revolutum, Glaux maritima, Heracleum maximum, Lupinus littoralis, Polypodium glycyrrhiza, Polystichum munitum, Populus balsamifera, Pteridium aquilinum, Rubus spectabilis, Zostera marina*
Vegetable: *Trifolium wormskioldii*
Winter Use Food: *Ribes bracteosum, Viburnum edule*

Kwakwaka'wakw
Unspecified: *Conioselinum gmelinii*

Laguna
Appetizer: *Rhus trilobata*
Beverage: *Yucca baccata*
Bread & Cake: *Yucca baccata*
Candy: *Asclepias speciosa, Populus deltoides*

Dried Food: *Amaranthus blitoides, A. hybridus, A. retroflexus, Opuntia imbricata, Prunus virginiana, Yucca baccata, Y. glauca*

Fruit: *Atriplex argentea, Ceanothus fendleri, Celtis laevigata, Juniperus monosperma, Opuntia engelmannii, Prunus virginiana, Ribes cereum, Yucca baccata, Y. glauca*

Porridge: *Cleome serrulata, Opuntia engelmannii, Prosopis glandulosa*

Preserves: *Ribes cereum, Yucca baccata*

Sauce & Relish: *Lycium pallidum, Yucca baccata*

Special Food: *Sophora nuttalliana*

Spice: *Agastache pallidiflora, Berlandiera lyrata, Juniperus monosperma, Monarda fistulosa, M. pectinata, Pectis angustifolia, Rhus trilobata*

Staple: *Amaranthus blitoides, Dalea candida, Quercus gambelii*

Starvation Food: *Juniperus monosperma, Opuntia clavata, Phoradendron juniperinum, Solanum triflorum, Yucca baccata*

Unspecified: *Abronia fragrans, Allium cernuum, Astragalus lentiginosus, Cyperus squarrosus, Lathyrus polymorphus, Opuntia imbricata, Plantago major, Prosopis glandulosa, Quercus gambelii, Ranunculus inamoenus, Tradescantia occidentalis, Typha latifolia, Vicia americana*

Vegetable: *Amaranthus blitoides, A. hybridus, A. retroflexus, Cymopterus bulbosus, Lactuca sativa, Portulaca oleracea*

Lakota

Beverage: *Agastache foeniculum, Amelanchier alnifolia, Ceanothus herbaceus, Coreopsis tinctoria, Juniperus virginiana, Mentha arvensis, Opuntia humifusa, Prunus virginiana, Rosa arkansana*

Candy: *Dalea purpurea*

Cooking Agent: *Asclepias speciosa, Humulus lupulus*

Dietary Aid: *Liatris punctata*

Dried Food: *Opuntia humifusa, Pediomelum esculentum, Rosa arkansana, Shepherdia argentea*

Fodder: *Astragalus canadensis, Equisetum hyemale, Populus ×acuminata*

Forage: *Artemisia cana, Clematis ligusticifolia, Oxytropis lambertii, Pascopyrum smithii, Populus deltoides*

Fruit: *Amelanchier alnifolia, Astragalus crassicarpus, Crataegus chrysocarpa, Fragaria vesca, Opuntia humifusa, Prunus americana, P. pumila, P. virginiana, Ribes americanum, R. aureum, R. missouriense, Rosa woodsii, Rubus occidentalis, Shepherdia argentea, Vitis vulpina*

Pie & Pudding: *Prunus virginiana*

Preserves: *Asclepias speciosa, Rosa arkansana*

Soup: *Allium textile, Hedeoma drummondii, Pediomelum esculentum, Quercus macrocarpa, Rosa arkansana*

Special Food: *Monarda fistulosa, Prunus virginiana, Vitis vulpina*

Spice: *Juniperus virginiana*

Staple: *Quercus velutina, Typha latifolia*

Starvation Food: *Amelanchier alnifolia, Helianthus tuberosus, Prunus americana, Ribes americanum, R. aureum, R. missouriense, Rosa arkansana*

Unspecified: *Acorus calamus, Allium drummondii, A. textile, Asclepias speciosa, Carya ovata, Cypripedium sp., Helianthus tuberosus, Juglans nigra, Lomatium orientale, Lygodesmia juncea, Nuphar lutea, Pediomelum esculentum, Polygonum amphibium, Quercus macrocarpa, Sagittaria latifolia, Scirpus tabernaemontani, Yucca glauca*

Vegetable: *Brassica oleracea, Chenopodium album*

Lillooet

Ice Cream: *Shepherdia canadensis*

Luiseño

Beverage: *Monardella lanceolata, Pellaea mucronata, Satureja douglasii*

Candy: *Asclepias eriocarpa, Eschscholzia californica*

Dried Food: *Heteromeles arbutifolia, Sambucus cerulea*

Fruit: *Arctostaphylos parryana, Carpobrotus aequilateralis, Prunus ilicifolia, P. virginiana, Rubus parviflorus, R. vitifolius, Sambucus cerulea, Vitis girdiana*

Porridge: *Prunus ilicifolia, Quercus agrifolia, Q. chrysolepis, Q. dumosa, Q. engelmannii, Q. kelloggii, Q. wislizeni, Rhus trilobata*

Staple: *Avena fatua, Prosopis glandulosa, Prunus ilicifolia, Quercus agrifolia, Q. chrysolepis, Q. dumosa, Q. engelmannii, Q. kelloggii, Q. wislizeni*

Substitution Food: *Quercus chrysolepis, Q. dumosa, Q. engelmannii, Q. wislizeni*

Unspecified: *Artemisia dracunculus, Bloomeria crocea, Boschniakia hookeri, Bromus diandrus, Calandrinia ciliata, Chenopodium californicum, Chlorogalum parviflorum, Cucurbita foetidissima, Dichelostemma pulchellum, Ericameria parishii, Gilia capitata, Helianthus annuus, Layia glandulosa, Lepidium nitidum, Malacothrix californica, Prunus ilicifolia, Salvia apiana, S. carduacea, S. columbariae, S. mellifera, Sarcostemma cynanchoides, Trifolium ciliolatum, T. gracilentum, T. microcephalum, T. obtusiflorum, T. willdenowii, Yucca schidigera, Y. whipplei*

Vegetable: *Apium graveolens, Brassica nigra, Calandrinia ciliata, Chenopodium album, Claytonia perfoliata, Eschscholzia californica, Hoita orbicularis, Lepidium nitidum, Lotus strigosus, Phacelia ramosissima, Portulaca oleracea, Rorippa nasturtium-aquaticum, Sidalcea malviflora, Solanum douglasii, Sonchus asper, Viola pedunculata*

Winter Use Food: *Quercus agrifolia, Q. chrysolepis, Q. dumosa, Q. engelmannii, Q. kelloggii, Q. wislizeni*

Lummi

Beverage: *Rosa nutkana*

Dried Food: *Amelanchier alnifolia, Rosa nutkana*

Fruit: *Oemleria cerasiformis, Ribes laxiflorum, Rubus spectabilis, Vaccinium parvifolium*

Unspecified: *Corylus cornuta, Lilium columbianum, Pteridium aquilinum, Rubus spectabilis*

Winter Use Food: *Sambucus cerulea*

Mahuna

Bread & Cake: *Prosopis glandulosa*

Dessert: *Quercus virginiana*

Dried Food: *Prosopis glandulosa*

Forage: *Kalmia latifolia*

Fruit: *Heteromeles arbutifolia, Prunus ilicifolia, P. serotina, Rhus integrifolia, R. trilobata, Ribes amarum, R. sanguineum, Rubus procumbens, Sambucus racemosa, Vitis vulpina*

Porridge: *Prosopis glandulosa, Salvia columbariae*

Sauce & Relish: *Yucca whipplei*

Unspecified: *Pteridium aquilinum, Quercus virginiana, Yucca whipplei*

Makah

Beverage: *Gaultheria shallon, Ledum groenlandicum, Rosa nutkana*

Bread & Cake: *Gaultheria shallon, Vaccinium ovalifolium, V. ovatum*

Candy: *Picea sitchensis*

Dessert: *Shepherdia canadensis*

Dietary Aid: *Polypodium glycyrrhiza*

Dried Food: *Gaultheria shallon, Sambucus racemosa, Shepherdia canadensis, Vaccinium ovalifolium*

Frozen Food: *Vaccinium parvifolium*

Fruit: *Arctostaphylos uva-ursi, Cornus canadensis, Fragaria chiloensis, Frangula purshiana, Gaultheria shallon, Malus fusca, Ribes bracteosum, R. divaricatum, R. laxiflorum, Rubus discolor, R. laciniatus, R. leucodermis, R. parviflorus, R. spectabilis, R. ursinus, Sambucus racemosa, Vaccinium ovalifolium, V. ovatum, V. oxycoccos, V. parvifolium*

Pie & Pudding: *Gaultheria shallon, Rubus laciniatus, R. leucodermis, R. ursinus, Vaccinium oxycoccos*

Preservative: *Rubus parviflorus*

Preserves: *Fragaria chiloensis, Gaultheria shallon, Mahonia aquifolium, M. nervosa, Malus fusca, Ribes laxiflorum, Rubus laciniatus, R. leucodermis, R. ursinus, Vaccinium oxycoccos*

Special Food: *Rubus spectabilis*

Spice: *Blechnum spicant, Gaultheria shallon, Polystichum munitum*

Unspecified: *Abronia latifolia, Allium cernuum,*

Angelica lucida, Argentina egedii, Camassia quamash, Equisetum telmateia, Heracleum maximum, Oxalis oregana, Phyllospadix scouleri, P. serrulatus, P. torreyi, Picea sitchensis, Polypodium glycyrrhiza, P. scouleri, Polystichum munitum, Pteridium aquilinum, Ranunculus reptans, Rosa nutkana, Rubus parviflorus, R. spectabilis, Tolmiea menziesii, Trifolium wormskioldii, Urtica dioica

Vegetable: *Lathyrus japonicus, Solanum tuberosum*

Winter Use Food: *Rubus spectabilis, Sambucus racemosa, Shepherdia canadensis, Vaccinium ovalifolium, V. oxycoccos, V. parvifolium*

Malecite

Beverage: *Ledum groenlandicum, Pyrola* sp.
Sauce & Relish: *Acer saccharum*
Spice: *Mentha canadensis*
Sweetener: *Acer saccharum*
Unspecified: *Helianthus tuberosus, Phytolacca americana, Taraxacum officinale*

Mandan

Staple: *Helianthus annuus*
Unspecified: *Helianthus annuus*

Maricopa

Beverage: *Carnegia gigantea, Prosopis glandulosa*
Dried Food: *Cucurbita moschata, Ziziphus obtusifolia*
Fruit: *Condalia hookeri, Cucurbita moschata, Lycium fremontii, Opuntia echinocarpa, O. engelmannii, Ziziphus obtusifolia*
Porridge: *Phoradendron californicum*
Staple: *Allenrolfea occidentalis*
Unspecified: *Opuntia acanthocarpa, Prosopis velutina*
Vegetable: *Cucurbita moschata*

Maricopa & Mohave

Fruit: *Ziziphus obtusifolia*

Mendocino Indian

Beverage: *Arctostaphylos manzanita, A. tomentosa*
Bread & Cake: *Boisduvalia densiflora, Quercus douglasii, Q. garryana, Q. kelloggii, Q. lobata, Umbellularia californica*
Cooking Agent: *Madia sativa*
Dried Food: *Juniperus californica, Prunus subcordata, Rubus leucodermis, R. vitifolius, Sambucus cerulea*
Fodder: *Hordeum marinum, Lathyrus jepsonii, Leymus triticoides, Plantago lanceolata, Vicia americana*
Forage: *Aesculus californica, Arbutus menziesii, Arctostaphylos manzanita, Asclepias eriocarpa, Brodiaea coronaria, Carex vicaria, Ceanothus cuneatus, Croton setigerus, Equisetum variegatum, Juncus effusus, Lupinus luteolus, Medicago polymorpha, Nuphar lutea, Orthocarpus lithospermoides, Pedicularis densiflora, Robinia pseudoacacia, Toxicodendron diversilobum*
Fruit: *Aesculus californica, Amelanchier alnifolia, Arctostaphylos manzanita, Fragaria vesca, Heteromeles arbutifolia, Prunus subcordata, Ribes californicum, R. divaricatum, Rubus leucodermis, R. parviflorus, R. vitifolius, Sambucus cerulea, Solanum nigrum, Taxus brevifolia*
Pie & Pudding: *Sambucus cerulea*
Porridge: *Rumex crispus*
Preserves: *Prunus virginiana, Sambucus cerulea, Vitis californica*
Sauce & Relish: *Armoracia rusticana, Umbellularia californica*
Soup: *Quercus douglasii, Q. garryana, Q. kelloggii*
Spice: *Perideridia kelloggii*
Staple: *Amaranthus retroflexus, Avena fatua, Boisduvalia densiflora, Bromus marginatus, Capsella bursa-pastoris, Clarkia purpurea, Hemizonia luzulifolia, Hordeum murinum, Layia platyglossa, Leymus triticoides, Madia gracilis, Perideridia kelloggii, Plagiobothrys fulvus, Ranunculus occidentalis, Thysanocarpus curvipes, Trifolium bifidum, T. dichotomum, Wyethia longicaulis*

lanatus, Corylus americana, Gymnocladus dioicus, Juglans nigra, Nelumbo lutea, Zea mays, Zizania aquatica

Vegetable: *Apios americana, Asclepias syriaca, Heracleum maximum, Lilium philadelphicum, Solanum tuberosum, Taraxacum officinale*

Winter Use Food: *Allium canadense, Apios americana, Asclepias syriaca, Carya ovata, Corylus americana, Cucurbita pepo, Juglans cinerea, Malus ioensis, Nelumbo lutea, Rubus allegheniensis, R. occidentalis, Sagittaria latifolia, Zea mays*

Mewuk

Beverage: *Arctostaphylos viscida*
Bread & Cake: *Quercus kelloggii*
Fruit: *Arctostaphylos viscida*
Porridge: *Quercus kelloggii*
Staple: *Madia elegans*
Unspecified: *Angelica tomentosa, Heracleum maximum, Pinus sabiniana, Quercus kelloggii*

Micmac

Beverage: *Abies balsamea, Acer pensylvanicum, A. saccharum, Acorus calamus, Aralia nudicaulis, Ledum groenlandicum, Mitchella repens, Picea glauca, P. mariana, Pinus strobus, Tsuga canadensis*
Sauce & Relish: *Acer saccharum*
Unspecified: *Helianthus tuberosus*
Vegetable: *Taraxacum officinale*

Midoo

Fruit: *Arctostaphylos patula, A. viscida, Rhus aromatica*

Miwok

Beverage: *Arbutus menziesii, Arctostaphylos manzanita, A. tomentosa, A. viscida, Castilleja applegatei, C. parviflora, Mentha spicata, Monardella odoratissima, Trifolium wormskioldii*
Bread & Cake: *Quercus douglasii, Q. kelloggii, Q. lobata, Q. wislizeni*
Cooking Agent: *Asclepias fascicularis, Darmera peltata, Lotus unifoliolatus*

Dried Food: *Chenopodium album, Heuchera micrantha, Hypericum scouleri, Pinus ponderosa, Trifolium ciliolatum*

Fruit: *Physocarpus capitatus, Ribes nevadense, R. roezlii, Solanum xantii*

Porridge: *Avena barbata, Quercus douglasii, Q. kelloggii, Q. wislizeni*

Sauce & Relish: *Lupinus latifolius*

Soup: *Aesculus californica, Avena barbata, Quercus douglasii, Q. kelloggii, Q. lobata, Q. wislizeni*

Staple: *Hypericum scouleri, Madia elegans, M. gracilis, Quercus lobata*

Substitution Food: *Perideridia bolanderi*

Sweetener: *Pinus lambertiana*

Unspecified: *Balsamorhiza sagittata, Boisduvalia densiflora, B. stricta, Brodiaea coronaria, Bromus diandrus, Calandrinia ciliata, Calochortus luteus, C. venustus, Chlorogalum pomeridianum, Clarkia amoena, C. biloba, C. purpurea, C. unguiculata, Claytonia perfoliata, Corylus cornuta, Dichelostemma pulchellum, Hemizonia fitchii, Juniperus occidentalis, Lathyrus vestitus, Lupinus densiflorus, Madia sativa, Navarretia sp., Orthocarpus attenuatus, Perideridia bolanderi, P. gairdneri, P. kelloggii, Pinus lambertiana, P. sabiniana, Ranunculus californicus, Trifolium ciliolatum, T. willdenowii, T. wormskioldii, Triteleia hyacinthina, T. ixioides, Veratrum californicum*

Vegetable: *Aquilegia formosa, Asclepias fascicularis, Chenopodium album, Clarkia purpurea, Conyza canadensis, Delphinium hesperium, Eriogonum nudum, Heuchera micrantha, Lathyrus vestitus, Mimulus guttatus, M. moschatus, Osmorhiza berteroi, Rumex acetosella, R. conglomeratus*

Winter Use Food: *Aesculus californica, Arbutus menziesii, Arctostaphylos manzanita, A. tomentosa, A. viscida, Chlorogalum pomeridianum, Lupinus latifolius, Quercus douglasii, Q. kelloggii, Q. lobata, Q. wislizeni, Trifolium willdenowii*

Modesse

Fruit: *Amelanchier alnifolia, Prunus subcordata, P. virginiana*

Staple: *Quercus kelloggii*
Starvation Food: *Aesculus californica*

Modoc
Unspecified: *Lomatium canbyi*

Mohave
Beverage: *Lycium andersonii, Prosopis pubescens, Salix gooddingii, Salvia columbariae*
Bread & Cake: *Olneya tesota, Prosopis glandulosa*
Dried Food: *Lycium andersonii, Olneya tesota, Prosopis glandulosa, Vigna unguiculata, Ziziphus obtusifolia*
Fruit: *Opuntia echinocarpa, O. engelmannii, Physalis hederifolia, P. pubescens, Yucca schidigera*
Porridge: *Quercus turbinella*
Staple: *Agastache pallidiflora, Agave americana, A. parryi, Allenrolfea occidentalis, Helianthus annuus, Salvia columbariae*
Starvation Food: *Baccharis salicifolia, Chloracantha spinosa, Parkinsonia florida, P. microphylla, Sisymbrium irio, Sonchus asper, Thelypodium integrifolium*
Unspecified: *Amaranthus caudatus, A. palmeri, Ammannia coccinea, Camissonia brevipes, Cyperus odoratus, Vigna unguiculata*
Vegetable: *Amaranthus caudatus, A. palmeri, Chenopodium fremontii, C. murale, Prosopis glandulosa, P. pubescens, Rumex crispus*
Winter Use Food: *Amaranthus caudatus, A. palmeri, Helianthus annuus*

Mohegan
Cooking Agent: *Apios americana*
Sweetener: *Acer saccharum*
Unspecified: *Apios americana, Asclepias syriaca, Caltha palustris, Chenopodium album, Phytolacca americana, Taraxacum officinale*
Vegetable: *Amaranthus retroflexus, Brassica nigra, Plantago major, Rumex crispus, Urtica dioica*

Montagnais
Beverage: *Aralia nudicaulis, Rhexia virginica*
Dietary Aid: *Betula papyrifera*

Forage: *Aralia nudicaulis, Sorbus americana, Streptopus amplexifolius*
Fruit: *Sorbus americana*
Spice: *Thalictrum pubescens*

Montana Indian
Beverage: *Amelanchier alnifolia, Mahonia repens, Prunus virginiana, Sambucus cerulea*
Bread & Cake: *Amelanchier alnifolia, Camassia quamash, Helianthus annuus, Lomatium cous, Pediomelum esculentum, Prunus virginiana, Tsuga heterophylla, Vaccinium membranaceum*
Cooking Agent: *Nuphar lutea, Pediomelum esculentum*
Dried Food: *Arctostaphylos uva-ursi, Lomatium cous, Opuntia polyacantha, Pediomelum esculentum, Shepherdia argentea, S. canadensis, Thuja plicata, Vaccinium membranaceum*
Fodder: *Claytonia lanceolata, C. multicaulis, Opuntia polyacantha, Pascopyrum smithii, Populus angustifolia, P. balsamifera, P. deltoides, P. tremuloides*
Forage: *Amelanchier alnifolia, Bouteloua gracilis, Claytonia lanceolata, Erythronium grandiflorum, Fritillaria pudica, Pascopyrum smithii*
Fruit: *Amelanchier alnifolia, Arctostaphylos uva-ursi, Crataegus columbiana, Elaeagnus commutata, Mahonia repens, Moneses uniflora, Opuntia polyacantha, Parthenocissus quinquefolia, Prunus virginiana, Rhus trilobata, Ribes americanum, R. aureum, R. cereum, R. hudsonianum, R. lacustre, R. oxyacanthoides, R. viscosissimum, Rosa acicularis, R. nutkana, R. woodsii, Rubus idaeus, R. leucodermis, Sambucus cerulea, Shepherdia argentea, S. canadensis, Vaccinium membranaceum*
Ice Cream: *Shepherdia canadensis*
Pie & Pudding: *Amelanchier alnifolia, Prunus virginiana, Sambucus cerulea, Vaccinium membranaceum*
Porridge: *Helianthus annuus, Lomatium cous, Nuphar lutea, Pediomelum esculentum*
Preserves: *Amelanchier alnifolia, Mahonia repens, Opuntia polyacantha, Prunus*

virginiana, Sambucus cerulea, Shepherdia argentea, Vaccinium membranaceum

Sauce & Relish: *Acer negundo, Claytonia cordifolia, C. parviflora, C. perfoliata, Scirpus acutus, Shepherdia argentea, Sium suave*

Snack Food: *Nuphar lutea*

Soup: *Amelanchier alnifolia, Arctostaphylos uva-ursi, Lomatium cous, Nuphar lutea, Prunus virginiana*

Staple: *Balsamorhiza sagittata, Camassia quamash, Chenopodium album, Lomatium ambiguum, L. cous, L. simplex, L. triternatum, Polygonum douglasii, Prunus virginiana, Scirpus acutus*

Starvation Food: *Alectoria fremontii, Arctostaphylos uva-ursi, Pinus contorta*

Substitution Food: *Pseudotsuga menziesii*

Sweetener: *Camassia quamash*

Unspecified: *Amaranthus blitoides, Astragalus crassicarpus, Balsamorhiza sagittata, Beckmannia syzigachne, Camassia scilloides, Claytonia lanceolata, C. multicaulis, Descurainia incana, Erythronium grandiflorum, Fritillaria pudica, Glycyrrhiza lepidota, Lewisia rediviva, Leymus condensatus, Lomatium ambiguum, L. cous, L. dissectum, L. simplex, L. triternatum, Matricaria discoidea, Mentzelia albicaulis, Microseris nutans, Nuphar lutea, Opuntia polyacantha, Oryzopsis hymenoides, Pediomelum esculentum, Perideridia gairdneri, Phragmites australis, Pinus albicaulis, P. flexilis, P. ponderosa, Populus angustifolia, P. balsamifera, P. deltoides, P. tremuloides, Pteridium aquilinum, Rubus parviflorus, Rumex aquaticus, R. crispus, R. salicifolius, Sagittaria cuneata, Scirpus acutus, S. robustus, Thuja plicata, Triglochin maritimum, Typha latifolia, Valeriana edulis, Vicia americana, Wyethia amplexicaulis, W. helianthoides*

Vegetable: *Amaranthus blitoides, Argentina anserina, Balsamorhiza sagittata, Chenopodium album, Cirsium undulatum, Heracleum maximum, Lomatium simplex, L. triternatum, Oxyria digyna, Pediomelum esculentum, Perideridia gairdneri, Rumex aquaticus, R. crispus, R. paucifolius, R. sal-*

icifolius, Sarcobatus vermiculatus, Urtica dioica

Winter Use Food: *Amelanchier alnifolia, Camassia scilloides, Crataegus columbiana, Lonicera involucrata, Pediomelum esculentum, Prunus virginiana, Shepherdia argentea, Vaccinium membranaceum*

Nanaimo

Dessert: *Shepherdia canadensis*

Navajo

Baby Food: *Calochortus nuttallii*

Beverage: *Anthemis sp., Arctostaphylos pringlei, Dalea purpurea, Ephedra torreyana, E. viridis, Lycium pallidum, Opuntia phaeacantha, Phoradendron juniperinum, Rhus trilobata, Salix exigua, Tragopogon porrifolius, Zea mays*

Bread & Cake: *Amaranthus retroflexus, Artemisia carruthii, Chenopodium fremontii, Cleome serrulata, Cupressus sp., Helianthus annuus, Opuntia phaeacantha, Oryzopsis hymenoides, Pinus edulis, Rhus trilobata, Sporobolus contractus, S. cryptandrus, Yucca baccata, Zea mays*

Candy: *Chloracantha spinosa, Dugaldia hoopesii, Hymenoxys richardsonii, Lactuca tatarica, Opuntia phaeacantha, Pinus edulis, Populus angustifolia, P. deltoides, Quercus pungens*

Cooking Agent: *Opuntia phaeacantha, Solanum elaeagnifolium*

Dessert: *Yucca baccata*

Dried Food: *Allium macropetalum, Amelanchier utahensis, Chenopodium album, Citrullus lanatus, Cleome serrulata, Cucumis melo, Cucurbita moschata, Cymopterus acaulis, Datura wrightii, Daucus pusillus, Lycium pallidum, Opuntia phaeacantha, Rhus trilobata, Shepherdia argentea, Yucca baccata*

Fodder: *Artemisia filifolia, Atriplex argentea, A. canescens, Avena sativa, Juniperus monosperma, Oryzopsis hymenoides, Salix exigua*

Forage: *Amaranthus blitoides, Atriplex argentea, A. canescens, Cercocarpus montanus,*

Chrysothamnus nauseosus, Dimorphocarpa wislizeni, Ipomopsis aggregata, Kochia scoparia, Krascheninnikovia lanata, Oryzopsis hymenoides, Portulaca oleracea, Purshia stansburiana, P. tridentata, Salix exigua, Sarcobatus vermiculatus, Sisymbrium officinale, Sophora nuttalliana, Sporobolus cryptandrus

Fruit: *Amelanchier alnifolia, A. utahensis, Arctostaphylos pringlei, Celtis laevigata, Cupressus* sp.*, Datura wrightii, Juniperus monosperma, Lycium pallidum, Opuntia phaeacantha, Phoradendron juniperinum, Physalis lanceolata, P. pubescens, P. subulata, Rhus trilobata, Ribes cereum, R. inerme, Rosa woodsii, Rubus arizonensis, Sarcobatus vermiculatus, Shepherdia argentea, Yucca baccata, Y. glauca*

Pie & Pudding: *Atriplex canescens*

Porridge: *Amaranthus blitoides, A. retroflexus, Arctostaphylos pringlei, Artemisia carruthii, Cupressus* sp.*, Descurainia pinnata, Helianthus annuus, Oryzopsis hymenoides, Pinus edulis, Prunus virginiana, Rhus trilobata, Rumex hymenosepalus, Sisymbrium altissimum, S. officinale, Suaeda moquinii, Yucca baccata, Zea mays*

Preserves: *Arctostaphylos pringlei, Cucurbita moschata, Opuntia phaeacantha, Physalis pubescens, Pinus edulis, Yucca baccata*

Sauce & Relish: *Allium cernuum, Cleome multicaulis, Cucumis melo, Cucurbita moschata, Yucca baccata*

Soup: *Allium cernuum, Cleome multicaulis, C. serrulata, Cymopterus acaulis, Lycium pallidum, Phaseolus vulgaris, Sisymbrium officinale*

Special Food: *Castilleja lineata, Cleome multicaulis, Dalea candida, Datura wrightii, Fragaria vesca, Lycium pallidum, Pinus edulis, Yucca baccata, Zea mays*

Spice: *Allium cernuum, Cleome serrulata, Cymopterus acaulis, C. purpureus*

Staple: *Amaranthus blitoides, A. palmeri, Chenopodium album, Opuntia phaeacantha, Oryzopsis hymenoides, Physalis pubescens, Pinus edulis, Rhus trilobata, Zea mays*

Starvation Food: *Calochortus nuttallii, Juniperus monosperma, Sphaeralcea coccinea*

Substitution Food: *Cymopterus montanus, Thelesperma longipes, T. megapotamicum*

Sweetener: *Amaranthus palmeri*

Unspecified: *Allium cepa, A. cernuum, A. macropetalum, Amaranthus retroflexus, Artemisia carruthii, Calochortus aureus, C. luteus, C. nuttallii, Capsicum annuum, Cercis canadensis, Cleome serrulata, Cuscuta* sp.*, Cymopterus montanus, Daucus pusillus, Eriogonum alatum, E. rotundifolium, Humulus lupulus, Juglans major, Lomatium orientale, Mentzelia multiflora, Neomammillaria* sp.*, Opuntia phaeacantha, Oryzopsis hymenoides, Panicum capillare, Pinus edulis, Populus angustifolia, P. deltoides, Portulaca oleracea, Quercus gambelii, Rumex hymenosepalus, Salsola australis, Sphaeralcea angustifolia, Verbesina encelioides, Zea mays*

Vegetable: *Allium cernuum, A. macropetalum, Amaranthus blitoides, A. retroflexus, Chenopodium album, Cleome multicaulis, C. serrulata, Cucurbita pepo, Cymopterus acaulis, Phaseolus vulgaris, Rumex hymenosepalus, Salsola australis, Solanum jamesii, Zea mays*

Winter Use Food: *Allium cepa, A. cernuum, A. macropetalum, Amaranthus retroflexus, Amelanchier utahensis, Cleome serrulata, Daucus pusillus, Lycium pallidum, Yucca baccata, Y. glauca*

Navajo, Kayenta

Beverage: *Sphaeralcea coccinea*

Candy: *Stephanomeria pauciflora*

Fruit: *Arctostaphylos patula, Mimulus eastwoodiae, Mirabilis linearis*

Porridge: *Eriogonum cernuum, Heliotropium convolvulaceum, Oxytropis lambertii, Plantago patagonica, Rumex maritimus*

Spice: *Encelia frutescens, Mentha arvensis*

Substitution Food: *Atriplex powellii*

Unspecified: *Artemisia campestris, Cercis canadensis, Chrysothamnus nauseosus, Comandra umbellata, Conioselinum scopulorum, Eriogonum racemosum, Gaura*

parviflora, Mirabilis linearis, Solidago
canadensis, Vulpia octoflora, Zigadenus
paniculatus
Vegetable: Antennaria parvifolia, Cymopterus
newberryi, Lygodesmia grandiflora, Mirabilis oxybaphoides, Phacelia heterophylla,
Phlox stansburyi, Streptanthus cordatus,
Zigadenus paniculatus

Navajo, Ramah

Beverage: Mirabilis multiflora, M. oxybaphoides, Thelesperma megapotamicum
Bread & Cake: Amaranthus retroflexus, Chenopodium album, C. incanum, Descurainia
pinnata, D. sophia, Prunus virginiana,
Yucca baccata
Candy: Lygodesmia juncea, Pinus edulis, Sene-
cio multicapitatus, Stephanomeria
pauciflora
Dried Food: Allium cernuum, Cleome serrula-
ta, Cymopterus bulbosus, Lycium pallidum,
L. torreyi, Machaeranthera gracilis, Opuntia
macrorhiza, Rhus trilobata
Fodder: Aristida purpurea, Atriplex canescens,
A. rosea, Avena sativa, Beckmannia syzigachne, Bromus anomalus, B. tectorum,
Chamaebatiaria millefolium, Cleome serrulata, Corydalis aurea, Cryptantha cinerea,
C. fendleri, Descurainia pinnata, D. sophia,
Echinochloa crus-pavonis, Elymus elymoi-
des, E. trachycaulus, Erodium cicutarium,
Helianthus annuus, Heliomeris longifolia,
H. multiflora, Heterotheca villosa, Lappula
occidentalis, Lepidium montanum, Marrubium vulgare, Medicago sativa, Monolepis
nuttalliana, Muhlenbergia filiformis, M.
mexicana, Oryzopsis hymenoides, Panicum
capillare, P. obtusum, Phaseolus vulgaris,
Poa fendleriana, Rorippa teres, Salsola australis, Sarcobatus vermiculatus, Stipa robusta, Tridens muticus, Triticum aestivum,
Zea mays
Forage: Astragalus mollissimus, Bouteloua
gracilis, B. simplex, Carex microptera,
Hilaria jamesii, Panicum obtusum
Fruit: Amelanchier utahensis, Echinocereus
coccineus, Juniperus deppeana, Lycium pallidum, L. torreyi, Opuntia macrorhiza, Par-

thenocissus vitacea, Physalis pubescens,
Prunus persica, P. virginiana, Rhus trilobata,
Ribes cereum, R. pinetorum, Rosa woodsii,
Yucca glauca
Pie & Pudding: Solanum tuberosum
Porridge: Atriplex rosea, Eriogonum alatum,
Oryzopsis hymenoides, Sporobolus cryptan-
drus, S. wrightii
Preserves: Pinus edulis, Yucca baccata
Special Food: Amaranthus retroflexus, Cheno-
podium album, C. incanum, Zea mays
Spice: Atriplex canescens, Capsicum annuum,
Cucurbita maxima, C. pepo, Portulaca
oleracea
Staple: Amaranthus albus, A. cruentus, Ment-
zelia multiflora, Quercus gambelii
Starvation Food: Pinus edulis, Populus tremu-
loides, Senecio multicapitatus
Unspecified: Allium cepa, A. cernuum, A.
drummondii, Calochortus aureus, C. gunnisonii, Ceanothus fendleri, Chenopodium
leptophyllum, C. watsonii, Citrullus lanatus,
Cleome serrulata, Cucumis melo, Cucurbita
maxima, C. pepo, Cymopterus bulbosus,
Eriogonum alatum, Fragaria vesca, Helianthus annuus, Juniperus monosperma,
Mammillaria wrightii, Orobanche fascicu-
lata, Phaseolus lunatus, Pinus ponderosa,
Pseudocymopterus montanus, Quercus grisea, Q. ×pauciloba, Rhus trilobata, Triticum
aestivum, Typha latifolia, Yucca glauca
Vegetable: Amaranthus retroflexus, Pisum sati-
vum, Portulaca oleracea, Solanum jamesii,
Zea mays
Winter Use Food: Amaranthus retroflexus,
Chenopodium album, C. incanum, Citrullus
lanatus, Cucurbita maxima, C. pepo,
Cymopterus bulbosus, Juniperus deppeana,
Opuntia macrorhiza, Phaseolus vulgaris,
Pinus edulis, Prunus virginiana, Solanum
jamesii, S. tuberosum, Zea mays

Neeshenam

Bread & Cake: Blennosperma nanum, Bromus
carinatus, Madia elegans, Quercus gambelii, Ranunculus californicus
Fruit: Heteromeles arbutifolia
Porridge: Blennosperma nanum, Bromus cari-

Chamaedaphne calyculata, Gaultheria procumbens, Juniperus horizontalis, Ledum groenlandicum, Mentha canadensis, Nepeta cataria, Prunus serotina, Rhus glabra, R. hirta, Thuja occidentalis, Tsuga canadensis

Bread & Cake: *Zizania aquatica*

Breakfast Food: *Zizania aquatica*

Cooking Agent: *Humulus lupulus*

Dietary Aid: *Asarum canadense*

Dried Food: *Allium tricoccum, Amelanchier laevis, Cucurbita maxima, C. pepo, Prunus americana, P. pensylvanica, P. pumila, P. serotina, P. virginiana, Ribes americanum, R. hudsonianum, R. missouriense, R. oxyacanthoides, R. rubrum, R. triste, Rubus idaeus, Typha latifolia, Vaccinium angustifolium, V. myrtilloides, Zea mays*

Fodder: *Equisetum arvense, Hydrophyllum virginianum, Lathyrus ochroleucus, L. palustris, Maianthemum racemosum*

Forage: *Erigeron philadelphicus, Sagittaria cuneata*

Fruit: *Amelanchier canadensis, Crataegus chrysocarpa, Empetrum nigrum, Fragaria virginiana, Gaultheria procumbens, Malus coronaria, Prunus americana, P. nigra, P. pensylvanica, P. pumila, P. serotina, P. virginiana, Ribes americanum, R. cynosbati, R. hudsonianum, R. missouriense, R. oxyacanthoides, R. rubrum, R. triste, Rubus canadensis, R. idaeus, R. occidentalis, Sorbus americana, Vaccinium angustifolium, V. macrocarpon, V. myrtilloides, V. oxycoccos, Viburnum lentago, V. opulus*

Preservative: *Betula papyrifera, Comptonia peregrina*

Preserves: *Fragaria virginiana, Prunus nigra, Ribes americanum, R. cynosbati, R. oxyacanthoides, R. triste, Rubus allegheniensis, R. idaeus, Viburnum lentago, Vitis vulpina*

Sauce & Relish: *Cardamine diphylla*

Soup: *Aster macrophyllus, Celastrus scandens, Prunus americana, P. pensylvanica, P. serotina, P. virginiana, Pteridium aquilinum, Quercus alba, Solanum tuberosum*

Sour: *Acer saccharum*

Special Food: *Parthenocissus quinquefolia, Zizania aquatica*

Spice: *Asarum canadense*

Staple: *Quercus rubra, Sagittaria cuneata, Typha latifolia, Zizania palustris*

Sweetener: *Acer nigrum, A. saccharinum, A. saccharum*

Unspecified: *Amphicarpaea bracteata, Asclepias syriaca, Aster macrophyllus, Caltha palustris, Carya ovata, Corylus americana, C. cornuta, Fagus grandifolia, Fraxinus pennsylvanica, Gaylussacia baccata, Juglans cinerea, Nelumbo lutea, Nymphaea odorata, Parthenocissus quinquefolia, Pinus strobus, Populus deltoides, P. grandidentata, Pteridium aquilinum, Quercus macrocarpa, Q. velutina, Rosa acicularis, R. virginiana, Sambucus racemosa, Sticta glomulifera, Typha latifolia*

Vegetable: *Allium cernuum, Amphicarpaea bracteata, Asclepias syriaca, Cardamine maxima, Chenopodium album, Cucumis sativus, Heracleum maximum, Lagenaria siceraria, Lathyrus ochroleucus, L. palustris, Maianthemum racemosum, Phaseolus lunatus, P. vulgaris, Solanum tuberosum, Taraxacum officinale, Zea mays*

Winter Use Food: *Asclepias syriaca, Fragaria virginiana, Rhus hirta, Rubus canadensis, R. occidentalis, Vaccinium angustifolium, V. myrtilloides*

Okanagan-Colville

Appetizer: *Trillium petiolatum*

Beverage: *Juniperus scopulorum, Ledum groenlandicum, Mentha arvensis, Monardella odoratissima, Picea engelmannii, P. glauca, Rhododendron albiflorum, Rhus glabra*

Bread & Cake: *Crataegus columbiana, C. douglasii, Lilium columbianum, Prunus virginiana, Ribes aureum, R. oxyacanthoides*

Candy: *Agoseris glauca, Larix occidentalis, Pinus ponderosa*

Dessert: *Rubus leucodermis*

Dried Food: *Allium cernuum, A. douglasii, A. geyeri, Amelanchier alnifolia, Balsamorhiza sagittata, Camassia quamash, Erythronium grandiflorum, Fritillaria pudica, Lewisia*

rediviva, *Lomatium ambiguum, L. canbyi,
L. cous, L. triternatum, Perideridia gairdneri, Ribes aureum, Rubus idaeus, R. leucodermis, Vaccinium cespitosum, V.
membranaceum*
Fodder: *Equisetum arvense, E. hyemale, E. laevigatum, Juncus effusus, Koeleria macrantha, Leymus cinereus, Sparganium
eurycarpum*
Forage: *Ceanothus sanguineus, C. velutinus,
Cornus sericea, Crataegus douglasii, Epilobium angustifolium, Larix occidentalis,
Lonicera ciliosa, L. involucrata, Lupinus
sericeus, L. sulphureus, L. wyethii, Lysichiton americanus, Nepeta cataria, Paxistima
myrsinites, Pinus contorta, Pseudoroegneria spicata, Purshia tridentata, Ribes cereum, R. oxyacanthoides, Rosa acicularis, R.
gymnocarpa, R. nutkana, R. woodsii, Symphoricarpos albus, Tragopogon pratensis,
Vaccinium cespitosum*
Frozen Food: *Amelanchier alnifolia, Pinus
ponderosa, Rubus idaeus, Sambucus
cerulea*
Fruit: *Amelanchier alnifolia, Arctostaphylos
uva-ursi, Cornus sericea, Crataegus columbiana, Elaeagnus commutata, Fragaria vesca, F. virginiana, Lonicera utahensis, Mahonia aquifolium, Prunus virginiana, Ribes
aureum, R. cereum, R. oxyacanthoides, Rubus idaeus, R. leucodermis, R. parviflorus,
Sambucus cerulea, Typha latifolia, Vaccinium cespitosum, V. membranaceum, V. scoparium, Viburnum edule*
Ice Cream: *Shepherdia canadensis*
Pie & Pudding: *Amelanchier alnifolia, Perideridia gairdneri*
Sauce & Relish: *Camassia quamash, Lomatium
dissectum*
Soup: *Opuntia fragilis, O. polyacantha*
Spice: *Lilium columbianum, Lomatium ambiguum, L. triternatum, Medicago sativa,
Rosa acicularis, R. gymnocarpa, R. nutka-
na, R. woodsii*
Starvation Food: *Rorippa
nasturtium-aquaticum*
Substitution Food: *Lomatium ambiguum,
L. triternatum*

Sweetener: *Amelanchier alnifolia, Comandra
umbellata*
Unspecified: *Astragalus miser, Balsamorhiza
hookeri, B. sagittata, Calochortus macrocarpus, Camassia quamash, Citrullus lanatus, Claytonia lanceolata, Cucumis melo,
Cucurbita pepo, Equisetum laevigatum,
Erythronium grandiflorum, Fritillaria pudica, Lewisia rediviva, Lilium columbianum,
Lomatium canbyi, L. cous, L. farinosum,
L. geyeri, L. macrocarpum, Maianthemum
racemosum, Matricaria discoidea, Opuntia
fragilis, O. polyacantha, Perideridia gairdneri, Physocarpus malvaceus, Pinus albicaulis, P. contorta, P. ponderosa, Pisum
sativum, Pseudotsuga menziesii, Rosa acicularis, R. gymnocarpa, R. nutkana, R.
woodsii, Sium suave, Triteleia grandiflora,
Triticum aestivum, Typha latifolia*
Vegetable: *Allium cernuum, A. douglasii, A.
geyeri, Brassica oleracea, B. rapa, Heracleum maximum, Rorippa nasturtium-aquaticum, Rumex acetosella, Taraxacum officinale, Urtica dioica*
Winter Use Food: *Amelanchier alnifolia, Claytonia lanceolata, Fragaria vesca, F. virginiana, Perideridia gairdneri, Pinus albicaulis, P. ponderosa, Prunus virginiana,
Pseudotsuga menziesii, Ribes oxyacanthoides, Rubus idaeus, Vaccinium cespitosum,
V. membranaceum, Valeriana edulis*

Okanagon
Beverage: *Shepherdia canadensis*
Bread & Cake: *Amelanchier alnifolia, Gaulthe-
ria shallon*
Dried Food: *Lomatium dissectum*
Forage: *Hydrophyllum fendleri*
Fruit: *Arctostaphylos uva-ursi, Crataegus co-
lumbiana, C. douglasii, Gaultheria shallon,
Lonicera involucrata, Maianthemum race-
mosum, M. stellatum, Ribes cereum, Rubus
spectabilis, Sambucus racemosa, Shepher-
dia canadensis, Sorbus sitchensis, Strepto-
pus amplexifolius, Viburnum opulus*
Soup: *Arctostaphylos uva-ursi*
Staple: *Allium cernuum, Amelanchier alnifolia, Arctostaphylos uva-ursi, Argentina*

anserina, Balsamorhiza sagittata, Calochortus macrocarpus, Camassia scilloides, Cirsium undulatum, Claytonia lanceolata, Comandra umbellata, Cornus sericea, Crataegus rivularis, Elaeagnus commutata, Erythronium grandiflorum, Ferula dissoluta, Fragaria vesca, Fritillaria lanceolata, F. pudica, Heracleum maximum, Hydrophyllum occidentale, Lewisia rediviva, Lilium columbianum, Lomatium macrocarpum, Lycopus uniflorus, Peucedanum sp., Pinus contorta, P. ponderosa, Prunus virginiana, Ribes cereum, R. lacustre, Rubus leucodermis, Shepherdia canadensis, Sium suave, Vaccinium membranaceum, V. myrtillus

Unspecified: Allium cernuum, Argentina anserina, Balsamorhiza sagittata, Calochortus macrocarpus, Camassia quamash, C. scilloides, Cirsium edule, C. hookerianum, Claytonia lanceolata, Corylus cornuta, Epilobium angustifolium, Erythronium grandiflorum, Fritillaria lanceolata, F. pudica, Heracleum maximum, Hydrophyllum fendleri, Lewisia rediviva, Lilium columbianum, Lithospermum incisum, Lomatium macrocarpum, Opuntia polyacantha, Osmorhiza berteroi, Pinus contorta, P. ponderosa, Pteridium aquilinum, Rubus leucodermis, R. spectabilis, R. ursinus, Tragopogon porrifolius, Triteleia grandiflora

Vegetable: Lomatium nudicaule

Winter Use Food: Lewisia columbiana, L. rediviva

Omaha

Beverage: Agastache foeniculum, Ceanothus americanus, Crataegus chrysocarpa, C. mollis, Mentha canadensis, Rubus idaeus, R. occidentalis, Sambucus canadensis, Verbena hastata, V. stricta

Bread & Cake: Prunus virginiana

Candy: Populus deltoides, Silphium laciniatum

Cooking Agent: Lithospermum canescens

Dried Food: Fragaria virginiana, Morus rubra, Pediomelum esculentum, Physalis heterophylla, Prunus americana, P. pumila, P. virginiana, Ribes missouriense, Rubus idaeus,

R. occidentalis, Shepherdia argentea, Vitis cinerea, V. riparia, V. vulpina

Fodder: Osmorhiza longistylis, Oxalis stricta, O. violacea

Fruit: Amelanchier alnifolia, Celtis occidentalis, Crataegus chrysocarpa, C. mollis, Fragaria vesca, F. virginiana, Helianthus tuberosus, Malus ioensis, Morus rubra, Prunus americana, P. pumila, P. virginiana, Ribes missouriense, Rubus idaeus, R. occidentalis, Sambucus canadensis, Shepherdia argentea, Smilax herbacea, Viburnum lentago, Vitis cinerea, V. riparia, V. vulpina

Preservative: Ulmus rubra

Sauce & Relish: Allium canadense, Physalis heterophylla, Prunus americana, P. pumila

Snack Food: Ulmus rubra

Soup: Carya ovata, Chenopodium album, Corylus americana, Juglans nigra, Nelumbo lutea, Pediomelum esculentum

Spice: Allium canadense, Ulmus rubra

Staple: Zea mays, Zizania aquatica

Starvation Food: Crataegus chrysocarpa, C. mollis, Rosa arkansana

Sweetener: Acer negundo, A. saccharinum, Agastache foeniculum, Carya ovata, Zea mays

Unspecified: Allium canadense, Amphicarpaea bracteata, Apios americana, Carya ovata, Corylus americana, Helianthus tuberosus, Juglans nigra, Lathyrus brachycalyx, Linum lewisii, Nelumbo lutea, Oxalis stricta, O. violacea, Pediomelum esculentum, Quercus macrocarpa, Q. rubra, Rumex crispus, Sagittaria latifolia, Ulmus rubra

Vegetable: Apios americana, Asclepias syriaca, Nelumbo lutea, Sagittaria latifolia

Winter Use Food: Amphicarpaea bracteata, Zea mays

Oregon Indian

Beverage: Shepherdia canadensis

Fruit: Crataegus columbiana

Soup: Lomatium cous

Oregon Indian, Warm Springs

Unspecified: Lewisia rediviva

Oweekeno

Beverage: *Camellia sinensis, Ledum groenlandicum, Rubus parviflorus*

Bread & Cake: *Porphyra abbottae*

Candy: *Picea sitchensis*

Dried Food: *Egregia menziesii, Macrocystis integrifolia, Porphyra abbottae, Sambucus racemosa, Tsuga heterophylla*

Forage: *Cornus unalaschkensis, Lysichiton americanus, Maianthemum dilatatum, Streptopus amplexifolius*

Fruit: *Amelanchier alnifolia, Arctostaphylos uva-ursi, Cornus unalaschkensis, Fragaria chiloensis, F. vesca, F. virginiana, Gaultheria shallon, Lonicera involucrata, Malus fusca, M. sylvestris, Ribes bracteosum, R. divaricatum, R. laxiflorum, Rubus idaeus, R. leucodermis, R. parviflorus, R. spectabilis, Shepherdia canadensis, Vaccinium cespitosum, V. ovalifolium, V. oxycoccos, V. vitis-idaea*

Preserves: *Fragaria chiloensis, F. vesca, F. virginiana, Gaultheria shallon, Rubus parviflorus, R. spectabilis, Sambucus racemosa, Viburnum edule*

Special Food: *Vaccinium cespitosum, V. membranaceum*

Unspecified: *Allium cepa, A. cernuum, Argentina egedii, Brassica rapa, Conioselinum gmelinii, Daucus carota, Egregia menziesii, Epilobium angustifolium, Fritillaria camschatcensis, Heracleum maximum, Macrocystis integrifolia, Nereocystis luetkeana, Oplopanax horridus, Oryza sativa, Populus balsamifera, Porphyra abbottae, Rubus parviflorus, R. spectabilis, Rumex aquaticus, Trifolium wormskioldii, Tsuga heterophylla, Urtica dioica, Zostera marina*

Vegetable: *Solanum tuberosum*

Winter Use Food: *Egregia menziesii, Macrocystis integrifolia, Nereocystis luetkeana, Rubus spectabilis, Shepherdia canadensis, Vaccinium ovalifolium, V. parvifolium, V. uliginosum*

Paiute

Beverage: *Balsamorhiza sagittata, Castanopsis chrysophylla, Descurainia sophia, Ephedra viridis, Mentha arvensis, M. canadensis, Prunus virginiana*

Bread & Cake: *Lomatium canbyi*

Candy: *Amelanchier alnifolia, Asclepias speciosa, Balsamorhiza sagittata, Chrysothamnus nauseosus, C. viscidiflorus, Juncus balticus, Larix occidentalis, Pinus ponderosa*

Dried Food: *Amelanchier alnifolia, A. utahensis, Balsamorhiza ×terebinthacea, Camassia quamash, Crataegus douglasii, Dichelostemma pulchellum, Frangula californica, Lewisia rediviva, Lomatium bicolor, L. canbyi, L. macrocarpum, Perideridia gairdneri, P. oregana, Pinus monophylla, P. ponderosa, Prunus virginiana, Ribes aureum, Sambucus cerulea, Shepherdia argentea, Vaccinium membranaceum, V. ovalifolium, V. parvifolium*

Fodder: *Juncus ensifolius*

Forage: *Arctostaphylos patula, Ceanothus velutinus, Ribes bracteosum*

Fruit: *Amelanchier alnifolia, A. utahensis, Arctostaphylos nevadensis, Crataegus douglasii, Frangula californica, Juniperus occidentalis, Prunus virginiana, Ribes aureum, R. cereum, R. sanguineum, Rubus parviflorus, R. spectabilis, Sambucus cerulea, Shepherdia argentea, Vaccinium cespitosum, V. membranaceum, V. ovalifolium, V. parvifolium*

Ice Cream: *Descurainia sophia*

Pie & Pudding: *Balsamorhiza sagittata, Camassia quamash, Shepherdia argentea*

Porridge: *Balsamorhiza sagittata, Cyperus rotundus, Helianthus annuus, Oryzopsis hymenoides, Pinus monophylla, Quercus dunnii, Q. kelloggii, Salvia columbariae, Stipa speciosa*

Preserves: *Vaccinium membranaceum, V. ovalifolium*

Sauce & Relish: *Allium acuminatum, A. bisceptrum, A. platycaule, A. pleianthum, Mentzelia albicaulis, M. laevicaulis, Oryzopsis hymenoides, Ribes lacustre*

Soup: *Pinus monophylla*

Spice: *Pseudotsuga menziesii*

Staple: *Agastache pallidiflora, Agave americana, A. parryi, Artemisia tridentata,*

Chenopodium album, C. nevadense, Descurainia sophia, Dichelostemma pulchellum, Helianthus annuus, Mentzelia albicaulis, Oryzopsis hymenoides, Pinus monophylla, Piptatherum miliaceum, Suaeda calceoliformis, Wyethia mollis

Starvation Food: *Artemisia tridentata, Lomatium grayi*

Sweetener: *Phragmites australis*

Unspecified: *Agropyron* sp., *Allium acuminatum, A. bisceptrum, A. platycaule, Asclepias fascicularis, A. speciosa, Balsamorhiza sagittata, B. ×terebinthacea, Bidens laevis, Calochortus macrocarpus, Camassia quamash, Chenopodium album, C. fremontii, Cirsium pastoris, C. tioganum, Comandra umbellata, Corylus cornuta, Crepis occidentalis, Cyperus rotundus, Dichelostemma pulchellum, Echinochloa crus-galli, Elaeagnus commutata, Eragrostis secundiflora, Fritillaria pudica, Haplopappus* sp., *Helianthus bolanderi, Juncus balticus, Lewisia rediviva, Leymus condensatus, Lilium parvum, Lomatium bicolor, L. canbyi, L. grayi, L. macrocarpum, L. piperi, Oenothera elata, Perideridia gairdneri, P. oregana, Pinus monophylla, P. monticola, P. ponderosa, Prosopis glandulosa, P. pubescens, Quercus garryana, Rorippa curvisiliqua, Rosa pisocarpa, Scorzonella* sp., *Spiranthes* sp., *Trifolium willdenowii, Triteleia hyacinthina, Typha latifolia, Valeriana edulis, Wyethia mollis, W. ovata*

Vegetable: *Allium acuminatum, Calochortus macrocarpus, Glyptopleura marginata, Lomatium nevadense, L. nudicaule, Trifolium willdenowii, T. wormskioldii, Triteleia hyacinthina*

Winter Use Food: *Amelanchier alnifolia, Balsamorhiza sagittata, Camassia quamash, Corylus cornuta, Helianthus annuus, Juniperus occidentalis, Lewisia rediviva, Lomatium watsonii, Perideridia gairdneri, Pinus monophylla, Prunus virginiana, Quercus dunnii, Q. kelloggii, Vaccinium cespitosum*

Paiute, Nevada
Unspecified: *Calochortus nuttallii*

Paiute, Northern
Beverage: *Descurainia incana, D. pinnata, D. sophia, Ephedra viridis, Juncus balticus*

Bread & Cake: *Allium anceps, Pinus monophylla, Prunus virginiana, Rumex crispus, Typha domingensis, T. latifolia*

Candy: *Artemisia tridentata, Chrysothamnus nauseosus, Phragmites australis, Pinus jeffreyi, P. monophylla*

Dried Food: *Allium parvum, Calochortus leichtlinii, C. nuttallii, Cyperus esculentus, Lycium andersonii, Mentzelia albicaulis, Pinus monophylla, Prunus virginiana, Ribes aureum, Sambucus racemosa, Shepherdia argentea, Typha domingensis, T. latifolia*

Fruit: *Juniperus occidentalis, Lycium andersonii, Prunus virginiana, Ribes aureum, Sambucus racemosa*

Ice Cream: *Pinus monophylla*

Porridge: *Atriplex argentea, Lycium andersonii, Mentzelia albicaulis, Oryzopsis hymenoides, Perideridia gairdneri, Prunus virginiana, Ribes aureum, Scirpus maritimus, S. pungens, Shepherdia argentea, Typha domingensis, T. latifolia, Wyethia mollis*

Soup: *Allium parvum, Calochortus leichtlinii, C. nuttallii, Oryzopsis hymenoides, Perideridia gairdneri, Pinus monophylla, Sambucus racemosa, Typha domingensis, T. latifolia*

Special Food: *Oryzopsis hymenoides*

Staple: *Chenopodium fremontii, Helianthus annuus, Oryzopsis hymenoides, Perideridia gairdneri, Quercus kelloggii, Typha domingensis, T. latifolia*

Starvation Food: *Rumex crispus*

Unspecified: *Allium anceps, A. nevadense, Balsamorhiza hookeri, Chenopodium nevadense, Claytonia umbellata, Cyperus esculentus, Descurainia incana, D. pinnata, D. sophia, Eleocharis palustris, Helianthus cusickii, Lewisia rediviva, Lomatium macrocarpum, L. nevadense, Opuntia polyacantha, Orobanche fasciculata, Perideridia gairdneri, Sagittaria cuneata, Scirpus acutus, S. maritimus, Suaeda calceoliformis, Typha domingensis, T. latifolia, Wyethia mollis*

Vegetable: *Calochortus leichtlinii, C. nuttallii, Claytonia perfoliata, Glyptopleura marginata, Lewisia rediviva*

Winter Use Food: *Descurainia incana, D. pinnata, D. sophia, Oryzopsis hymenoides, Pinus jeffreyi, Prunus virginiana, Scirpus maritimus, Wyethia mollis*

Paiute, Southern

Unspecified: *Leymus condensatus*

Papago

Beverage: *Baccharis sarothroides, Carnegia gigantea, Datura wrightii, Descurainia pinnata, Ephedra nevadensis, Ferocactus wislizeni, Opuntia engelmannii, Peniocereus greggii, Salvia columbariae, Stenocereus thurberi, Ziziphus obtusifolia*

Bread & Cake: *Carnegia gigantea, Stenocereus thurberi, Triticum aestivum*

Candy: *Encelia farinosa, Prosopis velutina, Quercus emoryi, Sarcostemma cynanchoides*

Cooking Agent: *Carnegia gigantea, Stenocereus thurberi*

Dried Food: *Amaranthus palmeri, Ambrosia tenuifolia, Carnegia gigantea, Cicer arietinum, Cucurbita moschata, C. pepo, Descurainia pinnata, Lens culinaris, Lepidium thurberi, Lycium fremontii, Monolepis nuttalliana, Olneya tesota, Parkinsonia aculeata, P. microphylla, Phaseolus acutifolius, P. vulgaris, Pholisma sonorae, Phoradendron californicum, Proboscidea louisianica, Prosopis velutina, Sporobolus wrightii, Stenocereus thurberi, Yucca baccata, Zea mays*

Fodder: *Carnegia gigantea, Stenocereus thurberi*

Fruit: *Carnegia gigantea, Celtis laevigata, Condalia globosa, Cucurbita maxima, C. moschata, C. pepo, Lycium fremontii, Yucca baccata, Y. schottii*

Porridge: *Yucca baccata*

Preserves: *Carnegia gigantea, Prosopis velutina, Stenocereus thurberi*

Sauce & Relish: *Carnegia gigantea, Opuntia engelmannii, Stenocereus thurberi, Ziziphus obtusifolia*

Soup: *Atriplex wrightii, Chenopodium album*

Special Food: *Capsicum annuum, Fouquieria splendens, Zea mays*

Spice: *Atriplex wrightii, Capsicum annuum, Suaeda suffrutescens*

Staple: *Agastache pallidiflora, Agave americana, A. parryi, Amaranthus palmeri, Ambrosia tenuifolia, Carnegia gigantea, Cucurbita pepo, Olneya tesota, Opuntia echinocarpa, O. engelmannii, O. fulgida, O. spinosior, O. versicolor, Parkinsonia microphylla, Phaseolus acutifolius, Pholisma sonorae, Prosopis glandulosa, P. velutina, Stenocereus thurberi, Triticum aestivum, Yucca baccata, Zea mays*

Unspecified: *Agave americana, A. deserti, A. palmeri, A. schottii, Allium unifolium, Amaranthus palmeri, Ambrosia tenuifolia, Atriplex lentiformis, Capsicum annuum, Carnegia gigantea, Chenopodium murale, Cicer arietinum, Descurainia pinnata, Dichelostemma pulchellum, Hordeum vulgare, Lens culinaris, Monolepis nuttalliana, Olneya tesota, Parkinsonia aculeata, P. microphylla, Peniocereus greggii, Phaseolus vulgaris, Pholisma sonorae, Pisum sativum, Proboscidea althaeifolia, P. louisianica, P. parviflora, Prosopis velutina, Quercus emoryi, Q. oblongifolia, Simmondsia chinensis, Stenocereus thurberi, Vigna unguiculata, Yucca baccata, Y. elata, Zea mays*

Vegetable: *Agave americana, Amaranthus palmeri, Ambrosia tenuifolia, Atriplex wrightii, Chenopodium murale, Dasylirion wheeleri, Ferocactus wislizeni, Opuntia echinocarpa, O. engelmannii, O. fulgida, O. imbricata, O. versicolor, Peniocereus greggii, Rumex hymenosepalus, Taraxacum officinale*

Papago & Pima

Beverage: *Stenocereus thurberi*

Candy: *Carnegia gigantea, Stenocereus thurberi*

Cooking Agent: *Pachycereus pringlei*

Fruit: *Carnegia gigantea, Machaerocereus eruca, M. gummosus, Myrtillocactus cochal, Peniocereus striatus, Stenocereus thurberi*

Porridge: *Stenocereus thurberi*
Preserves: *Carnegia gigantea, Stenocereus thurberi*
Sauce & Relish: *Carnegia gigantea, Stenocereus thurberi*

Pawnee

Beverage: *Agastache foeniculum, Ceanothus americanus, Mentha canadensis, Rubus idaeus, R. occidentalis, Sambucus canadensis, Vitis cinerea, V. vulpina*
Bread & Cake: *Prunus virginiana*
Candy: *Populus deltoides, Silphium laciniatum*
Dried Food: *Opuntia humifusa, Pediomelum esculentum, Physalis heterophylla, Prunus americana, P. pumila, P. virginiana, Rubus idaeus, R. occidentalis, Shepherdia argentea, Vitis cinerea, V. vulpina*
Fodder: *Oxalis stricta, O. violacea*
Forage: *Oxalis stricta*
Fruit: *Celtis occidentalis, Fragaria vesca, F. virginiana, Opuntia humifusa, Prunus americana, P. virginiana, Rubus idaeus, R. occidentalis, Sambucus canadensis, Shepherdia argentea, Viburnum lentago, Vitis cinerea, V. vulpina*
Sauce & Relish: *Allium canadense, Physalis heterophylla, Prunus americana, P. pumila*
Soup: *Carya ovata, Chenopodium album, Juglans nigra, Nelumbo lutea*
Spice: *Allium canadense*
Staple: *Zea mays*
Starvation Food: *Opuntia humifusa, Rosa arkansana*
Sweetener: *Acer negundo, Agastache foeniculum, Carya ovata, Zea mays*
Unspecified: *Allium canadense, Amphicarpaea bracteata, Apios americana, Carya ovata, Gymnocladus dioicus, Helianthus tuberosus, Juglans nigra, Linum lewisii, Nelumbo lutea, Nuphar lutea, Oxalis stricta, O. violacea, Pediomelum esculentum, Quercus macrocarpa, Q. rubra, Sagittaria latifolia*
Vegetable: *Asclepias syriaca*
Winter Use Food: *Zea mays*

Penobscot

Beverage: *Taxus canadensis*

Pima

Beverage: *Carnegia gigantea, Datura discolor, Ephedra fasciculata, Ferocactus cylindraceus, F. wislizeni, Lycium fremontii, Prosopis glandulosa, P. pubescens, P. velutina, Salvia columbariae, Yucca baccata*
Bread & Cake: *Atriplex nuttallii, A. polycarpa, Carnegia gigantea, Prosopis velutina, Rumex hymenosepalus, Triticum aestivum, Typha angustifolia, Yucca baccata, Zea mays*
Candy: *Agave deserti, Encelia farinosa, Ferocactus cylindraceus, F. wislizeni, Helianthus annuus, Populus deltoides, P. fremontii, Prosopis glandulosa, P. pubescens, P. velutina, Rumex hymenosepalus, Sarcostemma cynanchoides*
Cooking Agent: *Atriplex coronata, A. elegans, A. serenana*
Dessert: *Carnegia gigantea*
Dried Food: *Agave americana, Atriplex lentiformis, Carnegia gigantea, Cucurbita moschata, Descurainia pinnata, Olneya tesota, Opuntia imbricata, Yucca baccata*
Fodder: *Carnegia gigantea, Plantago ovata, Ziziphus obtusifolia*
Forage: *Atriplex polycarpa, Malva parviflora, Pluchea sericea, Prosopis pubescens, Sarcobatus vermiculatus*
Fruit: *Carnegia gigantea, Citrullus lanatus, Condalia hookeri, Cucurbita maxima, C. moschata, C. pepo, Echinocereus engelmannii, Lycium fremontii, Opuntia arbuscula, O. engelmannii, O. imbricata, O. leptocaulis, O. versicolor, Phoradendron californicum, Solanum elaeagnifolium, Yucca schottii, Ziziphus obtusifolia*
Pie & Pudding: *Rumex hymenosepalus*
Porridge: *Atriplex lentiformis, Carnegia gigantea, Prosopis velutina, Sisymbrium irio, Triticum aestivum, Typha angustifolia, Yucca baccata, Zea mays*
Preserves: *Sambucus cerulea*
Sauce & Relish: *Agave americana, Carnegia gigantea, Condalia hookeri, Ziziphus obtusifolia*
Spice: *Atriplex coronata, A. elegans, A. nuttal-*

lii, A. serenana, Capsicum annuum, Suaeda arborescens, S. suffrutescens

Staple: *Carnegia gigantea, Chenopodium murale, Descurainia pinnata, Helianthus annuus, Monolepis nuttalliana, Olneya tesota, Prosopis pubescens, P. velutina, Quercus oblongifolia*

Starvation Food: *Agave americana, Atriplex lentiformis, A. polycarpa, Sarcobatus vermiculatus*

Substitution Food: *Carnegia gigantea, Ferocactus wislizeni, Prosopis velutina, Solanum elaeagnifolium*

Sweetener: *Prosopis velutina*

Unspecified: *Acacia greggii, Agave deserti, Allenrolfea occidentalis, Amaranthus palmeri, Amsinckia spectabilis, A. tessellata, Atriplex coronata, A. elegans, A. nuttallii, A. serenana, Capsicum annuum, Carnegia gigantea, Cicer arietinum, Cucurbita foetidissima, C. pepo, Cyperus odoratus, Ferocactus cylindraceus, F. wislizeni, Helianthus annuus, Hoffmannseggia glauca, Hordeum vulgare, Lens culinaris, Malva nicaeensis, Monolepis nuttalliana, Opuntia engelmannii, O. phaeacantha, Orobanche ludoviciana, Parkinsonia florida, P. microphylla, Pisum sativum, Populus deltoides, Proboscidea parviflora, Prosopis velutina, Rumex hymenosepalus, Salix gooddingii, Sonchus asper, S. oleraceus, Triticum durum, T. polonicum, Typha angustifolia, Vigna unguiculata*

Vegetable: *Amaranthus palmeri, Atriplex wrightii, Hoffmannseggia glauca, Monolepis nuttalliana, Rumex crispus, R. hymenosepalus, Sonchus asper, Trianthema portulacastrum*

Winter Use Food: *Sisymbrium irio*

Pima, Gila River

Baby Food: *Dichelostemma pulchellum, Mammillaria grahamii, Physalis acutifolia, Sarcostemma cynanchoides, Washingtonia filifera*

Beverage: *Carnegia gigantea, Descurainia pinnata, Prosopis velutina, Salvia columbariae, Sambucus cerulea, Sisymbrium irio*

Bread & Cake: *Prosopis velutina*

Candy: *Agave deserti, Carnegia gigantea, Yucca baccata*

Dried Food: *Agave deserti, Amaranthus palmeri, Carnegia gigantea, Opuntia acanthocarpa, O. arbuscula*

Fruit: *Capsicum annuum, Opuntia engelmannii, O. leptocaulis, Phoradendron californicum, Sambucus cerulea, Yucca baccata, Ziziphus obtusifolia*

Porridge: *Carnegia gigantea, Descurainia pinnata, Salvia columbariae, Sisymbrium irio*

Preserves: *Carnegia gigantea*

Sauce & Relish: *Carnegia gigantea*

Snack Food: *Cucurbita digitata, Dichelostemma pulchellum, Echinocereus engelmannii, Mammillaria grahamii, Phoradendron californicum, Physalis acutifolia, Populus fremontii, Prosopis pubescens, P. velutina, Quercus turbinella, Sambucus cerulea, Washingtonia filifera*

Staple: *Agave deserti, Capsicum annuum, Carnegia gigantea, Descurainia pinnata, Opuntia acanthocarpa, Prosopis pubescens, P. velutina, Sisymbrium irio*

Starvation Food: *Acacia greggii, Allenrolfea occidentalis, Atriplex lentiformis*

Unspecified: *Allenrolfea occidentalis, Amaranthus palmeri, Amoreuxia palmatifida, Atriplex elegans, A. lentiformis, A. wrightii, Chenopodium album, C. pratericola, Descurainia pinnata, Eremalche exilis, Gossypium hirsutum, Hoffmannseggia glauca, Olneya tesota, Opuntia acanthocarpa, O. arbuscula, O. ×kelvinensis, Orobanche cooperi, Parkinsonia microphylla, Phalaris caroliniana, P. minor, Plantago ovata, P. patagonica, Portulaca oleracea, Rumex crispus, R. violascens, Salvia columbariae, Scirpus maritimus, Sisymbrium irio, Sonchus asper, S. oleraceus, Suaeda moquinii, Typha domingensis*

Vegetable: *Amaranthus palmeri, Eremalche exilis, Monolepis nuttalliana*

Winter Use Food: *Prosopis velutina*

Pima, Lehi

Beverage: *Ephedra fasciculata*

Poliklah

Bread & Cake: *Lithocarpus densiflorus*
Fruit: *Vaccinium ovatum, V. parvifolium*
Porridge: *Lithocarpus densiflorus*
Staple: *Lithocarpus densiflorus*

Pomo

Bread & Cake: *Lithocarpus densiflorus, Porphyra perforata, Quercus chrysolepis, Q garryana, Q. kelloggii, Q. lobata*
Dried Food: *Arctostaphylos tomentosa, Castanopsis chrysophylla, Porphyra perforata, Vaccinium ovatum*
Fruit: *Arbutus menziesii, Carpobrotus aequilateralus, Fragaria vesca, Gaultheria shallon, Heteromeles arbutifolia, Rubus leucodermis, R. parviflorus, R. spectabilis, Vaccinium ovatum, Vitis californica*
Pie & Pudding: *Vaccinium ovatum*
Porridge: *Arctostaphylos tomentosa, Lithocarpus densiflorus, Madia sativa, Melica bulbosa, Quercus chrysolepis, Q. garryana, Q. kelloggii, Q. lobata*
Soup: *Lithocarpus densiflorus, Quercus kelloggii, Q. lobata*
Spice: *Allium unifolium*
Staple: *Avena fatua, Boisduvalia densiflora, Hemizonia clevelandii, H. luzulifolia, Lolium temulentum, Madia capitata, M. elegans, M. gracilis, M. sativa, Perideridia gairdneri, P. kelloggii, Ranunculus occidentalis, Salvia columbariae, Wyethia angustifolia, W. longicaulis*
Unspecified: *Allium unifolium, Avena fatua, A. sativa, Brodiaea coronaria, Calochortus pulchellus, C. vestae, Castanopsis chrysophylla, Dichelostemma pulchellum, D. volubile, Lithocarpus densiflorus, Macrocystis luetkeana, Melica bulbosa, Pinus lambertiana, P. sabiniana, Postelsia palmaeformis, Quercus agrifolia, Q. garryana, Q. kelloggii, Sagittaria latifolia, Sanicula tuberosa, Scirpus acutus, Triteleia hyacinthina, T. laxa, T. peduncularis*
Vegetable: *Perideridia gairdneri, Scirpus acutus, S. robustus, Triteleia grandiflora, Typha latifolia*

Winter Use Food: *Avena fatua, Madia sativa, Porphyra perforata, Rubus leucodermis*

Pomo, Kashaya

Beverage: *Ledum ×columbianum, Satureja douglasii*
Candy: *Pinus lambertiana*
Dried Food: *Arctostaphylos glandulosa, Juglans hindsii, Lithocarpus densiflorus, Porphyra lanceolata, P. perforata, Postelsia palmaeformis, Quercus agrifolia, Q. garryana, Q. kelloggii, Umbellularia californica, Vaccinium ovatum*
Forage: *Lithocarpus densiflorus, Quercus dumosa*
Fruit: *Arbutus menziesii, Carpobrotus aequilateralus, Fragaria chiloensis, F. vesca, Gaultheria shallon, Heteromeles arbutifolia, Ribes californicum, Rosa californica, R. gymnocarpa, Rubus leucodermis, R. parviflorus, R. spectabilis, R. ursinus, Sambucus cerulea, Umbellularia californica, Vaccinium ovatum, V. parvifolium, Vitis californica*
Pie & Pudding: *Gaultheria shallon, Rubus ursinus, Vaccinium ovatum*
Porridge: *Lithocarpus densiflorus, Quercus agrifolia, Q. garryana, Q. kelloggii, Q. lobata, Triticum aestivum*
Sauce & Relish: *Rubus ursinus*
Sour: *Oxalis oregana*
Spice: *Lomatium macrocarpum, Ulva lactuca*
Staple: *Madia elegans, M. sativa, Pinus sabiniana, Wyethia angustifolia*
Sweetener: *Pinus lambertiana*
Unspecified: *Aesculus californica, Angelica tomentosa, Castanopsis chrysophylla, Heracleum maximum, Juglans hindsii, Lomatium macrocarpum, Nereocystis luetkeana, Perideridia kelloggii, Pinus lambertiana, P. muricata, P. sabiniana, Porphyra lanceolata, P. perforata, Postelsia palmaeformis, Trifolium albopurpureum, T. fucatum, T. variegatum, T. wormskioldii, Umbellularia californica, Wyethia glabra*
Vegetable: *Agaricus campestris, A. silvicola, Allium dichlamydeum, Boletus edulis, Brodiaea coronaria, Calochortus amabilis, C. luteus, C. tolmiei, C. vestae, Cantharellus*

*cibarius, Cyperus esculentus, Dentinum
repandum, Dichelostemma pulchellum,
Hericium coralloides, Peziza aurantia,
Piperia elegans, P. unalascensis, Pleurotus
ostreatus, Triteleia laxa*

Winter Use Food: *Arbutus menziesii, Castanopsis chrysophylla, Nereocystis luetkeana,
Pinus lambertiana, P. muricata, P. sabiniana, Rubus leucodermis, Umbellularia californica, Wyethia angustifolia*

Ponca

Beverage: *Agastache foeniculum, Ceanothus
americanus, Mentha canadensis, Rubus
idaeus, R. occidentalis, Sambucus
canadensis*

Bread & Cake: *Prunus virginiana*

Candy: *Dalea purpurea, Populus deltoides, Silphium laciniatum*

Cooking Agent: *Lithospermum canescens*

Dried Food: *Pediomelum esculentum, Physalis
heterophylla, Prunus americana, P. pumila,
P. virginiana, Rubus idaeus, R. occidentalis,
Shepherdia argentea, Vitis cinerea, V.
vulpina*

Fodder: *Osmorhiza longistylis, Oxalis stricta,
O. violacea*

Fruit: *Amelanchier alnifolia, Crataegus chrysocarpa, Fragaria vesca, F. virginiana, Malus
ioensis, Prunus americana, P. virginiana,
Ribes missouriense, Rubus idaeus, R. occidentalis, Sambucus canadensis, Shepherdia
argentea, Viburnum lentago, Vitis cinerea,
V. vulpina*

Sauce & Relish: *Allium canadense, Physalis
heterophylla, Prunus americana, P. pumila*

Soup: *Carya ovata, Corylus americana, Juglans nigra, Nelumbo lutea*

Spice: *Allium canadense*

Staple: *Zea mays, Zizania aquatica*

Starvation Food: *Crataegus chrysocarpa, Rosa
arkansana*

Sweetener: *Acer negundo, A. saccharinum,
Agastache foeniculum, Carya ovata, Zea
mays*

Unspecified: *Allium canadense, Amphicarpaea
bracteata, Apios americana, Carya ovata,
Corylus americana, Helianthus tuberosus,*

*Juglans nigra, Lathyrus brachycalyx, Linum
lewisii, Nelumbo lutea, Oxalis stricta, O.
violacea, Pediomelum esculentum, Quercus
macrocarpa, Q. rubra*

Vegetable: *Asclepias syriaca*

Winter Use Food: *Zea mays*

Potawatomi

Beverage: *Acer saccharum, Ledum groenlandicum, Prunus pumila, P. serotina*

Candy: *Acer saccharum*

Dessert: *Oxalis montana*

Dried Food: *Amelanchier stolonifera, Fragaria
vesca, Vaccinium myrtilloides, Zizania
palustris*

Fodder: *Larix laricina, Osmorhiza longistylis,
Pedicularis canadensis*

Fruit: *Amelanchier stolonifera, Aronia melanocarpa, Cornus canadensis, Crataegus chrysocarpa, Maianthemum canadense, Prunus
pensylvanica, P. serotina, P. virginiana,
Ribes cynosbati, Rubus allegheniensis,
R. idaeus, Vaccinium myrtilloides, V.
oxycoccos*

Pie & Pudding: *Zizania palustris*

Porridge: *Quercus rubra*

Preservative: *Myrica gale*

Preserves: *Ribes cynosbati, Rubus idaeus*

Soup: *Allium canadense, Aralia racemosa,
Asclepias syriaca, Parmelia physodes*

Sour: *Acer saccharum, Nemopanthus mucro-
natus, Rhus hirta*

Spice: *Asarum canadense*

Staple: *Zizania palustris*

Starvation Food: *Celastrus scandens*

Sweetener: *Acer saccharum*

Unspecified: *Arisaema triphyllum, Fagus grandifolia, Helianthus tuberosus, Nelumbo
lutea, Sagittaria latifolia, Taraxacum
officinale*

Vegetable: *Allium tricoccum, Apios americana,
Chenopodium album, Parmelia physodes,
Phaseolus vulgaris, Sagittaria latifolia*

Winter Use Food: *Amelanchier stolonifera,
Carya ovata, Corylus cornuta, Fragaria vesca, Juglans cinerea, Nelumbo lutea, Sagittaria latifolia, Zea mays*

Pueblo

Dried Food: *Descurainia pinnata, D. sophia, Monarda fistulosa, Polanisia dodecandra, Thelypodium wrightii, Yucca baccata, Y. glauca*

Fruit: *Celtis laevigata, Physalis longifolia, P. subulata, Prunus virginiana, Ribes inerme, Yucca baccata, Y. glauca*

Preserves: *Mahonia haematocarpa*

Soup: *Descurainia pinnata, D. sophia, Polanisia dodecandra, Thelypodium wrightii*

Special Food: *Polyporus harlowii, Zea mays*

Spice: *Allium geyeri, Atriplex argentea, Monarda fistulosa, Pectis angustifolia, P. papposa*

Staple: *Cleome serrulata*

Unspecified: *Descurainia pinnata, D. sophia, Helianthus annuus, Hoffmannseggia glauca, Pinus edulis, Polanisia dodecandra, Quercus gambelii, Solanum fendleri, Thelypodium wrightii*

Vegetable: *Amaranthus blitoides, A. retroflexus, Atriplex powellii, Chenopodium album, C. leptophyllum, Descurainia pinnata, D. sophia, Polanisia dodecandra, Thelypodium wrightii*

Puyallup

Fruit: *Rubus leucodermis*

Quileute

Beverage: *Rubus ursinus*

Bread & Cake: *Gaultheria shallon*

Dried Food: *Equisetum hyemale, E. laevigatum, Rubus ursinus, Vaccinium ovalifolium*

Fodder: *Equisetum telmateia*

Forage: *Lysichiton americanus*

Fruit: *Amelanchier alnifolia, Fragaria chiloensis, Gaultheria ovatifolia, G. shallon, Malus fusca, Ribes sanguineum, Rosa pisocarpa, Rubus idaeus, R. laciniatus, R. lasiococcus, R. leucodermis, R. nivalis, R. parviflorus, R. spectabilis, R. ursinus, Sambucus racemosa, Vaccinium deliciosum, V. myrtilloides, V. ovalifolium, V. ovatum, V. parvifolium*

Preserves: *Gaultheria ovatifolia, Mahonia nervosa, Prunus emarginata*

Sauce & Relish: *Gaultheria ovatifolia, Sambucus racemosa, Vaccinium deliciosum, V. myrtilloides, V. ovalifolium, V. ovatum, V. parvifolium*

Special Food: *Equisetum hyemale, E. laevigatum*

Spice: *Brassica nigra, Lysichiton americanus, Moricandia arvensis, Salix hookeriana, Sinapis alba*

Unspecified: *Allium acuminatum, A. cernuum, Argentina egedii, Athyrium filix-femina, Camassia quamash, Equisetum hyemale, E. telmateia, Heracleum maximum, Lepidium virginicum, Lilium columbianum, Lysichiton americanus, Oxalis oregana, Polystichum munitum, Pteridium aquilinum, Ranunculus reptans, Rubus spectabilis*

Vegetable: *Brassica nigra, Cirsium edule, Heracleum maximum, Lepidium virginicum, Moricandia arvensis, Sinapis alba, Urtica dioica*

Winter Use Food: *Ribes sanguineum, Rosa pisocarpa, Rubus idaeus, R. laciniatus, R. lasiococcus, R. leucodermis, R. nivalis, R. parviflorus, R. spectabilis, R. ursinus, Sambucus racemosa, Vaccinium deliciosum, V. myrtilloides, V. ovalifolium, V. ovatum, V. parvifolium*

Quinault

Beverage: *Vaccinium parvifolium*

Bread & Cake: *Gaultheria shallon*

Candy: *Picea sitchensis, Pseudotsuga menziesii*

Dried Food: *Vaccinium ovalifolium*

Fodder: *Equisetum telmateia*

Fruit: *Malus fusca, Oemleria cerasiformis, Rubus parviflorus, R. spectabilis, Vaccinium ovalifolium, V. ovatum, V. oxycoccos, V. parvifolium*

Preservative: *Ribes divaricatum*

Special Food: *Fragaria chiloensis*

Unspecified: *Allium cernuum, Athyrium filix-femina, Equisetum telmateia, Heracleum maximum, Lilium columbianum, Oxalis oregana, Polystichum munitum, Pteridium aquilinum, Rosa nutkana, Rubus spectabilis, Stachys mexicana*

Winter Use Food: *Sambucus cerulea, S. racemosa*

Rappahannock

Beverage: *Diospyros virginiana*
Candy: *Gnaphalium obtusifolium*
Snack Food: *Cucurbita pepo*

Ree

Staple: *Helianthus annuus*
Unspecified: *Helianthus annuus*

Rocky Boy

Fruit: *Rosa nutkana*
Preserves: *Rosa nutkana*

Round Valley Indian

Dried Food: *Prunus virginiana*
Fruit: *Prunus virginiana*
Spice: *Calocedrus decurrens*
Substitution Food: *Pseudotsuga menziesii*
Unspecified: *Camassia leichtlinii*

Saanich

Beverage: *Epilobium angustifolium, Ledum groenlandicum, Rubus ursinus, Satureja douglasii*
Candy: *Lonicera ciliosa*
Forage: *Stachys ciliata*
Fruit: *Amelanchier alnifolia, Oemleria cerasiformis, Rosa nutkana*
Spice: *Acer macrophyllum, Mentha arvensis, Zostera marina*
Unspecified: *Cirsium brevistylum, Daucus pusillus, Equisetum arvense, E. telmateia, Fritillaria lanceolata, Rorippa nasturtium-aquaticum, Rumex obtusifolius*
Vegetable: *Rumex acetosella, Urtica dioica*

Salish

Fruit: *Cornus canadensis, Vaccinium ovatum*
Unspecified: *Rosa nutkana*
Vegetable: *Camassia leichtlinii, C. quamash, Triglochin maritimum*

Salish, Coast

Beverage: *Fragaria chiloensis, F. vesca, F. virginiana, Ledum groenlandicum*
Bread & Cake: *Gaultheria shallon, Pinus contorta, Pteridium aquilinum, Ribes bracteosum, R. divaricatum, R. hudsonianum,*

R. lacustre, R. lobbii, R. sanguineum, Rubus leucodermis, R. parviflorus, R. ursinus
Dessert: *Shepherdia canadensis*
Dried Food: *Camassia leichtlinii, C. quamash, Pinus monticola, Polypodium virginianum, Thuja plicata, Tsuga heterophylla, Vaccinium ovalifolium, V. oxycoccos, V. parvifolium, V. uliginosum*
Fruit: *Amelanchier alnifolia, Arctostaphylos uva-ursi, Crataegus douglasii, Fragaria chiloensis, F. vesca, F. virginiana, Gaultheria shallon, Maianthemum dilatatum, Malus fusca, Rubus leucodermis, R. parviflorus, R. spectabilis, R. ursinus, Sambucus cerulea, Vaccinium ovalifolium, V. oxycoccos, V. parvifolium, V. uliginosum, Viburnum edule*
Preserves: *Mahonia aquifolium, M. nervosa*
Substitution Food: *Polypodium virginianum*
Unspecified: *Acer macrophyllum, Allium acuminatum, A. cernuum, Alnus rubra, Argentina egedii, Athyrium filix-femina, Corylus cornuta, Daucus pusillus, Dryopteris campyloptera, Fritillaria lanceolata, Glaux maritima, Heracleum maximum, Pinus contorta, P. monticola, Polypodium virginianum, Pteridium aquilinum, Quercus garryana, Rosa nutkana, Rubus parviflorus, R. spectabilis, Salicornia virginica, Thuja plicata*
Vegetable: *Camassia leichtlinii, C. quamash*

Salish, Straits

Unspecified: *Fritillaria camschatcensis*

Samish

Bread & Cake: *Gaultheria shallon*
Fruit: *Mahonia aquifolium, Malus fusca, Oemleria cerasiformis, Rubus parviflorus*
Unspecified: *Lilium columbianum, Rubus parviflorus*

Sanel

Substitution Food: *Brickellia californica*

San Felipe

Dried Food: *Prunus virginiana, Yucca baccata*
Fruit: *Juniperus deppeana, Opuntia engel-*

mannii, Physalis longifolia, Prunus virginiana, Ptelea trifoliata, Yucca baccata
Porridge: *Equisetum laevigatum, Opuntia engelmannii*
Special Food: *Sophora nuttalliana*
Staple: *Dalea candida, Quercus gambelii*
Starvation Food: *Platanthera sparsiflora*
Unspecified: *Cleome serrulata, Opuntia polyacantha, Portulaca oleracea, Quercus gambelii, Rumex venosus, Typha latifolia, Yucca baccata, Y. glauca*
Vegetable: *Portulaca oleracea, Rudbeckia laciniata*
Winter Use Food: *Opuntia polyacantha*

San Ildefonso
Fruit: *Juniperus monosperma*
Spice: *Monarda fistulosa*
Unspecified: *Dalea candida*

Sanpoil
Beverage: *Mentha arvensis*
Fruit: *Mahonia aquifolium*
Ice Cream: *Shepherdia canadensis*
Preserves: *Mahonia aquifolium*
Special Food: *Balsamorhiza sagittata, Lomatium dissectum*
Unspecified: *Lomatium macrocarpum*

Sanpoil & Nespelem
Beverage: *Mentha canadensis, Monardella odoratissima, Prunus virginiana*
Bread & Cake: *Amelanchier alnifolia, Prunus virginiana*
Dried Food: *Arctostaphylos uva-ursi, Crataegus douglasii, Daucus carota, Helianthus annuus, Opuntia polyacantha*
Fruit: *Amelanchier alnifolia, Cornus sericea, Crataegus columbiana, C. douglasii, Fragaria virginiana, Mahonia aquifolium, Prunus virginiana, Ribes cereum, R. oxyacanthoides, Rubus parviflorus, Sambucus cerulea*
Porridge: *Lewisia rediviva*
Soup: *Arctostaphylos uva-ursi*
Starvation Food: *Rosa woodsii*
Unspecified: *Corylus cornuta, Helianthus*

annuus, Larix occidentalis, Petasites frigidus, Pinus ponderosa, Valeriana edulis
Vegetable: *Daucus carota*
Winter Use Food: *Helianthus annuus*

Santa Clara
Special Food: *Dalea candida*

Seminole
Candy: *Ficus aurea*
Fodder: *Quercus virginiana*
Forage: *Licania michauxii*
Fruit: *Serenoa repens*
Spice: *Piloblephis rigida*
Starvation Food: *Sambucus canadensis*
Unspecified: *Allium cepa, Ananas comosus, Annona glabra, A. reticulata, Apios americana, Arachis hypogaea, Ardisia escallonoides, Brassica oleracea, Carica papaya, Celtis laevigata, Chrysobalanus icaco, Chrysophyllum oliviforme, Citrullus lanatus, Citrus aurantifolia, C. aurantium, C. limon, C. ×paradisi, C. reticulata, C. sinensis, Coccoloba diversifolia, Cocos nucifera, Colocasia esculenta, Cucumis melo, C. sativus, Cucurbita moschata, Diospyros virginiana, Ficus aurea, Fortunella sp., Lycopersicon esculentum, Mangifera indica, Manihot esculenta, Morus rubra, Musa sp., Oryza sativa, Peltandra virginica, Prunus persica, Psidium guajava, Pyrus communis, Quercus phellos, Q. pumila, Sabal palmetto, Saccharum officinarum, Sideroxylon foetidissimum, Thalia geniculata, Vaccinium myrsinites, Vitis aestivalis, V. munsoniana, Xanthosoma atrovirens, Ximenia americana, Zamia pumila, Zea mays*
Vegetable: *Ipomoea batatas, Solanum tuberosum*

Seri
Beverage: *Ferocactus coulteri, F. wislizeni*
Fruit: *Carnegia gigantea, Pachycereus pringlei, Stenocereus thurberi*
Porridge: *Acacia greggii, Carnegia gigantea, Olneya tesota, Pachycereus pringlei, Prosopis glandulosa, Stenocereus thurberi*
Staple: *Ruppia sp.*

Unspecified: *Hymenoclea monogyra, Jacquinia pungens*

Shasta

Bread & Cake: *Lithocarpus densiflorus, Pinus lambertiana, P. ponderosa, P. sabiniana, Quercus chrysolepis, Q. garryana, Q. kelloggii*
Dried Food: *Pinus lambertiana, P. ponderosa, P. sabiniana*
Fruit: *Oemleria cerasiformis*
Porridge: *Lithocarpus densiflorus, Quercus chrysolepis, Q. garryana, Q. kelloggii*
Soup: *Lithocarpus densiflorus, Quercus chrysolepis, Q. garryana, Q. kelloggii*
Staple: *Lithocarpus densiflorus, Quercus chrysolepis, Q. garryana, Q. kelloggii*
Unspecified: *Fritillaria recurva, Pinus lambertiana, P. ponderosa, P. sabiniana*

Shoshoni

Beverage: *Lithospermum incisum, Rhus trilobata*
Candy: *Asclepias speciosa*
Spice: *Allium falcifolium, Artemisia dracunculus, Osmorhiza occidentalis*
Starvation Food: *Leymus condensatus*
Unspecified: *Madia elegans, Pinus monophylla*
Winter Use Food: *Rhus trilobata*

Shuswap

Beverage: *Abies grandis, Ledum groenlandicum, Mentha arvensis, Prunus virginiana, Rosa nutkana, Shepherdia canadensis, Urtica dioica, U. urens*
Candy: *Abies grandis*
Dessert: *Shepherdia canadensis*
Dried Food: *Fragaria virginiana*
Fodder: *Medicago sativa, Phleum pratense, Trifolium pratense*
Forage: *Allium cernuum, Calochortus macrocarpus*
Fruit: *Amelanchier alnifolia, Cornus sericea, Disporum trachycarpum, Mahonia repens, Prunus emarginata, Ribes hudsonianum, R. lacustre, Rubus idaeus, R. leucodermis, R. parviflorus, Shepherdia canadensis, Vaccinium cespitosum, V. membranaceum, V. ovalifolium, Viburnum opulus*
Ice Cream: *Shepherdia canadensis*
Preservative: *Cornus sericea, Salix scouleriana*
Preserves: *Crataegus douglasii, Viburnum opulus*
Spice: *Allium cernuum, Angelica arguta, Cornus sericea, Lomatium macrocarpum*
Sweetener: *Pseudotsuga menziesii*
Unspecified: *Abies lasiocarpa, Argentina anserina, Balsamorhiza sagittata, Calochortus macrocarpus, Cirsium undulatum, Corylus cornuta, Fritillaria lanceolata, F. pudica, Heracleum maximum, Lewisia rediviva, Lilium columbianum, Lomatium dissectum, L. macrocarpum, Opuntia fragilis, Pinus contorta, P. monticola, Sium suave*
Vegetable: *Angelica arguta, Chenopodium album*
Winter Use Food: *Erythronium grandiflorum, Prunus virginiana*

Sia

Fruit: *Yucca baccata*
Staple: *Triticum aestivum, Zea mays*
Unspecified: *Amaranthus cruentus, Capsicum annuum, Citrullus lanatus, Cleome serrulata, Cucumis melo, Cucurbita maxima, C. moschata, Opuntia engelmannii, Pinus edulis*
Vegetable: *Amaranthus cruentus, Cleome serrulata, Phaseolus acutifolius, P. vulgaris, Solanum fendleri, S. jamesii, S. tuberosum, Vicia faba*

Sierra

Staple: *Pteridium aquilinum*

Sioux

Dried Food: *Vitis vulpina*
Fruit: *Symphoricarpos occidentalis, Vitis vulpina*
Sauce & Relish: *Polygonum amphibium*
Soup: *Pediomelum esculentum*
Staple: *Acer negundo*
Unspecified: *Helianthus maximiliani, Lygodesmia juncea, Scirpus acutus, Typha latifolia*
Winter Use Food: *Pediomelum esculentum*

Skagit

Beverage: *Rosa nutkana*
Bread & Cake: *Gaultheria shallon*
Dried Food: *Rubus ursinus*
Fruit: *Amelanchier alnifolia, Mahonia nervosa, Oemleria cerasiformis, Ribes laxiflorum, Rubus parviflorus, R. ursinus, Vaccinium parvifolium*
Preserves: *Mahonia nervosa*
Unspecified: *Corylus cornuta, Lilium columbianum, Pteridium aquilinum, Rosa nutkana, Rubus parviflorus*
Winter Use Food: *Sambucus cerulea, S. racemosa*

Skagit, Upper

Beverage: *Rosa nutkana*
Dried Food: *Amelanchier alnifolia, Gaultheria shallon, Mahonia aquifolium, M. nervosa, Rubus leucodermis, R. ursinus, Sambucus cerulea, S. racemosa, Vaccinium membranaceum*
Fruit: *Amelanchier alnifolia, Gaultheria shallon, Mahonia aquifolium, M. nervosa, Maianthemum racemosum, Malus fusca, Oemleria cerasiformis, Ribes divaricatum, R. lacustre, R. laxiflorum, R. sanguineum, Rubus leucodermis, R. parviflorus, R. spectabilis, R. ursinus, Sambucus cerulea, S. racemosa, Vaccinium membranaceum, V. parvifolium*
Spice: *Rosa nutkana*
Unspecified: *Alnus rubra, Camassia quamash, Corylus cornuta, Lilium columbianum, Perideridia gairdneri, Pteridium aquilinum, Rubus parviflorus, R. spectabilis, Urtica dioica*
Winter Use Food: *Corylus cornuta*

Skokomish

Bread & Cake: *Gaultheria shallon*
Fruit: *Arctostaphylos uva-ursi, Sambucus cerulea, Vaccinium parvifolium*
Unspecified: *Lilium columbianum, Lysichiton americanus, Oenanthe sarmentosa, Pteridium aquilinum, Rosa nutkana*
Winter Use Food: *Sambucus racemosa*

Snohomish

Bread & Cake: *Gaultheria shallon*
Fruit: *Mahonia aquifolium, Oemleria cerasiformis, Rubus parviflorus, Vaccinium parvifolium*
Unspecified: *Corylus cornuta, Pteridium aquilinum, Rosa nutkana*
Winter Use Food: *Sambucus racemosa*

Snuqualmie

Unspecified: *Juncus effusus, Oenanthe sarmentosa*

Southwest Indians

Beverage: *Yucca baccata, Y. schidigera*
Bread & Cake: *Dasylirion texanum, D. wheeleri, Yucca baccata*
Dessert: *Yucca baccata*
Dried Food: *Yucca baccata, Y. elata, Y. schidigera*
Fruit: *Carnegia gigantea, Yucca baccata, Y. brevifolia, Y. schidigera, Y. torreyi*
Preserves: *Yucca baccata*
Sauce & Relish: *Yucca glauca*
Staple: *Yucca baccata*
Starvation Food: *Yucca angustissima, Y. glauca, Y. harrimaniae*
Sweetener: *Yucca baccata*
Unspecified: *Prosopis glandulosa, Yucca baccata, Y. glauca*

Spanish American

Beverage: *Ribes leptanthum*
Candy: *Hymenoxys richardsonii*
Dried Food: *Monarda fistulosa*
Preserves: *Mahonia haematocarpa, Prunus virginiana, Ribes leptanthum*
Spice: *Monarda fistulosa*
Substitution Food: *Solanum elaeagnifolium*
Vegetable: *Amaranthus blitoides, A. retroflexus, Chenopodium album, C. leptophyllum*

Spokan

Fruit: *Arctostaphylos uva-ursi, Cornus sericea, Fragaria vesca, Prunus virginiana, Rubus leucodermis, Shepherdia canadensis, Vaccinium membranaceum*
Unspecified: *Alectoria jubata, Camassia scil-*

loides, *Cirsium undulatum*, *Fritillaria pudi-*
ca, *Heracleum maximum*, *Lewisia rediviva*,
Pinus albicaulis, *P. contorta*, *P. ponderosa*

Squaxin

Dried Food: *Rubus parviflorus*, *Symphoricar-*
pos albus
Fruit: *Arctostaphylos uva-ursi*, *Fragaria*
×ananassa, *Mahonia aquifolium*, *Oemleria*
cerasiformis, *Ribes sanguineum*, *Rubus*
parviflorus, *R. spectabilis*
Unspecified: *Corylus cornuta*, *Pteridium aqui-*
linum, *Quercus garryana*, *Rosa pisocarpa*,
Rubus spectabilis
Winter Use Food: *Sambucus cerulea*, *S.*
racemosa

Swinomish

Bread & Cake: *Gaultheria shallon*
Dried Food: *Amelanchier alnifolia*
Fruit: *Amelanchier alnifolia*, *Fragaria vesca*,
Mahonia aquifolium, *Malus fusca*, *Oemleria*
cerasiformis, *Ribes divaricatum*, *Rubus*
parviflorus, *R. spectabilis*, *Vaccinium*
parvifolium
Unspecified: *Alnus rubra*, *Corylus cornuta*,
Equisetum telmateia, *Juncus ensifolius*,
Lilium columbianum, *Pteridium aquili-*
num, *Rosa nutkana*, *Rubus parviflorus*,
R. spectabilis
Winter Use Food: *Sambucus cerulea*,
S. racemosa

Tanana, Upper

Beverage: *Andromeda polifolia*, *Hedysarum*
alpinum, *Ledum palustre*, *Rosa acicularis*,
Spiraea stevenii
Candy: *Picea glauca*
Fodder: *Boschniakia rossica*, *Epilobium*
angustifolium, *Picea glauca*
Frozen Food: *Allium schoenoprasum*, *Empe-*
trum nigrum, *Myriophyllum spicatum*, *Poly-*
gonum alpinum, *Rubus arcticus*, *R. chama-*
emorus, *R. idaeus*, *Rumex aquaticus*,
R. arcticus, *Vaccinium oxycoccos*, *V. vitis-*
idaea, *Viburnum edule*
Fruit: *Arctostaphylos rubra*, *A. uva-ursi*,
Elaeagnus commutata, *Empetrum nigrum*,

Ribes hudsonianum, *R. laxiflorum*, *R. triste*,
Rosa acicularis, *Rubus arcticus*, *R. cham-*
aemorus, *R. idaeus*, *Shepherdia canadensis*,
Vaccinium ovalifolium, *V. oxycoccos*,
V. uliginosum, *V. vitis-idaea*, *Viburnum*
edule
Pie & Pudding: *Empetrum nigrum*, *Rubus arcti-*
cus, *R. chamaemorus*, *R. idaeus*, *Vaccinium*
oxycoccos, *V. vitis-idaea*, *Viburnum edule*
Preservative: *Alnus viridis*, *Epilobium angusti-*
folium, *Populus tremuloides*
Preserves: *Empetrum nigrum*, *Ribes hudson-*
ianum, *Rosa acicularis*, *Rubus arcticus*,
R. chamaemorus, *R. idaeus*, *Vaccinium*
oxycoccos, *V. uliginosum*, *V. vitis-idaea*,
Viburnum edule
Soup: *Elaeagnus commutata*
Spice: *Ledum palustre*
Starvation Food: *Picea glauca*
Unspecified: *Allium schoenoprasum*, *Betula*
papyrifera, *Epilobium angustifolium*, *Equi-*
setum arvense, *Hedysarum boreale*, *Myrio-*
phyllum spicatum, *Picea glauca*, *Populus*
balsamifera, *P. tremuloides*, *Rosa acicu-*
laris, *Typha latifolia*
Vegetable: *Hedysarum alpinum*, *Polygonum*
alpinum, *Rumex aquaticus*, *R. arcticus*
Winter Use Food: *Arctostaphylos uva-ursi*,
Empetrum nigrum, *Hedysarum alpinum*,
H. boreale, *Rosa acicularis*, *Rubus arcticus*,
R. chamaemorus, *R. idaeus*, *Vaccinium*
oxycoccos, *V. uliginosum*, *V. vitis-idaea*,
Viburnum edule

Tewa

Beverage: *Thelesperma filifolium*, *T. mega-*
potamicum, *Zea mays*
Bread & Cake: *Zea mays*
Candy: *Hymenoxys richardsonii*
Dried Food: *Poliomintha incana*
Forage: *Equisetum arvense*, *Gutierrezia saro-*
thrae, *Zea mays*
Fruit: *Aster dumosus*, *Celtis laevigata*, *Junipe-*
rus monosperma, *J. scopulorum*, *Maianthe-*
mum racemosum, *Opuntia phaeacantha*,
Physalis subulata, *Prunus virginiana*, *Rhus*
trilobata, *Ribes cereum*, *Yucca baccata*,
Y. glauca

Spice: *Poliomintha incana*
Staple: *Phaseolus vulgaris, Zea mays*
Unspecified: *Allium cernuum, Amaranthus blitoides, A. retroflexus, Cleome serrulata, Liatris punctata, Pinus edulis, Poliomintha incana, Portulaca oleracea, Quercus gambelii, Thelypodium wrightii*
Vegetable: *Cleome serrulata, Solanum jamesii, Stanleya pinnata, Taraxacum officinale*

Tewa of Hano

Cooking Agent: *Atriplex canescens*
Fruit: *Opuntia imbricata*
Special Food: *Juniperus monosperma*
Unspecified: *Monarda fistulosa*

Thompson

Beverage: *Abies grandis, Amelanchier alnifolia, Arctostaphylos uva-ursi, Chimaphila umbellata, Geum triflorum, Juniperus communis, Ledum groenlandicum, Lomatium nudicaule, Penstemon confertus, Pinus contorta, Prunella vulgaris, Prunus virginiana, Ribes divaricatum, R. inerme, R. oxyacanthoides, Rosa acicularis, R. gymnocarpa, R. nutkana, R. pisocarpa, R. woodsii, Shepherdia canadensis, Spiraea betulifolia, S. ×pyramidata*
Bread & Cake: *Amelanchier alnifolia, Balsamorhiza sagittata, Claytonia lanceolata, Gaultheria shallon, Lewisia rediviva, Oemleria cerasiformis, Rubus idaeus, Shepherdia canadensis, Vaccinium ovalifolium, V. parvifolium*
Candy: *Agoseris glauca, Erythronium grandiflorum, Larix occidentalis, Lonicera ciliosa, Pinus contorta, Polypodium glycyrrhiza, P. hesperium, Shepherdia canadensis*
Dessert: *Balsamorhiza sagittata, Cornus sericea, Lycopus uniflorus, Opuntia fragilis, O. polyacantha, Prunus emarginata*
Dried Food: *Allium cernuum, Amelanchier alnifolia, Balsamorhiza sagittata, Cirsium edule, C. hookerianum, C. undulatum, C. vulgare, Cornus sericea, Crataegus douglasii, Erythronium grandiflorum, Fragaria vesca, F. virginiana, Fritillaria lanceolata, Heracleum maximum, Lewisia rediviva,*

Lilium columbianum, Lomatium dissectum, L. macrocarpum, L. nudicaule, Mahonia aquifolium, Nuphar lutea, Pinus albicaulis, P. contorta, Prunus virginiana, Ribes lacustre, R. sanguineum, Rubus idaeus, R. leucodermis, R. spectabilis, R. ursinus, Sagittaria latifolia, Sambucus cerulea, Sium suave, Sorbus sitchensis, Vaccinium cespitosum, V. deliciosum, V. membranaceum, V. ovalifolium, V. scoparium, Viburnum edule
Fodder: *Astragalus giganteus, A. miser, Carex atherodes, C. obnupta, C. rostrata, Castilleja miniata, Elymus trachycaulus, Epilobium angustifolium, Trifolium pratense, Vicia americana*
Forage: *Aquilegia formosa, Arctostaphylos uva-ursi, Astragalus purshii, Carex atherodes, C. obnupta, C. rostrata, Ceanothus velutinus, Hackelia diffusa, Heracleum maximum, Hydrophyllum fendleri, H. occidentale, Lathyrus nevadensis, Lonicera ciliosa, L. involucrata, Maianthemum racemosum, Oxytropis campestris, Paxistima myrsinites, Penstemon fruticosus, Phragmites australis, Populus balsamifera, P. tremuloides, Ribes hudsonianum, Rosa acicularis, R. woodsii, Shepherdia canadensis, Sium suave, Spiraea douglasii, Valeriana dioica, V. sitchensis*
Frozen Food: *Amelanchier alnifolia, Heracleum maximum, Lomatium nudicaule, Ribes lacustre, Rubus idaeus, Vaccinium membranaceum*
Fruit: *Amelanchier alnifolia, Arctostaphylos uva-ursi, Citrus limon, C. medica, C. sinensis, Cornus sericea, Crataegus columbiana, C. douglasii, Cucumis melo, Disporum hookeri, Fragaria vesca, F. virginiana, Gaultheria shallon, Lomatium nudicaule, Lonicera involucrata, Mahonia aquifolium, Maianthemum racemosum, M. stellatum, Malus fusca, Oemleria cerasiformis, Prunus emarginata, P. virginiana, Ribes cereum, R. divaricatum, R. hudsonianum, R. inerme, R. oxyacanthoides, R. sanguineum, Rosa gymnocarpa, Rubus idaeus, R. leucodermis, R. parviflorus, R. pedatus, R. spectabilis, R. ursinus, Sambucus cerulea, S. racemosa,*

Shepherdia argentea, S. canadensis, Sorbus sitchensis, Streptopus amplexifolius, Vaccinium membranaceum, V. myrtillus, V. ovalifolium, V. ovatum, V. oxycoccos, V. parvifolium, Viburnum edule, V. opulus

Pie & Pudding: Amelanchier alnifolia, Erythronium grandiflorum, Gaultheria shallon, Lewisia rediviva, Lomatium macrocarpum, Ribes divaricatum, R. inerme, R. oxyacanthoides, Vaccinium cespitosum, V. deliciosum, V. myrtilloides, V. scoparium

Porridge: Pinus albicaulis, P. ponderosa

Preservative: Rhododendron albiflorum

Preserves: Amelanchier alnifolia, Crataegus douglasii, Gaultheria shallon, Mahonia aquifolium, M. nervosa, Ribes lacustre, Rosa acicularis, R. woodsii, Rubus idaeus, Sambucus cerulea, Shepherdia canadensis, Vaccinium cespitosum, V. deliciosum, V. membranaceum, V. parvifolium, V. scoparium, Viburnum edule

Sauce & Relish: Acer macrophyllum, Prunus virginiana, Rosa acicularis, R. woodsii, Viburnum edule

Snack Food: Corylus cornuta

Soup: Arctostaphylos uva-ursi, Cirsium edule, Erythronium grandiflorum, Lilium columbianum, Sambucus racemosa, Sorbus sitchensis, Viburnum edule

Special Food: Allium cernuum, Lewisia rediviva

Spice: Amelanchier alnifolia, Fragaria vesca, Fritillaria lanceolata, Lilium columbianum, Lomatium macrocarpum, L. nudicaule, Maianthemum racemosum, Penstemon fruticosus, Ribes sanguineum, Sambucus cerulea, S. racemosa, Sorbus sitchensis

Staple: Balsamorhiza sagittata, Pteridium aquilinum

Starvation Food: Balsamorhiza sagittata, Opuntia fragilis, O. polyacantha

Sweetener: Amelanchier alnifolia, Pseudotsuga menziesii, Rubus parviflorus

Unspecified: Abies lasiocarpa, Acer macrophyllum, Alectoria jubata, Allium acuminatum, A. cernuum, Amelanchier alnifolia, Argentina anserina, Astragalus miser, Balsamorhiza sagittata, Calochortus macrocarpus,

Camassia quamash, C. scilloides, Carex rostrata, Cirsium edule, C. hookerianum, C. undulatum, C. vulgare, Claytonia lanceolata, Cornus sericea, Corylus cornuta, Crataegus columbiana, C. douglasii, Dryopteris arguta, D. expansa, Epilobium angustifolium, Erythronium grandiflorum, Fritillaria lanceolata, F. pudica, Heracleum maximum, Hieracium sp., Hydrophyllum fendleri, H. occidentale, Larix occidentalis, Lewisia columbiana, L. pygmaea, L. rediviva, Lilium columbianum, Lithospermum incisum, Lomatium dissectum, L. macrocarpum, L. nudicaule, Lycopus uniflorus, Maianthemum racemosum, Mentha arvensis, Opuntia fragilis, O. polyacantha, Osmorhiza berteroi, Peucedanum sp., Picea engelmannii, Pinus albicaulis, P. contorta, P. monticola, P. ponderosa, Polystichum munitum, Prunus virginiana, Pteridium aquilinum, Rosa acicularis, R. nutkana, R. pisocarpa, R. woodsii, Rubus leucodermis, R. occidentalis, R. parviflorus, R. spectabilis, R. ursinus, Rumex acetosella, Sagittaria latifolia, Sium suave, Tragopogon porrifolius, Triteleia grandiflora, Typha latifolia, Viburnum edule, Zizania aquatica

Vegetable: Acer macrophyllum, Capsella bursa-pastoris, Chenopodium album, Heracleum maximum, Lomatium nudicaule, Maianthemum racemosum, Urtica dioica

Winter Use Food: Amelanchier alnifolia, Claytonia lanceolata, Heracleum maximum, Lewisia columbiana, L. rediviva, Lomatium nudicaule, Opuntia fragilis, O. polyacantha, Pinus albicaulis, Prunus virginiana, Shepherdia argentea, Sorbus sitchensis, Vaccinium cespitosum, V. deliciosum, V. scoparium

Thompson, Lower
Ice Cream: Shepherdia canadensis

Thompson, Upper (Lytton Band)
Fruit: Ribes sanguineum
Unspecified: Triteleia grandiflora

Thompson, Upper (Nicola Band)

Unspecified: *Lewisia columbiana, Peucedanum* sp., *Tragopogon porrifolius*

Thompson, Upper (Spences Bridge)

Unspecified: *Tragopogon porrifolius, Triteleia grandiflora*

Tolowa

Beverage: *Ledum glandulosum, Satureja douglasii*
Bread & Cake: *Arctostaphylos ×cinerea, A. nevadensis, A. uva-ursi*
Dried Food: *Corylus cornuta, Vaccinium ovatum, V. parvifolium*
Fruit: *Fragaria chiloensis, Gaultheria shallon, Oemleria cerasiformis, Quercus kelloggii, Ribes lobbii, Rubus spectabilis, Umbellularia californica, Vaccinium ovatum, V. parvifolium*
Spice: *Ribes nevadense*
Staple: *Lithocarpus densiflorus*
Unspecified: *Castanopsis chrysophylla, Corylus cornuta, Heracleum maximum, Ligusticum californicum, Lysichiton americanus, Nuphar lutea, Oxalis oregana, Porphyra lanceolata, Rubus spectabilis*

Tsimshian

Fruit: *Empetrum nigrum, Rubus parviflorus, Vaccinium vitis-idaea*

Tubatulabal

Beverage: *Monardella candicans*
Candy: *Asclepias erosa*
Fruit: *Juniperus osteosperma, Lycium torreyi, Ribes quercetorum, Sambucus cerulea, Solanum nigrum, Vitis californica*
Unspecified: *Aesculus californica, Allium hyalinum, A. lacunosum, A. peninsulare, Calochortus palmeri, C. venustus, Cirsium occidentale, Coreopsis bigelovii, Distichlis spicata, Echinochloa crus-galli, Ephedra viridis, Heliotropium curassavicum, Lotus scoparius, Mentzelia albicaulis, M. gracilenta, Monardella candicans, Nolina bigelovii, Opuntia basilaris, O. caseyi, Pellaea mucro-*

nata, Pholistoma membranaceum, Pinus monophylla, P. sabiniana, Polypogon monspeliensis, Quercus chrysolepis, Q. douglasii, Q. dumosa, Q. kelloggii, Q. lobata, Q. wislizeni, Salvia carduacea, S. columbariae, Scirpus acutus, Sedum laxum, Sisymbrium officinale, Trifolium wormskioldii, Typha latifolia, Yucca brevifolia, Y. whipplei
Vegetable: *Rorippa nasturtium-aquaticum*

Umatilla

Unspecified: *Perideridia gairdneri*

Ute

Dried Food: *Amelanchier alnifolia*
Fruit: *Amelanchier alnifolia, Rhus trilobata, Ribes aureum, Rosa woodsii, Shepherdia argentea*
Staple: *Agastache pallidiflora, Agave americana, A. parryi*
Starvation Food: *Calochortus nuttallii*
Unspecified: *Allium acuminatum, A. bisceptrum, Balsamorhiza sagittata, Calochortus nuttallii, Claytonia caroliniana, Cymopterus longipes, Elymus canadensis, Fritillaria pudica, Perideridia gairdneri, Scirpus tabernaemontani, Taraxacum officinale*

Wailaki

Candy: *Pinus sabiniana*
Forage: *Robinia pseudoacacia, Trifolium ciliolatum*
Fruit: *Arbutus menziesii*
Unspecified: *Trifolium ciliolatum*

Walapai

Beverage: *Yucca baccata*
Dried Food: *Yucca baccata*

Warihio

Beverage: *Panicum sonorum*
Staple: *Panicum sonorum*

Washo

Dried Food: *Pinus monophylla*
Fruit: *Rosa nutkana*
Porridge: *Pinus monophylla*

Wet'suwet'en

Dried Food: *Pinus contorta*
Sweetener: *Tsuga heterophylla*
Unspecified: *Epilobium angustifolium, Heracleum maximum, Picea glauca, Pinus contorta, Sedum divergens, Tsuga heterophylla*
Winter Use Food: *Tsuga heterophylla*

Winnebago

Beverage: *Agastache foeniculum, Ceanothus americanus, Fragaria vesca, F. virginiana, Mentha canadensis*
Candy: *Silphium laciniatum*
Dried Food: *Pediomelum esculentum, Prunus americana, Shepherdia argentea, Vitis cinerea, V. vulpina*
Fruit: *Amelanchier alnifolia, Crataegus chrysocarpa, Fragaria vesca, F. virginiana, Prunus americana, Ribes missouriense, Shepherdia argentea, Viburnum lentago, Vitis cinerea, V. vulpina*
Sauce & Relish: *Allium canadense, Prunus americana*
Soup: *Carya ovata, Corylus americana, Juglans nigra, Nelumbo lutea*
Spice: *Allium canadense*
Staple: *Zizania aquatica*
Starvation Food: *Crataegus chrysocarpa*
Sweetener: *Acer negundo, A. saccharinum, Agastache foeniculum, Carya ovata*
Unspecified: *Allium canadense, Amphicarpaea bracteata, Apios americana, Carya ovata, Corylus americana, Erythronium mesochoreum, Gymnocladus dioicus, Helianthus tuberosus, Juglans nigra, Linum lewisii, Nelumbo lutea, Pediomelum esculentum, Quercus macrocarpa, Sagittaria latifolia*
Vegetable: *Asclepias syriaca*

Wintoon

Dried Food: *Quercus chrysolepis*
Fruit: *Arctostaphylos patula, A. viscida, Prunus subcordata, P. virginiana, Rhus trilobata, Rubus parviflorus, R. vitifolius, Sambucus cerulea, Vitis californica*
Unspecified: *Quercus chrysolepis, Q. lobata*

Yana

Bread & Cake: *Quercus douglasii*
Dried Food: *Quercus douglasii*
Porridge: *Quercus douglasii*
Spice: *Sidalcea malviflora*
Staple: *Aesculus californica, Quercus douglasii*
Unspecified: *Angelica tomentosa*, Apiaceae sp., *Brodiaea minor, Clarkia rhomboidea, Helianthella californica, Lilium pardalinum, Perideridia gairdneri, P. pringlei, Triteleia grandiflora*

Yaqui

Vegetable: *Sonchus oleraceus*

Yavapai

Beverage: *Arctostaphylos pungens, Carnegia gigantea, Juglans major, Juniperus deppeana, J. osteosperma, Psoralidium tenuiflorum, Rhus trilobata, Yucca baccata, Ziziphus obtusifolia*
Bread & Cake: *Carnegia gigantea, Juniperus deppeana, J. osteosperma, Olneya tesota*
Cooking Agent: *Quercus emoryi, Q. gambelii*
Dried Food: *Carnegia gigantea, Yucca baccata*
Fruit: *Arctostaphylos pungens, Carnegia gigantea, Echinocereus engelmannii, Mahonia fremontii, Morus microphylla, Opuntia chlorotica, O. echinocarpa, O. erinacea, Rhus ovata, Ribes aureum, Yucca baccata*
Preserves: *Simmondsia chinensis*
Snack Food: *Fouquieria splendens*
Staple: *Juniperus deppeana, J. osteosperma, Olneya tesota, Prosopis glandulosa*
Starvation Food: *Rumex crispus*
Unspecified: *Celtis laevigata, Cirsium neomexicanum, Cordylanthus sp., Echinocereus engelmannii, Juglans major, Prosopis glandulosa, Quercus gambelii, Rhus trilobata, Salvia columbariae, Yucca baccata*
Vegetable: *Scrophularia* sp.
Winter Use Food: *Juglans major, Quercus emoryi*

Yokia

Unspecified: *Asclepias fascicularis, Trifolium ciliolatum*
Vegetable: *Lathyrus jepsonii*

Yokut

Dried Food: *Sambucus cerulea*
Fruit: *Rhus trilobata*
Unspecified: *Quercus douglasii, Q. kelloggii, Q. lobata*
Winter Use Food: *Sambucus cerulea*

Yuki

Beverage: *Arctostaphylos manzanita, Mentha spicata*
Bread & Cake: *Hordeum vulgare, Lithocarpus densiflorus, Quercus kelloggii, Q. lobata*
Candy: *Pinus lambertiana*
Dried Food: *Rubus leucodermis, Sambucus cerulea*
Forage: *Chlorogalum pomeridianum*
Fruit: *Arbutus menziesii, Arctostaphylos manzanita, Prunus virginiana, Rubus leucodermis, Sambucus cerulea*
Porridge: *Lithocarpus densiflorus, Quercus kelloggii, Q. lobata*
Soup: *Lithocarpus densiflorus, Sambucus cerulea*
Spice: *Wyethia angustifolia*
Staple: *Arctostaphylos manzanita, Lolium temulentum, Pogogyne douglasii*
Substitution Food: *Hordeum vulgare, Linanthus ciliatus, Pseudotsuga menziesii*
Unspecified: *Aesculus californica, Allium unifolium, Calochortus tolmiei, Camassia leichtlinii, C. quamash, Corylus cornuta, Cynoglossum grande, Dichelostemma pulchellum, Dodecatheon hendersonii, Heracleum maximum, Lomatium californicum, Perideridia kelloggii, Triteleia laxa, Umbellularia californica*
Vegetable: *Plagiobothrys nothofulvus*

Yuma

Beverage: *Lycium exsertum, L. fremontii, Prosopis glandulosa, Salix gooddingii*
Bread & Cake: *Olneya tesota, Prosopis glandulosa, Typha latifolia*
Dried Food: *Cucurbita moschata, Lycium exsertum, L. fremontii, Olneya tesota, Prosopis glandulosa, Typha latifolia*
Fruit: *Physalis hederifolia, P. pubescens*
Porridge: *Atriplex lentiformis, Echinochloa crus-galli, Lycium exsertum, L. fremontii, Typha latifolia*
Spice: *Typha latifolia*
Staple: *Agastache pallidiflora, Agave americana, A. parryi, Allenrolfea occidentalis, Amaranthus palmeri, Echinochloa crus-galli, Panicum hirticaule, Prosopis glandulosa*
Starvation Food: *Baccharis salicifolia, Parkinsonia florida, P. microphylla*
Unspecified: *Amaranthus palmeri, Ammannia coccinea, Atriplex lentiformis, A. polycarpa, Echinochloa crus-galli, Hesperocallis undulata, Phragmites australis, Prosopis glandulosa, Salix gooddingii, Typha latifolia*
Vegetable: *Amaranthus palmeri*
Winter Use Food: *Amaranthus palmeri*

Yurok

Beverage: *Ledum glandulosum, Marah oreganus, Pseudotsuga menziesii, Rubus vitifolius*
Bread & Cake: *Lithocarpus densiflorus*
Candy: *Asclepias cordifolia, Pseudotsuga menziesii*
Cooking Agent: *Dryopteris arguta*
Fruit: *Arbutus menziesii, Arctostaphylos ×cinerea, A. uva-ursi, Fragaria chiloensis, F. vesca, Gaultheria shallon, Heteromeles arbutifolia, Prunus virginiana, Quercus kelloggii, Ribes roezlii, Rubus leucodermis, R. parviflorus, R. spectabilis, R. vitifolius, Sambucus cerulea, S. racemosa, Umbellularia californica, Vaccinium parvifolium, V. scoparium, Vitis californica*
Soup: *Lithocarpus densiflorus*
Staple: *Lithocarpus densiflorus*
Unspecified: *Aquilegia formosa, Armillaria ponderosa, Boschniakia strobilacea, Castanopsis chrysophylla, Claytonia sibirica, Corylus cornuta, Equisetum telmateia, Heracleum maximum, Lysichiton americanus, Oxalis oregana, Porphyra lanceolata, Umbellularia californica*
Vegetable: *Brodiaea elegans*

Yurok, South Coast (Nererner)

Staple: *Lithocarpus densiflorus*

Zuni

Beverage: *Coreopsis tinctoria, Ephedra nevadensis, Solanum elaeagnifolium, Triticum aestivum, Zea mays*

Bread & Cake: *Amaranthus blitoides, Artemisia carruthii, Chenopodium leptophyllum, Triticum aestivum, Xanthium strumarium, Zea mays*

Candy: *Chamaesyce serpyllifolia, Dalea lasiathera, Hymenopappus filifolius, Lactuca tatarica, Populus angustifolia, P. deltoides*

Cooking Agent: *Amaranthus cruentus*

Dried Food: *Astragalus lentiginosus, Cleome serrulata, Cucurbita pepo, Opuntia whipplei*

Forage: *Asclepias involucrata*

Fruit: *Lycium pallidum, Opuntia whipplei, Physalis longifolia, Ribes cereum, Yucca baccata*

Porridge: *Atriplex powellii, Cycloloma atriplicifolium, Opuntia whipplei, Zea mays*

Preserves: *Yucca baccata*

Sauce & Relish: *Coriandrum sativum, Physalis hederifolia, Solanum triflorum, Yucca baccata*

Snack Food: *Zea mays*

Special Food: *Cucurbita pepo*

Spice: *Dalea lasiathera*

Staple: *Cycloloma atriplicifolium, Oryzopsis hymenoides, Zea mays*

Sweetener: *Chamaesyce serpyllifolia, Yucca baccata*

Unspecified: *Artemisia carruthii, Asclepias subverticillata, Astragalus lentiginosus, Chenopodium leptophyllum, Cleome serrulata, Cucurbita pepo, Oenothera triloba, Oryzopsis hymenoides, Populus angustifolia, P. deltoides, Ribes cereum, Solanum fendleri, Yucca glauca*

Vegetable: *Chenopodium album, C. leptophyllum, Coriandrum sativum, Phaseolus vulgaris*

Winter Use Food: *Pinus edulis*

Index of Plant Usages

Plants are listed under the categories of food usage and then alphabetically by the particular usage. Plants are identified below to the level of genus. For all usages given below, check all entries under that genus in the Catalog of Plants. For example, one may find Fruit below and see that *Aronia* was used by the Abnaki and Potawatomi. The specific ethnobotanical information and the sources from which the information was obtained may be found by turning to *Aronia* in the Catalog of Plants and examining Fruit under the entries for that genus.

Appetizer

Asclepias: Chippewa
Mahonia: Kutenai
Rhus: Acoma; Laguna
Trillium: Okanagan-Colville

Baby Food

Calochortus: Navajo
Carya: Iroquois
Dichelostemma: Pima, Gila River
Juglans: Iroquois
Mammillaria: Pima, Gila River
Physalis: Pima, Gila River
Pinus: Cahuilla
Sarcostemma: Pima, Gila River
Washingtonia: Pima, Gila River
Zea: Iroquois

Beverage

Abies: Micmac; Shuswap; Thompson
Acer: Iroquois; Micmac; Ojibwa; Potawatomi
Achillea: Blackfoot
Acorus: Micmac
Agastache: Cheyenne; Cree, Woodlands; Dakota; Lakota; Omaha; Pawnee; Ponca; Winnebago

Agave: Apache, Western; Apache, White Mountain; Havasupai; Navajo; Yavapai
Alisma: Iroquois
Allenrolfea: Cahuilla
Aloysia: Havasupai
Amelanchier: Cheyenne; Lakota; Montana Indian; Thompson
Amorpha: Oglala
Anaphalis: Anticosti
Andromeda: Ojibwa; Tanana, Upper
Androsace: Isleta
Anthemis: Navajo
Arabis: Cheyenne
Aralia: Algonquin, Quebec; Bella Coola; Iroquois; Micmac; Montagnais
Arbutus: Miwok
Arctostaphylos: Atsugewi; Blackfoot; Cahuilla; Costanoan; Costanoan (Olhonean); Hualapai; Karok; Kawaiisu; Mendocino Indian; Mewuk; Miwok; Navajo; Thompson; Yavapai; Yuki
Artemisia: Apache, Chiricahua & Mescalero; Apache, White Mountain
Baccharis: Papago
Balsamorhiza: Paiute
Beta: Anticosti
Betula: Iroquois; Malecite; Ojibwa
Bidens: Hopi
Camassia: Flathead
Camellia: Haisla & Hanaksiala; Oweekeno
Carex: Klamath
Carnegia: Apache, Western; Maricopa; Papago; Pima; Pima, Gila River; Yavapai
Carya: Iroquois
Castanea: Iroquois
Castanopsis: Paiute
Castilleja: Miwok
Ceanothus: Dakota; Lakota; Menominee; Meskwaki; Omaha; Pawnee; Ponca; Winnebago

Chamaedaphne: Ojibwa
Chamaesyce: Apache, White Mountain
Cheilanthes: Apache, Chiricahua & Mescalero; Kawaiisu
Chimaphila: Thompson
Comarum: Eskimo, Alaska
Comptonia: Chippewa
Cordyline: Hawaiian
Coreopsis: Lakota; Zuni
Corylus: Iroquois
Crataegus: Omaha
Dalea: Navajo; Oglala
Dasylirion: Apache, Chiricahua & Mescalero; Apache, Mescalero
Datura: Apache, White Mountain; Papago; Pima
Descurainia: Havasupai; Kawaiisu; Paiute; Paiute, Northern; Papago; Pima; Pima, Gila River
Diospyros: Rappahannock
Distichlis: Kawaiisu
Echinocereus: Isleta
Elaeagnus: Cree
Empetrum: Koyukon
Ephedra: Apache, White Mountain; Cahuilla; Coahuilla; Havasupai; Kawaiisu; Navajo; Paiute; Paiute, Northern; Papago; Pima; Pima, Lehi; Shoshoni; Zuni
Epilobium: Clallam; Saanich
Equisetum: Blackfoot; Nitinaht
Eriodictyon: Cahuilla; Karok
Eriogonum: Blackfoot; Havasupai; Kawaiisu
Fagus: Iroquois
Ferocactus: Apache, San Carlos; Cahuilla; Papago; Pima; Seri
Ficus: Havasupai
Fouquieria: Cahuilla
Fragaria: Blackfoot; Cowlitz; Salish, Coast; Winnebago
Gaultheria: Abnaki; Algonquin, Quebec; Cherokee; Chippewa; Makah; Ojibwa
Geum: Thompson
Gleditsia: Cherokee
Gymnocladus: Meskwaki
Hamamelis: Cherokee
Hedeoma: Apache, Chiricahua & Mescalero
Hedysarum: Tanana, Upper
Holodiscus: Isleta
Hydrangea: Cherokee

Hymenopappus: Hopi; Isleta; Jemez
Hymenoxys: Hopi
Ilex: Comanche
Ipomopsis: Hopi
Iris: Eskimo, Alaska
Jacquemontia: Hawaiian
Juglans: Iroquois; Yavapai
Juncus: Paiute, Northern
Juniperus: Anticosti; Apache, Western; Havasupai; Jemez; Lakota; Ojibwa; Okanagan-Colville; Thompson; Yavapai
Kalmia: Hanaksiala
Larix: Anticosti
Lathyrus: Eskimo, Alaska
Ledum: Alaska Native; Algonquin, Quebec; Anticosti; Bella Coola; Chippewa; Cree; Cree, Woodlands; Eskimo, Alaska; Eskimo, Arctic; Eskimo, Inupiat; Haisla & Hanaksiala; Hesquiat; Kitasoo; Kwakiutl, Southern; Makah; Malecite; Micmac; Nitinaht; Ojibwa; Okanagan-Colville; Oweekeno; Pomo, Kashaya; Potawatomi; Saanich; Salish, Coast; Shuswap; Tanana, Upper; Thompson; Tolowa; Yurok
Lepidium: Kawaiisu
Lespedeza: Comanche
Lindera: Cherokee; Chippewa
Liquidambar: Cherokee
Lithospermum: Blackfoot; Shoshoni
Lomatium: Great Basin Indian; Thompson
Lycium: Havasupai; Kawaiisu; Mohave; Navajo; Pima; Yuma
Mahonia: Hualapai; Montana Indian
Maianthemum: Hanaksiala
Marah: Yurok
Martynia: Apache, Western
Mentha: Blackfoot; Cheyenne; Chippewa; Cree, Woodlands; Dakota; Gosiute; Kawaiisu; Klamath; Lakota; Miwok; Ojibwa; Okanagan-Colville; Omaha; Paiute; Pawnee; Ponca; Sanpoil; Sanpoil & Nespelem; Shuswap; Winnebago; Yuki
Mirabilis: Navajo, Ramah
Mitchella: Micmac
Monarda: Apache, Chiricahua & Mescalero; Iroquois
Monardella: Diegueño; Kawaiisu; Luiseño;

Miwok; Okanagan-Colville; Sanpoil & Nespelem; Tubatulabal

Morus: Cherokee

Nepeta: Ojibwa

Nicotiana: Cahuilla

Nuphar: Algonquin, Tête-de-Boule

Opuntia: Havasupai; Hualapai; Lakota; Navajo; Papago

Osmorhiza: Isleta

Panicum: Warihio

Paronychia: Kiowa

Parthenium: Apache, Chiricahua & Mescalero

Passiflora: Cherokee

Pellaea: Diegueño; Kawaiisu; Luiseño

Peniocereus: Papago

Penstemon: Navajo; Thompson

Pentaphylloides: Eskimo, Alaska; Eskimo, Arctic

Phoradendron: Cahuilla; Navajo

Phytolacca: Cherokee

Picea: Anticosti; Chippewa; Micmac; Okanagan-Colville

Pinus: Cahuilla; Hualapai; Micmac; Thompson

Plantago: Pima, Gila River

Platanus: Kawaiisu

Polygonum: Eskimo, Arctic; Eskimo, Inupiat

Prosopis: Apache, Chiricahua & Mescalero; Apache, Mescalero; Apache, Western; Cahuilla; Havasupai; Maricopa; Mohave; Pima; Pima, Gila River; Yuma

Prunella: Thompson

Prunus: Algonquin, Quebec; Blackfoot; Cherokee; Chippewa; Havasupai; Iroquois; Lakota; Menominee; Meskwaki; Micmac; Montana Indian; Ojibwa; Paiute; Potawatomi; Sanpoil & Nespelem; Shuswap; Thompson

Pseudocymopterus: Isleta

Pseudotsuga: Karok; Yurok

Psoralidium: Yavapai

Pyrola: Malecite

Quercus: Apache, White Mountain; Iroquois; Kiowa; Menominee; Meskwaki

Ratibida: Dakota; Oglala

Rhexia: Montagnais

Rhododendron: Okanagan-Colville

Rhus: Algonquin, Quebec; Apache, Western; Atsugewi; Cahuilla; Diegueño; Great Basin Indian; Havasupai; Hopi; Hualapai; Iroquois;

Keres, Western; Kiowa; Menominee; Meskwaki; Navajo; Ojibwa; Okanagan-Colville; Shoshoni; Yavapai

Ribes: Cree, Woodlands; Spanish American; Thompson

Robinia: Cherokee

Romneya: Cahuilla

Rosa: Alaska Native; Arapaho; Cahuilla; Eskimo, Inupiat; Haisla & Hanaksiala; Lakota; Lummi; Makah; Shuswap; Skagit; Skagit, Upper; Tanana, Upper; Thompson; Washo

Rubus: Cahuilla; Cherokee; Chippewa; Dakota; Haisla & Hanaksiala; Iroquois; Meskwaki; Omaha; Oweekeno; Pawnee; Ponca; Quileute; Saanich; Yurok

Rumex: Hanaksiala; Hualapai

Sadleria: Hawaiian

Salix: Eskimo, Inupiat; Mohave; Navajo; Yuma

Salvia: Cahuilla; Kawaiisu; Mohave; Papago; Pima; Pima, Gila River

Sambucus: Bella Coola; Cherokee; Dakota; Haisla & Hanaksiala; Montana Indian; Omaha; Pawnee; Pima, Gila River; Ponca

Sassafras: Cherokee; Chippewa

Satureja: Diegueño; Luiseño; Pomo, Kashaya; Saanich; Tolowa

Sedum: Eskimo, Alaska

Senna: Kiowa

Shepherdia: Flathead; Northwest Indian; Okanagon; Oregon Indian; Shuswap; Thompson

Simmondsia: Cahuilla; Coahuilla

Sisymbrium: Pima, Gila River

Solanum: Zuni

Sphaeralcea: Navajo, Kayenta

Sphagnum: Carrier

Spiraea: Abnaki; Tanana, Upper; Thompson

Stenocereus: Papago; Papago & Pima

Taraxacum: Iroquois

Taxus: Iroquois; Penobscot

Thelesperma: Apache, Chiricahua & Mescalero; Hopi; Isleta; Keres, Western; Keresan; Navajo, Ramah; Tewa

Theobroma: Haisla & Hanaksiala

Thuja: Chippewa; Ojibwa

Tragopogon: Navajo

Trichostema: Kawaiisu

Trifolium: Anticosti; Miwok

Triglochin: Klamath

Triticum: Zuni
Tsuga: Chippewa; Iroquois; Micmac; Ojibwa
Ulmus: Cheyenne; Kiowa
Umbellularia: Concow
Urtica: Shuswap
Vaccinium: Clallam; Eskimo, Arctic; Hesquiat; Quinault
Verbena: Omaha
Viburnum: Eskimo, Inupiat
Vitis: Apache, Western; Cahuilla; Cherokee; Hualapai; Pawnee
Washingtonia: Cahuilla; Cocopa
Yucca: Acoma; Apache; Apache, Mescalero; Havasupai; Hualapai; Keres, Western; Laguna; Pima; Southwest Indians; Walapai; Yavapai
Zea: Iroquois; Isleta; Menominee; Navajo; Tewa; Zuni
Ziziphus: Papago; Yavapai

Bread & Cake

Acacia: Havasupai
Acer: Iroquois
Aesculus: Kawaiisu
Agave: Apache, Mescalero
Allenrolfea: Cahuilla
Allium: Paiute, Northern
Amaranthus: Apache, Chiricahua & Mescalero; Havasupai; Navajo; Navajo, Ramah; Zuni
Amelanchier: Alaska Native; Iroquois; Montana Indian; Okanagon; Sanpoil & Nespelem; Thompson
Amphicarpaea: Cherokee
Amsinckia: Atsugewi
Anemopsis: Kamia
Apios: Delaware
Arctostaphylos: Atsugewi; Numlaki; Tolowa
Artemisia: Navajo; Zuni
Asimina: Iroquois
Atriplex: Pima
Balsamorhiza: Atsugewi; Thompson
Blennosperma: Neeshenam
Boisduvalia: Mendocino Indian
Bouteloua: Apache, White Mountain
Bromus: Neeshenam
Camassia: Blackfoot; Montana Indian; Sanpoil & Nespelem
Camelina: Apache, Chiricahua & Mescalero
Capsella: Apache, Chiricahua & Mescalero

Carnegia: Apache, San Carlos; Apache, Western; Papago; Pima; Yavapai
Carya: Iroquois
Castanea: Cherokee; Iroquois
Celtis: Apache, Chiricahua & Mescalero
Chenopodium: Atsugewi; Havasupai; Hopi; Navajo; Navajo, Ramah; Zuni
Cirsium: Apache, Chiricahua & Mescalero
Citrullus: Iroquois
Claytonia: Thompson
Cleome: Isleta; Jemez; Navajo
Coix: Cherokee
Corylus: Iroquois
Crataegus: Apache, Chiricahua & Mescalero; Chippewa; Coeur d'Alene; Iroquois; Okanagan-Colville
Cucumis: Cocopa; Iroquois
Cucurbita: Apache, White Mountain; Iroquois
Cupressus: Navajo
Cymopterus: Hualapai
Dasylirion: Apache, Chiricahua & Mescalero; Apache, Mescalero; Southwest Indians
Descurainia: Apache, Chiricahua & Mescalero; Atsugewi; Navajo, Ramah
Dyssodia: Apache, Chiricahua & Mescalero
Echinocereus: Isleta
Eriogonum: Hopi
Fagus: Iroquois
Fragaria: Iroquois
Gaultheria: Bella Coola; Clallam; Iroquois; Klallam; Makah; Okanagon; Quileute; Quinault; Salish, Coast; Samish; Skagit; Skokomish; Snohomish; Swinomish; Thompson
Gaylussacia: Cherokee; Iroquois
Gossypium: Papago
Helianthus: Apache, Chiricahua & Mescalero; Apache, Western; Havasupai; Montana Indian; Navajo
Hordeum: Yuki
Humulus: Algonquin, Quebec
Hymenopappus: Hopi
Juglans: Iroquois
Juniperus: Kawaiisu; Yavapai
Koeleria: Havasupai; Isleta
Lepidium: Havasupai
Lewisia: Thompson
Lilium: Okanagan-Colville

Breakfast Food

Candy

Amaranthus: Acoma; Laguna; Papago; Pima, Gila River

Ambrosia: Papago

Amelanchier: Alaska Native; Atsugewi; Blackfoot; Cahuilla; Carrier; Chippewa; Cree, Plains; Cree, Woodlands; Gosiute; Great Basin Indian; Hanaksiala; Iroquois; Karok; Lummi; Navajo; Ojibwa; Okanagan-Colville; Paiute; Potawatomi; Skagit, Upper; Swinomish; Thompson; Ute

Arbutus: Karok

Arctium: Iroquois

Arctostaphylos: Blackfoot; Cahuilla; Chinook, Lower; Coeur d'Alene; Costanoan; Hualapai; Karok; Kimsquit; Montana Indian; Paiute; Pomo; Pomo, Kashaya; Sanpoil & Nespelem

Argentina: Kwakiutl, Southern; Nitinaht

Asimina: Iroquois

Astragalus: Zuni

Atriplex: Pima

Balsamorhiza: Okanagan-Colville; Paiute; Thompson

Calochortus: Cheyenne; Gosiute; Paiute, Northern

Camassia: Klamath; Nisqually; Nitinaht; Okanagan-Colville; Paiute; Salish, Coast

Capsicum: Hopi

Carnegia: Apache, Western; Papago; Pima; Pima, Gila River; Yavapai

Carya: Cherokee

Castanopsis: Pomo

Celtis: Hualapai

Chamaesyce: Apache, White Mountain

Chenopodium: Eskimo, Inupiat; Miwok; Navajo

Cicer: Papago

Cirsium: Thompson

Citrullus: Cocopa; Iroquois; Navajo

Cleome: Navajo; Navajo, Ramah; Zuni

Cornus: Haisla & Hanaksiala; Thompson

Corylus: Tolowa

Costaria: Hesquiat

Crataegus: Cheyenne; Iroquois; Paiute; Sanpoil & Nespelem; Thompson

Cucumis: Cocopa; Hopi; Iroquois; Navajo

Cucurbita: Cahuilla; Cocopa; Havasupai; Hopi; Iroquois; Maricopa; Navajo; Ojibwa; Papago; Pima; Yuma; Zuni

Cymopterus: Navajo; Navajo, Ramah

Cyperus: Paiute, Northern

Dasylirion: Apache, Mescalero

Datura: Navajo

Daucus: Navajo; Sanpoil & Nespelem

Descurainia: Papago; Pima; Pueblo

Dichelostemma: Paiute

Echinocactus: Havasupai

Egregia: Bella Coola; Haisla & Hanaksiala; Oweekeno

Equisetum: Cowlitz; Hoh; Quileute

Eriodictyon: Diegueño

Eriogonum: Hopi

Eriophyllum: Kawaiisu

Erythronium: Kwakiutl; Kwakiutl, Southern; Okanagan-Colville; Thompson

Escobaria: Cheyenne

Ferocactus: Cahuilla; Hualapai

Ficus: Havasupai

Fragaria: Cowlitz; Iroquois; Omaha; Potawatomi; Shuswap; Skagit, Upper; Thompson

Frangula: Paiute

Fritillaria: Alaska Native; Hesquiat; Kwakiutl, Southern; Okanagan-Colville; Thompson

Fucus: Haisla & Hanaksiala; Yurok, South Coast (Nererner)

Gaultheria: Hesquiat; Iroquois; Kwakiutl, Southern; Makah; Nitinaht; Skagit, Upper

Gaylussacia: Iroquois

Gossypium: Pima

Helianthus: Havasupai; Hopi; Sanpoil & Nespelem

Heracleum: Thompson

Heteromeles: Costanoan; Luiseño

Heuchera: Miwok

Hypericum: Miwok

Juglans: Cherokee; Pomo, Kashaya

Juniperus: Apache, Western; Atsugewi; Cahuilla; Havasupai; Kawaiisu; Mendocino Indian

Lasthenia: Cahuilla

Lathyrus: Apache, Chiricahua & Mescalero

Lens: Papago

Lepidium: Papago

Lessoniopsis: Hesquiat

Lewisia: Blackfoot; Kutenai; Okanagan-Colville; Paiute; Thompson

Ligusticum: Cherokee

Lilium: Thompson

Lithocarpus: Pomo, Kashaya

Lomatium: Flathead; Klamath; Montana Indian; Okanagan-Colville; Okanagon; Paiute; Thompson

Lycium: Cahuilla; Havasupai; Kawaiisu; Mohave; Navajo; Navajo, Ramah; Paiute, Northern; Papago; Yuma

Lycopus: Chippewa

Machaeranthera: Navajo, Ramah

Macrocystis: Oweekeno

Mahonia: Skagit, Upper; Thompson

Malus: Cherokee; Hesquiat; Iroquois

Mammillaria: Apache, Chiricahua & Mescalero

Mentzelia: Hualapai; Paiute, Northern

Menyanthes: Alaska Native

Mitchella: Iroquois

Monarda: Hopi; Pueblo; Spanish American

Monolepis: Papago

Morus: Iroquois; Omaha

Nuphar: Cree, Woodlands; Klamath; Thompson

Oemleria: Cowlitz

Olneya: Mohave; Papago; Pima; Yuma

Opuntia: Acoma; Apache, Mescalero; Apache, White Mountain; Cahuilla; Cheyenne; Dakota; Diegueño; Havasupai; Hualapai; Laguna; Lakota; Luiseño; Montana Indian; Navajo; Navajo, Ramah; Papago; Pawnee; Pima; Pima, Gila River; Sanpoil & Nespelem; Yavapai; Zuni

Parkinsonia: Papago

Pectis: Hopi

Pediomelum: Blackfoot; Cheyenne; Dakota; Lakota; Montana Indian; Omaha; Pawnee; Ponca; Winnebago

Perideridia: Atsugewi; Cheyenne; Klamath; Okanagan-Colville; Paiute

Phaseolus: Iroquois; Papago

Pholisma: Cocopa; Papago

Phoradendron: Papago

Phyllospadix: Hesquiat

Physalis: Dakota; Iroquois; Omaha; Pawnee; Ponca

Phytolacca: Cherokee

Picea: Kitasoo

Pinus: Apache, Mescalero; Cahuilla; Miwok; Paiute; Paiute, Northern; Salish, Coast; Shasta; Thompson; Washo; Wet'suwet'en

Podophyllum: Iroquois

Polanisia: Pueblo

Poliomintha: Hopi; Tewa

Polygonum: Cocopa

Polypodium: Salish, Coast

Populus: Bella Coola; Clallam

Porphyra: Alaska Native; Bella Coola; Haisla & Hanaksiala; Kwakiutl, Southern; Oweekeno; Pomo; Pomo, Kashaya

Postelsia: Hesquiat; Pomo, Kashaya

Proboscidea: Havasupai; Papago

Prosopis: Apache, Chiricahua & Mescalero; Apache, Western; Cahuilla; Hualapai; Mahuna; Mohave; Papago; Yuma

Prunus: Acoma; Apache, Mescalero; Blackfoot; Cahuilla; Chippewa; Cochiti; Coeur d'Alene; Comanche; Dakota; Gosiute; Great Basin Indian; Havasupai; Hopi; Iroquois; Keresan; Klamath; Laguna; Mendocino Indian; Ojibwa; Omaha; Paiute; Paiute, Northern; Pawnee; Ponca; Round Valley Indian; San Felipe; Thompson; Winnebago

Pyrus: Iroquois

Quercus: Cahuilla; Kiowa; Pomo, Kashaya; Wintoon; Yana

Rhodymenia: Alaska Native

Rhus: Apache, Chiricahua & Mescalero; Atsugewi; Cahuilla; Havasupai; Navajo; Navajo, Ramah

Ribes: Cheyenne; Chippewa; Cowlitz; Gosiute; Iroquois; Kawaiisu; Klamath; Ojibwa; Okanagan-Colville; Omaha; Paiute; Paiute, Northern; Thompson

Robinia: Apache, Mescalero

Rosa: Lakota; Lummi

Rubus: Cahuilla; Chippewa; Coeur d'Alene; Cowlitz; Dakota; Diegueño; Haisla & Hanaksiala; Hesquiat; Iroquois; Klallam; Klamath; Kwakiutl, Southern; Mendocino Indian; Ojibwa; Okanagan-Colville; Omaha; Pawnee; Ponca; Quileute; Sanpoil & Nespelem; Skagit; Skagit, Upper; Squaxin; Thompson; Yuki

Rudbeckia: Cherokee

Sagittaria: Chippewa; Thompson

Sambucus: Bella Coola; Cahuilla; Chippewa; Haisla & Hanaksiala; Iroquois; Luiseño; Makah; Mendocino Indian; Oweekeno; Paiute; Paiute, Northern; Skagit, Upper; Thompson; Yokut; Yuki

Shepherdia: Carrier; Dakota; Haisla &

Hanaksiala; Lakota; Makah; Montana Indian; Navajo; Omaha; Paiute; Paiute, Northern; Pawnee; Ponca; Winnebago

Sium: Thompson

Sorbus: Thompson

Sporobolus: Papago

Stenocereus: Papago

Symphoricarpos: Squaxin

Thelypodium: Pueblo

Thuja: Montana Indian; Salish, Coast

Trifolium: Miwok; Nitinaht

Tsuga: Bella Coola; Haisla; Kitasoo; Oweekeno; Salish, Coast

Typha: Cree, Woodlands; Ojibwa; Paiute, Northern; Yuma

Umbellularia: Pomo, Kashaya

Vaccinium: Carrier; Chinook, Lower; Chippewa; Clallam; Coeur d'Alene; Hanaksiala; Iroquois; Kitasoo; Klallam; Klamath; Makah; Montana Indian; Nitinaht; Ojibwa; Okanagan-Colville; Paiute; Pomo; Pomo, Kashaya; Potawatomi; Quileute; Quinault; Salish, Coast; Sanpoil & Nespelem; Skagit, Upper; Thompson; Tolowa

Viburnum: Iroquois; Thompson

Vicia: Apache, Chiricahua & Mescalero; Papago

Vigna: Mohave

Vitis: Apache, Chiricahua & Mescalero; Apache, Western; Cahuilla; Comanche; Crow; Dakota; Diegueño; Hualapai; Iroquois; Kiowa; Menominee; Omaha; Pawnee; Ponca; Sioux; Winnebago

Washingtonia: Cahuilla

Yucca: Acoma; Apache, Chiricahua & Mescalero; Apache, Mescalero; Apache, San Carlos; Apache, Western; Apache, White Mountain; Cahuilla; Havasupai; Hualapai; Kawaiisu; Laguna; Navajo; Papago; Pima; Pueblo; San Felipe; Southwest Indians; Walapai; Yavapai

Zea: Delaware; Hopi; Ojibwa; Papago

Zizania: Potawatomi

Ziziphus: Maricopa; Mohave

Fodder

Acacia: Diegueño

Alectoria: Eskimo, Inuktitut

Aplectrum: Cherokee

Aristida: Navajo, Ramah

Artemisia: Navajo

Astragalus: Lakota; Thompson

Atriplex: Navajo; Navajo, Ramah

Avena: Navajo; Navajo, Ramah

Beckmannia: Navajo, Ramah

Boschniakia: Tanana, Upper

Bouteloua: Kiowa; Navajo

Bromus: Kiowa; Navajo, Ramah

Carex: Thompson

Carnegia: Papago; Pima

Castilleja: Thompson

Chamaebatiaria: Navajo, Ramah

Claytonia: Montana Indian

Cleome: Navajo, Ramah

Coleogyne: Havasupai

Cornicularia: Eskimo, Inuktitut

Corydalis: Navajo, Ramah

Croton: Hopi

Cryptantha: Navajo, Ramah

Cyperus: Apache, Chiricahua & Mescalero; Kiowa

Descurainia: Navajo, Ramah

Dichanthelium: Kiowa

Echinochloa: Navajo, Ramah

Elymus: Kiowa; Navajo, Ramah; Thompson

Elytrigia: Apache, White Mountain

Epilobium: Tanana, Upper; Thompson

Equisetum: Isleta; Lakota; Meskwaki; Ojibwa; Okanagan-Colville; Quileute; Quinault

Erodium: Navajo, Ramah

Geranium: Keres, Western

Helianthus: Hopi; Navajo, Ramah

Heliomeris: Navajo, Ramah

Heterotheca: Navajo, Ramah

Hordeum: Mendocino Indian

Hydrophyllum: Ojibwa

Juncus: Okanagan-Colville; Paiute

Juniperus: Navajo

Koeleria: Okanagan-Colville

Krascheninnikovia: Havasupai

Lappula: Navajo, Ramah

Larix: Potawatomi

Lathyrus: Mendocino Indian; Ojibwa

Lepidium: Navajo, Ramah

Leymus: Mendocino Indian; Okanagan-Colville

Linum: Dakota

Lotus: Diegueño

Lupinus: Thompson

Maianthemum: Ojibwa

Marrubium: Navajo, Ramah
Medicago: Navajo, Ramah; Shuswap
Monolepis: Navajo, Ramah
Muhlenbergia: Apache, White Mountain; Navajo, Ramah
Opuntia: Montana Indian
Oryzopsis: Apache, White Mountain; Navajo; Navajo, Ramah
Osmorhiza: Omaha; Ponca; Potawatomi
Oxalis: Omaha; Pawnee; Ponca
Panicum: Navajo, Ramah
Pascopyrum: Montana Indian
Paspalum: Kiowa
Pedicularis: Potawatomi
Phaseolus: Navajo, Ramah
Phleum: Shuswap
Phoradendron: Keres, Western
Picea: Tanana, Upper
Plantago: Mendocino Indian; Pima
Poa: Navajo, Ramah
Populus: Blackfoot; Cheyenne; Dakota; Lakota; Montana Indian
Prosopis: Kiowa
Quercus: Seminole
Rorippa: Navajo, Ramah
Salix: Navajo
Salsola: Navajo, Ramah
Sarcobatus: Navajo, Ramah
Sonchus: Houma
Sorghum: Kiowa
Sparganium: Okanagan-Colville
Sporobolus: Keres, Western; Kiowa
Stenocereus: Papago
Stipa: Navajo, Ramah
Tridens: Navajo, Ramah
Trifolium: Shuswap; Thompson
Triticum: Navajo, Ramah
Vicia: Mendocino Indian; Thompson
Zea: Kiowa; Navajo, Ramah
Ziziphus: Pima

Forage

Achillea: Haisla & Hanaksiala
Aesculus: Mendocino Indian
Alectoria: Hesquiat
Allium: Shuswap
Amaranthus: Navajo

Amelanchier: Havasupai; Hesquiat; Montana Indian
Anthoxanthum: Hesquiat
Aquilegia: Thompson
Aralia: Montagnais
Arbutus: Mendocino Indian
Arctostaphylos: Eskimo, Arctic; Mendocino Indian; Nitinaht; Paiute; Thompson
Artemisia: Blackfoot; Iroquois; Isleta; Lakota
Asclepias: Mendocino Indian; Zuni
Astragalus: Navajo, Ramah; Thompson
Atriplex: Keres, Western; Navajo; Pima
Blechnum: Haisla & Hanaksiala
Bouteloua: Hopi; Keres, Western; Montana Indian; Navajo, Ramah
Brodiaea: Mendocino Indian
Bromus: Thompson
Buchloe: Blackfoot
Calochortus: Shuswap
Carex: Blackfoot; Mendocino Indian; Navajo, Ramah; Thompson
Ceanothus: Karok; Mendocino Indian; Okanagan-Colville; Paiute; Thompson
Cercocarpus: Navajo
Chlorogalum: Yuki
Chrysothamnus: Blackfoot; Navajo
Cladonia: Abnaki
Claytonia: Montana Indian
Clematis: Lakota
Clintonia: Bella Coola
Cornus: Haisla & Hanaksiala; Okanagan-Colville; Oweekeno
Crataegus: Okanagan-Colville
Croton: Mendocino Indian
Dimorphocarpa: Navajo
Disporum: Karok; Nitinaht
Dryopteris: Haisla & Hanaksiala
Dyssodia: Dakota
Enteromorpha: Hesquiat
Epilobium: Okanagan-Colville
Equisetum: Haisla & Hanaksiala; Mendocino Indian; Tewa
Erigeron: Ojibwa
Erodium: Isleta; Kawaiisu
Erythronium: Montana Indian
Fritillaria: Hesquiat; Montana Indian
Gutierrezia: Tewa
Hackelia: Thompson

Hedysarum: Eskimo, Arctic
Heracleum: Anticosti; Hesquiat; Thompson
Hilaria: Navajo, Ramah
Hydrophyllum: Okanagon; Thompson
Ipomopsis: Navajo
Juncus: Mendocino Indian
Juniperus: Navajo
Kalmia: Mahuna
Kochia: Navajo
Koeleria: Havasupai
Krascheninnikovia: Keres, Western; Navajo
Larix: Okanagan-Colville
Lathyrus: Carrier; Thompson
Leymus: Blackfoot; Kawaiisu
Licania: Seminole
Lithocarpus: Pomo, Kashaya
Lonicera: Bella Coola; Hesquiat; Okanagan-
    Colville; Thompson
Lotus: Isleta
Lupinus: Mendocino Indian; Okanagan-
    Colville; Paiute
Lysichiton: Haisla & Hanaksiala; Hesquiat;
    Hoh; Okanagan-Colville; Oweekeno; Quileute
Maianthemum: Oweekeno; Thompson
Malus: Nitinaht
Malva: Pima
Medicago: Mendocino Indian
Melilotus: Jemez
Menyanthes: Hesquiat
Muhlenbergia: Blackfoot
Nemophila: Kawaiisu
Nepeta: Okanagan-Colville
Nuphar: Mendocino Indian
Oemleria: Karok
Orthocarpus: Mendocino Indian
Oryzopsis: Navajo
Oxalis: Pawnee
Oxytropis: Lakota; Navajo; Thompson
Panicum: Navajo, Ramah
Pascopyrum: Lakota; Montana Indian
Paspalum: Kiowa
Paxistima: Okanagan-Colville; Thompson
Pedicularis: Mendocino Indian
Penstemon: Navajo; Thompson
Petasites: Nitinaht
Phragmites: Thompson
Pinus: Okanagan-Colville
Pluchea: Pima

Populus: Dakota; Lakota; Thompson
Portulaca: Navajo
Potamogeton: Hesquiat
Prosopis: Pima
Prunus: Haisla & Hanaksiala
Pseudoroegneria: Okanagan-Colville
Purshia: Navajo; Okanagan-Colville
Quercus: Pomo, Kashaya
Ranunculus: Hesquiat
Ribes: Okanagan-Colville; Paiute; Thompson
Robinia: Mendocino Indian; Wailaki
Rosa: Hesquiat; Okanagan-Colville; Thompson
Rubus: Haisla & Hanaksiala
Sagittaria: Meskwaki; Ojibwa
Salix: Navajo; Thompson
Salsola: Havasupai
Sarcobatus: Keres, Western; Navajo; Pima
Scirpus: Hesquiat
Shepherdia: Blackfoot; Thompson
Sisymbrium: Navajo
Sium: Thompson
Sophora: Navajo
Sorbus: Heiltzuk; Montagnais
Spartina: Iroquois
Sphagnum: Haisla & Hanaksiala
Spiraea: Thompson
Sporobolus: Navajo
Stachys: Saanich
Stellaria: Iroquois
Streptopus: Hesquiat; Montagnais; Nitinaht;
    Oweekeno
Symphoricarpos: Haisla & Hanaksiala;
    Okanagan-Colville
Toxicodendron: Mendocino Indian
Tragopogon: Okanagan-Colville
Trifolium: Mendocino Indian; Wailaki
Usnea: Hesquiat
Vaccinium: Hesquiat; Okanagan-Colville
Valeriana: Thompson
Vicia: Thompson
Yucca: Isleta; Navajo
Zea: Tewa
Zostera: Hesquiat

Frozen Food
Allium: Tanana, Upper
Amelanchier: Okanagan-Colville; Thompson
Arbutus: Karok

Arctostaphylos: Eskimo, Inupiat
Chenopodium: Eskimo, Inupiat
Empetrum: Eskimo, Arctic; Tanana, Upper
Gaultheria: Nitinaht
Gaylussacia: Cherokee
Hedysarum: Eskimo, Inupiat
Heracleum: Thompson
Lomatium: Thompson
Myriophyllum: Tanana, Upper
Oxytropis: Eskimo, Inupiat
Pinus: Okanagan-Colville
Polygonum: Tanana, Upper
Ribes: Thompson
Rosa: Eskimo, Inupiat
Rubus: Alaska Native; Eskimo, Inuktitut; Eskimo, Inupiat; Okanagan-Colville; Tanana, Upper; Thompson
Rudbeckia: Cherokee
Rumex: Tanana, Upper
Sambucus: Okanagan-Colville
Sedum: Eskimo, Inupiat
Vaccinium: Alaska Native; Bella Coola; Cree, Woodlands; Eskimo, Arctic; Eskimo, Inupiat; Koyukon; Makah; Nitinaht; Tanana, Upper; Thompson
Viburnum: Cree, Woodlands; Eskimo, Inupiat; Koyukon; Tanana, Upper

Fruit

Aesculus: Costanoan; Mendocino Indian
Amelanchier: Abnaki; Alaska Native; Algonquin, Quebec; Bella Coola; Blackfoot; Cahuilla; Chehalis; Cherokee; Chippewa; Coeur d'Alene; Costanoan; Cree, Woodlands; Dakota; Gosiute; Great Basin Indian; Haisla; Hesquiat; Hoh; Iroquois; Isleta; Karok; Kawaiisu; Kitasoo; Klamath; Kwakiutl, Southern; Lakota; Mendocino Indian; Modesse; Montana Indian; Navajo; Navajo, Ramah; Ojibwa; Okanagan-Colville; Omaha; Oweekeno; Paiute; Ponca; Potawatomi; Quileute; Saanich; Salish, Coast; Sanpoil & Nespelem; Shuswap; Skagit; Skagit, Upper; Spokan; Swinomish; Thompson; Ute; Winnebago; Wintoon
Amphicarpaea: Chippewa
Arbutus: Costanoan; Karok; Pomo; Pomo, Kashaya; Wailaki; Yuki; Yurok

Arctostaphylos: Alaska Native; Blackfoot; Cahuilla; Carrier; Cherokee; Chinook, Lower; Coeur d'Alene; Costanoan; Cree, Woodlands; Diegueño; Eskimo, Alaska; Eskimo, Arctic; Eskimo, Inupiat; Hanaksiala; Hualapai; Karok; Kawaiisu; Klamath; Kwakiutl, Southern; Luiseño; Mahuna; Makah; Mendocino Indian; Mewuk; Midoo; Montana Indian; Navajo; Navajo, Kayenta; Nitinaht; Nuxalkmc; Okanagan-Colville; Okanagon; Oweekeno; Paiute; Salish, Coast; Skokomish; Spokan; Squaxin; Tanana, Upper; Thompson; Tubatulabal; Wintoon; Yavapai; Yuki; Yurok
Aronia: Abnaki; Potawatomi
Artocarpus: Hawaiian
Asclepias: Cheyenne; Kiowa
Asimina: Cherokee; Iroquois
Aster: Tewa
Astragalus: Apache, White Mountain; Lakota
Atriplex: Acoma; Cahuilla; Laguna
Berberis: Jemez
Canotia: Apache, San Carlos; Apache, Western
Capsicum: Pima, Gila River
Carica: Hawaiian
Carnegia: Apache, Chiricahua & Mescalero; Apache, San Carlos; Apache, Western; Apache, White Mountain; Papago; Papago & Pima; Pima; Seri; Southwest Indians; Yavapai
Carpobrotus: Luiseño; Pomo; Pomo, Kashaya
Ceanothus: Acoma; Keres, Western; Laguna
Celtis: Acoma; Apache, Chiricahua & Mescalero; Comanche; Hualapai; Keres, Western; Kiowa; Laguna; Navajo; Omaha; Papago; Pawnee; Pueblo; Tewa
Cereus: Apache, White Mountain
Citrullus: Apalachee; Cahuilla; Cocopa; Havasupai; Pima
Citrus: Haisla & Hanaksiala; Thompson
Clermontia: Hawaiian
Condalia: Maricopa; Papago; Pima
Cornus: Abnaki; Bella Coola; Blackfoot; Chippewa; Eskimo, Alaska; Flathead; Kitasoo; Kutenai; Kwakiutl, Southern; Makah; Nitinaht; Okanagan-Colville; Oweekeno; Potawatomi; Salish; Sanpoil & Nespelem; Shuswap; Spokan; Thompson
Corylus: Iroquois
Crataegus: Abnaki; Algonquin, Quebec;

Apache, Chiricahua & Mescalero; Bella Coola;
Blackfoot; Cherokee; Cheyenne; Coeur
d'Alene; Comanche; Haisla & Hanaksiala;
Iroquois; Kwakiutl, Southern; Lakota; Mesk-
waki; Montana Indian; Ojibwa; Okanagan-
Colville; Okanagon; Omaha; Oregon Indian;
Paiute; Ponca; Potawatomi; Salish, Coast;
Sanpoil & Nespelem; Spokan; Thompson;
Winnebago

Cucumis: Cocopa; Thompson

Cucurbita: Isleta; Maricopa; Papago; Pima

Cupressus: Navajo

Datura: Navajo

Dioscorea: Hawaiian

Diospyros: Cherokee; Comanche

Disporum: Blackfoot; Shuswap; Thompson

Echinocereus: Apache, Chiricahua & Mescalero;
Apache, Mescalero; Isleta; Keres, Western;
Navajo; Navajo, Ramah; Pima; Yavapai

Elaeagnus: Alaska Native; Blackfoot; Cree;
Montana Indian; Okanagan-Colville; Tanana,
Upper

Empetrum: Cree, Woodlands; Eskimo, Alaska;
Eskimo, Arctic; Eskimo, Inupiat; Ojibwa;
Tanana, Upper; Tsimshian

Escobaria: Blackfoot; Cheyenne; Crow

Ferocactus: Hualapai

Ficus: Havasupai

Forestiera: Apache, Chiricahua & Mescalero

Fragaria: Abnaki; Alaska Native; Algonquin,
Quebec; Algonquin, Tête-de-Boule; Apache,
Chiricahua & Mescalero; Bella Coola; Black-
foot; Cahuilla; Carrier; Chehalis; Cherokee;
Cheyenne; Chinook, Lower; Chippewa;
Clallam; Coeur d'Alene; Costanoan; Cowlitz;
Dakota; Diegueño; Gosiute; Haisla &
Hanaksiala; Hesquiat; Hoh; Iroquois; Isleta;
Karok; Kitasoo; Klallam; Klamath; Lakota;
Makah; Mendocino Indian; Menominee;
Montana Indian; Nisqually; Nitinaht; Ojibwa;
Okanagan-Colville; Omaha; Oweekeno;
Paiute; Pawnee; Pomo; Pomo, Kashaya; Ponca;
Puyallup; Quileute; Salish, Coast; Sanpoil &
Nespelem; Skagit, Upper; Skokomish; Spo-
kan; Squaxin; Swinomish; Thompson;
Tolowa; Winnebago; Yurok

Frangula: Atsugewi; Costanoan; Kawaiisu;
Makah; Paiute

Gaultheria: Alaska Native; Algonquin, Quebec;
Cherokee; Haisla & Hanaksiala; Hoh; Iro-
quois; Karok; Kitasoo; Makah; Nitinaht;
Ojibwa; Okanagon; Oweekeno; Pomo; Pomo,
Kashaya; Quileute; Salish, Coast; Skagit,
Upper; Thompson; Tolowa; Yurok

Gaylussacia: Cherokee; Iroquois

Geocaulon: Alaska Native

Helianthus: Omaha

Heteromeles: Cahuilla; Costanoan; Diegueño;
Karok; Mahuna; Mendocino Indian; Neeshenam; Pomo; Pomo, Kashaya; Yurok

Juniperus: Acoma; Apache; Apache, Chiricahua
& Mescalero; Apache, Mescalero; Apache,
White Mountain; Atsugewi; Cahuilla; Cochiti;
Comanche; Costanoan; Diegueño; Gosiute;
Hopi; Isleta; Jemez; Kawaiisu; Keresan;
Laguna; Navajo; Navajo, Ramah; Paiute;
Paiute, Northern; San Felipe; San Ildefonso;
Tewa; Tubatulabal

Lomatium: Thompson

Lonicera: Klamath; Okanagan-Colville; Okanagon; Oweekeno; Thompson

Lycium: Cahuilla; Hopi; Isleta; Jemez; Kawaiisu;
Maricopa; Navajo; Navajo, Ramah; Paiute,
Northern; Papago; Pima; Pima, Gila River;
Tubatulabal; Zuni

Lycopersicon: Haisla & Hanaksiala

Machaerocereus: Papago & Pima

Mahonia: Apache; Apache, Mescalero; Black-
foot; Cheyenne; Clallam; Coeur d'Alene;
Cowlitz; Flathead; Hualapai; Klallam;
Kwakiutl, Southern; Lummi; Montana Indian;
Okanagan-Colville; Samish; Sanpoil; Sanpoil
& Nespelem; Shuswap; Skagit; Skagit, Upper;
Snohomish; Spokan; Squaxin; Swinomish;
Thompson; Yavapai

Maianthemum: Bella Coola; Costanoan; Haisla
& Hanaksiala; Hesquiat; Kitasoo; Kwakiutl,
Southern; Okanagon; Potawatomi; Salish,
Coast; Skagit, Upper; Tewa; Thompson

Malus: Bella Coola; Cherokee; Chinook, Lower;
Clallam; Cowlitz; Haisla & Hanaksiala; Hoh;
Iroquois; Makah; Nitinaht; Ojibwa; Omaha;
Oweekeno; Ponca; Quileute; Quinault; Salish,
Coast; Samish; Skagit, Upper; Swinomish;
Thompson

Cowichan; Gosiute; Hesquiat; Hoh; Hopi;
Kawaiisu; Klamath; Koyukon; Lakota; Mon-
tana Indian; Navajo; Navajo, Ramah; Nitinaht;
Paiute; Pomo, Kashaya; Quileute; Rocky Boy;
Saanich; Spokan; Tanana, Upper; Thompson;
Ute; Washo

Rubus: Abnaki; Alaska Native; Algonquin, Que-
bec; Algonquin, Tête-de-Boule; Apache,
Chiricahua & Mescalero; Bella Coola; Black-
foot; Cahuilla; Carrier; Chehalis; Cherokee;
Cheyenne; Chinook, Lower; Chippewa; Clal-
lam; Coeur d'Alene; Costanoan; Cowlitz;
Cree, Woodlands; Dakota; Diegueño; Eskimo;
Eskimo, Alaska; Eskimo, Inuktitut; Eskimo,
Inupiat; Gosiute; Green River Group; Haisla &
Hanaksiala; Hesquiat; Hoh; Iroquois; Isleta;
Karok; Kitasoo; Klallam; Klamath; Koyukon;
Kwakiutl, Southern; Lakota; Luiseño; Lummi;
Mahuna; Makah; Mendocino Indian; Meno-
minee; Meskwaki; Montana Indian; Navajo;
Nisqually; Nitinaht; Ojibwa; Okanagan-
Colville; Okanagon; Omaha; Oweekeno; Pai-
ute; Pawnee; Pomo; Pomo, Kashaya; Ponca;
Potawatomi; Puyallup; Quileute; Quinault;
Salish, Coast; Samish; Sanpoil & Nespelem;
Shuswap; Skagit; Skagit, Upper; Snohomish;
Spokan; Squaxin; Swinomish; Tanana,
Upper; Thompson; Tolowa; Tsimshian; Win-
toon; Yuki; Yurok

Sambucus: Apache; Apache, White Mountain;
Cahuilla; Cherokee; Chippewa; Coeur d'Alene;
Costanoan; Dakota; Diegueño; Gosiute;
Haisla; Hanaksiala; Hesquiat; Hoh; Iroquois;
Karok; Kiowa; Klallam; Klamath; Luiseño;
Mahuna; Makah; Mendocino Indian; Mesk-
waki; Montana Indian; Nitinaht; Okanagan-
Colville; Okanagon; Omaha; Paiute; Paiute,
Northern; Pawnee; Pima, Gila River; Polik-
lah; Pomo, Kashaya; Ponca; Quileute; Salish,
Coast; Sanpoil & Nespelem; Skagit, Upper;
Skokomish; Spokan; Thompson; Tubatula-
bal; Wintoon; Yuki; Yurok

Sarcobatus: Navajo

Serenoa: Seminole

Shepherdia: Carrier; Coeur d'Alene; Dakota;
Gosiute; Kwakiutl, Southern; Lakota; Mon-
tana Indian; Navajo; Okanagon; Omaha;
Oweekeno; Paiute; Pawnee; Ponca; Shuswap;

Spokan; Tanana, Upper; Thompson; Ute;
Winnebago

Smilax: Meskwaki; Omaha

Solanum: Costanoan; Mendocino Indian;
Miwok; Pima; Tubatulabal

Sorbus: Algonquin, Quebec; Montagnais;
Ojibwa; Okanagon; Thompson

Stenocereus: Apache, Chiricahua & Mescalero;
Papago & Pima; Seri

Streptopus: Alaska Native; Okanagon;
Thompson

Symphoricarpos: Sioux

Taxus: Karok; Mendocino Indian

Typha: Havasupai; Okanagan-Colville

Umbellularia: Costanoan; Pomo, Kashaya;
Tolowa; Yurok

Vaccinium: Abnaki; Alaska Native; Algonquin,
Quebec; Algonquin, Tête-de-Boule; Bella
Coola; Chinook, Lower; Chippewa; Clallam;
Coeur d'Alene; Costanoan; Cree, Woodlands;
Eskimo, Alaska; Eskimo, Inuktitut; Eskimo,
Inupiat; Haida; Haisla & Hanaksiala;
Hanaksiala; Hesquiat; Hoh; Iroquois; Karok;
Kitasoo; Klallam; Klamath; Kwakiutl, South-
ern; Lummi; Makah; Menominee; Montana
Indian; Nitinaht; Ojibwa; Okanagan-Colville;
Oweekeno; Paiute; Poliklah; Pomo; Pomo,
Kashaya; Potawatomi; Quileute; Quinault;
Salish; Salish, Coast; Sanpoil & Nespelem;
Shuswap; Skagit; Skagit, Upper; Skokomish;
Snohomish; Spokan; Swinomish; Tanana, Up-
per; Thompson; Tolowa; Tsimshian; Yurok

Viburnum: Abnaki; Algonquin, Quebec; Dakota;
Eskimo, Inuktitut; Eskimo, Inupiat; Haisla &
Hanaksiala; Hesquiat; Iroquois; Menominee;
Meskwaki; Ojibwa; Okanagan-Colville;
Okanagon; Omaha; Pawnee; Ponca; Salish,
Coast; Shuswap; Tanana, Upper; Thompson;
Winnebago

Vicia: Kwakiutl, Southern

Vitis: Apache, Chiricahua & Mescalero; Apache,
Mescalero; Apache, Western; Cahuilla; Cher-
okee; Cheyenne; Chippewa; Comanche;
Costanoan; Crow; Dakota; Diegueño; Haisla
& Hanaksiala; Havasupai; Hualapai; Iroquois;
Isleta; Jemez; Karok; Keres, Western; Kiowa;
Lakota; Luiseño; Mahuna; Menominee;
Omaha; Pawnee; Pomo; Pomo, Kashaya;

Ponca; Sioux; Tubatulabal; Winnebago; Win-
toon; Yurok
Washingtonia: Cahuilla
Yucca: Acoma; Apache, San Carlos; Hopi;
Hualapai; Isleta; Kawaiisu; Keres, Western;
Keresan; Laguna; Mohave; Navajo; Navajo,
Ramah; Papago; Pima; Pima, Gila River;
Pueblo; San Felipe; Sia; Southwest Indians;
Tewa; Yavapai; Zuni
Ziziphus: Cahuilla; Maricopa; Maricopa &
Mohave; Pima; Pima, Gila River

Ice Cream
Anemone: Eskimo, Alaska
Arctostaphylos: Eskimo, Inupiat
Descurainia: Paiute
Dryopteris: Eskimo, Inuktitut
Empetrum: Eskimo, Alaska
Hippuris: Eskimo, Inuktitut
Honckenya: Alaska Native
Pinus: Paiute, Northern
Rosa: Eskimo, Inupiat
Rubus: Eskimo, Arctic; Eskimo, Inupiat
Rumex: Eskimo, Inuktitut
Shepherdia: Bella Coola; Carrier; Clallam;
Coeur d'Alene; Flathead; Haisla & Hanak-
siala; Kitasoo; Lillooet; Montana Indian;
Nitinaht; Okanagan-Colville; Sanpoil;
Shuswap; Thompson, Lower
Vaccinium: Eskimo, Inupiat
Viburnum: Eskimo, Inupiat

Pie & Pudding
Amelanchier: Alaska Native; Cheyenne; Flat-
head; Montana Indian; Okanagan-Colville;
Thompson
Atriplex: Hopi; Navajo
Balsamorhiza: Paiute
Camassia: Klamath; Paiute
Carnegia: Apache, Western
Carya: Iroquois
Castanea: Iroquois
Corylus: Iroquois
Cucurbita: Iroquois
Diospyros: Cherokee
Empetrum: Alaska Native; Eskimo, Inupiat;
Tanana, Upper
Erythronium: Thompson

Fagus: Iroquois
Gaultheria: Makah; Pomo, Kashaya; Thompson
Gaylussacia: Cherokee; Iroquois
Juglans: Iroquois
Lewisia: Thompson
Lomatium: Thompson
Pediomelum: Cheyenne
Perideridia: Nevada Indian; Okanagan-Colville
Pinus: Apache, Chiricahua & Mescalero
Polygonum: Alaska Native; Eskimo, Arctic
Prosopis: Apache, Chiricahua & Mescalero
Prunus: Cherokee; Cheyenne; Lakota; Montana
Indian
Quercus: Iroquois; Menominee
Rheum: Kitasoo
Ribes: Thompson
Rosa: Cheyenne
Rubus: Alaska Native; Cherokee; Iroquois;
Makah; Menominee; Meskwaki; Pomo,
Kashaya; Tanana, Upper
Rumex: Pima
Sambucus: Cherokee; Mendocino Indian; Mon-
tana Indian
Shepherdia: Cheyenne; Paiute
Solanum: Navajo, Ramah
Sporobolus: Hopi
Vaccinium: Alaska Native; Algonquin, Quebec;
Eskimo, Inupiat; Hesquiat; Iroquois; Makah;
Montana Indian; Nitinaht; Pomo; Pomo,
Kashaya; Tanana, Upper; Thompson
Viburnum: Tanana, Upper
Zea: Iroquois
Zizania: Potawatomi

Porridge
Acacia: Cahuilla; Seri
Agave: Navajo
Allenrolfea: Cahuilla
Amaranthus: Cahuilla; Havasupai; Hopi; Navajo
Amelanchier: Atsugewi
Anemopsis: Kamia
Arctostaphylos: Cahuilla; Navajo; Numlaki;
Pomo
Artemisia: Navajo
Atriplex: Cahuilla; Navajo, Ramah; Paiute,
Northern; Pima; Yuma; Zuni
Avena: Cahuilla; Diegueño; Miwok
Balsamorhiza: Paiute

Berberis: Yana
Blennosperma: Neeshenam
Bouteloua: Apache, Western; Apache, White
  Mountain
Bromus: Karok; Neeshenam
Calochortus: Cheyenne
Carex: Navajo, Kayenta
Carnegia: Apache, Western; Pima; Pima, Gila
  River; Seri
Celtis: Meskwaki
Chaenactis: Cahuilla
Chasmanthium: Cocopa
Chenopodium: Hopi; Navajo
Citrullus: Havasupai
Cleome: Acoma; Keres, Western; Laguna
Cucurbita: Cahuilla; Havasupai
Cupressus: Navajo
Cycloloma: Hopi; Zuni
Cyperus: Kamia; Paiute
Deschampsia: Kawaiisu
Descurainia: Gosiute; Navajo; Pima, Gila River
Echinocactus: Havasupai
Echinochloa: Cocopa; Yuma
Elymus: Karok; Kawaiisu
Equisetum: San Felipe
Eragrostis: Cocopa
Eriochloa: Cocopa
Eriogonum: Kawaiisu; Navajo, Kayenta; Navajo,
  Ramah
Ferocactus: Apache, San Carlos
Fouquieria: Cahuilla
Gaylussacia: Iroquois
Helianthus: Apache, Western; Montana Indian;
  Navajo; Paiute
Heliotropium: Navajo, Kayenta
Hirschfeldia: Cahuilla
Juglans: Cherokee
Juniperus: Cahuilla
Koeleria: Isleta
Lasthenia: Cahuilla
Layia: Cahuilla
Lewisia: Sanpoil & Nespelem
Leymus: Kawaiisu
Lithocarpus: Hahwunkwut; Hupa; Karok;
  Poliklah; Pomo; Pomo, Kashaya; Shasta; Yuki
Lomatium: Klamath; Montana Indian
Lycium: Hopi; Paiute, Northern; Yuma
Madia: Neeshenam; Pomo

Medicago: Cahuilla
Melica: Kawaiisu; Pomo
Mentzelia: Cahuilla; Hualapai; Paiute, Northern
Monolepis: Hopi
Muhlenbergia: Apache, Western; Apache, White
  Mountain
Nama: Kawaiisu
Nolina: Isleta
Nuphar: Klamath; Montana Indian
Olneya: Cocopa; Seri
Opuntia: Acoma; Apache, San Carlos; Apache,
  Western; Cahuilla; Laguna; San Felipe; Zuni
Oryzopsis: Apache, Western; Apache, White
  Mountain; Navajo; Navajo, Ramah; Paiute;
  Paiute, Northern
Oxytropis: Navajo, Kayenta
Pachycereus: Seri
Panicum: Cahuilla
Parkinsonia: Cahuilla; Cocopa
Pectis: Havasupai
Pediomelum: Montana Indian
Perideridia: Cheyenne; Paiute, Northern
Phaseolus: Havasupai
Phoradendron: Maricopa
Pinus: Apache, Western; Cahuilla; Hualapai;
  Kawaiisu; Navajo; Paiute; Thompson; Washo
Plantago: Havasupai; Navajo, Kayenta; Pima,
  Gila River
Polygonum: Klamath
Prosopis: Acoma; Apache, Western; Cahuilla;
  Kawaiisu; Keres, Western; Laguna; Mahuna;
  Pima; Seri
Prunus: Atsugewi; Diegueño; Gosiute; Luiseño;
  Navajo; Paiute, Northern
Quercus: Cahuilla; Concow; Diegueño; Hava-
  supai; Luiseño; Menominee; Meskwaki;
  Mewuk; Miwok; Mohave; Neeshenam; Paiute;
  Pomo; Pomo, Kashaya; Potawatomi; Round
  Valley Indian; Shasta; Yana; Yuki
Ranunculus: Neeshenam
Rhus: Cahuilla; Luiseño; Navajo
Ribes: Paiute, Northern
Rubus: Iroquois
Rumex: Kawaiisu; Mendocino Indian; Navajo;
  Navajo, Kayenta
Salvia: Cahuilla; Diegueño; Mahuna; Paiute;
  Pima, Gila River
Sambucus: Iroquois

Scirpus: Paiute, Northern
Shepherdia: Paiute, Northern
Sisymbrium: Navajo; Pima; Pima, Gila River
Sporobolus: Apache, Chiricahua & Mescalero;
Apache, Western; Apache, White Mountain;
Hopi; Navajo, Ramah
Stenocereus: Papago & Pima; Seri
Stipa: Paiute
Suaeda: Navajo
Trifolium: Cahuilla
Triticum: Cahuilla; Pima; Pomo, Kashaya
Typha: Cahuilla; Paiute, Northern; Pima; Yuma
Vaccinium: Iroquois
Vigna: Cocopa, Maricopa, Mohave & Yuma
Vitis: Cahuilla
Washingtonia: Cahuilla
Wyethia: Paiute, Northern
Yucca: Navajo; Papago; Pima
Zea: Cahuilla; Chippewa; Delaware; Havasupai;
Hopi; Iroquois; Isleta; Navajo; Pima; Zuni
Ziziphus: Cahuilla

Preservative

Achillea: Klamath
Alnus: Haisla & Hanaksiala; Karok; Tanana,
Upper
Amelanchier: Cree, Woodlands
Betula: Cree, Woodlands; Ojibwa
Comptonia: Ojibwa
Cornus: Shuswap
Epilobium: Tanana, Upper
Matricaria: Flathead
Monarda: Flathead
Myrica: Potawatomi
Populus: Cree, Woodlands; Tanana, Upper
Rhododendron: Thompson
Ribes: Quinault
Rubus: Makah
Salix: Shuswap
Ulmus: Omaha

Preserves

Amelanchier: Blackfoot; Montana Indian;
Thompson
Arctostaphylos: Diegueño; Navajo
Artemisia: Havasupai
Asclepias: Chippewa; Lakota

Carnegia: Apache, White Mountain; Papago;
Papago & Pima; Pima, Gila River
Celtis: Apache, Chiricahua & Mescalero
Cereus: Apache, White Mountain
Crataegus: Shuswap; Thompson
Cucurbita: Navajo
Descurainia: Havasupai
Echinocereus: Isleta
Empetrum: Alaska Native; Tanana, Upper
Fragaria: Alaska Native; Algonquin, Quebec;
Cherokee; Haisla & Hanaksiala; Makah;
Meskwaki; Ojibwa; Oweekeno
Gaillardia: Havasupai
Gaultheria: Hoh; Makah; Nitinaht; Oweekeno;
Quileute; Thompson
Gaylussacia: Cherokee
Gilia: Havasupai
Helianthus: Havasupai
Juniperus: Apache, Chiricahua & Mescalero
Lepidium: Havasupai
Lycium: Hopi
Mahonia: Apache, Chiricahua & Mescalero;
Hoh; Makah; Modesse; Montana Indian;
Pueblo; Quileute; Salish, Coast; Sanpoil;
Skagit; Spanish American; Thompson
Malus: Cherokee; Makah; Meskwaki
Mentzelia: Havasupai; Kawaiisu
Morus: Cherokee
Nolina: Isleta
Opuntia: Isleta; Kiowa; Montana Indian; Navajo
Physalis: Hualapai; Navajo
Pinus: Havasupai; Navajo; Navajo, Ramah
Podophyllum: Menominee; Meskwaki
Prosopis: Apache; Papago
Prunus: Algonquin, Quebec; Apache, Chiri-
cahua & Mescalero; Cahuilla; Cherokee;
Cree, Woodlands; Hoh; Kawaiisu; Mendocino
Indian; Menominee; Meskwaki; Montana
Indian; Ojibwa; Quileute; Spanish American;
Thompson
Quincula: Kiowa
Rhamnus: Cahuilla
Rheum: Kitasoo
Rhus: Apache, Chiricahua & Mescalero;
Atsugewi
Ribes: Acoma; Alaska Native; Algonquin,
Quebec; Anticosti; Apache, Chiricahua &
Mescalero; Carrier; Cree, Woodlands;

Sauce & Relish

Podophyllum: Iroquois
Polygonum: Eskimo, Inupiat; Sioux
Porphyra: Haisla & Hanaksiala
Prunus: Cree, Woodlands; Dakota; Iroquois;
    Omaha; Pawnee; Ponca; Thompson;
    Winnebago
Pyrus: Iroquois
Rhus: Isleta
Ribes: Bella Coola; Eskimo, Inupiat; Iroquois;
    Paiute
Rosa: Alaska Native; Eskimo, Inupiat;
    Thompson
Rubus: Iroquois; Pomo, Kashaya
Sambucus: Cahuilla; Hoh; Iroquois; Quileute
Scirpus: Montana Indian
Shepherdia: Montana Indian
Sium: Klamath; Montana Indian
Solanum: Zuni
Sorghum: Hopi
Stenocereus: Papago; Papago & Pima
Umbellularia: Mendocino Indian
Vaccinium: Alaska Native; Eskimo, Inupiat;
    Hoh; Iroquois; Quileute
Viburnum: Chippewa; Eskimo, Inupiat; Iro-
    quois; Thompson
Vitis: Iroquois
Yucca: Acoma; Apache; Apache, Mescalero;
    Apache, Western; Keres, Western; Laguna;
    Mahuna; Navajo; Southwest Indians; Zuni
Zea: Iroquois
Ziziphus: Papago; Pima

Snack Food

Amelanchier: Blackfoot; Cree, Woodlands
Chimaphila: Cherokee
Cornus: Algonquin, Quebec; Blackfoot; Cree,
    Woodlands
Corylus: Thompson
Cucurbita: Pima, Gila River; Rappahannock
Cyperus: Pima, Gila River
Dichelostemma: Pima, Gila River
Echinocereus: Pima, Gila River
Fouquieria: Yavapai
Fragaria: Cree, Woodlands
Gaultheria: Algonquin, Quebec
Ipomopsis: Klamath
Lilium: Cree, Woodlands
Mammillaria: Pima, Gila River

Nuphar: Montana Indian
Osmunda: Abnaki
Perideridia: Blackfoot
Phoradendron: Pima, Gila River
Physalis: Pima, Gila River
Populus: Blackfoot; Pima, Gila River
Porphyra: Alaska Native; Kwakiutl, Southern
Proboscidea: Pima, Gila River
Prosopis: Pima, Gila River
Quercus: Pima, Gila River
Rosa: Cree, Woodlands
Salix: Alaska Native
Sambucus: Pima, Gila River
Scirpus: Pima, Gila River
Ulmus: Omaha
Vaccinium: Cree, Woodlands
Viburnum: Cree, Woodlands
Washingtonia: Pima, Gila River
Zea: Iroquois; Zuni

Soup

Aesculus: Miwok
Agave: Navajo
Allium: Anticosti; Eskimo, Inupiat; Lakota;
    Navajo; Paiute, Northern; Potawatomi
Amaranthus: Havasupai
Amelanchier: Blackfoot; Montana Indian
Aralia: Potawatomi
Arctium: Iroquois
Arctostaphylos: Carrier; Coeur d'Alene; Mon-
    tana Indian; Okanagon; Sanpoil & Nespelem;
    Thompson
Asclepias: Blackfoot; Cheyenne; Menominee;
    Meskwaki; Potawatomi
Aster: Ojibwa
Atriplex: Papago
Avena: Miwok
Calochortus: Paiute, Northern
Camassia: Chehalis; Flathead
Capsicum: Keresan
Carya: Cherokee; Choctaw; Dakota; Iroquois;
    Omaha; Pawnee; Ponca; Winnebago
Castanea: Iroquois
Celastrus: Ojibwa
Chenopodium: Dakota; Omaha; Papago;
    Pawnee
Cirsium: Thompson
Claytonia: Alaska Native; Eskimo, Alaska

Cleome: Navajo
Corylus: Dakota; Iroquois; Omaha; Ponca; Winnebago
Cucurbita: Havasupai
Cymopterus: Hualapai; Navajo
Dasylirion: Apache, Mescalero
Descurainia: Pueblo
Dryopteris: Eskimo, Alaska
Elaeagnus: Blackfoot; Tanana, Upper
Erythronium: Blackfoot; Thompson
Fagus: Iroquois
Fritillaria: Alaska Native; Blackfoot
Gaillardia: Blackfoot
Gaylussacia: Iroquois
Hedeoma: Lakota
Heracleum: Blackfoot
Hippuris: Alaska Native; Eskimo, Alaska; Eskimo, Inuktitut
Juglans: Dakota; Iroquois; Omaha; Pawnee; Ponca; Winnebago
Juniperus: Acoma
Lilium: Blackfoot; Thompson
Lithocarpus: Pomo; Shasta; Yuki; Yurok
Lomatium: Montana Indian; Oregon Indian
Lycium: Navajo
Mentzelia: Havasupai
Nelumbo: Dakota; Omaha; Pawnee; Ponca; Winnebago
Nuphar: Montana Indian
Oenothera: Apache, Chiricahua & Mescalero
Opuntia: Apache, Western; Cahuilla; Cheyenne; Okanagan-Colville
Oryzopsis: Havasupai; Paiute, Northern
Osmunda: Menominee
Parmelia: Potawatomi
Parrya: Alaska Native
Pectis: Havasupai
Pediomelum: Lakota; Omaha; Sioux
Perideridia: Atsugewi; Blackfoot; Paiute, Northern
Phaseolus: Cherokee; Havasupai; Iroquois; Navajo
Pinus: Havasupai; Hualapai; Paiute; Paiute, Northern
Polanisia: Pueblo
Polygonum: Alaska Native; Blackfoot
Porphyra: Alaska Native

Prunus: Blackfoot; Coeur d'Alene; Iroquois; Montana Indian; Ojibwa
Pteridium: Ojibwa
Quercus: Havasupai; Hualapai; Iroquois; Lakota; Mendocino Indian; Miwok; Ojibwa; Pomo; Shasta
Ranunculus: Eskimo, Inuktitut
Rhodymenia: Alaska Native
Rhus: Cahuilla
Ribes: Blackfoot
Rosa: Lakota
Rubus: Coeur d'Alene; Iroquois
Salix: Eskimo, Inuktitut; Eskimo, Inupiat
Sambucus: Paiute, Northern; Thompson; Yuki
Sisymbrium: Navajo
Solanum: Ojibwa
Sorbus: Thompson
Thelypodium: Pueblo
Typha: Paiute, Northern
Vaccinium: Coeur d'Alene; Cree, Woodlands; Iroquois
Veratrum: Blackfoot
Viburnum: Thompson
Yucca: Apache; Apache, Chiricahua & Mescalero; Apache, Mescalero
Zea: Abnaki; Chippewa; Delaware; Havasupai; Iroquois

Sour

Acer: Ojibwa; Potawatomi
Nemopanthus: Potawatomi
Oxalis: Meskwaki; Pomo, Kashaya
Pedicularis: Eskimo, Alaska
Rhus: Potawatomi
Rumex: Hesquiat

Special Food

Allium: Thompson
Amaranthus: Navajo, Ramah
Amelanchier: Blackfoot; Cheyenne
Arctostaphylos: Bella Coola; Hanaksiala
Argentina: Kwakiutl, Southern
Balsamorhiza: Sanpoil
Camassia: Blackfoot; Cowichan
Capsicum: Papago
Carya: Iroquois
Castanea: Iroquois
Castilleja: Navajo

Chenopodium: Navajo, Ramah
Cirsium: Cheyenne
Citrullus: Iroquois
Cleome: Navajo
Cornus: Hesquiat
Corylus: Iroquois
Cucumis: Iroquois
Cucurbita: Hopi; Iroquois; Zuni
Dalea: Navajo; Santa Clara
Datura: Navajo
Equisetum: Hoh; Quileute
Fagus: Iroquois
Ferocactus: Pima, Gila River
Fouquieria: Papago
Fragaria: Apache; Cochiti; Isleta; Navajo;
    Quinault
Gaultheria: Kwakiutl, Southern
Helianthus: Apache, Western
Juglans: Iroquois
Juniperus: Tewa of Hano
Lewisia: Thompson
Lomatium: Sanpoil
Lycium: Jemez; Navajo
Malus: Kitasoo; Kwakiutl, Southern
Monarda: Lakota
Nuphar: Klamath
Oemleria: Kwakiutl, Southern
Oenothera: Apache, Chiricahua & Mescalero
Oryzopsis: Paiute, Northern
Parthenocissus: Ojibwa
Physalis: Apache, Chiricahua & Mescalero
Pinus: Apache, Chiricahua & Mescalero;
    Apache, Mescalero; Hopi; Navajo
Polyporus: Pueblo
Populus: Blackfoot
Prosopis: Apache, Chiricahua & Mescalero
Prunus: Blackfoot; Cheyenne; Lakota
Quercus: Cahuilla; Iroquois
Rhus: Apache, Chiricahua & Mescalero
Ribes: Kwakiutl, Southern
Rubus: Haisla & Hanaksiala; Iroquois; Isleta;
    Makah
Shepherdia: Haisla & Hanaksiala
Sophora: Acoma; Laguna; San Felipe
Vaccinium: Haisla & Hanaksiala; Kwakiutl,
    Southern; Nitinaht; Oweekeno
Viburnum: Kwakiutl, Southern
Vitis: Lakota

Yucca: Navajo
Zea: Iroquois; Menominee; Navajo; Navajo,
    Ramah; Papago; Pueblo
Zizania: Ojibwa
Zostera: Kwakiutl, Southern

Spice

Acer: Blackfoot; Cowichan; Saanich
Agastache: Acoma; Keres, Western; Laguna
Allium: Algonquin, Tête-de-Boule; Apache,
    Chiricahua & Mescalero; Blackfoot; Cahuilla;
    Cheyenne; Cree, Woodlands; Dakota; Eskimo,
    Inuktitut; Hopi; Keres, Western; Meskwaki;
    Navajo; Omaha; Pawnee; Pomo; Ponca;
    Pueblo; Shoshoni; Shuswap; Winnebago
Alnus: Paiute
Amelanchier: Chehalis; Thompson
Angelica: Shuswap
Apium: Shoshoni
Arctostaphylos: Chippewa
Arnoglossum: Cherokee
Artemisia: Apache, Chiricahua & Mescalero;
    Apache, White Mountain; Blackfoot; Hopi;
    Shoshoni
Asarum: Chippewa; Meskwaki; Ojibwa;
    Potawatomi
Asclepias: Blackfoot
Astragalus: Cahuilla; Shoshoni
Atriplex: Hopi; Navajo, Ramah; Papago; Pima;
    Pueblo
Berlandiera: Acoma; Keres, Western; Laguna
Blechnum: Makah
Brassica: Hoh; Quileute
Calocedrus: Round Valley Indian
Capsella: Cherokee
Capsicum: Hopi; Navajo, Ramah; Papago; Pima
Carum: Cree, Woodlands
Carya: Cherokee
Castanea: Iroquois
Celtis: Dakota
Cetraria: Eskimo, Inuktitut
Chenopodium: Cherokee; Hopi
Chrysothamnus: Hopi; Kawaiisu
Cleome: Navajo
Coriandrum: Hopi; Keresan
Cornus: Shuswap
Cucumis: Keresan
Cucurbita: Navajo, Ramah

Cymopterus: Apache, Chiricahua & Mescalero; Navajo
Dalea: Zuni
Descurainia: Cahuilla; Hopi
Distichlis: Cahuilla
Dracocephalum: Apache, Chiricahua & Mescalero
Encelia: Navajo, Kayenta
Eriogonum: Hopi
Eupatorium: Cherokee
Fragaria: Thompson
Fritillaria: Thompson
Gaultheria: Chippewa; Hesquiat; Makah; Nitinaht
Geranium: Blackfoot
Hedeoma: Apache, Chiricahua & Mescalero; Isleta
Humulus: Apache, Chiricahua & Mescalero
Juniperus: Acoma; Apache, Western; Keres, Western; Laguna; Lakota
Ledum: Eskimo, Alaska; Tanana, Upper
Ligusticum: Anticosti; Eskimo, Inupiat
Lilium: Okanagan-Colville; Thompson
Lindera: Cherokee; Chippewa
Lomatium: Okanagan-Colville; Pomo, Kashaya; Shuswap; Thompson
Lotus: Kawaiisu
Lygodesmia: Hopi
Lysichiton: Hoh; Quileute
Maianthemum: Thompson
Medicago: Okanagan-Colville
Mentha: Apache, Chiricahua & Mescalero; Blackfoot; Cherokee; Chippewa; Cree, Woodlands; Dakota; Hopi; Malecite; Navajo, Kayenta; Saanich
Monarda: Acoma; Apache, Chiricahua & Mescalero; Isleta; Keres, Western; Laguna; Pueblo; San Ildefonso; Spanish American
Moricandia: Hoh; Quileute
Osmorhiza: Shoshoni
Pectis: Acoma; Hopi; Keres, Western; Laguna; Pueblo
Penstemon: Thompson
Pentaphylloides: Blackfoot
Perideridia: Blackfoot; Mendocino Indian
Piloblephis: Seminole
Pinus: Havasupai
Piper: Cherokee; Haisla & Hanaksiala

Poliomintha: Hopi; Tewa
Polygonatum: Cherokee
Polygonum: Iroquois
Polystichum: Makah
Populus: Apache, Mescalero
Portulaca: Navajo, Ramah
Prosopis: Apache, Chiricahua & Mescalero
Prunus: Blackfoot
Pseudotsuga: Karok; Paiute
Pycnanthemum: Chippewa
Quercus: Apache, Chiricahua & Mescalero; Havasupai
Rhus: Acoma; Keres, Western; Laguna
Ribes: Thompson; Tolowa
Rorippa: Eskimo, Inuktitut
Rosa: Okanagan-Colville; Skagit, Upper
Rubus: Hesquiat
Rumex: Iroquois
Salix: Quileute
Salvia: Cahuilla; Diegueño
Sambucus: Thompson
Sassafras: Chippewa; Choctaw
Selaginella: Blackfoot
Sidalcea: Yana
Sinapis: Hoh; Quileute
Sorbus: Thompson
Sporobolus: Hopi
Stachys: Kawaiisu
Suaeda: Papago; Pima
Taraxacum: Apache, Chiricahua & Mescalero; Eskimo, Inuktitut
Thalictrum: Blackfoot; Montagnais
Tsuga: Cowlitz
Typha: Yuma
Ulmus: Omaha
Ulva: Pomo, Kashaya
Wyethia: Yuki
Zostera: Cowichan; Saanich

Staple

Acer: Sioux
Aesculus: Yana
Agastache: Apache; Comanche; Mohave; Paiute; Papago; Ute; Yuma
Agave: Apache; Comanche; Hualapai; Mohave; Paiute; Papago; Pima, Gila River; Ute; Yuma
Allenrolfea: Maricopa; Mohave; Yuma
Allium: Flathead; Kutenai; Okanogan

Nuphar: Klamath
Olneya: Cahuilla; Papago; Pima; Yavapai
Opuntia: Apache, San Carlos; Cahuilla; Luiseño; Navajo; Okanagon; Papago; Pima, Gila River
Oryza: Haisla & Hanaksiala
Oryzopsis: Havasupai; Hopi; Kawaiisu; Navajo; Paiute; Paiute, Northern; Zuni
Panicum: Hopi; Warihio; Yuma
Parkinsonia: Papago
Perideridia: Blackfoot; Mendocino Indian; Paiute, Northern; Pomo
Peucedanum: Okanagon
Phaseolus: Cocopa; Menominee; Papago; Tewa
Pholisma: Papago
Physalis: Navajo
Pinus: Apache, Western; Isleta; Navajo; Okanagon; Paiute; Pomo, Kashaya
Piptatherum: Paiute
Plagiobothrys: Mendocino Indian
Poa: Havasupai
Pogogyne: Numlaki; Yuki
Polygonum: Montana Indian
Prosopis: Apache, Mescalero; Apache, Western; Cahuilla; Comanche; Luiseño; Papago; Pima; Pima, Gila River; Yavapai; Yuma
Prunus: Blackfoot; Cahuilla; Luiseño; Montana Indian; Okanagon
Pteridium: Clallam; Sierra; Thompson
Quercus: Acoma; Choctaw; Cochiti; Diegueño; Isleta; Kawaiisu; Keres, Western; Laguna; Lakota; Luiseño; Menominee; Miwok; Modesse; Navajo; Navajo, Ramah; Ojibwa; Paiute, Northern; Pima; San Felipe; Shasta; Yana
Ranunculus: Mendocino Indian; Neeshenam; Pomo
Rhus: Apache; Navajo
Ribes: Okanagon
Rosa: Okanagon
Rubus: Okanagon
Rumex: Costanoan
Ruppia: Seri
Sagittaria: Ojibwa
Salvia: Cahuilla; Costanoan; Mohave; Pomo
Sambucus: Okanagon
Scirpus: Cahuilla; Montana Indian
Sedum: Eskimo, Inupiat
Shepherdia: Okanagon

Sisymbrium: Pima, Gila River
Sium: Okanagon
Stenocereus: Papago
Suaeda: Cahuilla; Paiute
Thysanocarpus: Mendocino Indian
Trifolium: Mendocino Indian
Triticum: Haisla & Hanaksiala; Papago; Sia
Tsuga: Gitksan; Haisla
Typha: Cahuilla; Lakota; Ojibwa; Paiute, Northern
Vaccinium: Okanagon
Verbena: Concow
Wyethia: Costanoan; Mendocino Indian; Paiute; Pomo; Pomo, Kashaya
Xanthium: Costanoan; Yavapai
Yucca: Apache, Mescalero; Hualapai; Papago; Southwest Indians
Zea: Dakota; Delaware; Havasupai; Hopi; Isleta; Keres, Western; Menominee; Navajo; Omaha; Papago; Pawnee; Ponca; Sia; Tewa; Zuni
Zizania: Dakota; Menominee; Ojibwa; Omaha; Ponca; Potawatomi; Winnebago
Ziziphus: Cahuilla

Starvation Food

Acacia: Pima, Gila River
Aesculus: Modesse
Agave: Pima
Alectoria: Montana Indian
Allenrolfea: Pima, Gila River
Allium: Havasupai
Amaranthus: Hopi
Amelanchier: Lakota
Apios: Huron
Arachis: Huron
Arctostaphylos: Montana Indian
Artemisia: Paiute
Atriplex: Pima; Pima, Gila River
Baccharis: Mohave; Yuma
Balsamorhiza: Thompson
Blechnum: Hesquiat; Nitinaht
Bromus: Cahuilla
Calochortus: Navajo; Ute
Celastrus: Menominee; Potawatomi
Chloracantha: Mohave
Cirsium: Havasupai
Crataegus: Omaha; Ponca; Winnebago
Gaultheria: Nitinaht

Substitution Food

Sweetener

Omaha; Pawnee; Ponca; Potawatomi; Winnebago

Agastache: Dakota; Omaha; Pawnee; Ponca; Winnebago

Agave: Hualapai

Alnus: Clallam

Amaranthus: Navajo

Amelanchier: Okanagan-Colville; Thompson

Camassia: Montana Indian

Carya: Dakota; Omaha; Pawnee; Ponca; Winnebago

Castilleja: Cahuilla; Paiute

Chamaesyce: Zuni

Comandra: Okanagan-Colville

Coreopsis: Kawaiisu

Dalea: Hopi; Keres, Western

Echinocereus: Hopi

Epilobium: Eskimo, Inupiat

Frasera: Arapaho

Justicia: Dieguño

Phragmites: Kawaiisu; Paiute

Pinus: Kawaiisu; Miwok; Pomo, Kashaya

Populus: Dakota

Prosopis: Pima

Pseudotsuga: Shuswap; Thompson

Rhus: Cahuilla

Rubus: Thompson

Salix: Eskimo, Inupiat

Sophora: Keres, Western

Tsuga: Gitksan; Haisla; Wet'suwet'en

Yucca: Southwest Indians; Zuni

Zea: Dakota; Hopi; Isleta; Omaha; Pawnee; Ponca

Unspecified

Abies: Haisla; Kitasoo; Shuswap; Thompson

Abronia: Acoma; Clallam; Klallam; Laguna; Makah

Acacia: Pima

Acer: Clallam; Costanoan; Salish, Coast; Thompson

Acorus: Abnaki; Dakota; Lakota

Adenostoma: Cahuilla; Coahuilla

Aesculus: Pomo, Kashaya; Tubatulabal; Yuki

Agaricus: Delaware

Agastache: Gosiute

Agave: Apache; Apache, Chiricahua & Mescalero; Apache, San Carlos; Apache, Western;

Apache, White Mountain; Cahuilla; Cocopa; Dieguño; Navajo; Papago; Pima; Yavapai

Agoseris: Gosiute; Ute

Agropyron: Paiute

Agrostis: Klamath

Alectoria: Coeur d'Alene; Spokan; Thompson

Allenrolfea: Pima; Pima, Gila River

Allium: Acoma; Alaska Native; Apache; Apache, White Mountain; Bella Coola; Cherokee; Cheyenne; Clallam; Comanche; Cree, Woodlands; Dakota; Gosiute; Great Basin Indian; Havasupai; Hoh; Hopi; Isleta; Karok; Klallam; Koyukon; Kwakiutl, Southern; Laguna; Lakota; Makah; Malecite; Mendocino Indian; Menominee; Navajo; Navajo, Ramah; Neeshenam; Nitinaht; Okanagon; Omaha; Oweekeno; Paiute; Paiute, Northern; Papago; Pawnee; Pomo; Ponca; Quileute; Quinault; Salish, Coast; Sanpoil & Nespelem; Seminole; Spokan; Tanana, Upper; Tewa; Thompson; Tubatulabal; Ute; Winnebago; Yuki

Alnus: Costanoan; Paiute; Salish, Coast; Skagit, Upper; Swinomish

Amaranthus: Apache, Chiricahua & Mescalero; Apache, White Mountain; Cocopa; Gosiute; Havasupai; Hopi; Jemez; Keres, Western; Klamath; Mohave; Montana Indian; Navajo; Papago; Pima; Pima, Gila River; Sia; Tewa; Yuma

Ambrosia: Papago

Amelanchier: Blackfoot; Klamath; Thompson

Ammannia: Mohave; Yuma

Amoreuxia: Pima, Gila River

Amphicarpaea: Cherokee; Chippewa; Dakota; Meskwaki; Ojibwa; Omaha; Pawnee; Ponca; Winnebago

Amsinckia: Gosiute; Mendocino Indian; Pima

Ananas: Seminole

Anemone: Alaska Native; Eskimo, Alaska

Angelica: Alaska Native; Bella Coola; Eskimo, Alaska; Eskimo, Inuktitut; Eskimo, Inupiat; Hanaksiala; Makah; Mendocino Indian; Mewuk; Pomo, Kashaya; Yana

Annona: Seminole

Apiaceae sp.: Yana

Apiastrum: Cahuilla

Apios: Cheyenne; Dakota; Delaware; Iroquois;

Chelone: Cherokee

Chenopodium: Apache, Chiricahua & Mescalero; Apache, Western; Apache, White Mountain; Cherokee; Dakota; Gosiute; Havasupai; Hopi; Klamath; Luiseño; Malecite; Mohegan; Navajo, Ramah; Paiute; Paiute, Northern; Papago; Pima, Gila River; Yavapai; Zuni

Chilopsis: Cahuilla

Chlorogalum: Costanoan; Karok; Luiseño; Mendocino Indian; Miwok; Neeshenam

Chrysobalanus: Seminole

Chrysophyllum: Seminole

Chrysothamnus: Apache, White Mountain; Navajo, Kayenta

Cicer: Papago; Pima

Cicuta: Eskimo, Inuktitut

Cinna: Gosiute

Cirsium: Apache, Chiricahua & Mescalero; Atsugewi; Blackfoot; Cahuilla; Cheyenne; Comanche; Costanoan; Cowichan; Flathead; Gosiute; Hesquiat; Houma; Kawaiisu; Kiowa; Kutenai; Nez Perce; Okanagon; Paiute; Saanich; Shuswap; Spokan; Thompson; Tubatulabal; Yavapai

Cistanthe: Kawaiisu

Citrullus: Cherokee; Hopi; Kamia; Meskwaki; Navajo, Ramah; Okanagan-Colville; Seminole; Sia

Citrus: Seminole

Clarkia: Miwok; Yana

Claytonia: Alaska Native; Costanoan; Eskimo, Alaska; Gosiute; Iroquois; Mendocino Indian; Miwok; Montana Indian; Okanagan-Colville; Okanagon; Paiute, Northern; Spokan; Thompson; Ute; Yurok

Cleome: Diegueño; Havasupai; Hopi; Kawaiisu; Keresan; Navajo; Navajo, Ramah; San Felipe; Sia; Tewa; Zuni

Coccoloba: Seminole

Cocos: Seminole

Colocasia: Hawaiian; Seminole

Comandra: Navajo, Kayenta; Paiute

Conioselinum: Haihais; Haisla; Haisla & Hanaksiala; Hanaksiala; Heiltzuk; Kwakwaka'wakw; Navajo, Kayenta; Nuxalkmc; Oweekeno

Cordylanthus: Yavapai

Cordyline: Hawaiian

Coreopsis: Tubatulabal

Coriandrum: Hopi

Cornus: Thompson

Corylus: Algonquin, Quebec; Chehalis; Cherokee; Chippewa; Costanoan; Cree, Woodlands; Dakota; Iroquois; Karok; Klamath; Lummi; Menominee; Meskwaki; Miwok; Ojibwa; Okanagon; Omaha; Paiute; Ponca; Salish, Coast; Sanpoil & Nespelem; Shuswap; Skagit; Skagit, Upper; Snohomish; Squaxin; Swinomish; Thompson; Tolowa; Winnebago; Yuki; Yurok

Crataegus: Thompson

Crepis: Gosiute; Paiute

Cucumis: Cocopa; Hopi; Kamia; Navajo, Ramah; Okanagan-Colville; Seminole; Sia; Thompson

Cucurbita: Apache, White Mountain; Cahuilla; Cherokee; Cocopa; Hopi; Kamia; Luiseño; Navajo, Ramah; Okanagan-Colville; Pima; Seminole; Sia; Zuni

Cuscuta: Navajo

Cycloloma: Hopi

Cymopterus: Apache, Chiricahua & Mescalero; Comanche; Gosiute; Hopi; Hualapai; Navajo; Navajo, Ramah; Ute

Cynoglossum: Yuki

Cyperus: Acoma; Apache, Chiricahua & Mescalero; Cocopa; Costanoan; Laguna; Mohave; Paiute; Paiute, Northern; Pima; Pima, Gila River

Cypripedium: Lakota

Dalea: Keresan; Kiowa; Paiute; San Ildefonso

Dasylirion: Apache, Chiricahua & Mescalero; Apache, Mescalero

Daucus: Clallam; Cowichan; Navajo; Oweekeno; Saanich; Salish, Coast

Dendromecon: Kawaiisu

Dentaria: Cherokee

Deschampsia: Gosiute

Descurainia: Apache, Chiricahua & Mescalero; Hopi; Klamath; Montana Indian; Paiute, Northern; Papago; Pima, Gila River; Pueblo; Tewa of Hano

Dichelostemma: Apache, San Carlos; Atsugewi; Cahuilla; Karok; Luiseño; Mendocino Indian; Miwok; Neeshenam; Paiute; Papago; Pomo; Yuki

Dioscorea: Hawaiian
Diospyros: Seminole
Diplazium: Hawaiian
Distichlis: Tubatulabal
Dodecatheon: Yuki
Dracocephalum: Gosiute
Dryopteris: Alaska Native; Bella Coola; Clallam; Costanoan; Cowlitz; Eskimo, Alaska; Hanaksiala; Kwakiutl, Southern; Oweekeno; Salish, Coast; Thompson
Dudleya: Cahuilla; Diegueño
Dyssodia: Apache, Chiricahua & Mescalero
Echinocereus: Cochiti; Isleta; Yavapai
Echinochloa: Cocopa; Paiute; Tubatulabal; Yuma
Egregia: Bella Coola; Kitasoo; Oweekeno
Elaeagnus: Paiute
Eleocharis: Paiute; Paiute, Northern
Elymus: Gosiute; Ute
Elytrigia: Apache, White Mountain; Gosiute
Ephedra: Kawaiisu; Tubatulabal
Epilobium: Alaska Native; Blackfoot; Eskimo, Alaska; Eskimo, Inuktitut; Eskimo, Inupiat; Gitksan; Haisla; Haisla & Hanaksiala; Karok; Okanagon; Oweekeno; Tanana, Upper; Thompson; Wet'suwet'en
Epixiphium: Apache, Chiricahua & Mescalero
Equisetum: Chinook, Lower; Clallam; Cowlitz; Eskimo, Alaska; Eskimo, Inupiat; Hoh; Klallam; Makah; Nitinaht; Okanagan-Colville; Quileute; Quinault; Saanich; Skagit, Upper; Swinomish; Tanana, Upper; Yurok
Eragrostis: Paiute
Eremalche: Pima, Gila River
Ericameria: Luiseño
Eriogonum: Blackfoot; Cahuilla; Karok; Kawaiisu; Kiowa; Mendocino Indian; Navajo; Navajo, Kayenta; Navajo, Ramah; Tubatulabal
Eriophorum: Alaska Native; Eskimo, Inuktitut; Eskimo, Inupiat
Erodium: Costanoan
Erythronium: Blackfoot; Kwakiutl; Kwakiutl, Southern; Montana Indian; Okanagan-Colville; Okanagon; Thompson; Winnebago
Exobasidium: Haisla & Hanaksiala
Fagus: Algonquin, Quebec; Chippewa; Iroquois; Ojibwa; Potawatomi
Ferocactus: Cahuilla; Pima; Pima, Gila River

Festuca: Gosiute
Ficus: Seminole
Fortunella: Seminole
Fouquieria: Cahuilla
Fragaria: Navajo, Ramah
Frasera: Apache; Yavapai
Fraxinus: Ojibwa
Fritillaria: Bella Coola; Blackfoot; Flathead; Gosiute; Haisla & Hanaksiala; Kitasoo; Montana Indian; Okanagan-Colville; Okanagon; Oweekeno; Paiute; Saanich; Salish, Coast; Salish, Straits; Shasta; Shuswap; Spokan; Thompson; Ute; Yana
Fucus: Eskimo, Alaska
Gaultheria: Cherokee
Gaura: Navajo, Kayenta
Gaylussacia: Cherokee; Ojibwa
Gilia: Luiseño
Glaux: Kwakiutl, Southern; Salish, Coast
Gleditsia: Cherokee
Glyceria: Crow; Klamath
Glycyrrhiza: Cheyenne; Montana Indian; Northwest Indian
Gossypium: Pima, Gila River
Gymnocladus: Meskwaki; Pawnee; Winnebago
Haplopappus: Paiute
Hedeoma: Isleta
Hedophyllum: Nitinaht
Hedysarum: Alaska Native; Tanana, Upper
Helenium: Mendocino Indian
Helianthella: Yana
Helianthus: Cheyenne; Chippewa; Costanoan; Dakota; Gosiute; Gros Ventre; Hopi; Hualapai; Iroquois; Kiowa; Lakota; Luiseño; Malecite; Mandan; Micmac; Navajo, Ramah; Omaha; Paiute; Paiute, Northern; Pawnee; Pima; Ponca; Potawatomi; Pueblo; Ree; Sanpoil & Nespelem; Sioux; Thompson; Winnebago
Heliomeris: Gosiute
Heliotropium: Tubatulabal
Hemizonia: Miwok
Heracleum: Alaska Native; Bella Coola; Blackfoot; Carrier; Coeur d'Alene; Costanoan; Cree, Woodlands; Gitksan; Haisla; Haisla & Hanaksiala; Hesquiat; Karok; Klamath; Kwakiutl, Southern; Makah; Mewuk; Nitinaht; Okanagon; Oweekeno; Pomo, Kashaya; Quileute; Quinault; Salish, Coast; Shuswap;

Spokan; Thompson; Tolowa; Wet'suwet'en;
Yuki; Yurok
Hesperocallis: Cahuilla; Yuma
Hieracium: Thompson
Hippuris: Eskimo, Inuktitut
Hoffmannseggia: Apache; Apache, Chiricahua
& Mescalero; Cocopa; Pima; Pima, Gila River;
Pueblo
Honckenya: Alaska Native; Eskimo, Alaska
Hordeum: Cahuilla; Kawaiisu; Papago; Pima;
Pomo, Kashaya
Humulus: Navajo
Hydrangea: Cherokee
Hydrophyllum: Cowlitz; Okanagon; Thompson
Hymenoclea: Seri
Ipomoea: Cherokee; Hawaiian
Jacquemontia: Hawaiian
Jacquinia: Seri
Jamesia: Apache, Chiricahua & Mescalero
Juglans: Algonquin, Quebec; Apache, Chirica-
hua & Mescalero; Apache, Mescalero;
Apache, Western; Cherokee; Comanche;
Costanoan; Dakota; Hualapai; Iroquois;
Kiowa; Lakota; Menominee; Meskwaki;
Navajo; Ojibwa; Omaha; Pawnee; Pomo,
Kashaya; Ponca; Winnebago; Yavapai
Juncus: Paiute; Snuqualmie; Swinomish
Juniperus: Miwok; Navajo, Ramah
Koeleria: Havasupai
Lactuca: Gosiute
Lagenaria: Cherokee
Laminaria: Nitinaht
Larix: Flathead; Sanpoil & Nespelem;
Thompson
Lathyrus: Acoma; Apache, Chiricahua & Mesca-
lero; Chippewa; Cochiti; Laguna; Miwok;
Omaha; Ponca
Layia: Luiseño
Lens: Papago; Pima
Lepidium: Cherokee; Havasupai; Hoh; Luiseño;
Quileute
Leucocrinum: Crow
Lewisia: Blackfoot; Kutenai; Montana Indian;
Okanagan-Colville; Okanagon; Oregon Indi-
an, Warm Springs; Paiute; Paiute, Northern;
Shuswap; Spokan; Thompson; Thompson,
Upper (Nicola Band)

Leymus: Klamath; Montana Indian; Paiute;
Paiute, Southern
Liatris: Blackfoot; Kiowa; Tewa
Ligusticum: Alaska Native; Apache, Chiricahua
& Mescalero; Cherokee; Tolowa
Lilium: Atsugewi; Blackfoot; Clallam; Cree,
Woodlands; Karok; Klallam; Lummi; Niti-
naht; Okanagan-Colville; Okanagon; Paiute;
Quileute; Quinault; Samish; Shuswap; Skagit;
Skagit, Upper; Skokomish; Swinomish;
Thompson; Yana
Linnaea: Carrier
Linum: Dakota; Omaha; Pawnee; Ponca;
Winnebago
Lithocarpus: Costanoan; Hupa; Mendocino
Indian; Pomo
Lithospermum: Blackfoot; Gosiute; Okanagon;
Pima; Thompson
Lobularia: Costanoan
Lomatium: Atsugewi; Blackfoot; Flathead;
Gosiute; Karok; Lakota; Mendocino Indian;
Modoc; Montana Indian; Navajo; Nez Perce;
Okanagan-Colville; Okanagon; Paiute; Paiute,
Northern; Pomo, Kashaya; Sanpoil; Shuswap;
Thompson; Yuki
Lonicera: Mendocino Indian
Lotus: Havasupai; Tubatulabal
Lupinus: Alaska Native; Haisla & Hanaksiala;
Kimsquit; Kitasoo; Kwakiutl; Kwakiutl, South-
ern; Luiseño; Miwok
Lycium: Hopi
Lycopersicon: Seminole
Lycopus: Thompson
Lygodesmia: Hopi; Lakota; Sioux
Lysichiton: Cowlitz; Quileute; Skokomish;
Tolowa; Yurok
Macrocystis: Haisla & Hanaksiala; Kitasoo;
Oweekeno; Pomo
Madia: Crow; Klamath; Miwok; Shoshoni
Maianthemum: Okanagan-Colville; Thompson
Malacothrix: Luiseño
Malus: Hopi
Malva: Cahuilla; Pima
Mammillaria: Apache, White Mountain;
Gosiute; Navajo; Navajo, Ramah; Tewa
Mangifera: Seminole
Manihot: Seminole
Marattia: Hawaiian

Phyllospadix: Hesquiat; Makah
Physalis: Dakota
Physocarpus: Okanagan-Colville
Phytolacca: Cherokee; Malecite; Mohegan
Picea: Eskimo, Inuktitut; Gitksan; Makah; Tanana, Upper; Thompson; Wet'suwet'en
Pinus: Apache, Chiricahua & Mescalero; Apache, Western; Apache, White Mountain; Blackfoot; Cheyenne; Cocopa; Coeur d'Alene; Costanoan; Cree, Woodlands; Diegueño; Flathead; Gitksan; Gosiute; Havasupai; Hopi; Hualapai; Iroquois; Isleta; Jemez; Karok; Kawaiisu; Keres, Western; Klamath; Kutenai; Mendocino Indian; Mewuk; Miwok; Montana Indian; Navajo; Navajo, Ramah; Ojibwa; Okanagan-Colville; Okanagon; Paiute; Pomo; Pomo, Kashaya; Pueblo; Salish, Coast; Sanpoil & Nespelem; Shasta; Shoshoni; Shuswap; Sia; Spokan; Tewa; Thompson; Tubatulabal; Wet'suwet'en
Pisum: Okanagan-Colville; Papago; Pima
Plagiobothrys: Mendocino Indian
Plantago: Acoma; Alaska Native; Keres, Western; Laguna; Pima, Gila River
Platanus: Costanoan
Pluchea: Cahuilla
Poa: Gosiute; Havasupai
Polanisia: Pueblo
Poliomintha: Hopi; Tewa
Polygonatum: Cherokee
Polygonum: Alaska Native; Cherokee; Cheyenne; Eskimo, Arctic; Eskimo, Inupiat; Koyukon; Lakota; Paiute
Polypodium: Kwakiutl, Southern; Makah; Salish, Coast
Polypogon: Tubatulabal
Polyporus: Isleta
Polystichum: Cherokee; Costanoan; Klallam; Kwakiutl, Southern; Makah; Nitinaht; Quileute; Quinault; Thompson
Populus: Apache, Chiricahua & Mescalero; Apache, White Mountain; Bella Coola; Blackfoot; Cheyenne; Clallam; Coeur d'Alene; Costanoan; Cree, Woodlands; Dakota; Flathead; Haisla; Haisla & Hanaksiala; Isleta; Jemez; Kutenai; Kwakiutl, Southern; Montana Indian; Navajo; Ojibwa; Oweekeno; Pima; Tanana, Upper; Zuni

Porphyra: Hesquiat; Kitasoo; Kwakiutl, Southern; Nitinaht; Oweekeno; Pomo, Kashaya; Tolowa; Yurok
Portulaca: Apache, Chiricahua & Mescalero; Hopi; Navajo; Pima, Gila River; San Felipe; Tewa
Postelsia: Pomo; Pomo, Kashaya
Proboscidea: Apache, Chiricahua & Mescalero; Cahuilla; Havasupai; Hualapai; Papago; Pima; Pima, Gila River
Prosopis: Acoma; Apache, Chiricahua & Mescalero; Cahuilla; Cocopa; Hualapai; Isleta; Kamia; Laguna; Maricopa; Paiute; Papago; Pima; Southwest Indians; Yavapai; Yuma
Prunus: Costanoan; Hopi; Luiseño; Seminole; Thompson
Pseudocymopterus: Navajo, Ramah
Pseudotsuga: Okanagan-Colville
Psidium: Seminole
Pteridium: Atsugewi; Bella Coola; Chehalis; Costanoan; Cowlitz; Green River Group; Hahwunkwut; Klallam; Kwakiutl, Southern; Lummi; Mahuna; Makah; Montana Indian; Nitinaht; Ojibwa; Okanagon; Quileute; Quinault; Salish, Coast; Skagit; Skagit, Upper; Skokomish; Snohomish; Squaxin; Swinomish; Thompson
Pterospora: Kawaiisu
Puccinellia: Gosiute
Pycnanthemum: Cherokee
Pyrrhopappus: Kiowa
Pyrus: Hopi; Seminole
Quercus: Acoma; Apache, Mescalero; Apache, Western; Apache, White Mountain; Chehalis; Cheyenne; Chippewa; Cochiti; Comanche; Costanoan; Cowlitz; Dakota; Gosiute; Havasupai; Hualapai; Iroquois; Karok; Keres, Western; Kiowa; Laguna; Lakota; Mahuna; Malecite; Mewuk; Navajo; Navajo, Ramah; Neeshenam; Nisqually; Ojibwa; Omaha; Paiute; Papago; Pawnee; Pomo; Ponca; Pueblo; Salish, Coast; San Felipe; Seminole; Squaxin; Tewa; Tubatulabal; Winnebago; Wintoon; Yavapai; Yokut
Ranunculus: Acoma; Alaska Native; Cherokee; Eskimo, Alaska; Gosiute; Iroquois; Keres, Western; Laguna; Makah; Miwok; Quileute
Raphanus: Costanoan

Rheum: Cherokee; Haisla & Hanaksiala
Rhododendron: Cherokee
Rhodymenia: Alaska Native
Rhus: Iroquois; Navajo, Ramah; Yavapai
Ribes: Eskimo, Alaska; Zuni
Robinia: Apache, Mescalero; Jemez
Rorippa: Gosiute; Havasupai; Karok; Kawaiisu; Paiute; Saanich
Rosa: Cahuilla; Cheyenne; Eskimo, Inupiat; Haisla & Hanaksiala; Makah; Montana Indian; Nitinaht; Ojibwa; Okanagan-Colville; Paiute; Quinault; Salish; Salish, Coast; Skagit; Skokomish; Snohomish; Squaxin; Swinomish; Tanana, Upper; Thompson
Rubus: Bella Coola; Chehalis; Cherokee; Chinook, Lower; Cowlitz; Cree, Woodlands; Green River Group; Hesquiat; Iroquois; Kitasoo; Klallam; Klamath; Kwakiutl, Southern; Lummi; Makah; Montana Indian; Nitinaht; Okanagon; Oweekeno; Quileute; Quinault; Salish, Coast; Samish; Skagit; Skagit, Upper; Squaxin; Swinomish; Thompson; Tolowa
Rudbeckia: Cherokee
Rumex: Anticosti; Apache, Chiricahua & Mescalero; Bella Coola; Chehalis; Cherokee; Cheyenne; Cocopa; Delaware; Eskimo, Alaska; Eskimo, Inuktitut; Hanaksiala; Heiltzuk; Kawaiisu; Klallam; Klamath; Koyukon; Montana Indian; Navajo; Omaha; Oweekeno; Pima; Pima, Gila River; Saanich; San Felipe; Thompson
Sabal: Seminole
Saccharum: Seminole
Sagittaria: Algonquin, Quebec; Cheyenne; Cocopa; Dakota; Great Basin Indian; Klamath; Lakota; Montana Indian; Omaha; Paiute, Northern; Pawnee; Pomo; Potawatomi; Thompson; Winnebago
Salicornia: Salish, Coast
Salix: Alaska Native; Blackfoot; Cocopa & Yuma; Eskimo, Alaska; Eskimo, Arctic; Eskimo, Inuktitut; Eskimo, Inupiat; Pima; Tanana, Upper; Yuma
Salsola: Navajo
Salvia: Diegueño; Luiseño; Pima, Gila River; Tubatulabal; Yavapai
Sambucus: Ojibwa
Sanicula: Mendocino Indian; Neeshenam; Pomo

Sarcostemma: Luiseño
Saxifraga: Alaska Native; Cherokee; Eskimo, Alaska; Eskimo, Inuktitut
Scirpus: Cheyenne; Chippewa; Costanoan; Cree, Woodlands; Dakota; Gosiute; Hopi; Kawaiisu; Keres, Western; Klamath; Lakota; Luiseño; Montana Indian; Paiute, Northern; Pima, Gila River; Pomo; Sioux; Thompson; Tubatulabal; Ute
Scorzonella: Paiute
Sedum: Alaska Native; Costanoan; Eskimo, Alaska; Eskimo, Inupiat; Gitksan; Haisla; Makah; Tubatulabal; Wet'suwet'en
Senecio: Eskimo, Alaska
Sideroxylon: Seminole
Silene: Eskimo, Inuktitut
Simmondsia: Cocopa; Papago
Sisymbrium: Pima, Gila River; Tubatulabal
Sium: Algonquin, Quebec; Bella Coola; Carrier; Cree, Woodlands; Okanagan-Colville; Shuswap; Thompson
Smilax: Cherokee
Solanum: Hopi; Iroquois; Pueblo; Zuni
Solidago: Gosiute; Navajo, Kayenta
Sonchus: Pima; Pima, Gila River
Sparganium: Klamath
Sphaeralcea: Navajo
Spiranthes: Paiute
Stachys: Gosiute; Quinault
Stanleya: Hopi
Stenocereus: Papago
Sticta: Ojibwa
Stipa: Kawaiisu
Streptopus: Cherokee
Strophostyles: Choctaw
Suaeda: Gosiute; Paiute, Northern; Pima, Gila River
Tacca: Hawaiian
Taraxacum: Eskimo, Alaska; Malecite; Mohegan; Potawatomi; Ute
Thalia: Seminole
Thelypodium: Pueblo; Tewa
Thlaspi: Havasupai
Thuja: Montana Indian; Salish, Coast
Tolmiea: Makah
Torreya: Mendocino Indian
Tradescantia: Acoma; Cherokee; Keres, Western; Laguna

Tragopogon: Cherokee; Okanagon; Thompson; Thompson, Upper (Nicola Band); Thompson, Upper (Spences Bridge)

Trifolium: Bella Coola; Costanoan; Haisla & Hanaksiala; Hesquiat; Kitasoo; Luiseño; Makah; Mendocino Indian; Miwok; Nitinaht; Nuxalkmc; Oweekeno; Paiute; Pomo, Kashaya; Round Valley Indian; Tubatulabal; Wailaki; Yokia; Yuki

Triglochin: Gosiute; Klamath; Montana Indian

Trisetum: Gosiute

Triteleia: Atsugewi; Karok; Mendocino Indian; Miwok; Neeshenam; Okanagan-Colville; Okanagon; Paiute; Pomo; Thompson; Thompson, Upper (Lytton Band); Thompson, Upper (Spences Bridge); Yana; Yuki

Triticum: Navajo, Ramah; Okanagan-Colville; Pima

Tsuga: Kitasoo; Nitinaht; Oweekeno; Wet'suwet'en

Typha: Acoma; Alaska Native; Apache; Apache, Chiricahua & Mescalero; Apache, Mescalero; Blackfoot; Carrier; Chehalis; Clallam; Costanoan; Cree, Woodlands; Gosiute; Hualapai; Kawaiisu; Keres, Western; Klamath; Laguna; Mendocino Indian; Montana Indian; Navajo, Ramah; Ojibwa; Okanagan-Colville; Paiute; Paiute, Northern; Pima; Pima, Gila River; Pomo, Kashaya; San Felipe; Sioux; Tanana, Upper; Thompson; Tubatulabal; Yuki; Yuma

Ulmus: Omaha

Umbellularia: Karok; Mendocino Indian; Midoo; Pomo; Pomo, Kashaya; Yuki; Yurok

Urtica: Alaska Native; Haisla & Hanaksiala; Makah; Oweekeno; Skagit, Upper

Ustilago: Apache, White Mountain; Hopi

Uvularia: Cherokee

Vaccinium: Algonquin, Tête-de-Boule; Iroquois; Seminole

Valeriana: Klamath; Montana Indian; Paiute; Sanpoil & Nespelem

Veratrum: Miwok

Verbesina: Navajo

Viburnum: Abnaki; Thompson

Vicia: Acoma; Apache, Chiricahua & Mescalero; Laguna; Montana Indian

Vigna: Cocopa; Kamia; Mohave; Papago; Pima

Vitex: Hawaiian

Vitis: Iroquois; Seminole

Vulpia: Gosiute; Navajo, Kayenta

Wislizenia: Hopi

Wyethia: Costanoan; Gosiute; Mendocino Indian; Montana Indian; Paiute; Paiute, Northern; Pomo, Kashaya

Xanthosoma: Seminole

Ximenia: Seminole

Yucca: Apache; Apache, Chiricahua & Mescalero; Apache, Mescalero; Apache, Western; Apache, White Mountain; Cahuilla; Cochiti; Diegueño; Isleta; Jemez; Kawaiisu; Keres, Western; Lakota; Luiseño; Mahuna; Navajo, Ramah; Papago; San Felipe; Southwest Indians; Tubatulabal; Yavapai; Zuni

Zamia: Seminole

Zea: Delaware; Hopi; Isleta; Kamia; Kiowa; Meskwaki; Navajo; Papago; Seminole

Zigadenus: Karok; Navajo, Kayenta

Zizania: Chippewa; Meskwaki; Thompson

Zostera: Bellabella; Hesquiat; Kwakiutl, Southern; Nitinaht; Oweekeno

Vegetable

Acacia: Cahuilla

Acer: Thompson

Agaricus: Pomo, Kashaya

Agave: Apache, Chiricahua & Mescalero; Papago

Agoseris: Kawaiisu

Aletes: Isleta

Allium: Apache, Chiricahua & Mescalero; Blackfoot; Cahuilla; Cherokee; Coeur d'Alene; Cree; Eskimo, Inupiat; Haisla & Hanaksiala; Hualapai; Iroquois; Isleta; Kawaiisu; Keres, Western; Montana Indian; Navajo; Ojibwa; Okanagan-Colville; Paiute; Paiute, Northern; Pomo, Kashaya; Potawatomi

Amaranthus: Acoma; Cahuilla; Cochiti; Cocopa; Havasupai; Hopi; Iroquois; Isleta; Keres, Western; Keresan; Laguna; Mohave; Mohegan; Montana Indian; Navajo; Navajo, Ramah; Papago; Pima; Pima, Gila River; Pueblo; Sia; Spanish American; Yavapai; Yuma

Ambrosia: Papago

Amphicarpaea: Cherokee; Ojibwa

Amsinckia: Kawaiisu; Pima, Gila River
Angelica: Alaska Native; Eskimo, Alaska; Eskimo, Greenland; Karok; Neeshenam; Shuswap
Antennaria: Navajo, Kayenta
Apios: Cherokee; Cheyenne; Chippewa; Menominee; Meskwaki; Omaha; Potawatomi
Apium: Cahuilla; Luiseño
Aquilegia: Miwok
Arabis: Alaska Native
Arctium: Iroquois
Argentina: Alaska Native; Montana Indian
Asclepias: Cahuilla; Chippewa; Iroquois; Meskwaki; Miwok; Ojibwa; Omaha; Pawnee; Ponca; Winnebago
Asparagus: Cherokee; Iroquois; Isleta
Aster: Algonquin, Quebec
Atriplex: Cochiti; Hopi; Isleta; Kawaiisu; Keres, Western; Papago; Pima; Pueblo
Balsamorhiza: Montana Indian
Barbarea: Alaska Native; Cherokee
Boletus: Pomo, Kashaya
Brassica: Cherokee; Diegueño; Haisla & Hanaksiala; Hoh; Iroquois; Kitasoo; Lakota; Luiseño; Mendocino Indian; Mohegan; Okanagan-Colville; Quileute
Brodiaea: Pomo, Kashaya; Yurok
Calandrinia: Luiseño
Calochortus: Paiute; Paiute, Northern; Pomo, Kashaya
Caltha: Abnaki; Chippewa; Iroquois; Menominee
Camassia: Coeur d'Alene; Haisla; Hesquiat; Karok; Nitinaht; Salish; Salish, Coast
Camissonia: Cahuilla
Cantharellus: Pomo, Kashaya
Capsella: Apache, Chiricahua & Mescalero; Cahuilla; Cherokee; Thompson
Cardamine: Cherokee; Menominee; Ojibwa
Carduus: Luiseño
Caulanthus: Kawaiisu
Chelone: Cherokee
Chenopodium: Alaska Native; Apache; Cahuilla; Cherokee; Cocopa; Diegueño; Eskimo, Inupiat; Hopi; Iroquois; Isleta; Kawaiisu; Keresan; Lakota; Luiseño; Mendocino Indian; Miwok; Mohave; Montana Indian; Navajo; Ojibwa; Papago; Pima; Potawatomi; Pueblo;

Shuswap; Spanish American; Thompson; Yaqui; Yavapai; Zuni
Chlorogalum: Cahuilla
Cirsium: Hoh; Montana Indian; Quileute
Citrullus: Iroquois
Clarkia: Miwok
Claytonia: Alaska Native; Algonquin, Quebec; Blackfoot; Cahuilla; Coeur d'Alene; Diegueño; Eskimo, Arctic; Kawaiisu; Luiseño; Mendocino Indian; Neeshenam; Paiute, Northern
Cleome: Apache, Western; Hopi; Isleta; Jemez; Keres, Western; Keresan; Navajo; Sia; Tewa
Cochlearia: Alaska Native
Colocasia: Hawaiian
Conioselinum: Kitasoo
Conyza: Miwok
Coreopsis: Kawaiisu
Coriandrum: Zuni
Crepis: Karok
Cucumis: Iroquois; Ojibwa
Cucurbita: Cherokee; Cocopa; Havasupai; Iroquois; Maricopa; Navajo
Cymopterus: Acoma; Cochiti; Keres, Western; Laguna; Navajo; Navajo, Kayenta
Cyperus: Keres, Western; Pomo, Kashaya
Darmera: Karok
Dasylirion: Apache, Chiricahua & Mescalero; Papago
Daucus: Haisla & Hanaksiala; Kitasoo; Sanpoil & Nespelem
Delphinium: Miwok
Dentinum: Pomo, Kashaya
Descurainia: Cahuilla; Cocopa; Hopi; Pueblo
Dichelostemma: Pomo, Kashaya
Dioscorea: Hawaiian
Dryopteris: Alaska Native; Kitasoo
Dudleya: Neeshenam
Dyssodia: Apache, Chiricahua & Mescalero
Echinocereus: Isleta
Epilobium: Alaska Native; Bella Coola; Eskimo, Arctic; Eskimo, Greenland; Eskimo, Inupiat
Equisetum: Hesquiat
Eremalche: Pima, Gila River
Eriogonum: Havasupai; Karok; Miwok
Erodium: Cahuilla; Diegueño
Eschscholzia: Luiseño; Mendocino Indian; Neeshenam
Ferocactus: Papago

Winter Use Food

Index of Common Names

Common plant names appearing in the original sources are listed alphabetically and are cross-referenced to the scientific names used in the Catalog of Plants. For brevity, we have not been able to list all common names. Plants are identified below to the level of species and a particular common name may apply only to a single subspecies or variety of that species. Word division as used in the original sources has been followed when possible, but indexing often required other word divisions. Some misspellings in the original sources have been corrected and some editorial conventions have been adopted to facilitate finding names in the index. Unlike scientific names, common plant names do not follow rules of nomenclature. This index is intended as a handy finding tool rather than as a consistently uniform catalog of common names.

Acacia: *Acacia* spp.
Acid Berry: *Rhus trilobata*
Adam and Eve: *Aplectrum hyemale*
Adelia: *Forestiera pubescens*
Adobe Yampah: *Perideridia pringlei*
Adonis Blazingstar: *Mentzelia multiflora*
Agave: *Agave* spp.
Air Yam: *Dioscorea bulbifera*
Ako-lea: *Phegopteris* sp.
Alaska Rein Orchid: *Piperia unalascensis*
Alaska Wild Rhubarb: *Polygonum alpinum*
Alder: *Alnus* spp., *Cornus sericea*
Alder, Green: *Alnus viridis*
Alder, Mountain: *Alnus rhombifolia, A. viridis*
Alder, Red: *Alnus rubra*
Alder, Sitka: *Alnus viridis*
Alder, White: *Alnus rhombifolia*
Alderleaf Mountain Mahogany: *Cercocarpus montanus*

Alfalfa: *Medicago sativa*
Alfilaria (or Alfileria): *Erodium cicutarium*
Alga, Tubular Green: *Enteromorpha intestinalis*
Algarrobo: *Prosopis chilensis*
Algerita: *Mahonia fremontii, M. haematocarpa*
Alkali Bulrush: *Scirpus robustus*
Alkali Buttercup: *Ranunculus cymbalaria*
Alkali Sacaton: *Sporobolus airoides*
Allegheny Blackberry: *Rubus allegheniensis*
Allegheny Serviceberry: *Amelanchier laevis*
Alligatorflag: *Thalia geniculata*
Alligator Juniper: *Juniperus deppeana*
Almond, Desert: *Prunus fasciculata*
Almond, Sweet: *Prunus dulcis*
Aloe: *Agave americana*
Alpine Bearberry: *Arctostaphylos alpina*
Alpine False Springparsley: *Pseudocymopterus montanus*
Alpine Fescue: *Festuca brachyphylla*
Alpine Laurel: *Kalmia microphylla*
Alpine Mountainsorrel: *Oxyria digyna*
Alpine Pennycress: *Thlaspi montanum*
Alpine Sweetvetch: *Hedysarum alpinum*
Alumroot, Crevice: *Heuchera micrantha*
Alumroot, Small Flowered: *Heuchera micrantha*
Alyssum, Desert: *Lepidium fremontii*
Amaranth: *Amaranthus* spp.
Amaranth, Bloodroot: *Amaranthus palmeri*
Amaranth, Fringed: *Amaranthus fimbriatus*
Amaranth, Green: *Amaranthus retroflexus*
Amaranth, Mat: *Amaranthus blitoides*
Amaranth, Palmer: *Amaranthus palmeri*
Amaranth, Powell's: *Amaranthus powellii*
Amaranth, Prostrate: *Amaranthus blitoides*
Amaranth, Purple: *Amaranthus cruentus*
Amaranth, Red: *Amaranthus cruentus*
Amaranth, Redroot: *Amaranthus retroflexus*
Amaranth, Sandhill: *Amaranthus arenicola*

Buffalograss: *Buchloe dactyloides*
Bugler, Scarlet: *Penstemon centranthifolius*
Bugleweed: *Lycopus asper, L. uniflorus*
Bulb Panicgrass: *Panicum bulbosum*
Bulbil Onion: *Allium geyeri*
Bulbous Springparsley: *Cymopterus bulbosus*
Bull Clover: *Trifolium fucatum*
Bull Kelp: *Nereocystis luetkeana*
Bull Mallow: *Malva nicaeensis*
Bull Thistle: *Cirsium vulgare*
Bulrush, Alkali: *Scirpus maritimus, S. robustus*
Bulrush, American: *Scirpus americanus*
Bulrush, Giant: *Scirpus tabernaemontani*
Bulrush, Great: *Scirpus acutus, S. tabernaemontani*
Bulrush, Hardstem: *Scirpus acutus*
Bulrush, Nevada: *Scirpus nevadensis*
Bulrush, Prairie: *Scirpus robustus*
Bulrush, Saltmarsh: *Scirpus maritimus*
Bulrush, Softstem: *Scirpus tabernaemontani*
Bum Branch: *Pinus edulis*
Bunchberry: *Cornus canadensis, C. suecica, C. unalaschkensis*
Bunchberry Dogwood: *Cornus canadensis*
Burclover: *Medicago polymorpha*
Burdock: *Arctium lappa, Xanthium strumarium*; see also Burrdock
Bur Oak: *Quercus macrocarpa*
Burr, Little: *Cardamine diphylla*
Burrdock: see also Burdock
Burrdock, Greater: *Arctium lappa*
Burrobush, Singlewhorl: *Hymenoclea monogyra*
Bush Morningglory: *Ipomoea leptophylla*
Bush Penstemon: *Penstemon fruticosus*
Bushy Blazingstar: *Mentzelia dispersa*
Butterbean: *Phaseolus lunatus*
Butterbur: *Petasites frigidus*
Buttercup: *Ranunculus reptans*
Buttercup, Alkali: *Ranunculus cymbalaria*
Buttercup, California: *Ranunculus californicus*
Buttercup, Creeping: *Ranunculus repens*
Buttercup, Five Petaled: *Ranunculus occidentalis*
Buttercup, Graceful: *Ranunculus inamoenus*
Buttercup, Lapland: *Ranunculus lapponicus*
Buttercup, Littleleaf: *Ranunculus abortivus*
Buttercup, Pallas: *Ranunculus pallasii*

Buttercup, Rocky Mountain: *Ranunculus cymbalaria*
Buttercup, Tall: *Ranunculus acris*
Buttercup, Western: *Ranunculus occidentalis*
Butterfly Mariposa Lily: *Calochortus venustus*
Butterfly Weed: *Gaura parviflora*
Butternut: *Juglans cinerea*
Butterweed: *Conyza canadensis*
Button Brittlebush: *Encelia frutescens*
Cabbage: *Brassica oleracea, Sabal palmetto*
Cabbage, Skunk: *Lysichiton americanus, Symplocarpus foetidus*
Cabbage, Squaw: *Caulanthus inflatus*
Cabbage, Wild: *Brassica oleracea, Caulanthus coulteri*
Cabbage Palmetto: *Sabal palmetto*
Cacao: *Theobroma cacao*
Cactus, Barrel: *Ferocactus coulteri, F. cylindraceus, F. wislizeni*
Cactus, Beavertail: *Opuntia basilaris*
Cactus, Brittle Prickly Pear: *Opuntia fragilis*
Cactus, Bunch: *Echinocereus engelmannii*
Cactus, Candy Barrel: *Ferocactus wislizeni*
Cactus, Cane: *Opuntia imbricata, O. whipplei*
Cactus, Chandelier: *Opuntia imbricata*
Cactus, Cholla: *Opuntia whipplei*; see also Cholla
Cactus, Christmas: *Opuntia leptocaulis*
Cactus, Cottontop: *Echinocactus polycephalus*
Cactus, Counterclockwise Nipple: *Mammillaria mainiae*
Cactus, Crimson Hedgehog: *Echinocereus coccineus*
Cactus, Cushion: *Escobaria missouriensis, E. vivipara*
Cactus, Fish Hook: *Ferocactus wislizeni, Mammillaria dioica, M. grahamii, Neomammillaria* sp.
Cactus, Gearstem: *Peniocereus striatus*
Cactus, Giant: *Carnegia gigantea, Pachycereus pringlei, Stenocereus thurberi*
Cactus, Graham's Nipple: *Mammillaria grahamii*
Cactus, Hedgehog: *Echinocereus engelmannii, E. fendleri, E. rigidissimus*
Cactus, Hedgewood: *Echinocereus coccineus*
Cactus, Horned Toad: *Mammillaria mainiae*
Cactus, Kingcup: *Echinocereus triglochidiatus*
Cactus, Many Spined: *Opuntia polyacantha*

Polypody: *Polypodium glycyrrhiza, P. virginianum*
Polypody, Leather Leaf: *Polypodium scouleri*
Polypody, Leathery: *Polypodium scouleri*
Polypody, Rock: *Polypodium virginianum*
Polypody, Western: *Polypodium hesperium*
Pomme Blanche: *Pediomelum esculentum*
Pomme de Prairie: *Pediomelum esculentum*
Pond Apple: *Annona glabra*
Pond Lily: *Nuphar lutea*
Pondlily, Rocky Mountain: *Nuphar lutea*
Pond Lily, Yellow: *Nuphar lutea*
Ponderosa Pine: *Pinus ponderosa*
Pondweed: *Menyanthes trifoliata*
Pond-weeds: *Potamogeton* sp.
Pony Beebalm: *Monarda pectinata*
Popcornflower, Fulvous: *Plagiobothrys fulvus*
Popcornflower, Rusty: *Plagiobothrys nothofulvus*
Poplar: *Liriodendron tulipifera, Populus grandidentata, P. tremuloides*
Poplar, Aspen: *Populus tremuloides*
Poplar, Balm (or Balsam): *Populus balsamifera*
Poplar, Carolina: *Populus deltoides*
Poppy, California: *Eschscholzia californica*
Poppy, Golden: *Eschscholzia californica*
Poppy, Matilija: *Romneya coulteri*
Poppy, Tree: *Dendromecon rigida*
Poppy, Yellow: *Eschscholzia californica*
Poque: *Boschniakia rossica*
Porter's Licoriceroot: *Ligusticum porteri*
Possumhaw: *Viburnum nudum*
Post Oak: *Quercus stellata*
Potato, Eskimo: *Claytonia tuberosa, Hedysarum alpinum*
Potato, Hog: *Hoffmannseggia glauca*
Potato, Indian: *Apios americana, Hoffmannseggia glauca, Solanum tuberosum*
Potato, Irish: *Solanum tuberosum*
Potato, James Wild: *Solanum jamesii*
Potato, Meskwaki: *Solanum tuberosum*
Potato, Native: *Solanum fendleri*
Potato, Ojibwe: *Solanum tuberosum*
Potato, Sweet: *Ipomoea batatas*
Potato, White: *Solanum tuberosum*
Potato, Wild: *Claytonia lanceolata, Hedysarum alpinum, Helianthus tuberosus, Oxypolis rigidior, Solanum fendleri, S. jamesii, S. triflorum, Triteleia grandiflora*

Potato Bean: *Apios tuberosum*
Povertyweed, Nuttall's: *Monolepis nuttalliana*
Powell's Amaranth: *Amaranthus powellii*
Powell's Saltweed: *Atriplex powellii*
Prairie Clover, Purple: *Dalea purpurea*
Prairie Clover, Slender White: *Dalea candida*
Prairieclover, Violet: *Dalea purpurea*
Prairie Clover, White: *Dalea candida*
Prairieclover, Woolly: *Dalea lanata*
Prairie Crabapple: *Malus ioensis*
Prairie Flax: *Linum lewisii*
Prairie Junegrass: *Koeleria macrantha*
Prairie Rose: *Rosa arkansana*
Prairiesmoke: *Geum triflorum*
Prairie Spiderwort: *Tradescantia occidentalis*
Prairie Sunflower: *Helianthus petiolaris*
Prairie Trefoil: *Lotus unifoliolatus*
Prester John: *Arisaema triphyllum*
Prettyface: *Triteleia ixioides*
Prickly Currant: *Ribes lacustre*
Pricklypear: *Opuntia humifusa, O. ×occidentalis*; see also Cactus, Prickly Pear
Pricklypear, Beavertail: *Opuntia basilaris*
Pricklypear, Brownspined: *Opuntia parryi*
Pricklypear, Dollarjoint: *Opuntia chlorotica*
Pricklypear, Golden: *Opuntia basilaris*
Pricklypear, Grizzlybear: *Opuntia erinacea*
Pricklypear, Hairspine: *Opuntia polyacantha*
Pricklypear, Kelvin's: *Opuntia ×kelvinensis*
Prickly Pear, Plains: *Opuntia polyacantha*
Prickly Pear, Tall: *Opuntia whipplei*
Pricklypear, Texas: *Opuntia engelmannii*
Pricklypear, Tulip: *Opuntia phaeacantha*
Pricklypear, Twistspine: *Opuntia macrorhiza*
Prickly Rose: *Rosa acicularis*
Prickly Russian Thistle: *Salsola australis*
Primrose, Brook Spike: *Boisduvalia stricta*
Primrose, Common Evening: *Oenothera biennis*
Primrose, Denseflower Spike: *Boisduvalia densiflora*
Primrose, Evening: *Boisduvalia densiflora, Calylophus lavandulifolius, Camissonia brevipes, C. claviformis, Musineon divaricatum, Oenothera* spp.
Primrose, Hooker's Evening: *Oenothera elata*